Modern Software Engineering Concepts and Practices:
Advanced Approaches

Ali H. Doğru
Middle East Technical University, Turkey

Veli Biçer
FZI Research Center for Information Technology, Germany

INFORMATION SCIENCE REFERENCE

Hershey · New York

Senior Editorial Director:	Kristin Klinger
Director of Book Publications:	Julia Mosemann
Editorial Director:	Lindsay Johnston
Acquisitions Editor:	Erika Carter
Development Editor:	Joel Gamon
Production Coordinator:	Jamie Snavely
Typesetters:	Keith Glazewski & Natalie Pronio
Cover Design:	Nick Newcomer

Published in the United States of America by
Information Science Reference (an imprint of IGI Global)
701 E. Chocolate Avenue
Hershey PA 17033
Tel: 717-533-8845
Fax: 717-533-8661
E-mail: cust@igi-global.com
Web site: http://www.igi-global.com

Library of Congress Cataloging-in-Publication Data

Modern software engineering concepts and practices : advanced approaches / Ali
H. Doğru and Veli Biçer, editors.
    p. cm.
  Includes bibliographical references and index.
  Summary: "This book provides emerging theoretical approaches and their
practices and includes case studies and real-world practices within a range of
advanced approaches to reflect various perspectives in the discipline"--
Provided by publisher.
  ISBN 978-1-60960-215-4 (hardcover) -- ISBN 978-1-60960-217-8 (ebook) 1.
Software engineering. I. Doğru, Ali H., 1957- II. Biçer, Veli, 1980-
  QA76.758.M62 2011
  005.1--dc22
                              2010051808

British Cataloguing in Publication Data
A Cataloguing in Publication record for this book is available from the British Library.

Table of Contents

Section 1
Introduction

Section 2
Software Architecture

Section 3
Software Services

Section 6
Parallel Applications and Multicore Software Engineering

Detailed Table of Contents

Section 1
Introduction

Chapter 1

    Bedir Tekinerdogan, Bilkent University, Turkey
    Mehmet Aksit, University of Twente, The Netherlands

Software engineering is, in essence, a problem-solving process, and to understand software engineering, it is necessary to understand problem-solving. To grasp the essence of problem-solving, we have provided an in-depth analysis of the history of problem-solving in mature engineering and software engineering. This has enabled us to position the software engineering discipline and validate its maturity level. To explicitly reason about the various problem-solving concepts in engineering, in section 2 we have presented the Problem-solving for Engineering Model (PSEM) that uniquely integrates the concepts of problem-solving, control and context. It appears that mature engineering conforms to the PSEM and this maturation process has been justified by a conceptual analysis from a historical perspective.

Chapter 2

    Kai Petersen, Blekinge Institute of Technology, Sweden & Ericsson AB, Sweden

This chapter compares two development paradigms (lean and agile development) which are of high relevance for industry because they focus on making companies agile in responding to changing market needs. The ability to respond quickly is essential in today's rapidly changing market. The result of the comparison is: (1) Agile and lean agree on the goals they want to achieve; (2) Lean is agile in the sense that the principles of lean reflect the principles of agile, while lean is unique in stressing the end-to-end perspective more; (3) Lean has adopted many practices known in the agile context, while stressing the importance of using practices that are related to the end-to-end flow. These practices are value-stream maps, inventory management, Kanban pull systems, and the use of a chief engineer. In addition, agile uses practices that are not found in lean. The practical implications are that: (1) Industry can potentially benefit from adopting lean practices related to flow, which helped to revolutionize manufacturing and product development; (2) Companies looking for evidence on lean will find important information in the agile literature as there is a high overlap between lean and agile. However, few papers are available that focus on the flow aspect in the software engineering context. The research implications are: (1) Research should focus on investigating which combination of practices should be recommended to industry depending on the industrial context, and (2) practices related to the E2E flow should be investigated to provide evidence for their benefit in the software engineering context.

Section 2
Software Architecture

Chapter 3

Jiehan Zhou, University of Oulu, Finland
Eila Ovaska, VTT Technical Research Centre of Finland, Finland
Antti Evesti, VTT Technical Research Centre of Finland, Finland
Anne Immonen, VTT Technical Research Centre of Finland, Finland

Ensuring software reliability prior to the development draws increasing attention, as the design decisions have direct impact on software system's capability to meet reliability requirements. In this chapter, Zhou, Ovaska, Evesti, and Immonen present the OntoArch method in order to create a reliability-aware architecture design. OntoArch incorporates quantitative reliability evaluation in software architecture design by the means of an ontology and the underlying tool. It incorporates quantitative software reliability measurement into software architecture design and enables reliability experts to formally conduct architecture modeling and reliability modeling in a unified environment. The approach is validated for a software architecture design, i.e. Personal Information Repository (PIR), with the use cases of software architecture knowledge management, software reliability profiling, and software architecture modeling and evaluation.

Chapter 4

Ricardo Pérez-Castillo, University of Castilla-La Mancha, Spain
Ignacio García-Rodríguez de Guzmán, University of Castilla-La Mancha, Spain
Mario Piattini, University of Castilla-La Mancha, Spain

One of the critical features of a software system is to support its evolution over time in order to adapt the system due to changes in technology and business. When such a feature is missing or not well-designed, a software system becomes subject to be outdated. Today, such systems, namely legacy systems, are critical problems as it is not so trivial for the enterprises to replace them, for economical and technical reasons. Software modernization mainly seeks the means to migrate a legacy system into a new form by examination, and modifications of system aspects. This chapter presents a recently adopted approach for software modernization, namely Architecture-Driven Modernization, which advocates carrying out reengineering processes, taking into account the principles and standards of model-driven development. An overview of ADM shows how it allows legacy information systems to evolve, making them more agile, preserving the embedded business knowledge, and reducing maintenance costs.

    Yujian Fu, Alabama A & M University, USA
    Zhijang Dong, Middle Tennessee State University, USA
    Xudong He, Florida International University, USA

Software architecture specifies a high-level abstraction of system topology, functionality, and behavior as a basis for system understanding and analysis. This chapter presents an architecture-centered verification approach to large scale complex software systems by integrating model checking with runtime verification. The approach aims at providing an analysis and verification of two different levels of software development process–design level and implementation level-and bridging the gap between software architecture analysis, verification, and the software product.

Section 3
Software Services

    Veli Biçer, FZI Forschungszentrum Informatik, Germany
    Stephan Borgert, TU Darmstadt, Germany
    Matthias Winkler, SAP Research CEC, Germany
    Gregor Scheithauer, OPITZ Consulting München GmbH, Germany
    Konrad Voigt, SAP Research CEC, Germany
    Jorge Cardoso, University of Coimbra, Portugal
    Erwin Aitenbichler, TU Darmstadt, Germany

The Internet revolutionizes deployment and delivery of software to a great extent. In this regard, the Internet of Services (IoS) is a new paradigm that introduces new requirements for service engineering in terms of addressing both business and technical perspectives. This chapter introduces a novel service engineering framework, Integrated Service Engineering (ISE) framework, and its ISE workbench in order to address these emerging requirements of IoS. The chapter provides a comprehensive overview of the foundations of IoS, and the principles on how the service engineering process can be conducted by applying separation of concerns. Additionally, three novel extensions are presented to the underlying ISE workbench in order to enrich the capabilities of the service modeling process.

Semantic service descriptions are shown to be useful to describe several service properties with rich semantics and expressive syntax. The expressiveness of these descriptions enables the automation of many service-related tasks (e.g. discovery, selection, composition), and leads the way to adopt many innovative techniques for a seamless interaction in a large service ecosystem. However, when a service is different from several other services in a dynamic fashion of a service ecosystem, the description of the service becomes a challenging task as many non-functional service aspects such as guarantees, pricing, payment, penalties, or delivery modes is hard to determine. This chapter provides an approach called Visual Semantic Analysis (VSA) in order to support semi-automatic modeling of semantic service descriptions.

Chapter 8

Software components are well-established techniques to facilitate the reuse and composition. Many techniques are proposed up to today that differ in terms of description, classification and discovery of components. In this chapter, Khemakhem, Drira and Jmaiel present a comparative study of component-based approaches and identify the key factors for a successful repository reuse. The comparison is based on search style, information type, comparison distance, and specification level, and highlights the importance of non-functional constraints in component descriptions, advantage of approximate comparison, and also tradeoff between the level of specification detail and the degree of difficulty to discover a component.

Section 4
Software Estimation and Metrices

Cost estimation is a challenging task for software engineers to estimate the time and cost of a software project, especially when the complexity and the size of the software is large. Recently the use of historical data along with statistical estimation techniques has gained special attention. A common problem in building software cost models is that the available datasets may contain projects with lots of missing categorical data. In this chapter, Angelis, Sentas, Mittas and Chatzipetrou present a comprehensive framework showing a combination of modern statistical and computational techniques can be used to compare the effect of missing data techniques on the accuracy of cost estimation. In addition, a recently proposed missing data technique, the multinomial logistic regression, is evaluated and compared with existing methods such as listwise deletion, mean imputation, expectation maximization, and regression imputation with respect to their effect on the prediction accuracy of a least squares regression cost model.

Chapter 10

Barış Özkan, Middle East Technical University, Turkey
Onur Demirörs, Middle East Technical University, Turkey

Software metrics are the key to quantitatively measure and estimate the software or its specification. Among the several software metrics, functional size, or function points, has been one of the most favored ones in the literature. Although it is recognized and applied in practice since introduced in 1979, Functional Size Measurement (FSM) has not been as widely practiced in software community as expected. The problems with FSM method structures and practices have been considered to be a major factor to explain the situation. This chapter presents a review and analysis of FSM approaches that propose solutions to the problems with FSM via formalization of FSM practices.

Chapter 11

Sanjay Misra, Federal University of Technology, Nigeria

A recent type of software measurement that is adopted from cognitive informatics is the cognitive complexity measure. Unlike the computational complexity, that deals with the algorithm complexity and evaluates time and memory needed to execute a program, cognitive complexity refers to the human effort needed to perform a task or the difficulty experienced in understanding the code. In recent years, several cognitive complexity measures based on CI have been proposed with varying advantages and disadvantages. This chapter presents a critical review on existing cognitive complexity measures and a comparative study based on some selected attributes of these measures.

Section 5
Software Process Improvement and Design Tools

Chapter 12

Minna Pikkarainen, University of Limerick, Ireland & VTT Technical Research Centre of
*   Finland, Finland*
Fergal McCaffery, Dundalk Institute of Technology, Ireland

In this chapter, Pikkarainen and McCaffery address the question of how to integrate agile practices with traditional plan-driven software process assessments. Assessments are critical within the organizations as they facilitate improvements in an organisation's software development and management processes by characterizing the current state of its software process and providing findings and recommendations to facilitate any improvement. Incorporating agile methods into software process assessments provides cost-effective and lightweight assessments that are highly desirable, especially, for small to medium sized enterprises. The authors introduce a method, namely Agile Hybrid Assessment Method for Automotive industry (AHAA), to enable the organizations to combine CMMI, agile practices and Automotive SPICETM approaches together. The method is also implemented and validated in the scope of two SMEs in Ireland.

Chapter 13

Nagehan Pala Er, ASELSAN Microelectronics, Turkey
Cengiz Erbaş, ASELSAN Microelectronics, Turkey
Bahar Çelikkol Erbaş, TOBB University of Economics and Technology, Turkey

This chapter addresses software development governance that is considered as the application of "governance" in software engineering in order to better manage the individual projects, as well as the organizations comprising many interrelated projects. It is an interdisciplinary perspective that adopts the principles from the field of Transaction Cost Economics. In this chapter, Pala, Erbas and Erbas analyze the organizations that aim to adapt the right governance structure for their projects based on their characteristics and the tools to be aligned with this structure. A novel Dependency Structure Matrix (DSM) is presented to utilize the mapping between governance structures and software modules and demonstrated with a successful integration using three broadly available tools in the software industry.

Chapter 14

Achilleas Achilleos, University of Cyprus, Cyprus
Nektarios Georgalas, British Telecom (BT) Innovate, UK
Kun Yang, University of Essex, UK
George A. Papadopoulos, University of Cyprus, Cyprus

As model-driven development techniques become widespread, the design tools that utilize domain-specific models to design and generate the software have also been a major prerequisite. The major predicament with these techniques is the complexity imposed when manually developing these domain-specific design tools. There is also a difficulty raised while integrating these design tools with model validation tools and code generators. This chapter presents a model-driven technique and its supporting model-driven environment to automate the tool development and integration. A formal parametric model is also proposed that allows evaluating the productivity impact in generating and rapidly integrating design tools.

Section 6
Parallel Applications and Multicore Software Engineering

Shang-Wei Lin, National Chung Cheng University, Taiwan
Chao-Sheng Lin, National Chung Cheng University, Taiwan
Chun-Hsien Lu, National Chung Cheng University, Taiwan
Yean-Ru Chen, National Taiwan University, Taiwan
Pao-Ann Hsiung, National Chung Cheng University, Taiwan

This chapter focuses on the development of multi-core embedded software. As multi-core processors are becoming prevalent rapidly in personal computing and embedded systems, it also becomes quite critical that the software to operate on a multi-core architecture is specifically designed; however, the current programming environment for multi-core processor based systems is still quite immature and lacks efficient tools. Lin, Lin, Lu, Chen, and Hsiung propose a new framework called VERTAF/Multi-Core (VMC) and show how software code can be automatically generated from high-level models of multi-core embedded systems. VMC aims to minimize the effort for developing embedded software for multi-core processors and to solve several of the issues related to model-driven development for multi-core embedded systems

Qichang Chen, University of Wyoming, USA
Liqiang Wang, University of Wyoming, USA
Ping Guo, University of Wyoming, USA
He Huang, University of Wyoming, USA

Concurrency is the major point of focus in parallel architectures as it introduces more fragility for programming errors than sequential programs. As multi-core/multi-processor hardware becomes more prevalent, detecting concurrency errors effectively and efficiently has become a research focus of software engineering in the recent years. This chapter presents the major concurrent programming models including multithreaded programming on shared memory and message passing programming on distributed memory and reviews the state-of-the-art approaches on detecting concurrency errors.

Foreword

American Association for the Advancement of Science initiated the Project 2061 to systematically identify science, mathematics, and technology themes and provide education recommendations. The processes, observations, and recommendations are documented in "Science for all Americans," published by Oxford University Press (ISBN 0-19-506771-1). In these wonderful guidelines, the "common themes" chapter starts like "some important themes pervade science, mathematics, and technology and appear over and over again, whether we are looking at an ancient civilization, the human body, or a comet. They are ideas that transcend disciplinary boundaries and prove fruitful in explanation, in theory, in observation, and in design." Furthermore, the committee stated that these thematic ideas are SYSTEMS, MODELS, CONSTANCY AND CHANGE, and SCALE.

While we were developing a modern and unifying approach to advanced software engineering education at the University of Texas, in 1995 in Austin, we had also identified four key thematic ideas underlying the foundations of modern software engineering–the engineering and technology of 21st century. We also claimed that these topics should be covered as core elements of software engineering and moved to develop these contents into four courses. One of the editors of Modern Software Engineering Concepts and Practices: Advanced Approaches, Dr. Ali Dogru had been instrumental in the development of these four thematic areas. These areas were SYSTEMS (Systems in Project 2061), DESIGN (Models in Project 2061), PROCESS (Constancy and Change in Project 2061), and METRICS/MEASUREMENTS (Scale in Project 2061). As can be readily observed, these four core themes of software engineering also correspond to the themes identified by Project 2061 as "transcending disciplinary boundaries," which is a testimony to the overarching comprehensiveness of modern software engineering beyond the common topics covered in popular software engineering books known as the software engineering body of Knowledge (SWEBOK). Therefore, I can safely claim that the book in your hand developed by two extraordinary software engineers and software engineering educators is not just another software engineering book regurgitating the material from SWEBOK and other related sources. This is a unique book looking into the complicated topic of software engineering with a fresh viewpoint.

If I may give a brief history of this development, I should start with our mentors Prof. Raymond T. Yeh and Prof. C. V. Ramamoorthy. Since the time of the establishment of IEEE Transactions of Software Engineering by Prof. Raymond T. Yeh in 1969 as the first software engineering journal and the subsequent expansion of it under Prof. C. V. Ramamoorthy's chief editorship, software engineering went through several major evolutionary transformations. During the 1980s, due to rapid advances in the applications of software to many disciplines, the systems view started taking root. At the same time, basic software engineering research started moving from universities to corporations, which had been the fate for hardware research during the 1970s. We witness during the 1990s the explosion of networking capabilities including Internet and World Wide Web, leading to the development of associated technologies related to systems integration. The first journal addressing to the issues of Systems Integration was initiated by our mentors Drs. Yeh and Ramamoorty again in collaboration with Dr. Peter Ng during early part of the 1990s. However, it was too early to introduce an applied systems integration journal since there have not been very urgent systems integration research problems yet. During 1995, Drs. Yeh and Ramamoorty, in collaboration with Dr. Herbert Simon and Dr. George Kozmetsky, spearheaded yet another development, the Society for Design and Process Science (www.sdpsnet.org) and the Transactions for society, as an archival journal, covering issues "transcending disciplinary boundaries." The later establishment of Software Engineering Society as a technology area in SDPS completed the revolutionary developments in the redefinition of software engineering research to achieve transformative goals by transdisciplinary means. Dr. Dogru has been one of the founders of these initiatives and cut his teeth among the pioneers in the development of fundamental ideas and themes of modern advanced software engineering. Superb selection of topics for this book reflects many of these experiences and developments.

Now, more than forty years after the recognition of Software Engineering as a discipline, considering software as a glue; systems integration issues are again in the forefront of problems we are facing – from health care, biological/medical application, popular networking application, to defense applications. Maturity of technological infrastructures including support for Service Oriented Architecture (SOA) prepared the way to develop systems applications with integration being the paramount issue. Now, we are facing the problem to address industry-wide practical as well as theoretical issues on Systems Integration. Many researchers are developing solutions using integration tools in all kinds of areas from all engineering disciplines. However, there is no book in advanced software engineering to prepare the interested groups to these current fundamental issues and themes. This book serves this purpose. Obviously, no single book can cover extremely broad area of advanced software engineering. The goal is to prepare the minds so that the techniques for further study and usage will be clear. Nobody expects to learn Electrical Engineering by simply studying a book claiming to contain the Electrical Engineering body of knowledge. The broader and youthful nature of software engineering makes it even harder to teach in one comprehensive compendium. Therefore, the right approach has been taken by the authors to limit their coverage by taking into account the main themes and technologies, and covering a significant amount of advanced topics in the profession of software engineering.

We should remember that the challenges in software development are well documented and software engineers are struggling to offer increasingly more effective techniques. The prior serious attempts in this struggle seem to be targeting improvements in orders of magnitude in development time, while utilizing revolutionary techniques usually based on composition and architecture centered paradigms. The main difficulty in the process of software development, however, is not just the selection of any technical paradigms. Another key difficulty is the fusion of different disciplines: social aspects need to be mastered besides the formalism behind the problem model. In other words, multidisciplinarity is inherent in today's software development. This book presents its content within this perspective, offering a coordinated mixture of different perspectives to address these frontiers. Practical techniques are also presented within this philosophy, adding to the value of the book in support of the multi-dimensional concern space. Get ready for the profession of the 21st century by studying the topics covered in this book.

Murat M. Tanik
October 2010, Birmingham, AL

Murat M. Tanik *is a professor at the University of Alabama (UAB) at Birmingham since 1998. Prior to joining the UAB faculty, he was an associate professor and the director of Software Systems Engineering Institute (SSEI) at the University of Texas at Austin and served as the director of Electronic Enterprise Engineering at NJIT. He is also the director and chief scientist of Process Sciences Laboratory, a think-tank of process-centered knowledge integration. Dr. Tanik has worked on related projects for NASA, Arthur A. Collins (developer of Apollo moon missions' tracking and communications systems), and ISSI. After Collins and ISSI, he joined SMU as an associate professor and the director of the Software Systems Engineering Technology (SEK) research group. Dr. Tanik is co-founder of the interdisciplinary and international society, Society for Design and Process Science. His publications include co-authoring six books, co-editing eight collected works, and more than 100 journal papers, conference papers, book chapters, and reports funded by various government agencies and corporations. Under his direction, more than 20 PhD dissertations and 25 M.S. theses have been completed. Dr. Tanik's research interests include philosophy of science, software systems engineering, embedded and intelligent software systems, wireless and time-critical software support, collaborative computing for domain specific applications, and integrated systems design and process engineering. His first principles research include the development of information theoretical foundations for computing.*

Preface

"Any intelligent fool can make things bigger and more complex... It takes a touch of genius - and a lot of courage to move in the opposite direction." – Albert Einstein

The ever-expanding field of Software Engineering continues its journey with the introduction of emerging topics and concepts in order to solve particular problems of the modern software industry. As one of the major fields, it has grown rapidly in recent years, in parallel with the complexity and scale of the software systems. Addressing a wide spectrum, from traditional engineering systems to the large, Web-scale architectures of today, customer requirements have always given rise to innovative approaches to be developed either through introducing new paradigms or extending the capabilities of well-established approaches. Therefore, a rapid explosion of advanced techniques, methodologies and tools has been witnessed in the recent years, especially when the well-established principles of the past are applied to today's upcoming challenges in order to build more reliable, evolving, and professional software systems.

A modern perspective to software engineering requires an outlook to understand those concepts and principles that have matured over the years as the field evolves. Actually, those principles are transferred from older terminology to newer ones: concepts such as abstraction, modularization, separation of concerns, composition, process improvement, adaptation, testing and so on have always been part of the life of a software engineer. What else shape and distinguish a modern perspective, in fact, are the key challenges facing software engineering. Being one of the major fields, software engineering research has expanded rapidly in recent years, in parallel with the complexity and scale of the software systems. As of today, software becomes an integral part of various systems including automobiles, aircrafts, World-Wide-Web, or even tiny devices. Therefore, many frontier approaches have either emerged as a remedy for the engineering needs of the software community or gained more momentum than they have in the past. The modern software engineer cannot afford to quest for incremental gains only–substantially different instruments are needed for a leap in the performance of the industry.

Whenever a new approach emerges, the software industry is also thirsty for an effective, yet simple and published method to safely utilize the approach. For this purpose, enactment of an emerging approach in the solution of a real world problem is as significant as the approach itself. The struggle is not merely for the sake of being up to date or feeling so; the software engineering world is really in need of approaches that are practically available to a broad range of practitioners. Real world practices, case studies, tools and development environments are all critical for the adoption of new techniques, in an effort to increase the quality of software.

In this book, we aim to provide an outlook to these recent concepts and approaches. There are two unique features of the book which deserve particular emphasis. The first is its broad coverage of the topics that provides a gateway to current directions in modern software engineering from both a researcher's and a practitioner's point of view. Even though it is impossible to cover all topics in the field, it combines various techniques into one coherent structure and presents them in a concise manner. Furthermore, the chapters devoted to the topics not only present the concepts, but also provide a clear outlook over their position in the field with its newly evolving personality.

Another important feature of the book is its new orientation that accommodates modern techniques. For this purpose, a range of new concepts occupying the literature are incorporated within a composition, enabling them to be accessible to engineers. Being more important than mere utilization of modern techniques, the long mentioned need in the software engineering world for this kind of composition is finally made practically available. Many authorities have been reporting the need for this kind of methodology, and many have proposed bits and pieces of this idea with different terminology. This line of thinking is also to show the expansion in the field and also indicates that they are not isolated islands but connected to a large body of land. We believe that the contribution of the book is unique in terms of compiling such approaches that will eventually find their way to the industry and change the course of software development drastically.

A MODERN PERSPECTIVE

A natural question arises: what does a modern perspective to software engineering constitute? A straightforward answer to this question could be to enumerate all recent topics that we deal in software engineering today. Such an answer might, however, be misleading without knowing how and why they have evolved. In the following, we discuss what the main drivers are, why they are critical to be a major motivation in a modern perspective, and how the emerging approaches contribute to the challenges we have today.

The Big Challenge

Despite being an essential asset in everyday life, software systems are still facing critical problems in terms of increasing size and complexity, overdue and over budgeted projects, or unreliable operation performance. According to statistics over software project failures, the Chaos Report by the Standish Group[1] states that, only in 1995, U.S. companies and government agencies spent $81 billion for canceled software projects and an additional $59 billion for software projects that were overdue. These figures have not improved so much over the last decade: According to the Chaos 2009 survey[2], there is a noticeable decrease in project success rates, with only 32% of all projects succeeding, and 68% of those are either challenged (late, over budget, or with less than the required features and functions) or failed.

The grounds yielding such an undermined picture could be many. One can directly relate it to inherent complexity of software systems to be the main reason, considering that today's systems need to operate in ever more pervasive environments in a highly distributed or embedded fashion. Software in such environments is often required to ensure reliability, security, and performance. There is, as well, an elevated demand for the software to be evolving and adaptive, complying with the changes in business, technology, or legal issues. Despite significant advances in programming languages and supporting integrated development environments (IDEs), the problem is more than merely code-centric, but involves architectural, operational, managerial, and organizational aspects. Nonetheless, most of these challenges are not quite addressable during the lifetime of an individual software project. Rather, well-established methodologies, mature tools, industrial best practices, and more importantly, theoretical research are required to pinpoint the problems and to offer innovative solutions.

Strive for Simplicity

The growing complexity of software systems is a key motivation behind the recent techniques to simplify design and development. On one hand, Model-Driven Engineering (MDE) evolved as an idea of creating models, or abstractions, concerning particular concepts and roles rather than directly modeling the code. This is intuitive when one considers the whole software design process as a concern-oriented, multi-leveled process where, in each level, engineers are supposed to transform problem-specific concerns into solution-specific ones. This simplifies the process of design as it provides a systematic transformation of problem-level abstractions to software implementations. Each level can also be supported with automation via tools, transformation and generators decreasing the complexity of bridging the gap between the levels. In such a vision of software development, models are the primary artifacts of development and lead the way also to higher level abstractions for domain-specific modeling.

On the other hand, lightweight methodologies (i.e. agile development) have gained more popularity in the last decade as a remedy to increased bureaucracy and slow pace of preceding methodologies. They work quite well, especially, when software project is not mission-critical, requirements change rapidly, and the development team is relatively small. The success of agile development has triggered some attempts in the software community to derive software development methods (e.g. Agile Unified Process) by incorporating the agile principles to well-known, plan-driven methodologies in order to create a synergy of both approaches. In addition, the agile principles are closely related to Lean Manufacturing and Six Sigma which are two widespread practices in operations management. Such an interdisciplinary approach can provide additional benefits for software development process as those principles of Lean Manufacturing and Six Sigma have already shown their applicability by helping to revolutionize the manufacturing process.

Predictable Economics

Economics is a significant determinant factor for the success of any software project and its value for a company. In order to maximize the Return of Investment (ROI) of a project, software engineers need to carefully consider and plan the cost of production. If not planned and foreseen beforehand, the cost can change exponentially and result in software project failures whose results might be devastating. In this regard, software economics appears as a field that seeks enabling improvements to software design and development via better predicting the size, complexity and cost of a software process, and enabling economic reasoning about the final product. Although it is a relatively mature sub-field with a significant amount of effort already spent, increasing demand for better cost predictions, and accurate scheduling still makes software economics a very active area.

A variety of advances took place that enable economic reasoning in a software project. Although these advances differ significantly in terms of the measures and parts that they improve in software project, their contribution to the decision-making in software economics is almost of equal importance. First, the size and complexity of software to be developed is a critical factor for ensuring an effective decision making and the focus of Software Cost Estimation (SCE), which predicts the effort and time required for a software project. SCE involves the construction of an estimation model which is mostly a statistical technique for a theoretical measurement and interpretation. These estimations are crucial for early design decisions and cost predictions, and, in turn, an essential input into any cost-benefit analysis.

Whereas size of software is crucial from an economical point of view, another point of research deals with Software Process Improvement (SPI) that explores the ways of improving the development process. In the last decade, we observed advances towards more managed processes and their widespread adoption in the organizations. The process and maturity models (e.g. CMMI, SPICE) developed for this purpose help the organizations to minimize risks and increase competitiveness. One challenge is to incorporate more agility and adaptability in a managed process constituting a crucial target for the research community. Another important focus is the development of effective design tools that increase the productivity and automation in a software process. Improvements in these directions have direct impact on making the software economics more predictable and to maximize the ROI of software projects.

Pushing the Limits

Recent advances in network technologies and the increasing popularity of the World Wide Web define new frontiers for software engineering. As the Web revolutionizes business and lifestyle with drastic changes, software engineering for Web-based applications is one of the limits that we have challenged in the recent years. From a design perspective, developing Web based applications involves significantly different practices when compared to developing traditional applications. Multi-users, scalability, flexibility, security, and trust are only some of the requirements that gain increasing importance when applications are developed and deployed for the Web. In addition, recent notions Software-as-a-Service and Cloud Computing offer a new perspective to consider the software not as a product, but as a service, to be deployed and used as a utility. Design and development of software for this purpose generates a number of difficulties that already find their way in challenging the software developers.

Another shift is taking place in the computer hardware field while the era of doubling performance periodically in the chip industry is about to come to an end. Multicore chips are emerging while pushing parallel computing into the mainstream. Due to the affordable prices and future predictions of chips with many cores, the embedded software to operate on these architectures is gaining significance in software industry. Unfortunately, one cannot rely solely on low level compilers to perform the parallelization; it is the parallelization of software that is noteworthy when performance is considered. Therefore, the challenge for software engineering becomes how to develop software to operate better on multicore architecture while minimizing design complexity resulting from parallelism.

BOOK ORGANIZATION

This book addresses many of the abovementioned topics in a modern perspective to software engineering and introduces and discusses concepts and practices for successful software development. In the remaining part of this preface, we briefly introduce summaries of the sixteen chapters of the book.

Chapter 1. A Comparative Analysis of Software Engineering with Mature Engineering Disciplines Using a Problem-Solving Perspective

Software engineering is in essence a problem-solving process, and to understand software engineering it is necessary to understand problem-solving. To grasp the essence of problem-solving, we have provided an in-depth analysis of the history of problem-solving in mature engineering and software engineering. This has enabled us to position the software engineering discipline and validate its maturity level. To explicitly reason about the various problem-solving concepts in engineering, we also introduce the Problem-solving for Engineering Model (PSEM) that uniquely integrates the concepts of problem-solving, control and context. It appears that mature engineering conforms to the PSEM and this maturation process has been justified by a conceptual analysis from a historical perspective.

Chapter 2. Is Lean Agile and Agile Lean? A Comparison between Two Software Development Paradigms

This chapter provides a comparative study of lean and agile development methodologies that are emerging as answers to agility needs of organizations. The study shows that the principles of these approaches agree on the goals to be achieved, while lean development stresses an end-to-end perspective. The chapter also indicates research implications to enable a synergy of both approaches and to maximize the benefits of industry by their adoption.

Chapter 3. OntoArch Reliability-Aware Software Architecture Design and Experience

Ensuring software reliability prior to the development draws increasing attention, as the design decisions have direct impact on software system's capability to meet reliability requirements. This chapter presents the OntoArch method in order to create a reliability-aware architecture design. OntoArch incorporates quantitative reliability evaluation in software architecture design by means of an ontology-based approach and the underlying tool. It incorporates quantitative software reliability measurement into software architecture design and enables reliability experts to formally conduct architecture modeling and reliability modeling in a unified environment. The approach is validated for a software architecture design, i.e. Personal Information Repository (PIR), with the use cases of software architecture knowledge management, software reliability profiling, and software architecture modeling and evaluation.

Chapter 4. Architecture-Driven Modernization

One of the critical features of a software system is to support its evolution over time in order to adapt the system to the changes in technology and business. When such a feature is missing or not well-designed, a software system becomes prone to be outdated. Today, such systems, namely legacy systems, pose a critical problem because it is usually not so trivial for the enterprises to replace them due to economical and technical reasons. Software modernization mainly seeks the means to migrate a legacy system into a new form by examination, and modifications of system aspects. This chapter presents a recently adopted approach for software modernization, namely Architecture-Driven Modernization, which advocates carrying out reengineering processes taking into account the principles and standards of model-driven development. An overview of Architecture Driven Modernization shows how it allows legacy information systems to evolve while making them more agile, preserving the embedded business knowledge, and reducing their maintenance costs.

Chapter 5. Architecture-Centered Integrated Verification

Software architecture specifies a high-level abstraction of system topology, functionality, and behavior as a basis for system understanding and analysis. This chapter presents an architecture-centered verification approach to large scale complex software systems by integrating model checking with runtime verification. The approach aims at providing analysis and verification in two different levels of software development process –design level and implementation level-hence, bridging the gap between software architecture analysis and verification and the software product.

Chapter 6. Modeling Services Using ISE Framework: Foundations and Extensions

The Internet revolutionizes deployment and delivery of software to a great extent. In this regard, the Internet of Services (IoS) is a new paradigm that introduces new requirements for service engineering in terms of addressing both business and technical perspectives. This chapter introduces a novel service engineering framework, Integrated Service Engineering (ISE) framework, and its ISE workbench in order to address these emerging requirements of IoS. The chapter provides a comprehensive overview of the foundations of IoS, and the principles on how the service engineering process can be conducted by applying separation of concerns. Additionally, three novel extensions are presented to the underlying ISE workbench in order to enrich the capabilities of the service modeling process.

Chapter 7. Visual Semantic Analysis to Support Semi-Automatic Modeling of Semantic Service Descriptions

Semantic service descriptions are shown to be useful to describe several service properties with rich semantics and expressive syntax. The expressiveness of these descriptions enables the automation of many service-related tasks (e.g. discovery, selection, composition), and leads the way to adopt many innovative techniques for a seamless interaction in a large service ecosystem. However, when a service is composed from several other services in a dynamic fashion of a service ecosystem, the description of the service becomes a challenging task as many non-functional service aspects such as guarantees, pricing, payment, penalties, or delivery modes are hard to determine. This chapter provides an approach called Visual Semantic Analysis (VSA) in order to support semi-automatic modeling of semantic service descriptions for addressing such issues.

Chapter 8. Description, Classification and Discovery Approaches for Software Components: A Comparative Study

Software components constitute a well-established technique to facilitate reuse and composition. Many techniques are proposed up to today that differ in terms of description, classification, and discovery of components. This chapter presents a comparative study of component-based approaches and identifies the key factors for a successful repository reuse. The comparison is based on search style, information type, comparison distance, and specification level, and highlights the importance of non-functional constraints in component descriptions, advantage of approximate comparison, and also trade-off between the level of specification detail and the degree of difficulty to discover a component.

Chapter 9. Methods for Statistical and Visual Comparison of Imputation Methods for Missing Data in Software Cost Estimation

Cost estimation is a challenging task for software engineers to estimate the time and cost of a software project, especially when the complexity and the size of the software is large. Recently, the use of historical data, along with statistical estimation techniques, has gained special attention. A common problem in building software cost models is that the available datasets may contain projects with lots of missing categorical data. This chapter presents a comprehensive framework showing that a combination of modern statistical and computational techniques can be used to investigate the effect of missing data on the accuracy of cost estimation. In addition, a recently proposed missing data technique, the multinomial logistic regression, is evaluated and compared with existing methods such as listwise deletion, mean imputation, expectation maximization, and regression imputation with respect to their effect on the prediction accuracy of a least squares regression cost model.

Chapter 10. Formalization Studies in Functional Size Measurement

Software metrics are the key to quantitatively measure and estimate the software or its specification. Among the several software metrics, functional size, or function points, has been one of the most favored ones in the literature. Although it is recognized and applied in practice since introduced in 1979, Functional Size Measurement (FSM) has not been as widely practiced in software community as expected. The problems with FSM method structures and practices have been considered to be a major factor to explain the situation. This chapter presents a review and analysis of FSM approaches that propose solutions to the problems with FSM via formalization of FSM practices.

Chapter 11. Cognitive Complexity Measures: An Analysis

A recent type of software measurement that is adopted from cognitive informatics is the cognitive complexity measure is presented. Unlike the computational complexity, that deals with the algorithm complexity and evaluates time and memory needed to execute a program, cognitive complexity refers to the human effort needed to perform a task or the difficulty experienced in understanding the code. In recent years, several cognitive complexity measures based on CI have been proposed with varying advantages and disadvantages. This chapter presents a critical review on existing cognitive complexity measures and a comparative study based on some selected attributes of these measures.

Chapter 12. Introducing Agility into Plan-Based Assessments

This chapter addresses the question of how to integrate agile practices with traditional plan-driven software process assessments. Assessments are critical within the organizations as they facilitate improvements in an organisation's software development and management processes by characterizing the current state of its software process and providing findings and recommendations to facilitate any improvement. Incorporating agile methods into software process assessments provides cost-effective and lightweight assessments that are highly desirable, especially for small to medium sized enterprises. The authors introduce a method, namely Agile Hybrid Assessment Method for Automotive industry (AHAA), to enable the organizations to combine CMMI, agile practices, and Automotive SPICE™ approaches together. The method is also implemented and validated in the scope of two SMEs in Ireland.

Chapter 13. Software Development Governance: A Case Study for Tools Integration

This chapter addresses software development governance that is considered as the application of "governance" in software engineering in order to better manage the individual projects, as well as the organizations involved in many interrelated projects. It is an interdisciplinary perspective that adopts the principles from the field of Transaction Cost Economics. This chapter analyzes the organizations that aim to adapt the right governance structure for their projects based on their characteristics and the tools to be aligned with this structure. A novel Dependency Structure Matrix (DSM) is presented to utilize the mapping between governance structures and software modules and is demonstrated with a successful integration using three broadly available tools in the software industry.

Chapter 14. A Software Cost Model to Assess Productivity Impact of a Model-Driven Technique in Developing Domain-Specific Design Tools

As model-driven development techniques become widespread, the design tools that utilize domain-specific models to design and generate software have also been a major prerequisite. The major predicament with these techniques is the complexity imposed when manually developing these domain-specific design tools. There is also a difficulty raised while integrating these design tools with model validation tools and code generators. This chapter presents a model-driven technique and its supporting model-driven environment to automate the tool development and integration. A formal parametric model is also proposed that allows evaluating the productivity impact in generating and rapidly integrating design tools.

Chapter 15. Model-Driven Development of Multi-Core Embedded Software

This chapter focuses on the development of multi-core embedded software. As multi-core processors are becoming prevalent rapidly in personal computing and embedded systems, it also becomes quite critical that the software to operate on a multi-core architecture is specifically designed; however, current programming environments for multi-core processor based systems are still quite immature and lack efficient tools. This chapter proposes a new framework called VERTAF/Multi-Core (VMC) and shows how software code can be automatically generated from high-level models of multi-core embedded systems. VMC aims to minimize the effort for developing embedded software for multi-core processors and to solve several of the issues related to model-driven development for multi-core embedded systems.

Chapter 16. Analyzing Concurrent Programs Title for Potential Programming Errors

Concurrency is the major point of focus in parallel architectures as it introduces more fragility for programming errors than sequential programs. As multi-core/multi-processor hardware becomes more prevalent, detecting concurrency errors effectively and efficiently has become a research focus of software engineering in the recent years. This chapter presents the major concurrent programming models including multithreaded programming on shared memory and message passing programming on distributed memory and reviews the state-of-the-art approaches on detecting concurrency errors.

Ali H. Doğru
Middle East Technical University, Turkey

Veli Biçer
FZI Research Center for Information Technology, Germany

ENDNOTES

[1]   http://www.projectsmart.co.uk/docs/chaos-report.pdf
[2]   http://www.standishgroup.com/newsroom/chaos_2009.php

Acknowledgment

The editors would like to acknowledge the contribution and effort of everybody involved in the writing, review, and production process of the book. We wish to thank the authors of each chapter for contributing the results of their work and enriching our knowledge related to modern software engineering topics.

We are also very grateful for the professional advice received from the members of the editorial board, in particular, Prof. Dr. Mehmet Aksit of the University of Twente, Prof. Dr. Fevzi Belli of the University of Paderborn, Prof. Dr. Jorge Cardoso of the University of Coimbra, Prof. Dr. Bernd Kraemer of the FernUniversität in Hagen, Prof. Dr. York Sure of the University of Koblenz, Prof. Dr. Murat Tanik of the University of Alabama, and Prof. Dr. Bedir Tekinerdogan of Bilkent University.

Most of the authors in this book served as reviewers, and so deserve a special "thank you." In addition, several external reviewers helped with the double-blind review of all chapters. Their dedication and willingness while working with very tight deadlines and short turnarounds contributed a lot to increase the quality of the work. Thanks go to all who provided comprehensive and constructive reviews.

Special thanks go to the publishing team at IGI Global, whose contributions throughout the whole process, from the commencement of initial idea to final publication, were precious. We would like to thank Joel Gamon, our development editor, for his unwavering assistance and support; Kristin Klinger, Jan Travers and Erika Carter for their invaluable thoughts in the development of initial idea and their confidence in this book. Their timely guidance and reminders have been instrumental in completing such a long and demanding project.

The editors also need to acknowledge with gratitude the support received from our respective institutions, Middle East Technical University and FZI Research Center for Information Technology, and from the THESEUS/TEXO research project. We are grateful to find the opportunity to complete the editorial task of putting this book together among our other daily duties of work. As such, the support and encouragement we receive for this project is greatly appreciated.

Finally, we would like to dedicate our efforts to our families. Without their patience and understanding, it may never be possible to reach a happy end in such a long journey.

Ali H. Doğru
Middle East Technical University, Turkey

Veli Biçer
FZI Research Center for Information Technology, Germany

Section 1
Introduction

Chapter 1
A Comparative Analysis of Software Engineering with Mature Engineering Disciplines Using a Problem–Solving Perspective

Bedir Tekinerdogan
Bilkent University, Turkey

Mehmet Aksit
University of Twente, The Netherlands

ABSTRACT

Software engineering is compared with traditional engineering disciplines using a domain specific problem-solving model called Problem-Solving for Engineering Model (PSEM). The comparative analysis is performed both from a historical and contemporary view. The historical view provides lessons on the evolution of problem-solving and the maturity of an engineering discipline. The contemporary view provides the current state of engineering disciplines and shows to what extent software development can actually be categorized as an engineering discipline. The results from the comparative analysis show that like mature engineering, software engineering also seems to follow the same path of evolution of problem-solving concepts, but despite promising advances it has not reached yet the level of mature engineering yet. The comparative analysis offers the necessary guidelines for improving software engineering to become a professional mature engineering discipline.

INTRODUCTION

Since the early history of software development, there is an ongoing debate what the nature of

DOI: 10.4018/978-1-60960-215-4.ch001

software engineering is. It is assumed that finding the right answer to this question will help to cope with the *software crisis*, that is, software delivered too late, with low quality and over budget (Pressman, 2008; Sommerville, 2007). The underlying idea behind this quest is that a particular view on software development directly has an impact on the software process and artifacts. Several researchers fairly stated that in addition to the question what software development currently is, we should also investigate what professional software development should be. The latter question acknowledges that current practices can be unprofessional and awkward and might require more effort and time to maturate. Although both the questions on what software development is and what professional software development should be are crucial, it seems that there are still no definite answers yet and the debate is continuing from time to time after regular periods of silence. Some researchers might consider this just as an academic exercise. Yet, continuing the quest for a valid view of software development and a common agreement on this is important for a profound understanding, of the problems that we are facing with, and the steps that we need to take to enhance software development.

The significant problems we may face, though, seem not to be easily solved at the level as they are analyzed in current debates. To be able to provide both an appropriate answer to what software engineering is, and what it should be, we must shift to an even higher abstraction level than the usual traditional debates. This view should be generally recognized, easy to understand and to validate and as such provide an objective basis to identify the right conclusions. We think that adopting a problem solving perspective provides us an objective basis for our quest to have a profound understanding of software development. Problem-solving seems to be ubiquitous that it can be applied to almost any and if not, according to Karl Popper (2001), to all human activities, software development included. But what is problem-solving actually? What is the state of software development from a problem-solving perspective? What needs to be done to enhance it to a mature problem solving discipline? In order to reason about these questions and the degree of problem-solving in software development we

have first to understand problem-solving better. Problem solving has been extensively studied in cognitive sciences such as (Newell et al., 1976; Smith et al., 1993; Rubinstein et al., 1980) and different models have been developed that mainly address the cognitive human problem solving activity. In this paper we provide the Problem Solving for Engineering Model (PSEM), which is a domain-specific problem solving model for engineering. This PSEM will be validated against the mature engineering disciplines such as civil engineering, electrical engineering and mechanical engineering. From literature (Ertas et al., 1996; Ghezzi et al., 1991; Wilcox et al., 1990; Shaw et al., 1990) it follows that engineering essentially aims to provide an engineering solution for a given problem, and as such, can be considered as a problem solving process. We could further state that mature engineering disciplines are generally successful in producing quality products and adopt likewise a mature problem-solving approach. Analyzing how mature engineering disciplines solve their problems might provide useful lessons for acquiring a better view on what software development is, that has not yet achieved a maturity level. Hence, we have carried out an in-depth comparative analysis of mature engineering with software engineering using the PSEM. In principle, every discipline can be said to have been immature in the beginning, and evolved later in time. Mature engineering disciplines have a relatively longer history than software engineering so that the various problem solving concepts have evolved and matured over a much longer time. Studying the history of these mature disciplines will justify the problem-solving model and allow deriving the concepts of value for current software engineering practices. Hence, our comparative study considers both the current state and the history of software development and mature engineering disciplines. Altogether, we think that this study is beneficial in at least from the following two perspectives. First, an analysis of software engineering from a problem-solving perspective will provide an innovative and refreshing view on the current analysis and debates on software development. In some perspectives it might be complementary to existing analyses on software development, and in addition since problem-solving is at a higher abstraction level it might also highlight issues that were not identified or could not have been identified before due to the limitations of the adopted models for comparison. Second, the study on mature engineering disciplines will reveal the required lessons for making an engineering discipline mature. The historical analysis of mature engineering will show how these engineering disciplined have evolved. The analysis on the current practices in these mature engineering disciplines will show the latest success factors of mature engineering. We could apply these lessons to software engineering to enhance it to a mature problem solving, and thus a mature engineering discipline. In short, this study will help us to show what software development currently is, and what professional software development should be.

The remainder of this paper is organized as follows: The second section presents the problem-solving for engineering model (PSEM). The model defines the fundamental concepts of problem-solving and as such allows to explicitly reason about these concepts. In the third section, we use the PSEM to describe the history of mature engineering. The fourth section reflects on the history of software engineering based on the PSEM model and compares software engineering with mature engineering. In the fifth section, we provide a discussion and the comparison of software engineering with mature engineering. The sixth section presents the related work and finally the last section presents the conclusions.

PROBLEM-SOLVING FOR ENGINEEING MODEL

Several survey papers (Deek et al., 1999; Rubinstein et al., 1980) represent a detailed analysis on

the various problem-solving models. While there are many models of problem-solving, none has been explicitly developed to describe the overall process of engineering and/or compare engineering disciplines in particular. There have been problem-solving models for representing design as problem-solving (Braha et al., 1997), but no broad general model has been proposed yet which encompasses the overall engineering process.

A common model that represents engineering from a problem-solving will specifically show the important features of engineering. In this context, we could come up with a very abstract model for problem-solving consisting essentially of two concepts: *Need* and *Artifact*. Given a particular need (*Problem*) an artifact (*Solution*) must be provided that satisfies the need. Because of its very abstract nature, all engineering disciplines, including software engineering, apply to this overly simple model. Of course, the counterpart of the abstract nature of the model is that it is less useful in identifying the differences between the existing engineering disciplines and for comparing these. Hence, we are interested in a concrete problem-solving model that describes the separate important concepts needed for understanding and expressing the concepts of engineering. To this aim, we propose the domain specific *Problem-Solving for Engineering Model (PSEM)*, which is illustrated in Figure 1. In the subsequent sections, PSEM will serve as an objective basis for comparing engineering disciplines.

This domain specific model has been developed after a thorough literature study on both problem-solving and mature disciplines. In addition to the before mentioned problem-solving literature, we have studied selected handbooks including chemical engineering handbook (Perry, 1984), mechanical engineering handbook (Marks, 1987), electrical engineering handbook (Dorf, 1997) and civil engineering handbook (Chen, 1998). Further we have studied several textbooks on the corresponding engineering methodologies of mechanical engineering and civil engineering (Cross,

Figure 1. Problem-solving for engineering model (PSEM)

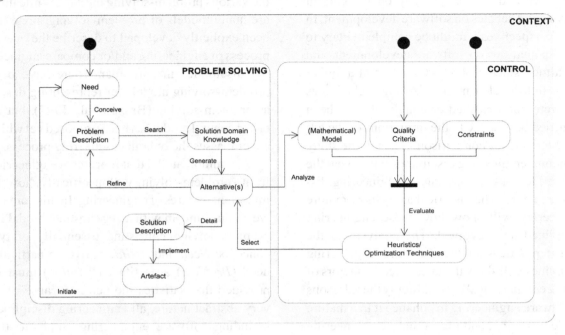

1989; Dunsheath, 1997; Shapiro, 1997), electrical engineering (Wilcox et al., 1990) and chemical engineering (Biegler, 1997).

The model is based on UML statecharts and consists of a set of states and transitions among these states. The states represent important concepts, the transitions represent the corresponding functions among these concepts. Concepts are represented by means of rounded rectangles, functions by directed arrows. The model consists of three fundamental parts: *Problem- Solving*, *Control* and *Context*. In the following, we will explain these parts in more detail.

Problem-Solving

The problem-solving part consists of six concepts: *Need, Problem Description, Solution Domain Knowledge, Alternative, Solution Description* and *Artifact*.

- *Need* represents an unsatisfied situation existing in the context. The function *Input* represents the cause of a need.
- *Problem Description* represents the description of the problem. The function *Conceive* is the process of understanding what the need is and expressing it in terms of the concept *Problem Description*.
- *Solution Domain Knowledge* represents the background information that is used to solve the problem. The function *Search* represents the process of finding the relevant background information that corresponds to the problem.
- *Alternative*, represents the possible alternative solutions. The function *Generate* serves for the generation of different alternatives from the solution domain knowledge. After alternatives have been generated, the problem description can be refined using the function *Refine*. The function *Detail* is used to detail the description of a selected alternative.

- *Solution Description* represents a feasible solution for the given problem.
- *Artifact* represents the solution for the given need. The function *Implement* maps the solution description to an artifact. The function *Output* represents the delivery and impact of the concept *Artifact* to the context. The function *Initiate* represents the cause of a new need because of the produced artifact.

Control

Problem-solving in engineering starts with the need and the goal is to arrive at an artifact by applying a sequence of actions. Since this may be a complex process, the concepts and functions that are applied are usually controlled. This is represented by the Control part in the model. A control system consists of a controlled system and a controller (Foerster, 1979). The controller observes variables from the controlled system, evaluates this against the criteria and constraints, produces the difference, and performs some control actions to meet the criteria. In PSEM, the control part consists of four concepts: *Representation of Concern, Criteria,* and *Adapter*.

- *(Mathematical) Model* represents a description of the concept Alternative. The function *Analyse* represents the process of analyzing the alternative.
- *(Quality) Criteria* represent the relevant criteria that need to be met for the final artifact. The function *Evaluate* assesses the alternative with respect to *(Quality) Criteria* and *Constraints*.
- *Constraints* represent the possible constraints either from the context or as described in *Problem* Statement.
- *Heuristics/Optimization Techniques* represents the information for finding the necessary actions to meet the criteria and constraints. The function *Select* selects

the right alternative or optimizes a given alternative to meet the criteria and the constraints.

Context

Both the control and the problem-solving activities take place in a particular context, which is represented by the outer rounded rectangle in Figure 1. Context can be expressed as the environment in which engineering takes place including a broad set of external constraints that influence the final solution and the approach to the solution. Constraints are the standards, the rules, requirements, relations, conventions, and principles that define the context of engineering (Newell et al., 1976), that is, anything, which limit the final solution. Since constraints rule out alternative design solutions they direct engineer's action to what is doable and feasible. The context also defines the need, which is illustrated in Figure 1 by a directed arrow from the context to the need concept. Apparently, the context may be very wide and include different aspects like the engineer's experience and profession, culture, history, and environment (Rubinstein et al., 1980).

HISTORICAL PERSPECTIVE OF PROBLEM-SOLVING IN MATURE ENGINEERING

In the following, we will explain PSEM from an engineering perspective and show how the concepts and functions in the model have evolved in history in the various engineering disciplines. While describing the historical developments we will indicate the related concepts of PSEM in italic format in the corresponding sentences.

Directly Mapping Needs to Artifacts

Engineering deals with the production of artifacts for practical purposes. Production in the early societies was basically done by hand and therefore they are also called craft-based societies (Jones et al., 1992). Thereby, usually craftsmen do not and often cannot, externalize their works in descriptive representations (Solution Description) and there is no prior activity of describing the solution like drawing or modeling before the production of the artifact. Further, these early practitioners had almost no knowledge of science (Solution Domain Knowledge), since there was no scientific knowledge established according to today's understandings. The production of the artifacts is basically controlled by tradition, which is characterized by myth, legends, rituals and taboos and therefore no adequate reasons for many of the engineering decisions can be given. The available knowledge related with the craft process was stored in the artifact itself and in the minds of the craftsman, which transmitted this to successors during apprenticeship. There was little innovation and the form of a craft product gradually evolved only after a process of trial and error, heavily relying on the previous version of the product. The form of the artifact was only changed to correct errors or to meet new requirements, that is, if it is necessary. To sum up, we can conclude that most of the concepts and functions of the problem-solving part in PSEM were implicit in the approach, that is, there was almost a direct mapping from the need to the artifact. Regarding the control part, the trial-and-error approach of the early engineers can be considered as a simple control action.

Separation of Solution Description from Artifacts

From history, we can derive that the engineering process matured gradually and became necessarily conscious with the changing context. It is hard to pinpoint the exact historical periods but over time, the size and the complexity of the artifacts exceeded the cognitive capacity of a single craftsman and it became very hard if not impos-

sible to produce an artifact by a single person. Moreover, when many craftsmen were involved in the production, communication about the production process and the final artifact became important. A reflection on this process required a fundamental change in engineering problem-solving. This initiated, especially in architecture, the necessity for drafting or designing (Solution Description), whereby the artifact is represented through a drawing before the actual production. Through drafting, engineers could communicate about the production of the artifact, evaluate the artifact before production and use the drafting or design as a guide for production. This enlightened the complexity of the engineering problems substantially. Currently, drafting plays an important role in all engineering disciplines. At this phase of engineering, the concepts of Problem Description and Solution Description became explicit.

Development of Solution Domain Knowledge

Obviously classical engineers were restricted in their accomplishments when scientific knowledge was lacking. Over time, scientific knowledge gradually evolved while forming the basis for the introduction of new engineering disciplines. New advancements in physics and mathematics were made in the 17th century (Solution Domain Knowledge). Newton, for example, generalized the concept of force and formulated the concept of mass forming the basics of mechanical engineering. Evolved from algebra, arithmetic, and geometry, calculus was invented in the 17th century by Newton and Leibniz. Calculus concerns the study of such concepts as the rate of change of one variable quantity with respect to another and the identification of optimal values, which is fundamental for quality control and optimization in engineering. The vastly increased use of scientific principles to the solution of practical problems and the past experimental experiences increasingly resulted in the production of new types of artifacts. The steam engine, developed in 1769, initiated the beginnings of the first Industrial Revolution that implied the transition from an agriculture-based economy to an industrial economy in Britain. In newly developed factories, products were produced in a faster and more efficient way and the production process became increasingly routine and specialized. In the 20th century the knowledge accumulation in various engineering disciplines has grown including disciplines such as biochemistry, quantum theory and relativity theory.

Development of Control Concepts and Automation

Besides of evolution of the concepts of the part Problem-Solving of Figure 1 one can also observe the evolution of the Control concepts. Primarily, mathematical modeling (Mathematical Model) seems to form a principal basis for engineering disciplines and its application can be traced back in various civilizations throughout the history. The development of mathematical modeling supported the control of the alternatives selection. Much later, this has led to automation, which is first applied in manufacture. The next step necessary in the development of automation was mechanization that includes the application of machines that duplicated the motions of the worker. The advantage of automation was directly observable in the increased production efficiency. Machines were built with automatic-control mechanisms that include a feedback control system providing the capacity for self-correction. Further, the advent of the computer has greatly supported the use of feedback control systems in manufacturing processes. In modern industrial societies, computers are used to support various engineering disciplines. Its broad application is in the support for drafting and manufacturing, that is, computer-aided design (CAD) and computer-aided manufacturing (CAM).

Contemporary Perspective of Problem-Solving in Mature Engineering

If we consider contemporary approaches in mature engineering then we can observe the following. First, the need concept in the PSEM plays a basic role and as such has directed the activities of engineering. In mature engineering, an explicit technical problem analysis phase is defined whereby the basic needs are mapped to the technical problems. Although initial client problems are ill-defined (Rittel, 1984) and may include many vague requirements, the mature engineering disciplines focus on a precise formulation of the objectives and a quantification of the quality criteria and the constraints, resulting in a more well-defined problem statement. The criteria and constraints are often expressed in mathematical formulas and equations. The quality concept is thus explicit in the problem description and refers to the variables and units defined by the International Systems of units (SI). From the given specification the engineers can easily calculate the feasibility of the end-product for which different alternatives are defined and, for example, their economical cost may be calculated.

Second, mature problem-solving also includes a rich base of extensive scientific knowledge that is utilized by a solution domain analysis phase (Arrango et al., 1994) to derive the fundamental solution abstractions. From our study it appears that each mature engineering is based on a rich scientific knowledge that has developed over several centuries. The corresponding knowledge has been compiled in several handbooks and manuals that describe numerous formulas that can be applied to solve engineering problems. The handbooks we studied contain a comprehensive coverage in-depth of the various aspects of the corresponding engineering field from contributions of dozens of top experts in the field. Using the handbook, the engineer is guided with hundreds of valuable tables, charts, illustrations, formulas, equations, definitions, and appendices containing extensive conversion tables and usually sections covering mathematics. Obviously, scientific knowledge plays an important role in the degree of maturity of the corresponding engineering.

Third, in mature engineering different alternatives are explicitly searched from the solution domain and often organized with respect to predetermined quality criteria. Hereby, the quality concept plays an explicit role and the alternatives are selected in an explicit alternative space analysis process whereby mathematical optimization techniques such as calculus, linear programming and dynamic programming are adopted. In case no accurate formal expressions or off-the-shelf solutions can be found heuristic rules (Coyne et al., 1990; Cross et al., 1989) are used.

In mature engineering the three processes of technical problem analysis, solution domain analysis and alternative space analysis are integrated within the so-called *synthesis* process (Maimon et al., 1996; Tekinerdogan et al., 2006). In the synthesis process, the explicit problem analysis phase is followed by the search for alternatives in a solution domain that are selected based on explicit quality criteria.

In the synthesis process each alternative is analyzed through generally representing it by means of mathematical modeling. A mathematical model is an abstract description of the artifact using mathematical expressions of relevant natural laws. One mathematical model may represent many alternatives. In addition different mathematical models may be needed to represent various aspects of the same alternative. To select among the various alternatives and/or to optimize the same alternative Quality Criteria are used in the evaluation process that can be applied by means of heuristic rules and/or optimization techniques. Once the 'best' alternative has been chosen it will be further detailed (Detailed Solution Description) and finally implemented.

Summary

Reflecting on the history of mature engineering disciplines, we can conclude that the separate concepts of PSEM have evolved gradually. Traditional engineering disciplines such as electrical engineering, chemical engineering and mechanical engineering can be considered mature because the maturity of each concept in the PSEM.

Figure 2 shows the historical snapshots from the evolution of problem-solving in PSEM. In section 3.1, we have seen that problem-solving at the early phases of the corresponding engineering disciplines was rather simple and consisted of almost directly mapping needs to artifacts. In Figure 2, this is represented as time Ta. Later on, the concepts of Problem Description and Solution Description evolved (time Tb), followed by the evolutions of Solution Domain Knowledge and Alternatives (Tc), and finally the control concepts (Td) leading to PSEM as presented in Figure 1. Figure 2 is an example showing several snapshots. In essence, for every engineering discipline we could define the maturity degrees of the problem-solving concepts throughout the history.

HISTORICAL PERSPECTIVE OF PROBLEM-SOLVING IN SOFTWARE ENGINEERING

We will now describe the historical development of problem-solving in software engineering. Although, the history of software engineering is relatively short and ranges only about a few decades, this study will illustrate the ongoing evolution of its concepts in PSEM and identify its current maturity level with respect to mature engineering disciplines.

Directly Mapping Needs to Programs

Looking back at the history we can assume that software development started with the introduction

Figure 2. Historical snapshots of the evolution of engineering problem-solving

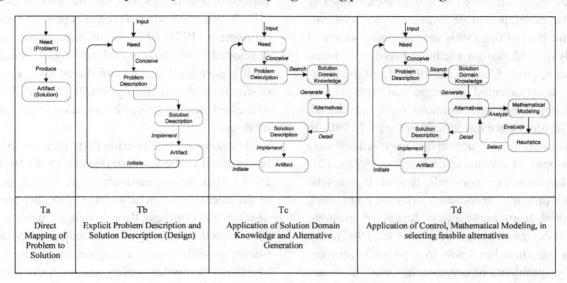

Ta	Tb	Tc	Td
Direct Mapping of Problem to Solution	Explicit Problem Description and Solution Description (Design)	Application of Solution Domain Knowledge and Alternative Generation	Application of Control, Mathematical Modeling, in selecting feasbile alternatives

of the first generation computers in the 1940s such as the Z3 computer (1941), the Colossus computer (1943) and the Mark I (1945) computer (Bergin et al., 1996). The first programs were expressed in machine code and because each computer had its own specific set of machine language operations, the computer was difficult to program and limited in versatility and speed and size (Need). This problem was solved by assembly languages. Although there was a fundamental improvement over the previous situation, programming was still difficult. The first FORTRAN compiler released by IBM in 1957 (Bergin et al., 1996) set up the basic architecture of the compiler. The ALGOL compiler (1958) provided new concepts that remain today in procedural systems: symbol tables, stack evaluation and garbage collection (Solution Domain Knowledge). With the advent of the transistor (1948) and later on the IC (1958) and semiconductor technology the huge size, the energy-consumption as well as the price of the computers relative to computing power shrank tremendously (Context). The introduction of high-level programming languages made the computer more interesting for cost effective and productive business use. When the need for data

processing applications in business was initiated (Need), COBOL (Common Business Oriented Language) was developed in 1960. In parallel with the growing range of complex problems the demand for manipulation of more kinds of data increased (Need). Later on the concept of abstract data types and object-oriented programming were introduced (Solution Domain Knowledge) and included in various programming languages such as Simula, Smalltalk, C++, Java and C#.

It appears that in the early years of computer science the basic needs did not change in variety and were directly mapped to programs. We can state that there was practically no design, no explicit solution domain knowledge and alternative analysis. In fact, this is similar to the early phases of mature engineering disciplines.

Separation of Solution Descriptions from Programs

The available programming languages that adopted algorithmic abstraction and decomposition have supported the introduction of many structured design methods (DeMarco, 1978; Jackson, 1975; Yourdon, 1979) during the 1970s, including different design notations to cope with the complexity of the development of large software systems. At the start of the 1990s several object-oriented analysis and design methods were introduced (Booch, 1991; Coad et al., 1991) to fit the existing object-oriented language abstractions and new object-oriented notations were introduced. CASE tools were introduced in the mid 1980s to provide automated support for structured software development methods (Chikofsky, 1998). This had been made economically feasible through the development of graphically oriented computers. Inspired from architecture design (Alexander, 1977) design patterns (Gamma et al., 1995) have been introduced as a way to cope with recurring design problems in a systematic way. Software architectures (Shaw et al., 1996) have been introduced to approach software development from the overall system structure. The need for systematic industrialization (Need) of software development has led to component-based software development (Solution Description) that aims to produce software from pre-built components (Szyperski, 1998). With the increasing heterogeneity of software applications and the need for interoperability, standardization became an important topic. This has resulted in several industrial standards like CORBA, COM/OLE and SOM/OpenDoc. The Unified Modeling Language (UML) (Rumbaugh et al., 1998) has been introduced for standardization of object-oriented design models.

Development of Computer Science Knowledge

The software engineering community has observed an emerging development of the solution domain knowledge (Solution Domain Knowledge). Simultaneously with the developments of programming languages, a theoretical basis for these was developed by Noam Chomsky (1965) and others in the form of generative grammar models (Solution Domain Knowledge). Knuth presented a comprehensive overview of a wide

variety of algorithms and the analysis of them (1967). Wirth introduced the concept of stepwise refinement (1971) of program construction and developed the teaching procedural language Pascal for this purpose. Dijkstra introduced the concept of structured programming (1969). Parnas (1972) addressed the concepts of information hiding and modules.

The software engineering body of knowledge has evolved in the last four decades (SWEBOK, 2004). This seems relatively short with respect to the scientific knowledge base of mature engineering. Nevertheless, there is now an increasing consensus that the body of knowledge is large and mature enough to support engineering activities. The IEEE Computer Society and the Association for Computing Machinery (ACM) have set up a joint project in which the so-called Software Engineering Body of Knowledge is developed (Bourque et al., 1999; SWEBOK, 2004) to characterize and organize the contents of the software engineering discipline.

Development of Control Concepts and Automation

The Control concepts have evolved in software engineering as well. Over the decades more and better case tools have been developed supporting software development activities ranging from architecture design to testing and software project management.

Mathematical modeling (Mathematical Model) and/or algebraic modeling is more and more integrated in software design. Empirical software engineering aims to devise experiments on software, in collecting data from the experiments, and in devising laws and theories from this data (Juristo et al., 2001). To analyze software systems, metrics are being developed and tested (Fenton et al., 1997).

Process improvement approaches such as, for example, the Capability Maturity Model Integration (CMMI) is proposed and applied (Boehm et al., 2003). In parallel to these plan-based approaches agile software development has been advocated as an appropriate lightweight approach for high-speed and volatile software development (Boehm et al., 2003).

Currently the so-called model-driven software development (MDSD) aims to support the automation of software development (Stahl et al., 2006). Unlike conventional software development, models in MDSD do not constitute mere documentation but are considered executable similar to code. MDE aims to utilize domain-specific languages to create models that express application structure and behavior in a more efficient way. The models are then (semi)automatically transformed into executable code by model transformations.

The above developments are basically related to the enhancement of control in software engineering. Although this has not yet completed we can state that it follows similar path as in mature engineering.

Contemporary Perspective of Problem-Solving in Software Engineering

We have analyzed a selected set of textbooks on software engineering (Ghezzi et al., 2002; Pressman, 2004; Sommerville, 2007). In software engineering, the phase for conceiving the needs is referred to as requirements analysis, which usually is started through an initial requirement specification of the client. In mature engineering we have seen that the quality concept is already explicit in the problem description through the quantified objectives of the client. In software engineering this is quite different. In contrast to mature engineering disciplines, however, constraints and the requirements are usually not expressed in quantified terms. Rather the quality concern is mostly implicit in the problem statement and includes terms such as 'the system must be adaptable' or 'system must perform well' without having any means to specify the required degree of adaptability and/

or the performance. Of course, the importance of requirements engineering has seriously changed over the last decade. There is an IEEE conference on Requirements Engineering, which has been running successfully since 1993, a Requirements Engineering journal, several serious textbooks on requirements engineering and a lot of research, which deals with both formalizing and measuring functional and non-functional requirements. Although we can observe substantial progress in this community it is generally acknowledged that the aimed state of mature engineering is unfortunately not reached yet.

A similar development can be observed for the organization and the use of knowledge for software engineering. The field of software engineering is only about 50 to 60 years old and obviously is not as mature as in the traditional engineering disciplines. The basic scientific knowledge, on which software engineering relies, is mainly computer science that has developed over the last decades. Progress is largely made in isolated parts, such as algorithms and abstract data types (Shaw, 1990; Shaw et al., 1996).

One of the interesting developments is the increasing size of pattern knowledge. The goal of patterns is to create a body of literature, similar to the mature engineering disciplines, to help software developers resolve common difficult problems encountered throughout all of software engineering and development. Several books have been written including many useful patterns to support to design and implementation. Nevertheless, if we relate the quantity of knowledge to the supporting knowledge of mature engineering disciplines, the available knowledge in software engineering is still quite meager. The available handbooks of software engineering (Ghezzi et al., 2002; Pressman, 2004; Sommerville, 2007) are still not comparable to the standard handbooks of mature engineering disciplines. Moreover, on many fundamental concepts in software engineering consensus among experts has still not been reached yet and research is ongoing.

In other engineering disciplines at phases when knowledge was lacking we observe that the basic attitude towards solving a problem was based on common sense, ingenuity and trial-and-error. In software engineering it turns out that this was not much different and the general idea was that requirements have to be specified using some representation and this should be refined along the software development process until the final software is delivered.

Regarding alternative space analysis we can state that the concept of Alternative(s), is not explicit in software engineering. The selection and evaluation of design alternatives in mature engineering disciplines is based on quantitative analysis through optimization theory of mathematics. This is not common practice in software engineering. No single method we have studied applies mathematical optimization techniques to generate and evaluate alternative solutions. Currently, the notion of quality in software engineering has more an informal basis. There is however, a broad agreement that quality should be taken into account when deriving solutions. As in other engineering disciplines, in software engineering the quality concept is closely related to measurement, which is concerned with capturing information about attributes of entities (Fenton et al., 1997).

DISCUSSION

Since the introduction of the term software engineering in 1968 the NATO Software Engineering Conference, there has been many debates on the question whether software development is an engineering discipline or not. We can identify different opinions in this perspective. Some authors view software engineering as a branch of traditional engineering often believe that concepts from traditional engineering need to apply to software development. For example, Parnas (1998) argued that software engineering is a "an element of the set, {Civil Engineering, Mechanical Engineer-ing, Chemical Engineering, Electrical Engineer-ing,....}." Others argue that software engineering is not an engineering discipline, but that it should be (McConnell, 2003). Again others claim that software is fundamentally different from other engineering artifacts and as such can and should not be considered as an engineering discipline.

Based on our historical analysis we argue that currently software engineering shows the characteristics of an engineering discipline, but has not evolved yet to the maturity level of the traditional engineering disciplines. If we would characterize the current state of software engineering based on Figure 2, then it would be somewhere between T_b and T_c. Obviously it is not possible to define the exact characterization in terms of crisp values simply because each concept in the PSEM might have a maturity degree of progress that cannot be expressed as yes or no. Table 1 presents an analytical overview in which the different properties of both software engineering and mature engineering are shown. The properties (left column) are derived from the PSEM. For each property, we have provided a short explanation derived from our analysis as described in the previous sections. Based on this we can identify the concrete differences of software engineering with mature engineering and are better able to pinpoint what needs more focus to increase the maturity level of software engineering.

In the coming years we expect that each of these concepts will further evolve towards a mature level. This can be observed if we consider the current trends in software development in which the concepts are developing in a relatively high pace. By looking at the concepts in Table 1 we can give several examples in this perspective.

For example, Michael Jackson (2000) provides in his work on so-called problem-frames an explicit notion of problem in requirements engineering. In the aspect-oriented software development community the notion of concern has been introduced and several approaches are proposed to identify, specify and compose concerns (Filman

Table 1. Comparison of mature engineering with software engineering

	Mature Engineering	Software Engineering
Technical Problem Analysis	Explicit problem description specified with quantified metrics. Well-defined problems.	Usually implicitly defined as part of the requirements and usually no quantification of required solution. Ill-defined problems.
Availability of Domain Knowledge	Very extensive solution domain knowledge compiled in different handbooks.	Basically knowledge for isolated domains in computer science. Increasing number of pattern catalogs
Application of Domain Knowledge	Explicit domain analysis process for deriving abstractions from solution domain.	Solution domain analysis not a common practice. In general applied in case reuse is required.
Solution Description	Rich set of notations for different problems.	Various design notations. Still lack of global standards.
Alternative Analysis	Explicit alternative space analysis; optimization techniques for defining the feasible alternatives	Implicit. Almost no systematic support for alternative space analysis.
Quality Measurement	Explicit quality concerns both for development and evaluation.	Quality is usually implicit. No systematic support for measuring quality in common software practices
Application of Heuristics	Explicitly specified in handbooks as a complementary means to mathematical techniques for defining feasible solutions.	Implicit in software development methods.

et al., 2004). In a sense, concerns can be viewed as similar to the notion of technical problem that we have defined in this paper.

The organization and modeling of domain knowledge has been addressed, for example, in SWEBOK (2004) and other work on taxonomies (Glass et al., 1995). In parallel with this we can see the increasing number of publication of different pattern catalogs for various phases of the software life cycle. Also we observe that textbooks on software engineering provide a broader and more in-depth analysis of software engineering and related concepts, which is reflected by the large size of the volumes.

The application of domain knowledge to derive the abstractions for software design is represented in the so-called domain analysis process that was first introduced in the reuse community and software product line engineering (Clements et al., 2002). Currently we see that it is also being gradually integrated in conventional software design methods, which are indicating on the use of domain-driven approaches (Evans, 2004).

Regarding design notations we can state that the software engineering community is facing a continuous evolution of design notations and the related tools (Budgen, 2003).

Alternative analysis is not really explicitly addressed but there are several trends that show directions towards this goal. In software product line engineering variability analysis is an important topic and the process for application engineering is applied to develop different alternative products from a reusable asset base (Clements et al., 2002). The case of quality measurement has been explicitly proposed in the work on software measurement and experimentation (Fenton et al., 1997).

RELATED WORK

Several publications have been written on software engineering and the software crisis. Very often software engineering is considered fundamentally different from traditional engineering and it is claimed that it has particular and inherent complexities that are not present in other traditional engineering disciplines. The common cited causes of the software crisis are the complexity of the problem domain, the changeability of software, the invisibility of software and the fact that software does not wear out like physical artifacts (Booch, 1991; Budgen, 2003; Pressman, 2004). Most of these studies, however, lack to view software engineering from a broader perspective and do not attempt to derive lessons from other mature engineering disciplines.

We have applied the PSEM for describing problem-solving from a historical perspective. Several publications consider the history of computer science providing a useful factual overview of the main events in the history of computer science and software engineering. The paper from, for example, Shapiro (1997) provides a very nice historical overview of the different approaches in software engineering that have been adopted to solve the software crisis. Shapiro maintains that due to the inherently complex problem-solving process and the multifaceted nature of software problems from history it follows that a single approach could not fully satisfy the fundamental needs and a more pluralistic approach is rather required.

Some publications claim in accordance with the fundamental thesis of this paper that lessons of value can be derived from other mature engineering disciplines. Petroski (1992) claims that lessons learned from failures can substantially advance engineering. Baber (1997) compares the history of electrical engineering with the history of software engineering and thereby focuses on the failures in both engineering disciplines. According to Baber software development today is in a pre-mature phase analogous in many respects to the pre-mature phases of the now traditional engineering discipline that had also to cope with numerous failures. Baber states that the fundamental causes of the failures in software development today are the same as the causes of the failures in electrical engineering 100 years ago, that is, lack of scientific mathematical knowledge or the failure to apply whatever such basis may exist. This is in alignment with our conclusions. Shaw (1990) provides similar conclusions. She presents a model for the evolution of an engineering discipline,

which she describes as follows: "Historically, engineering has emerged from ad hoc practice in two stages: First, management and production techniques enable routine production. Later, the problems of routine production stimulate the development of a supporting science; the mature science eventually merges with established practice to yield professional engineering practice". Using her model, she compares civil engineering and chemical engineering and concludes that these engineering disciplines have matured because of the supporting science that has evolved. Shaw distinguishes between craft, commercial and professional engineering processes. These distinct engineering states can be each expressed as a different instantiation of the PSEM. The immature craft engineering process will lack some of the concepts as described by the PSEM. The mature professional engineering process will include all the concepts of the PSEM.

Several authors criticize the lack of well-designed experiments for measurement-based assessment in software engineering (Fenton et al., 1997). They state that currently the evaluation of software engineering practices depend on opinions and speculations rather than on rigorous software-engineering experiments. To compare and improve software practices they argue that there is an urgent need for quantified measurement techniques as it is common in the traditional scientific methods. In the PSEM measurement and evaluation is represented by the control part. As we have described before, mature engineering disciplines have explicit control concepts. The lack of these concepts in software engineering indicates its immature level.

CONCLUSION

Software engineering is in essence a problem-solving process and to understand software engineering it is necessary to understand problem-solving. To grasp the essence of problem-solving we have provided an in-depth analysis of the history of problem-solving in mature engineering and software engineering. This has enabled us to position the software engineering discipline and validate its maturity level. To explicitly reason about the various problem-solving concepts in engineering, in section 2 we have presented the Problem-solving for Engineering Model (PSEM) that uniquely integrates the concepts of problem-solving, control and context. It appears that mature engineering conforms to the PSEM and this maturation process has been justified by a conceptual analysis from a historical perspective.

The PSEM and the analysis have provided the framework and the context for the debates on whether software development should be considered as an engineering discipline or not. From our conceptual analysis we conclude that software engineering is still in a pre-mature engineering state. This is justified by the fact that it lacks several concepts that are necessary for effective problem-solving. More concretely, we have identified the three processes of technical problem analysis, solution domain analysis and alternative space analysis that are not yet complete and fully integrated in software development practices. Nevertheless, despite the differences between software engineering and mature engineering, one of the key issues in this analysis is that software development does follow the same evolution of the problem-solving concepts that can also be observed from the history of mature engineering disciplines. Although it has not yet achieved the state of a professional mature engineering discipline the consciousness on the required concepts is increasing. With respect to the developments in other engineering disciplines, our study shows even a higher pace of the evolution of problem-solving concepts in software engineering and we expect that it will approach mature engineering disciplines in the near future.

REFERENCES

Alexander, C., Ishikawa, S., Silverstein, M., Jacobson, M., Fiksdahl-King, I., & Angel, S. (1977). *A pattern language: Towns, buildings, construction*. New York: Oxford University Press.

Arrango, G. (1994). Domain analysis methods. In Schäfer, R., Prieto-Díaz, R., & Matsumoto, M. (Eds.), *Software reusability*. Ellis Horwood.

Baber, R.L. (1997). Comparison of electrical engineering of Heaviside's times and software engineering of our times. *IEEE Annals of the History of Computing archive, 19*(4), 5-17.

Bergin, T. J., & Gibson, R. G. (Eds.). (1996). *History of programming languages*. Addison-Wesley.

Biegler, L. T., Grossmann, I. E., & Westerberg, A. W. (1997). *Systematic methods of chemical process design*. Prentice Hall.

Boehm, B., & Turner, R. (2003). *Balancing agility and discipline*. Addison-Wesley.

Booch, G. (1991). *Object-oriented analysis and design, with applications*. Redwood City, CA: The Benjamin/Cummins Publishing Company.

Bourque, P., Dupuis, R., & Abran, A. (1999). The guide to the software engineering body of knowledge. *IEEE Software, 16*(6), 35–44. doi:10.1109/52.805471

Braha, D., & Maimon, O. (1997). The design process: Properties, paradigms, and structure. *IEEE Transactions on Systems, Man, and Cybernetics, 27*(2).

Brooks, F. (1975). *The mythical man-month*. Reading, MA: Addison-Wesley.

Budgen, D. (2003). *Software design* (2nd ed.). Addison-Wesley.

Chen, W. F. (1998). *The civil engineering handbook*. CRC Press.

Chikofsky, E. J. (1989). *Computer-Aided Software Engineering (CASE)*. Washington, D.C.: IEEE Computer Society.

Chomsky, N. (1965). *Aspects of the theory of syntax*. MIT Press.

Clements, P., & Northrop, L. (2002). *Software product lines: Practices and patterns*. Addison-Wesley.

Coad, P., & Yourdon, E. (1991). *Object-oriented design*. Yourdon Press.

Colburn, T. R. (2000). Philosophy of computer science, part 3. In *Philosophy and Computer Science* (pp. 127–210). Armonk, USA: M.E. Sharpe.

Coyne, R. D., Rosenman, M. A., Radford, A. D., Balachandran, M., & Gero, J. S. (1990). *Knowledge-based design systems*. Addison-Wesley.

Cross, N. (1989). *Engineering design methods*. Wiley & Sons.

Deek, F. P., Turoff, M., & McHugh, J. A. (1999). A common model for problem solving and program development. *IEEE Transactions on Education, 4*, 331–336. doi:10.1109/13.804541

DeMarco, T. (1978). *Structured analysis and system specification*. Yourdon Inc.

Diaper, D. (Ed.). (1989). *Knowledge elicitation*. Chichester, UK: Ellis Horwood.

Dijkstra, E. W. (1969). *Structured programming, software engineering techniques*. Brussels: NATO Science Committee.

Dorf, R. C. (1997). *The electrical engineering handbook*. New York: Springer Verlag.

Dunsheath, P. (1997). *A history of electrical engineering*. London: Faber & Faber.

Ertas, A., & Jones, J. C. (1996). *The engineering design process*. Wiley.

Evans, E. (2004). *Domain-driven design: Tackling complexity in the heart of software*. Addison-Wesley.

Fenton, N. E., & Phleeger, S. L. (1997). *Software metrics: A rigorous & practical approach*. PWS Publishing Company.

Filman, R.E. Elrad, T., Clark, S. & Aksit, M. (2004). *Aspect-oriented software development*. Pearson Eduction.

Gamma, E., Helm, R., Johnson, R., & Vlissides, J. (1995). *Design patterns: Elements of reusable object-oriented software*. Reading, MA: Addison-Wesley.

Ghezzi, C., Jazayeri, M., & Mandrioli, D. (2002). *Fundamentals of software engineering*. Prentice-Hall.

Glass, R. L., & Vessey, I. (1995). Contemporary application domain taxonomies. *IEEE Software, 12*(4), 63–76. doi:10.1109/52.391837

Jackson, M. (1975). *Principles of program design*. Academic Press. Jackson, M. (2000). *Problem frames: Analyzing and structuring software development problems*. Addison-Wesley.

Jacobson, I., Booch, G., & Rumbaugh, J. (1999). *The unified software development process*. Addison-Wesley.

Jones, J. C. (1992). *Design methods: Seeds of human futures*. London: Wiley International.

Juristo, N., & Moreno, A. M. (2001). *Basics of software engineering experimentation*. Kluwer Academic Publishers.

Knuth, D. (1967). *The art of computer programming*. Addison-Wesley.

Knuth, D. (1974). Computer programming as an art. *Communications of the ACM, 17*(12), 667-673. Transcript of the 1974 Turing Award lecture.

Maimon, O., & Braha, D. (1996). On the complexity of the design synthesis problem. *IEEE Transactions on Systems, Man, and Cybernetics, 26*(1).

Marks, L. S. (1987). *Marks' standard handbook for mechanical engineers.* McGraw-Hill.

McConnell, S. (2003). *Professional software development: Shorter schedules, better projects, superior products, enhanced careers.* Boston: Addison-Wesley.

Newell, N., & Simon, H. A. (1976). *Human problem solving.* Englewood Cliffs, NJ: Prentice-Hall.

Parnas, D. L. (1972). On the criteria to be used in decomposing systems into modules. *Communications of the ACM, 15*(12). doi:10.1145/361598.361623

Parnas, D. L. (1998). Software engineering programmes are not computer science programmes. *Annals of Software Engineering*, 19–37. doi:10.1023/A:1018949113292

Perry, R. (1984). *Perry's chemical engineer's handbook.* New York: McGraw-Hill.

Petroski, H. (1992). *To engineer is human: The role of failure in successful design.* New York: Vintage Books.

Popper, K. (2001). *All life is problem solving.* Routledge.

Pressman, R. S. (2008). *Software engineering: A practitioner's approach.* McGraw-Hill.

Rapaport, B. (2006). *Philosophy of computer science: What I think it is, what I teach, & how I teach it. Herbert A. Simon Keynote Address.* NA-CAP Video.

Rittel, H. W., & Webber, M. M. (1984). Planning problems are wicked problems. *Policy Sciences, 4*, 155–169. doi:10.1007/BF01405730

Rubinstein, M. F., & Pfeiffer, K. (1980). *Concepts in problem solving.* Englewood Cliffs, NJ: Prentice-Hall.

Rumbaugh, J., Jacobson, I., & Booch, G. (1998). *The unified modeling language reference manual.* Addision-Wesley.

Shapiro, S. (1997). Splitting the difference: The historical necessity of synthesis in software engineering. *IEEE Annals of the History of Computing, 19*(1), 20–54. doi:10.1109/85.560729

Shaw, M. (1990). Prospects for an engineering discipline of software. *IEEE Software*, 15–24. doi:10.1109/52.60586

Shaw, M., & Garlan, D. (1996). *Software architecture: Perspectives on an emerging discipline.* Prentice Hall.

Smith, A. A., Hinton, E., & Lewis, R. W. (1983). *Civil engineering systems analysis and design.* Wiley & Sons.

Smith, G. F., & Browne, G. J. (1993). Conceptual foundations of design problem solving. *IEEE Transactions on Systems, Man, and Cybernetics, 23*(5). doi:10.1109/21.260655

Sommerville, I. (2007). *Software engineering.* Addison-Wesley.

Stahl, T., & Völter, M. (2006). *Model-driven software development.* Wiley.

SWEBOK. (2004). *Guide to the software engineering body of knowledge.*

Szyperski, C. (1998). *Component software: Beyond object-oriented programming.* Addison-Wesley.

Tekinerdoğan, B., & Akşit, M. (2006). Introducing the concept of synthesis in the software architecture design process. *Journal of Integrated Design and Process Science, 10*(1), 45–56.

Upton, N. (1975). *An illustrated history of civil engineering*. London: Heinemann.

von Foerster, F. (1979). Cybernetics of cybernetics. In Krippendorff, K. (Ed.), *Communication and control in society*. New York: Gordon and Breach.

Wilcox, A. D., Huelsman, L. P., Marshall, S. V., Philips, C. L., Rashid, M. H., & Roden, M. S. (1990). *Engineering design for electrical engineers*. Prentice-Hall.

Williams, M. R. (1997). *A history of computing technology*. IEEE Computer Society.

Wirth, N. (1971). Program development by step-wise refinement. *Communications of the ACM, 14*(4), 221–227. doi:10.1145/362575.362577

Yourdon, E., & Constantine, L. L. (1979). *Structured design*. Prentice-Hall.

Chapter 2
Is Lean Agile and Agile Lean?
A Comparison between Two Software Development Paradigms

Kai Petersen
Blekinge Institute of Technology, Sweden & Ericsson AB, Sweden

ABSTRACT

Lean and agile development are two development paradigms that were proposed to help dealing with highly dynamic markets and the resulting rapid changes in customer needs. As both paradigms address a similar problem, it is interesting to compare them and by that, determine what both paradigms can learn from each other. This chapter compares the paradigms with regard to goals, principles, practices, and processes. The outcome of the comparison is: (1) both paradigms share the same goals; (2) the paradigms define similar principles, with one principle ("see the whole") being unique to lean; (3) both paradigms have unique as well as shared principles; (4) lean does not define processes, while agile has proposed different ones such eXtreme programming and SCRUM.

INTRODUCTION

The nature of software development has changed in recent years. Today, software is included in a vast amount of products, such as cars, mobile phones, entertainment and so forth. The markets for these products are characterized as highly dynamic and with frequent changes in the needs of the customers. As a consequence, companies have to respond rapidly to changes in needs requiring them to be very flexible.

Due to this development, agile methods have emerged. In essence agile methods are light-weight in nature, work with short feedback and development cycles, and involve the customer tightly in the software development process. The main principles that guided the development of different agile practices such as eXtreme programming (Beck 2000) and SCRUM (Schwaber 2004) are summarized in the agile manifesto (AgileManifesto). As shown in a systematic review by (Dybå and Dingsøyr 2008) agile has received much attention from the research community.

DOI: 10.4018/978-1-60960-215-4.ch002

While agile became more and more popular lean software development has emerged with the publication of the book (Poppendieck and Poppendieck 2003), which proposes ways of how practices from lean manufacturing could be applied in the software engineering context. Lean has a very strong focus on removing waste from the development process, i.e. everything that does not contribute to the customer value. Furthermore, according to lean the development process should only be looked at from an end-to-end perspective to avoid sub-optimization. The aim is to have similar success with lean in software development as was the case in manufacturing. That is, delivering what the customer really needs in a very short time.

Both development paradigms (agile and lean) seem similar in their goal of focusing on the customers and responding to their needs in a rapid manner. Though, it is not well understood what distinguishes both paradigms from each other. In order to make the best use of both paradigms it is important to understand differences and similarities for two main reasons:

- Research results from principles, practices, and processes shared by both paradigms are beneficial to understand the usefulness of both paradigms. This aids in generalizing and aggregating research results to determine the benefits and limitations of lean as well as agile at the same time.
- The understanding of the differences shows opportunities of how both paradigms can complement each other. For instance, if one principle of lean is not applied in agile it might be a valuable addition.

The comparison is based on the general descriptions of the paradigms. In particular, this chapter makes the following contributions:

- Aggregation of lean and agile principles and an explicit mapping of principles to practices.
- A comparison showing the overlap and differences between principles regarding different aspects of the paradigms.
- A linkage of the practices to the principles of each paradigm, as well as an investigation whether the practices are considered part of either lean or agile, or both of the paradigms.

The remainder of the chapter is structured as follows: Section 2 presents background on lean and agile software development. Section 3 compares the paradigms with respect to goals, principles, practices, and processes. Section 4 discusses the findings focusing on the implications on industry and academia. Section 5 concludes the chapter.

BACKGROUND

Plan-driven software development is focused on heavy documentation and the sequential execution of software development activities. The best known plan-driven development model is the waterfall model introduced by Royce in the 1970s (Royce 1970). His intention was to provide some structure for software development activities. As markets became more dynamic companies needed to be able to react to changes quickly. However, the waterfall model was built upon the assumption that requirements are relatively stable. For example, the long lead-times in waterfall projects lead to a high amount of requirements being discarded as the requirements became obsolete due to changes in the needs of the customers. Another problem is the reduction of test coverage due to big-bang integration and late testing. Testing often has to be compromised as delays in earlier phases (e.g. implementation and design) lead to less time for testing in the end of the project.

In response to the issues related to plan-driven approaches agile software development emerged in the late 1990s and early 2000s. Agile software development is different from plan-driven development in many ways. For example, a plan-driven project contains detailed planning of the time-line with clearly defined products and documentation to be delivered while agile focuses on a high-level plan for the overall product development life-cycle with detailed plans only for the current iterations. Another difference is the way requirements are specified. That is, in plan-driven development there is a clearly defined specification phase where the complete requirements specification is created, the specification representing the contract. Hence, a change in requirements is a formal and work intensive process. On the other hand, agile welcomes changing requirements leading to continuous evolution. Consequently, change requests are handled through a more relaxed change request process. With regard to other activities (such as programming and testing) waterfall development concentrated these activities on one specific phase of development, while in agile development the activities are conducted throughout the overall development life-cycle (Hirsch 2005). The most prominent descriptions of agile software development process are eXtreme Programming (XP) (Beck 2000) and SCRUM (Schwaber 2004). Each of these processes contains a high-level description of the work-flow and a set of agile software development practices. A mapping of the practices and a description of the work-flows of different agile processes (including eXtreme Programming and SCRUM) can be found in (Koch 2005) and (Larman 2004).

Lean software development is inspired by ideas that have been used in the context of manufacturing and product development. Lean manufacturing led to tremendous performance improvement in the context of manufacturing cars at Toyota, the approach being referred to as the Toyota Production System. The lean manufacturing approach allowed delivering high quality products with fewer resources and in shorter time. The improvements were achieved by continuously improving processes through a systematic analysis focusing on waste identification; waste being everything that does not contribute to customer value. The ideas of lean manufacturing were put forward in the book The Machine that Changed the World (cf. (Womack 2007)). In lean manufacturing the main focus was on optimizing the shop floor. Car manufacturers today have implemented the lean principles in their shop floors, i.e. the use of lean manufacturing does not lead to a competitive advantage anymore. Hence, to achieve further improvements the ideas behind lean have been extended to the overall product development life-cycle and the whole research & development organization. This includes the disciplines purchasing, sales and marketing, product planning, people management, and so forth. This view is more relevant for software development than the pure manufacturing view as in software engineering the overall development cycle should be in focus when improving software processes. The extensions to incorporate the whole of product development are known as the Toyota Product Development System (cf. (Morgan and Liker 2006)). The Poppendiecks translated the lean principles and practices known from manufacturing and product development to software engineering. Mary Poppendick stated that they were motivated to translate the practices when she heard about the waterfall model of software development, believing that software development would largely benefit from lean principles and practices, which helped product development in creating a flexible organization. The references from Mary and Tom Poppendieck (cf. (Poppendieck and Poppendieck 2003)(Poppendieck and Poppendieck 2007)(Poppendieck and Poppendieck 2009)) are the main sources of how to interpret lean practices in the context of developing software. Hence, their books are used as the main sources for the identification of goals, principles, practices, and processes of lean software development. In comparison to agile, there are very few studies with an explicit focus on lean software development. The lack of empirical evidence for lean software development means that the comparison is focused on the generic descriptions provided in books.

In the following section the goals, principles, practices, and processes of the development paradigms are described and compared.

COMPARISON

The comparison focuses on different facets of the paradigms, namely goals, principles, practices, and processes.

- Goals state what should be achieved by the paradigm. Hence, they present the rationale for why the principles, practices, and processes should be applied. In other words, goals represent the "why".
- Principles are rules that should be followed while using the paradigms. A rule of agile, for example, says that one should achieve technical excellence. Rules represent the "What".
- Practices are the implementation of the principles. For example, in order to implement technical excellence eXtreme programming uses pair programming to reduce the number of faults introduced into the code due to the continuous peer review process. Practices represent the "How".
- Processes describe the workflow and artifacts produced. That means the process is a representation of "when" an activity is done, and in which order (Subsection 2.4).

Each of the subsections of the comparison follows a similar pattern. First, the goals/principles/practices are introduced and thereafter the comparison is made.

Goals

Description of Goals

Goals describe why we should care about agile and lean; they provide a rational for software companies to adapt the paradigms. The following goals are identified for agile and lean:

- **Goal agile:** Agile (in comparison to traditional approaches such as plan-driven development) has the goal of delivering working software continuously that can be demonstrated to the customers to illustrate the latest status checking whether the software fulfills the customers' needs. Thus, the customers can provide feedback early and by that make sure that a product fulfills the needs of the customers. The goal becomes clear from the statement that working software is the primary measure of progress that should be delivered on regular bases in short cycles (AgileManifesto) (Beck 2000)(Larman 2004)(Koch 2005).
- **Goal lean:** The goal of lean software development focuses on creating value for the customer rapidly and not spending time on activities that do not create value (Poppendieck and Poppendieck 2003). Value in this case has to be seen through the glasses of the customer (Morgan and Liker 2006). If there is an activity that is not of value for the customer then it is considered waste.

Comparison

Both goals have the focus on the customer in common. In the case of agile the customers are in focus as they should regularly receive working software. Lean adds the notion of value which was not as explicitly expressed in agile as it was in lean (see Table 1). Value has many different meanings and is a whole research field on its own,

Table 1. A comparison of goals for lean and agile

Aspect	Lean	Agile
Customer	Create *value* for the customer and thus only focus on value-adding activities	Have a working product that fulfills the customers' *needs*
Development Speed	Rapid value creation and short cycle times	Continuous delivery of working software

referred to as value-based software engineering (Biffl et al. 2005). One example of a definition of value in the lean context is that one should focus on everything that delights the customer, which is not necessarily what the customer wants or asks for (Poppendieck and Poppendieck 2003) (Morgan and Liker 2006). In the agile context, the needs of the customer are in the center, i.e. what the customer wants and requires. This is not in conflict with value, however, the notion of value puts more emphasis on exciting and delighting the customers and surprising them positively, which goes beyond satisfying the customers' needs.

Both development paradigms also share the goal of having frequent and rapid deliveries to the customer (see row Development Speed in Table 1). They are very similar in the sense that new and changed features should be made usable for the customer as fast as possible. This is a lesson learned from waterfall-oriented projects where all requirements are elicited, developed, tested, and finally delivering together based on a well defined plan. Waterfall development leads to a number of issues which were the reasons for the movement towards agile. The main issues are: (1) planned and validated requirements become obsolete as waterfall is inflexible in responding to changes; (2) reduction of test coverage due to limited and late testing; (3) the amount of faults increases with late testing; and (4) faults found late are hard and expensive to fix (Petersen et al. 2009b). In contrast, delivering fewer requirements/features more frequently avoids that requirements become obsolete, and allows for much earlier feedback from testing and customers (Andersen and Fagerhaug 2000).

The goals that we identified drive the principles by which lean and agile work. The principles of both development paradigms are analyzed in the following section.

Principles

Description of Principles

The principles constitute the rules that, according to the general descriptions of the methods, should be followed to achieve the goals (see Section 2.1). The principles for agile and lean are explicitly defined for both paradigms. The agile manifesto states four values and twelve related principles of agile development. In the lean context seven principles have been defined. For each principle we assigned a unique ID which eases the mapping and comparison between lean and agile, and also to make it easier to connect the principles to the practices implementing them. The following four values are presented in the agile manifesto (AgileManifesto):

- **V1:** Individuals and interactions over processes and tools.
- **V2:** Working software over comprehensive documentation.
- **V3:** Customer collaboration over contract negotiation.
- **V4:** Responding to change over following a plan.

The agile manifesto states that the statements on the left have a higher value than the ones on the right. For example, agile does not say that there is no value in processes. However, as (Koch 2005) points out processes can be harmful if they are misused and hinder people in working together, drain people's enthusiasm and excitement, and require more investment in maintaining them than they help in working more effectively and efficiently. The 12 principles are based on the values and can be related to them. For each of the principles (AP01 to AP12) we state to which value the principle relates (cf. (AgileManifesto)).

- **AP01—Customer satisfaction**: The satisfaction of the customer should have the highest priority. To achieve this, software needs to be delivered early and continuously (i.e. software fulfilling the customer needs as stated in the goals). (V3)
- **AP02—Welcome change:** Changes should be welcomed by software developers, no matter if they come in early or late. The ability to react to late changes is seen as a competitive advantage. (V4)
- **AP03—Frequent deliveries:** Working software should be delivered frequently to the customer. Deliveries should happen within a couple of months or weeks. The manifesto stresses that preference should be given to the shorter time-scale. (V2)
- **AP04—Work together:** Developers (i.e. technicians) and business people (i.e. product managers, administration, management, etc.) are required to work together on a daily basis throughout projects. (V2)
- **AP05—Motivated individuals:** Motivated individuals are a prerequisite for successful projects and hence projects should be built around them. Building projects around them means to provide them with environments (e.g. tools and workspace) and to support them (e.g. project managers could help in avoiding unnecessary project disturbances). Furthermore, the project teams should be trusted to be

successful in achieving the project goals. (V1)
- **AP06—Face-to-face conversation:** Face-to-face communication is seen as the most efficient way of exchanging information (e.g. in comparison to e-mail and telephone conversation). This is true within a development team, but also between teams and other relevant stakeholders of the project. (V1)
- **AP07—Working software:** The progress of software development should be measured through working software. Hence, working software is more important than detailed documentation, as was expressed in the second value of agile software development (V2).
- **AP08—Sustainable pace:** Everyone involved in the project (developers, software users, sponsors, managers, etc.) should be able to work indefinitely in a continuous pace. A process supporting the achievement of sustainable pace is referred to as sustainable development. (V1)
- **AP09—Technical excellence:** Agile requires discipline in focusing on technical excellence and good design. Having a high quality product and a good design allows for easy maintenance and change, making a project more agile. (V2)
- **AP10—Simplicity:** The agile manifesto defines simplicity as *"the art of maximizing the amount of work not done – and is essential"*. (V4)
- **AP11—Self-organizing teams:** Teams organizing themselves (e.g. picking their own tasks, and taking responsibility for completing the tasks) leads to the best requirements, architectures, and designs. (V1)
- **AP12—Continuous reflection:** Teams should reflect on their work continuously and think about how to become more efficient. Improvements should be imple-

mented according to the discoveries made during the reflection. (V4)

Lean is based on seven principles, which are explained in more detail as they are not as self-contained as the ones presented for the agile manifesto.

- **LP01—Eliminate waste:** Waste in lean is everything that does not contribute to the value for the customer, i.e. everything that does not help to fulfill the needs of the customer or does delight the customer. Seven types of waste were identified in manufacturing and mapped to software development (see Table 2). The left column of the table describes the wastes in manufacturing and the right column the corresponding wastes in software engineering (cf. (Poppendieck and Poppendieck 2003)). Each waste related to software development has an ID which is used to reference the wastes in the text. The wastes slow down the development flow and thus should be removed to speed up value creation.
- **LP02—Amplify learning:** Software development is a knowledge-intensive process where learning happens during the whole development lifecycle and needs to be amplified. Learning includes getting a better understanding of the customer needs, potential solutions for architecture, good testing strategies, and so forth. Thus, the processes and practices employed in a company should support learning.
- **LP03—Defer commitment:** A commitment should be delayed as far as possible for irreversible decisions. For example, a tough architectural decision might require some experimentation and therefore should not be committed early. Instead, the option for change should be open for as long as possible. (Poppendieck and Poppendieck 2003) point out that not all decisions are ir-

reversible and thus do not have to be made late as they can be changed.

- **LP04—Deliver as fast as possible:** Lean has a strong focus on short cycle times, i.e. to minimize the time from receiving a request for a feature to the delivery of the feature. The reason for the strong focus on cycle time is that while a feature is under development it does not create value for the customer.
- **LP05—Respect people:** (Poppendieck and Poppendieck 2003) provide three principles that were used in the context of the Toyota Product Development System fostering the respect for people: (1) *Entrepreneurial leadership:* People that are led by managers who trust and respect them are more likely to become good leaders themselves. This helps in creating a management culture facilitating committed and independent people in an organization. (2) *Expert technical workforce:* Successful companies help building expertise and managers in these companies make sure that the necessary expertise for achieving a task is within the teams. (3) *Responsibility-based planning and control:* Management should trust their teams and not tell them how to get the job done. Furthermore, it is important to provide the teams with reasonable and realistic goals.
- **LP06—Build quality in:** Quality of the software product should be built in as early as possible, and not late in development by fixing the defects that testing discovered. In result the integrity of the software in development should be high at any point in time during the development lifecycle. As (Poppendieck and Poppendieck 2003) point out, a prerequisite for achieving integrity is very high discipline. For example, if a defect is discovered early in the development process the ongoing work must be stopped and the defect fixed.

Table 2. Wastes in lean software engineering and their mapping to manufacturing (cf. (Poppendieck and Poppendieck 2003))

Manufacturing	Software Engineering
Inventory: Intermediate work-products and work in process	**W1—Partially Done Work:** Work-in-process that does not have value until it is completed (e.g. code written, but not tested)
Over-Production: The number of produced items is higher than the number of demanded items (inventory in this case is "dead capital"	**W2—Extra Features:** Functionality that has been developed, but does not provide value to the customer
Extra Processing: Extra work is created in the production due to e.g. poor set-up of machines	**W3—Extra processes:** Process steps (e.g. creation of documentation that is not really needed) that can be removed
Transportation: Transport of intermediate work-products (e.g. due to a poor layout of the production line)	**W4—Handovers:** Many handovers (e.g. documentation) create overhead
Motion: People and machines are moved around instead of being used to create value.	**W5—Motion/Task Switching:** People have to move to identify knowledge (e.g. team members that work together are not co-located) or have many disturbances in their work
Waiting: A machine with free capacity is waiting for input	**W6—Delays:** There are delays in development that, for example, cause waiting times within a development team (team idles)
Defects: Fixing of problems in the products	**W7—Defects:** Fixing of problems in the products

- **LP07—See the whole:** When improving the process of software development the whole value-stream needs to be considered end to end (E2E). For example, there is no point in sub-optimizing the requirements process and by that increase the speed of the requirements flow into coding and testing if coding can only implement the requirements in a much slower pace.

Comparison

Figure 1 shows a mapping of the principles related to lean and agile. The identified principles were grouped into seven aspects (people management and leadership; quality of the product; release of the product; flexibility; priority of the customer needs/value; learning; and E2E flow). Each aspect contains a set of principles for lean and agile. If principles from the lean and agile paradigms respectively are stated in the same row then they are related and their relationship is explained further. For example, AP11 (self-organizing teams) and LP05 (respect people) are related within the aspect "people management and leadership". We can also see that there exists an N to N relationship

between the principles of both paradigms, e.g. AP07 (working software) can be related to LP01 (eliminate waste) and LP06 (build quality in). Vice versa the principle LP01 (eliminate waste) relates to several agile principles (e.g. AP03 – frequent deliveries and AP01 – customer satisfaction). If only one column states a principle then the principle is only explicitly referred to in one of the development paradigms, such as LP07 (see the whole). For LP01 (eliminate waste) we also state which waste is concerned in the comparison. In the following paragraphs we explain why and how the principles in Figure 1 are related to each other. The IDs in Figure 1 (AP01 to AP12 and LP01 to LP07) refer to the detailed descriptions of the principles provided earlier.

People management and leadership: This aspect contains all principles that are related to leading and managing people in a project. As can be seen in Figure 1 for each of the principles of agile a corresponding principle of lean development can be identified.

- **Relation of AP05 (motivated individuals), AP08 (sustainable pace), and AP11 (self-organizing teams) to LP05 (respect**

Figure 1. Mapping of agile and lean principles

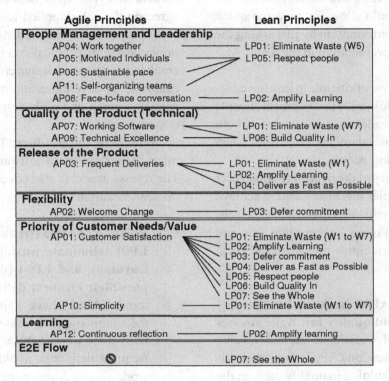

people): Respecting people (LP05) is facilitated by trusting the team to find a solution for a given task (Responsibility-Based Plan and Control). This is the same as self-organizing teams (AP11) who take on the responsibility for solving a task in agile development. Respecting people (LP05) is also connected to sustainable pace (AP08) as self-organized teams that are trusted and empowered are more motivated over a long period of time (AP05 - motivated individuals) and thus it can be expected that they are working productively in a continuous manner.

- **Relation of AP06 (face-to-face conversation) to LP02 (amplify learning):** Face-to-face conversation (AP06) allows for direct and instant communication to resolve misunderstandings and thus amplifies learning (LP02). For example, informal communication taking place in coffee

corners is considered an important part of information exchange allowing people to share knowledge (DeMarco and Lister 1999).

- **Relation of AP04 (work together) to LP01 (eliminate waste "motion/task switching"):** Agile raises the importance of different groups of people (e.g. technical developers and business/marketing) to work closely together (AP04). Close cooperation between people of different competence areas (LP01 - eliminate waste) helps in making their competence more easily accessible which reduces the time to find the information. Consider the example of a developer who should decide which requirement to implement next based on its importance to the market. Without cooperation the developer would have to spend time searching for documentation and/or the right person to ask. Having cooperation between marketing and development in the first place would allow for easy and quick access to the information by just asking the marketing-representative in the team.

Comparison: Every principle in lean has a corresponding principle in agile for the aspect "People Management and Leadership". In conclusion both paradigms very much share the same rules when it comes to managing people.

Technical quality of the product: This aspect contains the principles that are related to achieve a working product with high quality from a technical perspective. Figure 1 shows that lean and agile both apply principles related to technical product quality.

- **Relation of AP09 (technical excellence) to LP06 (build quality in):** Agile stresses that technical excellence should receive continuous attention (AP09). In lean this is achieved by building in quality early in the development process, and not by testing for and fixing defects later (LP06). Thus, LP06 fulfills the principle of having a continuous focus on building technically excellent products.

- **Relation of AP07 (working software) to LP01 (eliminate waste) and LP06 (build quality in):** The rule of having working software (AP07) throughout development enforces that the quality of the software has to be ensured throughout the whole development lifecycle. For example, having mechanisms in place to increase the quality of code while it is written (LP01 - eliminate waste) helps to achieve the goal of working product with few defects (LP06, W7).

Comparison: Both paradigms stress the continuous attention to quality and technical excellence. A consequence of this attention is a working software product throughout the development lifecycle. Thus, both paradigms strongly agree on the rules applied to the quality of the software product. A small distinction is made in principle AP09 (technical excellence) where agile emphasizes that good design enhances agility. For example, an easy extension of the architecture enables a rapid and agile response to changing customer needs.

Release of the product: The release aspect refers to the delivery of software to the customer. The release aspect is also covered in both development paradigms.

- **Relation of AP03 (frequent deliveries) to LP01 (eliminate waste), LP02 (amplify learning), and LP04 (deliver as fast as possible):** Frequent deliveries to the customer (AP03) have a positive effect on the elimination of waste concerning partially done work (LP01). That is, enforcing frequent deliveries avoids that completed work (e.g. adding a new feature) stays within the development organization without being made available to the customer. Frequent deliveries also amplify learning (LP02) as they allow the customer to provide regular feedback on the latest status of the product. Thereby, the development organization can learn about the needs of the customers and what features excite them. In addition AP03 influences the speed of delivery (LP04) positively. In waterfall development the delivery of the overall scope is done in the end which means that all features together have a very long lead-time. Frequent deliveries, however, imply that less software is delivered at once, but much more frequently and with shorter lead-time (Petersen and Wohlin 2009a).

Comparison: There is a clear relation between the principles of the release aspect between lean and agile, i.e. both paradigms are in strong agreement on this.

Flexibility: Flexibility is the ability to react on changes that impact the development of the software product. The most common is the change in the needs of the customer reflected in changing requirements. Other changes are timeline changes (e.g. deadlines), changes of rules and regulations (law) that affect development, or innovations in technology.

- **Relation of AP02 (welcome change) to LP03 (defer commitment):** Agile stresses that software organizations should welcome change instead of fighting it (AP02) as being able to deliver what the market needs today determines the success of products. The principle refers to the attitude that one should have when developing software. Lean adds to that by providing a rule that supports the attitude of welcoming change, i.e. to defer commitment (LP03). Deferring commitment means to decide as late as possible. For example, a company should not decide of an overall release scope early on in development (early decision), but instead decide whether a feature should be included into the scope as late as possible (deferred commitment).

Comparison: Both paradigms address flexibility, but describe it in a different way. In lean one should defer commitment, i.e. decide as late as possible. However, software organizations that are generally driven by plans, scopes, and deadlines have to change their attitude towards harnessing change as this is a prerequisite to implement late decisions. Hence, the principles of the two development paradigms complement each other very well as accepting and harnessing change in the process is a pre-requisite to defer commitment.

Priority of customer needs/value: This aspect contains principles that stress the priority of the customer in software development over other focuses (such as the focus on documentation).

- **Relation of AP01 (customer satisfaction) to LP01 (eliminate waste, all wastes in Table 2):** The priority of the customer (AP01) is reflected in all the principles that are stated for lean (LP01-LP07). This is very clear for the wastes (LP01) as the waste is identified from the point of view of the customer. Amplify learning (LP02) puts high priority on customers' needs as it is about learning the needs of customers and what delights them. The same holds for deferred commitment (LP03) as this enables a flexible reaction to customer change requests that are due to a change in needs. Delivering fast (LP04) implies that the needs of the customer are realized quickly as soon as they are articulated. The respect for people (LP05) can also be related to the customer focus as happy employees are an important factor for project success (DeMarco and Lister 1999). Furthermore, technical quality (LP06) is a prerequisite to deliver valuable software (e.g. if the software is not stable then the customer cannot make sufficient use of its functionality). Finally, see the whole (LP07) implies that one should not put too much effort in sub-optimization of the process as this is does not lead to significant improvements for the customer. Thus, the improvement effort would be wasted.

- **Relation of AP10 (simplicity) to LP01 (eliminate waste, all wastes in Table 2):** Simplicity is about maximizing the amount of work not done (AP10). In that sense it is very strongly related to wastes (LP01) as the elimination of waste leads to a reduction of work. This includes unnecessary work that can be easily avoided (e.g. documentation never used) or reduction of rework (e.g. defects).

Comparison: The comparison indicates that customer priority in agile is related to all principles in lean. As we have shown the principles in lean are also linked to the principles in agile other than AP10 we conclude that AP10 is the very central principle of both development paradigms.

Learning: This aspect is about gaining new knowledge (e.g. about customer needs, ways of working, etc.) and is addressed in both paradigms.

- **Relation of AP12 (continuous reflection) to LP02 (amplify learning)):** Continuous reflection allows time for the team to reflect on how to improve the ways of working to become more efficient (AP12). Thus, the learning focus is on identifying improvement potential for efficiency. In lean the learning focus has a broader perspective by emphasizing learning in general, not with a specific focus on efficiency. Learning in general includes, for example, gaining new knowledge about customer needs and market trends.

Comparison: Both paradigms focus on learning, while lean takes a more general perspective.

E2E flow: The E2E flow includes principles that emphasize the focus on the overall flow of value (i.e. from the very beginning when a need for a feature enters the organization till it is delivered). The principle related to the E2E flow is "see the whole" (LP07). When comparing the principles within the aspect "priority of customer needs/value" LP07 is related to the prioritization of the customer needs (AP01 - customer satisfaction). However, the E2E flow aspect is not considered in the principles of agile and thus is what sets lean and agile apart when looking at the principles.

Overall, the comparison shows which principles are the same, complement each other, or are new to either one of the two paradigms.

- **Same:** For the aspects people management and leadership, technical quality of the product, and release of the product both paradigms strongly agree on the principles.

That is, they mean the same, but only express it in different words.

- **Complementary:** The paradigms complement each other with regard to the aspects flexibility, priority of customer needs/value, and learning. For flexibility lean emphasizes deferred commitment, while agile stresses the attitude a company must have to be willing to defer commitments. For priority of customer needs/value lean complements agile by concretizing what does not contribute positively to the value for the customer in the form of the seven wastes of software development (see Table 2).
- **New:** The need to look at the development and value flow from an end to end perspective is unique for lean and therefore is what clearly distinguishes both paradigms from each other.

Regarding the question whether lean development is agile and agile development is lean we can provide the following answer for the principles: Lean is agile as it includes all the principles of agile. However, agile is not lean as it does not emphasize the E2E focus on flow in its principles.

In the next section we analyze the practices which implement the principles of lean and agile development. A proposition based on the similarities is that both paradigms also propose similar practices. However, this proposition has to be investigated as:

- Agile and lean might propose different practices ("How") in order to fulfill the practices they agree on ("What").
- Lean is unique in its E2E focus and hence we can expect to identify practices that are not already proposed in the agile context.

Furthermore, it is interesting to investigate which principles are covered by which practices, as this investigation shows the coverage of practices through principles.

Practices

Practices describe how the principles are implemented by the development paradigms. Therefore, we first present the practices for lean and agile and link each of the different practices to the principles. After that we make a comparison between the paradigms.

In total we identified 26 principles by looking at the literature describing lean (Poppendieck and Poppendieck 2003) and agile software development (Beck 2000)(Schwaber 2004)(Larman 2004) (Koch 2005), as well as lean product development (Morgan and Liker 2006). The principles are described and for each principle it is stated whether literature connects it to lean, agile, or both paradigms. The principles are grouped as being related to requirements engineering, design and implementation, quality assurance, software releases, project planning, team management, and E2E flow. First, a comparison of practices in each group is made, and thereafter we provide an overall comparison.

Requirements Engineering

P01—On-site customer: Representatives of the customer are located at the development site to allow for immediate feedback on the product (AP02 – welcome change). At the same time the customer always knows about the progress of the development (AP01 – customer satisfaction). The co-location also allows the developers to interact with the customer to ask questions and clarify requirements, which avoids implementation of features not needed by the customer (LP01 – eliminate waste "extra features"). Furthermore, a regular face-to-face communication between the team and the customer is ensured (AP05 - face-to-face conversation).

P02—Metaphors and user stories: A metaphor is a very high level requirement outlining the purpose of the system and characterizes what the system should be like. The purpose on the high level should be stable. The metaphor is broken down into more detailed requirements to be used in the development project. These are feature descriptions (FDD) or user stories (XP and SCRUM). The features/user stories should be used to track the progress and apply the pull concept (see P26 – Kanban pull-system). Having the metaphor defined also avoids the inclusion of irrelevant user stories (LP01 – eliminate waste "extra features") and describes what should be developed to provide value to the customer (AP01 – customer satisfaction). That is, if a user story cannot be linked to the metaphor then it should not be included in the product.

Comparison: Table 3 shows the principles related to the requirements practices, and whether the principles are considered in lean and agile development. Metaphors and user stories have been recognized in agile as well as lean software development. However, the on-site customer is not part of the lean practices, but is a key practice in agile software development. Both practices support lean and agile principles.

Design and Implementation

P03—Refactoring: Refactoring is the continuous improvement of already working code with respect to maintainability, readability, and simplification of code (AP10 - simplicity) which has a positive effect on understanding the code (LP02 - amplify learning). When code is being worked on over a long period of time the assumptions that were made in the past while writing the code might not be true in the end. For example, a class that was written in the beginning of a project might have to be restructured in order to fit the latest version of the overall product in a better way, e.g. removing duplicated code, changing code to improve readability, or changing the structure of the class

Table 3. Comparison for requirements practices

	AP01: Customer prio	AP02: Welcome change	AP03: Frequent del.	AP04: Work together	AP05: Motivated individ.	AP06: Face-to-face conv.	AP07: Working software	AP08: Sustainable pace	AP09: Technical excel.	AP10: Simplicity	AP11: Self-org. teams	AP12: Continuous refl.	LP01: Eliminate waste	LP02: Amplify learning	LP03: Defer commit.	LP04: Deliver fast	LP05: Respect people	LP06: Build quality in	LP07: See the whole	Used in lean SE	Used in agile SE
P01: On-site customer	√					√							√	√							√
P02: Metaphors/Stories	√												√							√	√

to fit a certain design pattern (cf. (Andersen and Fagerhaug 2000)). It is important to mention that changing the external structure (e.g. interfaces and their parameters) should be avoided as this might be harmful for the integrity of the overall system. The simple and clear structure of the code helps new developers to become more productive in delivering value (AP01 – customer satisfaction).

P04—Coding standards: Coding standards make sure that developers structure and write code in the same way. This is important to assure that everyone can understand the code (AP01 – customer satisfaction, LP02 - amplify learning). Furthermore, a common understanding on how to code avoids unnecessary discussions in pair programming. Examples for coding standards for Java are (Sun):

- File organization (e.g. package statements before import statements)
- Interface declarations (public before protected before private variable declarations)
- Wrapping lines
- Rules for formatting if-else, try-catch, loop-statements, etc.
- Naming conventions (packages, classes, interfaces, methods, etc.)

Understandability and maintainability can be improved further by applying good programming practices in addition to the rules for formatting and naming. For the Java Code Convention different rules apply for programming practices (e.g. one should avoid to use an assignment operator in a place where it can be confused with an equality operator; one should not assign a value to several variables at once; always use parentheses with mixed operators; only use return once in a method; etc.).

P05—Team code-ownership: The code written by an individual is not owned by that individual. Instead, everyone in the team owns the code and is allowed to make changes. Team code ownership is also related to the concept of egoless programming (Weinberg 1999) where the success as a team is more important than promoting the status of the team member with the strongest ego. The team factor is a driver for motivation (AP01- customer satisfaction, AP05 - motivated individuals) and gives credit to each member of the team for the achieved result (LP05 - respect people).

P06—Low dependency architecture: This type of architectures clearly encapsulates functionality into components that can be developed independently, i.e. the delivery of one component does not depend on the delivery of another component (Poppendieck and Poppendieck 2009). That way the functionality provided by the components can be delivered to the customer as soon as they are ready (AP01 – customer satisfaction, AP03 - frequent deliveries) and by that reduce the amount of partially done work (LP01 - eliminate waste). Furthermore, the architecture becomes easier to

Table 4. Comparison for design and implementation practices

	AP01: Customer prio	AP02: Welcome change	AP03: Frequent del.	AP04: Work together	AP05: Motivated individ.	AP06: Face-to-face conv.	AP07: Working software	AP08: Sustainable pace	AP09: Technical excel.	AP10: Simplicity	AP11: Self-org. teams	AP12: Continuous refl.	LP01: Eliminate waste	LP02: Amplify learning	LP03: Defer commit.	LP04: Deliver fast	LP05: Respect people	LP06: Build quality in	LP07: See the whole	Used in lean SE	Used in agile SE
P03: Refactoring	√									√				√						√	√
P04: Coding standards	√	√																			√
P05: Team-Code Own.	√				√												√				√
P06: Low Dep. Arch.	√	√	√							√				√		√				√	

change (AP03 - frequent deliveries) as the change impact is more isolated with few dependencies.

Comparison: Table 4 shows the principles linked to the design and implementation practices, and whether the principles are considered in lean and agile development. Refactoring has been considered in lean as well as agile (cf. (Poppendieck and Poppendieck 2003))). Coding standards and team-code ownership are unique to agile software development (Koch 2005), while low dependency architecture is a principle unique to lean (Poppendieck and Poppendieck 2009). All practices identified for design and implementation are linked to lean as well as agile principles.

Quality Assurance

P07—Test-driven development and test automation: In test-driven development (TDD) (Beck 2003) the test cases for unit tests are written before the implementation takes place. The test cases are to be implemented (e.g. JUnit (Beck 2004) is a test framework supporting the implementation in Java) so that they can verify the implementation as soon as it is finished (AP07 - working software, AP09 - technical excellence, L06). Thereby, defects are caught early (LP01 – eliminate waste "delays"), which results in higher quality software for the customer (AP01 – customer satisfaction). When-

ever the implementation is changed the test cases can be re-run as they are already implemented. This aids in automation of regression tests. After the test is completed the code is refactored (see P03 - refactoring).

P08—Pair-programming: In pair programming two developers share one workstation. One of the developers is actively developing the test cases and writing the code. The second developer should reflect on what the first developer is doing and act as a reviewer thinking about the impact (e.g. how does the implementation affect other parts of the system) and the quality (e.g. is the code defective, or are any important unit test cases missing). The review allows to detect defects in the code immediately after their introduction (AP09 - technical excellence, LP01 – eliminate waste "defects", LP06 - build quality in) improving the quality for the customer early on in the coding process (AP01 – customer satisfaction). The second developer can improve the work by asking questions and providing feedback on the work done. Agile recommends to continuously changing pairs throughout a project to improve knowledge transfer (LP02 - amplify learning).

P09—Continuous integration: Features that are developed as increments for a product should be integrated into the overall product as soon as possible after they are finalized, making every extension to the product deliverable (AP01 – customer satisfaction, AP03 - frequent deliveries, LP01 – eliminate waste "partially done work"). That way, problems in integration are discovered early and can be fixed close to their discovery (AP07 - working software, AP09 - technical excellence, LP01 – eliminate waste "partially done work", and LP06 - build quality in). Furthermore, integrating a large scope at once often leads to unpredictable results in terms of quality and schedule (Petersen et al. 2009b).

P10—Reviews and inspections: Inspections are a visual examination of any software artifact (requirements, code, test cases, etc.) allowing the detection of defects early in the process (AP01 – customer satisfaction, AP07 - working software, AP09 - technical excellence, LP01 – eliminate waste "defects", and LP06 - build quality in). Fagan introduced a very formal inspection process in 1976 (Fagan 1976). However, the formality requirements are not given in the agile context, i.e. different agile methods use reviews and inspections in a different way. The inspection in Feature Driven Development (FDD) (Koch 2005) is a relatively rigorous peer review. Furthermore, post-mortems are used in FDD where completed development activities are reviewed to identify improvement potential for upcoming iterations. SCRUM also uses reviews after each 30 day sprint where the work product of the sprint is reviewed by all relevant stakeholders during a meeting (Schwaber 2004).

P11—Configuration management: The goal of configuration management is to achieve consistency between versions of software artifacts and thus to achieve system integrity (Leon 2005). Different software artifacts linked to a configuration item should be consistent in the sense that requirements, code, and test cases match and represent the same version of the system. For example, an inconsistent situation would be if test cases are derived from a specific requirements specification, but are linked to an older version of the requirements specification within

the configuration. The negative consequence is that the wrong things would be tested. In order to achieve and maintain consistency configuration management has mechanism for version control and change processes. Configuration management is not explicitly acknowledged in most of agile process models, only FDD has configuration management as one of its practices (Koch 2005). The benefits of configuration management are: (1) create transparency in terms of status and progress of configuration items to be reported to the customer (AP01 – customer satisfaction); (2) the knowledge about status avoids making the wrong decisions causing waiting (LP01 – eliminate waste "delays"), quality problems (AP07 - working software, AP09 - technical excellence, LP01 – eliminate waste "defects", and LP06 - build quality in); and (3) the information of configuration items aids in communication and reflection (AP12 - continuous reflection).

Comparison: Table 5 shows the principles linked to the quality assurance practices, and whether the principles are considered in lean and agile development. All principles have been considered in lean as well as agile (cf. (Poppendieck and Poppendieck 2003)(Larman 2004)(Koch 2005))). Furthermore, all quality assurance practices are linked to lean as well as agile principles.

Software Releases

P12—Incremental deliveries to the customer: New functionality is delivered continuously as an increment of the previous software version to the customer. The increments go through a development lifecycle consisting of the activities requirements elicitation, design and integration, implementation, testing, and release. The flow of activities (e.g. order of activities, branching, merging, and loop-backs) depends on the process model used. Frequent deliveries help to achieve customer satisfaction as the customer receives value continuously (AP01 – customer satisfaction, LP01 – eliminate waste "partially done work")

Table 5. Comparison for quality assurance practices

	AP01: Customer prio	AP02: Welcome change	AP03: Frequent del.	AP04: Work together	AP05: Motivated individ.	AP06: Face-to-face conv.	AP07: Working software	AP08: Sustainable pace	AP09: Technical excel.	AP10: Simplicity	AP11: Self-org. teams	AP12: Continuous refl.	LP01: Eliminate waste	LP02: Amplify learning	LP03: Defer commit.	LP04: Deliver fast	LP05: Respect people	LP06: Build quality in	LP07: See the whole	Used in lean SE	Used in agile SE
P07: TDD	√						√		√				√	√				√		√	√
P08: Pair-programming	√								√				√	√				√		√	√
P09: Continuous Int.	√		√				√		√				√		√					√	√
P10: Reviews/Insp.	√						√		√				√					√		√	√
P11: CM	√						√		√				√					√		√	√

and speed up deliveries of value (AP03 - frequent deliveries, LP04 - deliver as fast as possible). Furthermore, incremental deliveries assure that a working system is build continuously with each new increment (AP07 - working software, LP06 - build quality in). Learning is amplified as increments allow the customer to provide feedback on the integration of each new feature (LP02 - amplify learning). As features are developed rapidly after requesting them the risk of features not needed is reduced (LP01 – eliminate waste "extra features").

P13—Separation between internal and external releases: Internal releases are baselines of the software product that have the quality to be released to the market, but are not. One reason to not releasing them could be that the market window is not right from a marketing strategy. The internal release makes sure that there is a continuous attention to quality as baselines should be releasable (AP01 – customer satisfaction, AP09 - technical excellence, LP01 – eliminate waste "defects", and LP06 - build quality in). An example of the implementation of internal and external releases in a market-driven context can be found in (Petersen and Wohlin 2009a).

Comparison: Table 6 shows the comparison of software release practices. The principles can be found in both paradigms (cf. (Poppendieck and Poppendieck 2003)(Larman 2004)(Koch 2005))). Furthermore, the practices fulfill principles of lean and agile.

Table 6. Comparison for software release practices

	AP01: Customer prio	AP02: Welcome change	AP03: Frequent del.	AP04: Work together	AP05: Motivated individ.	AP06: Face-to-face conv.	AP07: Working software	AP08: Sustainable pace	AP09: Technical excel.	AP10: Simplicity	AP11: Self-org. teams	AP12: Continuous refl.	LP01: Eliminate waste	LP02: Amplify learning	LP03: Defer commit.	LP04: Deliver fast	LP05: Respect people	LP06: Build quality in	LP07: See the whole	Used in lean SE	Used in agile SE
P12: Inc. Del.	√		√				√						√	√		√		√		√	√
P13: Int./Ext. Rel.	√								√				√					√		√	√

Project Planning

P14—Short iterations: Within an iteration the product is further improved and enhanced based on regular feedback and planning of the iteration (see e.g. sprints in SCRUM (Schwaber 2004)). For example, a feature is delivered to the customer to receive feedback, the feedback being that the feature needs to be improved. Based on the feedback from the customer the feature goes into another iteration to incorporate the feedback (AP02 - welcome change). When the customer is satisfied (AP01 – customer satisfaction, AP07 - working software) no further iteration is required. The iteration cycles should be short (no more than a month with a preference for a shorter scale) to allow continuous feedback (AP02 – welcome change) to improve the product (AP09 - technical excellence, LP06 - build quality in, LP01 – eliminate waste "defects"). The feedback allows the team to learn about the needs of the customer (LP02 - amplify learning). The shortage of the iteration assures that work is completed and made available to the customer in a rapid manner (LP01 – eliminate waste "partially done work").

P15—Adaptive planning with highest priority user stories / requirements: A list of requirements is maintained which shows the priority of the requirements, the requirements that are more important for the customer being higher ranked in the list (AP01 - customer satisfaction). The priority of the requirements is important to indicate which requirement should be implemented next. The list is the backlog of work. Adaptive planning means that the priority of requirements can be changed in the backlog and there is flexibility in choosing work-tasks for the next iteration (AP02 - welcome change, LP03 - defer commitment). Furthermore, adoption avoids delivering features the customer does not need (LP01 – eliminate waste "extra features") while learning more about the customers' needs (LP02 - amplify learning).

P16—Time-boxing: Fixed start and end dates are set for iterations and projects. SCRUM, for example, proposes to have 30 day sprints in which the next increment has to be completed (Schwaber 2004). In consequence the scope of development (i.e. how much to implement in a project) has to be decided based on the maximum duration of the project. Hence, time-boxing forces new functionality to be delivered within one cycle speeding up value creation (AP01 - customer satisfaction) and the rate in which new functions can be delivered (AP03 - frequent deliveries,LP01 – eliminate waste "partially done work").

P17—The planning game: In the planning game the next iteration of the project is planned. Different stakeholders have to be involved in the planning game, namely the customer, developers, and managers. The game is usually organized in a workshop setting and allows the participants, that are not on-site during the whole development time, to meet all important stakeholders (AP05 - face-to-face conversation, LP01 - eliminate waste "extra processes") (Koch 2005). Furthermore, the meeting is used to resolve conflicts and assures that the right feature is developed in the next iteration (LP01 – eliminate waste "extra features"). It can also be used to reflect on the previous iteration as the baseline for the next one (AP12 - continuous reflection) and by that supports learning (LP02 - amplify learning). A regular planning game meeting allows the customer to suggest changes to the plan (AP02 - welcome change).

Comparison: Table 7 shows the comparison of project planning practices. The practices short iterations, adaptive planning, and time-boxing can be found in both paradigms (cf. (Poppendieck and Poppendieck 2003)(Larman 2004)(Koch 2005))). The planning game is unique to agile, the practice being used in Scrum (Schwaber 2004). Furthermore, the practices fulfill principles of lean and agile.

Team Management

P18—Co-located development: People from different disciplines should be located together to

Table 7. Comparison for project planning practices

	AP01: Customer prio	AP02: Welcome change	AP03: Frequent del.	AP04: Work together	AP05: Motivated individ.	AP06: Face-to-face conv.	AP07: Working software	AP08: Sustainable pace	AP09: Technical excel.	AP10: Simplicity	AP11: Self-org. teams	AP12: Continuous refl.	LP01: Eliminate waste	LP02: Amplify learning	LP03: Defer commit.	LP04: Deliver fast	LP05: Respect people	LP06: Build quality in	LP07: See the whole	Used in lean SE	Used in agile SE
P14: Short iterations	√	√	√				√		√					√	√			√		√	√
P15: Adaptive Planning	√	√												√	√	√				√	√
P16: Time-boxing	√				√															√	√
P17: Planning game	√	√				√						√	√	√							√

ease communication. Direct communication can replace documentation that otherwise would have to written and handed over between disciplines, which reduces the number of handovers and extra processes to create the documentation (LP01 – eliminate wastes "extra processes" and "handovers") (Petersen and Wohlin 2009a). An additional benefit is that people do not have to move around or wait to discuss (motion/task-switching), which eases learning from each other (LP02 - amplify learning). With the removal of this waste one can concentrate on value-adding activities instead (AP01 - customer satisfaction). The continuous discussions between team members also aid in the continuous reflection with regard to the ways of working (AP12 - continuous reflection).

P19—Cross-functional teams: Teams need to be cross-functional so that they gather the competence needed to develop a feature. Two situations are shown in Figure 2. In the first situation (top of the figure) a development-centric organization is shown where other disciplines, such as requirements and testing, exchange information with the development team. There is also information exchange between each of the disciplines, which is not included in the figure for simplification. The separation of the development team (coding) from other disciplines hinders the exchange of information (e.g. in the form of barriers and lack of understanding for each other) (cf.

(Petersen and Wohlin 2009a)(Dybå and Dingsøyr 2008)). Consequently, it is beneficial to create cross-functional teams where each discipline has at least one representative in the team (see bottom of the figure) (Morgan and Liker 2006)(Karlsson and Ahlström 2009). The representation of different disciplines helps them in learning from each other (LP02 - amplify learning), and assures that business and technical people work together and develop an understanding for each other's work (AP04 - work together). Furthermore, people do not have to search long to find the right competence (LP01 – eliminate waste "motion/task switching") and do not have to rely on handovers and documentation (LP01 – eliminate wastes "extra processes" and "handovers"). Overall, the avoid-

Figure 2. Cross-functional teams

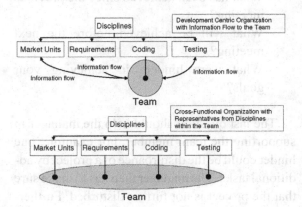

ance of handovers and extensive documentation frees resources for value-adding activities (AP01 - customer satisfaction).

P20—40-hour week: Overtime should be avoided as rested people produce better work and are more concentrated, reducing the number of mistakes made (AP09 - technical excellence, LP01 – eliminate waste "defects", LP06 - build quality in),. Thus, the working time in the projects should be limited to approximately 40 hours. If developers do overtime in one week they are not allowed to do overtime in the week after that. Koch (Koch 2005) distinguishes between forced and voluntary overtime and states that voluntary overtime should be tolerated. Rested developers can produce quality over a long period of time, while overworked developers might end up in a burnout situation. The avoidance of burnouts aids in achieving a sustainable pace (AP08). Furthermore, ongoing deliveries to the customer are assured (AP01 - customer satisfaction).

P21—Standup-meeting: This meeting takes place daily and is a place for the whole team to communicate and reflect on the completed and ongoing work (AP12 - continuous reflection). The discussions in the meeting should aid in becoming more efficient. The meeting should not last longer than 15 minutes. Participants are standing during the meeting to ensure that the meeting is kept short. Every team member has to answer three questions:

- What has been achieved since the previous meeting?
- What will be achieved before the next meeting?
- What were hinders in achieving your goals?

The last question should help the manager in supporting the team member. For example, one hinder could be the disturbance of a project by additional tasks. The manager then has to make sure that the project is not further disturbed. Further-

more, wastes like waiting times could be raised. Hence, stand-up meetings aid in the discovery of the different wastes not generating value (AP01 - customer satisfaction, LP01 – eliminate waste).

P22—Team chooses own tasks: Teams should be able to choose their own tasks, which increases the commitment to the task (AP05 - motivated individuals, LP05 - respect people). For example, from a number of features to be developed a team can choose which feature to implement, given some restrictions regarding the priority of the features. The choice is also influenced by the competencies in the team so that the task is implemented in the most efficient way for the customer (AP01 - customer satisfaction). The team takes the responsibility to complete the task (A11 - self-organizing teams).

Comparison: Table 8 shows the comparison of project planning practices. Three practices are shared between lean and agile, namely co-located development, cross-functional teams, and team chooses own tasks (cf. (Poppendieck and Poppendieck 2003)(Larman 2004)(Koch 2005))). The 40-hour week (Beck 2000) and stand-up meetings (Schwaber 2004) are unique to agile. The practices fulfill principles of lean and agile.

E2E Flow

P23—Value-stream mapping: A value-stream map visualizes the end-to-end flow of the overall development lifecycle (Morgan and Liker 2006), i.e. the emphasis is on seeing the whole (LP07). The map shows the activities and lead-times. The lead-times are separated into processing time and waiting time. Processing time means that work is done during that time (e.g. a requirement is implemented). Waiting time means that nobody works on the requirement (e.g. the requirement has been implemented and is waiting to be tested). The processing time value is added to the product while waiting time is non-value adding. The overall lead time is the sum of all waiting and processing times. The map should help in identifying everything that

Table 8. Comparison for team management practices

	AP01: Customer prio	AP02: Welcome change	AP03: Frequent del.	AP04: Work together	AP05: Motivated individ.	AP06: Face-to-face conv.	AP07: Working software	AP08: Sustainable pace	AP09: Technical excel.	AP10: Simplicity	AP11: Self-org. teams	AP12: Continuous refl.	LP01: Eliminate waste	LP02: Amplify learning	LP03: Defer commit.	LP04: Deliver fast	LP05: Respect people	LP06: Build quality in	LP07: See the whole	Used in lean SE	Used in agile SE
P18: Co-loc. develop.	√					√						√	√	√						√	√
P19: Cross-func. teams	√			√									√	√						√	√
P20: 40-hour week	√							√	√									√			√
P21: Stand-up meeting	√										√	√									√
P22: Team chooses T.	√	√			√						√						√			√	√

does not contribute to the value of the customer (AP01 - customer satisfaction). A value-stream map analysis is conducted in four steps:

- **Create current-state value-stream map:** First, the value-stream map is created by following the steps a single work product (e.g. requirements, test cases, change requests, etc.). The data is collected through interviews across the lifecycle of the work product. If lead time measurements are available then these should be considered as well.
- **Analyze current-state value-stream map:** The map is analyzed by looking at critical wastes as those have the largest improvement potential. The criticality of lead times from an end to end perspective can be determined by calculating the ratio of non-value adding time and overall lead time.
- **Identify reasons for waiting times and propose improvements:** The reasons for waiting times and long processing times are identified in workshops and discussions with practitioners, e.g. in form of a root cause analysis (Andersen and Fagerhaug 2000). During the root cause analysis all types of waste can be discovered by hav-

ing a dialogue about the map. For example, by asking an engineer why a certain activity takes so long the engineer can pinpoint many types of waste (LP01 – eliminate wastes W1 to W7). Depending on the nature of the problems for long processing and waiting times the value stream map can potentially pinpoint to reasons that, when being addressed, fulfill any of the principles of agile and lean development (AP01 to AP12 and LP01 to LP07)

- **Create future-state map:** Solutions are proposed for the identified problems and the potential of the solution candidates in reducing the waiting and processing times is evaluated. Based on the assessment of the improvement suggestions a new map (future-state map) can be constructed. The future-state map provides an indication of the overall improvement potential in terms of lead-time when implementing the solutions.

An example of an analysis of a software process for product customizations with value-stream maps and the notation to illustrate them can be found in (Mujtaba 2010).

P24—Inventory management with queuing theory and theory of constraints: Inventory is the work in process that is not completed and thus does not provide value to customers. High inventory levels have a negative impact on the performance of software development for multiple reasons: (1) Inventory hides defects (hinders fulfilling AP07 - working software, AP09 - technical excellence, LP01 – eliminate waste "defects", and LP06 - build quality in); (2) Time and effort has been spent on the artifacts in the inventory and when not making them available to the market they might become obsolete (hinders fulfilling AP03 - frequent deliveries, LP01 – eliminate waste "partially done work", and LP04 - deliver as fast as possible) (Petersen et al. 2009b); (3) Inventory creates waiting and slows down the development flow (hinders fulfilling AP03 - frequent deliveries, LP01 – eliminate waste "delays", and LP04 - deliver as fast as possible). Point (3) can be related to queuing theory where one can calculate the work-in-process and the time work stays in process based on arrival distributions and processing times (distribution of time needed for the server, e.g. a development team, to complete a task), and by that identify overload situations. An example of identifying overload situations with queuing theory based on real world data for a requirements process is shown in (Höst et al. 2001). In order to achieve a continuous flow of development the workload should be below the capacity of the development organization (Petersen and Wohlin 2010). Being below the capacity also allows for emergency situations (e.g. customer faults, emerging high priority requirements).

The theory of constraints (TOC) also helps to reduce inventory levels. TOC consists of five steps: (1) Identify the system constraint; (2) Decide candidate solutions of how to remove the constraint; (3) Select candidate solution that is focused on constraint; (4) Remove constraint with selected solution; (5) go to step (1) to see whether a new system constraint has become visible (Anderson 2003). The constraint can be identified by looking at processing times of different steps in the development flow. For example, how many require-

ments are processed per time unit (e.g. weeks) in different phases (e.g. requirements specification, design, implementation, testing, and release)? If the processing time for test produces the least amount of requirements per time unit then this is the constraint. As the constraint produces at a slower rate than the other activities inventories that are inputs to the constraint will grow. A method for integrated analysis of multiple inventories is presented in (Petersen and Wohlin 2010). As in value-stream maps the focus has to be on the end-to-end flow to avoid sub-optimization (LP07) and to achieve a continuous flow of customer value (AP01 - customer satisfaction).

P25—Chief engineer: The chief engineer is one person that is accountable for the success and failure of the development teams. The chief engineer has a wide range of responsibilities (voice of the customer, product concepts and requirements, product architecture and performance, product planning) and requires special abilities (feeling for the needs of customers, exceptional engineering skills, intuition, hard driving teacher and motivator, patient listener, exceptional communicator, etc.) (Morgan and Liker 2006). At the same time the chief engineer does not have formal authorities over the teams. Overall, the chief engineer is an important driving force in optimizing value creation which makes him an initiator to any potential improvement towards agile (AP01 to AP12) or lean (LP01 to LP07).

P26—Kanban pull-system: In a push system requirements are pushed from the requirements activity into the development organization, e.g. by defining a requirements roadmap and assigning time slots for each requirement. The push approach is likely to result in an overload situation. The Kanban approach, on the other hand, is a pull approach that avoids planning too far ahead (AP02 - welcome change, LP03 - defer commitment). When a work team (or machine in the manufacturing context) has free capacity a signal is given that the next work task can be taken. For software engineering this means that

Figure 3. Kanban Board

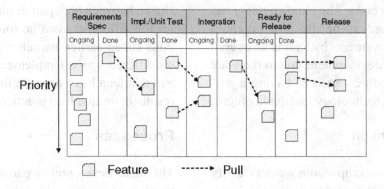

the development systems would pull requirements from a prioritized requirements list when they have enough free capacity. However, teams should not pull new work if there is not enough capacity as this would result in an overload situation creating inventory (LP01 – eliminate waste "partially done work"). Furthermore, if possible they should pull work that has highest priority to the customer (AP01 - customer satisfaction). This strategy might not always be possible due to complex dependencies between features. The management of Kanban is supported by a so-called Kanban board (see Figure 3). The Kanban board also shows the progress of development, which fulfills the call of FDD for a progress measure visualizing what has been achieved.

Comparison: Table 9 shows the comparison of E2E flow practices. All practices presented in the table are unique to lean as the "see the whole" principle is the driver for their usage. For the value-stream map and the chief engineer all principles of lean and agile are ticked. That does not mean that the approaches guarantee the fulfillment of all principles. However, the value-stream map is a tool that can potentially drive the implementation of practices that fulfill the principles. For example, if the value-stream map helps to discover that long waiting times are due to overload situation then the improvement could be to apply the techniques related to inventory management, as well as to implement a Kanban pull approach. Another discovery through value-streams might be long processing times due to a lack of motiva-

Table 9. Comparison for E2E flow practices

	AP01: Customer prio	AP02: Welcome change	AP03: Frequent del.	AP04: Work together	AP05: Motivated individ.	AP06: Face-to-face conv.	AP07: Working software	AP08: Sustainable pace	AP09: Technical excel.	AP10: Simplicity	AP11: Self-org. teams	AP12: Continuous refl.	LP01: Eliminate waste	LP02: Amplify learning	LP03: Defer commit.	LP04: Deliver fast	LP05: Respect people	LP06: Build quality in	LP07: See the whole	Used in lean SE	Used in agile SE
P23: Value-Stream M.	√	√	√	√	√	√	√	√	√	√	√	√	√	√	√	√	√	√	√	√	
P24: Inventory Mgt.	√		√			√		√					√			√		√	√	√	
P25: Chief Engineer	√	√	√	√	√	√	√	√	√	√	√	√	√	√	√	√	√	√	√	√	
P26: Pull-Systems	√	√											√		√					√	

tion, which could lead to the practice of teams choosing their own tasks. The chief engineer has all principles ticked as he/she is a potential driver for the improvements by having an overall picture of product development due to the wide range of responsibilities, such as having a customer, architecture, technology, and quality focus.

Overall Comparison

Based on the previous comparisons we can identify which principles are the same for both paradigms, and which are unique for one of them.

- **Same:** Quality assurance practices and software release practices are the same for both paradigms. Hence, for these practices lean is agile and agile is lean. All other groups contain practices that are either unique to agile or lean. In total 15 practices are shared between lean and agile.
- **Unique to agile:** The following practices have been identified as unique to agile: on-site customer, coding standards, team-code ownership, planning game, 40 hour week, and stand-up meetings. In consequence for the practices the conclusion is that lean is not agile. However, all practices identified for agile support lean principles and hence are potentially valuable to lean software development.
- **Unique to lean:** One principle in the group "design and implementation" is unique to lean, namely low dependency architecture. Furthermore, all principles connected to the E2E perspective can only be found in the lean context. This is due to the principle "see the whole" that distinguishes lean from agile regarding the principles.

Overall, the analysis shows that lean as well as agile have unique practices (lean has five, and agile has six). Hence, when it comes to practices the statement lean is not agile, and agile is not lean is partially true. The majority of practices are shared between both paradigms. The explanation for the differences can be found in the propositions stated earlier, namely that both paradigms see different ways of implementing their practices, and that lean has a specific focus on E2E which results in unique lean practices.

Processes

The agile development paradigm consists of a number of instantiations in the form of agile processes. The most famous representatives are eXtreme programming (XP) and SCRUM. Both paradigms consist of a set of principles, but also describe a workflow and artifacts that are produced in the process. Detailed descriptions of the processes can be found in (Schwaber 2004) for SCRUM and in (Beck 2000) for XP. However, lean software development does not propose a workflow or the production of specific artifacts. Rather lean states principles and provides analysis tools for processes to guide engineers in improving their processes to achieve a good flow of value. An advantage of not providing a process is that the approaches of lean become more generally applicable, while an agile process often needs tailoring to a specific context. That is, the general agile process models are often not applied exactly as they are described in the books, but are tailored to the specific needs of the context in which they are used (Petersen and Wohlin 2009a).

DISCUSSION

Practical Implications

Potential benefit of E2E perspective in agile: The lean practices (value-stream mapping, inventory management, chief engineer, and pull-systems) are potentially strong tools to support the E2E flow of agile software development. When not having the E2E focus in mind there is, for example, a risk that agile is only implemented in implementation projects and not in the overall development lifecycle. Though, the benefits of agile cannot be leveraged when not focusing on the overall development lifecycle and balancing the flow of work across the complete development lifecycle. Hence, when moving towards agile it is not enough to make the projects agile, as this is likely to result in a sub-optimization of the actual implementation and testing part of development. An additional risk is that the overall flow of requirements is not continuous due to coordination problems when developing large systems with many teams (Petersen and Wohlin 2009a). How well the flow actually works can be evaluated with value stream maps and inventory management as shown in (Mujtaba 2010)(Petersen and Wohlin 2010). Vice versa, lean could also benefit from the principles unique to agile.

Looking for evidence: Companies are interested in research results that show which practices are most successful in specific contexts. A company wanting to know about the benefits of lean practices should turn to the agile literature due to the large overlap between lean and agile principles. We also have shown that agile principles positively influence the principles of lean as well. Only very little is known about the principles and practices that are related to "see the whole", thus companies looking for information related to principles with an E2E focus will not find much information in the software engineering literature. The high overlap between lean and agile also means that companies having adopted agile practices are not too far away from having a lean software process, given that they add the flow and E2E perspective on-top of their current practices.

Research Implications

Combination of practices: The agile community often states that an agile process only works if all its principles are implemented. However, there is little empirical evidence for this state-ment. In particular, there is little evidence for which combinations of practices work well in which context (e.g. large-scale vs. small-scale, telecommunication vs. information systems, and so forth). Hence, future research should focus on figuring out which combinations of practices are most beneficial, depending on the context. For example, different practices contribute to the quality related principles. Hence, it is interesting to know which combination of quality assurance practices is most cost efficient, which calls for further empirical evidence.

Investigate practices related to E2E flow: Several books describe lean practices related to the end to end flow of software development. Though, no research (industrial case studies, experiments, or simulations) document the benefits and challenges related to their usage. For example, further case studies are needed that apply value-stream maps in practice. In addition, little work is done on inventory management and Kanban implementations in software development. We believe that the evaluations will aid in driving the technology transfer of value-stream maps, inventory management, and Kanban.

Overall, lean software development is a research area with great promise and little work done, making it an attractive field for software engineering research.

CONCLUSION

This chapter compares two development paradigms (lean and agile development) which are of high relevance for industry due to that they focus on making companies agile in responding to changing market needs. The ability to respond quickly is essential in today's rapidly changing market. The result of the comparison is: (1) Agile and lean agree on the goals they want to achieve; (2) Lean is agile in the sense that the principles of lean reflect the principles of agile, while lean is unique in stressing the end-to-end perspective more; (3) Lean has adopted many practices known in the agile context, while stressing the importance of using practices that are related to the end-to-end flow. These practices are value-stream maps, inventory management, Kanban pull systems, and the use of a chief engineer. In addition, agile uses practices that are not found in lean. The practical implications are that: (1) Industry can potentially benefit from adopting lean practices related to flow, which helped to revolutionize manufacturing and product development; (2) Companies looking for evidence on lean will find important information in the agile literature as there is a high overlap between lean and agile. However, few papers are available that focus on the flow aspect in the software engineering context. The research implications are: (1) Research should focus on investigating which combination of practices should be recommended to industry depending on the industrial context, and (2) practices related to the E2E flow should be investigated to provide evidence for their benefit in the software engineering context.

REFERENCES

Andersen, B., & Fagerhaug, T. (2000). *Root cause analysis: Simplified tools and techniques.* Milwaukee: ASQ Quality.

Anderson, D. (2003). *Agile management for software engineering: Applying the theory of constraints for business results.* Prentice Hall.

Beck, K. (2000). *Extreme Programming explained: Embrace change.* Reading, MA: Addison-Wesley.

Beck, K. (2003). *Test-driven development: By example.* Boston: Addison-Wesley.

Beck, K. (2004). *JUnit pocket guide.* Sebastopol, CA: O'Reilly.

Beck, K., et al. (2001). *Manifesto for agile software development.* Retrieved from http://agilemanifesto.org

Beecham, S., Baddoo, N., Hall, T., Robinson, H., & Sharp, H. (2008). Motivation in software engineering: A systematic literature review. *Information and Software Technology, 50*(9-10), 860–878. doi:10.1016/j.infsof.2007.09.004

Biffl, S., & Aurum, B. B. A. (2005). *Value-based software engineering.* New York: Springer.

DeMarco, T., & Lister, T. (1999). *Peopleware: Productive projects and teams.* New York: Dorset House Publishing.

Dybå, T., & Dingsøyr, T. (2008). Empirical studies of agile software development: A systematic review. *Information and Software Technology, 50*(9-10), 833–859. doi:10.1016/j.infsof.2008.01.006

Fagan, M. E. (1976). Design and code inspections to reduce errors in program development. *IBM Systems Journal, 15*(3), 182–211. doi:10.1147/sj.153.0182

Hirsch, M. (2005). Moving from a plan driven culture to agile development. In *proceedings of the 27th International Conference on Software Engineering (ICSE 2005)*, (p. 38).

Höst, M., & Regnell, B., och Dag, J. N., Nedstam, J. & Nyberg, C. (2001). Exploring bottlenecks in market-driven requirements management processes with discrete event simulation. *Journal of Systems and Software, 59*(3), 323–332. doi:10.1016/S0164-1212(01)00072-3

Karlsson, C., & Ahlström, P. (2009). The difficult path to lean product development. *Journal of Product Innovation Management, 13*(4), 283–295. doi:10.1016/S0737-6782(96)00033-1

Kerievsky, J. (2005). *Refactoring to patterns.* Boston: Addison-Wesley.

Koch, A. S. (2005). *Agile software development: Evaluating the methods for your organization.* Boston: Artech House.

Larman, C. (2004). *Agile and iterative development: A manager's guide.* Boston: Addison-Wesley.

Leon, A. (2005). *Software configuration management handbook.* Boston: Artech House.

Morgan, J. M., & Liker, J. K. (2006). *The Toyota product development system: Integrating people, process, and technology.* New York: Productivity Press.

Petersen, K., & Wohlin, C. (2009). A comparison of issues and advantages in agile and incremental development between state of the art and an industrial case. *Journal of Systems and Software, 82*(9), 1479–1490. doi:10.1016/j.jss.2009.03.036

Petersen, K. & Wohlin, C. (2010). Software process improvement through the lean measurement (SPI-LEAM) method. *Journal of Systems and Software.*

Petersen, K., Wohlin, C., & Baca, D. (2009). The waterfall model in large-scale development. In *proceedings of the International Conference on Product-Focused Software Process Improvement (PROFES 2009)*, (pp 386-400).

Poppendieck, M., & Poppendieck, T. (2003). *Lean software development: An agile toolkit.* Boston: Addison-Wesley.

Poppendieck, M., & Poppendieck, T. (2007). *Implementing lean software development: From concept to cash.* Boston: Addison-Wesley.

Poppendieck, M., & Poppendieck, T. (2009). *Leading lean software development.* Boston: Addison-Wesley.

Royce, W. (2009). Managing the development of large software systems: Concepts and techniques. In *Proceedings IEEE WESCOM.* IEEE Computer Society.

Schwaber, K. (2004). *Agile project management with Scrum.* Redmond, WA: Microsoft Press. Mujtaba, S., Feldt, R. & Petersen, K. (2010). Waste and lead time reduction in a software product customization process with value stream maps. *Proceedings of the Australian Software Engineering Conference (ASWEC 2010).*

Sun Microsystems. (1999). *Java code conventions.* Retrieved from http://java.sun.com/docs/codeconv/

Weinberg, G. M. (1999). Egoless programming. *IEEE Software, 16*(1). doi:10.1109/MS.1999.744582

Womack, J. P. (2007). *The machine that changed the world.* London: Simon & Schuster.

KEY TERMS AND DEFINITIONS

Agile Manifesto: The agile manifesto describes the values and principles behind agile practices, and allows supporters to sign the manifesto to express their support for the agile values and principles.

Project Planning: The planning of the project is mainly concerned with defining a schedule and the scope for the project.

Quality Assurance: Quality assurance comprises all activities to evaluate and improve the quality of the software product; the most commonly known activities are testing, reviews, and inspections.

Software Architecture: The architecture of a software system describes its structure; this includes components, interfaces, and communication between interfaces.

Software Based Software Engineering: Value-based software engineering is concerned with expressing value for different aspects of software, e.g. quality attributes, process activities (value of testing activities) etc. Value here does not only constitute money, and what value means is still vaguely defined.

Software Development Lifecycle: The software lifecycle refers to all stages a software product goes through, from the creation of the basic concept till its market release and maintenance.

Team Management: Team management focuses on people and is concerned with supporting and motivating the team members, as well as selecting them.

Section 2
Software Architecture

Chapter 3
OntoArch Reliability–Aware Software Architecture Design and Experience

Jiehan Zhou
University of Oulu, Finland

Eila Ovaska
VTT Technical Research Centre of Finland, Finland

Antti Evesti
VTT Technical Research Centre of Finland, Finland

Anne Immonen
VTT Technical Research Centre of Finland, Finland

ABSTRACT

Reliability-aware software architecture design has recently been gaining growing attention among software architects. This chapter tackles the issue by proposing an ontology-based, reliability-aware software architecture design and evaluation approach, called OntoArch, which incorporates quantitative reliability evaluation in software architecture design by the means of the OntoArch ontology and the OntoArch tool. The OntoArch approach is characterized by: (1) integration of software reliability engineering and software architecture design; (2) proposing a reliability-aware software architecture design process model; (3) developing the OntoArch ontology in the context of software architecture design and software reliability engineering; and (4) the OntoArch tool not only enabling software architects to design architectures and model reliabilities, but also functioning as a knowledge management platform relying on reliability-aware software architecture design. The OntoArch approach is validated for a software architecture design; for example, Personal Information Repository (PIR), with the use cases of OntoArch-based software architecture knowledge management, software reliability profiling, and software architecture modeling and evaluation.

DOI: 10.4018/978-1-60960-215-4.ch003

INTRODUCTION

Reliability evaluation taking place prior to software development has been attracting a growing attention among software architects and reliability experts. In particular, software architecture design has been regarded as the first phase of evaluating reliability in the development of software systems. Software architectural decisions (i.e. architecture design) have a direct impact on such system aspects as cost, time-to-market, and quality. This consideration results in software reliability evaluation in the phase of software architecture design (i.e. software architecture-based reliability evaluation and reliability evaluation at software architecture level) (Goseva-Popstojanova, Mathur, & Trivedi, 2001; Wang, Pan, & Chen, 2006) (Roshandel & Medvidovic, 2004). We use the term of reliability-aware software architecture design and evaluation, which aims to obtain software architecture design in the context of reliability measurement and evaluation.

This paper is based on our previous work (Zhou & Niemelä, et al. 2008) in terms of reliability-aware software architecture, especially extending the scope of the OntoArch ontology design and its usage in PIR prototype implementation. Our contribution is proposing an ontology-based software architecture design and evaluation method, i.e., the OntoArch method. The method integrates software reliability engineering, quality driven software architecture design and quality evaluation approaches. The method embodies reliability engineering in the OntoArch ontology, which is used and exploited in software architecture design and reliability evaluation.

The remainder of the paper is organized as follows. The second section addresses the motivations of creating a reliability-aware software architecture ontology, i.e., the OntoArch ontology. The third section presents the OntoArch engineering process. The fourth section examines knowledge domains of reliability-aware software architecture design and develops the OntoArch ontology. The fifth section presents the experiences on the development of the OntoArch tool and validates the OntoArch method within the PIR system architecture design in the use cases of PIR architecture knowledge management, reliability profiling, architecture modeling, and architecture evaluation. The sixth section reviews related work and outlines our future work. The final section draws a conclusion.

BACKGROUND AND MOTIVATIONS

Traditionally, reliability analysis is performed after system's implementation, when corrections are difficult and modifications are time consuming and expensive. Currently the interest of reliability evaluation has turned to quality evaluation at the software architecture level. Several proposals have been made to predict reliability at the architecture level. In (Immonen & Niemelä, 2007) we compare six most promising reliability evaluation methods, i.e. the methods from Cortellessa et al. (Cortellessa, Singh, & Cukic, 2002), Rodrigues et al. (Oreizy & Taylor et al., 1999), Yacoub et al. (Yacoub, Cukic, & Ammar, 1999), Reussneer et al. (Reussner, Schmidt, & Poernomo, 2003), and Wang et al. (Wang, Pan, & Chen, 1999) from the viewpoint of software architecture. In summary, all the surveyed methods require additional work, especially in the development of the analysis model and application of mathematical algorithms. Although many of these methods have been created for years ago, only few evidences of their maturity are available; i) the methods have been experimented only in laboratory settings by the authors; ii) no comparison of the predicted and measured reliability values exists; and iii) no cost estimation of using the methods could be found. The above mentioned methods are targeted to system architects, software architects, software integrators or service assemblers. It is also common to these methods that traceability of reliability requirements to software architecture is missing.

Moreover, most of these methods lack tool support for reliability evaluation. Thus, we conclude the main findings as a motivation for our approach; methods that apply UML, like (Cortellessa et al., 2002; Rodrigues et al., 2005; Yacoub et al., 1999), in reliability analysis models have several benefits; (i) no additional learning effort because architects are familiar with UML, (ii) no extra modeling cost because no specific analysis model is required, and (iii) open source and commercial tools are available. Therefore, our approach heavily relies on the use of common and widely accepted modeling constructs in architecture models that are extended with required and measured reliability values (Ovaska & Evesti et al., 2010).

Our methodology, Quality driven Architecture Design and quality Analysis (QADA) (Ovaska & Evesti et al., 2010; Matinlassi, Niemelä & Dobrica, 2002; Niemelä, Kalaoja & Lago, 2005), includes two methods and a tool environment that helps in reliability-aware software architecture design and evaluation. The Quality Requirements of a software Family (QRF) method (Niemelä & Immonen, 2006) specifies, how quality requirements have to be defined, represented and transformed to architectural models. The Reliability and Availability Prediction (RAP) method (Ovaska & Evesti et al., 2010; Immonen, 2006) represents the reliability properties in the architectural models using UML profiles and assists in evaluating measured reliability values from architecture models with the help of the method and supporting tool and measuring the reliability values from source code by using the ComponentBee tool for testing (Ovaska & Evesti et al., 2010).

To our knowledge our approach (Ovaska & Evesti et al., 2010) is the only approach that uses the reliability metrics ontology for defining reliability requirements and measures. However, the OntoArch ontology presented in this chapter has a broader scope; besides the reliability metrics ontology the OntoArch defines the whole reliability-aware software architecting process in the form of ontology. Thus, it provides a metamodel for systematic engineering of reliable software systems, from which our methodology is an instance verified and validated in a set of case studies summarized in (Ovaska & Evesti et al., 2010).

Due to the complicated nature of today's systems and the shortcomings of the existing reliability prediction methods, an ontology-based method is required to support reliability-aware architecture design and evaluation. The OntoArch method takes the advantages of QADA, QRF and RAP and integrates architecture design and reliability engineering with respects to software reliability modeling and software architecture modeling and evaluation. The reliability-aware architecture ontology is intended to be used in the following aspects:

- Management and development of reliability-aware software architecture knowledge in the software architect community. The reliability-aware architecture ontology allows end users to better understand software architecture and reliability terminologies, assess software reliability, and communicate effectively with the architect. The ontology further allows the architect to make appropriate decisions in context of architecture modeling, resource usage and schedules through monitoring the reliability-aware architecture design process. Once a reliability-aware architecture ontology is built into the traditional computer-aided architecture design and reliability evaluation programs (i.e. ontology-based reliability-aware architecture design), the programs will be enhanced in terms of ontology-guided architecture design and reliability evaluation. To our knowledge, there are no existing tools in the publications so far. The OntoArch supports the systematic use of the predefined knowledge of reliability in different phases of the software life cycle. The use of reliability ontology improves software quality and makes it possible to handle quality properties during software execution as well.

- Support for service-oriented architecture design in the foreseeable service-intensive business. The service-oriented software development has already emerged for SOA (Service-Oriented Architecture) -based applications integration (Barry, 2003; Marks & Michael, 2006). Non-functional requirements of services, including reliability, are playing an important role in quantitative architecture reliability evaluation. Research (Keller & Ludwig, 2002; Wada & Suzuki, 2006; Zhou & Niemelä, 2006) on QoS (Quality of Service) -aware Web service architectures tries to extend the W3C-defined SOA model (W3C-WSA, 2004) by integrating QoS in Web services. A comparison of existing service description ontologies has been given in (Kantorovitch &Niemelä, 2008). Reliability-aware architecture ontology aims to provide the reliability-aware architect community with a common reliability data communication platform, and to facilitate reliability-aware component/service discoveries and compositions.

In this chapter, we focus on the first aspect. To validate it, we use the OntoArch method in the PIR case study, introduced in detail hereafter.

THE ONTOARCH ENGINEERING PROCESS

Ontology engineering aims to design a subject ontology in order to facilitate knowledge management within internal and external communities and support computer-aided knowledge management and automation of networked knowledge management, e.g. knowledge acquisition, knowledge storage, and knowledge exchange. Based on the

Figure 1. Domains in reliability-aware architecture design

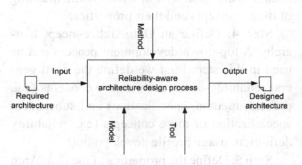

summary of ontology engineering methods (Zhou & Dieng, 2004) and a typical process of ontology engineering given in (Noy & McGuinness, 2006), we refine the ontology engineering steps for creating the OntoArch ontology as follows:

Step 1. Determine the domain for the OntoArch ontology. The OntoArch ontology covers concepts from the areas of software architecture and software reliability, and the aspects of process, methods, models, specifications, tools, and organizations. The OntoArch ontology is designed for the purposes of architecture design, failure data collection, architecture reliability modeling, reliability-aware architecture evaluation, decision guidance, and architecture transformations. The domain in the aspect of organization is not taken into account in the current version of the OntoArch ontology (Figure 1).

Step 2. Consider reusing existing reliability-aware architecture ontologies. Unfortunately, there are no existing ontologies reported for software architecture or software reliability so far. The knowledge body for reliability-aware architecture design has been distributed in textbooks and research publications in terms of software architecture design and reliability engineering.

Step 3. Determine the key concepts related to reliability-aware architecture design. It is advisable to start with classic textbooks in the fields of software architecture and reliability engineering, and to compile a list of all the concepts that the reliability-aware architect community is likely to need. Further, we need to examine the meaning of these concepts and their properties.

Step 4. Define an OntoArch concept hierarchy. A top-down development process can be used in this step. First we define the most general reliability-aware architecture concepts (e.g. process, method, specification) and subsequent specialization of these concepts (e.g. reliability definition, usage profile development).

Step 5. Define the properties of the OntoArch concepts. The OntoArch properties represent the relationships between the OntoArch concepts. In general, there are two types of OntoArch properties: internal and external. The internal properties indicate properties owned by the concepts themselves, such as the name of a process. The external properties indicate the relationships between concepts, such as the method of a process.

Step 6. Define additional OntoArch properties (e.g., cardinality, bidirectional/inverse, etc.). As an example of fine tuned properties, it is possible for a reliability-aware architecture design process to involve one or several methods; and, conversely, a method must be associated with a process.

Step 7. Create OntoArch axioms/rules. OntoArch axioms/rules are a kind of special properties. Defining rule types helps us reduce the workload of formalizing the OntoArch ontology. For example, we define the rule of subProcessTransitivity to denote that the process 'failure severity definition' is a sub-process of the reliability definition process.

Step 8. Create OntoArch instances. We define specific OntoArch instances in terms of its concepts and its properties. For example, we can build the PIR architecture instance to represent a specific application architecture.

ONTOARCH DESIGN

To realize OntoArch, we follow the refined ontology engineering steps for creating the OntoArch ontology. The first step is to determine the knowledge domain for the OntoArch ontology. This section will discover concepts and relationship in context of software architecture and software reliability.

OntoArch Domains

We describe reliability-aware architecture design as a series of interrelated architecture design and reliability prediction processes, through which the reliability-aware architecture knowledge body is organized in terms of methods, tools, models, and the specifications of input and output (Figure 1). The OntoArch processes refer to reliability-aware architecture design and evaluation processes, consisting of five main activities, which are functional-based architecture design, reliability definition, usage profile development, reliability modeling, and failure data interpretation.

The OntoArch method identifies a way for the organization to conduct reliability-aware architecture design processes paying attention to cost-efficiency and purpose-specification. For example, in the failure data interpretation process, there are such methods as reliability trend estimation and reliability chart demonstration. The architect can choose either or both of them for interpreting the architecture reliability.

The OntoArch models are chosen and used in any given applications depending on the specific application purposes or requirements. A software reliability model usually takes the form of a random process that describes the behaviour of failures over a period of time. For example, the first-order Markov chain model (Musa, 1998) assumes that the next component to be executed will probabilistically depend on the present component only and will thus be independent of the past history.

The OntoArch tools refer to computer programs used for software architecture design and/or reliability evaluation. Examples of this kind of software reliability tools are CASRE (Lyu & Nikora, 1992) and SMERFS (Wright, 2006). Among the tools for architecture modeling are

ADLs (Medvidovic, Dashofy & Taylor, 2007), and Stylebase (Matinlassi, 2006). Tools are explained in more detail in the section of tool concepts specification. However, no tools exist in the sense of ontology-based reliability-aware architecture design so far.

The OntoArch specifications refer to the input and output of the OntoArch processes. This data may take the form of tables, files, and graphics.

OntoArch Concept Hierarchy

The OntoArch concept hierarchy is a hierarchical concept classification showing the concept relationships between the knowledge domains of reliability-aware architecture design (Figure 2). This section describes these concepts in detail.

Process Concepts Specification

The OntoArch process model presented below is developed based on the quality-attribute-oriented software architecture design method (Bosch, 2000), the quality-driven architecture design and quality analysis (QADA®[1]) methodology (Matinlassi, Niemelä & Dobrica, 2002; Niemelä et al. 2005; Purhonen, Niemelä & Matinlassi, 2004), the general architecture-based reliability estimation processes surveyed in (Popstojanova & Trivedi, 2001) and a method for predicting reliability and availability at the architecture level (Immonen, 2006) which is one of the methods of QADA®. The proposed OntoArch process model (see Figure 2) has the following features:

- It incorporates quantitative reliability engineering in software architecture design.
- It combines qualitative architecture reliability evaluation and quantitative architecture reliability prediction.
- It employs software architecture views as the primary input/output specifications of reliability modeling.

- It is capable of being customized by the reliability-aware architect community

Process 1: Architecture design. Generally, an architecture design process starts with the functional requirements determined through a requirement specification process (Bosch, 2000). The reliability requirements are not explicitly addressed at this stage. The result is a first version of the application architectural design. Architectural description languages (ADLs) and formal modeling notations are used to enable critical analyses of software architecture designs. This process concludes four core sub-processes: select an architecture style, design a structure view, design a scenario view, and design a development view.

(1) **Select an architecture style.** An architecture style must be selected at the beginning of the architecture design phase. Style is typically associated with certain software quality attributes; for example, a layered architecture style increases the flexibility of the software by defining several levels of abstraction, while it will also generally decrease the performance of the resulting system. This step helps us make an initial architecture decision from the viewpoint of qualitative evaluation.

Input: software quality requirement specification
Output: architecture styles. The architecture styles will be used for selecting style-based software reliability models.
Tool: Stylebase (Merilinna & Niemelä, 2005) that provides guidance for architects in qualitative mapping between quality attributes and architecture styles.

(2) **Design a structure view.** The structure view is one of the core architecture designs, describing the software system in terms of its major components and the relationships between them.

Input: software functional requirement specification, architecture styles
Output: a structure view

Figure 2. OntoArch concept hierarchy

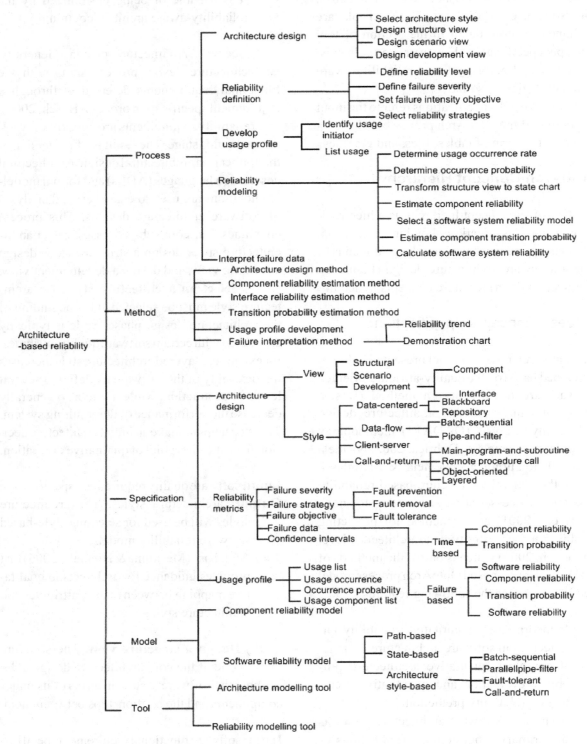

(3) **Design a scenario view.** Designing a scenario view is the second important process in architecture design. The scenario view is a collection of use cases, describing a series of specific, time ordered interactions between the software system, components and end users.

Input: software functional requirement specification, a structure view
Output: a scenario view

(4) **Design a development view.** The development view presents the components, their relationships to each other and the actors responsible for their development. The relationships between two components are specified as a collection of interfaces, interactions, a collection of parameters, a set of files, or as any combination of them.

Input: software requirement specification, a structure view
Output: a development view
Process 2: Architecture reliability definition specifies the required reliability for software architecture in quantitative terms, consisting of four sub-processes:

(1) **Define architecture reliability levels.** The architecture reliability levels indicate how important reliability is to the software system compared with the importance of other factors, such as time-to-market, cost, and manpower.

Input: software quality requirement specification
Output: architecture reliability levels, e.g. high, medium, low

(2) **Define failure in terms of severity classes.** The failure severity classes definition process consists of outlining users' negative requirements for each severity class in a system-specific fashion.

Input: impact criteria, e.g. economic loss and human life

Output: failure severity classes

(3) **Set failure intensity objectives.** The failure intensity objectives are derived from the quality requirement analysis and existing associated software system reliability.

Input: existing associated software system reliability and the capabilities of competing software systems
Output: failure intensity objectives

(4) **Select reliability strategies.** There are three principal reliability strategies: fault prevention, fault removal, and fault tolerance.

Default output: a fault prevention strategy
Process 3: Developing usage profiles; addresses how users will employ the software being designed. By using usage profiles, we can substantially improve the efficiency of both the development and testing of software (Musa, 1998). The development process consists of the following sub-processes:

(1) **Identify the initiators of operations.** While software end users are the most common initiators, machine entities (e.g. software components) may also initiate software operations. To identify the initiators, we first determine the expected end user types based on an architecture scenario view and then determine the end user types.

Input: a scenario view and a development view
Output: initiators of use

(2) **List the modes of operation, for each initiator.** The conceptual architecture (structure and scenario views) provides the most useful information source for this task. Note that each instance of program use is associated with a software operation.

Input: a structure view and a scenario view

Output: list of modes of operation

Process 4: Architecture reliability modeling. Architecture reliability depends on the specific reliabilities of the associated components, interfaces, but also on component transition probabilities. The process of modeling architectural reliability consists of the following sub-processes.

(1) **Determine the occurrence rate for the different modes of operation.** You might collect the data from the previous versions of the same or similar software.

Input: legacy data from previous versions of the same or similar software

Output: occurrence rate for modes of operation

(2) **Determine occurrence probabilities.** To do this, you divide the occurrence rate for each usage by the total occurrence rate of all use instances.

Input: occurrence rates for modes of operation.

Output: occurrence probabilities for operation modes

(3) **Transform the structure view to a state chart.** The state chart represents the execution of components and the transition from one state to another. A style-based transformation from a conceptual architecture to a state view is introduced in (Wang et al., 2006).

Input: a structure view, an architecture style

Output: a state view

(4) **Estimate component reliability.** When using existing components (e.g. from the repository or third parties), the specific component reliability may already be known, based on prior execution of the components. Several techniques (Everett, 1999; Thomason & Whittaker, 1999; Voas, 1998)

have been proposed for estimating the reliability of newly developed components.

Input: a structure view, usage occurrence probabilities, a component reliability estimation model

Output: component reliabilities

(5) **Estimate component transition probability.** Component transition probability is estimated based on the type of component connection (i.e. local/remote, wired/wireless, etc.).

Input: a development view and a usage profile

Output: transition probabilities

(6) **Selecting a software system reliability model.** The general selection strategies (Musa, Iannino, & Okumoto, 1987) favor methods that are: simple and easy to understand; thoroughly developed and widely applied to actual projects; its parameters should also have a clear physical interpretation; and it should be capable of handling evolving systems.

Input: failure strategies

Output: reliability models

(7) **Calculating software system reliability.** This step makes the use of the component reliability values obtained from component reliability measurements to predict the overall software system reliability in a compositional manner.

Input: reliability models, component reliabilities and transition probabilities

Output: an architecture reliability estimate or a chart demonstration of architecture reliability.

Process 5: Interpret failure data. The predicted architecture reliability is compared with the set architecture reliability objectives. If the estimated reliability is good or better than required, the given architecture design version is accepted. If not, the architect can choose either to retain the architecture and downgrade the reliability objectives, or to change the architecture styles.

Specification of Method Concepts

A method describes how to conduct a process efficiently and effectively. The OntoArch method mainly consists of the methods used in the OntoArch processes, i.e. the architecture modeling and evaluation methods (see Figure 2).

Architecture modeling methods provide software architects with architecture design guidelines for turning the software requirement specification into the form of an architecture, identifying the potential risks and verifying software requirements that have been addressed in the architecture design. Architecture design methods concentrate on architecture views, e.g. the 4 views method (Hofmeister, Nord, & Soni, 2000), the 4+1 views method (Kruchten, 1995), the 3+1 views method (Jaaksi, Aalto, Aalto, & Vatto, 1999) or/and quality driven architecture design, e.g. ABD (Bachmann, Bass, Chastek et al., 2000), and QASAR (Bosch, 2000) and QADA® (Matinlassi et al., 2002; Niemelä et al., 2005; Purhonen et al., 2004).

There are also a number of architecture analysis methods available (Dobrica & Niemelä, 2002), including the scenario-based architecture analysis method (SAAM) (Kazman, Abowd, Bass, & Clements, 1996) and its three particular extensions, one founded on complex scenarios (SAAMCS) (Lassing, Rijsenbrij, & Vliet, 1999), and two designed for reusability, ESAAMI (Molter, 1999) and SAAMER (Lung, Bot, Kalaichelvan, & Kazman, 1997), an architecture trade-off analysis method (ATAM) (Kazman et al., 1998), scenario-based architecture reengineering (SBAR) (Bengtsson & Bosch, 1998), architecture level prediction of software maintenance (ALPSM)(Bengtsson & Bosch, 1999), and a software architecture evaluation model (SAEM) (Duenas, Oliveira, & Puente, 1998). Usage profile development meth-

ods include tabular representation and graphical representation. Tabular representation is generally better suited for systems whose usages have few (often one) attributes. The graphical representation is generally more suitable for software the operations of which involve multiple attributes (Musa, 1998).

Component reliability estimation methods include independent component reliability estimation and dependent component reliability estimation. In independent component estimation, a component is considered as an independent unit, while dependent component estimation regards the component as a dependent unit; its reliability is affected by the surrounding components.

Interface reliability estimation methods. Explanations and analyses regarding the interfaces between components have been presented by Voas et al. (Voas, Charron, & Miller, 1996). In addition, there is a method for integration testing, which has been proposed by Delamaro et al. (Delamaro, Maldonado, & Mathur, 1996), and which seems promising for estimating interface reliabilities.

Transition probability estimation methods. There are two approaches for estimating transition probabilities: the Scenario-Based method (Yacoub et al., 1999), which first works out an estimate of the probabilities of execution of different scenarios based on the usage profile. Then, using the analysis scenarios, the transition probabilities are calculated. In (Gokhale, Wong, Trivedi, & Horgan, 1998), the transition probabilities are computed based on the execution counts extracted from the (Automatic Test Analyzer in C) trace files obtained during coverage testing.

Failure interpretation methods. There are two approaches for interpreting architecture reliability: architecture reliability trend and architecture reliability chart demonstration. The failure intensity trend method estimates the failure intensity over all severity classes and across all operational modes against time. The reliability chart method is used in certification testing, where each failure is plotted and labelled with its severity class (Musa, 1998).

Input/Output Specification

OntoArch specifications are used as input or output for the OntoArch processes and sub-processes. For example, a software requirement is an input specification for software architecture design. The OntoArch specifications are divided into the main categories of architecture design and reliability metrics (see Figure 2).

Architecture design field. The software requirement specification is used as an input for software architecture design. The software requirement consists of functional requirements and quality requirements. The functional requirements are related to the domain-specific functionalities of the application.

Software architecture is defined as the structures of the system, consisting of software components, externally visible properties of those components, and the relationships between them (IEEE, 2000; Bass, Clements, & Kazman, 1998).

Architecture style is a description of component types and their runtime control and/or data transfer pattern. An architecture style is determined by a set of component types, a topological layout of the components, a set of semantic constraints and a set of connectors (Bass et al., 1998) (Buschmann, Meunier, Rohnert, Sommerlad, & Stal, 1996). Architecture styles (Bass et al., 1998) include data-centred, data-flow, and call and return styles.

An architecture view is defined to be a representation of a whole system from the perspective of a related set of concerns (IEEE, 2000). The structure view describes the system in terms of its major design elements and the relationships between them. The scenarios view illustrates the collaboration of these components in different use situations. The development view describes the software's static organization in its development environment. There are also a number of other architecture views, such as logical, module, execution, code, conceptual, behaviour, and deployment views (Hofmeister et al., 2000; Immonen, 2006; Jaaksi et al., 1999; Matinlassi et al., 2002). For the first version of OntoArch ontology, we only select the core architecture views that are useful and closely related to quantitative architecture reliability modeling.

Software component is a unit of composition with contractually specified, provided, and required configuration interfaces, quality attributes, and explicit context dependencies (Szyperski, 1997). There are three levels of software component reuse: component reuse over subsequent versions of a software product, reuse over product versions and various products, and reuse over product versions, various products and different organizations (Bosch, 2000).

Reliability metrics field. Software reliability is the probability of failure-free operation of a computer program in a specified environment for a specified time (Standard, 1991; Lyu, 1995; Musa, 1998).

A failure is the departure of program behaviour during execution from user requirements; it is a user-oriented concept. A fault is the defect in the program that causes the failure when executed; it is a developer-oriented concept. A confidence interval represents a range of values within which we expect a parameter to lie with a certain statistical degree of confidence.

A failure objective is the failure intensity degree of satisfaction with customers. Note that there are tradeoffs among a failure intensity objective, required development time and required cost (Musa, 1998; Musa et al., 1987).

A failure severity is a set of failures that affect users to the same degree or level. The severity is often related to the criticality of the operation that fails. Common classification criteria include impacts on human life, cost, and operations. In general, the classes are widely separated regarding impact because one cannot estimate impact with high accuracy (Musa, 1998; Musa et al., 1987).

Failure strategies include fault prevention, fault removal, and fault tolerance. Fault prevention uses requirement management, design, and coding technologies and processes, as well as requirements and design reviews, to reduce the number of faults. Fault removal uses design reviews, code inspection and testing to remove faults in the code once it is written. Fault tolerance reduces the number of failures that occur by detecting deviations in program execution that may lead to failures (Musa, 1998).

A usage profile is a usage scenario that describes the typical uses for the system, where the use scenarios are evaluated with respect of the component reliabilities, resulting in use scenario reliabilities. A usage list is a tabular or graphical representation on the operations each initiator produces.

A usage occurrence refers to the occurrence rates of operation scenarios. The occurrence rates of operations are commonly measured with respect to time. Occurrence probability, again, is the ratio of a specific operation to the total occurrence rate. The total occurrence rate is the sum of all operation occurrence rates. A usage component list is a tabular representation of the components used by each usage scenario.

Component reliability is the probability that the component operates correctly (free of failures) in the course of its execution (Musa, 1998; Yacoub et al., 1999).

A transition is a passage from one state to another, whose transition probability is the probability of this transition taking place (Wang et al., 2006). Transition probability is the probability at which data sent from one component to another component will be delivered error-free. This probability includes possible interface errors and possible channel delivery errors (Yacoub et al., 1999).

Model Concepts Specification

A reliability model usually has the form of a failure process that describes the behaviour of failures over time, also called failure random process. There are two equivalent ways of describing the failure random process: the time of failures and the number of failures in a given period of time. The possibilities for different mathematical forms to describe the failure process are almost limitless (Musa, 1998). Note that there is no clear borderline between the different reliability models. Some well-known reliability models proposed in the literature are presented in the following (see Figure 2).

Component Reliability Estimation Model

Component reliability models refer to models applied for exploring software component reliability. Examples of the component reliability model include: the Hyperexponential model (Kanoun & Sabourin, 1987), the enhanced NHPP model (Gokhale et al., 1998). The Hyperexponential model (Kanoun & Sabourin, 1987) is based on a non-homogeneous Poisson process, and it is used for estimating the stationary failure rates of components. The enhanced NHPP model (Gokhale et al., 1998) was proposed as a method for determining the time-dependent failure intensity of components based on block coverage measurement during the testing.

Software Reliability Estimation Models

State-based model. This class of models uses the control flow graph to represent the architecture of the system. It is assumed that the transfer of control between components has a Markov property, which means that given the knowledge of the component in control at any given time, the future behaviour of the system is conditionally independent of the past behaviour (Thomason & Whittaker, 1999). The state-based models consist of states, i.e. externally visible modes of operation that must be maintained and state transitions labelled with system inputs and transition probabilities. State-based models can be used even if the source code of the component is not available. The state-based model instances include: the Littlewood model (Littlewood, 1979), the Cheung model (Cheung, 1980), the Laprie model (Laprie, 1984), the Kubat model (Kubat, 1989), and the Ledoux model (Ledoux, 1999).

Path-based model. This class of models is based on the same common steps as the state-based models, except that the approach taken to combine the software architecture with the failure behaviour can be described as a path-based one since the system reliability is computed taking into account the possible execution paths of the program either experimentally by testing or algorithmically (Popstojanova & Trivedi, 2001). In addition, the path-based models enable one to specify, with the help of the simulation, the reliability estimations of components (Immonen, 2006). The path-based model instances include: the Shooman model (Shooman, 1976), the Krishnamurthy and Mathur model (Krishnamurthy & Mathur, 1997), and the Yacoub et al. model (Yacoub et al., 1999).

Architecture style-based model. This class of models takes the characteristics of architectural styles into account, including batch-sequential style-based, parallel/pipe-filter style-based, fault-tolerant architectural style-based, and call-and-return style-based. The detail about these models is given in (Bass et al., 1998; Buschmann et al., 1996; Wang et al., 2006).

Tool Concepts Specification

Tools are categorized into architecture design tools and reliability modeling tools.

Architecture Modeling Tools

Architecture modeling tools refer to those that are used for abstracting architecture views, describing software architectures, supporting the mapping between architecture styles and quality requirements, and supporting the transformation between architecture documents and programming languages. In the following, some tools applied in the architecture modeling process are presented:

The modeling tools used for extracting a dynamic view of the software architecture are: the GNU profiler gprof (GNU gprof.2006), ATAC (Horgan & London, 1992), and Dali workbench (Dali, 2006).

The NFR framework is a tool designed for software architects for conducting a trade-off between various conflicting quality attributes and for evaluating the criticality of quality requirements (Chung, Nixon, Yu, and Mylopoulos, 2000). Using the NFR framework, the quality requirements can be renegotiated with the affected stakeholders to find a solution that provides an acceptable trade-off for all of the stakeholders.

Architecture description language (ADL) tools are used for describing software architecture. The ADL tool instances include e.g. Wright (developed by Carnegie Mellon) (Wright, 2006).

UML is a general language for software architecture design. An UML architecture model usually contains diagrams for software structure, behaviour, and interaction (Unified, 2006).

Reliability Modeling Tools

This section briefly summarizes some reliability modeling tools addressing their key properties. However, their usage for architecture level reliability modeling and estimation has to be evaluated.

SMERFS (Statistical Modeling and Estimation of Reliability Functions for Systems) (Lyu, 1995) offers flexibility in data collection and provides multiple time-domain (e.g. Littlewood and Musa basic execution time) and interval-domain (e.g. nonhomogeneous Poisson and generalized Poisson) models.

CASRE (Computer Aided Software Reliability Estimation) (AT&T, 2006; Lyu & Nikora, 1992) is a software reliability modeling tool, which guide the user through selecting a set of failure data and executing a model by selectively enabling pull-down menu options.

SoRel (Kanoun, Kaaniche, Laprie, & Metge, 1993) is a tool for software (and hardware) reliability analysis and prediction, which makes combined use of trend tests and reliability growth models.

AgenaRisk (AgenaRisk, 2006) is a risk assessment and risk analysis tool. It arms users with the latest algorithms for quantifying uncertainty

Figure 3. OntoArch property definition

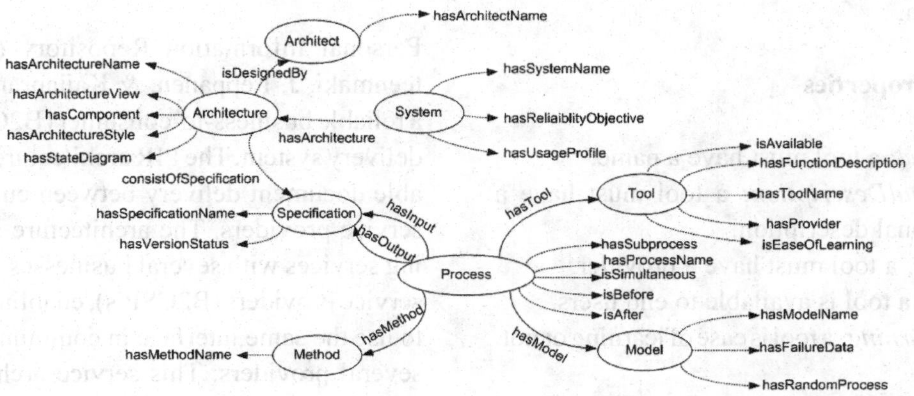

and producing models for prediction, estimation and diagnosis.

OntoArch Properties

We divide the OntoArch properties into internal and external. An internal property describes the internal structure and the attributes of concepts, whereas an external property describes the relationships between concepts. For an internal property, we must determine which concept it describes; for instance, specificationName is one of the internal properties of the concept Specification. For an external property, we must determine the class(es) which the values of the property will be members of and the class(es) that will have the property as a member; for instance hasMethod is an internal property between concepts of Method and Process. The initial OntoArch properties are defined in Figure 3.

• **System properties**

hasSystemName: a system has a name.
hasArchitecture: a system has an architecture.
hasUsageProfile: a system has a usage profile.
hasReliabilityObjective: a system has a reliability objective.

• **Architecture properties**

hasArchitectureName: an architecture has a name.
hasArchitectureView: an architecture has at least one architecture view.
hasComponent: an architecture consists of at least one component.
hasArchitectureStyle: an architecture has at least one architecture style.
hasStateChart: an architecture has at least one state chart.
isDesignedBy: an architecture is designed by at least one architect.
consistOfSpecification: an architecture consists of at least one specification.

• **Process properties**

hasProcessName: a process has a name.
hasSubProcess: a process could have two or more sub-processes.
isBefore/isAfter/isSimutaneous: a process can occur before/after/simultaneously with at least one other process.
hasMethod: a process could have a method.
hasTool: a process could have a supporting tool.
hasModel: a process could have a model.
hasInput: a process could have an input specification.

hasOutput: a process could have an output specification.

- **Tool Properties**

hasToolName: a tool must have a name.
hasFunctionalDescription: a tool must have a functional description.
hasProvider: a tool must have a provider.
isAvailable: a tool is available to end users.
isEaseOfLearning: a tool is ease of learning or not.

- **Model properties**

hasModelName: a model must have a name.
hasFailureDate: a model must have failure data.
hasRandomProcess: a model must have a random process.

- **Specification properties**

hasSpecificationName: a specification must have a name.
hasVersionStatus: a specification has a version status.

- **Method Properties**

hasMethodName: a method must have a name.

EXPERIENCE ON ONTOARCH METHOD

In this section, we present our experiences gained in developing the OntoArch tool and its applications, including the Personal Information Repository (PIR) system examination, OntoArch system requirement analysis, the OntoArch technical features and case demonstrations related to PIR system architecture design.

PIR Examination

Personal Information Repository (PIR) (Lahteenmaki, J. Leppanen, & Kaijanranta, 2007) is a reliable business-to-consumer (B2C) document delivery system. The PIR architecture is for a reliable document delivery between customers and service providers. The architecture allows sharing services with several businesses to consumer service providers (B2CSP's), enabling customers to use the same interface in communicating with several providers. This service architecture approach also enables information to be accessed and used by other applications.

PIR automatically retrieves the required information from service providers' servers and organises the information in the user's information storage. PIR supports structured and semantic information to be sent, which enables automatic processing of the received documents (e.g. producing summary reports and graphics). Some examples of delivery documents are: invoices; health care documents; taxation documents.

Currently, the main function of the PIR system (Figure 4) is to transmit health care information between hospitals (service providers) and customers (patients). The most important components of the PIR system are Document Service for Customer, PIR Case, Browser, and identification through the NetBank component. The Document Service for Customer component works as a temporal data store, mediating documents between customers and B2CSP's. It offers message based and browser based connection to the stored documents. In both cases, data is transmitted using the HTTPS protocol from service providers to customers and vice versa. The component also maintains lists of subscribed B2CSP's and takes care of establishing and maintaining document exchange connections between the B2CSP's and their customer. The Browser or the locally installed PIR case software is used by the customers for accessing the Document Service for Customer. The both components include functionalities for sending, receiving and

Figure 4. Component view of the PIR system

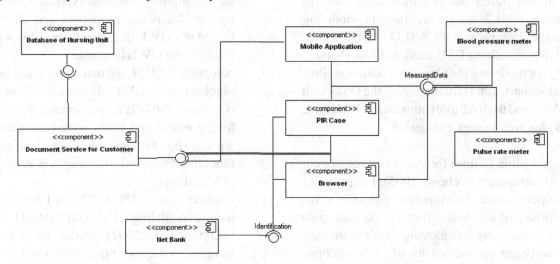

managing documents while PIR Case also provides support for local document management and encryption. The identification service makes it possible to authenticate the service user, for example using the own network bank account.

It is extremely important that PIR system is of high reliability. The identified reliability requirements are: the system probability of failure must be close on 0; the system availability should be close on 100%; data cannot be lost in error situations or must be restored after the errors; if breakdown occurs, mean down time should be less than a minute; system data must always be correct; and system must detect and handle errors.

The PIR system has been validated in a user trial in Finnish hospitals and health centres. At the moment the PIR system is in pilot use in one hospital and two health centres in Finland. The experiments from the pilot use are positive; there would be a demand for having a PIR system available more broadly in hospitals and health centres.

OntoArch System Requirements

In order to identify how the OntoArch tool works for reliability-aware architecture design and evaluation, we take the PIR system architecture

design as an example. To provide the required PIR system functionalities and fulfil the high reliability requirements, the architects and reliability experts expect to use the OntoArch tool to facilitate the processes of system architecture design and reliability evaluation. First, the OntoArch tool is expected to guide the architect through a number of selections concerning PIR system architecture styles and the design of its conceptual structural view, scenarios view and development view, which have to be made with respect to the PIR requirement specification. Then the OntoArch tool is expected to guide the reliability experts through collecting failure data based on architecture views and legacy failure data in previous or similar systems, and estimating the reliabilities of the system components, interfaces and the probabilities of the component transitions. Further, the OntoArch tool is expected to guide the architect in the tasks of selecting software reliability prediction models, and interpreting the simulation results.

OntoArch-Based PIR Design

In the implementation of the OntoArch system, we explore and adopt the following techniques apart from the OntoArch ontology design, i.e., Eclipse for an integrated development environment, Eclipse's UML2 for an architecture modeling language, Eclipse's TOPCASED (TOPCASED, 2007) for visualizing UML models, OWL (Sandia, 2005) for modeling the OntoArch ontology, Protégé (Gennari, 2003) for managing the OntoArch ontology, and the RAP tool (Immonen & Niskanen, 2005) for architecture evaluation.

- Adopting Eclipse for the OntoArch system development (Eclipse, 2005). Eclipse is an open source development platform comprised of extensible frameworks and tools for building, deploying and managing software throughout its lifecycle. Eclipse possesses a powerful modeling framework and code generation facility (i.e. Eclipse Modeling Framework (EMF)). EMF provides the foundation for interoperability with other EMF-based tools and applications.
- Adopting UML2 (UML2, 2006) for software architecture modeling. UML2 is an EMF-based implementation of the UML 2.x metamodel for the Eclipse platform, which implements the UML 2 standards defined by the OMG (Object Management Group) and tools for viewing and editing UML models.
- Adopting OWL (Web Ontology Language) (Sandia, 2005) for OntoArch ontology modeling. OWL provides greater machine interpretability of Web content than XML, RDF, or RDF Schema. OWL also offers additional vocabulary along with formal semantics and provides qualifiers, such

as disjointness, cardinality, and symmetry, for describing properties and classes. OntoArch OWL documents are files written with the OWL language.

- Adopting Protégé for managing OntoArch ontology and OWL documents. Protégé (Gennari, 2003) is a free, open source ontology editor and knowledge-base framework. The Protégé platform facilitates modeling OntoArch ontology via Protégé-OWL editors.
- Adopting the TOPCASED tool for architecture modeling. The TOPCASED tool (TOPCASED, 2007) works on top of Eclipse UML2 and it facilitates visualizing software architecture diagrams.
- Integrating the RAP tool for architecture evaluation. The RAP tool (Immonen & Niskanen, 2005) was independently developed by us before and it is integrated to the OntoArch tool for software architecture evaluation.

Figure 5 presents a workflow used in the OntoArch-based PIR design – containing techniques listed above. Rounded rectangles present utilised tools (capital letters) and high-level mapping to concept hierarchy presented in Figure 2 (italic letters). Rectangles at the bottom show information set produced by each tool and a format used to store and exchange this information.

Some screenshots developed within the OntoArch-based PIR system architecture design are presented in the following, including OntoArch-aided architecture knowledge management, OntoArch-aided reliability profiling, OntoArch-

Figure 5 Workflow of OntoArch-based PIR design

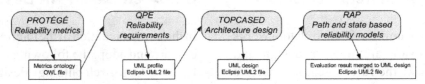

Figure 6. Reliability ontology development under Protégé

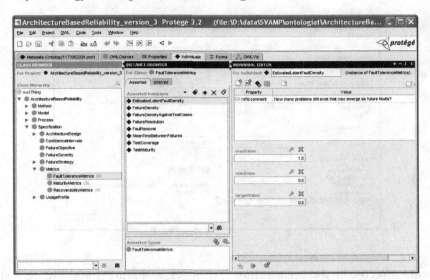

aided architecture modeling, and OntoArch-aided architecture evaluation. Presentation follows the same order presented in the previous workflow figure.

OntoArch-aided architecture knowledge management. Figure 6 shows how reliability metric is defined in the OntoArch ontology by utilizing Protégé ontology tool. Reliability metrics can be found from the OntoArch concept hierarchy in Figure 2. Each metric has maxValue and minValue, which represents range of the metric, and targetValue that shows best value of the metric. Metric's description is written in the comment field of the instance. When the ontology is defined it is stored in the OWL format for the further usage. Reliability metric definition can be thought as a community level activity – producing reusable metrics. However, software companies can also define metrics for their own purposes. In the PIR design we utilized reliability metrics from the existing standards like ISO/IES 9126 (ISO/IEC, 1997)

OntoArch-aided reliability profiling. Figure 7 shows the Quality Profile Editor (QPE) in the OntoArch tool. Using this tool, the architect can define requirements for the designed architecture.

The earlier defined OWL formatted metric ontology acts as an input to this tool. With the QPE tool the architect defines reliability requirements for the PIR system and selects an appropriate reliability metric for each requirement. Thus, architects are able to understand reliability requirements in a similar fashion.

The New Requirement field is used to entering requirements, these requirements appear to the Identified requirements group that makes it possible to connect requirement to the metric from the Quality Metrics Browser group. The Quality Metrics Browser group contains the metrics defined in the OntoArch ontology. The field of the Dependencies to Other Profiles makes it possible to define dependencies between new and earlier defined requirements. Tool automatically compares requirement's value to the range of the selected metric – defined in the ontology – and asks a new value if an inappropriate value is tried to use (Evesti, 2007). As a conclusion, using the OntoArch ontology during this phase makes it possible to define quality requirements as a uniform way. The Quality Profile Editor stores defined requirements and selected metrics in a UML profile form, which makes it possible to utilise

Figure 7. Quality profile editor in the OntoArch tool

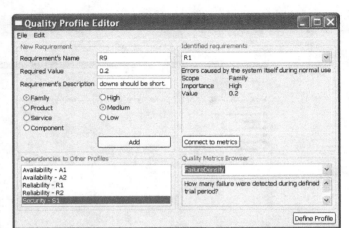

these requirements directly in the architecture design phase.

OntoArch-aided architecture design. In this application, the OntoArch tool invokes UML2 to enable architects to create a reliability-aware PIR architecture – i.e. architecture design concept in the OntoArch concept hierarchy. Figure 8 shows the case where the architect has made a component diagram of the architecture and reliability requirements are connected to the components. Therefore, each component has a set of quality requirements that has to be fulfilled in the selected component. This ensures that the place for each reliability requirement is clearly stated in the architecture design. The Quality Profile Editor stores reliability requirements in a UML stereotype format and these stereotypes can be handled using normal operations that TOPCASED UML tool (Sandia, 2005) offers. The content of reliability requirements defined for the PIR case component is shown in the property view on the bottom of the figure. Thus, the property view shows all content entered by architect in the Quality Profile Editor – including metric selected from the ontology. The architect can modify some attributes of reliability by normal UML tool operations, like dropdown menu shown in the Figure 8. At this time, PIR architecture is described in the high

level, as Figure 4 and Figure 8 shows, in order to exemplify the OntoArch approach. However, behind of these high level structures different architectural styles are used, for instance Model View Controller.

OntoArch-aided architecture evaluation. Figure 9 shows how the PIR architecture is evaluated against reliability requirements. In this application, the RAP tool is used as appeared on the bottom of the figure. The RAP tool is based on the RAP method, tool takes the architectural model – made in the previous step – as an input. RAP tool analyses reliability based on component failure probabilities, i.e. a state-based analysis, and system execution paths, i.e. path-based analysis. Both, state and path based analysis are represented under the Software reliability model in the OntoArch concept hierarchy (c.f. Figure 2). The RAP tool contains a usage profile editor. Thus, the architect is able to create different usage profiles for the PIR system and evaluate reliability with these different usages. The usage profile editor reads execution paths (sequence diagrams) from the architecture design and the architect give execution times for each execution path. The architect uses the RAP tool to address each execution path and path's failure probability, how many times each component is executed and what fail-

Figure 8. Architecture modeling with reliability requirements within the OntoArch

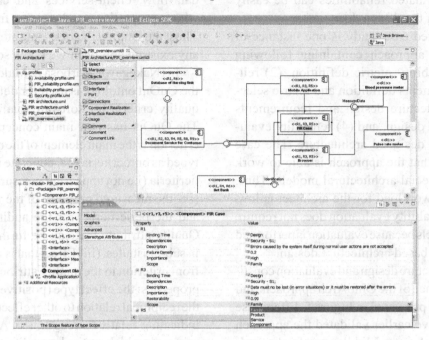

ure probability each component has in the PIR system. On the right bottom corner the failure probability for the whole system is calculated by

the RAP tool. The RAP tool stores evaluation results to the architecture design. Hence, the re-

Figure 9. PIR architecture reliability evaluation

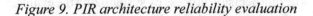

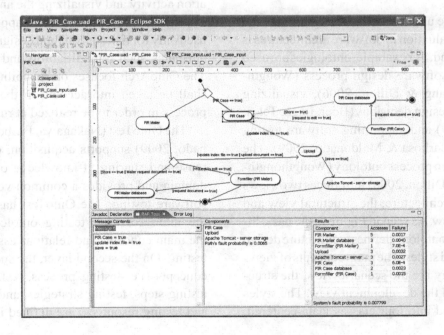

quired and evaluated reliabilities can be easily compared from the design documents.

The presented case study is one instance of the OntoArch approach containing following steps: (1) reliability metric definition, (2) reliability requirements definition and metric selection, (3) architecture design and requirements mapping to the design, and (4) reliability evaluation from the designed architecture. The case study showed that the approach is able to work without any special architectural models. Thus, the additional workload for the architect is low. In addition, reliability evaluation does not require additional models because evaluation is performed from the UML based architecture design.

Each architecture design and evaluation constitutes own instance of the OntoArch approach, and thus, workflow presented in Figure 5 differs case by case. We have earlier validated the approach in the SMEPP (Secure Middleware for Embedded Peer to Peer Systems) case study (Ovaska & Evesti et al., 2010) that presented a different instantiation from the approach.

RELATED AND FUTURE WORK

Nowadays, the use of ontology orientation in the design and evaluation of software architectures is a common trend. For example, ontologies are used for defining software design process (Wongthongtham, Chang & Dillon, 2006), visualizing architecture design decisions (Boer, Lago, Telea, & Vliet, 2009) and supporting software testing (Nakagawa, Barbosa & Maldonado, 2009). The software design process ontology (Wongthongtham, Chang & Dillon, 2006) introduces two views of software architecture; the structural view and behavioral view. As seen in Figure 2, the basic hierarchy of our ontology defines architecture design with views and styles. The main concepts of views in our ontology are the scenario view, the structural view and the development view. The styles are categorized into four classes: data-centered,

data-flow, client-services and call-and-return, whose properties are thereafter further defined. Thus, the OntoArch goes some steps further than any existing approach we know so far.

In (Nakagawa, Barbosa & Maldonado, 2009), the QuOnt ontology is used for defining reusable quality criteria for software quality evaluation. The QuOnt has four main concepts. (i) Quality criterion is the main element of the ontology that is typed as ontocriteria (i.e. concrete measures), anticriteria (i.e not appearing measures), diacriteria (i.e. the measured property of the whole system) and the pericriteria (for the audit process). (ii) Quality attribute that can be further specialized in sub-attributes. (iii) Effect that is reified relation from criterion to the quality attribute, having two properties: the effect type (positive/negative) and the reciprocal relation to other effect relationships, indicating relative strength. (iv) Audit defines a process in which particular quality criteria are used to assess a set of quality attributes. The use of the QuOnt is exemplified by applying the scenario based evaluation method for trade-off analysis, impact analysis and if-then analysis. The main contribution of this approach is on its help in the design decision process by systemizing the evaluation activity and visualizing the analysis results in a tabular format. Thus, this approach can be used only for risk analysis and design time quality attributes, such as modifiability and extensibility. The OntoArch focuses on reliability and how it shall be taken into account in the engineering process in order to be realized at run time.

The OntoTest (Nakagawa, Barbosa & Maldonado, 2009) supports acquisition, organization, reuse and sharing of knowledge on the testing domain and provides a common vocabulary for software testing. The OntoTest has two layers; the main software testing ontology provides the main concepts and relations associated with testing. On the second layer, the specific testing concepts (i.e. testing process, testing artifacts, testing steps, testing strategies, and procedures, and testing resources) are defined in detail. The approach has similarities to ours but focuses on the testing domain in the context of aspect oriented programming. Our approach focuses on reliability in the context of the model and quality driven architecture development.

As illustrated with the examples of related work, the current trend is on merging ontology orientation with different kinds of software engineering activities. Currently, we are working for developing a cross domain innovation platform for smart spaces that exploits ontology orientation in achieving interoperability between different industry domains and making end-user application development easy. Because smart spaces are heavily dynamic and quality attributes such as security and performance besides reliability are the interest of smart space owners and users, we have extended our scope from reliability to other execution qualities. Thus, we are currently applying the enhanced approach to designing and managing the security and performance properties of services and applications in a situation based manner in smart spaces. Due to the dynamic nature of smart spaces our focus is on how to manage quality properties of dynamic systems with an appropriate and feasible way. Therefore, we aim to extend our approach with the capabilities of autonomic computing for achieving self-adaptive and self-organizing software systems. Thus, merging ontology orientation with software engineering is a necessary step in order to develop more sophisticated and intelligent service systems.

CONCLUSION

Reliability-aware software architecture design and evaluation aims to measure software reliability at the software architecture level. In order to achieve this goal, we introduced the OntoArch, an ontology-based reliability-aware architecture design and evaluation approach, along with the OntoArch tool development. The OntoArch approach incorporates quantitative software reliability measurement in software architecture design. Making use of the OntoArch ontology, the OntoArch tool enables software architects and reliability experts to formally, explicitly, and coherently conduct architecture modeling and reliability modeling in a unified computer-aided environment.

In this chapter, the concepts related to ontology-based reliability-aware architecture design and evaluation were defined first. The motivation was examined for getting insight into applying the OntoArch method and exploring the objectives of creating a reliability-aware architecture ontology. Then the process of creating the OntoArch ontology was presented. We also identified the knowledge scopes of reliability-aware architecture design and evaluation, and then designed the OntoArch ontology primarily with respect to the OntoArch concepts and OntoArch properties. The experience on the development of the OntoArch tool was presented, including a description of the requirements specification, and the application of the OntoArch approach into the PIR system design with the use cases of OntoArch-based architecture knowledge management, reliability profiling, architecture design and evaluation.

REFERENCES

W3C-WSA. (2004). *Web services architecture*. Retrieved May 25, 2010, from http://www.w3.org/TR/ws-arch/#whatis

AgenaRisk. (2006). *Bayesian network and simulation software for risk analysis and decision support*. Retrieved May 25, 2010, from http://www.Agenarisk.Com/

AT&T. (2006). *SRE toolkit*. Retrieved May 25, 2010, from http://www.Cse.Cuhk.Edu.hk/~lyu/book/reliability/sretools.Html

Bachmann, F., Bass, L., Chastek, G., Donohoe, P., & Peruzzi, F. (2000). *The architecture-based design method*. Unpublished Technical Report 2000-TR-001, CMU/SEI.

Barry, D. K. (2003). *Web services and service-oriented architectures: The savvy manager's guide*. San Francisco: Morgan Kaufmann Publishers.

Bass, L., Clements, P., & Kazman, R. (1998). *Software architecture in practice*. Boston: Addison-Wesley.

Bengtsson, P. O., & Bosch, J. (1998). Scenario-based architecture reengineering. *Proceedings Fifth International Conference on Software Reuse (ICSR 5)*. (pp. 308).

Bengtsson, P. O., & Bosch, J. (1999). Architecture level prediction of software maintenance. *Third European Conference on Software Maintenance and Reengineering*, (pp. 139-147).

Boer, R. C. D., Lago, P., Telea, R., & Vliet, H. V. (2009). *Ontology-driven visualization of architectural design decisions* (pp. 51–60). Cambridge, UK: WICSA/ECSA.

Bosch, J. (2000). *Design & use of software architectures-adopting and evolving a product line approach*. Addison-Wesley.

Buschmann, F., Meunier, R., Rohnert, H., Sommerlad, P., & Stal, M. (1996). *Pattern-oriented software architecture: A system of patterns*. New York: Wiley.

Cheung, R. C. (1980). A user-oriented software reliability model. *IEEE Transactions on Software Engineering*, 6(2), 118–125. doi:10.1109/TSE.1980.234477

Chung, L., Nixon, B. A., Yu, E., & Mylopoulos, J. (2000). *Non-functional requirements in software engineering*. Kluwer Academic Publishing.

Cortellessa, V., Singh, H., & Cukic, B. (2002). *Early reliability assessment of UML-based software models*. Paper presented at the Third International Workshop on Software and Performance, (pp. 302-309).

Dali. (2006). The Dali workbench. Retrieved May 25, 2010, from http://www.Cs.Cmu.edu/afs/cs/project/tinkerrch/www/html/1998/Lectures/25.RevEng/base.007.Html

Delamaro, M., Maldonado, J., & Mathur, A. P. (1996). *Integration testing using interface mutations*. Paper presented at The Seventh International Symposium on Software Reliability Engineering (ISSRE'96), (pp. 112–121).

Dobrica, L., & Niemelä, E. (2002). A survey on software architecture analysis methods. *IEEE Transactions on Software Engineering*, 28(7), 638–653. doi:10.1109/TSE.2002.1019479

Duenas, J. C., Oliveira, W. L. D., & de la Puente, J. A. (1998). *A software architecture evaluation model*. Paper presented at the Second Int'l ESPRIT ARES Workshop, (pp. 148-157).

Eclipse. (2005). *Home page*. Retrieved May 25, 2010, from http://www.eclipse.org/

Everett, W. (1999). *Software component reliability analysis*. Paper presented at the Symposium on Application-Specific Systems and Software Engineering Technology (ASSET'99), (pp. 204–211).

Evesti, A. (2007). *Quality-oriented software architecture development* (p. 79). Espoo: VTT Publications.

Gennari, J. H. (2003). The evolution of protégé: An environment for knowledge-based systems development. *International Journal of Human-Computer Studies*, 58, 89–123. doi:10.1016/S1071-5819(02)00127-1

GNU. (2006). *The GNU profiler*. Retrieved 25 May, 2010, from http://www.Cs.Utah.edu/dept/old/texinfo/as/gprof_toc.html

Gokhale, S., Wong, W. E., Trivedi, K., & Horgan, J. R. (1998). *An analytical approach to architecture based software reliability prediction.* Paper presented at the Third International Computer Performance and Dependability Symposium (IPDS'98), (pp. 13-22).

Goseva-Popstojanova, K., Mathur, A. P., & Trivedi, K. S. (2001). *Comparison of architecture-based software reliability models.* Paper presented at the 12th International Symposium on Software Reliability Engineering, (p. 22).

Hofmeister, C., Nord, R., & Soni, D. (2000). *Applied software architecture.* Addison-Wesley.

Horgan, J. R., & London, S. (1992). *ATAC: A data flow coverage testing tool for C.* Paper presented at the Second Symposium on Assessment of Quality Software Development Tools, (pp. 2–10).

IEEE. (2000). *IEEE recommended practice for architectural description of software-intensive systems.* IEEE Std-1471-2000.

Immonen, A. (2006). A method for predicting reliability and availability at the architectural level. In Kakola, T., & Duenas, J. C. (Eds.), *Research issues in software product-lines-engineering and management* (pp. 373–422). Berlin, Heidelberg: Springer Verlag.

Immonen, A., & Niemelä, E. (2007). Survey of reliability and availability prediction methods from the viewpoint of software architecture. *Software and Systems Modeling, 7*(1), 49–65. doi:10.1007/s10270-006-0040-x

Immonen, A., & Niskanen, A. (2005). *A tool for reliability and availability prediction.* Paper presented at the 31st Euromicro Conference on Software Engineering and Advanced Applications, (p. 416).

ISO/IEC. (1997). *ISO/IEC CD 9126-1: Software quality characteristics and metrics, part 1: Quality characteristics and sub-characteristics.*

Jaaksi, A., Aalto, J., Aalto, A., & Vatto, K. (1999). *Tried & true object development, industry-proven approaches with UML.* Cambridge University Press.

Kanoun, K., Kaaniche, M., Laprie, J., & Metge, S. (1993). *SoRel: A tool for reliability growth analysis and prediction from statistical failure data.* Paper presented at The Twenty-Third International Symposium on Fault-Tolerant Computing, (p. 654).

Kanoun, K., & Sabourin, T. (1987). Software dependability of a telephone switching system. Paper presented at the 17th International Symposium on Fault-Tolerant Computing (FTCS'17), (pp. 236–241).

Kantorovitch, J., & Niemelä, E. (2008). Service description ontologies. *Encyclopedia of information science and technology, second edition,* (pp. 3445-3451).

Kazman, R., Abowd, G., Bass, L., & Clements, P. (1996). Scenario-based analysis of software architecture. *IEEE Software, 13*(6), 47–55. doi:10.1109/52.542294

Kazman, R., Klein, M., Barbacci, M., Lipson, H., Longstaff, T., & Carriere, S. J. (1998). *The architecture tradeoff analysis method.* Paper presented at the Fourth International Conference Eng. of Complex Computer Systems (ICECCS '98).

Keller, A., & Ludwig, H. (2002). The WSLA framework: Specifying and monitoring of service level agreements for web services. *Journal of Network and Systems Management, 11*(1), 57–81. doi:10.1023/A:1022445108617

Krishnamurthy, S., & Mathur, A. P. (1997). On the estimation of reliability of a software system using reliabilities of its components. *Proceedings of the Eighth International Symposium on Software Reliability Engineering,* (pp. 146-155).

Kruchten, P. B. (1995). The 4+1 view model of architecture. *IEEE Software, 12*(6), 42–50. doi:10.1109/52.469759

Kubat, P. (1989). Assessing reliability of modular software. *Operations Research Letters, 8*(1), 35–41. doi:10.1016/0167-6377(89)90031-X

Lahteenmaki, J., Leppanen, J., & Kaijanranta, H. (2007). *Document-based service architecture for communication between health and wellness service providers and customers.* (pp. 275-278). ICHIT2007.

Laprie, J. C. (1984). Dependability evaluation of software systems in operation. *IEEE Transactions on Software Engineering, 10*(6), 701–714. doi:10.1109/TSE.1984.5010299

Lassing, N., Rijsenbrij, D., & Vliet, H. v. (1999). *On software architecture analysis of flexibility, complexity of changes: Size isn't everything.* Paper presented at the Second Nordic Software Architecture Workshop (NOSA '99), (pp. 1103-1581).

Ledoux, J. (1999). Availability modeling of modular software. *IEEE Transactions on Reliability, 48*(2), 159–168. doi:10.1109/24.784274

Littlewood, B. (1979). Software reliability model for modular program structure. *IEEE Transactions on Reliability, 28*(3), 241–246. doi:10.1109/TR.1979.5220576

Lung, C., Bot, S., Kalaichelvan, K., & Kazman, R. (1997). An approach to software architecture analysis for evolution and reusability. *Proceedings of CASCON '97*, (pp.15).

Lyu, M. R. (1995). *Handbook of software reliability engineering.* McGraw-Hill.

Lyu, M. R., & Nikora, A. (1992). *CASRE: A computer-aided software reliability estimation tool.* Paper presented at the Fifth International Workshop on Computer-Aided Software Engineering, (pp. 264-275).

Marks, E., & Michael, B. (2006). *Service oriented architecture: A planning and implementation guide for business and technology.* Hoboken, NJ: John Wiley & Sons.

Matinlassi, M. (2006). *Quality driven software architecture model transformation towards automation.* Espoo, Finland: VTT Publications.

Matinlassi, M., Niemelä, E., & Dobrica, L. (2002). *Quality-driven architecture design and quality analysis method: A revolutionary initiation approach to a product line architecture.* Espoo, Finland: VTT Publications.

Medvidovic, N., Dashofy, E. M., & Taylor, R. N. (2007). Moving architectural description from under the technology lamppost. *Information and Software Technology, 49*(1), 12–31. doi:10.1016/j.infsof.2006.08.006

Merilinna, J., & Niemelä, E. (2005). A stylebase as a tool for modelling of quality-driven software architecture. *Proceedings of the Estonia Academy of Sciences Engineering, Special Issue on Programming Languages and Software Tools, 11*(4), 296-312.

Molter, G. (1999). Integrating SAAM in domain-centric and reuse-based development processes. *Proceedings of the Second Nordic Workshop on Software Architecture (NOSA '99)*, (pp. 1103-1581).

Musa, J. (1998). *Software reliability engineering, more reliable software faster development and testing.* McGraw-Hill.

Musa, J. D., Iannino, A., & Okumoto, K. (1987). *Software reliability: Measurement, prediction, application.* McGraw-Hill.

Nakagawa, E. Y., Barbosa, E. F., & Maldonado, J. C. (2009). *Exploring ontologies to support the establishment of reference architectures: An example on software testing* (pp. 249–252). Cambridge, UK: WICSA/ECSA.

Niemelä, E., & Immonen, A. (2006). Capturing quality requirements of product family architecture. *Information and Software Technology, 49*(11-12), 1107–1120. doi:10.1016/j.infsof.2006.11.003

Niemelä, E., Kalaoja, J., & Lago, P. (2005). Toward an architectural knowledge base for wireless service engineering. *IEEE Transactions on Software Engineering, 31*(5), 361–379. doi:10.1109/TSE.2005.60

Noy, N. F., & McGuinness, D. L. (2006). *Ontology development 101: A guide to creating your first ontology*. Retrieved May 25, 2010, from http://ksl.Stanford.edu/people/dlm/papers/ontology101/ontology101-Noy-Mcguinness.Html

Oreizy, L. P., Taylor, R. N., Heimbigner, D., Johnson, G., Medvidovic, N., & Quilici, A. (1999). Self-adaptive software: An architecture-based approach. *IEEE Intelligent Systems, 14*(3), 54–62. doi:10.1109/5254.769885

Ovaska, E., Evesti, A., Henttonen, K., Palviainen, M., & Aho, P. (2010). Knowledge based quality-driven architecture design and evaluation. *Information and Software Technology, 52*(6), 577–601. doi:10.1016/j.infsof.2009.11.008

Popstojanova, K. G., & Trivedi, K. S. (2001). Architecture-based approach to reliability assessment of software systems. *Performance Evaluation, 45*(2), 179–204. doi:10.1016/S0166-5316(01)00034-7

Purhonen, A., Niemelä, E., & Matinlassi, M. (2004). Viewpoints of DSP software and service architectures. *Journal of Systems and Software, 69*(1), 57–73. doi:10.1016/S0164-1212(03)00050-5

Reussner, R., Schmidt, H., & Poernomo, I. (2003). Reliability prediction for component-based software architectures. *Journal of Systems and Software, 66*(3), 241–252. doi:10.1016/S0164-1212(02)00080-8

Rodrigues, G., Rosenblum, D., Uchitel, S., Bt, W., & Rh, S. (2005). *Using scenarios to predict the reliability of concurrent component-based software systems*. FASE 2005 – LNCS 3442, (pp. 111-126).

Roshandel, R., & Medvidovic, N. (2004). Toward architecture-based reliability estimation. *Proceedings from The International Conference on Dependable Systems and Networks*.

Sandia, N. L. (2005). Java expert system shell (JESS). Retrieved May 25, 2010, from http://herzberg.ca.sandia.gov/jess/

Shooman, M. (1976). Structural models for software reliability prediction, (pp. 268–280). Paper presented at the Second International Conference on Software Engineering.

Standard. (1991). *Standard glossary of software engineering terminology*.

Szyperski, C. (1997). *Component software, beyond object-oriented programming*. New York: Addison Wesley Longman Ltd.

Thomason, M. G., & Whittaker, J. A. (1999). *Rare failure-state in a Markov chain model for software reliability*, (pp. 12-19). Paper presented at the 10th International Symposium on Software Reliability Engineering.

TOPCASED. (2007). *Home page*. Retrieved May 25, 2010, from http://topcased-mm.Gforge.Enseeiht.fr/website/index.Html

UML2. (2006). *Home page*. Retrieved May 25, 2010, from http://www.Eclipse.org/uml2/

Unified. (2006). *Unified modeling language*. Retrieved May 25, 2010, from http://en.Wikipedia.org/wiki/Unified_Modeling_Language.

Voas, J., Charron, F., & Miller, K. (1996). Robust software interfaces: Can COTS-based systems be trusted without them? (pp. 126–135). Paper presented at the 15th International Conference on Computer Safety.

Voas, J. M. (1998). Certifying off-the-shelf software components. *IEEE Comput., 31*(6), 53–59.

Wada, H., & Suzuki, J. (2006). Modeling non-functional aspects in service oriented architecture, (pp. 222-229). Paper presented at the IEEE International Conference on Service Computing.

Wang, W., Pan, D., & Chen, M. (1999). An architecture-based software reliability model. *In Proceedings of the Pacific Rim International Symposium on Dependable Computing (PRDC'99),* (pp. 143-150).

Wang, W., Pan, D., & Chen, M. (2006). Architecture-based software reliability modeling. *Journal of Systems and Software, 79*(1), 132–146. doi:10.1016/j.jss.2005.09.004

Wongthongtham, P., Chang, E., & Dillon, T. (2006). Software design process ontology development. In *On the move to meaningful internet systems* (pp. 1806–1813). Berlin, Heidelberg: Springer.

Wright. (2006). The Wright architecture description language. Retrieved May 25, 2010, from http://www.Cs.Cmu.edu/afs/cs/project/able/www/wright/index.Html

Yacoub, S., Cukic, B., & Ammar, H. (1999). *Scenario-based reliability analysis of component-based software,* (pp. 22-31). Paper presented at the 10th International Symposium on Software Reliability Engineering (ISSRE'99).

Zhou, J., & Dieng, R. (2004). A semantic knowledge management system for knowledge-intensive manufacturing, (pp. 114-122). Paper presented at the 2004 IADIS International Conference of e-Commerce.

Zhou, J., & Niemelä, E. (2006). *Toward semantic QoS-aware web services: Issues, related studies and experience.* Paper presented at the IEEE/WIC/ACM International Conference on Web Intelligence.

Zhou, J., Niemelä, E., Evesti, A., Immonen, A., & Savolainen, P. (2008). *OntoArch approach for reliability-aware software architecture development* (pp. 1228–1233). Turku, Finland.

KEY TERMS AND DEFINITIONS

Software Architecture: Includes multiple views that describe the software entities and their relationships in three dimensions: abstraction, dynamism and aggregation. Architectural principles define the style that design and evolution of software entities are to follow.

Software Reliability: The probability of the failure-free operation of a software system for a specified period of time in a specified environment.

Service Reliability: Extends the software reliability definition, requiring that either the software system does not fail at all for a given period or it successfully recovers state information after a failure for a system to resume its service as if it had not been interrupted.

Reliability-Aware Architecture Design: Provides a systematic and managed way to guaranteeing that reliability requirements are taken into account in architecture design and evaluation.

Ontology Oriented Design: Aims at representing, structuring and managing topic knowledge shared across people, organizations, computers and software.

ENDNOTE

[1] Trademark of VTT Technical Research Center of Finland.

Chapter 4
Architecture–Driven Modernization

Ricardo Pérez-Castillo
University of Castilla-La Mancha, Spain

Ignacio García Rodríguez de Guzmán
University of Castilla-La Mancha, Spain

Mario Piattini
University of Castilla-La Mancha, Spain

ABSTRACT

Legacy information systems can be a serious headache for companies because, on the one hand, these systems cannot be thrown away since they store a lot of valuable business knowledge over time, and on the other hand, they cannot be maintained easily at an acceptable cost. For many years, reengineering has been a solution to this problem because it facilitates the reuse of the software artifacts and knowledge embedded in the system. However, reengineering often fails due to the fact that it carries out non-standardized and ad hoc processes. Currently, software modernization, and particularly ADM (Architecture-Driven Modernization), standardized by the OMG, is proving to be an important solution to that problem, since ADM advocates carrying out reengineering processes taking into account the principles and standards of model-driven development. This chapter provides an overview of ADM and shows how it allows legacy information systems to evolve, making them more agile, preserving the embedded business knowledge, and reducing maintenance costs. Also, this chapter presents the software archeology process using ADM and some ADM success stories.

INTRODUCTION

According to the Lehman's first law, an information system must continually evolve or it will become progressively less suitable in real-world environments (Lehman et al., 1998). Indeed, companies count on a vast number of large legacy systems which are not immune to software erosion and software ageing, i.e., legacy information systems that become progressively less maintainable (Polo et al., 2003). Nevertheless, software erosion is due to maintenance itself and the evolution of

DOI: 10.4018/978-1-60960-215-4.ch004

the system over time. It is possible to measure this erosion using different metrics (Visaggio, 2001), e.g., dead code, clone programs, missing capacities, inconsistent data and control data (coupling), among others.

The successive changes in an information system degrade its quality, and thus, a new and improved system must replace the previous one. However, the wholesale replacement of these systems from scratch is risky since it has a great impact in technological, human and economic terms (Koskinen et al., 2004; Sneed, 2005). The technological and human point of view is affected since replacement would involve retraining all the users in order to understand the new system and the new technology, or the new system may lack specific functionalities that are missing due to the technological changes. Moreover, the economic point of view is also affected since the replacement of an entire legacy system implies a low Return of Investment (ROI) in that system. In addition, the development or purchase of a new system could exceed a company's budget.

For example, let us imagine a transmission belt in a car engine which deteriorates over use and over time. When this piece is damaged, it must be replaced, and then the engine operates normally. This example is easy, but an information system used in a company is more difficult. When this system ages, it cannot simply be replaced by another new system for two important reasons: (i) a belt costs a few dollars while an enterprise information system costs thousands of dollars, but in addition (ii) the aged system embeds a lot of business knowledge over time that is lost if it is replaced, thus the company with a new system may not operate normally like the car engine.

When companies are faced with the phenomenon of software erosion, evolutionary maintenance is a better solution to obtain improved systems, without discarding the existing systems, thus minimizing the software erosion effects. Evolutionary maintenance makes it possible to manage controllable costs and preserves the valuable busi-ness knowledge embedded in the legacy system, since 78% of maintenance changes are corrective or behaviour-preserving (Ghazarian, 2009).

Over the last two decades, reengineering has been the main tool for addressing the evolutionary maintenance of legacy systems (Bianchi et al., 2003). Reengineering preserves the legacy knowledge of the systems and makes it possible to change software easily, reliably and quickly, resulting in a maintenance cost that is also tolerable (Bennett et al., 2000).

The reengineering is the examination and alteration of a subject system to reconstitute it in a new form and the subsequent implementation of the new form [...] This may include modifications with respect to new requirements not met by the original system.(Chikofsky et al., 1990)

Nevertheless, a 2005 study states that over 50% of reengineering projects fail (Sneed, 2005). This is due to the fact that in most cases the reengineering usually has two main problems when dealing with specific challenges at this point in time:

- the reengineering of large complex legacy information systems is very difficult to automate (Canfora et al., 2007), therefore the maintenance cost grows significantly.
- the traditional reengineering processes lacks formalization and standardization (Kazman et al., 1998), and thus different reengineering tools that address specific tasks in the reengineering process cannot be integrated or reused in different reengineering projects.

For these reasons, the software industry is demanding reengineering processes that enable the evolutionary maintenance of legacy systems in an automatic and standardized way. The typical reengineering concept has shifted to so-called Architecture-Driven Modernization (ADM) as a solution to those demands.

ADM is the concept of modernizing existing systems with a focus on all aspects of the current system's architecture and the ability to transform current architectures to target architectures. (OMG, 2006a)

ADM advocates carrying out reengineering processes following the MDA (Model-Driven Architecture) standard (Miller et al., 2003), i.e., it becomes possible to model all the legacy software artifacts as models and establishes model transformations between the different MDA abstraction levels. The model-driven principles assist in solving the standardization and automation problems inherent in traditional reengineering processes. In this way, ADM addresses the software erosion phenomenon by modernizing legacy systems. This software modernization can be considered as a kind of software evolution. Its main purposes are (OMG, 2007a):

- Software improvement
- Interoperability
- Migration
- Refactoring
- Restructuring
- Enterprise application integration
- MDA migration

In addition to software erosion management, ADM provides other important benefits such as (OMG, 2007a):

- Revitalizing legacy information systems, making them more agile.
- Reducing maintenance and development costs
- Extending the useful life of legacy information systems, also improving the ROI of those systems.
- Easy integration with other systems and other environments like Service-Oriented Architecture (SOA).

The objective of this chapter is to provide an overview of the emerging concepts and standards related to ADM, and show the way in which these elements are able to solve a typical problem in the software industry: modernizing legacy and ageing systems in companies.

The rest of this paper is organized as follows. The second section summarizes the state-of-the-art of software modernization as well as the most important works related to the concepts in this chapter. The third section gives a detailed account of software evolution by means of the possibilities offered by ADM. Following this, the fourth section presents software archeology as an emerging stage within software modernization processes, focusing on understanding and recovering specific knowledge from existing software assets. The fifth section shows a concrete real world case study in order to clarify the concepts presented previously. The sixth section briefly presents some projects and tools where the ADM approach has successfully been applied. Finally, the last section presents a summary of the chapter and future and emerging trends related to software modernization.

BACKGROUND

This section discusses the main concepts related to this chapter in detail: firstly, it defines legacy systems and their problems; secondly, it presents the reengineering process and its stages; and finally, it shows the ADM approach, its history and the standards that it defines.

Legacy Information Systems

Most companies have existing information systems considered to be *legacy systems* because the code in these systems was written long ago and may now be technologically obsolete. According to (Paradauskas et al., 2006), *"a legacy information system is any information system that significantly resists modification and evolution to meet new and constantly changing business requirements"*. (Ulrich, 2002) states that *"legacy systems are defined as any production-enabled software, regardless of the platform it runs on, language it's written in, or length of time it has been in production"*. (Hunt et al., 2002) go further to state that the *"code becomes legacy code just about as soon as it's written"*.

Software vendors have cultivated a belief that *"anything new is beautiful and that everything old is ugly"* and we have become *"victims of a volatile IT industry"* (Sneed, 2008). Despite the fact that legacy systems may be obsolete, this kind of system usually has a critical mission within the company and represents a valuable asset for companies, since legacy systems embed a lot of business logic and business rules that are not present elsewhere (Sommerville, 2006). The business knowledge embedded in the legacy systems results from the fact that companies maintain their legacy systems over time. This maintenance adds increasingly more functionalities to legacy systems, supporting the company's operation and activities. Therefore, the companies cannot discard their legacy systems, although for this reason, they must deal with the underlying problems of software erosion in the legacy systems (Paradauskas et al., 2006):

- Typically, legacy systems are implemented with obsolete technology which is difficult and expensive to maintain.
- The lack of documentation leads to a lack of understanding of the legacy systems, making the maintenance of these systems a slow and expensive process.
- A great effort must be made to integrate a legacy system together with other systems in the company, since the interfaces and boundaries of the legacy system are not usually well defined.

Reengineering

Two decades ago, the reengineering of legacy systems became one of the most successful practices for dealing with software erosion problems in this type of system. A reengineering process does not discard the whole system, and the enhanced system that it obtains preserves most of the business knowledge embedded in the legacy system. Therefore, the reengineering processes make it possible to carry out evolutionary maintenance of the legacy systems assuming low risks and low costs (Sneed, 2005).

The reengineering process consists of three stages: reverse engineering, restructuring and forward engineering (Chikofsky et al., 1990). The first stage is the reverse engineering process which analyzes the legacy system in order to identify the components of the system and their interrelationships. Then, the reverse engineering stage builds one or more representations of the legacy system at a higher level of abstraction. The second stage is the restructuring process which takes the previous system's representation and transforms it into another at the same abstraction level. This stage preserves the external behavior of the legacy system. Finally, the third stage of the reengineering process is forward engineering, which generates physical implementations of the target system at a low abstraction level from the previous restructured representation of the system.

According to (Kazman et al., 1998), the whole reengineering process can be viewed as a horseshoe model. The reverse engineering stage that increases the abstraction level represents the left side of the horseshoe; the restructuring stage preserves the same abstraction level, thus it represents the curve of the horseshoe; and the last part on the right side of the horseshoe is the forward engineering stage that instantiates the target system.

Applications of Reengineering

Reengineering practices have been applied to several fields in addition to software engineering, such as the hardware industry and business process management. Specifically, the software industry has successfully applied reengineering to many domains. Some examples of these domains are the following:

- Traditionally, reengineering has been used to carry out technological changes or migrations to another program language. One example is the transformation of a legacy system that was developed following a structured paradigm into an object-oriented system. This reengineering process also involves rewriting the code written in a structured programming language such as COBOL or C into other object-oriented language such as JAVA or C++.
- Reengineering has also been used to modify the design of a legacy system in order to improve its maintainability, efficiency, and other system features. For example, imagine a legacy information system based on JAVA technology. In the reverse engineering stage we could analyze the legacy source code and recover the design of the legacy systems, i.e., a set of class diagrams that depict the system. After that, in the restructuring stage, we can modify the design of the systems by adding well-defined design patterns such as the patterns proposed by (Gamma et al., 1995), which improve the maintainability of the system. Finally, the forward engineering stage generates the new source code from the improved class diagrams.
- Another broad field where reengineering has been applied within the software industry is database reengineering. In this respect, (Hainaut et al., 1996) propose reengineering as a mechanism to design relational databases. While the forward engineering of a database requires conceptual design, logical design and physical design, the reengineering approach only needs data structure extraction and data structure conceptualization. This approach makes it possible to migrate towards a relational data model from any kind of data model.

Limitations of Reengineering

Reengineering has been a successful practice in the software industry, but currently more than half of the traditional reengineering projects fail when dealing with specific challenges (Sneed, 2005). The most important problems are the standardization and automation of the reengineering process.

Firstly, standardization constitutes a problem since the reengineering process is typically carried out in an *ad hoc* manner. Thus reengineering projects must focus their efforts on a better definition of the process. Furthermore, the code cannot be the only software asset that the standardization covers, since *"the code does not contain all the information that is needed"* (Müller et al., 2000). The reengineering process must be formalized to ensure an integrated management of all of the knowledge involved in the process such as source code, data, business rules, and so on.

Secondly, automation is also a very important problem. In order to prevent failure in large complex legacy systems, the reengineering process must be more mature and repeatable (Canfora et al., 2007). In addition, the reengineering process needs to be aided by automated tools so that companies can handle the maintenance cost (Sneed, 2005). Moreover, automation can be considered as a problem derived from the standardization problem, since standardization and the formalization of the process are necessary requirements to provide tools to automate the process, which can be reused for several reengineering projects.

Figure 1. Horseshoe modernization model

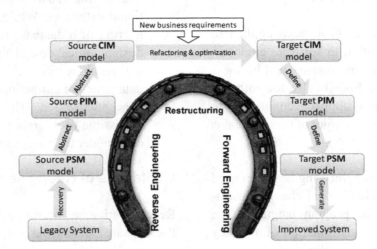

Architecture-Driven Modernization

The software modernization paradigm, and particularly ADM as defined by the OMG, can be considered as a mechanism for software evolution, i.e., it makes it possible to modernize the legacy information systems and eradicates, or at least minimizes, the software erosion problem in legacy systems. According to (OMG, 2003b), ADM *"is the process of understanding and evolving existing software assets. ADM restores the value of existing applications"*.

ADM solves the problems of traditional reengineering since it carries out reengineering processes taking *model-driven* principles into account. However, ADM does not replace reengineering, but ADM improve it. The MDA (Model-Driven Architecture) standard proposed by OMG defines two main principles: (i) modeling all the artifacts as models at different abstraction levels; and (ii) establishing model transformations between them (Miller et al., 2003).

The horseshoe reengineering model has been adapted to ADM and it is known as the horseshoe modernization model (see Figure 1). There are three kinds of models in the horseshoe model (Miller et al., 2003):

- **Computation Independent Model (CIM)** is a view of the system from the computation independent viewpoint at a high abstraction level. A CIM does not show details of the system's structure. CIM models are sometimes called domain models and play the role of bridging the gap between the domain experts and experts in the system design and construction.
- **Platform Independent Model (PIM)** is a view of a system from the platform independent viewpoint at an intermediate abstraction level. A PIM has a specific degree of technological independence in order to be suitable for use with a number of different platforms of a similar type.
- **Platform Specific Model (PSM)** is a view of a system from the platform specific viewpoint at a low abstraction level. A PSM combines the specifications in the PIM with the details that specify how that system uses a particular type of platform or technology.

ADM solves the formalization problem since it represents all the artifacts involved in the reengineering process as models. Therefore,

ADM treats them homogenously, i.e., as models, meaning that ADM can establish model transformations between them. Those transformations are formalized by means of the QVT (Query / Views / Transformations) standard proposed by the OMG (OMG, 2008b). The QVT specification consists of two distinct but related languages: (i) *QVT-Operational* language, which is procedural in nature, and (ii) *QVT-Relations*, a declarative language. QVT makes it possible to define deterministic transformations between models at the same abstraction level or at a different level. As a consequence, the model transformations can be automated. Furthermore, the model-driven development principles make it possible to reuse the models involved in the ADM projects, since several PIM models can be generated from a CIM model, and in turn, several PSM models can be obtained for each PIM model. Therefore, the automation problem can be also solved due to the automated transformations together with the reuse of the models.

So far, model-driven development principles have been usually used in the forward engineering stage. Model-driven, generative techniques are used in that stage to obtain source code from different kinds of models, for instance UML models. Indeed, some researchers consider model-driven engineering only applicable for forward engineering. However, model-driven development principles can be applied to the reverse engineering and restructuring stages in an effective way.

In reverse engineering stage, the information recovered from software artifacts can be represented in models according to certain metamodels. In addition, restructuring and refactoring techniques can be applied on models. Thus, it consists of a transformation from the input model (as is) to obtain a target model (as be). Model-based restructuring has some advantages with respect to the traditional restructuring: (i) the model-based one allow researchers to define language- and platform-independent refactoring

techniques; (ii) a restructuring transformation could be implemented as a model it-self, thus the transformation can be reused; (iii) the model-based refactoring makes it possible to define generic or domain-specific refactoring techniques in an easy manner; (iv) it improves the feature location since the traceability throughout corresponding models at different abstraction levels is better; (v) and so on.

ADM Standards

ADM not only adopts other existing standards like MDA and QVT, it has also spearheaded the development of a set of standards to address the different challenges that appear in the modernization of legacy information systems (OMG, 2009b).

In June 2003, the OMG formed a Task Force for modeling software artifacts in the context of legacy systems. Initially, the group was called the Legacy Transformation Task Force and was then renamed the Architecture-Driven Modernization Task Force (ADMTF). In July 2003, the ADMTF issued a software modernization whitepaper (OMG, 2003b). In November 2003, the ADMTF issued the request-for-proposal of the Knowledge Discovery Metamodel (KDM) specification. KDM aims to be an initial metamodel that allows modernization tools to exchange application metadata across different applications, languages, platforms and environments. The objective of this initial metamodel was to provide a comprehensive view of the application structure and data, but does not represent software below the procedure level. The request-for-proposal stated that the KDM metamodel:

- represents artifacts of legacy software as entities, relationships and attributes
- includes external artifacts with which software artifacts interact
- supports a variety of platforms and languages

- consists of a platform and language in-dependent core, with extensions where needed
- defines a unified terminology for legacy software artifacts
- describes the physical and logical structure of legacy systems
- can aggregate or modify, i.e. refactor, the physical system structure
- facilitates tracing artifacts from logical structure back to physical structure
- represents behavioral artifacts down to, but not below, the procedural level.

In May 2004, six organizations responded to the request-for-proposal. However, throughout 2004 and 2005 more than 30 organizations from 5 different countries have collaborated in the development and review of the KDM standard. In May 2006, KDM was adopted by the OMG and moved into the finalization stage in the adoption process. In March of 2007, the OMG presented the recommended specification of KDM 1.0. In April 2007, the OMG started ongoing maintenance of the KDM specification. In January 2009, the recommended specification of KDM 1.1 became available in the OMG (OMG, 2009a), and in turn, the OMG started the revision of this version. Recently, in March 2009, KDM was recognized as a draft international standard, specifically ISO/IEC 19506 (ISO/IEC, 2009).

KDM is the first fulfilled standard and is the cornerstone of the set of standards proposed by the ADMTF of the OMG. However, the ADMTF is defining the rest of the standards planned around the KDM, although some of these standards are still in the approval or development stage. The set of ADM specifications is (OMG, 2009b):

- **Abstract Syntax Tree Metamodel (ASTM)** is a specification built under KDM to represent software below the pro-cedural level by means of abstract syntax tree models. The ASTM and the KDM are two complementary modeling specifications to fully represent applications and facilitate the exchange of granular metadata across multiple languages. In 2009 the ADMTF proposed the first specification of ASTM 1.0.
- **Software Metrics Metamodel (SMM)** defines a metamodel for representing measurement information related to software, its operation, and its design. The specification is an extensible metamodel for exchanging software-related measurement information concerning legacy software artifacts: designs, implementations, or operations. Also in 2009, the ADMTF proposed the first specification of SMM 1.0.
- **ADM Pattern Recognition specification** aims to be a standard to facilitate the examination of structural metadata with the intent of deriving patterns about legacy systems. These patterns can be used to determine refactoring and transformation requirements and opportunities that could be applied to one or more systems. This specification was issued in 2009.
- **ADM Visualization specification** focuses on the different ways to show application metadata stored within the KDM models. In 2009 there was no target date for this proposal.
- **ADM Refactoring specification** seeks to define ways in which the KDM specification can be used to refactor applications by means of structuring, rationalizing, modularizing, and so on. In 2009 there was no target date for this proposal.
- **ADM Transformation specification** seeks to define mappings between KDM, ASTM and target models. Also, in 2009 there was no target date for this proposal.

Software Evolution through ADM

Software evolution is a kind of software maintenance which is also called evolutionary maintenance. In general, the maintenance process can perform four categories of modifications in the existing software (ISO/IEC, 2006):

- **Corrective maintenance** modifies a software product performed after delivery in order to correct discovered problems.
- **Preventive maintenance** modifies a software product after delivery to detect and correct latent faults in the software product before they become effective faults.
- **Adaptive maintenance** modifies a software product performed after delivery to keep a software product usable in a changed or changing environment;
- **Perfective maintenance** modifies a software product after delivery in order to improve the performance or the maintainability.

Evolutionary maintenance is a specific maintenance process that focuses on adaptive and perfective modifications. Indeed, (Mens et al., 2008) states that a legacy system must be evolved when it *"operates in or addresses a problem or activity of the real world. As such, changes in the real world will affect the legacy system and require adaptations to it"*.

Software evolution can be considered as a process to enhance legacy information systems in order to deal with software erosion problems. Nevertheless, the software erosion phenomenon is due to the maintenance process itself. Thus, according to the software entropy law, evolutionary maintenance could trigger more software erosion problems over the long term (Jacobson et al., 1992).

"The software entropy law states that a closed system's disorder cannot be reduced, it can only remain unchanged or increase. A measure of this disorder is entropy. This law also seems plausible for software systems; as a system is modified, its disorder, or entropy, always increases. This is known as software entropy". (Jacobson et al., 1992)

Therefore, evolutionary maintenance should generate new improved versions of legacy systems while minimizing the negative effects of the maintenance. Software modernization, and in particular ADM itself, can be seen as a kind of evolutionary maintenance, which is based on the reengineering process and follows a model-driven approach. Due to the fact that ADM advocates carrying out model-driven processes, automation and reuse (based on abstract models) are ensured. Thus, the outcomes of the ADM-based processes are not only the improvement or evolution of a specific legacy system, but also that the legacy system is represented through a set of models at different abstraction levels that can be reused in future maintenance processes. Therefore, the software entropy problem is minimized with software evolution by means of ADM.

According to the horseshoe model, the ADM-based process can be categorized into three kinds of modernization processes (Khusidman et al., 2007). These depend on the abstraction level reached in the reverse engineering stage in the horseshoe model, and thus each kind of modernization process defines a specific modernization curve (see *Figure 2*).

Depending on the abstraction level reached (see *Figure 2*), the knowledge and models available to the restructuring stage may be different. Usually, a higher abstraction level implies a greater amount of knowledge and rich information that provides more restructuring possibilities to the modernization process. The three kinds of modernization processes are the following:

- **Technical Modernization.** This kind of modernization considers the lowest ab-

Figure 2. Horseshoe modernization model

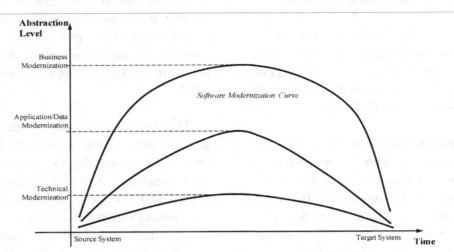

straction level and is historically the most commonly applied to legacy systems. A company carries out a technical modernization project when it wants to deal with platform or language obsolescence, new technical opportunities, conformance to standards, system efficiency, system usability or other similar modernization factors. This type is sometimes not considered strictly as a modernization process since it only focuses on corrective and preventive modifications, but in any case it addresses adaptive or perfective modifications according to the modernization definition.

- **Application/Data Modernization.** This kind of modernization considers an intermediate abstraction level since it focuses on restructuring a legacy system at the level of application and data design to obtain the target system. This kind of modernization is driven by several modernization factors such as improving the system reusability, reducing the delocalized system logic or system complexity, and applying design patterns. There is a fine line between this kind of modernization and the previous one, but that line is crossed when there is some impact on the system design level.

- **Business Modernization.** This kind of modernization increases the abstraction level to the maximum. Thus, the restructuring stage is done at the level of business architecture, i.e., the business rules and processes that govern a legacy system in the company. This kind of modernization incorporates, apart from technical models and application/data models, business semantic models that are a key asset (i) to preserve the business knowledge embedded in legacy systems; and (ii) to align the business requirements of the company with the future target systems.

Business modernization is probably the most important kind of modernization since changes in business processes are one of the most important software modernization decision criteria according to (Koskinen et al., 2005). However, not many modernization attempts have achieved the business abstraction level in the reverse engineering stage so far. This could be due to the fact that the mapping paradigms between business and IT lack the standardization to modernize legacy systems.

For this reason, the standardization effort by the ADMTF is so important. As a consequence, the ADM standards make it possible to deal with this kind of modernization processes at this time.

Modernization Scenarios

Each kind of modernization process makes it possible to modernize certain legacy systems under specific modernization scenarios. A modernization scenario provides templates that define project objectives, tasks and their related deliverables, the role of each ADM standard, and so on.

"A modernization scenario can be defined as an initiative, such as the ongoing task of portfolio management, a project, such as migrating from one platform to another, or a series of project phases (i.e., a super project) as would be the case when consolidating, redesigning and redeploying an application in a model-driven architecture". (OMG, 2006b)

According to (OMG, 2006b), there are thirteen different modernization scenarios that can be applied to legacy systems:

1. **Application Portfolio Management.** Companies have several applications and information systems which are grouped together under the name application portfolio. The application portfolio should be managed as business assets, meaning that this scenario aims to capture and expose a repository of cross-systems and cross-platform application metadata in a company's systems. This is due to the fact that legacy systems are usually poorly documented and this scenario addresses this shortcoming. This scenario is applied within application/data or business modernization processes.

2. **Application Improvement.** This scenario aims to improve the robustness, integrity, quality, consistency and/or performance of applications, but it does not involve an architecture transformation effort. The scenario can be thought of as a super scenario that consists of several sub-scenarios such as the correction of system flaws, source code restructuring, source code rationalization and other refactoring activities. This scenario is only applied within technical modernization processes.

3. **Language-to-Language Conversion.** This scenario deals with the conversion of one or more information systems from one programming language to another. The scenario can be motivated by the obsolescence of a language, or by the existence of a requirement to enhance a functionality not supported in the current language, and so on. However, this scenario does not involve a redesign of the system functionality. Thus, it is applied within technical modernization processes.

4. **Platform Migration.** This scenario moves systems from one platform to another because of the platform's obsolescence or to standardize the system to an organizational standard. The scenario is usually carried out together with a language-to-language conversion. This scenario is also applied throughout technical modernization processes.

5. **Non-Invasive Application Integration.** This scenario is triggered when there is a need to bring legacy user interfaces to end users by replacing the legacy front-ends with other front-ends like Web-based interfaces. Thus, the users gain value through replacing legacy front-ends while leaving the core functionality of the system untouched. This scenario is only carried out within technical modernization processes.

6. **Service Oriented Architecture Transformation.** This scenario takes the legacy systems that usually embed their functionality monolithically and segregates that functionality into services according

to SOA principles. The scenario not only modifies the front-end interfaces, but it also requires the redesign and componentization of the whole legacy system. In the scenario, the KDM standard identifies and tracks relationships between the physical system, program functionality, data usage and user interfaces. This scenario needs to be applied within application/data modernization processes.

7. **Data Architecture Migration.** This scenario moves one or more data structures to another, for instance, moving from a non-relational file or database to the relational data architecture. ADM also facilitates this scenario because the KDM metamodel assists with tracking and refactoring artifacts such as program-based data definitions, data access logic, and so on. The scenario must be applied within application/data modernization processes.

8. **System and Data Architecture Consolidation.** This scenario is motivated by the need to build a single system from multiple standalone systems that perform the same basic functions. The scenario aims to eradicate the redundant systems and data structures, inconsistencies, redundant business processes, and so on, in order to minimize excessive maintenance workloads. It can be combined with other scenarios such as model-driven transformation (see number 12), language change or platform migration. This scenario is applied throughout application/data modernization processes.

9. **Data Warehouse Deployment.** This scenario builds a common repository or a data warehouse of business data as well as the different ways to access this data. The KDM standard facilitates data analysis and data capture from legacy systems. In addition, the Common Warehouse Model (CWM) (OMG, 2003a), another OMG standard but outside the ADMTF, can be used together with KDM to represent data from different data sources in order to build and maintain the data warehouse. This scenario is usually carried out within application/data modernization processes, but it can be applied within business modernization processes as well.

10. **Application Package Selection and Deployment.** This scenario is aimed at third party application components. It defines how legacy systems are to be retired, integrated or retooled to work with a specific component. Furthermore, it helps to determine which portions of a component need to be implemented, integrated, discarded or updated. This scenario is exclusively applied within application/data modernization processes.

11. **Reusable Software Assets / Component Reuse.** This modernization scenario helps to identify, capture, streamline and prepare functionality and information assets of legacy systems for reuse. The ADM standards facilitate the identification of specific software artifacts based on data usage, transaction access, and other criteria. This scenario is also applied within application/data modernization processes.

12. **Model-Driven Architecture (MDA) Transformation.** This scenario converts a non-model-driven environment into a model-driven environment. Moving to MDA requires transforming legacy systems into a set of models that can be used to generate replacement systems. This scenario is applied within application/data modernization processes.

13. **Software Assurance.** This scenario aims to measure trustworthiness with regard to established business and security objectives. The KDM standard makes it possible to verify and measure software attributes across a variety of platforms and languages. Also, SMM can be used to define, evaluate and visualize different software metrics about legacy systems. This scenario can be

applied within application/data or technical modernization processes.

Toward Software Archeology

The reverse engineering stage is probably the most important stage in the horseshoe modernization process. This is due to the fact that this activity conditions the abstraction level achieved in each kind of modernization process and therefore the resources and possibilities to restructure the legacy systems. The reverse engineering stage is the key activity especially when a business modernization process is being carried out. In the third kind of modernization process, the reverse engineering stage must obtain business process models, business rules and any other business semantics from the legacy systems. However, there is a large conceptual gap between business processes and legacy systems that needs to be gradually reduced. Therefore, specific business knowledge must be extracted, although in many cases, it must be also inferred or deduced from previous knowledge.

Therefore, the reverse engineering stage can also be seen as a software archeology process in modernization processes. Real archeologists investigate several artifacts and situations, trying to understand what they are looking at, i.e., they must understand the cultural and civilizing forces that produced those artifacts. In the same way, a software archeologist analyzes different legacy artifacts such as source code, databases and user interfaces and then tries *"to understand what they were thinking to understand how and why they wrote the code the way they did"* (Hunt et al., 2002). Therefore, the software archeology process consists of analyzing different software artifacts by means of reverse engineering techniques and tools in order to obtain very abstract models that depict not only the legacy systems, but also the company and/or the company operation supported by this system, e.g., business process models.

ADM facilitates the software archeology process by means of KDM, since this standard makes it possible to represent all software artifacts involved in a certain legacy system in an integrated and standardized way. KDM can be compared with the UML standard (OMG, 2009c): UML is used to generate new code in a top-down manner; but in contrast, a process involving KDM starts from the existing code and builds a higher level model in a bottom-up manner (Moyer, 2009).

KDM Metamodel

The goal of the KDM specification (OMG, 2009a) is to represent legacy information systems as a whole and not just their source code (Khusidman, 2008). The KDM metamodel provides a comprehensive high-level view of the behavior, structure and data of systems, but it does not represent the procedural models of the systems.

The KDM metamodel is divided into layers representing both physical and logical software artifacts of information systems at several abstraction levels (OMG, 2008a). It separates knowledge about legacy information systems into various orthogonal concerns that are known in software engineering as architecture views (see Figure 3).

The KDM metamodel consists of four abstraction layers, each based on a previous layer. Furthermore, each layer is organized into packages that define a set of metamodel elements whose purpose is to represent a specific independent facet of knowledge related to legacy systems:

- **Infrastructure Layer** defines a small set of concepts used systematically throughout the entire KDM specification. It has three packages: Core, KDM and Source. The Core and KDM packages define the common metamodel elements that constitute the infrastructure for other packages. The Source package enumerates the artifacts of the legacy system and defines traceability links between the KDM elements and their original representation in the legacy source code.

Figure 3. Layers, packages and concerns in KDM (Adapted from (OMG, 2008a)).

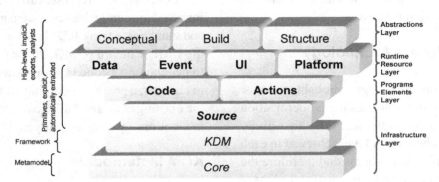

- **Program Elements Layer** aims to provide a language-independent intermediate representation for various constructs determined by common programming languages. There are only two packages in this layer: Code and Action. The Code package represents the named items from the source code and several structural relationships between them and the Action package focuses on behavior descriptions and control- and data-flow relationships determined by them.
- **Runtime Resource Layer** enables the representation of high-value knowledge about legacy systems and their operating environment, i.e., this layer focuses on those things that are not contained within the code itself. It has four packages: Data, Event, UI and Platform. The Data package defines the persistent data aspects of a legacy system; the Event package defines a common concept related to event-driven programming; the UI package represents the user interface aspects; and finally, the Platform package defines artifacts related to the run-time platform and environment of a legacy system.
- **Abstraction Layer** defines a set of metamodel elements whose purpose is to represent domain-specific knowledge as well as to provide a business-overview of legacy information systems. This layer has

three packages: Conceptual, Structure and Build. The Conceptual package represents the domain-specific elements of a legacy system; the Structure package represents the architectural components of legacy systems like subsystems, layers, packages and so on; and the Build package defines the artifacts related to engineering legacy systems such as roles, development activities or deliverables.

Throughout the software archeology process, the Infrastructure layer is not used to represent any specific model since the elements of this layer are used by other layers. The following KDM layers, Program Elements layer and Runtime Resource layer are used for modeling explicit knowledge of the legacy systems. Therefore the models built according to the packages of these layers can be obtained automatically through specific tools. For instance, imagine a tool that analyzes a database schema and directly represents a KDM data model from the recovered information. The last layer, the Abstraction layer, is used when the software archeologist finds himself full-on interpreting intent (Moyer, 2009). That is, this layer focuses on representing the implicit knowledge of the legacy systems. For this purpose, the models built according to this layer are obtained by means of the analysis of the explicit knowledge of the previous layers as well as the help of domain experts.

Figure 4. Software archeology tools: silo solutions (left) and KDM ecosystem (right)

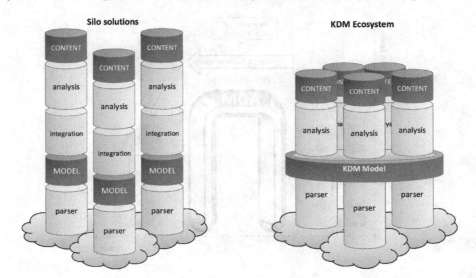

The KDM Ecosystem

Legacy information systems are becoming more and more complex, and the development and management of these systems already require an important effort. However, the software archeology processes as a part of an ADM-based process involve, perhaps, even greater effort in order to modernize or simply understand the complex legacy systems. Therefore, the software archeology processes (or most parts of them) must be automated by means of reverse engineering tools.

In this respect, the KDM standard enables the automation of the software archeology processes since it defines the items that a reverse engineering tool should discover and a software analysis tool can use; the KDM standard, then, has been designed to enable knowledge-based integration between tools.

The KDM standard changes the way in which reverse engineering tools are built and used. Traditional reverse engineering tools have been built as silos where each tool recovers and analyzes different proprietary content in a single silo (see Figure 4, left). For instance, suppose that we are carrying out an archeology process of a legacy

enterprise application. We would use a reverse engineering tool for the source code and another tool for the legacy database. As a consequence, at the end of the process, we would have two proprietary and independent models, a source code model and a database model, which must be also analyzed independently.

The KDM standard also makes it possible to build reverse engineering tools in a KDM ecosystem (see Figure 4, right). Here, the reverse engineering tools recover different knowledge related to different artifacts, but this knowledge is represented and managed in an integrated and standardized way through KDM. Thus, the software analysis tools can analyze the KDM repository and generate the new knowledge. Furthermore, in the future more software analysis tools can be plugged in to the KDM models homogeneously, to generate ever more valuable knowledge.

A MODERNIZATION CASE STUDY

This section shows a case study that applies an ADM-based process for modernizing legacy

Figure 5. An ADM-based process form modernizing relational databases

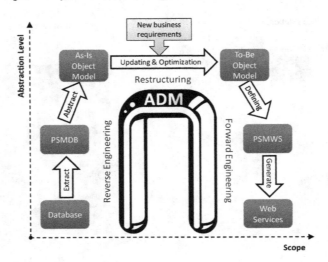

databases toward SOA environments. The case study consists on a real modernization project (Pérez-Castillo et al., 2009b) which was jointly carried out by the University of Castilla-La Mancha and Indra Software Labs (a multinational software development company) in the context of the "Catedra Indra" (CI hereinafter), a R+D centre located in Spain and devoted to carry out research projects in a close cooperation between industry and university.

Context of the Case Study

CI needed to develop a corporate website in order to support all the information related to the cooperation of industry & university. For instance, the site should contain information about conferences, lectures, courses, offered grants, events, awards, published papers, journals and so on. Thus, the website could be used by academics, researchers, PhD candidates and students.

The CI website must be built using a standard Web architecture based on the Microsoft.NET platform, and it uses Microsoft SQL Server 2000 as RDBMS (Relational Data Base Management System).

Moreover, CI was using at that moment an existing database created long time ago, which was used to register the some information related to the CI. However, the data stored in database was not being managed by any application. In this context, it is possible to find the suitable conditions for implementing a modernization project, since the CI's database is considered as a legacy system which can be exposed as web services in order to integrate in a SOA environment. Therefore, a modernization process based on ADM was proposed to obtain a set of web services from the legacy database to manage the access to the data, and then integrate the web services into the CI website.

The Proposed Modernization Process

The process aims to establish guidelines to allow the generation of Web services from relational databases through a set of model transformations. Figure 5 represents the proposed modernization process. Firstly, a PSM model, according to SQL-92 meta-model (ISO/IEC, 1992), is obtained from the legacy database through reverse engineering. Secondly, the PSM is transformed to PIM model

Figure 6. Fragment of the legacy database schema modernized in the case study

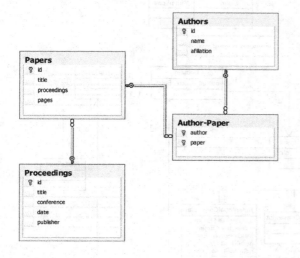

which raises the abstraction level of the system. This PIM model is represented in terms of UML2 meta-model (OMG, 2007b). Thirdly, the restructuring stage can modify the object model in order to add new business requirements. Fourthly, the process generates through forward engineering a certain PSM model that depicts the web services at higher abstraction level. Finally, the source code of the web services is generated from the PSM model, thus the abstraction level is reduced again.

The modernization process (see Figure 5) is explained in the following subsections in detail. In addition, an example will be developed to clarify each stage in the process. The example considers only a small fragment of the legacy database of CI (see Figure 6). The database fragment consists of four tables: *Proceedings*, *Papers*, *Authors* and *Author-Paper*. The proceedings have several papers, which are written by several authors in turn. The table *Author-Paper* relates each paper with the authors.

Reverse Engineering Stage

The first stage is the database reverse engineering, which aims to recover the relational database design and create a PSM model that represents the input database. The metadata recovered from the database is represented in a PSM model according to the SQL-92 metamodel (see Figure 7).

The metadata needed to build the database schema model can be taken through *INFORMATION_SCHEMA* (Melton et al., 1993). This is a standardized mechanism from SQL-92 standard that identifies a set of views. These views return metadata in a standardized way and in a RDBMS-independent manner.

Moreover, the built model can be made persistent through XMI (*XML Metadata Interchange*) (Grose et al., 2001), which defines the manipulation, persistence and interchange of models through XML. In the example, the database model is recovered and written in XMI format (see Figure 8). In this model, there is an element for each table and constraint in database schema according to the proposed metamodel. There are four instances of the *BaseTable* metaclass to represent the four tables. Also, the different constrains are modelled as instances of the *PrimaryKey* and *ReferentialConstraint* metaclass (see Figure 8).

After database design is recovered, the outgoing PSM model is transformed into a PIM model that represents the database information in a platform-independent manner. Thus, in this step an object model is generated, which will be afterward the basis to generate Web Services in following stages.

The object model is represented according to UML2 metamodel (OMG, 2007b) and the transformation is defined by means of QVT. Figure 9 shows a QVT fragment of the transformation. This fragment presents two relations: the first one transforms each database schema into a code package, and the second one generates instances of the *Class* metaclass for each instance of the *Table* metaclass of the PSM model.

The object model obtained in the example consists of four objects, one object for each table in database model: *Proceedings*, *Papers*, *Authors*, *Author-Paper*. These classes conforms the so-

Figure 7. SQL-92 meta-model

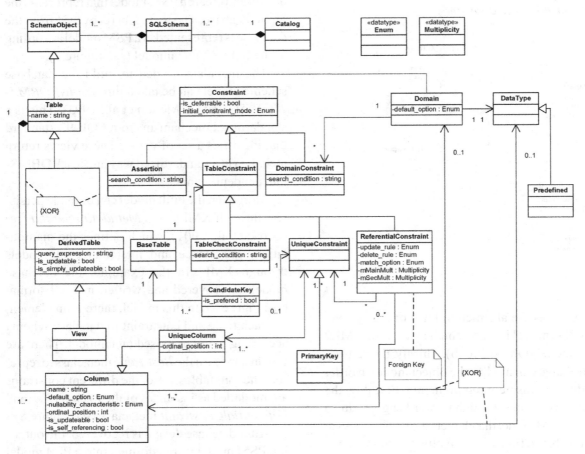

called *business layer* according to the three-tier architecture (see Figure 10), which contains all business knowledge of the future web services. The remaining layers are addressed in following stages of the modernization process.

Restructuring Stage

The restructuring stage is in charge of transform the PIM model into another improved PIM model at the same abstraction level. This stage adds the auxiliary objects to support the persistence layer of the object model (see Figure 10).

In addition, the restructuring stage discovers the potential services from the information recovered from the database. For this purpose,

the modernization process defines a set of patterns, which are sought in the recovered database schema. In turn, each pattern defines a template to create well known services. Figure 11 details the patterns as well as the services that can be derived from each pattern. On the one hand, there are simple services involving only a single table. These services are directly obtained from database scheme and matched with *CRUD* operations (*Create / Read / Update / Delete*) as well as *getters & setters* methods for handling the different columns on each table. And on the other hand, advanced services involve several tables of schema (see Figure 11). In this case, services may be directly obtained from views, or on the contrary, services can be obtained from the following patterns that

Figure 8. Database model (in XMI representation) obtained in the modernization case study

```xml
<?xml version="1.0" encoding="utf-8" ?>
- <xmi:XMI xmi:version="2.0" xmlns:xmi="http://www.omg.org/XMI">
  - <xmi:Documentation>
      <exporter>PRECISO</exporter>
      <exporterVersion>0.5</exporterVersion>
    </xmi:Documentation>
  - <Schema name="Conferences">
    - <SchemaObjects>
      - <Tables xmi:id="_0">
        + <BaseTable name="Papers" xmi:id="_1.0">
        - <BaseTable name="Proceedings" xmi:id="_1.1">
          - <Columns>
            + <Column name="id" xmi:id="_1.1.0" ordinal_position="1"
                is_nullable="NO">
            + <Column name="title" xmi:id="_1.1.1" ordinal_position="2"
                is_nullable="NO">
            + <Column name="conference" xmi:id="_1.1.2"
                ordinal_position="3" is_nullable="NO">
            + <Column name="date" xmi:id="_1.1.3" ordinal_position="4"
                is_nullable="NO">
            + <Column name="publisher" xmi:id="_1.1.4"
                ordinal_position="5" is_nullable="NO">
            </Columns>
          </BaseTable>
        + <BaseTable name="Authors" xmi:id="_1.2">
        + <BaseTable name="AuthorPaper" xmi:id="_1.3">
        + <BaseTable name="sysdiagrams" xmi:id="_1.4">
        </Tables>
      - <Constraints xmi:id="_1">
          <Assertions />
        - <TableConstraints>
          - <UniqueConstraints>
            + <UniqueConstraint name="UK_principal_name" xmi:id="_2.8">
            </UniqueConstraints>
          + <PrimaryKeyConstraints>
          - <ReferentialConstraints>
            + <ReferentialConstraint name="FK_Paper_Proceedings"
                xmi:id="_2.4" update_rule="NO ACTION" delete_rule="NO
                ACTION" match_option="SIMPLE"
                xmlns="FK_Paper_Proceedings">
            + <ReferentialConstraint name="FK_Author-Paper_Author"
                xmi:id="_2.5" update_rule="NO ACTION" delete_rule="NO
                ACTION" match_option="SIMPLE" xmlns="FK_Author-
                Paper_Author">
            + <ReferentialConstraint name="FK_Author-Paper_Paper"
                xmi:id="_2.6" update_rule="NO ACTION" delete_rule="NO
                ACTION" match_option="SIMPLE" xmlns="FK_Author-
                Paper_Paper">
            </ReferentialConstraints>
            <TableCheckConstraints />
          </TableConstraints>
          <DomainConstraints />
        </Constraints>
        <Domains />
      </SchemaObjects>
    </Schema>
  </xmi:XMI>
```

are recognized in the relational database scheme: (1) *referenced table*, when there is a foreign key among two tables; (2) *combined table*, when there are two or more foreign keys from one table to other; and finally (3) *observed table*, which searches two or more foreign keys in different tables to a table.

According to the example, the process adds four objects to support the persistence layer: *Procedings_persistent*, *Papers_persistent*, *Author_persistent* and *AuthorPaper_persistent* (see Figure 10). In addition, several services are discovered by means of the proposed patterns. Let us pay attention to the table *Author-Paper*, which

Figure 9. QVT fragment to transform a database model (PSM) into an object model (PIM)

```
transformation rdbms2uml(rdbms:SimpleRDBMS, uml:SimpleUML) {
  -- map each schema to a package
  top relation SchemaToPackage {
    pn : String;
    checkonly domain rdbms s : RdbmsSchema {
      rdbmsName = pn
    };
    enforce domain uml p : UmlPackage {
     umlName = pn
    };
  }
  -- map each table to a class
  top relation TableToClass {
    cn : String;
    checkonly domain uml t : RdbmsTable {
      rdbmsSchema = s : RdbmsSchema {},
      rdbmsName = cn
    };
    enforce domain rdbms c : UmlClass {
      umlNamespace = p : UmlPackage {},
      umlName = cn
    };
    when {
      SchemaToPackage(s, p);
    }
    where {
      -- Call to ColumnToAttribute relation for each column in each class
      t.rdbmsColumn->forAll(cl:RdbmsColumn | cl.oclIsUndefined()
        implies ColumnToAttribute(t, c, cl));
    }
  }
  ...
}
```

Figure 10. Object model obtained in the modernization case study

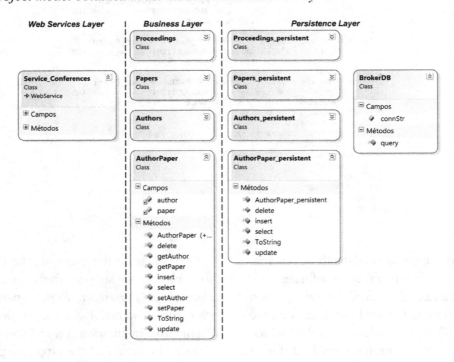

94

Figure 11. Patterns and service templates used in the modernization case study

Simple Services	Tables	CRUD operations	
		Getters & Setters Operations	
	Views	Queries	
Advanced Services	Patterns in database schema	*Referenced Table*	Select_A_of_B (pkB) Select_B_for_A (pkA) 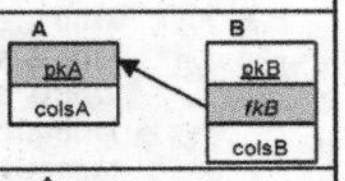
		Combined Table	Select_A_for_B (pkB) Select_A_for_B_filtered (pkB, colsM) Exists_A_related_with_B (pkA, pkB) Select_A_for_B_and_C (pkB, pkC) Select_A_for_B_and_C_filtered(pkB, pkC, colsM) Exists_A_related_with_B(pkA, pkB, pkC) 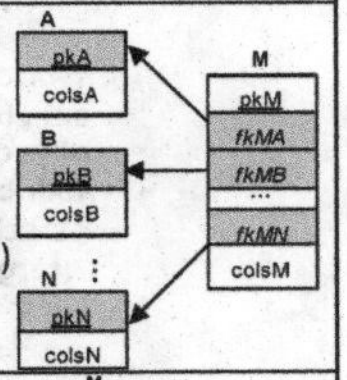
		Observed Table	Select_A_for_B (pkB) Select_B_for_A (pkA) 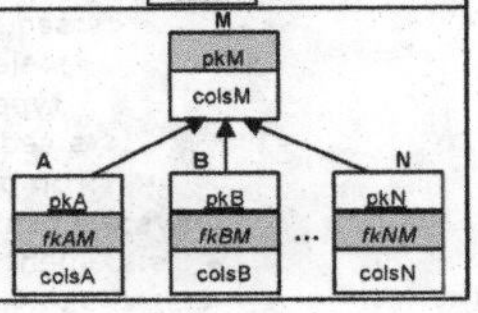

have two foreign keys to the tables *Authors* and *Papers* (see Figure 6). The *'Combined Tables'* pattern is recognized in that structure of the database schema, therefore predefined services could be built from the detected pattern instance (see Figure 12). The service templates to select tuples filtering data are not instantiated in this example because the table *Author-Paper* has not additional columns a part from the columns involved in the primary key (see Figure 6).

Forward Engineering Stage

The third stage aims to obtain by means of forward engineering a set of web services that manage the access to the data stored in the input database. Firstly, the last PIM model (transformed after restructuring stage) is transformed into a PSM model that represent the service interfaces of the future web services. This model is represented according to the WSDL metamodel (Web Services Description Language) (W3C, 2007).

In the example, it focuses again on the instance of the *'Combined Tables'* pattern that was discovered, and in particular it shows the results for the service *'selectAuthors_for_Papers (int id_paper)'*. Figure 13 shows the WSDL segment generated for this service by means of the process from Service Discovery and Object Model Transformation tasks.

Finally, the last step is the generation of the source code to support: (i) the object model obtained in previous stages, as well as (ii) the implementation of the web services from the WSDL model.

Figure 12. Services obtained from an instance of 'Combined Tables' pattern

```
Author selectAuthors_for_Papers(int id_paper)
Boolean existsAuthors_rel_Papers(int id_author, int id_paper)
Paper selectPapers_for_Authors(int id_author)
Boolean existsPapers_rel_Authors(int id_paper, int id_author)
```

Figure 13. The WSDL segment generated to support a service in the modernization case study

```
<?xml version="1.0" encoding="utf-8" ?>
- <wsdl:definitions xmlns:soap="http://schemas.xmlsoap.org/wsdl/soap/"
    xmlns:tm="http://microsoft.com/wsdl/mime/textMatching/"
    xmlns:soapenc="http://schemas.xmlsoap.org/soap/encoding/"
    xmlns:mime="http://schemas.xmlsoap.org/wsdl/mime/"
    xmlns:tns="http://Conferences.org/"
    xmlns:s="http://www.w3.org/2001/XMLSchema"
    xmlns:soap12="http://schemas.xmlsoap.org/wsdl/soap12/"
    xmlns:http="http://schemas.xmlsoap.org/wsdl/http/"
    targetNamespace="http://Conferences.org/"
    xmlns:wsdl="http://schemas.xmlsoap.org/wsdl/">
    <wsdl:documentation xmlns:wsdl="http://schemas.xmlsoap.org/wsdl/">Web
      service for testing access to database by means of Conferences
      objects.</wsdl:documentation>
  - <wsdl:types>
    - <s:schema elementFormDefault="qualified"
        targetNamespace="http://Conferences.org/">
      - <s:element name="selectAuthors_for_Papers">
        - <s:complexType>
          - <s:sequence>
              <s:element minOccurs="1" maxOccurs="1" name="paper"
                type="s:int" />
            </s:sequence>
          </s:complexType>
        </s:element>
        + <s:element name="selectAuthors_for_PapersResponse">
      </s:schema>
    </wsdl:types>
  + <wsdl:message name="selectAuthors_for_PapersSoapIn">
  - <wsdl:message name="selectAuthors_for_PapersSoapOut">
      <wsdl:part name="parameters"
        element="tns:selectAuthors_for_PapersResponse" />
    </wsdl:message>
  - <wsdl:portType name="Service_ConferencesSoap">
    - <wsdl:operation name="selectAuthors_for_Papers">
        <wsdl:documentation
          xmlns:wsdl="http://schemas.xmlsoap.org/wsdl/">Return the
          object list correspond to the pattern "COMBINED TABLE" to
          relationship "selectAuthors_for_Papers"</wsdl:documentation>
        <wsdl:input message="tns:selectAuthors_for_PapersSoapIn" />
        <wsdl:output message="tns:selectAuthors_for_PapersSoapOut" />
      </wsdl:operation>
    </wsdl:portType>
  + <wsdl:binding name="Service_ConferencesSoap"
      type="tns:Service_ConferencesSoap">
  + <wsdl:binding name="Service_ConferencesSoap12"
      type="tns:Service_ConferencesSoap">
  + <wsdl:service name="Service_Conferences">
  </wsdl:definitions>
```

In the example, the classes shown in Figure 10 are written in physical files according to a certain programming language that supports Web Services technology as *Java*, *C#*, and so on. In this case study, the web services are written in *C#*. Finally, the obtained web services are deployed moving them to production stage they are integrated into the CI website. Thus, the web services become in fully operational services that wrap the legacy database and provides a modernized data access in a SOA environment.

Obtained Results

In order to support the modernization process, an ad hoc tool was developed to carry out the modernization of the legacy database. The tool made a selective publication and deployment of some services from the entire set of web services discovered from the database. Figure 14 summarizes the performance of the services used in the CI website. This table considers (1) the different types of services according to the set of patterns; (2) services generated for each type; (3) the number of services (for each type) included in the CI website; and (4) the percentage of services included.

Figure 14. Performance of services published in CI website

Kind of Service	Candidate Services	Published Services	Performance	
insert	13	11		85%
update	13	11		85%
delete	13	11		85%
select	13	12		92%
setters	56	0		0%
getters	56	0		0%
show	13	0		0%
views	4	4		100%
referenced tables	24	12		50%
combined tables	32	8		25%
observed tables	8	4		50%
TOTAL	245	73		30%

The percentage of services that was published to support the functionalities of the CI website was 30%. This percentage included 73 services on a total of 245 candidate services. In addition, the development staff noticed that the non-selected web services would be very useful for future developments. Since these non considered services were identified and collected, it would be easy to deploy and integrate them into the CI website for the implementation of additional features. The tool keeps information of the modernization project, that is, the object model, configuration of the generated services, services deployed and services available. Thus, we only need to load the project of the current case study to deploy new web services to fulfill new information requirements.

The development staff took advantages from the availability of the required information to improve the development process: since all the required information was available as services, the staff could work with real data when developing the website. The staff could put all their effort into the development of the web interface. Furthermore, since the required information was available from the first, all the features of the CI site could be tested with the real information of the database. It allowed the staff to accelerate the testing process, because web developers could build the necessary web interfaces which in turn will use the aforementioned web services, and will properly display the information.

ADM Success Stories

In spite of the fact that ADM is a relatively new approach, it has acquired great relevance not only within the academic community but also within the industrial community. Currently, there are several international projects as well as tools that address modernization challenges.

Modernization Projects

Several meaningful and international projects such as MOMOCS (MOMOCS, 2008) and ModelWare (ModelWare, 2006) aim to lead ADM industrialization and also ensure its successful adoption by the industry. Both projects are funded by the European Commission under the Information Society Technologies in the 6th Framework Program. These projects combine innovations in modeling technologies, engineering processes and methodologies, tool development, standardization, experimentations and change management.

The MOMOCS project studies how complex legacy systems can be modernized with a focus on some of their specific software portions, with the goal of *"keeping up with a very fast changing business and technical environment taking human beings as the centre of the interaction"* (MO-

MOCS, 2008). The MOMOCS project defines a modernization methodology that is applied to complex systems and makes it possible to reengineer software architectures, data heterogeneities and processes in order to make system behavior more predictable in terms of performance, stability and maintainability.

The ModelWare project has developed a complete infrastructure required for the large-scale deployment of model-driven development strategies, validating this infrastructure in several business domains including the modernization of legacy systems (ModelWare, 2006). While the ModelWare project focuses on most parts of model-driven development, the MOMOCS project particularly addresses the activities and techniques of the software modernization approach.

Moreover, in 2009 the OMG organized an *Architecture Driven Modernization Case Studies Workshop*. Some relevant works were presented in this event, which consist of real world case studies involving the automated transformation of information systems from legacy source code into modernized languages and platforms. For instance, *DelaPeyronnie et al.* (DelaPeyronnie et al., 2010) present an ADM-based project for modernizing the EATMS system, an air traffic management system used at 280 airports worldwide. This project was carried out in a platform migration scenario, since the main objective was the transformation of the legacy system from the *Ada* language into the high-performance, real-time *Java* language. Another successful case study was the modernization project presented by *Barbier et al.* (Barbier et al., 2010), which focuses on how PIM models can be automatically generated from COBOL-based legacy systems.

Modernization Tools

At this time, some tools are available to deal with some ADM challenges. KDM SDK 2.0 is an Eclipse™ EMF plug-in which provides a set of tools for working with KDM. KDM SDK 2.0 is an adoption kit to help understand the KDM specification that facilitates mapping design from proprietary internal representation in the KDM metamodel and jump starts development of the KDM tools (KDMAnalytics, 2008).

MoDisco is another important tool that consists of an Eclipse™ plug-in for model-driven reverse engineering. With MoDisco, practical extractions of models can be made from various kinds of legacy systems. In addition, MoDisco proposes a generic and extensible metamodel-driven approach to model discovery (MoDisco, 2008).

Agility™, from the Obeo company, is a tool that can be used to re-document, migrate, refactor or redesign any kind of program. Agility™ supports Ada, Java, C, C++, Forte, Cobol, Oracle Forms and Visual Basic, among others type of programs (Obeo, 2007b). Furthermore, Obeo offers Acceleo™, another commercial tool that can be used together with Agility™. Acceleo™ is a code generator for transforming models into code following the MDA approach (Obeo, 2007a). Therefore, this tool makes it possible to complete a whole modernization process based on the horseshoe model.

Modernization Workbench™ makes it possible to extract technical and business knowledge from existing application portfolios. This tool creates a centralized, always-current warehouse of business and technical intelligence about the applications that run in the business (Micro Focus, 2009).

BLU AGE™ (BLU AGE, 2010) focuses on the reverse engineering and forward engineering stages. On the one hand, this tool facilitates the generation of PIM models from different platforms and languages. And on the other hand, it provides a module to generate automatically the source code of modernized systems.

Another core concept of ADM is transformation between models. There are many tools that make it possible to transform models using QVT: Medini QVT (ikv++, 2008) is an Eclipse™ application to transform models using QVT Relation, the declarative language of QVT; another tools is

SmartQVT (France Telecom R&D, 2008), which provides an Eclipse™ plug-in to perform transformations according to QVT Operational (this tool was partly financed by the ModelWare project). These tools are not alone, since many other similar tools exist. Indeed, there are other tools that enable model transformations following other transformation languages, such as ATL (ATLAS Transformation Language) (INRIA, 2005), TXL (Turing eXtender Language) (Queen's University et al., 2009), among others.

Finally, MARBLE, a non-commercial tool based on the Eclipse™ platform, can also be used to recover business processes from legacy systems in order to carry out business modernization processes (Pérez-Castillo et al., 2009a). This tool obtains business processes through three transformations: firstly, the tool recovers PSM models from different legacy software artifacts; secondly, the tool integrates those models into a single PIM model according to the KDM metamodel; and finally, MARBLE recovers a business process model by applying a set of business patterns in the KDM model (Pérez-Castillo et al., 2010).

CONCLUSION

As the history of software engineering reveals, information systems are not static entities that are unchangeable over time. Information systems degrade and age, which is known as the software erosion problem. This problem can be compared with the degradation of any material thing that deteriorates over use and over time. However, the nature of software makes it impossible to replace an information system in the same way that a material thing can be replaced. In fact, the wholesale replacement of a legacy information system has devastating economic and technical consequences.

Therefore, legacy information systems must evolve to enhanced versions of themselves, preserving the embedded business knowledge in order to extend the lifespan and improve the ROI of these legacy systems. This process is known as software modernization and the main effort to standardize this process is Architecture-Driven Modernization (ADM), as defined by the OMG.

ADM advocates carrying out reengineering processes, but treats each involved artifact as a model and establishes transformations between the models through the horseshoe model, i.e., ADM can be seen as a reengineering process that follows MDA principles. Furthermore, the ADM specification defines a wide set of standards to deal with specific modernization challenges. The standardization effort of the ADM initiative of the OMG solves the two main problems of traditional reengineering, the previous alternative to software modernization: (i) the formalization of the process in order to the modernization project can be repeatable and reusable, and (ii) the automation of the process in order to address the modernization of large complex legacy systems.

ADM can be seen as a set of standards for software modernization. The first and most important ADM standard is KDM, which offers a metamodel to represent all the software artifacts involved in a legacy system according to different views of the system and different abstraction levels. KDM facilitates the software archeology process, especially when a legacy system must be represented at a higher abstraction level, for instance in a business modernization process, since it reduces the gap between the legacy source code and high-level models like business process models.

ADM and software modernization in general have acquired a certain degree of importance within the academic and industrial communities. Indeed, there are already many ongoing modernization projects and there is a significant market for modernization tools. In addition, the main conferences on reverse engineering and software maintenance present increasingly more papers related to software modernization.

RESEARCH DIRECTION

In the future, software modernization will need *"to be addressed as a business issue as well as a technology issue, and therefore it is fundamentally interdisciplinary"* (Bennett et al., 2000). ADM will change how software and society interact, how software will be used, how software will behave, and how software will be developed. However, the biggest challenge for ADM currently is more widespread adoption in the software industry. Indeed, modernization tools cannot be effective if they are not used.

Therefore, while the launch of a modernization effort is important, the sustainability and business adoption of these efforts are equally important. Thus, the communication of the added value of a certain modernization effort is also a main challenge (Ulrich, 2010).

Moreover, in the software industry at this time, *"there is a pressing need for software on demand. This means that the basic functionality should be available before it is even required"* (Sneed, 2008). SOA environments can help to provide software as services on demand, but the problem is that a whole legacy system cannot be thrown away, and thus it must be migrated toward a SOA environment. ADM will be the cornerstone to SOA transformations since the ADM standards help in the following way (OMG, 2006b):

- They facilitate identification of redundant, inconsistent and segregated functionalities that need to be refactored to create services.
- They also identify the interfaces that could serve as prototypes for creating a service that wraps a legacy system.
- They can discover and extract business logic from legacy systems as service candidates.
- They enable necessary refactoring across multiple platforms and languages.

In another research direction, ADM will take on the most important challenges in software archeology processes, the problems of *delocalization* and *interleaving*. These problems lie in the fact that pieces of knowledge are usually scattered between many legacy systems and a single legacy system contains several pieces of knowledge (Ratiu, 2009). Therefore, in the future, KDM should support the recovery, management and deduction of different knowledge from several legacy systems in an integrated and homogeneous way.

REFERENCES

W3C. (2007). *WSDL in Web Services description working group*. Retrieved August 1, 2008, from http://www.w3.org/2002/ws/desc/

Barbier, F., Eveillard, S., Youbi, K., Guitton, O., Perrier, A., & Cariou, E. (2010). Model-driven reverse engineering of COBOL-based applications. In Ulrich, W. M., & Newcomb, P. H. (Eds.), *Information Systems transformation: Architecture-driven modernization case studies* (pp. 283–299). Burlington, MA: Morgan Kauffman.

Bennett, K. H., & Rajlich, V. T. (2000). Software maintenance and evolution: A roadmap. *Proceedings of the Conference on The Future of Software Engineering*. Limerick, Ireland: ACM.

Bianchi, A., Caivano, D., Marengo, V., & Visaggio, G. (2003). Iterative reengineering of legacy systems. *IEEE Transactions on Software Engineering, 29*(3), 225–241. doi:10.1109/TSE.2003.1183932

BLU AGE. (2010). *BLU AGE - agile model transformation*. Netfective Technology S.A.

Canfora, G., & Penta, M. D. (2007). *New frontiers of reverse engineering. 2007 Future of Software Engineering*. IEEE Computer Society.

Chikofsky, E. J., & Cross, J. H. (1990). Reverse engineering and design recovery: A taxonomy. *IEEE Software, 7*(1), 13–17. doi:10.1109/52.43044 de la Peyronnie, J., Newcomb, P. H., Morillo, V., Trimech, F., Nguyen, L., & Purtill, M. (2010). Modernization of the Eurocat Air Traffic Management System (EATMS). In Ulrich, W. M., & Newcomb, P. H. (Eds.), *Information Systems Transformation: Architecture driven modernization case studies* (pp. 91–131). Burlington, MA: Morgan Kauffman.

France Telecom R&D. (2008). *SmartQVT: An open source model transformation tool implementing the MOF 2.0 QVT-Operational language*. Retrieved from http://smartqvt.elibel.tm.fr/.

Gamma, E., Helm, R., Johnson, R., & Vlissides, J. (1995). *Design patterns: Elements of reusable object-oriented software*. Boston: Addison Wesley Longman Publishing Co.

Ghazarian, A. (2009). A case study of source code evolution. In R. Ferenc, J. Knodel and A. Winter (Eds.), *13th European Conference on Software Maintenance and Reengineering (CSMR'09)*. (pp. 159-168). Kaiserslautern, Germany, IEEE Computer Society.

Grose, T. J., Doney, G. C., & Brodsky, S. A. (2001). *Mastering XMI: Java programming with XMI, XML, and UML*. John Wiley & Sons.

Hainaut, J.-L., Henrard, J., Hick, J.-M., Roland, D., & Englebert, V. (1996). Database design recovery. *Proceedings of the 8th International Conference on Advances Information System Engineering*, (pp. 463-480). Springer-Verlag.

Hunt, A., & Thomas, D. (2002). Software archaeology. *IEEE Software*, *19*(2), 20–22. doi:10.1109/52.991327

ikv++. (2008). *Medini QVT*. Retrieved from http://www.ikv.de/index.php?option=com_content&task=view& id=75&Itemid=77, ikv++ technologies

INRIA. (2005). *ATL transformation description template, version 0.1*. ATLAS group. Retrieved from http://www.eclipse.org/m2m/atl/doc/ATL_Transformation_Template%5Bv00.01%5D.pdf

ISO/IEC. (1992). *ISO/IEC 9075*, Database Language SQL.

ISO/IEC. (2006). *ISO/IEC 14764*, Software engineering-software life cycle processes- Maintenance. ISO/IEC. Retrieved from http://www.iso.org/iso/catalogue_detail.htm?csnumber=39064

ISO/IEC. (2009). *ISO/IEC DIS 19506*, Knowledge Discovery Meta-model (KDM), v1.1. Retrieved from http://www.iso.org/iso/catalogue_detail.htm?csnumber=32625

Jacobson, I., Christerson, M., Jonsson, P., & Övergaard, G. (1992). *Object-oriented software engineering: A use case driven approach*. Boston: Addison-Wesley.

Kazman, R., Woods, S. G., & Carrière, S. J. (1998). Requirements for integrating software architecture and reengineering models: CORUM 2. *Proceedings of the Working Conference on Reverse Engineering (WCRE'98)*, (pp. 154-163). IEEE Computer Society.

KDMAnalytics. (2008). *Knowledge Discovery Metamodel (KDM) software development kit 2.0 eclipse plugin*. Retrieved from http://www.kdmanalytics.com/kdmsdk/KDMSDK_brochure.pdf, Hatha Systems.

Khusidman, V. (2008). *ADM transformation White Paper. DRAFT V.1*. Retrieved from http://www.omg.org/docs/admtf/08-06-10.pdf

Khusidman, V., & Ulrich, W. (2007). *Architecture-driven modernization: Transforming the enterprise. DRAFT V.5*. Retrieved from http://www.omg.org/docs/admtf/07-12-01.pdf

Koskinen, J., Ahonen, J., Lintinen, H., Sivula, H., & Tilus, T. (2004). *Estimation of the business value of software modernizations.* Information Technology Research Institute, University of Jyväskylä.

Koskinen, J., Ahonen, J. J., Sivula, H., Tilus, T., Lintinen, H., & Kankaanpää, I. (2005). Software modernization decision criteria: An empirical study. *European Conference on Software Maintenance and Reengineering,* (pp. 324-331). IEEE Computer Society.

Lehman, M. M., Perry, D. E., & Ramil, J. F. (1998). Implications of evolution metrics on software maintenance. *Proceedings of the International Conference on Software Maintenance*, (pp. 208-217). IEEE Computer Society.

Melton, J., & Simon, A. R. (1993). *Understanding the new SQL: A complete guide.* USA: Morgan Kaufmann Publishers, Inc.

Mens, T., & Demeyer, S. (2008). *Software Evolution.* Berlin, Heidelberg: Springer-Verlag.

Micro Focus. (2009). *Modernization Workbench™.* Retrieved from http://www.microfocus.com/products/modernizationworkbench/

Miller, J., & Mukerji, J. (2003). *MDA Guide Version 1.0.1.* Retrieved from www.omg.org/docs/omg/03-06-01.pdf

ModelWare. (2006). *MODELWARE.* Retrieved August 24, 2009, from http://www.modelware-ist.org/

MoDisco. (2008). *KDM-to-UML2 converter.* Retrieved from http://www.eclipse.org/gmt/modisco/toolBox/KDMtoUML2Converter/

MOMOCS. (2008). *MOdel driven MOdernisation of Complex Systems is an EU-Project.* Retrieved from http://www.momocs.org/. 2008, from http://www.momocs.org/

Moyer, B. (2009). Software archeology: Modernizing old systems. *Embedded Technology Journal, 1*, 1-4.

Müller, H. A., Jahnke, J. H., Smith, D. B., Storey, M.-A., Tilley, S. R., & Wong, K. (2000). Reverse engineering: A roadmap. *Proceedings of the Conference on The Future of Software Engineering.* Limerick, Ireland: ACM.

Obeo. (2007a). *Acceleo™.* Retrieved from http://www.obeo.fr/pages/acceleo/en

Obeo. (2007b). *Agility™.* Retrieved from http://www.obeo.fr/pages/agility/en

OMG. (2003a). *CWM. Common Warehouse Metamodel, v1.1 Specification.* Retrieved from http://www.omg.org/spec/CWM/1.1/PDF/

OMG. (2003b). *Why do we need standards for the modernization of existing systems?* OMG ADM task force.

OMG. (2006a). *ADM Glossary of Definitions and Terms.* Retrieved from http://adm.omg.org/ADM_Glossary_Spreadsheet_pdf.pdf

OMG. (2006b). *Architecture-driven modernization scenarios.* Retrieved November, 2, 2009, from http://adm.omg.org/ADMTF_Scenario_White_Paper%28pdf%29.pdf

OMG. (2007a). *ADM task force by OMG.* Retrieved June 15, 2009, 2008, from http://www.omg.org/

OMG. (2007b). *Unified modeling language: Superstructure, version 2.0.* Retrieved August 16, 2007, from http://www.omg.org/docs/formal/05-07-04.pdf

OMG. (2008a). *Architecture-Driven Modernization (ADM): Knowledge Discovery Meta-Model (KDM), v1.0.* Retrieved from http://www.omg.org/docs/formal/08-01-01.pdf

OMG. (2008b). *QVT. Meta Object Facility (MOF) 2.0 query/vew/transformation specification.* Retrieved from http://www.omg.org/spec/QVT/1.0/PDF

OMG. (2009a). *Architecture-Driven Modernization (ADM): Knowledge Discovery Meta-Model (KDM), v1.1.* Retrieved from http://www.omg.org/spec/KDM/1.1/PDF/

OMG. (2009b). *Architecture-Driven Modernization standards roadmap.* Retrieved October 29, 2009, from http://adm.omg.org/ADMTF%20Roadmap.pdf

OMG. (2009c). *UML (Unified Modeling Language) superstructure specification. Version 2.2.* Retrieved June 24, 2009, from http://www.omg.org/spec/UML/2.2/Superstructure/PDF/

Paradauskas, B., & Laurikaitis, A. (2006). Business knowledge extraction from legacy Information Systems. *Journal of Information Technology and Control, 35*(3), 214–221.

Pérez-Castillo, R., García-Rodríguez de Guzmán, I., Ávila-García, O., & Piattini, M. (2009a). MARBLE: A modernization approach for recovering business processes from legacy systems. *International Workshop on Reverse Engineering Models from Software Artifacts (REM'09)*, Lille, France.

Pérez-Castillo, R., García-Rodríguez de Guzmán, I., Ávila-García, O., & Piattini, M. (2010). Business process patterns for software archeology. *25th Annual ACM Symposium on Applied Computing (SAC'10)*. Sierre, Switzerland: ACM.

Pérez-Castillo, R., García Rodríguez de Guzmán, I., Caballero, I., Polo, M., & Piattini, M. (2009b). PRECISO: A reengineering process and a tool for database modernisation through Web services. *24th Annual ACM Symposium on Applied Computing. Track on Service Oriented Architectures and Programming (SOAP 2009),* (pp. 2126-2133). Waikiki Beach, Honolulu, Hawaii: ACM.

Polo, M., Piattini, M., & Ruiz, F. (2003). *Advances in software maintenance management: Technologies and solutions*. Hershey, PA: Idea Group Publishing.

Queen's University. NSERC & IBM. (2009). Turing eXtender Language (TXL). Retrieved from http://www.txl.ca/

Ratiu, D. (2009). Reverse engineering domain models from source code. *International Workshop on Reverse Engineering Models from Software Artifacts (REM'09)*. Lille, France.

Sneed, H. M. (2005). *Estimating the Costs of a Reengineering Project*. IEEE Computer Society.

Sneed, H. M. (2008). *Migrating to Web services. Emerging Methods, Technologies and Process Management in Software Engineering* (pp. 151–176). Wiley-IEEE Computer Society Pr.

Sommerville, I. (2006). *Software Engineering*. Addison Wesley.

Ulrich, W. M. (2002). *Legacy systems: Transformation strategies*. Prentice Hall.

Ulrich, W. M. (2010). Launching and sustaining modernization initiatives. In Ulrich, W. M., & Newcomb, P. H. (Eds.), *Information Systems Transformation: Architecture driven modernization case studies* (pp. 403–418). Burlington, MA: Morgan Kauffman.

Visaggio, G. (2001). Ageing of a data-intensive legacy system: Symptoms and remedies. *Journal of Software Maintenance, 13*(5), 281–308. doi:10.1002/smr.234

ADDITIONAL READING

Newcomb, P. (2005). Architecture-Driven Modernization (ADM). Proceedings of the 12th Working Conference on Reverse Engineering, IEEE Computer Society. Heuvel, W.-J. v. d. (2006). Aligning Modern Business Processes and Legacy Systems: A Component-Based Perspective (Cooperative Information Systems), The MIT Press.

Ulrich, W., & Newcomb, P. (2010). *Information Systems Transformation. Architecture Driven Modernization Case Studies*. Burlington, MA: Morgan Kauffman.

Chapter 5
Architecture–Centered Integrated Verification

Yujian Fu
Alabama A & M University, USA

Zhijang Dong
Middle Tennessee State University, USA

Xudong He
Florida International University, USA

ABSTRACT

This chapter presents an architecture-centered verification approach to large scale complex software systems by integrating model checking with runtime verification. A software architecture design provides a high-level abstraction of system topology, functionality, and/or behavior, which provides a basis for system understanding and analysis as well as a foundation for subsequent detailed design and implementation. Therefore, software architecture plays a critical role in the software development process. Reasoning and analysis of software architecture model can detect errors in an early stage, further reduce the errors in the final product and highly improve the software quality. First identified are the two main streams of software architecture research groups–the groups that work on the architectural abstraction and semantic foundation, and the group works on the framework using object oriented concepts. Problematically, both architecture designs cannot generate correct products due to two reasons. On one hand, not all properties can be verified at design level because of the state space explosion problem, verification costs, and characteristics of open-system. On the other hand, a correct and valid software architecture design does not ensure a correct implementation due to the error-prone characteristics of the software development process.

The approach aims at solving the above problems by including the analysis and verification of two different levels of software development process–design level and implementation level-and bridging the gap between software architecture analysis and verification and the software product. In the architecture design level, to make sure the design correctness and attack the large scale of complex systems, the compositional verification is used by dividing and verifying each component individually

DOI: 10.4018/978-1-60960-215-4.ch005

and synthesizing them based on the driving theory. Then for those properties that cannot be verified on the design level, the design model is translated to implementation and runtime verification technique is adapted to the program. This approach can highly reduce the work on the design verification and avoid the state-explosion problem using model checking. Moreover, this approach can ensure both design and implementation correctness, and can further provide a high confident final software product. This approach is based on Software Architecture Model (SAM) that was proposed by Florida International University in 1999. SAM is a formal specification and built on the pair of component-connector with two formalisms – Petri nets and temporal logic. The ACV approach places strong demands on an organization to articulate those quality attributes of primary importance. It also requires a selection of benchmark combination points with which to verify integrated properties. The purpose of the ACV is not to commend particular architectures, but to provide a method for verification and analysis of large scale software systems in architecture level. The future research works fall in two directions. In the compositional verification of SAM model, it is possible that there is circular waiting of certain data among different component and connectors. This problem was not discussed in the current work. The translation of SAM to implementation is based on the restricted Petri nets due to the undecidable issue of high level Petri nets. In the runtime analysis of implementation, extraction of the execution trace of the program is still needed to get a white box view, and further analysis of execution can provide more information of the product correctness.

INTRODUCTION

A software architecture (SA) design provides a high-level abstraction of system topology, functionality, and/or behavior ((Shaw, M. and Garlan, D., 1996), (Perry, D. E. and Wolf, A. L.,1992), (Taylor, R. N. et al., 2009)), which provides a basis for system understanding and analysis as well as a foundation for subsequent detailed design and implementation. Therefore, software architecture plays a critical role in the software development process. In the past decade, tremendous research ((Luckham, D., et al., 1995), (Taylor, R. N., et al., 1996), (Roshandel, R., et al.,2004),(Medvidovic, N., et al., 1996,2002,200,2006),(He, X., et al.,2002,2004),(Fu, Y., et al.,2007)) has been done on software description languages and their analysis.

There are two main research groups in the field of software architectures: one group has focused on the architectural abstraction, and semantic analysis of architectures, while the other present a framework adopting object oriented reuse concepts for software architectures. The first group has focused on architectural design abstractions called styles and the semantics underpinning (Shaw, M. and Garlan, D., 1996). Various formal architecture description languages (ADLs) ((Luckham, D., et al.,1995),(Allen, R. J., 1997), (Taylor, R. N., et al., 1996),(Lu L., et al., 2002), (Vestal, S., 1998)) and their supporting tools ((Medvidovic, N., et al., 1996), (Vestal, S., 1998) have emerged from this body of research over the decades (N. Medvidovic & R.N. Taylor, 2000). To date, most architectural tools have focused on the simulation and analysis of architectural models to exploit the semantic power of ADLs. However, the analysis and verification of various ADLs are still a very challenging issue due to syntax and semantics problems ((Clarke, E.M., et al., 2000), (Pnueli, A.,1985)). In other words, it is not enough to generate correct products.

The second group has focused on providing software frameworks, often through object-oriented reuse techniques such as design patterns and object hierarchies. A framework is a skeleton set of software modules that may be tailored for building domain-specific applications, typically resulting in increased productivity and faster time-to-market (Fregonese, G., et al., 1999). This approach has lead to creation of a variety of mediate techniques and associated commercial technologies for component-based development ((Shannon, B., et al., 2000), (Williams, S. & Kindel, C., 1994), (Discussion of the Object Management Architecture, 1997)). However, software implementations resulting from such use of frameworks often differ widely from conceptual models and lack adequate semantic underpinnings for analytic purposes.

Analysis of software architecture is not enough to generate correct product due to two reasons. On one hand, not all properties can be verified at design level because of the state space explosion problem, verification costs and characteristics of open-system. On the other hand, a correct and valid software architecture design does not ensure a correct implementation due to the error-prone characteristics of the software development process. At the same time, insufficient progress has been made on supporting implementation of applications based ADL models (Medvidovic, N. & Taylor, R.N., 2000).

A major focus of our work has been precisely on alleviating and attacking these problems, and bridging the two approaches described above. By analyzing automatically constructed implementations, the properties that cannot be verified at the design level can be checked to increase confidence on the correctness of software architecture. Additionally, the correctness of implementations can be validated, which is necessary since "architectural analysis in existing ADLs may reveal important architectural properties, those properties are not guaranteed to hold in the implementations" (Aldrich, J., et al., 2002). This chapter describes our design of and our experience in developing an integrated verification for architecture verification supporting automatic implementation and compositional verification of large scale software applications built on an architecture specification – SAM (Wang, J., et al., 1999), a general formal specification for specifying and analyzing

software architectures. Thus we will provide an architecture-centered verification method (ACV) for large scale safety- and mission-critical systems and used it to evaluate large scale software architectures. This method is based upon a common understanding and representation for architectures and formal analysis approaches, and can dramatically increase the verification capability of system scales in design model by integration of decomposition and shifting to implementation.

COMPOSITIONAL VERIFICATION

To analyze large scale software systems and ensure high quality of software products, several software architecture description languages have been proposed such an Wright (Allen, R.J., 1997), Rapide (Luckam, D., et al., 1995), MetaH (Vestal, S.,1998), C2 (Taylor, R.N., 1996), etc. The main stream methodology to verify and validate architecture specifications is formal analysis, including model checking and theorem proving. Model checking is an automated verification technique that can be used to determine whether a concurrent system satisfies certain properties by exhaustively exploring all its possible executions. It is typically applied to components of a larger system in order to obtain high quality. Recently model checking has gained popularity due to its increasing use for software system verification even in industrial contexts ((Chan, W., et al., 1998), (Dingel, J., 2003)). However the application of model checking techniques is still suffering the notorious state explosion problem. State explosion occurs either in systems composed of many interacting components, or in systems where data structures assume many different values. The number of global states easily becomes exponential and intractable with the increment of the system size. Considering theorem proving, two weak points of theorem proving are it is hard to be automatic and it requires expert knowledge of notations.

To solve these problems, many methods have been developed by exploiting different approaches (Clarke, E.M., et al., 2000). They can be logically classified into two disjoint groups. The first group, we named technique methods, considers algorithms and techniques used internally to the model checker in order to efficiently represent transition relations between concurrent states, such as Binary Decision Diagrams (Bryant, R.E., 1986) and Partial Order Reduction ((Katz, S. & Peled, D.,1989), (Holzmann, G.J.)) techniques. The second group, that we call system methods investigates the system or model which model checker operates on. Generally this group can be used in conjunction with technique methods. Typical examples in this group are Abstraction (Clarke, E.M., et al., 2000), Symmetry (Clarke, E.M., et al., 2000) and Compositional Reasoning ((Abadi, M. & Lamport, L.,1989), (Pnueli, A.,1985), (Ostroff, J.S., 1999)). In fact, compositional verification is to break up the verification tasks into smaller ones by using "divide-and-conquer". In particular, Compositional Reasoning aims at decomposing a global system property specification into local properties that hold on small sub-parts of the system. This decomposition is meaningful if we have the knowledge that the conjunction of the local properties on the system sub-parts implies the global property on the entire system. This suggests the use of software architectures as suitable system abstractions to efficiently carry on Compositional Reasoning.

Our goal is to efficiently integrate compositional verification techniques, like model checking, with the software architecture model verification in order to improve the overall software quality of large scale software products. In this sense we have to consider two crucial folds that we will fully motivate later on. One is related to the software architecture model we want to verify, i.e. SAM. The other is on the verification technique we decide to apply, i.e. compositional model checking. Both have an implication on the applicability of the verification technique.

Model checking is an automated verification technique that can be used to determine whether a concurrent system satisfies certain properties by exhaustively exploring all its possible executions. It is typically applied to components of a larger system in order to obtain high quality. Recently model checking has gained popularity due to its increasing use for software system verification even in industrial contexts ((Chan, W., et al., 1998), (Dingel, J., 2003)). However the application of model checking techniques is still suffering the notorious state explosion problem. State explosion occurs either in systems composed of many interacting components, or in systems where data structures assume many different values. The number of global states easily becomes exponential and intractable with the increment of the system size.

To solve this problem, many methods have been developed by exploiting different approaches (Clarke, E.M., et al., 2000). In order to efficiently represent transition relations between concurrent states, Bryant proposed Binary Decision Diagrams (BDD) (Bryant, R.E., 1986), Holzmann and Katz et.al. proposed Partial Order Reduction (POR) ((Katz, S. & Peled, D. 1989),(Holzmann, G.J., 1997)) techniques. To structurally conquer this issue, Abstraction (Clarke, E.M., et al., 2000),], Symmetry (Clarke, E.M., et al., 2000), and Compositional Reasoning ((Abadi, M. & Lamport, L.,1989), (Pnueli, A.,1985), (Ostroff, J.S., 1999)) are proposed and these methods usually integrate with either BDD or POR. In fact, compositional verification is to break up the verification tasks into smaller ones by using "divide-and-conquer". In particular, Compositional Reasoning aims at decomposing a global system property specification into local properties that hold on small sub-parts of the system. This decomposition is meaningful if we have the knowledge that the conjunction of the local properties on the system sub-parts implies the global property on the entire system. This suggests the use of software architectures as suitable system abstractions to efficiently carry on Compositional Reasoning.

SOFTWARE ARCHITECTURE MODEL (SAM)

SAM (Software Architecture Model) ((Wang, J., et al., 1999),(He, X., et al., 2002)), an architectural description language, not only provides means to define structure and behavior of software architecture, but also provide means to specify behavioral properties for components and connectors that should hold in the architecture by Petri nets.

Predicate Transition Nets

Predicate Transition (PrT) net (Aldrich, J., et al., 2002) is a high level Petri net. A PrT has a net structure: (P,T,F), where P is a set of places represented by circles, T is a set of transitions represented by rectangles and T is disjoint from P, and F is a relation between P and T represented by arcs. Each place is assigned a sort indicating what kind of tokens it can contain. The tokens in a place can be viewed as a multi-set over the sort. A marking of a PrT net is a function that assigns tokens to each place. A label is assigned to each arc to describe types and numbers of tokens that flow along this arc. Each transition has a boolean expression called guard, which specifies the relationship among arcs related with the transition. A transition is enabled if there is an assignment to all variables occurred in arcs related with the transition such that each incoming place contains the set of tokens specified by the label of the arc, and the guard of the transition is satisfied. An enabled transition is fired under an assignment by removing tokens from incoming places and adding tokens to outgoing places.

Temporal Logic

Temporal logic (Manna, Z. & Pnueli, A., 1992) defines four future-time (past-time) operators in addition to the propositional logic operators. They are

- Always in the future (past), symbolized as a box $\square$ ($\boxdot$).
- Sometime in the future (past), symbolized as a diamond $\lozenge$ ($\blacklozenge$).
- Until for the future (Since for the past), U (S).
- Next (Previous) for the future (past), $\circ$($\odot$)

Let p and q be any formula, an example of a temporal logic formula $\square(p \rightarrow \lozenge q)$ indicates that predicate p implies eventually q always happen.

FORMAL VERIFICATION

To ensure the correctness and reliability of large scale, complex and disconcurrent systems, computer-assisted mathematical based formal verification methodologies become a necessary step in the design process. The state-of-art techniques of formal verification on the software architecture model are model checking and theorem proving. The goal of theorem proving is to prove whether a model satisfies given properties. The approach of theorem proving is to prove $M \vdash p$ by mathematical deduction where M is a model of a program given as characteristic statements on the program and p is a property. A weak point of theorem proving is that theorem proving is undecidable as many logic systems are, so that it is hard to be automatic. The goal of model checking is similar to that of theorem proving – to prove whether a model satisfies given properties. However, the approach of model checking is different from that of theorem proving. A model checker provides a *design specification language* for describing a model of a system, which is similar to a programming language but simplified. Also, a model checker provides a *property specification language* for describing desired properties. A property specification language may be the same as the design specification language. A model checker generates and explores all possible/reachable states of the model and checks whether all the states satisfy the given properties. A disadvantage of model checking is that tractable reachability testing algorithms exist for only very simple systems ((Clarke, O.G.E & Long, D., 1994),(Kurshan, R.P., 1994)). In many cases, even those simple systems require large amount of computational resources. This is called state explosion problem. There has been active research on the state reduction technique (Kurshan, R.P., 1987), such as symbolic model checking ((Burch, J.R., et al., 1990), (McMillan, K.L., 1992)) binary decision diagram reduction (Bryant, R.E., 1986), partial order reduction (Holzmann, G.J., 1997). Symbolic representations are mainly used for the hardware verification, while partial order reduction is good at the loosely coupled systems. However, symbolic representation is very sensitive to the order of variables. In this work, we introduce a logic based model checking technique named Maude (Clavel, P.L.M. et al., 1996).

Maude (Luckham, D. et al., 1995) is a freely distributed high-performance system, supporting both rewriting logic and membership equational logic. Because of its efficient rewriting engine and its metalanguage features, Maude turns out to be an excellent tool to create executable environments for various logics, theorem provers, and even programming languages.

Rewriting logic (First Workshop on Runtime Verification, 2001) is a logic for concurrency. A rewrite theory R is a tuple $(\sum, E, L, R)$, where $(\sum, E)$ is an equational logic, L is set of labels, and R is a set of rewrite rules. A rewrite $P: M \rightarrow N$ means that the term M rewrites to the term N modulo ER, and this rewrite is witnessed by the proof term P. Apart from general (concurrent) rewrites $P: M \rightarrow N$ that are generated from identity and atomic rewrites by parallel and sequential composition, rewriting logic classifies its most basic rewrites as follows: a one-step (concurrent) rewrite is generated by parallel composition from identity and atomic rewrites and contains at least one atomic rewrite, and a one-step sequential

rewrite is a one-step rewrite containing exactly one atomic rewrite. We often write

$$l : [s] \rightarrow [t] \text{ if } [\vec{u}] \rightarrow [\vec{v}] \text{ for } l : [s] \rightarrow [t]$$
$$\text{if } [u_1] \rightarrow [v_1] \wedge ... \wedge [u_k] \rightarrow [v_k]$$

In Maude (Clavel, P.L.M. et al., 1996) the basic units are functional modules and system modules. A functional module is an equational style functional program with user-definable syntax in which a number of sorts, their elements, and functions on those sorts are defined. A system module is a declarative style concurrent program with user-definable syntax.

A functional module is declared in Maude using the keywords

```
fmod <ModuleName> is
    <DeclarationsAndStatements>
endfm
```

The <DeclarationsAndStatements> includes signatures (e.g. sorts, subsorts, kinds etc.), operations, and equations. In Maude, functional modules are equational theories in membership equational logic satisfying some additional requirements. Computation in a functional module is accomplished by using the equations as rewrite rules until a canonical form is found. This is the reason why the equations must satisfy the additional requirements of being Church-Rosser, terminating, and sort decreasing.

A system module is declared in Maude using the keywords

```
mod <ModuleName> is
    DeclarationsAndStatements>
endm
```

The <DeclarationsAndStatements> includes sorts and subsorts, operation, equation, rules, etc.. declaration.

Conditional rules has the form of

Figure 1. Overview of architecture-centered verification

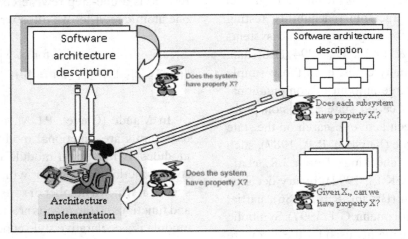

```
crl [label]: <left term> => <right
term> if <condition or set of condi-
tions>.
```

While unconditional rules has the form of

```
rl [label]: <left term> => <right
term>.
```

ARCHITECTURE-CENTERED VERIFICATION

Over the past decade, changes in the software architecture characterize the advances in support environments for the development of user interfaces. However, it is often difficult to assess a developer's claims of qualities inherent in a software architecture. By integrating design verification with implementation verification we can verify large scale software products in design model. In addition to it, to improve the state space we can reach in the design level, we investigate and develop a modular verification on the design model. As the top abstraction of the system description, software architecture description has played a key role in the large scale software development process. It is important to detect and reveal errors in an early stage of software development process (Pressman, R., 2009). Therefore, our integrated framework (Figure 1.) is proposed to center on the architecture model as the target specification.

Software architecture model represents the first complete system description in the software development lifecycle. It provides not only a high-level behavioral abstraction of components but also their interactions (connectors), as well as a description of the static structure of the system. Since we are interested in verification of behavioral properties, we concentrate on the architecture behavioral descriptions. Behavioral properties are usually specified by using Temporal Logic formulas, and in particular Linear Temporal Logic (LTL) (Manna, Z. & Pnueli, A., 1992). Because temporal logic is part of the SAM architecture description, it is easy to integrate the description of the architecture behavior property.

Composition Verification of Software Architecture Model

The Compositional Verification key idea is to decompose the system specification into properties that describe the behavior of a systems subset. In general checking local properties over subsystems does not imply the correctness of the entire system.

Figure 2. Generic software architecture in SAM

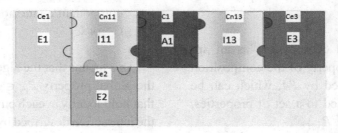

The problem is due to the existence of mutual dependencies among components.

Components are usually designed with some assumptions over the behavior of their environment. Thus, in order to guarantee that a component satisfies its local properties, it is necessary that its environment satisfies some assumptions. This strategy is called assume-guarantee and was introduced by Amir Pnueli (Dingel, J., 2003). The notation used by Pnueli is the following: $< \varphi > M < \psi >$

The common reading is "if the environment of M satisfies φ, then M in this environment satisfies ψ". Below we show the classical reasoning chain:

$$< > M < \varphi >$$

$$< \varphi > M' < \psi >$$

$$< > M \| M' < \psi >$$

Its interpretation is: if M satisfies φ and M', over an environment that satisfies ψ, satisfies then $M \| M'$ will satisfies ψ, where $\|$ is a suitable composition operator. In the scope of this work M and M' model components behaviors while φ and ψ are LTL formulae.

In SAM architecture model, it is a key issue to identify how to deploy compositional verification among components and connectors. As shown in previous section, SAM model consists of communication pair and requires disjoint communication between components and connectors. In addition, except for behavior model of each component/connector is described by Petri Nets, property description is considered in SAM model. Therefore, a decomposition of each property among components/connectors is necessary. In this work, we present how to distribute SAM properties among components by viewing a certain component as an application.

We consider an application and a certain kind of its environment as components in the SAM model (Fu, Y., et al., 2009). The connector in SAM can be used to model interface component. An application A is composed of several components $A_i \in A$ that interact with several environment components $E_j \in E$ through interface components $I_i \in I$. This scenario can be represented in the Figure 2.

In Figure 2, the investigated component C_i represents application A, while all other components that are connected with connectors are considered as environment E of C_i. In SAM model, all components cannot communicate with each other directly, this communication must be done through connector(s). In this sense, we concern connectors that have direct connection with component C_i as interface component I_i.

The behavior of each investigated component $C_i \in A$ is represented by a Petri net N_{Ci}, which denotes an application A_i. The behavior of an environment component $C_j \in E$ is captured by a Petri net N_{Cj}, which denotes an entity component of environment E_i. All C_i, C_j and I_i compose the SAM model, which denoted by a composition C. This composition C describes the behavior of an application A on a certain kind of environment E.

We consider the architecture of a composition C, in which we identify:

1. each investigated composition as an application. The property of the composition satisfied is denoted by PA, which can be further decomposed to a set of properties, e.g., $P_A = \{P_{c1}, ..., P_{cm}\}$.
2. the connected component/connector as the environment E of the investigated composition;
3. the connectors as the Interface components I of the investigated application. The synchronization between two communicated ports is obtained by the message passing and the same port identification. The properties satisfied by E are given in a set $P_E = \{P_{e1}, ..., P_{en}\}$.

Before introducing the SAM-AG-decomposition theorem, let us introduce the steps the theorem is built on:

a. Let P_A be the set of properties $P_A = \{P_{C1}, ..., P_{Cm}\}$. P_A is the global properties satisfied by the application A. Let S be the system that composed of A working under environment E, e.g., $S = A + E$. We want to prove that S satisfies P_A.
b. For each component C_m ($C_m \in C$) and connector C_n ($C_n \in C$), we apply the algorithm $A_{subfma\_Gen\_A}$ that given a C and C_m/C_n as input, return a set Q of set Q_i where Q_i contains local properties related to each P_{Ci}, where P_{Ci} represents the global properties of C_i, where C_i denotes C_{mi} or C_{ni}.

$$A_{sub\,fma\_Gen\_A}: PCi \rightarrow \{Q_{A1}, ..., Q_{Am}\}$$

and such that

$$\forall i(N_C \models P_{Ci}) \rightarrow (N_{Ci} \models Q_i),$$

where N_{Ci} denotes the behavior model of a component/connector $_{Ci}$, which can be either C_{mi} or C_{ni}.

This means that the algorithm A_1 decomposes the global property $P_{Ci} \in PA$ in local properties that hold locally at each environment involved in the interaction described by Petri net N_{Ei}, which is a behavior model of environment component E_i.

Let us now consider the set $P_E = \{P_{e1}, ..., P_{en}\}$ of standard properties of E which comes with a set of constraints $X = \{x_1, ..., x_r\}$. X assesses the correct usage of E by the application A. This means that E satisfies P_E, under the assumptions expressed by X. All the local properties that related investigated application component and its environment component are in the set X, and generated by algorithm $A_{fma\_Gen\_X}$. The set X is needed to ensure the validity of the property P_E in E. In fact they specify how P_E should be used in order to correctly work. In particular X must be satisfied by the interfaces components.

However, SAM does not have an Interface Component concept. We refer connector as interface component I between investigated components and its environment components. They are connected through ports and messages in ports which is the atomic predicates in the constraints.

There is not interaction between ports and internal components, thus there is no interaction between interface component and investigated component C_i. All properties of each composition can be expressed by atomic entity $P_i(tk)$ with logic connections. Thus we have $< A > I < E >$.

For each $P_{Ei} \in P_E$ we apply the algorithm $A_{subfma\_Gen\_E}$ that, given N_{Cj} as input, extracts a set P_{Er} of behavioral properties that E must hold in order to satisfy N_{Cj} according to the property P_A, where N_{Cj} denotes the behavior model of component/connector C_j:

$$A_{sub\,fma\_Gen\_E}: N_{Cj} \rightarrow \{P_{Er1}, ..., P_{Erv}\} \text{ and such that:}$$

$(A \models P_{Ai}) \rightarrow (E \models P|)$

P_{Er} represents the set of expected behaviors of the environment needed in order to satisfy N_{Cj}.

For each $P_{Ai} \in P_A$ apply the algorithm $A_{subprop}$ in order split the N_{Ci} into a conjunction of sub-properties that must hold locally on the system components. More precisely

$Asubprop\_Gen$: $N_{Ci} \rightarrow \{a_{i1}, ..., a_{ip}\}$ such that:

$A \models P_{Ai} \rightarrow (P_{Ai} \rightarrow a_{i1} \wedge ... \wedge a_{ip})$

$\forall i (\exists k ((a_{iv} \in Q_k) \vee (a_{iv} \in X) \vee (a_{iv} \in P_{Er})))$

This last step is needed in order to ensure the global consistency of all the previous steps.

The algorithms are listed as follows.

The algorithm $A_{sub\_fma\_A\_Gen}$ is used to distribute the property P_A into the components that constitute the composition. The idea of the algorithm $A_{sub\_fma\_A\_Gen}$ is to discrete P_{Ai} on the ports of a composition C in order to obtain the set of properties Q_i. This algorithm is shown in the Figure 3.

In our case, we consider connector as an interface component. The algorithm $A_{fma\_Gen\_X}$ constructs the set X_i that the connector I_{ij} must satisfy. Focusing on a generic component C_i, the algorithm idea is to generate, for each outgoing and incoming message, a translation rule that must be verified by the connector I_{ij}.

Figure 3. Algorithm for generation of Q_i

1. According to the output ports in P_{Ai}, find corresponding input ports
2. Based on the hierarchical mapping function f find the corresponding ports of each internal components/connectors
3. Construct sub–formulae according to the relation in each component/connector
4. Repeat step 1–3 until no further subcomponent/connector

We get a theorem for property distribution in SAM model based on Figure 2 and the above steps (Fu, Y., et al., 2009).

Theorem 1. (*SAM-Property Distribution*) *Let* $C = C_1, ..., C_m$ *be an application composed of n compositions (including components and connectors) that satisfies a set of properties P_A. Let E, I, X, P_E be defined as above. Then, for each P_{Ai} let:*

- $Q = A_{sub\_fma\_Gen\_A}(N_{Ci})$
- $PEr = A_{sub\_fma\_Gen\_E}(N_{Cj})$
- $a_{i1} \wedge ... \wedge a_{ip} = A_{subprop\_Gen}(N_{Ci})$,

Under the following hypothesis:

1. $\diamond C < Q_{Ai}>$, $\forall C_i \in C$
2. $\diamond I_i < X>$, $\forall i$
3. $< X > E < P_E >$
4. $\diamond I_i \| E < P >$ *for each component in C*
5. $\Gamma(P_{Er}) \preccurlyeq \Gamma(P_E)$: *E contains all behaviors specified by the properties contained in P_{Er}*
6. *Algorithm* $A_{subprop\_Gen}$ *decomposes p_a into the following:* $p_a = a_1 \wedge ... \wedge a_p$

Then we have

$\diamond C_i \| I_i \| E_i < p_a >$

Next, we discuss each algorithm in the following steps.

1. Let P_A be the set of properties $P_A = \{P_{C1}, ..., P_{Cm}\}$. P_A is the global properties satisfied by the application A. Let S be the system that composed of A working under environment E, e.g., $S = A + E$. We want to prove that S satisfies P_A.
2. For each component C_m ($C_m \in C$) and connector C_n ($C_n \in C$), we apply the algorithm $A_{sub\_fma\_Gen\_A}$ (Figure 3.) that given a C and C_m / C_n as input, return a set Q of set Q_i where Q_i contains local properties related to each P_{Ci}, where P_{Ci} represents the global properties of C_i. $A_{sub\_fma\_Gen\_A}$: $P_{Ci} \rightarrow \{Q_{A1}, ..., Q_{Am}\}$

Figure 4. Algorithm for generation of X

```
X = ∅;
X_AE = X_EA = ∅;
InPorts = all input ports of I;
OutPorts = all output ports of I;

Let     M_AE be the set of messages from A to E,
        M_AE be the set of messages from E to A

for each port p_i ∈ Inports {
        find its corresponding output ports p_o ∈ OutPorts
        for all message m,m' ∈ M_AE,
        X_AE = X_AE ∪ {□ p_i(m) →? p_o(m'))}
}

for each port p_i ∈ Inports {
        find its corresponding output ports p_o ∈ OutPorts
        for all message m,m' ∈ M_EA,
        X_EA = X_EA ∪ {□ p_i(m) →? p_o(m'))}
}

X = XAE ∪ XEA
Return X;
```

and such that $\forall i(N_C \models P_{Ci}) \rightarrow (N_{Ci} \models Q_i)$. This means that the algorithm $A_{sub\_fma\_Gen\_A}$ decomposes the global property $P_{Ci} \in P_A$ in local properties that hold locally at each environment involved in the interaction described by Petri net N_{Ei}.

3. Let us now consider the set $P_E = \{P_{e1}, ..., P_{en}\}$ of standard properties of E which comes with a set of constraints $X = \{x_1, ..., x_r\}$. X assesses the correct usage of E by the application A. This means that E satisfies P_E, under the assumptions expressed by X. All the local properties that related investigated application component and its environment component are in the set X, and generated by algorithm $A_{fma\_Gen\_X}$ (Figure 4.).

They are connected through ports and messages in ports which is the atomic predicates in the constraints. There is not interaction between ports and internal components, thus there is no interaction between interface component and investigated component C_i. All properties of each composition can be expressed by atomic entity $Pt(tk)$ with logic connections. Thus we have $<A> I < E >$.

For each $P_{Ei} \in P_E$ we apply the algorithm $A_{sub\_fma\_Gen\_E}$ (Figure 5.) that, given N_{Cj} as input, extracts a set P_{Er} of behavioral properties that E must hold in order to satisfy N_{Cj} according to the property P_A:

$A_{sub\_fma\_Gen\_E}: N_{Cj} \rightarrow \{P_{Er1}, ..., P_{Erv}\}$ and such that:

$$(A \models P_{Ai}) \rightarrow (E \models P_{Er})$$

P_{Er} represents the set of expected behaviors of the environment needed in order to satisfy N_{Cj}.

5. For each $P_{Ai} \in P_A$ apply the algorithm $A_{subprop}$ in order split the N_{Ci} into a conjunction of subproperties that must hold locally on the system components. This last step is needed in order to ensure the global consistency of all the previous steps.

The algorithm $A_{sub\_fma\_A\_Gen}$ is used to distribute the property P_A into the components that constitute the composition. The idea of the algorithm $A_{sub\_fma\_A\_Gen}$ is to discrete P_{Ai} on the ports of a composition C in order to obtain the set of properties Qi. This algorithm is shown in the Figure 3.

In our case, we consider connector as an interface component. The algorithm $A_{fma\_Gen\_X}$ constructs the set X_i that the connector I_{ij} must satisfy. Focusing on a generic component C_i, the algorithm idea is to generate, for each outgoing and incoming message, a translation rule that must be verified by the connector I_{ij}.

Referring to Figure 2, let us suppose, without loss of generality, that m_1 is a message sent from A_1 to E_1, and m_2 is a message sent from E_1 to A_1. The generated formulae for the connector I_{11} are $\square(p_{inA}(m_1) \rightarrow \lozenge p_{outA}(m_1'))$ and $\square(p_{inB}(m_2) \rightarrow \lozenge p_{outB}(m_2'))$, where m_1' and m_2' are the original data with the augmented information such as security

Figure 5. Algorithm of generating P_{Er}

```
Set  P_{E_R} = Φ;
for each component  C_j ∈ E  {
    let m be the messsage received from  A_i ;
    let m' be the messsage send to  A_i ;
    let PtE be the set of ports that received messages from    A_i
    for each port p_t ∈ PtE  {
        P_{E_R} = P_{E_R} ∪ {□(p_{t_R}(m) → ◇p_{t_S}(m'))}
    }
}
```

or acknowledgement data. Based on this idea, we have the algorithm in Figure 5.

The algorithm $A_{sub\_fma\_E\_Gen}$ constructs the set of properties P_{ER} that the environment E must satisfy based on the property P_{Ai}. For each incoming message of the environment E $send(p_{ti})$, a property $□(receive(p_{ti}) → ◇send(p_{ti}))$ is added to P_{Er}. This algorithm is shown in Figure 5.

Since these subformulae generated from $A_{fma\_Gen\_X}$ and $A_{sub\_fma\_E\_Gen}$ are responsive properties, considering the mapping function f that connected the ports hierarchically and algorithm $A_{subfma\_A\_Gen}$, it is easy to get the $A_{subprop}$ which is the conjunction of all these formulae.

The purpose of Theorem SAM-Property Distribution is to reduce verification of global properties to local properties given some assumptions.

Runtime Verification on the Implementation Model

Runtime verification (Workshop on Runtime Verification, 2001, 2002, 2003, 2004, 2005, 2006, 2007, 2008, 2009) has been proposed as a lightweighted formal method applied during the execution of programs. It can be viewed as a complement to traditional methods of proving design model or programs correct before execution. Aspect-oriented software engineering ((Ossher, H. & Kiczales, G., 2002), (Griswold, W.G. & Akit, M., 2003), (Murphy G. & Lieberherr, K., 2004)) and

aspect-oriented programming (Elrad, T., et al., 2001) were proposed to separate concerns during design and implementation. Aspect-Oriented Programming complements OO programming by allowing the developer to dynamically modify the static OO model to create a system that can grow to meet new requirements. In other words, it allows us to dynamically modify models or implementations to include code required for secondary requirements (in our case, it is runtime verification) without modifying the original code.

Figure 6 is the overview of the structure of our methodology. Our method has three levels: design level, tool support level and implementation level, in terms of data flowing.

Design level handles the SAM model and its input format. Two different types of input are specified: SAM XML and PNML (Petri Net Markup Language). SAM models are expressed in an XML-based interchange format (e.g. SAM XML), which specifies the SAM structure, property specifications for components or connectors. Behavior model (Petri nets) are defined as PNML (Petri Net Markup Language) (Billington, J., et al., 2003) files, which specify Petri nets in an XML-based interchange format. Although SAM supports any temporal logic and any kinds of Petri nets, here only linear temporal logic and high level Petri nets are considered.

SAM Parser and the logic server, the tools we developed, fall in the tool support level. The purpose of SAM Parser is to take the design level as input, by communicating through logic server and generate the function and monitoring code to be executed. This level will be discussed in detail in the next subsection. All generated code forms the implementation level. They work together for an integrated system of architecture realization and runtime monitoring. Their output results, the runtime verification of architecture model against system properties in the implementation level, are used to analyze the architecture implementation and guide the application of the system design.

Figure 6. Overview of runtime verification technology

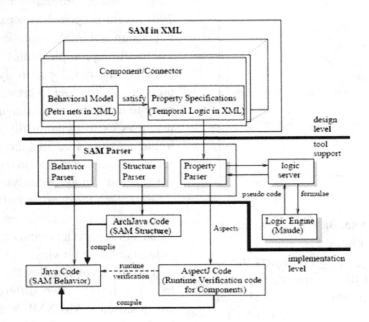

The SAM parser (Fu, Y., et al., 2009) generates runtime verification code automatically and weaves it into functionality code seamlessly without side effects on the functionality code. In order to generate monitoring codes for properties (linear temporal formulae), a logic server, Maude (Clavel, P.L.M., et al., 1996) in our case, is necessary. Maude, acting as the main algorithm generator in the framework, constructs an efficient dynamic programming algorithm (i.e. monitoring code) from any LTL formula (Rosu, G. & Havelund, K., 2004). The generated algorithm can check if the corresponding LTL formula is satisfied over an event trace.

The SAM parser (Fu, Y., et al., 2009) weaves monitoring code into functionality code by integrating them as aspects. In aspect-oriented programming, AspectJ (AspectJ Project) in our case, aspects wrap up *point cuts*, *advice*, and *inter-type declarations* in a modular unit of crosscutting implementation where *point cuts* pick out certain join points in the program flow, *advice* brings together a pointcut (to pick out join points) and a

body of code (to run at each of those join points), and *Inter-type declarations* are declarations that cut across classes and their hierarchies. In our case, for each component or connector, *point cuts* specify time spots: whenever a port sends or receives a message; pieces of code brought together by *advice* with *point cuts* are the generated monitoring code; and *Inter-type declaration* specifies helper variables and methods. Currently the SAM parser can handle future time linear temporal formulae as well as past time linear temporal formulae.

By combining runtime verification and automated implementation of software architecture, we can obtain the following benefits:

- The transformation from design models to implementations is generally informal, therefore error-prone. Automated implementation provide a means to prevent man-made errors, and runtime verification can validate transformation indirectly.

- Runtime verification at implementation level is a natural complement to analysis techniques of design level. Not all properties can be verified against a design model either due to the state space explosion problem or due to characteristic of open-systems. In either case, runtime verification can be explored to verify the correctness of design models.

- Runtime verification provides a mechanism to handle exceptions of implementations that are not detected during development or testing.

CASE STUDY

In this section we present an application of our approach to the basic pervasive health care system on a novel middleware – communication virtual machine – which was developed by FIU in 2007. Our approach is domain independent, i.e. it is based on fundamental definitions of an ontology that captures what a component and a connector are.

Pervasive healthcare system (PHS) (Burkhardt, J. et al., 2002, Hansmann, U., et al., 2001) is a novel computer aided healthcare technology that healthcare professionals should be able to maintain and observe the patient records at the current time, wherever they go. Thus, up-to-date information about patients, diagnoses, treatment plans, medication etc. would always be available at any time, in any given situation. The challenge seen from an IT perspective is to develop computer support for such new ways of working, and one potential approach is to exploit pervasive and mobile computing.

UCM is introduced to provide a high-level unified user-centric communication abstraction which can be shared across communication applications design and development. Under this unified high-level abstraction, internally UCM utilizes the underlying network infrastructure, systems and libraries to ensure that basic communication tasks are carried out smoothly. By separating the application dependent business logic from the network-level communication services, it makes the UCM reusable across the communication applications and increases the portability of the communication applications. To satisfy the communication needs, UCM should support multiple user sessions. A user session is defined as a communication process that involves a number of participants, who can be added or removed dynamically. Within a user session, each participant can send media to all the other session participants. Another requirement is that UCM should allow the upper-layer application to be notified of the communication states. Further, in some applications, the user may desire to dynamically control the behavior of UCM in session control and media delivery.

SAM Model of Pervasive Healthcare System (PHS) on CVM

The top topology of a PHS system specified in SAM model is demonstrated in Figure 7. Each description block is captured in a component (or a composition). At the top level, there are three compositions and two connectors. The first composition, *Distance Devices*, is use to represent any electronic instruments that can be used to send the information to the clinic office or pharmacy, such devices as computers, mobile diagnostic device, and work stations etc.. It is not necessary for these devices to locate in the hospital or clinic that required these information, but they can be used to represent the devices in the hospital too. There are two components and one connectors included in this composition. *Interface Component* represents the interface devices, graphic design, web browser that can be used to interact with patient. While *Controller Component* represents the data and signal process of the interface of the computer. In the case study, we just model a simplified case, a home computer with the clinic and pharmacy information that can be used to send information to the clinic office. The second composition is a middleware composition, Communication Virtual Machine, which is used to describe the communication middleware, which includes three components and two connectors. We just reused the model developed by Sun et al. (Sun, W., et al., 2006) due to the same middleware. The third composition, *Clinic Clerk*, is to describe the clinic office that used by doctors and nurses. This composition includes three components (*Check-in*, *ICU*, and *Device Monitor*) and three connectors. *Check-in* is used for inputting necessary data, records, automatically update the database. *ICU* is used to describe emergency conditions. *Device Monitor* updates the information from distance devices.

The basic requirements for the PHS system are correctness, robustness and reliability. For instance, if a patient request to a prescription medicine from a pharmacy, after a proper process, the system should make this medicine to be able for the patient to pick up at the pharmacy. If this medicine cannot be available in that pharmacy, a rearrangement to an alternative pharmacy should be provided. The process of the request, process, response and deliver should be properly recorded and sent to the doctor. In the architecture model shown in Figure 7, this can be represented by following data flows in the SAM model (Figure 7): a request with the signal (s), user ID (u), and request message (req) is sent from port *sigIC-O(s,u,req)*, then eventually there will be a response (res) received from the port *sigIC-I(s,u,res)of* the composition *Diagnostic Device*, a display information (rec) to the doctor (d) and nurse to the port *MMCin(s,u,rec,d)* of component *Device Monitor*, and a record will be kept in the port *CiMout(s,u,rec,d)* of component *Check-In* in the composition *Clinic Clerk*. The information flow passed through the middleware, some data used for session, server of the middleware was ignored in the composition *Clinic Clerk*. Using temporal logic, this example can be denoted by following formula:

$$\forall s,u,d,req.\,\square\,(sigIC\text{-}O(s,u,req) \rightarrow \Diamond\,sigIC\text{-}I(s,u,req) \wedge (DMout(s,u,rec,d) \wedge Ciout(s,u,rec,d))) \tag{1}$$

Property shown in formula (1) spans ten compositions and six connectors in two different levels. Depends on the complexity of each composition, it is a common case that the time consuming for the verification of each component is proportional to the number of compositions, components and connectors. In the following sections, we first illustrate how to use modular verification of SAM model of PHS system and then we demonstrate the runtime verification of the property of SAM model of PHS system.

Modular Verification of PHS on CVM

In this section we present the modular verification of PHS using property (1). In the SAM architecture model, the interface component (I) usually is a connector. Since we consider the investigated component (composition) as the application component (A), all components (compositions) and connectors that communicate with that interface component are considered as environment (E) of the application component (A) in the first step. In the property (1), the application component is called *Interface Component*. What we expect from the component is

$$\forall s, u, d, req.\,\square\,(sigIC\text{-}O(s,u,req) \rightarrow \Diamond\,sigIC\text{-}I(s,u,req)) \tag{2}$$

To verify property (2), we can generate a set of formulae using modular verification and verify each subformula to avoid performance trouble of model checker. Use property (1), by following the SAM property distribution theorem, we can prove the property in the following steps:

1. The property that we need to verify is (1), which can be decomposed to following properties:

For composition *Diagnostic Device*, property (2);

For component $\forall$s, u, d, req. $\square$ (*sigIC-O(s,u,req)* $\rightarrow \lozenge$ *sigIC-I(s,u,req)*)   (3)

$\forall$s, u, d, req. $\square$ (*sigIC-O(s,u,req)* $\rightarrow \lozenge$ *sigIC-I(s,u,req)*)   (2)

For each composition, we find the sub-properties Q_i of the investigated composition A, i.e., *Diagnostic Device*.

$\forall$s, u, d, req. $\square$ (*sigIC-O(s,u,req,d)* $\rightarrow \lozenge$ *IC-CC-sigO(s,u,req,d)*)   (4)

This property ensures any signal that goes out from component *Interface Component* will signal the information to the *Controller Component* for process and update.

$\forall$s, u, d, req. $\square$ (*IC-CC-sigO(s,u,req,d)* $\rightarrow \lozenge$ *IC-CC-SO(s,u,req,d)*)   (5)

This property denotes that any information from component *Interface Component* will be conveyed to the the input port of *Controller Component*.

$\forall$s, u, d, req. $\square$ (*IC-CC-SO(s,u,req,d)* $\rightarrow \lozenge$ *CC-IC-SO(s,u,req,d)*)   (6)

This property describes after process of *Controller Component*, there should be data output from *Controller Component* to update the *Interface Component*.

Similar as (5) and (6), we have

$\forall$s, u, d, req. $\square$ (*CC-IC-SO(s,u,req,d)* $\rightarrow \lozenge$ *CC-IC-sigI(s,u,req,d)*)   (7)

This property denotes that update information flows back to *Interface Component*. For mobile devices, usually we need to have following property to update data to users:

$\forall$s, u, d, req. $\square$ (*CC-IC-SO(s,u,req,d)* $\rightarrow \lozenge$ *CC-IC-sigI(s,u,req,d)*)   (8)

The above properties from (4) to (8) can be able to ensure the correct behavior of composition *Dianostic Devices*. It is worth to notice that different devices may have different model. Moreover, for the computer with browser surfing, there is not Controller Component.

3. Find the set of constraints of interface component I. In the SAM model of PHS system (Figure 7), the connector of components and compositions are simply the transitions with truth conditions. This indicates that all data with any types will be conveyed to the next composition or component. The set of constraints X can be simply defined as X = {true}.

4. For the environment component, we can get the set of P_{Ei} as follows by using $A_{subfma\_Fen\_E}$.

The compositions *Communication Virtual Machine* and *Clinic Clerk* and connector between them are considered as environment components of *Distance Devices*. Concerning property (1), we can have following property for the set of P_{Ei}:

Let *ReqType=CMD× CRED× Session× USER× Media × String×String×} (USER)×} (Media)*

Φ(*UAPIReq*) = Φ(*UAPIRes*) = Φ(*UCMReq*) = Φ(*UCMRes*) = *ReqType*

$\forall$reqtype. $\square$ (*UAPIReq-DD(reqtype)* $\wedge$ *UCMReq-DD(reqtype)* $\rightarrow \lozenge$ *SigMSend-DD(reqtype)*)   (9)

$\forall$reqtype. $\square$ (*SigMSend-DD(reqtype)* $\rightarrow \lozenge$ *SigM-Rev-CC(reqtype)*)   (10)

$\forall$reqtype. $\square$ (*SigMRev-CC(reqtype)* → $\lozenge$ *UAPIRes-CC(reqtype)* $\wedge$ *UAPIRes-CC(reqtype)*) (11)

$\forall$reqtype. $\square$(*UAPIReq-CC(reqtype)* $\wedge$ *UCMReq-CC(reqtype)* → $\lozenge$ *SigMSend-CC(reqtype)*) (12)

$\forall$reqtype. $\square$ (*SigMSend-CC(reqtype)* → $\lozenge$ *SigMRev-DD(reqtype)*) (13)

$\forall$reqtype. $\square$ (*SigMRev-DD(reqtype)* → $\lozenge$ *UAPIRes-DD(reqtype)* $\wedge$ *UAPIRe-DDs (reqtype)*) (14)

Since all message are encoded in the ReqType, so there is an automatic decoding of the message in the Clinic Clerk composition. Due to limitation, we do not discuss the message type interpretation in this chapter.

$\forall$s,u,d,req,reqtype. $\square$ (*UAPIRes-DD(reqtype)* →

$\lozenge$ ($Ccin(s,u,d,req)$ $\vee$ $ICUin(s,u,d,req)$ $\vee$ $DMin(s,u,d,req)$)) (15)

$\forall$s,u,d,req. $\square$ ($Ccin(s,u,d,req)$ → $Ciout(s,u,d,req)$) (16)

$\forall$s,u,d,req,reqtype. $\square$ ($ICUin(s,u,d,req)$ → $\lozenge$ $ICUout(s,u,d,req)$) (17)

$\forall$s,u,d,req. $\square$ ($DMin(s,u,d,req)$ → $\lozenge$ *DMout(s,u,d,req)*) (18)

5. The ports of each component (N_{Ci}) can be mapped to a place in the Petri Nets N_{Ci}. The formulae that shown in step 2 and 3 are the formulae of P_{Ai}.

After running Maude on each set of formulae, we can show the sets of properties I_{AE}, I_{EA}, X_{AE}, X_{EA}, P_{Er} hold. Therefore, we can say that the property

(1) holds. The model checker we use is a high performance declarative programming language Maude (Clavel, P.L.M., et al., 1996) introduced in Section 2. To translate the SAM model to the Maude programming language, we developed an algorithm that maps SAM specification to Maude (Fu, Y., et al., 2008).

Runtime Verification of PHS on CVM

Since the property (1) was proved to hold, it is not necessary to have it run on the runtime checker. In the case of the any subformula generated by SAM distribution theorem cannot be verified by model checker, a shift to runtime checker is needed. As we have done several examples on our runtime checker ((Fu, Y., et al., 2007), (Fu, Y., et al., 2006)), we are confidently to say that the shift from model checker to runtime verification is feasible and temporal properties can be verified with few scalability problem.

CONCLUSION

In this chapter, we have provided an architecture-centered verification method (ACV) for large scale safety- and mission-critical systems and used it to evaluate large scale software architectures. This method is based upon a common understanding and representation for architectures and formal analysis approaches, and can dramatically increase the verification capability of system scales in design model by integration of decomposition and shifting to implementation. This method permits the separation of architectures and conversion between design and implementation, split of systems, and transformation from design to implementation. The separations of verification and implementation have been hitherto quite difficult.

Another strong point of ACV method is decomposition of software architecture model based on the behavior model and property specification and synthesization of behavior model and properties to be verified. Decomposition of software architecture is a key issue and properties are considered. Another group using algebraic approach to describe software architecture model can avoid the challenge of decomposition of properties. For example, in (Ding, Z., & Liu, J., 2009), an architecture behavior can be modeled by a group of ordinary differential equations containing some control parameters, where the control parameters are used to represent deterministic/ nondeterministic choices. Property analysis is based on the equation solutions. A disadvantage is loss visualization comparing to graphic behavior model (Petri Nets) used in SAM. However, a weak point of our decomposition approach is semantics of each component/connector are not formally defined, therefore, the current work is based on the flattened SAM model. The future work for the compositional model checking of SAM is extending SAM model with refinement analysis and investigating the more interesting properties such as deadlock freedom.

Runtime verification has been more and more popular due to its scalability. Recently, some research work performs runtime verification on the component systems (Belhaouari, H. & Peschanski, F., 2008). However, there is still few approach that applies runtime checking on the software architecture model. Although the runtime verification provides an alternative verification technique of architecture model, it is hard to say the validity of the property on all execution paths due to the incompleteness. Currently, we can track the different execution branches by investigating the extracted event trace and identify the coverage and loss of execution. The future work would be extending the current version with execution path analysis using state update information.

The ACV approach places strong demands on an organization to articulate those quality attributes of primary importance. It also requires a selection of benchmark combination points with which to verify integrated properties. The purpose of the ACV is not to commend particular archi-

tectures, but to provide a method for verification and analysis of large scale software systems in architecture level.

REFERENCES

Abadi, M., & Lamport, L. (1989). Composing specifications. In de Bakker, J. W., de Roever, W.-P., & Rozenberg, G. (Eds.), *Stepwise refinement of distributed systems-models, formalisms, correctness (Vol. 430*, pp. 1–41). Berlin: Springer-Verlag.

Aldrich, J. Chambers, C. & Notkin, D. (2002). Archjava: Connecting software architecture to implementation. In *International Conference on Software Engineering,* Orlando,FL.

Allen, R. J. (1997). *A formal approach to software architecture*. Unpublished doctoral thesis.

Aspect, J. Project. (2004). AspectJ project. Retrieved from http://eclipse.org/aspectj/

Belhaouari, H., & Peschanski, F. (2008). A lightweight container architecture for runtime verification. In *proceedings of 8th international runtime verification workshop*, LNCS 5289. (pp. 173–187). Springer-Verlag.

Billington, J., Christensen, S., et al. (2003). The Petri Net Markup Language: Concepts, technology, and tools. In *Proceedings of the 24th International Conference on Applications and Theory of Petri Nets (ICATPN 2003)*, LNCS 2679, (pp. 483–505). Springer-Verlag.

Bryant, R. E. (1986). Graph-based algorithms for Boolean function manipulation. *IEEE Transactions on Computers, C-35*(8), 677–691. doi:10.1109/TC.1986.1676819

Burch, J. R., Clarke, E. M., McMillan, K. L., Dill, D. L., & Hwang, L. J. (1990). Symbolic model checking: 10^{20} states and beyond. In *Proceedings of the Fifth Annual IEEE Symposium on Logic in Computer Science*, (pp.1–33). Washington, D.C.: IEEE Computer Society Press.

Burkhardt, J., Henn, H., & Hepper, S. Rintdorff, K. & Sch¨ack, T. (2002). *Pervasive computing–technology and architecture of mobile internet applications*. Addison-Wesley.

Chan, W., Anderson, R. J., Beame, P., Burns, S., Modugno, F., & Notkin, D. (1998). Model checking large software specification. *IEEE Transactions on Software Engineering, 24*(7), 498–520. doi:10.1109/32.708566

Clarke, E. M., Grumberg, O., & Peled, D. A. (2000). *Model checking*. The MIT Press.

Clarke, O. G. E., & Long, D. (1994). Verification tools for finite-state concurrent systems. In *Proceedings of In A Decade of Concurrency–Reflections and Perspectives*, LNCS 803.

Clavel, P. L. M., Eker, S., & Meseguer, J. (1996). Principles of Maude. Vol. 4. *Electronic Notes in Theoretical Computer Science*. Elsevier Science Publishers.

Ding, Z., & Liu, J. (2009). An improvement of software architecture verification. In *Proceedings of the 2nd International Workshop on Harnessing Theories for Tool Support in Software (TTSS 2008), 243*, 49-67.

Dingel, J. (2003). Computer-assisted assume/guarantee reasoning with Verisoft. In *ICSE '03: Proceedings of the 25th International Conference on Software Engineering*, (pp. 138–148). Washington, DC: IEEE Computer Society.

Discussion of the Object Management Architecture. (1997). *OMG Document 00-06-41*.

Eighth Workshop on Runtime Verification (2008). *Lecture Notes in Computer Science, 5289*.

Elrad, T., Filman, R. E., & Bader, A. (2001). Aspect-oriented programming: Introduction. *Communications of the ACM, 44*(10), 29–32. doi:10.1145/383845.383853

Fifth Workshop on Runtime Verification (2005). *Electronic Notes in Theoretical Computer Science, 144*.

First Joint Workshop on Formal Aspects of Testing and Runtime Verification (2006). *Lecture Notes in Computer Science, 4262*.

First Workshop on Runtime Verification (2001). *Electronic Notes in Theoretical Computer Science, 55*(2).

Fourth Workshop on Runtime Verification (2004). *Electronic Notes in Theoretical Computer Science, 113*.

Fregonese, G. Zorer, A. & Cortese, G. (1999). Architectural framework modeling in telecommunication domain. In *ICSE'99: Proceedings of the 21st international conference on Software engineering*, (pp. 526–534). Los Alamitos, CA: IEEE Computer Society Press.

Fu, Y. Dong, Z. & He, X. (2006). A method for realizing software architecture design. In *Proceedings of QSIC06: Sixth International Conference on Quality Software*, Beijing, China, October 26 - 28.

Fu, Y., Dong, Z., Ding, J., & He, X. (2008). *Towards rewriting semantics of a Software Architecture Model*. Paper presented at The 8th International Conference of Quality Software, Oxford UK, Aug 12-13.

Fu, Y., Dong, Z., Ding, J., He, X., & Atluri, V. (2009). A modular analysis of Software Architecture Model. In *Proceedings of The Nineth International Conference on Software Engineering and Research Practice (SERP'09)*, Las Vegas, USA.

Fu, Y., Dong, Z., & He, X. (2007). A translator of software architecture design from SAM to Java. *International Journal of Software Engineering and Knowledge Engineering, 17*(6), 1–54. doi:10.1142/S0218194007003483

Griswold, W. G., & Akit, M. (Eds.). (2003). *Proceedings of the 2nd International Conference on Aspect-oriented Doftware Development*. ACM Press.

Hansmann, U., Merk, L., Nicklous, M. S., & Stober, T. (2001). *Pervasive computing handbook*. Springer Verlag.

He, X., Ding, J., & Deng, Y. (2002). Model checking software architecture specifications in SAM. In *Proceedings of the 14th international conference on Software engineering and knowledge engineering (SEKE'02)*, volume 27 of *ACM International Conference Proceeding Series*, (pp. 271–274). New York: ACM Press.

He, X., Yu, H., Shi, T., Ding, J., & Deng, Y. (2004). Formally analyzing software architectural specifications using SAM. *Journal of Systems and Software, 71*(1-2), 11–29. doi:10.1016/S0164-1212(02)00087-0

Holzmann, G. J. (1997). The model checker SPIN. *IEEE Transactions on Software Engineering, 23*(5). doi:10.1109/32.588521

Katz, S., & Peled, D. (1989). An efficient verification method for parallel and distributed programs. In *Linear time, branching time and partial order in logics and models for concurrency, school/workshop* (pp. 489–507). London: Springer-Verlag. doi:10.1007/BFb0013032

Kurshan, R. P. (1987). *Reducibility in analysis of coordination*. (pp. 19–39). LNCS 103.

Kurshan, R. P. (1994). *Computer-aided verification of coordinating processes: The automata-theoretic approach*. Princeton, NJ: Princeton University Press.

Lu, L., Li, X., Xiong, Y., & Zhou, X. (2002). Xmadl: An extensible markup architecture description language. In *IEEE*, (pp. 63–67). IEEE Press.

Luckham, D., & Kenney, J. L.A., et al (1995). Specification and analysis of system architecture using Rapide. In *IEEE Transactions on Software Engineering, 21*, 336–355.

Luckham, D., Kenney, J. J., Augustin, L. M., Vera, J., Bryan, D., & Mann, W. (1995). Specification and analysis of system architecture using Rapide. *IEEE Transactions on Software Engineering, 21*(4), 336–353. doi:10.1109/32.385971

Manna, Z., & Pnueli, A. (1992). *Temporal logic of reactive and concurrent systems*. Springer.

McMillan, K. L. (1992). *Symbolic model checking: An approach to the state explosion problem*. Unpublished doctoral thesis, Carnegie Mellon University.

Medvidovic, N., & Jakobac, V. (2006). Using software evolution to focus architectural recovery. *Automated Software Engineering, 13*(2), 225–256. doi:10.1007/s10515-006-7737-5

Medvidovic, N., Malek, S., & Mikic-Rakic, M. (2003). Software architectures and embedded systems. In *Proceedings of the Monterey Workshop on Software Engineering for Embedded Systems (SEES 2003)*, (pp. 65–71).

Medvidovic, N., Oreizy, P., et al. (1996). Using object-oriented typing to support architectural design in the C2 style. In *Proceedings of the 4th ACM SIGSOFT Symposium on Foundations of Software Engineering*, (pp 24–32).

Medvidovic, N., & Taylor, R. N. (2000). A classification and comparison framework for software architecture description languages. *Software Engineering, 26*(1), 70–93. doi:10.1109/32.825767

Murphy, G., & Lieberherr, K. (Eds.). (2004). *Proceedings of the 3rd International Conference on Aspect-oriented Software Development*. ACM Press.

Ninth Workshop on Runtime Verification (2009). *Lecture Notes in Computer Science, 5779*.

Ossher, H., & Kiczales, G. (Eds.). (2002). *Proceedings of the 1st International Conference on Aspect-oriented Software Development*. ACM Press.

Ostroff, J. S. (1999). Composition and refinement of discrete realtime systems. *ATSEM, 8*(1), 1–48.

Perry, D. E., & Wolf, A. L. (1992). Foundations for the study of software architecture. *ACM SIGSOFT Software Engineering Notes, 17*(4), 40–52. doi:10.1145/141874.141884

Petri Net Markup Language. (2009). *About*. Retrieved from http://www2.informatik.hu-berlin.de/top/pnml/about.html

Pnueli, A. (1985). *In transition from global to modular temporal reasoning about programs* (pp. 123–144).

Pressman, R. (2009). *Software engineering: A practitioner's approach* (7th ed.). McGraw-Hill Companies.

Roshandel, R., Hoek, A. V. D., Mikic-Rakic, M., & Medvidovic, N. (2004). Mae—a system model and environment for managing architectural evolution. *ACM Transactions on Software Engineering and Methodology, 13*(2), 240–276. doi:10.1145/1018210.1018213

Rosu, G. & Havelund, K. (2004). Rewriting-based techniques for runtime verification. *Journal of Automated Software Engineering*.

Second Workshop on Runtime Verification (2002). *Electronic Notes in Theoretical Computer Science, 70*(4).

Seventh Workshop on Runtime Verification (2007). *Lecture Notes in Computer Science, 4839*.

Shannon, B., Hapner, M., Matena, V., Davidson, J., Davidson, J., & Cable, L. (2000). *Java 2 platform, enterprise edition: Platform and component specifications*. Pearson Education.

Shaw, M., & Garlan, D. (1996). *Software architecture: Perspectives on an emerging discipline*. Prentice Hall.

Sun, W., Shi, T., Argote-Garcia, G., Deng, Y., & He, X. (2006). Achieving a better middleware design through formal modeling and analysis. In the *proceedings of SEKE'06: The 18th International Conference of Software Engineering and Knowledge Engineering*, San Francisco Bay, July 5–7.

Taylor, R. N., Medvidovic, N., Anderson, K. M., Whitehead, E. J. Jr, Robbins, J. E., & Nies, K. A. (1996). A component and message-based architectural style for GUI software. *IEEE Transactions on Software Engineering, 22*(6), 390–406. doi:10.1109/32.508313

Taylor, R. N., Medvidovic, N., & Dashofy, E. M. (2009). *Software architecture: Foundations, theory, and practice*. Wiley.

Third Workshop on Runtime Verification (2003). *Electronic Notes in Theoretical Computer Science, 89*(2).

Vestal, S. (1998). *MetaH user's manual*.

Wang, J., He, X., & Deng, Y. (1999). Introducing software architecture specification and analysis in SAM through an example. *Information and Software Technology, 41*(7), 451–467. doi:10.1016/S0950-5849(99)00009-9

Williams, S., & Kindel, C. (1994). *The component object model: Technical overview*. Dr. Dobbs Journal.

Section 3
Software Services

Chapter 6
Modeling Services Using ISE Framework:
Foundations and Extensions

Veli Bicer
FZI Forschungszentrum Informatik, Germany

Stephan Borgert
TU Darmstadt, Germany

Matthias Winkler
SAP Research CEC, Germany

Gregor Scheithauer
OPITZ Consulting München GmbH, Germany

Konrad Voigt
SAP Research CEC, Germany

Jorge Cardoso
University of Coimbra, Portugal

Erwin Aitenbichler
TU Darmstadt, Germany

ABSTRACT

The Internet of services introduces new requirements for service engineering in terms of addressing both business and technical perspectives. The inherent complexity of the new wave of services that is emerging requires new approaches for an effective and efficient service design. In this chapter a novel service engineering framework is introduced: the Integrated Service Engineering (ISE) framework. With its ISE workbench, it can address the emerging requirements of Internet of services. The chapter presents the foundations on how the service engineering process can be conducted by applying the separation of concerns to model different service dimensions within various layers of abstraction. Additionally, three novel extensions are presented to the aforementioned ISE workbench in order to enrich the capabilities of the service modeling process.

DOI: 10.4018/978-1-60960-215-4.ch006

INTRODUCTION

Several advances have been made to describe and model Web services. Examples of proposed approaches include the use of ontologies to describe services and interfaces (Kerrigan, 2005) (Paolucci & Wagner, 2006), the semantic annotation of Web services (Paolucci & Wagner, 2006) (Cardoso & Sheth, 2003), and the use of UML and UML extensions for Web service modeling (Lopez-Sanz, Acuna, Cuesta, & Marcos, 2008) (Sadovykh, Hahn, Panfilenko, Shafiq, & Limyr, 2009) (Dumez, Gaber, & Wack, 2008). All these approaches targeted the modeling of a relatively simple artifact: a Web service interface which was composed of data inputs, data outputs, and operations names. While some approaches (e.g. (Paolucci & Wagner, 2006) (Kerrigan, 2005)) went a step further and have also modeled goals, precondition, participants, control, etc., their scope and technical orientation have delimited their use outside the research community.

Web services (such as WSDL or REST services) are seen as IT entities. Nevertheless, the Internet of Services (IoS) also embrace what we call IoS-based services (Cardoso, Voigt, & Winkler, 2009) and requires combining and correlating business and operational descriptions with existing IT-based descriptions. While Web services define the pipeline between two companies and semantics Web services look into and explain what goes down the pipeline, IoS-based services provide capabilities to describe the business added-value of the pipeline itself.

When contrasted to Web services, modeling IoS-based services is a more complex undertaking since they are multi-faceted and must account for aspects such as legal regulations, community rating, service level agreements, pricing models, and payment need to be factored in to design a tradable entities (Cardoso, Voigt, & Winkler, 2008).

Due to the multifaceted nature of IoS-based services, their design is inherently complex. To cope with this density of facets, we conceptualize and implement the Integrated Service Engineering (ISE) framework (Cardoso, Voigt, & Winkler, 2009) (Kett, Voigt, Scheithauer, & Cardoso, 2009) and its software workbench (Scheithauer, Voigt, Bicer, Heinrich, Strunk, & Winkler, 2009) to enable the modeling and design of IoS-based services. By covering business, operational and technical perspectives, ISE provides a structured approach for service engineering. The structuring is achieved by following a separation of concerns (inspired in the Zachman framework (Zachman, 1987)) and a model-driven design.

In this chapter we present the ISE framework as two main parts. In the first part, we discuss the main characteristics of IoS-based services as an underlying motivation for the approach. Mainly, it is derived from the service concept that spans the definitions in various domains such as marketing, operations research, and information technology. The service concept allows to a generic service provisioning process that involves the actors interacting to achieve a common service goal. Then, we present the basics of the ISE framework in terms of different service dimensions and aspects required in an engineering process. ISE workbench is introduced as an instantiation of ISE framework with specific model editors and model transformations.

In the second part, we present three advanced extensions for ISE with novel techniques to guide service engineering. In this part, our contributions include: (1) techniques to model service processes using pattern matching, (2) modeling of service context, and (3) Service Level Agreement (SLA) management of composite services. The process pattern matching approach allows generating these service compositions semi-automatically by aligning business and IT. Furthermore, the semantic context modeling and service description approach provides a mechanism to enable complex service descriptions to be specified and interpreted based on context since services are subject to a vast amount of contextual information emerging dynamically during service procurement. Finally, service composition results generally in more complexity in terms of functionality, resource, time and location aspects, and quality. The approach to dependency and SLA management for composite services (Winkler & Schill, 2009) supports providers to manage dependencies between services in their composition to assure its proper execution. Finally, the last two sections give an overview of the related work in service engineering and conclude our contribution with prospects about the future work.

FOUNDATIONS

Internet of Services (IoS)

This section introduces ideas and concepts that are related with the Internet of Services. It is important to note that the term Internet of Services (IoS) spans ideas that are borrowed from other approaches with varying terminology. In this work, the terms (Web) Service Ecosystems and Digital Ecosystems are used synonymously to IoS.

Tertiarisation describes a structural change in developed countries concerning the sectoral composition. Countries shift from an industry economy toward a service economy. Drivers of this change include globalization, technological change, and an increasing demand for services (Peneder, Kaniovski, & Dachs, 2003). Considering this trend, it becomes clear that services and the service economy play an important role in today's and tomorrow's business. In line with this trend, Internet marketplaces for services emerge, such as Google Base, SalesForce.com, and SAP Business by Design.

The vision of IoS is an evolution of service orientation and takes services from merely integration purposes to the next level by making them available as tradable products on service delivery platforms (Barros & Dumas, 2006). They aim at trading services over the Internet between different legal bodies, compose complex services from

Figure 1. Service trade

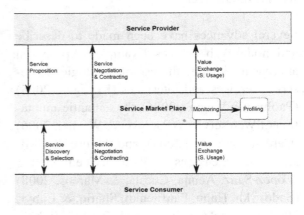

existing ones, and IT-supported service provisioning (Janiesch, Niemann, & Repp, 2009).

Figure 1 depicts the steps involved in service trade: (1) service proposition, (2) service discovery & selection, (3) service negotiation & contracting, and (4) service monitoring & profiling.

Midst service proposition, service providers advertise their services toward potential consumers, whereas during discovery and selection, service consumers specify their service preferences toward providers. In case a service consumer selects an appropriate service, providers and consumers negotiate and finally agree on service levels (SLA) which are monitored throughout value exchange. In the event service levels are not met, compensations must be triggered. During service profiling, valuable information on services' performance is stored, which is gathered while value exchange and monitoring.

The rest of this section follows this structure: the next subsection introduces a service taxonomy that distinguishes between services in a general sense as well as their electronic counterpart and implementation. While the subsequent subsections outline the Internet of Services as an evolution of service-orientation, the following subsection introduces actor roles for the IoS. Additionally, IoS requirements or impediments will be discussed. The final subsection delineates a life cycle concept for services

Service Taxonomy

Before diving into definitions for IoS, this section outlines a comprehensive service taxonomy. The concept of a service is investigated in different research communities and is subject of different domains. This leads to different interpretations of the concept of a service in these fields. More precisely, it is defined differently in business science, information science and computer science. Baida et al. (Baida, Gordijn, & Omelayenko, 2004) surveys different definitions of the service leading to a taxonomy that distinguishes business services, eServices, and technical services. They directly relate to the service concepts that are in the focus of the three research fields mentioned above.

Distinguishing between business services, eServices, and technical services is useful because it directly relates to the process of transforming requirements derived in the business domain into software artifacts in the IT domain. Moreover, it will help to understand, which business services are amendable to be implemented as technical services. The remainder of this section will survey them more closely.

Business Services. A large variety of definitions for business services exist. The concept of a business service is not only a concept from a research perspective, but economists categorize companies according to this definition. Classically, services were defined as one of the three sectors in an economy: agriculture, manufacturing, and services, where services are everything that is neither considered as agriculture nor manufacturing (Sampson & Froehle, 2006) (Teboul, 2005). Thus, services were defined as a residual of concepts. In recent years, this residual has contributed an ever larger part of the total economic value creation and employed an increasing percentage of people. Another common classification for business services is to distinguish between Business-to-Business services (e.g. financing or logistics), Consumer services (banking, insurance, or education), and Self services (washing salons).

E-Services. The definitions of a service are largely developed in the business sciences. The scope of these definitions of services includes a large variety of economic fields including public services, health care services, transportation, or travel industry. Information sciences investigate how business services in these economic fields relate to information technology and refer to this subset of services as *e-services* (Baida, Gordijn, & Omelayenko, 2004).

Technical Services. The first two types of services in the classification taxonomy specify the service concept from a high-level point of view, especially with the interpretations in business science and information technology. Technical services, on the other hand, are described as an aggregation of the functionality specified in the other types and as the *realizations* by an underlying technological platform, e.g. Web services. Therefore, they can be regarded as an extension of the interdisciplinary service concept into computer science (Baida, Gordijn, & Omelayenko, 2004). According to the W3C Web Services Architecture Group (Booth, et al., 2004), a service is defined as *"an abstract resource that represents a capability of performing tasks that form a coherent functionality from the point of view of providers entities and requesters entities. To be used, a service must be realized by a concrete provider agent."* As a specific incarnation of a service, they define a Web Service as *"a software system designed to support interoperable machine-to-machine interaction over a network. It has an interface described in a machine-processable format (specifically WSDL). Other systems interact with the Web service in a manner prescribed by its description using SOAP-messages, typically conveyed using HTTP with an XML serialization in conjunction with other Web-related standards."* These definitions of a technical service, in particular a Web Service, is consistent with other definitions (Papazoglou, Traverso, Dustdar, Leymann, & Kramer, 2008) (Kopecky, Vitvar, Bournez, & Farrell, 2007) (Preist, 2004). A service description is based on the assessment the goals the service aims to achieve. These goals include non-functional properties, key performance indicators (KPI), or legal aspects which are related to the business level of a service. But the service description also needs to provide a description of its technical interface, message formats, and semantics of operations. This functional and technical perspective is linked to the technical *realization* of the service.

Internet of Services as an Evolution of SoA toward Marketplaces

In general, IoS comprises two main concepts. Firstly, it is a network architecture that tells how actors or peers or services interact with each other. Secondly, it is a marketplace that shows how to trade services over the Internet.

(Barros & Dumas, 2006) see Web Service Ecosystems (WSE) as an evolution of Service-oriented Architecture (SoA). The authors describe SoA as a novel paradigm in order to combine legacy applications, automate business processes as well as foster technical integration between different legal bodies. Contrary to implementing business logic into hard-wired applications, software developers define technical services as fine-grained, reusable, loosely coupled functionality, which in turn can be wired according to actual business requirements. Barros and Dumas refer to WSE "... *as a logical collection of web services ...*" Recent developments show that once companies adapt to this paradigm, services are treated as valuable assets which can be exposed to other companies. Companies may offer and procure, and hence, trade these assets beyond organizational boundaries.

(Chang & West, 2006) on the other hand, who relate to the term Digital Ecosystems (DE), address the way of how actors interact with each other. The authors ascribe that this new development will shift the business to business interaction from "...*centralized, distributed or hybrid models into an open, flexible, domain cluster, demand-driven, interactive environment.*"

(Briscoe & De Wilde, 2006) see potential for optimization in the current way companies conduct their business in that they relate biological ecosystems to business ecosystems. Furthermore, the authors attribute the Internet as an enabler for this optimization.

(Janiesch, Niemann, & Repp, 2009) define IoS as service networks where a service is provided by different actors. The authors acknowledge that realization of such networks involves business services as well as technical details involving web service technology. Internet of services' main aims is foster service trade, ability to bundle services, which in turn open new markets for small and medium enterprises, so the authors say.

Actors in Service Trade

Following the discussion of different views on IoS this section outlines diverse players in service trade. Existing literature reviews in the area of service ecosystems (Barros & Dumas, 2006) (Riedl, Bohmann, Leimeister, & H, 2009) (Blau, Kramer, Conte, & van Dinther, 2009), business value webs (Tapscott, Ticoll, & Lowy, 2000) **and** IoS (Janiesch, Niemann, & Repp, 2009) find evidence for different roles for actors. All the same, actors may play more than one role in service trade. Table 1 gives an overview of different actor roles.

(Tapscott, Ticoll, & Lowy, 2000) distinguish between consumer, context provider, content provider, commerce service provider, and infrastructure provider. *Consumers* demand and consume goods and services. *Context providers*

Table 1. Overview of actors

Tapscott et al.		Barros and Dumas	
Consumer	Provider	Consumer	Provider
• Service consumer	• Context provider • Content provider • Commerce service provider • Infrastructure provider	• Service consumer	• Service provider • Mediator • Broker

provide a single face to the customer. They lead the process of value creation, in terms of orchestrating IoS in such a way that value meets consumer needs. They also provide a set of rules for each stakeholder in IoS. *Content providers* are the main value contributors. They actually design, create, and deliver goods and services to meet customer needs. *Commerce service providers* offer services with a cross sectional character. These services include financial management, security, logistics, and monitoring for example. They enable the stream of value creation in IoS. *Infrastructure providers*, finally, offer services in terms of communication platforms, computing, buildings, networks, facilities, and roads.

(Barros & Dumas, 2006) on the other hand, identify next to service consumers three different roles for actors in service ecosystems. *Service providers*, who provide services in the first place. *Service brokers* offer services from different providers. Their business model is to bring providers and consumers together, or enhance services with delivery functions for convenient service provisioning. *Service mediators*, on the other hand, generate value by customizing provider's standard services toward consumer's needs.

Requirements / Infrastructure and the Internet of Services

While the previous text outlines the IoS as a means for trading services over the internet, the following paragraphs elaborate on current impediments for realizing a successful IoS. (Barros & Dumas, 2006) for example outline the following issues: service discovery, conversational multiparty interactions, and service mediation and adaption.

Barros and Dumas pinpoint that the current *service discovery* process depends on keyword-based searches. It is assumed that service providers as well as consumers use the same keywords for describing and discovering them. According to the authors, this works well in closed environments but not for multi-actor marketplaces. Barros and

Dumas advocate a combination of a free-text and ontology-based search.

Additionally, while trading services over the Internet, interactions between actors will exceed traditional request-response patterns. In consequence, IoS must support *multiparty interactions* as well as a formalization for defining them. Barros and Dumas foster two technical specifications for this: firstly, the Business Process Execution Language (BPEL) and secondly, the Web Service Choreography Description Language (WS-CDL).

Another challenges lies in integrating purchased services into companies' internal service systems. In the scope of IoS, services may be used in contexts that were not initially considered by service providers, and hence, provide an interface that is inappropriate for others, including service mediators and brokers. This fact makes it necessary to *mediate* between services' given interface and an expected interface.

Service Lifecycle in the Internet of Services

A service runs through a number of states during its lifecycle. In general, the two states design time and run time can be distinguished. While during service engineering service ideas are transformed into operational and technical service implementations, during service execution services are consumed. This general distinction can be further refined into four phases in order to enable a fine-granulated management of these phases as well as transitions between them. Service design may be refined into *service innovation* and *service design*. Service execution on the other hand, may be refined into the stages *service usage* and *monitoring and evolution*. Figure 2 displays the four different stages.

Innovation processes in a service system may be quite different to the ones we know from dealing with (software) products because of the inherently different nature of services in comparison to products. In this section, we argue that cus-

Figure 2. IoS lifecycle

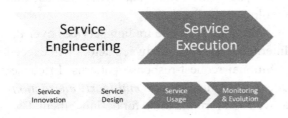

tomer input required during service provisioning is the main opportunity but also the main challenge for innovation in the services sector. An innovation usually implies the novelty of an idea linked to its (successful) realization. Today, the link between the innovation phase and its realization in the engineering phase is established in an ad-hoc way. Proprietary tools for brainstorming, idea evaluation and idea documentation are used. Successful service innovators rely on a collaboration tools and innovation processes which interlink the proprietary innovation tools using SOA technology.

Service engineering for both, service-oriented architectures and evolving service marketplaces in the Internet is still a challenge due to dynamic environments, high uncertainties, and increasing coopetition of market participants. An approach must supports service engineering in terms of planning, designing and implementing services, which are traded over the Internet, in addressing stakeholders from business & IT, acknowledgement of different service aspects, and utilization of model-driven architectures. This approach should not be limited to computing services; rather, it also should target business services, e.g., insurance & financial services, civil services, marketing services, and telecommunication services.

Service usage as the third phase relies on an expressive service description and embodies the following sub-phases: service discovery, service selection, and composition of services. The first step to realize services is to express them in terms of service descriptions in order to expose the functionalities and capabilities to the service

consumer (e.g. human or software agent). The initial attempt in this direction has been to provide a service interface - borrowing the idea from previous component-oriented approaches (Herzum & Sims, 2000). This enables the software artifacts to be abstracted in a well-defined, platform independent way and hides the implementation details to achieve a loosely-coupled architecture (Booth, et al., 2004). As a common standard, Web Service Description Language (WSDL) (Christensen, Curbera, Meredith, & Weerawarana, 2001) fulfils this need by describing service operations, input and output parameters, and endpoints. The services, expressed through service descriptions, need to be discovered by potential consumers to whom they offer a business value. Technically, this is initially addressed by the Web service registries, namely UDDI (Bellwood, et al., 2002) and ebXML (Fuger, Najmi, & Stojanovic, 2005). They enable the service providers to publish the service grounding to a central repository and annotate it within a basic classification scheme. The consumer can then select a service suitable to her needs. In fact, both Web service registries are basic implementations of a broader conceptual component that is called *discovery framework* (Studer, Grimm, & Abecker, 2007). It is a harmony of all the mechanisms and tools required to utilize discovery. Basically, a discovery framework relies on three essential elements: capability descriptions of services, request descriptions of consumers, and comparison mechanisms to match the capabilities and requests. For the instance of ebXML registry, an external WSDL document, registry information model, or filter queries can be stated as the examples of such mechanisms. The usage of Web service registries are often limited for the service discovery although there are some approaches to extend them with semantics (Dogac, Kabak, Laleci, Mattocks, Najmi, & Pollock, 2005).

While *service monitoring* IT services (such as WSDL or REST web services) are usually seen mainly as a technological problem, the monitoring of business services adds the requirement of

Figure 3. Service perspectives and aspects in the integrated service engineering (ISE) framework

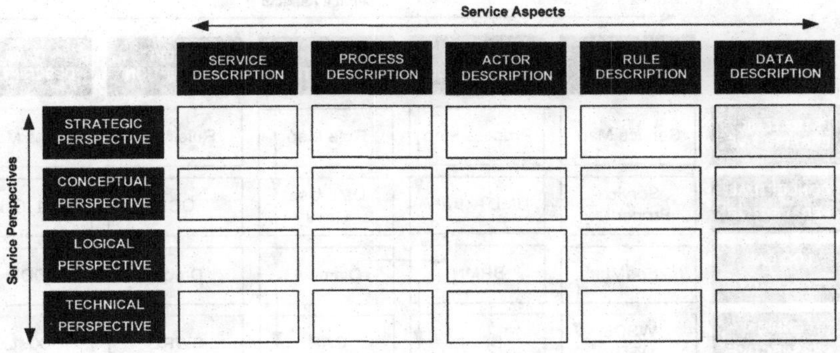

also monitoring business aspects. Monitoring IT services usually targets to measure network attributes such as latency, packet loss, throughput, link utilization, availability and connectivity, one-way delay, one-way packet loss, round trip delay, delay variation, and bulk transfer capacity. (Moser, Rosenberg, & Dustdar, 2008) recognize that web services currently lack monitoring mechanisms and they provide a solution based on the interception of SOAP messages exchanged during runtime. The emphasis is on technical aspects. On the other hand, the monitoring of business services can only achieve its full potential when it addresses the business level and accounts for organizations' strategies. Compared to IT monitoring, business monitoring is more complex since services are intangible, often inseparable, immersive, and bipolar.

ISE Framework

Based on a state-of-the-art study of existing frameworks, (Kett, Voigt, Scheithauer, & Cardoso, 2009) argued that existing frameworks for service engineering either address the business perspective or the technical perspective. To overcome the gap between these approaches, the ISE Framework is introduced as depicted in Figure 3. The framework builds on the Zachman framework (Zachman,

1987) and a service engineering methodology for service products (Bullinger H., 2003). The vertical axis shows four perspectives of the engineering process and is named *service perspectives*. Each perspective relates to a specific role with appropriate skills and offers different sets of tools and methods. It also implies the chronology of the framework for they are linked to phases of the service engineering process. The horizontal axis shows five different *descriptions of a service*. Each description is valid for each perspective. Each intersection in the matrix is placeholder for a meta model, a notation, and activities, which are appropriate for the respective perspective and the modeling aspect.

Service Perspectives

Business strategists pick up new service ideas and focus on requirement analysis in the *strategic perspective*. (Kett, Voigt, Scheithauer, & Cardoso, 2009) depicted a basic underlying model for this perspective: the Business Model Ontology (BMO). Eventually, a decision is made whether to implement a new service or not. The *conceptual perspective* focuses on operationalizing and implementation of strategic artifacts from the owner's perspective. The final artifact is a service design which is neither technical nor platform-

Figure 4. The integrated service engineering (ISE) workbench implementing the ISE framework

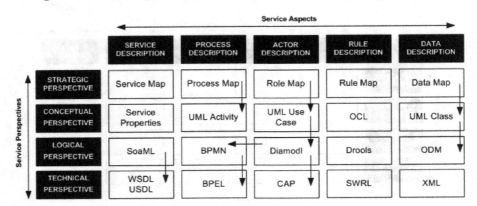

specific. Conceptual artifacts are transformed into formal models during the *logical perspective* by IT analysts. This perspective offers a bridge between service design and technical service implementation. Finally, the IT developer transforms the logical artifacts into platform-dependent software artifacts, e.g., BPEL (Alves, et al., 2007) and WSDL (Christensen, Curbera, Meredith, & Weerawarana, 2001), etc., during the *technical perspective.*

Service Aspects

The *service description* embodies services' value proposition toward potential customers. This includes functional, financial, legal, marketing, and quality of service properties as well as other meta data for service proposition, discovery, selection, contracting, and monitoring. The *process description* addresses services' behavioral aspect, which includes core capabilities and sequence flows. The *actor description* offers means to model and to refine human resources, and to assign tasks. Intangible assets, terms, and concepts as well as their relationships are defined in the *data description*. The *rule description* addresses organizational rules. These are defined to elicit and formalize domain knowledge to guide services' behavior.

ISE Workbench

The Integrated Service Engineering (ISE) Workbench implements the ISE Framework (cf. Figure 4) and supports an interdisciplinary structured service engineering process to develop services that can be traded over the Internet. The work on the workbench started in April 2008 and is a prototype, which is still under development. Developers add new features as well as improve existing ones. For example, the business rule aspect is not implemented, yet. The ISE Workbench builds on Eclipse's Rich Client Platform (RCP), which allows an integration of existing tools as well as offers a platform for novel tool development. The workbench embodies a total number of 20 editors in order to model the five service aspects for each of the four perspectives. OMG's Query View Transformation (QVT) specification is the basis for model transformation implementation, e.g. BPMN (White, 2004) to BPEL (Alves, et al., 2007).

Main Functionality & Notations

In order to support the ISE Framework with its 20 intersections, available notations were analyzed. Figure 4 depicts the resulting 20 modeling notations. This set of notations is only one possible selection. For each chosen notation, a suitable editor was integrated into the workbench to design all service aspects from different angles. The *strategic perspective* uses the mind map notation to elicit the information. The *conceptual perspective* employs mostly the UML diagrams, a semi-formal graphical notation. Whereas, the *logical perspective* makes use of formal notations, the *technical perspective* applies formal languages, such as BPEL and WSDL.

Next to existing notations, new languages were developed, where necessary. The *service property* notation is a domain-specific language and describes services from a provider's perspective in a non-technical fashion and includes information about capabilities, price & payment, delivery channels, rating, legal aspects, and provider details in order to facilitate service discovery. The *Universal Service Description Language (USDL)* (Cardoso, Winkler, & Voigt, A Service Description Language for the Internet of Services, 2009) is a XML specification that holds facts about business information, operational information, and technical information related to the service. The *Canonical Abstract Prototypes* (*CAP*) editor provides an abstract description of a user interface structure. Finally, the *service archive (SAR)* is an XML schema and denotes how to bundle technical models for deployment.

Model Transformations

The ISE Workbench offers model transformation for flexibility, speed, and accuracy in design. Since the union of all models defines a service they need to be integrated and synchronized. This integration task is facing major challenges because of the various people involved within the development process and the rising complexity of the models. To cope with these challenges we propose to integrate the models automatically by model transformations.

The ISE models contain artifacts representing a service's five dimensions: service, process,

actor, rule, and data. Furthermore, each of these models is divided into four layers (levels) of abstraction. This leads to multiple representations of information on different layers of abstraction in the corresponding dimensions. Changes in one model have to be propagated into the affected models holding the overlapping information. This is a time-consuming and challenging task since each of the models has to be aware of changes and needs to be adjusted. For a structured approach we separate the dependencies between models into two classes: vertical and horizontal.

Vertical dependencies cover the synchronization of dependencies between models on different layers of abstraction in one dimension. It represents the bridging of layers of abstraction by transforming between multiple representations of artifacts.

Horizontal dependencies define the synchronization of models on the same layer of abstraction. This describes dependencies between models of different dimensions which refer to artifacts of other dimensions. This also includes multiple representations of an artifact on the same layer of abstraction.

These dependencies form the integration of the models and have to be implemented manually or by automatic support. Being more precise, a dependency is defined by a mapping. Formally a mapping assigns to a set of artifacts a set of artifacts; where one sets corresponds to the other. That means the different representations of information are assigned to each other. To illustrate the dependencies, Figure 5 Example for vertical and horizontal model transformation. Figure 5 shows an example which depicts the dependencies between two layers of abstraction as well as between models on the same layer but of different dimensions. The process dimension shown is specified regarding the conceptual and logical layers. The conceptual layer is represented by an UML activity diagram. The Business Process Modeling Notation (BPMN) is used to represent the logical layer. The arrows depict artifacts that

Figure 5. Example for vertical and horizontal model transformation

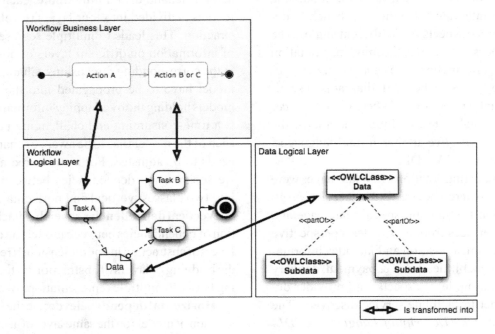

need to be synchronized and are mapped onto each other.

The Actions modeled in the activity diagram are again represented in BPMN as tasks. Therefore, *Action A* needs to be synchronized with *Task A*. That means that UML actions need to be mapped to BPMN tasks. The *XOR* between *Task B* and *Task C* of the BPMN model is mapped from *Action B or C* of the UML model. Furthermore, the *Information I* artifact used in the workflow is defined in the OWL-model (i.e., it depends on it). When one model changes (e.g. renaming or deletion), the depending models have to be updated. These updates can be done manually or by providing an automatic support. One solution to enable an automatic approach is by using model transformations for implementing mappings.

The first step to enable the implementation of model transformations is to define one common formal representation of models. This can be done using ontology formalism or more mature concepts like the Meta Object Facility (MOF). Based on this formalism, a domain specific language for model

transformation can be used to define rules and apply them to the models. During the last years many model transformation languages have been proposed, both by academia and industry. For an overview, we refer to Czarnecki and Helsens classification of today's approaches (Czarnecki & Helsen, 2006). The two most prominent proposals in the context of Model Driven Architecture (MDA) are Query, View and Transformation (QVT) and the ATLAS Transformation Language (ATL).

We have chosen to rely on MDA to support model transformations because of matured concepts, well established infrastructure for model management and transformation, and available OMG standards. A model transformation is the process of converting one model to another model of the same system. Thus a model transformation is an implementation of a mapping (model dependency specification). We follow Kleppe and Warmer (Kleppe & Warmer, 2003) refining this definition to an automatic generation of a target model from a source model, following a transfor-

Figure 6. Architecture of ISE workbench

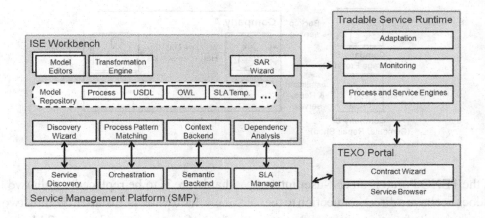

mation definition. A transformation definition is a set of rules describing formally how a source model can be transformed into a target model. Using a rule-based language like QVT to define model transformations executed by an engine allows for incremental and traceable transformations.

For automatic model integration we argue for model transformations as the implementation of mappings. Using and applying these concepts enables automatic model synchronization. This supports both the implementation of vertical and horizontal dependencies, thus reducing the complexity, effort and errors in modeling a service using ISE.

The ISE Workbench also offers deployment capabilities for seamless service execution. The service archive (SAR) is an XML schema and denotes how to bundle technical models. After service design with the ISE Workbench, the tool generates a SAR file and deploys it on a service runtime environment.

ISE Architecture

The ISE workbench is a part of larger TEXO service ecosystem architecture as depicted in Figure 6 in detail. The overall architecture mainly includes four components including the ISE workbench to

perform further operations for a seamless service provisioning. The ISE workbench component is built on an Eclipse[1] platform and has several internal building blocks: Model editors, model repository and model transformation engine enables to develop services in a model-driven way as introduced in the ISE matrix above. Specifically, we have 20 separate models each of which is associated with the corresponding editors and transformation among them.

In addition, SAR wizard interacts with the Tradable Service Runtime (TSR) which is a component to handle deployment and execution of a service in the Service Execution phase of the service lifecycle. It mainly includes Adaptation, Monitoring and Process/Service Engines required for runtime functionality. Besides, there are other blocks included in the ISE Workbench to enable the service engineer to interact with Service Management Platform (SMP) for further service related tasks. Discovery Wizard enables the service engineer to interact with Service Discovery that, in turn, searches the repository to discover available services to be composed into the service. Process Pattern Matching, Context Backend and Dependency Analysis are all special extensions to the ISE workbench which will be explained in detail in the subsequent sections.

Figure 7. Overall process of hardware maintenance service

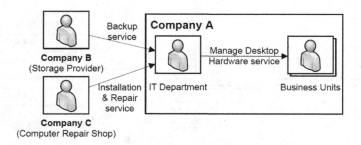

Finally, the TEXO Portal is an end-user interface which does not have a direct connection to the ISE workbench, but its functionality to negotiate service agreements, to search for available services and to test and execute them is very crucial in the architecture. It allows the end-users to use the services engineered in the ISE workbench with the help of the TSR and SMP components. Currently, the ISE workbench employs some well-known editors for service engineering, which are widely adopted by Eclipse community. These include the WSDL editor or the BPEL editor. Some other editors are also developed from scratch such as the SLA model editor or the context modeler.

MODELING EXTENSIONS

Running Example

This section introduces an example that is utilized throughout the rest of the chapter to motivate the three advanced modeling ISE extensions. Figure 1 shows three companies. Company A's IT department offers the Manage Desktop Hardware (MDH) service, that allows outsourcing the purchase and the maintenance of computer hardware. The service's target customers are company A's own business units who pays for computer hardware leasing. The benefits for business units include lower transaction costs, lower labor costs, lower IT costs, and latest hardware. The MDH service is provided with four service levels: (1) out of order

hardware is to be replaced within two hours, (2) new hardware is installed within two working days after ordering, (3) every 24 hours a backup is performed, and (4) backups can be played back within 30 minutes. The price that business units need to pay for the MDH service depends on contextual information, including business units' location, usage data, and whether business units are standard or premium customers. The IT department itself utilizes two services in order to offer desktop hardware management. Company B, a storage provider, performs a backup service and company C, a computer repair shop, conducts installations as well as repair services at business units' location.

In order to develop the MDH service, service provider (i.e. IT department) needs to deal with some challenges in terms of realizing a service composition, describing the realized service and ensuring its proper functioning. First, the service provider should be supported to identify suitable services that can be reused for realizing the MDH service. This is especially important to assign concrete services to high-level business tasks for an executable process realization. Furthermore, there is a need for a mechanism to describe the service in such a way that service context is taken into account. Specifically, some service properties (e.g. service price) cannot be determined in advance due to the dynamicity and dependency on the context. Another challenge for service provider is to manage the interplay of services for a proper functioning. Here, SLA

Figure 8. Transformation from BPMN to BPEL

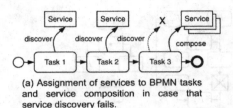 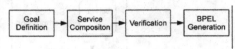

(a) Assignment of services to BPMN tasks and service composition in case that service discovery fails.

(b) Automatic service composition: steps from goal definition to executable process.

compatibility comes into play since different problems may occur due to SLA incompatibility such as violations (e.g. negotiated composite QoS (new hardware in 24 hours) cannot be met due to negotiated atomic QoS (backup data, replace hardware, and restore data).

Service Composition by Process Pattern Matching

To manage the transition from the business perspective to the technical perspective (Cardoso, Voigt, & Winkler, 2009) (Kett, Voigt, Scheithauer, & Cardoso, 2009), ISE supports the transformation of BPMN models to executable BPEL models. As shown in Figure 8(a), two different methods are supported to assign services to BPMN tasks. The first method is a direct transformation, where the designer statically assigns a set of existing atomic or composite services to a task. Alternatively, if a suitable service does not already exist, the designer can add a goal specification to the task which is represented by a fragmented process model constructed by process patterns. This specification can then be used by the automatic service composition component to automatically compose services that satisfy the given specification.

The automatic service composition component applies process pattern matching to identify suitable services. An important foundation for this action is the use of a formal description language for processes with well-defined semantics. For that reason, we have chosen the Parallel Activities Specification Scheme (PASS) (Fleischmann, 1994) as a description language. PASS graphs

allow to model processes in a subject oriented way, which is also well-suited for SOA. Subject-orientation introduces an approach that gives a balanced consideration to the actors in business processes (persons and systems as subjects), their actions (predicates), and their goals or the subject matter of their actions (objects). It is based on the fact that humans, machines and services can be modeled in the same manner. All receive and deliver information by exchanging messages. Humans, e.g., exchanges emails, office documents, or voice messages. Furthermore, the subject-oriented modeling approach enables the modeling of business processes in any arbitrary size because of the feature of composing services which is provided by the underlying model.

Reusability is one of the main motivations for the SOA paradigm and in the context of TEXO, the reusable modules are web services. In the case of a large number of services, automatic composition methods gain importance and one requirement for automatic composition approaches is the use of formal service descriptions.

The formalism of PASS is founded on top of the process algebra CCS (Milner, 1995) (Calculus of Communicating Systems) and the language constructs of PASS can be transformed down to pure CCS. Process algebras provide a suitable means for modeling distributed systems. They offer well-studied algorithms for verification and formalisms, e.g., for defining behavioral equivalences. In addition, the CCS hiding operator facilitates a hierarchization and modularization of the model, allowing to handle business processes of arbitrary size.

Figure 9. Parallel activities specification scheme (PASS) models

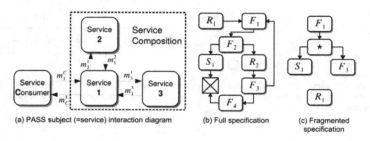

(a) PASS subject (=service) interaction diagram   (b) Full specification   (c) Fragmented specification

Figure 8(b) shows the most important steps of our service composition method. In the following, we briefly describe each of these steps.

Defining a Goal for Business Tasks

In order to add a goal specification to a BPMN task, we extended the BPMN editor by an additional property sheet to create a goal for each task, but this is only necessary if no suitable service could be found.

To specify goals, we have integrated the jPASS editor from jCOM1[2] into the ISE workbench. Figure 9 shows the basic concepts of the specification scheme. The two model levels, subject interactions and internal behavior of service, are available to specify a valid goal. Figure 9(a) depicts the subject interaction level and Figure 9(b) and Figure 9(c) depict examples for the internal behavior of services. The relationships between subjects and the types of exchanged messages are defined on the subject interaction level. The description of service behavior is explained in more detail below.

In accordance to our motivating scenario, the Service Consumer represents the Business Units, Service 1 the IT department, and Services 2 and 3 the Backup Service and the Installation & Repair Service. We assume that the IT department conducts the most maintenance and backup work by itself, but in certain cases it is dependent on both external services. How to model the internal behavior of each service is shown in the Figure 9(b) and 4(c). It is modeled using three different basic types of activities:

1. Send message.
2. Receive message.
3. Function (= F Figure 9 (b), (c))

The first two types enable services to exchange messages, and the function activity allows to call internal functions. The ⊠ symbol marks the end of the process description. To make the matching of activities work, it is vitally important that the activities in the search pattern and in the process description of a service are modeled using the same vocabulary. To ensure this, an activity catalogue is also introduced.

To describe process patterns, the PASS language was extended. Figure 9(c) shows a process pattern. In contrast to regular PASS graphs, process patterns do not have to be fully connected graphs and may contain the _ wildcard operator. This operator is a place holder for arbitrary subgraphs and is part of the fragment depicted in Figure 9(c). The process patterns are used for service matching and their modeling differs from that of fully-specified processes in the following two aspects:

1. In the model of the composite service, only activities which are essential for the process are specified. This simplifies modeling since the service engineer does not have to specify all functionalities and does not have to take care about each detail activity. E.g., he could omit modeling the payment branch in the process. If services have such branches, they would still be included, unless the engineer

explicitly models the exclusion of certain behavior.

2. The order of activities can be defined in a more general way as in traditional process models. The ~ operator can be used in conjunction with multiple isolated subgraphs to express an order between activities, instead of a single sequential order. This is useful, e.g., to enforce a certain behavior or communication pattern, while only concentrating on the essential parts of a process.

Service Composition

The first step in a composition is to find matching service candidates. To match goal specifications with service descriptions, we use the programmed graph rewriting system GRL. GRL stands for Graph Rewrite Library and is a Java library that provides the core functions of a graph rewriting system by supporting queries and rewrite operations. Rewrite rules are described in the declarative language GRL RDL (Rule Description Language). GRL operates on directed, attributed graphs, whose data structures are defined by the respective application. Nodes and edges of the graph can be attributed by arbitrary Java objects. Its basic building blocks are predicates (tests) and productions (rewrite rules). Rewrite rules are specified textually Complex attribute tests and transformations can be performed by calling Java methods from inside RDL programs. RDL programs are compiled, optimized using heuristics, and then executed on a virtual machine. Hence, GRL provides highly efficient graph matching. The rule description language RDL is nondeterministic.

The service descriptions are used as work graphs and the goal specifications are translated into query expressions in the language GRL-RDL. To match the pattern with services, it is required that each service comes with a fully-specified PASS description. Applying graph algorithms leads to candidate lists for each specified pattern or goal.

Verification

The graph-based representation is suitable for finding candidate services, but it is not directly suitable for verification, because it lacks a theoretical foundation. For this purpose, we transform a graph into a CCS description and use this formal representation for advanced validation.

We currently use the CWB-NC Workbench[3] which supports various behavioral equivalences as well as features such as model checking. The model checking rules are described with the μ-calculus, which is temporal logic. Firstly, this allows to identify services that expose equivalent behavior. At runtime, such services might be used as replacements in case the original service fails. Secondly, a choreography conformance check can be performed. In a valid composition, it must be ensured that the involved services are able to communicate with each other. For this purpose, we have developed a method for checking the communication of each pair of services. Two requirements have to be fulfilled: First, the statical interfaces of both services have to match and second, the dynamic interfaces have to match, i.e., the communication pattern has to match.

BPEL Generation

To determine all possible combinations of services, the first step was to discover all candidate services using process graph pattern matching. Next, these combinations were checked in the verification step and all incorrect combinations were discarded. Finally, for each valid combination, an executable BPEL process is generated, which orchestrates the constituent services.

In order to deploy a process on a process execution engine, several additional files are needed beside the main BPEL file describing the process. Figure 10 shows how business, technical, and deployment concerns are separated and how the different description files are interrelated.

Figure 10. Separation of concerns in BPEL processes

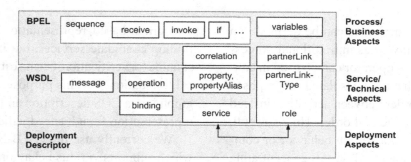

The generation of BPEL starts from the subject interaction diagram as shown in Figure 9(a). In the previous processing steps, a list of candidate services has been generated for each subject in the diagram. If existing services are used, then the corresponding WSDL files, which describe the technical interface, already exist. Alternatively, if a subject has a fully specified PASS graph, then an executable BPEL process together with a WSDL interface description can be automatically generated for the subject. This involves the following parts:

- *Process:* To generate the main flow of the process, the elements of the PASS description are processed according to the control flow and corresponding BPEL elements are generated.
- *Variables* hold the state information associated with each instance of a process. Because the generator generates code to orchestrate existing services with given WSDL files, it has to generate message mediation code translating web service requests and replies to the types of the process instance variables as well.
- *Correlations* are needed during asynchronous interactions with services. When the process invokes a service and later receives the reply, it must be able to identify the correct process instance to which the incoming message belongs. The set of key

variables used to uniquely identify a process instance is defined in correlation sets.

- *Properties and PropertyAliases* define mappings from the properties in variables to the properties in service-specific messages. They allow to describe which properties of different message types are equivalent, despite their different names.
- *PartnerLinks* describe the possible interactions between every interacting pair of services and defines their roles in the interaction.
- *PartnerLinkTypes* map from roles to port types and thereby define the message types exchanged during the interaction between partners.

Our generator supports ActiveBPEL and Apache ODE as output formats. While the BPEL and WSDL parts are standardized and (in principle) portable, the different engines require some proprietary supplemental files, which concern deployment aspects:

- *Deployment Descriptor* (for Apache ODE): The deployment descriptor defines which services a process provides and which services a process uses. This is done by linking the PartnerLinkType tags defined in the WSDL of the process to the Service tags defined in the WSDL files of the corresponding services. This simple deployment descriptor only points to the services of the first valid composition.

- *Process Deployment Descriptor* (for ActiveBPEL): Similar to above, this file defines which services a process provides and which services it uses, but in a different format. This simple deployment descriptor only points to the services of the first valid composition.
- *Catalog* (for ActiveBPEL): The catalog file lists all references to the WSDL files used by the process.
- *Endpoints File* (for Theseus/TEXO): The endpoints file lists the service candidates for all valid service compositions. When the process is deployed on a suitable process engine, this information can be used to bind or replace services at runtime.

Semantic Context Modeling and Service Descriptions

Another important extension of ISE is its support to annotate services semantically with the incorporation of context information emerging from service environment. Services need to operate in a knowledge-intensive environment that, in turn, affects the service provisioning and procurement process. The information captured from the environment is also known as context. The techniques that enable the exploitation of contextual information in services are generally known as "context handling" techniques, while the use of context to provide relevant information and/or services to the user, where relevancy depends on the users task, is known as "context-awareness". Context handling is of vital importance for developers and service architects since it provides dynamic service behaviour, content adaptation and simplicity in service usage.

Let us consider service price as an example. Due to the dependency on many context dimensions, it is hard to determine a fixed price for a service, especially at the time of service design.

This is mostly regarded as price discrimination in the business literature (Lehmann & Buxmann, 2009), where the determination of price can be based on relevant information such as user's location, service agreement, usage data, temporary discounts, surcharges, etc., which we regard as context in this work. In such a setting, different price values can show up by the emergence of dynamic context data. Therefore, it becomes a challenging issue to obtain a consistent service description – e.g. to specify what is the price of a service – with the incorporation of this context data.

Figure 11 illustrates our approach for interpreting context information within semantic service description. All collected information conforms to a service ontology which is explained in Section "Service Ontology". Semantic IoS-based service description includes static service information (e.g. service name, provider, parameters, etc.) as well as viewpoints that are defined at design time to incorporate different perceptions of service based on possible contexts. At runtime, emerging context information is interpreted by these viewpoints to incorporate specific views during runtime procedures – e.g. service discovery, agreement, or execution.

Service Ontology

In order to capture both service descriptions and context information semantically, we rely on the service ontology which was previously introduced in detail in (Oberle, Bhatti, Brockmans, Niemann, & Janiesch, 2009). It provides a consistent and holistic way of capturing information by defining different aspects of a service and service related concepts as well as any relevant information that emerges as context.

Figure 12 presents an excerpt of service ontology for the purposes of this chapter (see (Oberle, Bhatti, Brockmans, Niemann, & Janiesch, 2009) for a detailed description). The concepts in the upper part are based on the DOLCE founda-

Figure 11. Overview of viewpoints and interpretation of context information

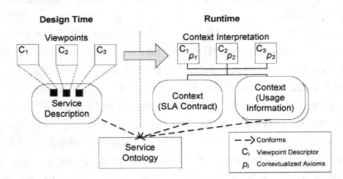

tional ontology (Oltramari, Gangemi, Guarino, & Masolo, 2002) providing us with a generic set of concepts and relations as well as ontology design patterns. Based on this upper part, several concepts are introduced to prescribe service information common to every service (e.g., service description, provider or parameters such as quality of service). This allows to capture service descriptions as a set of axioms within a knowledge-base (KB). For example, the MDH service in our scenario has the following ontological (assertion) axioms based on the concepts and relations in the service ontology:

ServiceDescription(#MDH),
hasParam(#MDH;#MDH$_{Price}$),
provides(#CompA;#MDH)

Similarly, context information is captured as axioms based on the ontology. Although, from an

ontological point of view, there is no distinction between the axioms describing services and context, in the course of service offering, context information dynamically emerges from various sources and is incorporated into KB as depicted in Figure 11. For example, information about service consumers' profile, or service contracts of a consumer for particular services can all be obtained from, e.g., Service Management Platform (see Figure 6) and be represented as axioms similar to the following:

ServiceConsumer(#BusU$_A$),
hasAddress(#BusU$_A$;#Germany)
hasSLA(#BusU$_A$;#SLA$_1$),
serviceType(#SLA$_1$;#Premium)

The central notion about using a service ontology to maintain all this information is to address

Figure 12. An excerpt of service ontology

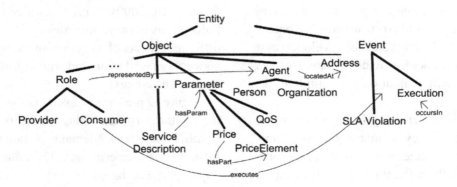

the information integration challenge that emerges from the existence of several components in the design and offering of IoS-services. However, dynamic context information in the KB may result in different interpretations of a service description that requires the introduction of viewpoints as elaborated in the followings.

Viewpoints and Rules

According to the context information collected in the KB based on the service ontology, we can determine the subparts of service description, e.g. service price, tax rates, discounts etc., by using ontology-based rules. However, since all these information is managed in one KB for our service management platform, we need to create different viewpoints for different users in order to provide individualized values based on context. For example, to associate the German tax value for the business units in Germany, the following rule was defined for the MDH service:

$C1: \text{ServiceConsumer}(?c) \wedge \text{hasAddress}(?c, \#\text{Germany}) \wedge \text{consume}(?c, \#\text{MDH})$

$\wedge \text{ hasParam}(\#\text{MDH}, ?p) \wedge \text{Price}(?p) \rightarrow \text{hasPart}(?p, \#\text{GermanTax})$

Similar rules can also be specified to associate further contextual information with the service descriptions such as offering discounts for SLA violations or different price values for standard and premium contracts. What is crucial in our approach is that every rule is associated with a viewpoint identifier (e.g. C1) that parameterizes the result of a rule into different viewpoints. Context modeler utilizes a reasoning mechanism defined in (Baader, Knechtel, & Penaloza, 2009) at the backend to generate different, e.g., pricing schemes for the same service.

SLA Management of Composite Services

ISE supports composite service providers when creating service compositions using existing services from the TEXO service marketplace. This is achieved by the functionality provided by the process modeling tools as shown in Figure 6. Atomic services are composed to collaboratively achieve tasks of higher complexity. The execution of atomic and composite services is regulated by service level agreement (SLA). SLAs regulate the tasks of the service, required and provided resources (i.e. what the service requires to execute and what it provides as result), different quality of service (QoS) and legal aspects, and start and end times of a service.

We developed an approach to support composite service providers to manage interdependencies between services in service compositions which they are offering. The approach is based on the assumption that information regarding dependencies between services is implicitly contained in the composite service process description and the SLAs negotiated between the composite service provider, atomic service providers, and the service consumer. We will now outline the approach and its integration into the ISE Workbench and illustrate its use based on the MDH scenario.

Dependency Management Approach

In order to manage the dependencies in service compositions, we developed an approach which captures dependencies between services in a dependency model. The model contains information about the different services involved in a service composition, the SLAs negotiated for the atomic services, the service composition, and a detailed description of the different dependencies between the dependant that depends on one or more antecedents (Winkler & Schill, 2009). This model is created at design time by a semi-automatic approach. At runtime it is used to

Table 2. Service dependencies of the MDH scenario

Antecedent	Dependency	Dependant
Backup Data	finish-to-start	Replace Hardware
Replace Hardware	finish-to-start	Restore Data

support the composite service provider to handle the dependencies.

The lifecycle associated with dependency model consists of four phases. During the creation and re computation phase the dependency model is created based on the composite service process description and SLA information. The created dependency model can be extended manually with dependency information, which cannot be detected automatically. The model needs to be recalculated if conflicts are detected with respect to the dependencies, SLAs change, or the process description is adapted. In the MDH scenario different time dependencies are discovered (see Table 2). The Backup Data service needs to finish before Replace Hardware can start. Replace Hardware needs to finish before Restore Data can start.

The validation phase is necessary to ensure that the created dependency model is valid. It is also necessary to validate the negotiated SLAs, which can be supported by the dependency model. In the case that problems are detected the model needs to be re-computed. In our scenario it is necessary to schedule the different services according to the dependency model, i.e. the backup of data is scheduled before the replacement of hardware and the restoring of data afterwards. During the usage phase, the dependency model supports runtime dependency evaluation tasks such as the determination of SLO (Service Level Objective) violation effects or handling SLA renegotiation requests. In the case of renegotiation, the model may need to be adapted accordingly. In our scenario company C needs to renegotiate the scheduled data for hardware re-

Figure 13. Architecture for SLA dependency management

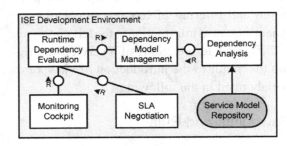

placement due to availability problems of the hardware. The request is evaluated based on the dependency model and a conflict is detected with the scheduled time for the service for restoring data. Thus, a new slot needs to be arranged for restoring the data. During the retirement phase, the dependency model is discarded when is not used or referenced.

Architecture and Integration with ISE

The functionality for the handling of dependencies is provided by three main components, which are integrated into the ISE workbench (see Figure 13). They implement the lifecycle presented above. The Dependency Analysis component is used for the semi-automatic dependency analysis at design time and the recomputation of the dependency model at runtime, i.e. the first phase of the lifecycle. For the creation of the dependency model, the BPMN process description and the SLA information for the different services are analysed. Both are requested from the Service Model Repository. Temporal relationships between services are detected based on the process description. Resource and location dependencies are discovered based on the negotiated SLAs. QoS and price dependencies are calculated based on SLA information as well as the composite service process structure. While various dependencies can be discovered automatically, there is a need for extending the generated dependency model with information which cannot be discovered. This is achieved by a dependency model editor, which is part of the Dependency Analysis component. Upon changes to the SLAs related to the composite service and the business process itself, the dependency model needs to be re-computed using the semi-automatic approach presented.

The Dependency Model Management component manages different instances of dependency models and is responsible for model creation, storage, retrieval, and removal. It is integrated with the Dependency Analysis and Runtime Dependency Evaluation components to support their work at design time and runtime. Furthermore, the validation of dependency models and the associated SLAs is realized by the Dependency Model Management component. It assures that only validated dependency models are used for runtime evaluation. It also detects conflicts between different SLAs (e.g. start/end time) based on the dependency model. Thus, while supporting the Dependency Creation & Recomputation and Usage phases, it realizes the Validation and Retirement lifecycle phases.

The Runtime Dependency Evaluation component implements the Usage phase. It uses the dependency model at runtime to evaluate the dependencies that take effect e.g. when a SLA shall be renegotiated. The evaluation of dependencies is triggered by the SLA Negotiation component upon SLA renegotiation requests. The dependency evaluation can also be initiated by the Monitoring Cockpit upon receiving information about SLO violations.

RELATED WORK

WSMF, WSML, WSMT, and WSMO provide frameworks, tools and an integrated modeling environments (see (Kerrigan, 2005) and (Paolucci & Wagner, 2006)) to describe semantic Web services. Compared to ISE, these approaches concentrate their attention on the use of ontologies to enhance the expressiveness of descriptions of technical Web services and their interfaces (i.e. WSDL). While ISE also relies on ontologies, their use is not limited to the interfaces of services and can be also used to increase the expressiveness of the organizational and IS models that can be found, for example, in the business rule and human resource aspects.

SoaML (Sadovykh, Hahn, Panfilenko, Shafiq, & Limyr, 2009), MIDAS (Lopez-Sanz, Acuna, Cuesta, & Marcos, 2008), and UML-S (Dumez, Gaber, & Wack, 2008) also follow an MDA approach for service modeling but target the development of SOA-based solutions and Web information systems. In contrast to ISE, these approaches rely uniquely on UML models and UML extensions for service modeling. The inexistence of organizational and IS perspectives, and the purely UML-based approach difficult the participation of business stakeholders (e.g. CEO, CTO, CIO) when defining IoS- based services. Furthermore, advanced modelling mechanisms, such as business process design based on patterns and context-based modeling were not yet explored. One interesting aspect of UML-S is the provision of transformation rules between UML-S and adapted Petri nets to solve to verify and validate the models created. ISE relies on the use of CCS (Milner, 1995) since it has proven to provide a suitable means for modeling business processes.

Commercial applications that target the use of multiple models to design services or SOA-based architectures are currently available from several companies. For example, Select Architect[4], Business Architect[5], and Enterprise Architect[6] typically rely on business motivation modeling, business process modeling, component-based models, and corporate data models to design IS/IT. While they rely on MDA approaches for code generation, they lack precise mapping and synchronization techniques between models. Furthermore, since these tools mainly target the design of IS/IT solutions, and do not directly target business services, important aspects of services such as pricing models and marketing channels models are not available.

CONCLUSION

In this chapter, we presented ISE framework and its three advanced extensions to meet the requirements emerging from the inherent complexity of IoS-based services. ISE framework utilizes separation of concerns and model-driven techniques to overcome the inherent complexity in a service engineering process. The process pattern matching approach provides a semi automatic means to identify suitable services for the assignment to particular business tasks while constructing executable service compositions. Furthermore, semantic context modeling and service description extension enables an ontology-based approach to specify the service context and descriptions and to define dynamic service properties by incorporating the changes in context. Finally, the SLA management approach supports service providers to manage dependencies between the services in their composition to assure a proper execution. Future work includes further case studies to improve the modeling experience and to gather requirements from different business service domains.

REFERENCES

Alves, A., Arkin, A., Askary, S., Barreto, C., Bloch, B., Curbera, F., et al. (2007). *Web services business process execution language, version 2.0 (OASIS Standard)*. WS-BPEL TC OASIS. Retrieved from http://docs.oasis-open.org/wsbpel/2.0/wsbpel-v2.0.html

Baader, F., Knechtel, M., & Penaloza, R. (2009). *A generic approach for large-scale ontological reasoning in the presence of access restrictions to the ontology axioms* (p. 49).

Baida, Z., Gordijn, J. & Omelayenko, B. (2004). A shared service terminology for online service provisioning.

Barros, A., & Dumas, M. (2006). The rise of Web service ecosystems. *IT Professional*, 31–37. doi:10.1109/MITP.2006.123

Bellwood, T., Clement, L., Ehnebuske, D., Hately, A., Hondo, M., & Husband, Y. L. (2002). *UDDI Version 3.0. Published specification*. Oasis.

Blau, B., Kramer, J., Conte, T., & van Dinther, C. (2009). Service value networks. *Proceedings of the 11th IEEE Conference on Commerce and Enterprise Computing*.

Booth, D., Haas, H., McCabe, F., Newcomer, E., Champion, M., Ferris, C., et al. (2004). Web Services Architecture. *W3C Working Group Note, 11*(1).

Briscoe, G., & De Wilde, P. (2006). Digital ecosystems: Evolving service-orientated architectures. In *Bio-inspired models of network, information and computing systems,* (pp. 1-6).

Bullinger, H. (2003). Service engineering–methodical development of new service products. *International Journal of Production Economics*, 275–287. doi:10.1016/S0925-5273(03)00116-6

Cardoso, J., & Sheth, A. (2003). Semantic e-workflow composition. *Journal of Intelligent Information Systems, 21*, 191–225. doi:10.1023/A:1025542915514

Cardoso, J., Voigt, K., & Winkler, M. (2008). *Service engineering for the Internet of Services* (pp. 17–25). Springer.

Cardoso, J., Voigt, K., & Winkler, M. (2009). *Service engineering for the Internet of Services* (pp. 15–27). Berlin, Heidelberg: Springer.

Cardoso, J., Winkler, M., & Voigt, K. (2009). A service description language for the Internet of Services. *Proceedings First International Symposium on Services Science (ISSS'2009)*. Berlin: Logos Verlag.

Chang, E., & West, M. (2006). Digital ecosystems a next generation of the collaborative environment. *Proceedings from the Eight International Conference on Information Integration and Web-Based Applications & Services*, (pp. 3-24).

Christensen, E., Curbera, F., Meredith, G. & Weerawarana, S. (2001). *Web Services Description Language (WSDL) 1.1.*

Czarnecki, K., & Helsen, S. (2006). Feature-based survey of model transformation approaches. *IBM Systems Journal, 45*(3). doi:10.1147/sj.453.0621

Dogac, A., Kabak, Y., Laleci, G. B., Mattocks, C., Najmi, F., & Pollock, J. (2005). Enhancing ebXML registries to make them OWL aware. *Distributed and Parallel Databases, 18*, 9–36. doi:10.1007/s10619-005-1072-x

Dumez, C., Gaber, J., & Wack, M. (2008). *Model-driven engineering of composite web services using UML-S* (pp. 395–398). ACM.

Fleischmann, A. (1994). *Distributed systems: Software design and implementation.* Springer.

Fuger, S., Najmi, F. & Stojanovic, N. (2005). *ebXML registry information model, version 3.0.*

Herzum, P., & Sims, O. (2000). *Business component factory.* New York: John Wiley.

Janiesch, C., Niemann, M., & Repp, N. (2009). Towards a service governance framework for the Internet of Services. *Proceedings of the 17th European Conference on Information Systems.* Verona, Italy.

Kerrigan, M. (2005). *Web Service Modeling Toolkit (WSMT).* Techreport.

Kett, H., Voigt, K., Scheithauer, G. & Cardoso, J. (2009). *Service engineering for business service ecosystems.*

Kleppe, A., & Warmer, J. (2003). *MDA rxplained. The model driven architecture: Practice and promise.* Addison-Wesley.

Kopecky, J., Vitvar, T., Bournez, C., & Farrell, J. (2007). SAWSDL: Semantic annotations for WSDL and XML schema. *IEEE Internet Computing, 11*, 60–67. doi:10.1109/MIC.2007.134

Lehmann, S., & Buxmann, P. (2009). Pricing strategies of software vendors. *Journal of Business and Information Systems Engineering, 6*, 1–10.

Lopez-Sanz, M., Acuna, C. J., Cuesta, C. E., & Marcos, E. (2008). *Defining service-oriented software architecture models for a MDA-based development process at the PIM level* (pp. 309–312). IEEE Computer Society.

Milner, R. (1995). *Communication and concurrency.* Prentice Hall PTR.

Moser, O., Rosenberg, F., & Dustdar, S. (2008). Non-intrusive monitoring and service adaptation for WS-BPEL. *Proceedings of the World Wide Web Conference,* (pp. 815-824). New York: ACM.

Oberle, D., Bhatti, N., Brockmans, S., Niemann, M., & Janiesch, C. (2009). Countering service information challenges in the Internet of Services. *Business and Information Systems Engineering, 1*, 370–390. doi:10.1007/s12599-009-0069-9

Oltramari, A., Gangemi, A., Guarino, N., & Masolo, C. (2002). *Sweetening ontologies with DOLCE.* Springer.

Paolucci, M., & Wagner, M. (2006). *Grounding OWL-S in WSDL-S* (pp. 913–914). IEEE Computer Society.

Papazoglou, M. P., Traverso, P., Dustdar, S., Leymann, F., & Kramer, B. J. (2008). Service-oriented computing: A research roadmap. *International Journal of Cooperative Information Systems, 17*, 223–255. doi:10.1142/S0218843008001816

Peneder, M., Kaniovski, S., & Dachs, B. (2003). What follows tertiarisation? Structural change and the role of knowledge-based services. *The Service Industries Journal, 23*, 47–66. doi:10.10 80/02642060412331300882

Preist, C. (2004). *A conceptual architecture for semantic Web services* (pp. 395–409). Springer.

Riedl, C., Bohmann, T., Leimeister, J. M., & Krcmar, H. (2009). A framework for analysing service ecosystem capabilities to innovate. *Proceedings of 17th European Conference on Information Systems.*

Sadovykh, A., Hahn, C., Panfilenko, D., Shafiq, O., & Limyr, A. (2009). *SOA and SHA tools developed in SHAPE project* (p. 113). University of Twente.

Sampson, S. & Froehle, C. (2006). Foundations and implications of a proposed unified services theory. *Production and Operations Management.*

Scheithauer, G., Voigt, K., Bicer, V., Heinrich, M., Strunk, A. & Winkler, M. (2009). *Integrated service engineering workbench: Service engineering for digital ecosystems.*

Studer, R., Grimm, S., & Abecker, A. (2007). *Semantic Web services: Concepts, technologies, and applications. New York.* Secaucus, NJ: Springer-Verlag Inc.

Tapscott, D., Ticoll, D., & Lowy, A. (2000). *Digital capital: Harnessing the power of business Webs.* Harvard Business School Press.

Teboul, J. (2005). *Service is in front stage.*

White, S.A. (2004). Introduction to BPMN. *IBM Cooperation*, 2008-029.

Winkler, M., & Schill, A. (2009). *Towards dependency management in service compositions* (pp. 79–84).

Zachman, J. A. (1987). A framework for information systems architecture. *IBM Systems Journal, 26*, 276–292. doi:10.1147/sj.263.0276

ENDNOTES

[1] http://www.eclipse.org/

[2] http://www.jcom1.com

[3] http://www.cs.sunysb.edu/_cwb/

[4] http://www.selectbs.com/adt/analysis-and-design/select-architect

[5] http://www.ids-scheer.com/en/Software/ARISSoftware/ARISBusinessArchitect/3731.html

[6] http://www.sparxsystems.com.au/

Chapter 7
Visual Semantic Analysis to Support Semi-Automatic Modeling of Semantic Service Descriptions

Nadeem Bhatti
Fraunhofer IGD, Germany

Dieter W. Fellner
TU Darmstadt, Graphisch-Interaktive Systeme & Fraunhofer IGD, Germany

ABSTRACT

The service-oriented architecture has become one of the most popular approaches for distributed business applications. A new trend service ecosystem is merging, where service providers can augment their core services by using business service delivery-related available functionalities like distribution and delivery. The semantic service description of services for the business service delivery will become a bottleneck in the service ecosystem. In this chapter, the Visual Semantic Analysis approach is presented to support semi-automatic modeling of semantic service description by combining machine learning and interactive visualization techniques. Furthermore, two application scenarios from the project THESEUS-TEXO (funded by German federal ministry of economics and technology) are presented as evaluation of the Visual Semantic Analysis approach.

INTRODUCTION

As the web service infrastructures matures and standards facilitating web service-enabled applications, the Service-oriented Architecture (SOA) is becoming one of the most popular approach

DOI: 10.4018/978-1-60960-215-4.ch007

for the design of IT landscape. A new trend in service-orientation is merging, which allow web service providers to interconnect their offerings in unforeseen ways (Barros, A. & Dumas, M (2006)). This phenomenon is captured as service ecosystem.

A Web Service Ecosystem is a logical collection of Web services whose exposure and access are subject to constraints characteristic of business service delivery (Barros, A. & Dumas, M ((2006)).

In the service ecosystem, service providers could augment their core services by using available service ecosystem functionalities like distribution and delivery. For example, the service provider can use payment facility provided by service ecosystem to extend the functionality of their core services. As service ecosystem grows, service provider can outsource the "front desk" role to service broker in order to increase service procurement through different markets. A service broker is responsible for delivering services according to provider's constraints, such as authentication, payment, timelines and enforcement of penalties. Service brokers bring service providers and service consumers closer. They can integrate a service with certain delivery functionality like authentication and payment or combine services offered by one or more service providers to create new value added services. They can provide these integrated services or value added service to service consumers to meet their demand (Barros, A. & Dumas, M (2006); Barros, A. & Dumas, M (2005)). Routing between service broker and single/multiple service providers is another issue. Service brokers should focus on their own competency and outsource routing to service mediator. Service mediators offer translation between different service formats and other routine functions.

Basole and Rouse introduce value networks, i.e., complex networks of social and technological resources that create economic value, also on the web (Basole, R.C. & Rouse, W.B. (2008); Speiser, S, Blau, B., Lamparter, S. & Tai, S. (2008); Vervest, P.H.M (2005)). Such occurrences of value networks are often called Future Business Value Networks or Business Webs (Kagermann, H. & Österle, H.(2006)). The platform for the realization of business webs is called Internet of Services (IoS) (Heuser, L., Alsdorf, C. & Woods, D.(2008)). The IoS allows offering services and selling services. As a result services become tradable goods.

The Internet of Services can be considered as infrastructure for Web service ecosystem, where services are deployed, published, discovered and delivered via different business channels (Cardoso, J., Winkler, M. & Voigt, K.(2009); Barros, A. & Dumas, M (2006); Rai, A, Sambamurthy, V. (2006); Oberle, D., Bhatti, N., Brockmans, S., Niemann, M. & Janiesch, C. (2009); Jensen, J. B., Kletzer, L. G.(2005); Papazoglou, M.P. (2003); Rust, R. T., Kannan, P. K. (2003)).

Barros and Dumas (Barros, A. & Dumas, M (2006)) identified three major challenges for service ecosystem flexible service discovery, conversational multiparty interactions and, service mediation and adaptation. To offer flexible service discovery, service providers must describe non functional service properties e.g. guarantees, pricing, payment, penalties and delivery modes. The service description with rich semantic will help service consumer to find services easily. Conversational multiparty interaction has to be supported in emerging service ecosystems. Single request-response transactions give way to multiparty, pull-oriented and stream based interaction e.g. auctions, voting and RSS feeds. For the Service mediation and adaption, the aspects not only from structural perspective like schema-mapping and transformation language, but also from behavioral and policy perspective have to be address. According to Barros and Dumas (Barros, A. & Dumas, M (2006)), the explicit and formalized Semantic Service Description, which includes of non-functional aspects of such as guarantees, pricing, payment, penalties, and delivery modes, will become a bottleneck for service ecosystems.

In this book chapter, the Visual Semantic Analysis (VSA) approach is introduced to support semi-automatic modeling of SSD. First, the fundamentals and related work related to services and semantic analysis are introduced. Afterwards, a generic process model and a conceptual framework for VSA are presented. Finally, two application scenarios from the project THESEUS-TEXO[1] (funded by German federal ministry of economics and technology) are presented as evaluation of the VSA approach.

SERVICES AND SEMANTIC ANALYSIS

This section gives a detailed overview of fundamentals related to services, semantic analysis and visualization techniques for the semantic analysis.

Services

The terms "Service" and "Web service" are often used synonymously in computer science. The differences between these terms are often discussed and still there are different definitions of both terms in the research community. The definitions of "Service" and "Web service" according to (Preist, C. (2004)) are:

- **Service:** A service is defined as the provision of a concrete product or abstract value in some domain.
- **Web service:** Web services are defined as computational entities accessible over the Internet (using Web service standards and protocols) via platform- and programming-language-independent interfaces.

An example describes the both terms "Service" and "Web services". Let us consider a person want to book a flight from Frankfurt to Madrid. The provision of service and contractual issues related to it is independent of how the supplier and the provider interact. It is not relevant, if the person goes to airline ticket office or uses airline website to book the ticket. In this example, provision of value is considered as service. An airline can offer a software component accessible via Web service standards to request a service i.e. Web service to request the booking of a flight. Thus, Web service means to consume an actual service or place a contract for actual service. Both services and

Web services will be considered in this research work from different perspectives e.g. technical and business perspective.

Semantic Service Description

The service discovery, selection and negotiation as it is described in the service matchmaking phase of the service lifecycle require description of functional and nonfunctional parameters e.g. price, general terms and availability. The functional description is not sufficient for the service discovery and selection in today´s applications. Particularly price and Quality of Service parameters (QoS) e.g. availability are most important. Typically, users will not decide for a service - even if it fulfils their functional requirements - if it cannot meet their requirements about price or QoS parameters. They may compromise on their functional requirement rather than on nonfunctional requirements (Hamdy, M., Koenig-Ries, B.& Kuester, U. (2007)).

A separate consideration of functional and nonfunctional requirements is not the best way to approach problem service discovery, selection and negotiation. The distinction between functional and nonfunctional attributes of a service is artificial and often arbitrary. Should price regarded as functional or nonfunctional parameter? Consider two offers, both offer maps download for German cities. Offer A offers maps download in resolution of 1:10,000 over a slow network connection far a price of 0,50 Euro per map. Offer B offers maps download in resolution of 1: 15,000 over a fast connection for a price of 0,60 Euro per map. The decision for functional and nonfunctional parameters is not clear. The name of the city is undoubtedly functional parameter. The both other parameters resolution and price can be considered either functional or nonfunctional parameters. This example shows also that just functional parameters are not sufficient for service consumers to decide for a service. The functional and nonfunctional parameters are important to offer flexible service discovery to service consumers (Hamdy, M., Koenig-Ries, B.& Kuester, U. (2007); Berbner, R. (2007)).

According to (Hamdy, M., Koenig-Ries, B.& Kuester, U. (2007)), there are three different categories of functional and nonfunctional attributes.

- Static attributes
- Dynamic attributes within the influence of service provider
- Dynamic attributes beyond the influence of service provider

The value of static attributes does not change over time and static attributes can be static part of the service description. Static attributes can be functional e.g. types of notebooks sold by an online trader or nonfunctional e.g. price per picture offered by a photo printing service, the resolution offered by a printer and the delivery time offered by a shipment company.

The value of dynamic attributes change over time. The dynamic attributes are either within the influence or beyond the influence of service provider. The dynamic attributes within influence of serviced provider allow offering configurable services. The price attribute for airline reservation services is an example for dynamic attributes within the influence of service provider. The price of airline reservation may change over time depending on holiday's season or current booking status of flights. These attributes can again be functional or nonfunctional.

Dynamic attributes beyond the influence of service provider are most challenging. The value of these dynamic attributes change over time. Examples for such attributes are available bandwidth, response time or reputation of the service provider. The attributes of this category are typically characterized as QoS parameters. They can be defined by service provider as estimated values, but the real values of these parameters can be provided by monitoring service of service provider. Typically, functional attributes do not belong to this category.

Semantic Analysis

The manual semantic description of information artifacts e.g. services is still tedious and cumbersome task, which can result in a knowledge acquisition bottleneck. The usage of semantic description for information artifacts requires quickly and easily completion of semantic description. The semantic analysis, which is also cited in literature as ontology learning, aims at facilitating the construction of semantic descriptions by using machine learning techniques. The vision of the semantic analysis is to support semi-automatic semantic analysis process by using unstructured, semi-structured and structured data, because the fully automated semantic building process remains in the distant future (Maedche, A. (2002)).

The paradigm *balanced cooperative modeling* relies on a coordinated interaction between human modeler and learning algorithms for the semantic analysis (Maedche, A. (2002)). According to this approach, semantic analysis support cooperation between knowledge experts and machine learning algorithms. It deals also with learning techniques and algorithms that can be applied for an efficient support of semantic description by using data from available knowledge sources e.g. Web. Furthermore, it addresses refinement of semi-automatic generated semantic description of information artifacts. There are different semantic analysis process models, which will be discussed later briefly.

Semantic Extraction Algorithms

The main semantic extraction algorithms are classified in four different categories statistics based, rule-based, hybrid (statistics and rule based) and Formal Concept Analysis (FCA) (Sabou, M. & Pan, J. (2007); Zhou, L. (2007); Cimiano, P.,

Table 1. The main semantic extraction algorithms

Category	Algorithms
Statistics-based	Mutual information, MLE
	Clustering
	MDL, Simulated annealing
	Naive Bayes, concept mapping
	Correlation analysis
Rule-based	Heuritic pattern
	Dependency analysis
	Syntactic and semantic/verb frame
	Information extraction, heuristics, dictionary
	ArkRank, dictionary
	A-Box Mining, concept induction
	Information extraction, WordNet, semantically tagged corpus
Hybrid (statistics-based and rule-based)	Heuristic patterns, clustering
	Syntax regularity/phrase chunker, clustering
	Parsing, association rule analysis
	Lexico-syntactic pattern, GermaNet, clustering
	Lexico-syntactic pattern, mutual information
	Lexical knowledge, decision tree
	Syntactic/dependency analysis, cosine
Formal	Formal Concept Analysis

Hotho, A. & Staab, S. (2005); Maedche, A. (2002)) as depicted in Table 1.

Semantic extraction techniques are mostly unsupervised learning because the training data with background knowledge is not available. Therefore, statistical techniques are often used for the semantic extraction. A statistical model represents probabilistic dependencies between random variables. The concepts and relations are extracted by using statistical information, which are calculated by observing frequencies and distribution of the terms in corpus. The rule-based techniques are pattern-based approaches and use heuristic methods using regular expressions. The pattern based approaches for extraction of semantic structures is introduced by Maedche (Maedche, A. (2002)). The hybrid approaches combine the strength of the both techniques statistics-based

and rule-based techniques. Formal Concept Analysis (FCA) is an unsupervised learning technique for the semantic extraction. The semantic extraction techniques, which are supported in this research work, are described in the following sections.

Lexical Entry and Concept Extraction

The lexical entry and concept extraction is baseline method to acquire lexical entries and corresponding concepts. Web documents have to be morphologically process by using text pre-processing techniques which are described below. The semantic analysis process may be applied without pre-processing, but additional linguistic pre-processing is used to enhance semantic analysis process. The POS-Tagging determines the part of speech tag for each term e.g. noun, verb and adjective. Based on the observation that the concepts in domain ontologies are usually nouns in the extracted information (Cimiano, P., Hotho, A. & Staab, S. (2005); Hotho, A., Nürnberger, A. & Paass, G.(2005)).

The stop words like articles and other terms that do not constitute the idea and concepts of documents can be eliminated. For example the words such as "a", "an" and "the" can be eliminated from the extracted information. The preposition and conjunction should not eliminated, because they allow the usage of phrases within semantic analysis process (Maedche, A. (2002); Pan, T.& Fang, K.(2009)). The extracted information may conclude different writing styles or variations of the words to define one concept. The usage of plurality, verbal nouns and tenses can alter from the basic form of a word. In the task stemming, the different forms of the words are replaced by their root word. For example, the words "Fish", "Fishes" "Fishing" and "Fished" are replaced by "Fish" (Maedche, A. (2002); Pan, T.& Fang, K.(2009)).

The lexical analysis converts the extracted information into "n-gram", i.e. arbitrary strings of n consecutive terms. This can be done by moving a window of n terms through extracted information. The n-gram models with n= 1 to 6 can be used to enhance the semantic analysis process. The lexical analysis allows not only the terms, but also phrases for the semantic analysis. (Pan, T.& Fang, K.(2009); Greengrass, E. (2000)).

After the lexical analysis, the extracted terms and documents related to terms can be inserted in document term matrix that contains documents, terms and term frequency inverted document frequency (*tf idf*). The *tfidf* weighs the lexical entry in documents and used to evaluate how important word is to a document in a collection or corpus. The *tfidf* defined is given by (Maedche, A. (2002)):

$$tfidf_{l,d} = lef_{l,d} + \log\left(\frac{|D|}{df_l}\right)$$

where $lef_{l,d}$ is the lexical entry frequency of the lexical entry l in a document d, d_{fl} is the overall document frequency of lexical entry l and D is the set of documents in the corpus.

Dictionary Parsing

The existing domain knowledge (Fellbaum, C. (1998)) can be exploited for the extraction of domain conceptualization. For example, WordNet is a network of semantic relations among English words. It allows extraction of synonyms by using the basic synset relation of WordNet. In addition to synonyms, the different semantic relations e.g. hyponymy, meronymy and troponomy help to extract real concepts of a word. These semantic relations allow mapping of words to more general concepts or merging synonyms (Wermter, S., Hung, C. (2002)). For Example, two terms "car" and another one "truck" can be mapped to "vehicles" by using WordNet.

The pattern matching heuristic can be applied to extract lexical entries from morphological processing of text to identify semantic relations. For example, the dictionary from insurance company contains following entry (Maedche, A., & Staab, S. (2001)):

- **Automatic Debit Transfer:** Electronic service arising from a debit authorization of the Yellow Account holder for a recipient to debit bills that fall due direct from the account.

A simple heuristic relates definition term "automatic debit transfer" with the first noun phrase in the definition "Electronic Service". It means both concepts are linked in the concept hierarchy.

Formal Concept Analysis

Formal Concept Analysis (FCA) is an unsupervised learning technique to form structures from data, which is based on the creation of natural clusters of objects and attributes. The purpose of the FCA is to offer data mining operations against

Table 2. Real estate domain context

Objects	Attributes					
	Real estate	Family house	Country house	Summer house	Blockhouse	Skyscraper
A1	x	x				
A2	x	x	x	x		
A3	x		x			
A4	x				x	x
A5	x				x	
A6	x			x		

data collection to analyze semantics within data collections (Ducrou, J. (2007); Priss, U. (2006)). The Formal Concept Analysis (FCA) is a technique for data analysis, knowledge presentation and information management proposed by Wille (Wille, R. (1982)) and formalized by Wille and Ganter (Ganter, B., & Wille, R. (1999)).

Philosophically, a concept is a unit of human thoughts. A concept can be defined by all attributes which describes the concept (the intent), or all objects which are members of the concept (the extent). Numerous objects and attributes can be used to define real world concepts, which make the representation of the real world units of thoughts difficult. That is why Formal Concept Analysis works within a *context*, which has fixed objects and attributes (Ducrou, J. (2007)).

The Table 2 depicts an example of formal context of real estate domain (Haav, H.-M.(2004)). The objects of the context are real estate objects and attributes are real estate specific attributes like family house, country house or summer house etc. The rows represent objects and columns represent attributes in the formal context of real estate domain. The "x" in Table 2 indicates, which attributes describe an object (represented by a row) or which objects has an attribute (represented by a column).

The formal context can be defined as $K(G, M, I)$ where G is set of objects, M is set of attributes and $I \subseteq G \times M$. A formal concept of the context $K(G, M, I)$ is defined as pair (A,B). For $A \subseteq G$ and $B \subseteq M$:

$$A' = \left\{ m \in M \left(\forall g \in A \right) g \operatorname{Im} \right\}$$
$$B' = \left\{ g \in G \left(\forall m \in B \right) g \operatorname{Im} \right\}$$

The A' is the set of attributes, which is common to all objects in A and B' is the set of objects, which is common to all attributes in B. The concept of the context $K(G, M, I)$ is (A,B), where $A \subseteq G$, $B \subseteq M$, $A'=B$ and $A=B'$. The extent of the concept (A,B) is A and its intent is B.

For the concepts (A_1, B_1) and (A_2, B_2) from the set S of all the concepts *of* $K(G, M, I)$:

$$(A_1, B_1) \leq (A_2, B_2) \Leftrightarrow A_1 \subseteq A_2$$

It is also equivalent to:

$$(A_1, B_1) \leq (A_2, B_2) \Leftrightarrow B_2 \subseteq B_1$$

The relation $\leq$ is an order on S e.g. the concept (A_1, B_1) is less general as compared to the concept (A_2, B_2), if the extant of the concept (A_1, B_1) is contained by (A_2, B_2).

The complete set of concepts S of a context $K(G, M, I)$ and the order between concepts $(S(K), \leq)$ is a complete lattice and it is known as concept lattice of the context $K(G, M, I)$ as shown in

Figure 1. The concept lattice of the real estate domain

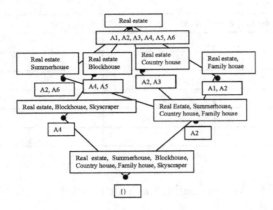

(Ganter, B., Stumme, G. & Wille, R. (2005)). The concept lattice of the context of real estate domain as depicted in the Table 2 is shown in the Figure 1.

The formal concepts are represented by nodes and sub- and super-concept relationships are represented by edges in the lattice (see Figure 1) For example, one of the formal concept in the lattice is {*A4*} x {*Real estate, Blockhouse, Skyscraper*}. The set {*A4*} is extent of the concept and the set {*Real estate, Blockhouse, Skyscraper*} is its intent. The formal concept {*A5*} × {*Real Estate, Blockhouse*} is its sub-concept. The extent of the bottom concept is empty, because there is no any object that has all the attributes.

Information Visualization for Semantic Analysis

Visual techniques take into account human perceptual capabilities to detect patterns and outliers in visual information. They can facilitate experts' understanding about complex data, structures, hierarchy and relations in semantic analysis process (Sabou, M. (2005)). These techniques can support domain experts with less semantic modeling background knowledge to deal with extracted semantic (Bhatti, N. & Weber, S. H. (2009); Bhatti, N. (2008)). Sabou has presented the "Cluster Map" technique to support semantic

analysis process specific tasks (e.g., evaluation). She purposes investigation of new visual techniques for semantic analysis and their integration in semantic analysis process (Sabou, M. (2005)).

Information visualization is derived from several communities. Playfair (1786) is seemed to be among earliest, who uses abstract visual properties such as line and area to represent data visually. Since then the classical data plotting methods have been developed. Bertin published his theory of graphics in 1967. This theory identified basic elements of diagrams and described a framework for the design of diagrams. Tufte (1983) introduced his theory of data graphics that highlighted maximizing density of useful information. Both well-known theories from Bertin and Tufte led to the development of information visualization as discipline (Card, S., Mackinlay, J. D. & Shneiderman, B. (1999)).

Foyel (Foley, J. D. & Ribarsky, W. (1994)) has defined visualization as follows:

A useful definition of visualization might be the binding (or mapping) of data to a representation that can be perceived. The types of binding could be visual, auditory, tactile, etc. or a combination of these (Card, S., Mackinlay, J. D. & Shneiderman, B. (1999)).

The main focus of Foyel's definition of visualization is the mapping of data to visual forms to improve understanding of users about data. The visualization can be seen as communication medium between data and users according to Foyel's definition. The definition of visualization provided by Card et al. (Card, S., Mackinlay, J. D. & Shneiderman, B.(1999)) underlined the objectives of visualization:

The use of computer-supported, interactive, visual representations of data to amplify cognition (Card, S., Mackinlay, J. D. & Shneiderman, B.(1999)).

According to (Card, S., Mackinlay, J. D. & Shneiderman, B.(1999)), the visualization can be categorized into two subfields scientific visualization and information visualization. This categorization is based on the type of data to be visualized. Scientific visualizations are based on physical data e.g. human body, the earth, molecules etc. The physical data allows spatial mapping e.g. ozone concentration in the atmosphere cab be visualized on a physical 3D representation of the earth. The non-physical data such as financial data, business information, collection of documents and abstract conceptions does not have an obvious spatial mapping. The visualization of non-physical data has two major problems visualization of objects´ properties and mapping of non-spatial abstractions into effective visual form. Therefore, the information visualization is defined by as follows:

The use of computer-supported, interactive, visual representations of abstract data to amplify cognition (Card, S., Mackinlay, J. D. & Shneiderman, B.(1999)).

According to (Godehardt, E. (2009); Domik, G (2000); Card, S., Mackinlay, J. D. & Shneiderman, B. (1999)), the objectives of information visualization can be summarized as:

- Improvement of exploration/exploitation of data and information by using visualization.
- Enhance understanding of concepts and processes by using knowledge and process visualization
- Gaining new (unexpected, profound) insights with the help of visualization techniques
- Making invisible visible
- Effective presentation of significant features by using visual forms

- Increasing scientific productivity by assisting experts with visual techniques
- Improving communication / collaboration by using visualization as medium

Visual Analytics for Semantic Analysis

The field of visual analytics (Keim, D., Andrienko, G., Fekete, J. D., Görg, C., Kohlhammer, J., & Melancon, G. (2008)) proposes combination of automated data analysis and interactive visualizations to support effective understanding, reasoning and decision making on the base of very large and complex data sets. Visual analytics allows users to enter into a loop and inactively manipulate data to gain insight on the data and the representation itself. The visual analytics approaches plays also an important role in the semi-automatic semantic analysis.

According Keim, D., Andrienko, G., Fekete, J. D., Görg, C., Kohlhammer, J., & Melancon, G. (2008) visual analytics is defined as:

Visual analytics combines automated analysis techniques with interactive visualizations for an effective understanding, reasoning and decision making on the basis of very large and complex data sets (Keim, D., Andrienko, G., Fekete, J. D., Görg, C., Kohlhammer, J., & Melancon, G. (2008)

The goals of visual analytics is to provide techniques to enable people to (Keim, D., Andrienko, G., Fekete, J. D., Görg, C., Kohlhammer, J., & Melancon, G. (2008):

- Analyze massive, dynamic, ambiguous, and often conflicting data to synthesize information and derive insight.
- Pattern analysis and matching to detect the expected and discover the unexpected.
- Formal data analysis methods to provide timely, defensible, and understandable assessments.
- Better presentation to communicate assessment effectively for action.

The difference between visual analytics and information visualization is not clear to people, because there is certainly some overlay and some information visualization task are related to visual analytics. Visual analytics is more than visualization. It is an integral approach to combine visualization, human factor and data analysis. The challenge is to develop a solution by combining best fit automated analysis algorithms and visualization and interaction techniques. The application of advanced knowledge discovery algorithms in information visualization community has been limited. Visual analytics tries to solve the problem that cannot be solved automatically and provide solutions to problems that we were not able to solve before.

The process of producing views and creating valuable interaction techniques for a given class of data were main objectives of information visualization. The tuning of underlying analytical processes was less in focus. Visual analytics aims to give higher priority to data analytics from the start and through all iterations. The learning form users' behavior and effective use of the visualization should play an important role in the analytical process (Keim, D., Andrienko, G., Fekete, J. D., Görg, C., Kohlhammer, J., & Melancon, G. (2008)). Visual analytics proposes intelligent combination of analytical approaches and advanced visualization techniques, which may play an important role for the semantic analysis.

SEMANTIC SERVICE DESCRIPTION APPROACHES AND SEMANTIC ANALYSIS PROCESS MODELS

This section describes the related work to semantic service description, semi-automatic modeling of semantic service description and semantic analysis Process Models in detail.

Related Work to Semantic Service Description

The modeling of semantic service descriptions is challenging task. It covers different aspects regarding the content level e.g. legal information comprising general terms and conditions or technical information contains in WSDL description. Different user roles provide and use different aspects for describing service. Legal experts might provide the general terms and condition and business experts provide the pricing information. The different kind of information are created and used in different phases of the service lifecycle. General terms and conditions and pricing information might exist as soon as the service is offered, broker might add special kind of quality of parameters later. The users' feedback can be available only after service usage. The service description related information might be spread throughout the Internet of services. Quality of service parameter may reside centrally on a platform or users' feedback may reside on consumers' community portal. The different kind of service description related information might available in different structures and unstructured formats. The variety of tools might be available to capture service description related information for different aspects and different roles. A software engineer might use Eclipse to create WSDL file for a Web service, but Eclipse tool is not desired tool for legal or business experts (Papazoglou, M.P. (2003)). The following eight challenges are identified by (Barrett, M., Davidson, E., Middleton, C., De-Gross, J. I.(2008); Basole, R.C. & Rouse, W.B. (2008); Nadhan, E. G. (2004); Petrie, C., Margaria, T., Lausen, H., Zaremba, (2008); Heck, E., Vervest, P.(2007)) for the modeling of semantic service description.

- Modeling
- Documentation
- Interlinkage
- Interoperability

- Querying
- Compliance
- Inconsistency
- Cooperation

The modeling of semantic service description should be in a holistic and consistent way and enable traceability of modeling decision. Domain experts can ground their modeling decision in scientific literature of the corresponding domain. For example, the modeling expert and business experts are needed to model pricing schemes for services. The business expert can just justify how a pricing scheme must look like. The *documentation* of the modeled information without media bread is also an important issue. This includes formal knowledge representation, natural language description and UI labels in multiple languages.

Because of the different roles, phases, locations and structures, the modeled information have to be *interlinked* with each other. For example, users' feedback on the community portal should be linked to service offering information on the service broker's site. Different user roles use heterogeneous tools along the service lifecycle to model different aspects of semantic service description, which raise the *interoperability* issues. The obtaining of information should be available e.g. "give me all services, which are cheaper than 5 Euro, and have at least an average of 3 star rating". The modeled semantic service description should be *compliance* with (international) specifications or policies, standard or laws.

Different users may introduce same kind of information independently and differently during the modeling different aspects of semantic service description. A sensible information management is needed to avoid *inconsistenc*. The information has to be modularized to allow different user roles to maintain and contribute information corresponding to different aspects in different phases of service lifecycle. Although pricing model and technical description belong to same service, but business expert may not interested in technical

description. The support for *cooperative* modeling is one of the most import issues to allow different user roles to model different aspects of service in the different phase of service lifecycle.

There are many approaches for the modeling of semantic service descriptions. These approaches are analyzed according to five criteria as shown in the Table 3. First criterion is black box or glass box view. The black box view based efforts focus on the aspects related to data and control flow considering mainly Web services. The glass box view based approaches describes the internal structure such as service level agreements and non-functional attributes. Second, approaches present just a model or the corresponding method as well. Most approaches present just model without describing method. Third, interdisciplinary means, if the semantic service description covers single domain or experts from different domains e.g. legal and price plan experts are involved in the modeling. The fourth criterion best practices indicates the usage of foundation ontology as sound modeling starting point and the usage of ontology patterns to avoid arbitrariness in modeling (Gangemi, A., Guarino, N, Masolo, C., Oltramari, A., Schneider, L.(2002))}. In fact, best practice is not often applied in existing approaches. The last criterion reflects whether W3C Semantic Web recommendations are used for the modeling of semantic service description.

The semantic service description approaches are grouped in five categories. The first category represents approached in the field of semantic Web services. The most prominent efforts e.g. OWL-S (Ankolekar A, Hobbs, J.R, Lassila, O., Martin, D.L. McIlraith, S.A. Narayanan, S.,Paolucci, M.,Payne, T.R.,Sycara, K.P. &Zeng H (2001)) and WSMO (Roman, D., Bruijn, J. de, Mocan,A.,Lausen,H.,Domingue,J., Bussler, C.,Fensel,D.(2006)) are just listed in the Table 3. Many other approaches are available in literature. According to the black box view, the purpose of these approaches is to automate tasks such as discovery and composition.

Table 3. The related work to semantic models for services

Effort	Glass Box	Method	Interdisciplinary	Best practice	W3C Semantic Web
Service Ontology	Yes	Yes	Yes	Yes	Yes
1. Semantic Web Services					
OWL-S	No	No	No	No	Yes
WSMO	No	No	No	No	No
...					
2. Other Service-related Ontologies					
OASIS Reference Ontology	No	No	No	No	Yes
The Open Group SOA Ontology	Yes	No	No	No	Yes
Ferrario and Guarino (2008)	Yes	No	No	Yes	Yes
Core Ontology of Web Services	No	No	No	Yes	Yes
OBELIX ontology	Yes	Yes	No	No	Yes
e³Service ontology	Yes	Yes	No	No	Yes
3. UML-based Efforts					
Service Network Notation	Yes	Yes	No	N/A	N/A
UPMS	Yes	Yes	No	N/A	N/A
SOAML	Yes	Yes	No	N/A	N/A
4. XML-based Efforts					
SML	Yes	No	No	N/A	N/A
USDL	Yes	No	No	N/A	N/A
DIN PAS 1018 (2002)	Yes	No	No	N/A	N/A
Emmrich (2005)	Yes	No	No	N/A	N/A
WS*	No	No	No	N/A	N/A
5. Informal Efforts					
Alter (2008)	Yes	No	No	N/A	N/A
O'Sullivan (2006)	Yes	No	No	N/A	N/A
Baida et al. (2001)	Yes	No	No	N/A	N/A

The second category shows other service-related ontologies outside the field of semantic Web dervices. The OASIS reference ontology for Semantic Service Oriented Architectures (Domingue, J., Zaremba, M.(2007)) is however not built on best practices and in a very early stage. Similarly, The Open Group ontology for Service-Oriented Architectures (SOA Ontology) (Harding, C.(2010)) covers both aspects business and technical perspectives. The approach presented by Ferrario et al. (Ferrario, R., Guarino, N.(2008)) is based on basic ontological analysis.

This effort captures an ontologically sound glass box view on a service. Oberle et al. (Oberle, D., Lamparter, S., Grimm, S., Vrandecic, D., Staab, S., & Gangemi A (2006)) has introduced a black box ontology "Core Ontology of Web Services" based on best practices and Semantic Web standards. The OBELIX ontology (Akkermans, H., Baida, Z., Gordijn, J., Pena, N., Altuna, A., Laresgoiti, I.(2004)) focuses on the ecosystem and value chain relationships between services and it is based on best practices. The approaches (De Kinderen, S., Gordijn, J. (2008a); De Kinderen, S., Gordijn, J.

(2008b)) introduces e3Service ontology to model services from the perspective of the user needs. The main focus of this approach is to generate service bundles under the consideration of user needs. The approach Service ontology proposed by Oberle et al. (Oberle, D., Bhatti, N., Brockmans, S., Niemann, M., & Janiesch, C. (2009)) follows a glass box view of services with their internal structure, service level agreements and non-functional attributes. It proposes also Semantic Business Web approach as method and service governance framework. The Service Ontology is constructed by interdisciplinary team of experts from different domain such as legal, rating, business model etc. It is build by applying best practices and W3C semantic Web recommendations.

UML-based efforts aim to support model-driven software engineering for services. Bitsaki et. al. (Bitsaki, M., Danylevych, O., Heuvel, W. van d., Koutras, G., Leymann, F., Mancioppi, M., Nikolaou, C., Papazoglou, M.(2008)) presents Service Network Notion (SNN), which covers similar aspects as e3Service ontology. The UML profile and Metamodel for services (UPMS) (Berre, A.J. (2008)) is an OMG (Object Management Group) to support top down and bottom up modeling and utilizes UMK collaboration diagrams. It is also liked with business modeling framework with business process modeling (BPMN) and goal modeling (BMM). The Service-oriented architecture Modeling Language (SoaMAL) (Berre, A.J. (2008)) for UPML describes a UML profile and metamodel for the design of services in SOA. The main goal of SoaML is to support activities of service modeling and model-driven development approach (Berre, A.J. (2008)). The survey UML-based Modeling of Web Service Composition (WSC) presents different approaches e.g. structure-based WSC Modeling, behavior-base WSC Modeling and hybrid WSC modeling. A UML based approach presented by Emmerich (Emmerich, A. (2005)) covers product related services such as maintenance without considering model-driven software engineering.

Service Modeling Language (SML) (Pandit, B., Popescu, V., Smith, V.(2010)) is the most prominent XML based effort. SML offers support to build a rich set of constructs for creating and constructing models of complex IT services and systems. A SML-Model consist of interrelate XML documents containing information about parts of IT services and constraints. The SML model could contain information about parts of IT services e.g. configuration, deployment, monitoring and capacity planning etc. The Universal Service Description Language (USDL) (Cardoso, J., Winkler, M. & Voigt, K.(2009)) covers technical, business and operation perspective. This approach defines and formalizes a metamodel Meta Object Facility (MOF) for the USDL to support model-driven service engineering. \'OSullivan (O'Sullivan, J.(2006)) analyzes a set of existing informal service descriptions to identify functional properties of a service. For the sake of completeness, WS-* specification such as WSDL or WS-BPEL are also mentioned, but they consider just Web services and have black box view.

Furthermore, the informal efforts such as Alter's approach (Alter, S.(2008)) Baid et al. approach (Baida, Z.,Gordijn,J.(2001)) or DIN PAS 1018 (DIN PAS 1018 (2002)) are listed in the Table 3. They capture a glass box view from business perspective. For example, the German norm PAS1018 (Public Available Specification) describes elements e.g. service, provider, category, location, etc.

Related Work to Semi-Automatic Modeling of Semantic Service Description

Different approaches for semantic description of software components were already explored to supports aspects like program understanding (Biggerstaff, T., Mitbander, B., Webster, D.(1993)) or reusable software libraries. The acquisition of semantic was always a critical issue. The survey of software reuse libraries (Mili, A., Mili, R.,

Mittermeir, R. (1998)) concludes that the use of ad-hoc and low tech methods more practical than semantically sophisticated methods. Several approaches to acquire semantics automatically were introduced such as (Maarek, Y., Berry, D., Kaiser., G.(1991); Helm, R., Maarek, Y.(1991); Mili, H., Ah-Ki, E., Godin, R., Mcheick, H.(1997)).

The GURU tool introduced by (Maarek, Y., Berry, D., Kaiser., G.(1991)) uses software documentation as knowledge source and use hierarchical agglomerative cluster method to extract hierarchy of terms contained in the software documentation. Helm et al. (Helm, R., Maarek, Y.(1991)) have combined this approach with code analysis methods. Milli et al. (Mili, H., Ah-Ki, E., Godin, R., Mcheick, H.(1997)) has introduced Information Retrieval (IR) based approach, that use noun phrases in the corpus and extract semantic by using co-occurrence of terms in some documents.

A subtopic of acquisition of semantic for software is the acquisition of semantics for Web services, which is a time consuming and complex task. The automation of semantic acquisition task is desirable as it is mentioned in the research work of (Wroe, C., Goble, C., Greenwood, M., Lord, P., Miles, S., Papay, J., Payne, T., Moreau, L.(2004); Sabou, M. (2005); Sabou, M.(2006); Sabou, M. & Pan, J. (2007)). The four research teams have introduced semi-automatic semantic acquisition techniques for Web services. Hess and Kushmerick (Hess, A., Kushmerick, N.(2003); Hess, A., Johnston, E., Kushmerick, N(2004); Hess, A., Kushmerick, N.(2004)) employ Naive Bayes and SVM machine learning methods to WSDL files. They have also introduced a tool that allows users to assign classes and properties to operations, parameters and complex types. The machine learning algorithms suggest probable classification to users to annotate Web services.

Patil et al. (Patil, A., Oundhakar, S., Sheth, A., Verma, K.(2004)) has introduced an interesting semi-automatic semantic acquisition technique that allow matching of WSDL file with relevant ontologies. The conversion of WSDL and ontology formats to a common representation format SchemaGraph to facilitate better matching. The common representation format SchemaGraph allows the usage of different ontology formats DAML, RDF-S or OWL. The mapping between WSDL concepts and ontology was achieved by applying match score techniques. Both techniques Hess and Kushmerick (Hess, A., Kushmerick, N.(2003); Hess, A., Johnston, E., Kushmerick, N.(2004); Hess, A., Kushmerick, N.(2004)) and Patil et al. (Patil, A., Oundhakar, S., Sheth, A., Verma, K.(2004)) use existing domain ontologies.

Sabou (Sabou, M. (2005); Sabou, M. (2006); Sabou, M. & Pan, J. (2007)) has presented a semi-automatic semantic acquisition of Web service. She used textual description of Web Services as knowledge source and deployed pattern based extraction rules (lexical analysis) for the semantic acquisition. She observed that noun phrases in the textual description of Web services denote the parameters of services and the verbs indicate the functionality of services. For example, the noun phrases image and url address denote parameter and verbs extract indicate the functionality of the service with the textual description "Extract images from a giver url address".

Wei et al. (Wei, D., Wang, T. Wang, J., & Chen, Y (2008)) has deployed heuristic rules to extract semantic constraint from description text of services. The constraint types were defined to extract semantic constraint from the text description of services. For example, a constraint type is {A, isPropertyObjectof, B} means concept A is a property object of concept B. According to this constraint type the constraint {Price, isPropertyObjectOf, Book} can be extracted from the text description of a service "The service returns the price of the book published by Springer". Furthermore, Constraint Graph Matching was used for the service discovery.

Related Work to Semantic Analysis Process Models

The Most prominent process models based semantic analysis approaches are discussed briefly in this section. These semantic analysis approaches do not deals directly with the semi-automatic modeling of semantic service description, but they may provide a solid scientific base to derivate a process model for the Visual Semantic Analysis to support semi-automatic modeling of semantic service descriptions. The usage of information visualization techniques for these process model based semantic analysis approaches will also be discussed briefly.

Maedche et al. (Maedche, A., & Staab, S. (2001); Maedche, A. (2002)) has presented ontology learning process model (or semantic analysis process model) with four steps import / reuse, extraction, prune and refine. First, the available knowledge sources with their (schema) structures imported and merged together by defining mapping rules. Second, semantic is extracted by using different learning techniques e.g. lexical entry \& concept extraction, clustering and association rules. Third, the extracted semantic is pruned to adjust extracted semantic to it prime purpose. Fourth, the refinement profits from pruned semantic, but complete pruned semantic at fine granularity. Finally, more iteration of process can be performed to include new domains into extracted and refined semantic and maintain its scope. The information visualization technique e.g. graph visualization is used to visualize the results of semantic analysis, but the visualization technique does not allow interactive analysis or refinement.

Cimiano et al. (Cimiano, P., Hotho, A., Stumme, G., Tane, J.(2004)) used existing ontologies and extracted instances from a given set of domain specific text documents by applying Natural Language Processing (NLP) techniques. The concepts of the ontologies are assigned to text documents. In this way, a number of context information can be derived. The documents and concepts of different ontologies define the context information. The FCA merging techniques allow semantic extraction form domain specific text documents by using different existing ontologies. Finally, the semantic can be generated form extracted semantic information. Cimiano et al. (Cimiano, P., Hothos, A., & Staab, S. (2005)) has also introduced another process model to extract semantics from the text without using existing ontologies. This process model describes NLP process steps in detail. The both process models use classical lattice visualization to visualize the results of semantic analysis process.

The Rapid Ontology Development (ROD) approach (Zhou, L. Booker, Q., & Zhang, D. (2002); Zhou, L. (2007)) combines top down and bottom up approach for the semantic extraction. First, the top level ontology is crafted manually from existing resources and then semantic is extracted automatically from textual resources. This approach applies statistical and extraction technique to filter term candidates, estimating similarity between terms and extracting and ranking terms related to semantic extraction. Finally, the learned semantic is mapped to high level semantic manually.

PACTOLE methodology (Bendaoud, R., Toussaint, Y., & Napoli, A. (2008)) allows semi-automatic semantic acquisition from astronomical texts. The first step is the NLP to extract pairs (object, property). In the second step, the Formal Concept Analysis is used to extract hierarchy of concepts from the pairs (object, property). The third step converts the existing knowledge sources e.g. dictionary/data base into concept hierarchy by using FCA. In the fourth step, both semantic models (from the text and from existing knowledge sources) are merged together and enriched. During the fifth step, the semantic is generated from lattice and formalized. This semantic analysis method uses also lattice visualization to visualize the extracted semantic.

Pan et al. (Pan, T., & Fang, K. (2009)) has introduced a semantic analysis process model for the radiology reports. This approach was developed for the Picture Archiving and Communication system (PACS) to improve image diagnosis accuracy and reducing patients' radiation exposure. In the first step, radiologists create radiology report text during diagnosis of medical images. After the term parsing process, FCA was applied to extract semantic from radiology report text. Finally, the extracted semantic is compared with related ontologies by using distance measurement method. The lattice visualization is also used by Pan et al. (Pan, T., & Fang, K. (2009)) to visualize the extracted semantic.

Jia et al. (Jia, H., Newman, J., & Tianfield, H. (2008)) has introduced a process model to extract semantic from the domain specific scientific documents semi-automatically. In the first step, keywords extraction from the research corpus takes place. The keywords, which were semantically similar, are clustered together. After the statistical filtering and NLP processing, formal context is generated. Then the FCA is applied to extract lattice structure. Finally, the semantics can be extracted from the lattice structure. Havre (Havre, S., Hetzler, B. (2000)) used also similar approach to extract semantic from domain specific text. This approach introduce additionally rules and facts to enrich the semi-automatically extracted semantic. The lattice visualization was also used by Jia et al. to visualize extracted semantic.

AS it is already discussed, Visual techniques plays an important role for the semantic analysis approaches. The process models which deals with visualization techniques for data analysis are also described here to consider visualization techniques for the semantic analysis as it is also proposed by Sabou (Sabou, M. (2005)).

Card et al. (Card, S., Mackinlay, J. D. & Shneiderman, B.(1999)) has introduced a simple reference model for the information visualization to map row data to visual forms. User can transform the row data to accomplish a desired task. Raw data can consist of various forms e.g. spreadsheets or text. The usual strategy is to map the row data into a relation or set of relations that are more structured. The data transformation facilitates the transformation of various forms of row data to more structured forms like data tables. The visual mapping data tables into visual structures that combine spatial substrates (such as x- and y-coordinates), marks (points, lines and areas) and graphical properties (color, size and texture). Finally, the view transformation generates views by specifying graphical parameters of visual structures such as position, scaling and clipping. User can control the parameters of the transformations e.g. restricting the view to certain data ranges. The information visualization, user interaction and transformation facilitate users to perform a desire task.

May et al. (May, Thorsten, Kohlhammer, Jörn (2008)) has presented process model to combine statistical data classification and interactive visualization technique in order to group data items into categories. This approach extends information visualization reference process (Card, S., Mackinlay, J. D. & Shneiderman, B. (1999)) as discussed above and establish an iterative cyclic process. A single cycle starts with selection of data, proceed with the update of the classifier and ends with the visual feedback of the new categories by using KV-Map. The user may continue iterative refinement process by modifying selection and analyzing visual feedback.

Keim et al. (Keim, D., Andrienko, G., Fekete, J. D., Görg, C., Kohlhammer, J., & Melancon, G. (2008)) has introduced the visual analytics process that is based on the simple model of visualization. According to Keim, this process model has to be evaluated and measured in terms of efficiency of knowledge gained. After initial data analysis by using statistical and mathematical techniques, the initial data analysis results can be visualized with appropriate visualization and interaction techniques. After initial analysis, users can enter into a loop to gain knowledge on the data and drive the system towards more focused analysis and adequate analytical techniques. The interaction on the visual representation facilitates users to gain a better understanding of visualization itself. Different views help them to go beyond visual representation and confirm or reject hypotheses of previous iteration. They can keep analyzing data within this loop till they find answers to their question or task from dataset understudy. Visualization techniques such as (Card, S., Mackinlay, J. D. & Shneiderman, B.(1999); May, Thorsten, Kohlhammer, Jörn (2008)) and Visual Analytics mostly deal with interactive data analysis, but semantic analysis can also profit from these techniques to support interactive semi-automatic semantic analysis.

A GENERIC PROCESS MODEL FOR THE VISUAL SEMANTIC ANALYSIS

A generic process model for the Visual Semantic Analysis (VSA) approach to support semi-automatic modeling of SSD is described briefly. First, the requirements analysis is performed to define requirements for the VSA approach. After the requirements analysis, the comparison of related approaches, which are already presented above, is presented. The comparison of related approaches with the Visual Semantic Analysis presents also the positioning of VSA approach to related work. Afterwards, a generic process model for VSA developed on the base of requirements analysis is presented in detail.

Requirements Analysis

A study was conducted to derive requirements for the VSA. The knowledge experts from different domains were interviewed in this study. The requirements for the VSA were derived from these interviews. The following sections give an overview of requirements from users' perspective,

semantic analysis perspective and SSD modeling perspective.

Requirements from Users' Perspective

The semantic service description contains non-functional parameters e.g. price plan, QoS parameters, legal aspects and key words etc. The modeling of semantic service description is a complex and interdisciplinary task, where knowledge experts from different domains take part. For example, modeling of a movie rental service with a price plan (e.g. 1,99 €/day or 2,99€/day with HD-Format) and legal aspects (e.g. copyright issues). The pricing model experts, legal experts and QoS parameters experts besides service engineers have to take part in the modeling task. The market competitive pricing and QoS parameters can have an impact on the modeling of price plan for a service. Furthermore, the context information e.g. student rebate can make the pricing plan modeling more complex task. The most important users' requirement is to have a semantic analysis approach to compare existing semantic service descriptions e.g. price plans on service market place during the modeling.

The semantic analysis approach should also allow experts to check the competitiveness of their modeled services with the offered services on service market places. First the experts should be able to perform semantic analysis for extracting semantic information from semantic service descriptions and then model their new service. Later, the re-analysis of new-modeled services with the existing services should facilitate experts to view changes in the semantics. Finally, the comparison of new-modeled services with the existing services should allow experts to check the competitiveness of their new-modeled service with the existing services on the market places. The experts should be able to iterate this process until they are satisfied with the modeling of new service.

The semantic analysis can lead to information overload e.g. irrelevant semantic information or inappropriate semantic presentation. The visualization technique should support effective understanding, reasoning and decision-making based on very large and complex semantic information (Keim et al.). For example, the visual support for the price plan analysis should visualize context information of price plans and semantic analysis of different price plans. The semantic analysis approach should help users to avoid information overload und to have better understandings of semantics in the semantic service descriptions. The interactive visualization techniques should facilitate experts to focus on their point of interest to avoid information overload (e.g. price plan can be point of interest for the pricing model experts).

The semantic analysis tool should propose the semantically most similar semantic service descriptions, which can be used as template to model new services. It will support users not to model whole service, but reuse or adapt existing parts of semantic service descriptions. The visualization techniques should also support users to find out semantically similar services by using different semantic analysis techniques and pattern matching techniques.

The interdisciplinary tasks of the semantic service description modeling demand multiple perspectives. The users want to have multiple perspectives to analyze the different aspects such as price plan, QoS parameters and legal aspects separately or together. They should also be able to filter data of their interest and analyze separately. For example, users should be able to perform semantic analysis of price plan, QoS parameters and legal aspects for all movie rental services in separate perspectives or just in one. The price plan analysis in one perspective can give deep insight into semantics of price plans. If the price plans are QoS parameters dependent, then is important to analyze price plans and QoS parameters in one perspective simultaneously. The users should be able to decide for the data of their interest and choose different perspectives to analyze it.

Requirements from Semantic Analysis Perspective

The semantic analysis process models present different abstraction level as discussed above. An abstract process model is necessary to consider different process steps and different semantic analysis aspects presented by different semantic analysis process models. It will also help to have a use case independent process model and adapt different process models in an abstract semantic analysis process model. The process model abstraction for the visual semantic analysis process model is one of the most important requirements to achieve a generic process model for the visual semantic analysis.

The visual techniques in the semantic analysis can facilitate experts' understanding about complex data, structures, hierarchy and relations in semantic descriptions Sabou (Sabou, M. (2005);. Keim et al. (Keim, D., Andrienko, G., Fekete, J. D., Görg, C., Kohlhammer, J., & Melancon, G. (2008)) proposes visual analytics as combination of interactive visualization and data analysis for the understanding and reasoning about data. The application of user interfaces for semantic analysis in the real world should not be underestimated. The presentation of the results generated by semantic analysis algorithms should provide graphical means (Maedche, A. (2002))The visual techniques can play a key role to facilitate knowledge experts in semantic analysis process. The visualization of knowledge base and results generated by semantic analysis algorithms can provide better understanding about knowledge sources and extracted semantics to knowledge experts. The knowledge base contains feathers extracted from structured, semi-structured or unstructured data and serves as basis for the semantic analysis process. The visualization of results generated by semantic analysis algorithms can give an overview of complex semantic structures extracted from the data.

Semantic analysis aims at the integration of multitude of disciplines e.g. machine learning and semantic modeling to facilitate semi-automatic construction of semantics. It relies on the *balanced cooperative modeling* paradigm, which is defined as cooperated interaction between human modeler and learning algorithms (Maedche, A (2002)). Cimiano et al. mentions that they do not believe in fully automatic semantic extraction without any user involvement. Users can be involved in the automatic semantic extraction by keeping their involvement in the process as minimum as possible (Cimiano, P., Hothos, A., & Staab, S. (2005)). It demands support for the *balances cooperative modeling* paradigm by using semantic analysis algorithms and human interaction. The interactive visualization techniques as human interaction may support knowledge experts to focus on their point of interest in data or semantics to have better understanding of semantic analysis process. Knowledge experts may reduce or extend the dimensionality of knowledge base to improve the semantic analysis process. They may also refine the results of semantic analysis process by using interactive techniques and use the refined semantic to reanalyze the semantic in order to improve overall results of the semantic analysis process. Therefore, the interactive visualization techniques are the most important requirement for the visual semantic analysis.

Requirements from Semantic Service Description Modeling Perspective

The modeling of semantic service description is an interdisciplinary task, where the experts from different domains such as price plan experts, legal experts etc, take part. For example, the price plan and legal aspects modeling of a service requires price plan experts and legal experts. The knowledge expert can only justify how a sensible price plans or legal aspects can look like. Similarly, it

holds also for other domains as well. A modularization approach is used to define modules for different domains expert, where domain experts are responsible for domain specific modules (Oberle, D., Bhatti, N., Brockmans, S., Niemann, M. & Janiesch, C. (2009); Cardoso, J., Winkler, M. & Voigt, K. (2009)). For example, price plan experts can be responsible for the pricing module in the semantic service description. This approach is also called as roles based modeling of semantic service description. A governance team, where knowledge experts and domain experts work hand-in-hand, monitors the modeling activities to assure the consistency. These aspects lead to the requirement that semantic analysis should support modular approach to support roles based of semantic service description and governance process. Visual semantic analysis should support collaborative modeling of semantic service description, where the knowledge experts from different domains model SSD by using different tools. The governance team assures consistency and monitor if the modeling guidelines are followed.

Different tools can be used for the SSD modeling knowledge experts. For example, technical expert can model services with Eclipse-based tools or modeling tools, but legal experts or price plan experts can model services with easy to use tools e.g. a simple form based editor etc. The interdisciplinary modeling and heterogeneous tools stipulate that visual semantic analysis approach should support different standards to assure interoperability and interlinkage.

According to Barros and Dumas (Barros, A. & Dumas, M (2006)), the SSD modeling will become a bottleneck for service ecosystems. The semi-automatic semantic acquisition techniques have to be introduced to facilitate modeling of semantic service description as it already discussed above. The extension of semantic analysis process to facilitate semi-automatic modeling of semantic service description is one of the most important requirements for the visual semantic analysis. The semantic service description may contain static attributes, dynamic attributes within the influence of service provider and dynamic attributes beyond the influence of service provider as discussed above. It contains also unstructured data e.g. textual description of services. The formalization of semantic service description can be in different formats e.g. XML, UML or ontologies. It demands that the semantic analysis process should also support these formats. Furthermore, the extension of semantic analysis process for the SSD modeling should also take into consideration the governance guidelines to face the modeling challenges like consistency and cooperation.

The SSD modeling and governance efforts can be at risk if the semantic presentation and interactive manipulation cannot be accomplished in an intuitive and user-friendly way (Oberle, D., Bhatti, N., Brockmans, S., Niemann, M. & Janiesch, C. (2009)). The complex SSD modeling task demands innovative visualization techniques to present semantic in a personalized and interactive manner, where experts from different domains e.g. price plan experts or legal experts can model the SSD.

Requirements from Technological Perspective

The extensibility is the main requirement for the VSA approach from the technological perspective, which demands support for different data input formats, flexible usage of further semantic analysis algorithms and visualization techniques.

The structured, semi-structured and unstructured data e.g. textual description of services, WSDL and USDL can be considered as knowledge sources for the visual semantic analysis process. It requires that semantic analysis approach should support different formats for the context acquisition. After the context acquisition, the data transformation to prepare for the presentation is also one of the most important issues. The choice of visualization is very challenging task and depend upon data types, task and target groups (Card, S.,

Mackinlay, J. D. & Shneiderman, B. (1999)). The visual semantic analysis approach should provide a possibility to use different visualization techniques for the presentation of data and semantics to improve the understanding of knowledge experts about them.

Different semantic analysis algorithms cannot perform always the best results. The combination of different semantic analysis algorithms as multi-strategy seems to be a promising approach (Maedche, A (2002)). The visual semantic analysis approach should allow the integration of more semantic analysis algorithms. The support for different input formats, flexible data transformation techniques and flexible usage of different visualization techniques and semantic analysis algorithms may help users to improve semantic analysis process (Maedche, A (2002)).

Requirements Overview

The Table 4 gives an overview of concrete requirements derived from the requirements as described above. The requirements are grouped to nine requirements categories. They are later used in this research work to compare visual semantic analysis approach with related efforts. They are assigned further to two main category types semantic analysis and SSD modeling.

The category type semantic analysis consists of six requirements categories as shown in the Table 4. The "process model/method for semantic analysis" indicates the need for process or method based approach and comprises all requirements that are directly related to semantic analysis process. The requirements data sources related requirements for the semantic analysis are represented by the categories "support for unstructured data" and "support for semi-structured or structured data". The semantic analysis algorithms related requirements are depicted by the category "multiple semantic analysis algorithms". The categories "visual context analysis" and "visual semantic analysis" capture requirements

Table 4. The requirements overview for the visual semantic analysis

Category types	Requirements categories	Requirements	Perspective
Semantic analysis	Process model/method for semantic analysis	Process model abstraction for the semantic analysis to achieve a generic process model	Semantic analysis
		Support for balanced cooperative modeling	Semantic analysis
		Extension of visual semantic analysis approach with further visualization techniques	Technical
		Interactive visualization approaches to improve semantic analysis process	Semantic analysis
	Support for unstructured data	Support for different data input formats	Technical
	Support for semi-structured or structured data	Support for different data input formats	Technical
	Multiple semantic analysis algorithms	Flexible usage of different semantic analysis algorithms	Technical
	Visual Context Analysis	Visual support for the context analysis	Semantic analysis
	Visual Semantic Analysis	Visual support for the semantic analysis	Semantic analysis
SSD modeling	Process model/ Method for the SSD modeling	Extension of semantic analysis process for the service modeling	SSD modeling
		Semantic analysis support during the modeling of semantic service description	User
		Modularization approach to support role based SSD modeling	SSD modeling
		Support for different SSD modeling languages	SSD modeling
		Collaborative modeling support	SSD modeling
		Multiple tools support for SSD modeling	SSD modeling
		Governance support for the visual semantic analysis approach to support collaborative modeling	SSD modeling
	Visual support for SSD Modeling	Visual support for the semantic service description modeling	User/ SSD modeling
		Interactive visualization techniques to visualize the semantics of semantic service description	User
		Multiple perspectives to support role based modeling of semantic service description	User
	Analyze – Visualize –Model – Reanalyze	Comparison of new modeled services with existing services	User
		Reusability for the modeling of semantic service description	User

related to the usage of visualization techniques for the context and semantic analysis in order to improve semantic analysis process.

Three requirements categories are assigned to the category type SSD modeling as depicted in the Table 4. The "process model/ Method for the SSD modeling" represents all requirements to extend semantic analysis process with modeling specific aspects. The "visual support for SSD modeling" manifests the need of visualization for the SSD modeling to support knowledge experts. The requirement category "Analyze – Visualize – Model – Reanalyze" demonstrates the need of techniques for knowledge experts to analyze data, visualize analysis results, model services and re-analyze modeled services with the analyzed data.

Comparison of Visual Semantic Analysis Approach with Related Efforts

There are four approaches that deal with semi-automatic semantic service description modeling directly. Further semantic analysis and visualization supported semantic analysis approaches are also related to this research work. The nine distinguishing requirements categories as discussed above set our Visual Semantic Analysis approach apart from related efforts. The comparison of Visual Semantic Analysis Approach with related efforts according to nine requirements categories is presented in the Table 5.

The Visual Semantic Analysis is process model based approach for the semantic analysis and SSD modeling. It support unstructured, semi-structured and structured data sources for the semantic analysis and allow usage of different semantic analysis algorithms in the process model. The interactive visualization techniques are used to support both the semantic analysis and SSD modeling. For example, interactive visualization techniques facilitate knowledge experts to analyze context information extracted from different data sources and semi-automatic extracted

semantic and model SSD. The Analyze – Visualize – Model – Reanalyze enables knowledge experts to use semantic analysis methods during modeling of services and comparison of modeled services with existing services. The requirements category Analyze – Visualize – Model – Reanalyze is the most prominent difference between Visual Semantic Analysis and other related efforts, which is just supported by the Visual Semantic Analysis.

The approaches 2 to 5 supports both semantic analysis and SSD modeling, but they are not process model/method based approaches. The approach offered by Hess and Kushmerick (Hess, A., Kushmerick, N. (2003)) supports just unstructured data for the semantic analysis. It employs Naive Bayes and SVM machine learning methods to extract semantic from WSDL files. The approach of Patil et al. (Patil, A., Oundhakar, S., Sheth, A., Verma, K.(2004)) supports unstructured, semi-structured and structured data for the semantic analysis. This approach presents conversion of WSDL and exiting ontology formats to a common representation format SchemaGraph and then maps the WSDL concepts to existing ontologies by applying match score techniques. The both approached do not allow the combination of different semantic analysis algorithms and offer visualization techniques to support SSD modeling. The approaches proposed by Sabou (Sabou, M. (2005); Sabou, M. (2006); Sabou, M. & Pan, J. (2007)) and Wei et al. (Wei, D., Wang, T. Wang, J., & Chen, Y (2008)) both support unstructured data for semantic analysis. The both techniques used lexical analysis technique for the semantic extraction and do not allow the combination of different semantic analysis algorithms. Wei et al. do not offer any visualization technique, but Sabou offers visualization technique to improve semantic analysis.

The approaches 6 to 16 allow process model based semantic analysis and do not deal with the SSD modeling. Maedche et al. (Maedche, A., & Staab, S. (2001); Maedche, A. (2002)), Cimiano et al. (Cimiano, P., Hotho, A., Stumme, G.,Tane,

Table 5. The comparison of the visual semantic analysis with the related efforts

Nr.	Approaches	Semantic Analysis						Semantic Service Description Modeling		
		Process model/Method	Support for unstructured data	Support for semi-structured or structured data	Multiple semantic analysis algorithms	Visual Context Analysis	Visual Semantic Analysis	Process model/Method based	Visual support for SSD Modeling	Analyze –Model– Reanalyze
1	Visual Semantic Analysis approach	++	++	++		++	++	++	++	++
2	Hess and Kushmerick	-	++	-	-	-	-	-	-	-
3	Patil et al.	-	++	++	-	-	-	-	-	-
4	Sabou	-	++	-	-	-	+	-	-	-
5	Wei et al.	-	++	-	-	-	-	-	-	-
6	Maedche et al.	++	++	++	++	-	+	-	-	-
7	Cimiano et al.	++	++	++	++	-	+	-	-	-
8	Cimiano et al.	++	++	++	-	-	+	-	-	-
9	ROD Methodology	++	++	++	-	-	-	-	-	-
10	PACTOLE methodology	++	++	++	++	-	+	-	-	-
11	Pan et al.	++	++	++	++	-	+	-	-	-
12	Jia et al.	++	++	-	-	-	+	-	-	-
13	Haav	++	++	++	-	-	+	-	-	-
14	Card et al.	++	++	++	-	++	+	-	-	-
15	May et al.	++	++	++	++	+	+	-	-	-
16	Keim et al.	++	++	++	++	+	++	-	-	-

J.(2004)) and Cimiano et al. (Cimiano, P., Hothos, A., & Staab, S. (2005)). facilitate usage of different data format such as unstructured, semi-structured and structured data. The approach offered by Maedche et al. supports multiple semantic analysis algorithms and combination of different algorithms to improve semantic extraction. The both approaches from Cimiano et al. apply Formal Concept Analysis (FCA) for the semantic extraction and do not allow the combination of different semantic analysis algorithms. These three semantic analysis techniques offer visual support e.g. graph visualization or lattice visualization to improve semantic extraction, but they do not exploit different interactive techniques for the semantic analysis.

The approaches ROD (Zhou, L. Booker, Q., & Zhang, D. (2002); Zhou, L. (2007)), PACTOLE (Bendaoud, R., Toussaint, Y., & Napoli, A. (2008)) and Pan et al. (Pan, T., & Fang, K. (2009)) allow different data formats and combination of different semantic analysis algorithms. The approaches of Jia et al. (Jia, H., Newman, J., & Tianfield, H. (2008)) and Havre (Havre, S., Hetzler, B. (2000)) supports just unstructured data and do not support multiple semantic analysis algorithms. The methodology Rod does not offer visual support, but the other approaches PACTOLE, Pan et al. Jia et al. and Havre offer lattice visualization without using sophisticated interactive visualization techniques for the exploration of extracted semantic.

The approaches introduced by Card et al. (Card, S., Mackinlay, J. D. & Shneiderman, B.(1999)), May et al. (May, Thorsten, Kohlhammer, Jörn (2008)) and Keim et al. (Keim, D., Andrienko, G., Fekete, J. D., Görg, C., Kohlhammer, J., & Melancon, G. (2008)) propose visualization techniques as essential part of data analysis. Card et al. propose usage of visualization technique for data to have better understanding about data and discuss visualization issues like overview, zoom and level of details with handling semantic analysis issues. May et al. and Keim et al. suggest that the visualization techniques and data analysis have to go hand in hand to achieve better data analysis results. These both approaches originate from visual analytics, which focuses more on the data analysis rather than semantic analysis. The usage of visualization techniques for the data analysis presented by Card et al., May et al. and Keim et al. play an important role for the Visual Semantic Analysis approach.

Visual Semantic Analysis Process Model

A generic process model for the Visual Semantic Analysis is developed on the base of the requirements analysis. The generic VSA process model is divided in two parts: semantic analysis specific sub process and SSD modeling specific sub process as shown in Figure 2. The semantic analysis spe-

Figure 2. A generic process model for the visual semantic analysis

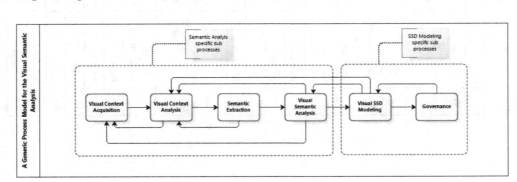

cific sub processes include sub processes "visual context acquisition", "visual context analysis", "semantic extraction" and visual semantic analysis". And SSD modeling specific sub processes covers sub process "visual SSD modeling" and "governance". The sub processes are described briefly in the following sections.

Semantic Analysis Specific Sub Processes

Different semantic analysis process models are already discussed briefly in this chapter. They consist of different tasks with different abstraction levels. The VSA process model considers an abstract semantic analysis process model, where different tasks with different abstraction levels can be presented. The semantic analysis specific sub processes in the generic VSA process model is described below.

Visual Context Acquisition

The context acquisition is an essential part of all semantic analysis approaches. All semantic analysis approaches support unstructured, semi-structured and/or structured data input formats as it is also perceptible from the Table 5. The sub process visual context acquisition allows context acquisition from unstructured, semi-structured and structured data input formats e.g. textual description of services, service documentation, monitoring information of QoS parameters, WSDL, USDL and service ontology. The context extraction from these data input formats can be achieved by using

different Natural Language Processing (NLP) and parsing techniques. Knowledge experts may use techniques like text/XML parser, stemming, POS tagging, stemming, stop words elimination and *tfidf* value calculation etc. to extract context information as it is already discussed above.

The sub process visual context extraction consists of two process steps context extraction and conceptual scaling. The context can be extracted from the unstructured, semi-structured and structured data in the process step context extraction. The textual information can be extracted from the unstructured data such as services descriptions in WSDL files and service documentation by using text/XML parser techniques. This extracted textual information serves as text corpus for the visual semantic analysis process. After the extraction of text corpus, the tasks POS-tagging, reduction of stop words, stemming, lexical analysis and document term matrix generation are performed. The result of this process step is a context table. One example of the context table is depicted in the Table 6, where the rows and columns represent services and attributes (terms extracted from unstructured data) respectively. The entries in the Table 6 indicate, which service (represented by a row) owns attributes (represented by column). The values in this table are the *tfidf* values of attributes in the text corpus.

The context extraction from semi-structured or structured data such as monitoring information of QoS parameters, WSDL, USDL and service ontology is also supported in this process step by using text/XML parser techniques. The result of

Table 6. One example of context table for the unstructured data

	Car	Car rental	Navigation	Navigation system
7th car rental	2.32	4.52	1.23	3.34
BW car rental	2.21	6.21	1.11	4.23
World car rental	1.23	7.23	1.52	4.56
Rent-me Car rental	2.34	5.32	1.43	5.12
Lunge car rental	1.54	6.34	1.21	4.35

Table 7. One example of context table for the semi-structured or structured data

	Rent per day	**Price per day for Navigation system**
7th car rental	57€	5€
BW car rental	41€	3€
World car rental	55€	4€
Rent-me Car rental	50€	8€
Lunge car rental	45€	4€

this process step is also a context table. One example of context information extracted from the semi-structured or structured data is presented in the Table 7. The rows and columns depict services (e.g. car rental services) and attributes (car rental services specific attributes) and entries in the table represent attributes values.

The context extracted from unstructured (see Table 6) and semi-structured and structured data (see Table 7) can be merged together to achieve the overall context information.

In the case of semi-structured or structured data, the context information are mostly complex. Application of semantic analysis techniques to complex context is very difficult. For example, non- functional parameters of services (attributes) like pricing model, legal aspects and QoS parameters can be very complex. In this case, the knowledge experts can transform complex context information into suitable context information. The context transformation takes place in the process step conceptual scaling. The complex non-functional parameters of service (attributes)

are considered as objects that are described by new scale attributes. The transformation is not unique and allows different interpretations and views of knowledge experts (conceptual scaling 2 papers). The conceptual scaling can be done with different levels of details or granularity. For example, the conceptual scaling of the context is depicted in Table 8. The columns represent price ranges. The entries "1" shows that the prices of rental services are between these price ranges. The output of the sub process visual context acquisition is such type of context tables (context matrixes) as shown in the Table 8.

Visual Context Analysis

Knowledge experts can prune or refine the extracted context matrix in the sub process visual context analysis. The pruning or refinement of the context can be achieved by using dictionary parsing technique e.g. WordNet (Fellbaum, C. (1998)). It allows the extraction of synonyms by using the basic synset relation of WordNet. In addition to synonyms, several different semantic

Table 8. One example of conceptual scaling

	Rent per day: from 40€ to 50€	**Rent per day: from 51€ to 60€**	**Price per day for Navigation system: from 1€ to 5€**	**Price per day for Navigation system: from 6€ to 10€**
7th car rental	0	1	0	1
BW car rental	1	0	0	1
World car rental	0	1	0	1
Rent-me Car rental	1	0	0	1
Lunge car rental	1	0	1	0

relations e.g. hyponymy help to extract real concepts of a word. These semantic relations allow pruning or refinement of context by mapping of words to more general concepts or more specific concepts (Wermter, S., Hung, C. (2002)). For example, one document contains the attribute "beef" and another one "lamb", but "beef" and "lamb" will be considered as unrelated attributes. By using WordNet, these both attributes can be mapped to "meat". The visual context analysis offers visualization of attributes from the context and their synset, hypernyms and hyponyms. The knowledge experts can decide to merge synset of attributes in the context or extend or reduce context information by using hypernyms and hyponyms.

The lexical analysis by means of lexical pattern matching leads to refinement of knowledge base. The multi-word terms (phrases) are more important to identify concepts (attributes). For example, the phrase "unemployment benefit" consists of two terms "unemployment" and "benefit", where "benefit" is more general than "unemployment benefit". The lexical patterns can be identified by using POS-tagging e.g. Noun-Noun patterns or Noun-Preposition-Noun in the n-gram model (Maedche, A. (2002); Wei, D., Wang, T. Wang, J., & Chen, Y (2008)). Knowledge experts can choose the parameters like *tfidf* threshold or different n-gram model to choose terms and phrases with specific *tfidf* threshold. Additionally, they can apply lexical pattern matching to extract important multi-word terms (attributes) by using different pattern matching.

Visual context analysis offers different interactive visualization techniques to visualize context in order to detect expected and discover unexpected facts or patterns. It supports the visual analytics approaches as described by Keim et al. (Keim, D., Andrienko, G., Fekete, J. D., Görg, C., Kohlhammer, J., & Melancon, G. (2008))). The interactive visualization techniques help knowledge experts to see the density of the context matrix. The reduction of dimensionality can also be achieved by clustering similar services or similar attributes.

The knowledge experts can also choose the parts of context matrix as point of interest by using interactive visualization techniques for the next sub process semantic extraction.

Knowledge experts can select attributes from the context matrix to see semantic neighbors, which are related to selected attributes or belong to the semantic space of the attributes. For example, they can select the attribute "meat" from the context matrix to see semantic neighbors of services that own attributes meat, lamb, beef and butcher shops. They can also sort attributes according to their occurrence frequency in the context matrix to see frequent or rare terms in the context. The knowledge experts can additionally add their own knowledge to the context in order to enhance semantic analysis process.

The visual context base analysis offers different perspectives for pruning and refinement of the context matrix. After pruning and refinement, knowledge experts can create new perspectives of the context and compare these with the last perspectives or original perspectives of the context. This approach helps them to understand the context better and to provide both explicit and implicit learning with the context matrix. For example, they can see changes in the context, when they are using WordNet to find synonyms, general concepts or more specific concepts. The output of this sub process is modified context matrix after pruning and refinement of the context generated by the sub process visual context analysis.

Semantic Extraction

The main semantic analysis algorithms can be classified in four different categories statistics based, rule-based and hybrid (statistics and rule based) and formal concept analysis (Sabou, M. & Pan, J. (2007); Zhou, L. (2007); Cimiano, P., Hotho, A. & Staab, S. (2005); Maedche, A. (2002)) as discussed above. The visual semantic approach offers a bundle of semantic algorithms in the sub process semantic extraction to knowledge experts, which may produce results with varying quality.

Knowledge experts can combine these algorithms to compensate advantages or disadvantages of each technique. They can compare the results of different techniques or combine them to improve the results.

The sub process visual context analysis uses different semantic extraction techniques e.g. lexical pattern matching, dictionary parsing or clustering, which are offered by the sub process semantic extraction. The feedback loop between the sub processes visual context analysis and semantic extraction allow knowledge experts to use automatic semantic extraction techniques. For example, the knowledge experts can use dictionary parsing and clustering techniques to prune or refine the context information. By using dictionary parsing, they can use WordNet functionality like synset or pattern matching techniques to prune or refine context information. The clustering techniques allow them to reduce the dimensionality of context information by clustering similar services or attributes.

The output of this sub process depends on the semantic extraction algorithms, which are used for the semantic analysis process. For example, dictionary parsing provides synonyms by using synset functionality, lexical pattern matching offers a list of multi-words terms (phrases), clustering techniques cluster similar attributes or services or the formal concept analysis generates conceptual hierarchy and semantic relations. The most important issue is that knowledge experts should be able to use either a single or a combination of semantic extraction algorithms within sub processes like visual context analysis and visual semantic analysis. It is also very important that these sub processes can also process output of this sub process.

Visual Semantic Analysis

The issue usability of semantic knowledge arises as large number of concepts and relations are extracted from the semantic analysis process. The extracted semantic has to be adapted and ex-

tended according application scenarios (Zhou, L. (2007); Cimiano, P., Hotho, A. & Staab, S. (2005); Maedche, A. (2002)). Cimiano et al. (Cimiano, P., Hotho, A. & Staab, S. (2005)) mention that they do not believe in fully automatic semantic extraction without any user involvement. Cimanto et al. (Cimiano, P., Hotho, A. & Staab, S. (2005)) purpose also the user involvement in the automatic semantic analysis process for validation. According to ((Maedche, A. (2002)), the extracted semantic has to be inspected by domain experts during the semantic analysis process for the validation. The domain expert can prune or refine extracted semantic as desired in this sub process.

The visual semantic analysis offers different interactive visualization techniques to support knowledge experts by exploring the extracted semantic. These visualization techniques enable knowledge experts to explore through the concept hierarchy in order to review extracted semantic. They can not only have an overview of the extracted semantic, but also analyze specific parts of extracted semantic. The interactive visualization facilitate knowledge experts to have better understanding about extracted semantic and validate extracted semantic.

Knowledge experts can analyze extracted semantic and enrich the extracted semantic by adding new attributes or clustering attributes. The feedback loop between visual semantic analysis and the visual context analysis facilitates the synchronization of context information with the enrichment of extracted semantic. Knowledge experts can also model their own domain knowledge e.g. concepts, attributes and semantic relations manually in this sub process. The feedback loop between visual semantic analysis and the visual context analysis allows also the merging of automatically extracted semantic and manual generated semantic by using semantic merging techniques.

The result of this sub process is semantic that can be represented by different semantic languages like RDF(S) or OWL. This output contains extracted semantic, enrichment of extracted semantic and manually generated domain knowledge.

SSD Modeling Specific Sub Process

The sub processes SSD modeling and governance are the extension of semantic analysis process to support semi-automatic modeling of SSD modeling by using semantic analysis and visualization techniques. It supports knowledge experts during the SSD modeling by offering extracted semantic and visualization techniques. It helps them not only to rely on their own view of the domain, but also use semi-automatically extracted semantic during the SSD modeling. The following sections describe SSD modeling specific sub process.

Visual SSD Modeling

The sub process Visual SSD modeling allows knowledge experts to analyze existing services, model own services and compare them with existing services. This sub process contains five process tasks as described below:

1. Analyze existing services
2. Visualization of extracted semantic
3. Abstract modeling of new services
4. Reanalyze existing services with modeled services
5. Concrete modeling of new services

One example of price plan modeling for car rental service describes these five tasks. Knowledge experts can analyze price plans of the existing car rental services e.g. offered cars, price range etc. by using semantic analysis techniques as it is described above. After the price plan analysis of existing services, knowledge experts can visualize extracted semantic to have an overview of price plans of the existing services. Now they can model their own new car rental service on the abstract level by defining prices ranges (e.g. car rental price = 30€ - 35€ per day). Afterwards, they can reanalyze the existing car rental services

with the new-modeled service by using feedback loop between SSD modeling and visual context analysis to compare them and check the market competiveness of new-modeled service. The abstract modeling by defining price ranges helps knowledge experts to compare the modeled service with the existing services. They can iterate these three tasks until they are satisfied with the modeled price plan of new service. Finally, they can model new service with concrete data (e.g. car rental price = 32€ per day) according to a specific SSD schema and modeling language e.g. XML or USDL.

The reanalysis of modeled service with existing services may also help knowledge experts to find the most similar services to the new-modeled service. The most similar services can be used as template for the concrete modeling of new service. This approach facilitates the reuse of existing services for the SSD modeling. The knowledge experts can use existing service descriptions as templates and model their new service.

The knowledge experts from different domain e.g. legal experts or pricing models experts may have different IT-expertise, therefore user friendly interactive visualization techniques should facilitate them to perform SSD modeling tasks. In such a way, the combination of semantic analysis techniques and interactive visualization techniques supports semi-automatic SSD modeling. Knowledge experts can use semi-automatic semantic analysis techniques and interactive visualization techniques to model SSD.

The role based semantic modeling allows knowledge experts to model the modules of SSD, which are only related to their own domain. For example, legal experts want to model only the legal aspects related modules of SSD. The role based visualization techniques offers the SSD modules to knowledge experts, which are related to their domain. The role based visualization techniques reduce complexity of SSD modeling by visualizing only role's related SSD modules to knowledge experts e.g. legal experts can see just legal domain specific SSD modules.

The collaborative modeling mechanism supports knowledge experts to model different modules of service in a collaborative manner as it is proposed by Oberle et al. (Oberle, D., Bhatti, N., Brockmans, S., Niemann, M., & Janiesch, C. (2009)). This sub process offer collaboration support and allows domain experts to model the SSD modules collaboratively. The knowledge experts from different domain can model SSD modules and collaboration server synchronizes all modules and merges them together as SSD. The result of this sub process is SSD of a service, which can be represented by different SSD languages e.g. USDL or service ontology. Therefore, the output of this sub process may have different formats.

Governance

Governance is a holistic long-term management model to exercise control and mitigate risk. It establishes organizational structures, processes, policies, and metrics to ensure that the adoption, implementation, operation and evolution of the subject is in line with the organization's strategies and objectives and complies with laws, regulations, standards, and best practices(Oberle, D., Bhatti, N., Brockmans, S., Niemann, M., & Janiesch, C. (2009)).

The service governance framework (Oberle, D., Bhatti, N., Brockmans, S., Niemann, M., & Janiesch, C. (2009)) takes care of changes and maintenance of the semantic service description in a collaborative and distributed environment. The focus of sub process governance is to synchronize the feedback of the service governance framework during the modeling. The modeling of SSD has to follow the governance guidelines to assure consistency during the modeling.

The knowledge experts from different domain take part in the modeling of SSD, which can lead to inconsistency. The governance framework defines guideline and monitoring mechanisms to avoid

the inconsistency. A governance team monitors the SSD modeling activities. The governance team can accept or reject the change requests of knowledge experts. The knowledge experts have to change the SSD until governance team accepts it. Furthermore, the governance framework monitors also roles restrictions of knowledge experts during the modeling of SSD as well. For example, the legal experts are allowed to change only legal aspects. This sub process synchronizes SSD modeling activities and visualizes the feedback of governance process in the visual SSD modeling via feedback loop. The visualization of governance process feedback supports knowledge experts to check consistency of modeled service.

A CONCEPTUAL FRAMEWORK FOR THE VISUAL SEMANTIC ANALYSIS

The Figure 3 depicts a conceptual framework for the Visual Semantic Analysis (VSA). The VSA conceptual framework consists of two client applications semantic analysis client and SSD modeling client. These client applications use different platform services of service platform for the semantic analysis and SSD modeling. For example, the client applications use platform services monitoring, service discovery to collect textual descriptions, statistic and dynamic non-functional parameters of services from the semantic service descriptions and monitoring information. The communication components of the both clients facilitate the usage of platform services for the semantic analysis and SSD modeling.

The semantic analysis client collect the textual descriptions and statistic and dynamic non-functional parameters of services and use context acquisition to extract context by applying Natural Language Processing (NLP) and conceptual scaling techniques. The semantic analysis client offers different perspectives for the semantic analysis, which allow knowledge experts to analyze different context information or different parts of

Figure 3. A conceptual framework for the visual semantic analysis

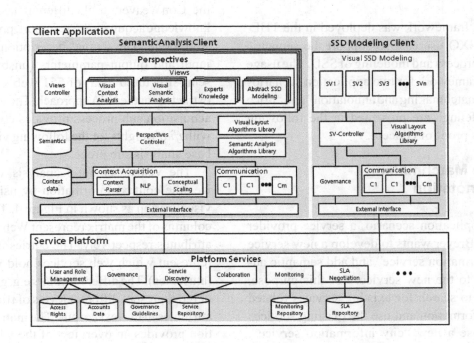

context information simultaneously. For example, knowledge experts can use two perspectives for price plans and legal aspects related context information to perform semantic analysis for both aspects simultaneously. Each perspective offers three different views visual context analysis, visual semantic analysis and experts knowledge. Each view offers different visualization techniques available in the visual layout algorithms library. The views visual context analysis and visual semantic analysis supports knowledge experts to analyze context information and semantics by using different semantic analysis algorithms available in semantic analysis algorithms library. The expert's knowledge view allows knowledge experts to model their own knowledge and semantic service description on the abstract level. The expert's knowledge can be merged to the context information and extracted semantic by using merging techniques from the semantic analysis algorithms library. After the semantic analysis, knowledge experts can save the enriched seman-

tic and extracted semantic information in repositories semantics and context data. They can export semantic analysis results to collaboration service of the platform by using the communication components.

The SSD modeling client can import the semantic analysis results and service schema from the collaboration service of the platform by using communication components. The knowledge experts can view both by using visual SSD modeling component. Knowledge experts can use different visualization techniques to visualize the semantic analysis results and service schema by using different layout algorithms from visual layout algorithms. After visual analysis, knowledge experts can perform concrete modeling of SSD according to the service schema. The semantic analysis results and visualization techniques support them to model the SSD semi-automatically. Finally, the governance component use governance service of the service platform to check the SSD of the modeled service.

APPLICATION SCENARIOS

The VSA framework was deployed in the THE-SEUS-TEXO use case to support the semantic analysis process and modeling of SSD. The usage of VSA framework for two application scenarios "service matchmaking and annotation" and "price plan modeling" are presented in the following section as proof of concept.

Service Matchmaking and Annotation

In this application scenario, a service provider Matthias Breyer wants to develop a new service "city information service" and add semantic annotations to the new service. For this purpose, he wants to search for existing services related to city information and use the existing services to compose a new "city information service". Furthermore, he wants to add semantic annotations to the new service according to extracted semantic from the existing services.

For this application scenario, the OWL-S MX v2[2] collection of web services was selected as the data source. It consists of 551 web services from 7 domains. By using visual workflow of the ConWeaver[3] tool, different tasks of visual knowledge acquisition e.g. import, pre-processing were done. The textual descriptions as well as input and output parameters (unstructured and semi-structured data) of 551 web services were extracted for the VSA approach. The visual context acquisition sub process provides context matrix with *tfidf* weights for the following visual context base analysis sub process.

The visual semantic analysis view visualizes the context information by using a matrix visualization as shown in Figure 4. The rows and columns of the matrix represent Web services and attributes respectively. The entries in the matrix represent which web services hold which terms (attributes). The different colors e.g. green, yellow or red represent different levels of tfidf-weight of attributes in the text corpus. The matrix visualization provides an overview of the whole context information, density of context matrix, and relevance of attributes in text corpus at a glance. It contains 551 Web services (rows), 1194 attributes (columns) and 5392 entries.

Then Matthias performs semantic analysis by applying FCA and sees the extracted semantics

Figure 4. Visual context analysis for the service matchmaking and annotation

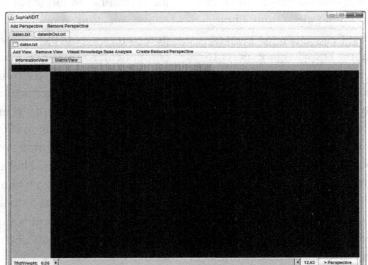

Figure 5. Visual semantic analysis for service matchmaking and annotation

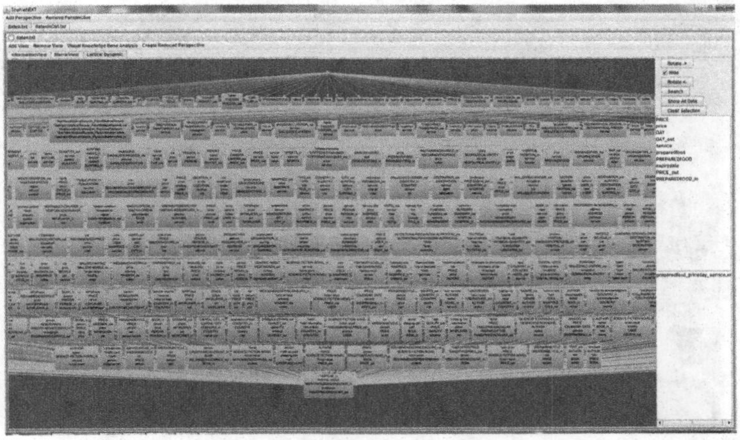

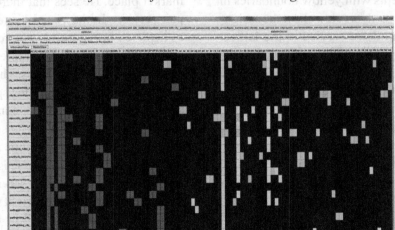

in the visual semantic analysis view as shown in Figure 5. He realizes that he has to reduce the dimensionality of the context in order to get readable extracted semantic.

To reduce the dimensionality of the context matrix, Matthias uses the semantic neighbors functionality to search for semantic neighbors with the context space "city". After finding the semantic neighbors, he creates a new perspective, which contains only semantic neighbors for the context space "city". It contains 24 services, 95 attributes and 274 entries. Additionally, he per-

forms the semantic analysis again to extract semantics from the reduced context. The reduced context and extracted semantics from the reduced context are visualized in Figure 6 and Figure 7. The yellow colored concepts in the visual semantic analysis view contain the "city" attribute and the blue colored concepts with yellow boundary contain the "city" attribute as well as the "city hotel service" instance. Now he can explore the extracted semantics to get a better understanding about them.

Figure 6. The reduced context information for service matchmaking and annotation

Figure 7. The extracted semantics from reduced context information for servcie matchmaking and annotation

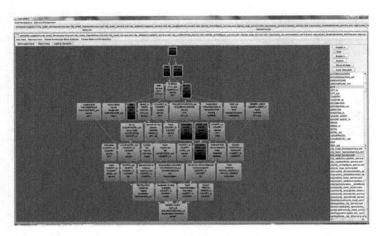

After the semantic analysis and the visualization of semantic analysis results, he wants to model his own new service "City information service". He models his own service by defining attributes from the context information as shown in

Figure 8. The modeled service is added to the context matrix with its attributes as it is depicted in Figure 9. The last row with green background represents new modeled service and the red colored entries are its attributes. After the modeling of the new service, he can reanalyze the semantics to see the assignment of his new service in the extracted semantics as shown in Figure 10. The blue colored concepts with yellow boundaries in the visual semantic analysis view show the assignment of his new modeled service in the lattice. All other services which are also assigned to the blue colored concepts with yellow boundaries are the candidates that can be used to compose the new service "city information service". The input, output and functionality of these services have to be examined in detail to check if they can really be used for the service composition.

Price Plan Analysis

In this application scenario, the service provider Franz Kriewitz is owner of a car repair shop. He wants to offer his car repair service on the TEXO service market place, which is specially designed for motor insurance companies. Franz wants to model a price plan for his car repair service and compare it with competitors before he publishes his car repair service onto the TEXO service market place.

He uses the Visual Semantic Analysis Framework "Sophie" and searches for car repair services, which are already published on the TEXO service market place. He sees that there are four car repair services in the visual context analysis view as depicted in Figure 11. The rows and columns of the matrix visualization represent services and price plan specific attributes. The entries indicate which services hold price plan specific attributes. Then he applies FCA to the context information to extract semantics. Now he sees extracted semantics in the visual semantic analysis view as presented in the Figure 12. He is interested in the "Schwarz car glass repair" service as it is shown on the bottom panel on the right side in Figure 12. The blue concepts with yellow boundaries show that this service is assigned to them. The upper

Figure 8. The service modeling for service matchmaking and annotation (I)

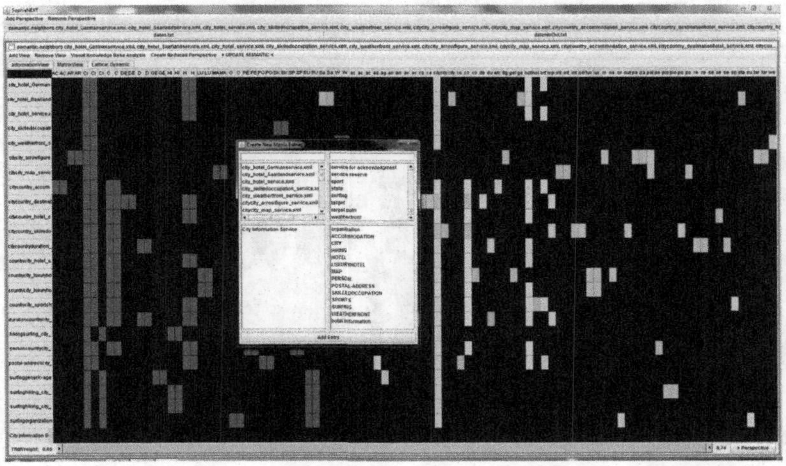

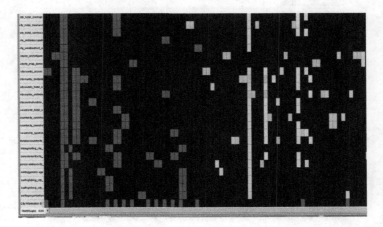

Figure 9. The service modeling for service matchmaking and annotation (II)

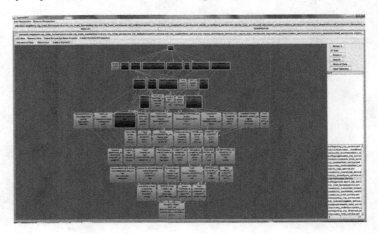

Figure 10. The reanalysis for the service matchmaking and annotation after service modeling

Figure 11. Visual context analysis for the price plan analysis

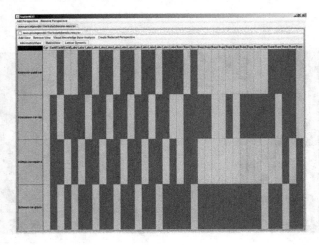

Figure 12. Visual semantic analysis for the price plan analysis

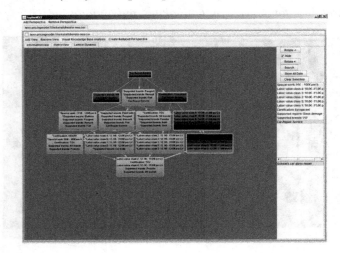

Figure 13. Knowledge expert's view to model new service for the price plan analysis

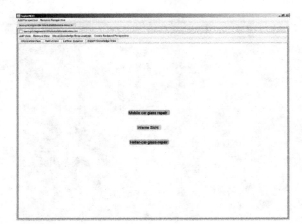

Figure 14. The Price plan modeling for the price plan analysis (I)

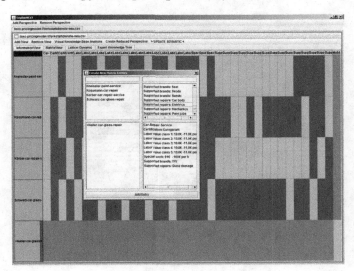

panel on the right side presents the attributes of the "Schwarz car glass repair" service e.g. the price value class 1 is between 10€ and 11€. He realized also that it does contain the attribute "Mobile car glass repair". He decides to model a new service "Heller car glass repair" with a unique offer "Mobile car glass repair" as shown in Figure 13.

Franz wants to offer the new service in the price segment as "Schwarz car glass repair" with an additional service attribute "Mobile car glass repair". He uses the experts view to add a new service and an attribute as depicted in Figure 13. Then he adds this new service to the context information as shown at the bottom of the Figure 14. Additionally, he adds also further attributes e.g. "supported brands: VW" to the new service as shown in Figure 14. The new modeled service is shown at the bottom of the Figure 15.

After the modeling of the new service, Franz performs a reanalysis and sees in the visual se-

Figure 15. The Price plan modeling for the price plan analysis (II)

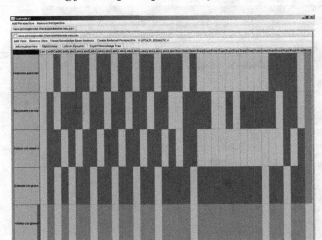

Figure 16. Reanalysis for the price plan analysis (I)

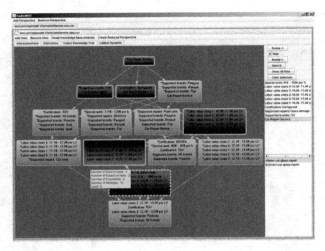

mantic analysis view that "Heller car glass repair" is assigned to concepts with blue color and yellow boundary as shown in Figure 16. He can also see that "Schwarz car glass repair" is a competitor service to his service as it is shown in the bottom panel on the right side of the Figure 16. He can also see that both services have the same attributes as it shown in the upper panel on the right side of the Figure 16. Franz can also see that his service

with the additional attribute "mobile car glass repair" does not have any competitors as it is shown upper and bottom panel on the right side of the Figure 17. Now he is satisfied with his new-modeled service.

Franz has modeled the new service on an abstract level. Now, he wants to model the service with concrete price values instead of price ranges. For this purpose, he uses the visual SSD

Figure 17. Reanalysis for the price plan analysis (II)

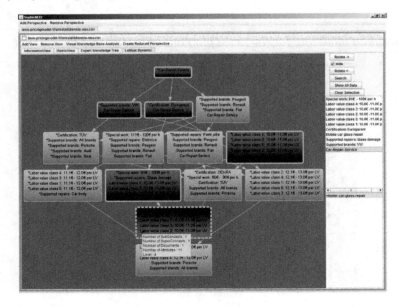

Figure 18. Concrete modeling of price plan (I)

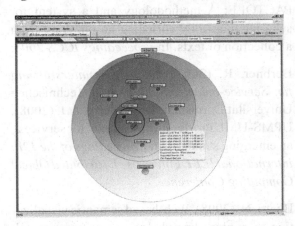

modeling view, which is developed on the base of Semantic Visualization Framework (SemaVis) (Bhatti, N. & Weber, S. H. (2009); Nazemi, K.; Breyer, M.; & Hornung, C. (2009); Nazemi, K., Breyer, M., Burkhardt, D., Stab, C., Hofmann, C.; Hornung, C. (2009)), and sees the semantic analysis information as shown in Figure 18. Now, he selects the most similar service "Schwarz car glass repair" and generates a new template for his service "Heller car glass repair" as depicted in Figure 19 and Figure 20. Now he models the new service with concrete values with the help of semantic analysis information as it is shown in Figure 19 and Figure 20.

CONCLUSION AND FUTURE WORK

The VSA approach to combine visual and semantic analysis techniques to support modeling of semantic models is introduced. A generic process model for VSA is also presented. To evaluate the VSA approach, the VSA framework was applied to two THESEUS-TEXO use cases.

The future work will focus on the analysis of further aspects of SSD modeling e.g. legal aspects and Service Level Agreements (SLA) and how VSA can support the modeling of these aspects. The data contained in the SSDs will be analyzed with semantic analysis techniques to analyze conceptual facts, which will help domain experts to identify similar services. This approach will help domain experts to use existing SSD of services as templates to model new services.

Furthermore, it will also be analyzed, how the existing semantic knowledge e.g. personal domain knowledge of domain experts can be used for the analysis of SSDs. This approach will allow domain experts to perform personalized analysis of SSDs. It can be very helpful for domain experts during the modeling of SSDs. It will also help them during the composition of web services and composition of SSDs

Figure 19. Concerate modeling of price plan (II)

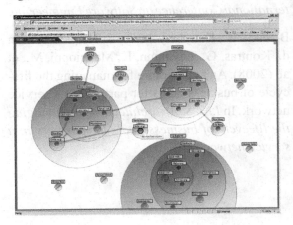

Figure 20. Concerate modeling of price plan (III)

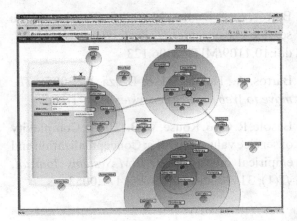

ACKNOWLEDGMENT

The project was funded by means of the German Federal Ministry of Economy and Technology under the promotional reference "01MQ07012". The authors take the responsibility for the contents.

REFERENCES

Akkermans, H., Baida, Z., Gordijn, J., Pena, N., Altuna, A., & Laresgoiti, I. (2004). Using ontologies to bundle real world services. *IEEE Intelligent Systems, 19*, 57–66. doi:10.1109/MIS.2004.35

Alter, S. (2008). Service system fundamentals: Work system, value chain, and life cycle. *IBM Systems Journal, 47*, 71–85. doi:10.1147/sj.471.0071

Ankolekar, A., Hobbs, J. R., Lassila, O., Martin, D. L., McIlraith, S. A., Narayanan, S., et al. (2001). DAML-S: semantic markup for Web services. *In proceedings of the first Semantic Web Working Symposium (SWWS)*, (p. 4). Stanford University.

Baida, Z., Gordijn, J. & Akkermans, H. (2001). *Service ontology*. OBELIX Deliverable 6.1 / Free University Amsterdam–Forschungsbericht.

Barrett, M., Davidson, E., Middleton, C., & DeGross, J. I. (2008). *Information Technology in the service economy: Challenges and possibilities for the 21st Century*. Springer Publishing Company. doi:10.1007/978-0-387-09768-8

Barros, A., & Dumas, M. (2006). The rise of Web service ecosystems. *IT Professional, 8*, 31–37. doi:10.1109/MITP.2006.123

Barros, A., Dumas, M. & Bruza, P. (2005). *The move to Web service ecosystems*. BPTrends.

Basole, R. C., & Rouse, W. B. (2008). Complexity of service value networks: Conceptualization and empirical investigation. *IBM Systems Journal, 47*(1), 31–37. doi:10.1147/sj.471.0053

Bendaoud, R., Toussaint, Y., & Napoli, A. (2008). PACTOLE: A methodology and a system for semi-automatically enriching an ontology from a collection of texts. In *proceedings ICCS 2008*.

Berbner, R. (2007). *Dienstgüteunterstützung für Service-orientierte Workows*, Technischen Universität Darmstadt, Diss., Berre, A.J. (2008). UPMS-UML Pro-le and metamodel for services–an emerging standard. In *Proceedings of the 12th international IEEE Enterprise Distributed Object Computing Conference*.

Bhatti, N. (2008). Web-based semantic visualization to explore knowledge spaces-an approach for learning by exploring. In J. Luca & Weippl, E.R. (Eds.), *Association for the Advancement of Computing in Education (AACE): Proceedings of ED-Media 2008 World Conference on Educational Multimedia, Hypermedia & Telecommunications*, (pp. 312-317).

Bhatti, N., & Weber, S. H. (2009). Semantic visualization to support knowledge discovery in multi-relational service communities. In Cruz-Cunha, M. M., de Oliveira, E. F., Tavares, A. J. V., & Ferreira, L. G. (Eds.), *Handbook of research on social dimensions of semantic technologies and Web services*. Hershey, PA: IGI Global. doi:10.4018/9781605666501.ch014

Biggerstaff, T., Mitbander, B., & Webster, D. (1993). The concept assignment problem in program understanding. In *Proceedings of the 15th International Conference on Software Engineering*.

Bitsaki, M., Danylevych, O., & Heuvel, W. van d., Koutras, G., Leymann, F., Mancioppi, M., et al. (2008). An architecture for managing the lifecycle of business goals for partners in a service network. In *LNCS: An architecture for managing the lifecycle of business goals for partners in a service network*.

Brambilla, M., Celino, I., Ceri, S., Cerizza, D., Valle, E. V., & Facca, F. M. (2006). A software engineering approach to design and development of semantic Web service applications. In the *proceedings of the 5th International Semantic Web Conference, ISWC 2006*, Athens, Georgia.

Card, S., Mackinlay, J. D., & Shneiderman, B. (1999). *Readings in information visualization: Using vision to think. San Fransisco.* Morgan Kaufmann Publishers, Inc.

Cardoso, J., Winkler, M., & Voigt, K. (2009). A service description language for the internet of services. In *Proceedings first international symposium on services science (ISSS'09).* Logos, Berlin

Christensen, E., Curbera, F., Meredith, G., & Weerawarana, S. (2001). *Web Services Description Language (WSDL)*. Retrieved October 10, 2009, from http://www.w3.org/TR/wsdl

Cimiano, P., Hotho, A., Stumme, G., & Tane, J. (2004). *Conceptual knowledge processing with formal concept analysis and ontologies.* Berlin/Heidelberg: Springer. Retrieved from http://www.springerlink.com/content/ 4r62l72l3baayxdu/?p =d23d0d6442a244d8a6872c1f3813e8b2&pi=0.

Cimiano, P., Hothos, A., & Staab, S. (2005). Learning concept hierarchies from text corpora using formal concept analysis. *Journal of Artificial Intelligence Research, 24,* 305–339.

Cimiano, P., Hothos, A., Stumme, G., & Tane, J. (2009). *Conceptual knowledge processing with formal concept analysis and ontologies.* Retrieved October 10, 2009, from http://www.aifb.uni-karlsruhe.de/WBS/pci/icfca04.pdf

Connolly, D., Harmelen, F., Horrocks, I., McGuiness, D., Patel-Schneider, P. F., & Stein, L. A. (2001). *Annotated DAML+OIL ontology markup.* Retrieved October 10, 2009, from http://www.w3.org/TR/daml+oil-walkthru/#1

De Kinderen, S., & Gordijn, J. (2008a). e3Service-a model-based approach for generating needs-driven e-service bundles in a networked enterprise. In: *Proceedings of 16th European Conference on Information Systems.*

De Kinderen, S., & Gordijn, J. (2008b). e3Service-an ontological approach for deriving multi-supplier IT-service bundles from consumer needs. In: *Proceedings of the 41st Annual Hawaii International Conference on System Sciences.*

Dinger, U., Oberhauser, R., & Reichel, C. (2006). SWS-ASE: Leveraging Web service-based software engineering. In the *proceedings of the IEEE International Conference on Software Engineering Advances, ICSEA 06,* Papeete, Tahiti, French Polynesia.

(2002). *DINPAS 1018.* Berlin: Grundstruktur für die Beschreibung von Dienstleistungen in der Ausschreibungsphase.

Domik, G. (2010). *Computer-generated visualization, the need for visualization.* Universität Paderborn. Retrieved April 2010, from http://cose.math.bas.bg/SciVisualization/compGenVis/download/chapter1.pdf

Domingue, J., & Zaremba, M. (2007). *Reference ontology for semantic service oriented architectures.* OASIS working draft 0.1. Retrieved April, 2010, from http://www.oasis-open.org

Ducrou, J. (2007). *Design for conceptual knowledge processing: Case studies in applied formal concept analysis.* Unpublished doctoral dissertation, University of Wollongong.

Emmrich, A. (2005). *Ein Beitrag zur systematischen Entwicklung produktorientierter Dienstleistungen.* Paderborn: University of Paderborn.

Fellbaum, C. (1998). *WordNet–an electronic lexical database.* Cambridge, MA/London: MIT Press.

Ferrario, R., Guarino, N. (2008): *Towards an ontological foundation for services science*.

Foley, J. D., & Ribarsky, W. (1994). Next-generation data visualization tools. In: *Scientific visualization: Advances and challenges*.

Gangemi, A., Guarino, N., Masolo, C., Oltramari, A., & Schneider, L. (2002). Sweetening ontologies with DOLCE. In: *Proceedings of the EKAW*.

Ganter, B., Stumme, G., & Wille, R. (2005). Formal concept analysis–foundations and applications. In *Lecture Notes in Computer Science, Lecture Notes in Artificial Intelligence, 3626*. Heidelberg: Springer Verlag.

Ganter, B., & Wille, R. (1999). *Formal concept analysis, mathematical foundations*. Berlin: Springer Verlag.

Godehardt, E. (2009). *Kontextualisierte Visualisierung am Wissenintensiven Arbeitsplatz*. Unpublished doctoral dissertation, Technische Universität Darmstadt.

Greengrass, E. (2000). *Information retrieval: A survey*. Retrieved October 10, 2009, from http://clgiles.ist.psu.edu/IST441/materials/texts/IR.report.120600.book.pdf

Haav, H. M. (2004). A semi-automatic method to ontology design by using FCA. In: *proceedings of the International Workshop on Concept Lattices and their Applications (CLAS)*, (p. 23-24).

Hamdy, M., Koenig-Ries, B., & Kuester, U. (2007). Non-functional parameters as first class citizens in service description and matchmaking-an integrated approach. In *Proceeding International Conference on Service Oriented Computing*.

Hamp, B., & Feldweg, H. (1997). Germanet–a lexical-semantic net for German. In *proceedings of the ACL Workshop on Automatic Information Extraction and Building of Lexical Semantic Resources for NLP Applications*, Madrid.

Harding, C. (2010). *Service-oriented architecture ontology*. The open group draft 2.0. Retrieved April, 2010, from http://www.opengroup.org/projects/soa-ontology/

Harris, Z. (1968). *Mathematical structures of language*. Wiley.

Havre, S., Hetzler, B., & Nowell, L. (2000). Visualizing theme changes over time. In *IEEE Symposium on Information Visualization*.

Heck, E., & Vervest, P. (2007). Smart business networks: How the network wins. *Communications of the ACM, 6*, 28–37. doi:10.1145/1247001.1247002

Helm, R., & Maarek, Y. (1991). Integrating information retrieval and domain specific approaches for browsing and retrieval in object-oriented class libraries. In *proceedings of Object-oriented Programming Systems, Languages, and Applications*.

Hess, A., Johnston, E., & Kushmerick, N. (2004). A tool for semi-automatically annotating semantic Web Services. In *Proceeding third International Semantic Web Conference*.

Hess, A., & Kushmerick, N. (2003). Learning to attach semantic metadata to Web Services. In: *Proceedings Second International Semantic Web Conference*.

Hess, A., & Kushmerick, N. (2004). Machine learning for annotating semantic Web Services. In *AAAI Spring Symposium on Semantic Web Services*.

Heuser, L., Alsdorf, C., & Woods, D. (2008). *Proceedings of the International Research Forum 2007*. Evolved Technologists Press.

Hotho, A., Nürnberger, A., & Paaß, G. (2005). A brief survey of text mining. *GLDV Journal for Computational Linguistics and Language Technology, 20*(1), 19–62.

Jensen, J. B., & Kletzer, L. G. (2005). *Understanding the scope and impact of services outsourcing*. Social Science Research Network.

Jia, H., Newman, J., & Tianfield, H. (2008). A new formal concept analysis-based learning approach to ontology building. In *Metadata and semantics*. US: Springer.

Kagermann, H., & Österle, H. (2006). *Wie CEOs Unternehmen transformieren*. Frankfurter Allgemeine Buch.

Katifori, A., Halatsis, C., Lepouras, G., Vassilakis, E., & Giannopoulou, E. (2007). Ontology visualization methods-a survey. In *ACM Computational survey*. New York: ACM.

Keim, D., Andrienko, G., Fekete, J. D., Görg, C., Kohlhammer, J., & Melancon, G. (2008). Visual analytics: Definition, process, and challenges. In *Journal Information Visualization*. Springer Verlag. doi:10.1007/978-3-540-70956-5_7

Maarek, Y., Berry, D., & Kaiser, G. (1991). An information retrieval approach for automatically constructing software libraries. *IEEE Transactions on Software Engineering, 17*(8), 800–813. doi:10.1109/32.83915

Maedche, A. (2002). *Ontology learning for the Semantic Web*. Boston: Kluwer Academic Publishers.

Maedche, A., & Staab, S. (2001). Ontology learning for the Semantic Web. *IEEE Intelligent Systems, 16*(2), 72–79. doi:10.1109/5254.920602

May, T., & Kohlhammer, J. (2008). Towards closing the analysis gap: Visual generation of decision supporting schemes from raw data. *Computer Graphics Forum, 27*, 911–918. doi:10.1111/j.1467-8659.2008.01224.x

McGuinness, D., & van Harmelen, F. (2004). *OWL web ontology language overview*. W3C recommendation. Retrieved February 10, 2004, from http://www.w3.org/TR/owl-features/

McIlraith, S., Son, T. C., & Zeng, H. (2001). Semantic Web services. *IEEE Intell. Syst. Special Issue Semantic Web, 16*(2), 46–53.

Mili, A., Mili, R., & Mittermeir, R. (1998). A survey of software reuse libraries. *Annals of Software Engineering, 5*, 349–414. doi:10.1023/A:1018964121953

Mili, H., Ah-Ki, E., Godin, R., & Mcheick, H. (1997). Another nail to the coffin of faceted controlled-vocabulary component classification and retrieval. In *SIGSOFT Software Engineering Notes, 22*, 89 – 98.

Nadhan, E. G. (2004). Service-oriented architecture: Implementation challenges. In *Microsoft Architect Journal, 2*.

Nazemi, K., Breyer, M., Burkhardt, D., Stab, C., Hofmann, C. & Hornung, C. (2009). *D.CTC.5.7.1: Design und Conceptualization Semantic Visualization*.

Nazemi, K., Breyer, M., & Hornung, C. (2009). SeMap: A concept for the visualization of semantics as maps. In *HCI International 2009. Proceedings and Posters (DVD-ROM), with 10 further associated conferences*. Berlin, Heidelberg, New York: Springer.

Oberle, D., Bhatti, N., Brockmans, S., Niemann, M., & Janiesch, C. (2009). Countering service information challenges in the Internet of Services. In *Journal Business & Information Systems Engineering – Special issue Internet of Services*.

Oberle, D., Lamparter, S., Grimm, S., Vrandecic, D., Staab, S., & Gangemi, A. (2006). *Towards ontologies for formalizing modularization and communication in large software systems*. Applied Ontology.

OSullivan, J. (2006). *Towards a precise understanding of service properties*. Queensland University of Technology.

Pan, T., & Fang, K. (2009). Ontology-based formal concept analysis in radiology report impact by the adoption of PACS. In *proceedings of ICFCA 2009*.

Pandit, B., Popescu, V., & Smith, V. (2010). *SML service modeling language*. Retrieved April, 2010, from http://www.w3.org/TR/sml/. Accessed 2009-06-15

Papazoglou, M. P. (2003). Service-oriented computing: Concepts, characteristics and directions. In *proceedings of the Web Information Systems Engineering (WISE)*.

Patil, A., Oundhakar, S., Sheth, A., & Verma, K. (2004). METEOR-S Web service annotation framework. In *Proceedings of the 13th International World Wide Web Conference (WWW 04)*.

Perez, A.G.D. & Mancho, D.M. (2003). *A survey of ontology learning methods and techniques*. OntoWeb Delieverable 1.5.

Petrie, C., Margaria, T., Lausen, H., & Zaremba, M. (2008). *Semantic Web Services challenge: Results from the first year*. Springer Publishing Company.

Preist, C. (2004). A conceputal architecture for semantic web services. In *Proceedings Third International Semantic Web Conference*.

Priss, U. (2006). Formal concept analysis in Information Science. In B. Cronin (Ed.), *Annual Review of Information Science and Technology*, 521-543.

Priss, U. (2009). Formal concept analysis software. Retrieved October 10, 2009, from http://www.upriss.org.uk/fca/fcasoftware.html

Roman, D., de Bruijn, J., Mocan, A., Lausen, H., Domingue, J., Bussler, C., et al. (2006). WWW: WSMO, WSML, and WSMX in a nutshell. In *Proceedings of the XIX. International conference of RESER*.

Rust, R. T., & Kannan, P. K. (2003). E-service a new paradigm for business in the electronic environment. *Communications of the ACM, 46*(6), 36–42. doi:10.1145/777313.777336

Sabou, M. (2004). From software APIs to Web service ontologies: A semi-automatic extraction method. In the *proceedings of the Third International SemanticWeb Conference, ISWC 04*, Hiroshima, Japan.

Sabou, M. (2005). Visual support for ontology learning: An experience report. In the *proceedings of the Ninth International Conference on Information Visualization*.

Sabou, M. (2006). Building Web Service ontologies. Unpublished doctoral dissertation, Dutch Graduate School for Information and Knowledge Systems.

Sabou, M., & Pan, J. (2007). Towards semantically enhanced Web service repositories. In *Web Semantics*. Sci. Services Agents World Wide Web.

Sabou, M., Wroe, C., Goble, C., & Mishne, G. (2005). Learning domain ontologies for Web service descriptions: An experiment in bioinformatics. In the *proceedings of the 14th International World Wide Web Conference*, Chiba, Japan.

Sabou, M., Wroe, C., Goble, C., & Stuckenschmidt, H. (2005). Learning domain ontologies for Semantic Web service descriptions. *Journal of Web Semantics, 3*(4). doi:10.1016/j.websem.2005.09.008

Speiser, S., Blau, B., Lamparter, S., & Tai, S. (2008). Formation of service value networks for decentralized service provisioning. In *proceedings of the 6th International Conference on Service Oriented Computing*.

Tetlow, P., Pan, J. Z., Oberle, D., Wallace, E., Uschold, M., & Kendall, E. (2006). *Ontology driven architectures and potential uses of the Semantic Web in systems and software engineering.* Retrieved August 2009, from http://www.w3.org/2001/sw/BestPractices/SE/ODA/

van Wijk, J. J. (2005). The value of visualization. In *IEEE Visualization, 11.*

Vervest, P. H. M. (2005). *Smart business networks.* Heidelberg, Berlin: Springer. doi:10.1007/b137960

Wei, D., & Wang, T. Wang, J. & Chen, Y. (2008). Extracting semantic constraint from description text for semantic Web services discovery. In *Proceedings 7th International Semantic Web Conference, ISWC 2008.* Karlsruhe, Germany.

Wermter, S., & Hung, C. (2002). Self-organizing classification on the Reuters news corpus. In *Proceedings of the 19th International Conference on Computational Linguistics, 1.* ACM.

Wersig, G. (1985). *Thesaurus-Leitfaden.* München.

Wille, R. (1982). Restructuring lattice theory: An approach based on hierarchies of concepts. In *Ordered sets. Boston.* Dordrecht: Reidel.

Wroe, C., Goble, C., Greenwood, M., Lord, P., Miles, S., & Papay, J. (2004). Automating experiments using semantic data on a bioinformatics grid. *IEEE Intelligent Systems, 19*(1), 48–55. doi:10.1109/MIS.2004.1265885

Zhou, L. (2007). Ontology learning: State of the art and open issues. In *Springer Science.* Business Media.

Zhou, L., Booker, Q., & Zhang, D. (2002). ROD–towards rapid ontology development for underdeveloped domains. *In proceedings 35th Hawaii International Conference on System Sciences,* Hawaii, USA.

ENDNOTES

[1] http://www.theseus-programm.de/en-us/theseus-application-scenarios/texo/default.aspx

[2] http://www-ags.dfki.uni-sb.de/~klusch/owls-mx/

[3] http://www.conweaver.de

Chapter 8
Description, Classification and Discovery Approaches for Software Components:
A Comparative Study

Sofien Khemakhem
CNRS, LAAS, & Université de Toulouse, France; University of Sfax, Tunisia

Khalil Drira
CNRS, LAAS, & Université de Toulouse, France

Mohamed Jmaiel
University of Sfax, Tunisia

ABSTRACT

The successfulness of the Component-Based Development (CBD) process relies on several factors, including: the structuration of the component repositories, and the comparison procedures for interface exploring while comparing the expected and the provided services. Both functional and non-functional features should be considered. This chapter presents three key factors to guarantee the successfulness of the repository reuse: the description, the classification and the discovery of components. Through this study, first, the type of information is specified. Next, the style of adopted search is indicated, and then the type of comparison, and the level of specification. Then, the chapter analyzes the importance of non-functional constraints in the description of the components, and studies the advantages and the disadvantages of existing techniques.

DOI: 10.4018/978-1-60960-215-4.ch008

INTRODUCTION

Component-based and service-oriented software architectures are likely to become widely used technologies in the future distributed system development. Component reuse is a crucial requirement for the development process of component-based and service-oriented software.

Components are developed as important and big autonomous and customizable software units. The successfulness of the reuse is important and depends on the efficiency of the search procedure. The search step is essential in the development process, since the developer is generally faced with a significant number of various component types. The search step may fail if the explored component repositories are not appropriately structured or if the required and the provided services are not correctly compared. The use of a component repository, having a well-defined structure, is crucial for the efficiency of the CBD approach. This allows the developer to easily seek and select the component which perfectly meets his/her needs.

Through this study, we analyze the key factors that are necessary for obtaining a well-organized software component repository and software components having a pertinent description for the search procedures (see Figure 1). These factors act not only on the precision of the specified request but also on the component resulting from the search process.

For component description, two generation approaches of description are distinguished:

Manual generation (Erdur & Dikenelli, 2002) and automatic generation. The automatic generation is relying on different methods such as introspection (Sessions, 1998), (ONeil & Schildt, 1998), trace assertion (Whaley et al., 2002) and invariant detection (Perkins & Ernst, 2004).

The second part identifies and describes five categories of methods for representing component classification. The first is the adhoc method, called also behavioral method (Podgurski & Pierce,

Figure 1.

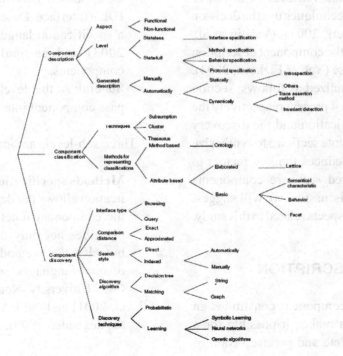

1992), (Atkinson & Duke, 1995). The second is based on the semantic characteristics of the component (Penix & Alexander, 1999). The third uses the facet classification (Damiani et al., 1999), (Ostertag et al., 1992), (Vitharana et al., 2003), (Ferreira & Lucena, 2001). The fourth method is based on the lattice (Fischer, 2000). Finally, the fifth method applies the notion of ontology (Erdur & Dikenelli, 2002), (Meling et al., 2000) to describe and classify components. Different techniques are used to organize components in repository: the cluster technique (Nakkrasae et al., 2004), the thesaurus technique (Liao et al., 1997) and the subsumption technique (Napoli, 1992).

The third part addresses the component discovery techniques related to classification methods. A successful adequation between the description and the classification methods should provide a powerful discovery service. This allows the developer to easily discover the appropriate component that meets his/her needs. The most popular discovery techniques are based on: genetic algorithms (Xie et al., 2004), neural networks (Nakkrasae et al., 2004), symbolic learning (Utgoff, 1989) and probabilistic information retrieval (Yunwen & Fischer, 2001). These techniques use the decision tree algorithm (Ruggieri, 2004), (Vasiliu et al., 2004) or unification of the component description in the comparison phase (Yao & Etzkorn, 2004).

This chapter is organized as follows: section 2, section 3 and section 4 present respectively the description, the classification and the discovery techniques. We will devote section 5 to synthesize our study. Section 6 deduces the key factors to obtain a well-structured software components repository through a discussion, we will suggest some openings and prospects related to this study.

COMPONENT DESCRIPTION

The description of a component constitutes an effective means which makes it possible for a user to obtain a complete and precise vision of the component. The component specification aims to provide a basis for the development, management and use of components. It has four aspects. First, there is *level description* of the component, which can be stateful or stateless next aspect of component specification concerns the *description generation*, including automatic generation and manually generation. The third aspect of component specification is *description aspects*. It describes the characterization of the component in terms of their non-functional properties or quality attributes and their functional properties. The *composability* property of the service model class can have values denoting possible ways for service composition.

Description Levels and Description Aspects

In the description levels we distinguishes two classes:

1. Stateless: includes the service signature, its attributes, component identification and the exceptions. Different approaches propose IDL (Interface Description Language) as a specification language (Fetike and Loos 2003) and particularly address COTS components.
2. Stateful: At this level, descriptions encompass component internal characteristics.

Three sub-levels are identified:

•   **Methods specification:** The method specification allows the developer to understand the component functionalities in detail. It describes not only the methods signature but also the method body. The majority of used languages are formal such as the Oslo University Notation (OUN) (Ryl et al. 2001) and the LARCH notation (Penix & Alexander, 1999).

- **Component behavior specification:** it is usually defined in terms of pre-condition, post-condition of the operations, and invariants. This level of specification was described by several languages such as XML, Eiffel style in (Cicalese & Rotenstreich, 1999), LARCH in (Zaremski & Wing, 1995) and Linear Temporal Logic (LTL) in (Nakajima & Tamai, 2001).

- **Protocol specification:** The protocol describes the component states when we execute component methods. Finite State Machines (Yellin & Strom, 1997), Petri Net (Bastide et al., 1999) and π-calculus (Canal et al. 2000) are the most often used. This level of specification is applied, not only for classification, but also for checking, substitution, composition of components (Faras & Y.Guhneuc, 2003) and analysis of compatibility between protocols (Yellin & Strom, 1997).

In the specification of a software component, two different aspects are considered:

1. **Functional aspect:** It identifies the functionalities of the component that should provide. The methods of a component are an example of this type of information. The approach in (Khemakhem et al., 2002) specifies the static part of the functional aspect through the service interface and the dynamic part through the invocation interface.

2. **Non-functional aspect:** It specifies the component properties. They include properties of safety, and fault tolerance as well as quality of service. The approach presented in (Sun, 2003) classifies the non-functional information into two categories:

Dynamic constraints and static constraints. This distinction is related to the degree of constraint change at the run-time in different operating system and application server.

Generation Techniques for Component Description

Recent works propose tools which automatically generate specifications based on program runs (Whaley et al. 2002), (Ammons et al. 2002). These tools allow programmers to benefit from formal specifications with much less effort. Other works specify the component description manually. These approaches are hard to apply if there are a large number of components in the repository.

The component can be specified at design-time by developers via interfaces. Such specifications may also be generated for already implemented components. The IDL specification for object and WSDL for Web services are two examples of description which may be generated after component implementation.

Several works specify the component description manually via an interface. This description is stored as elements of databases (Braga et al., 2001), as an XML file, as ontologies (Paez & Straeten, 2002) or as elements of knowledge base.

In (Erdur & Dikenelli, 2002), components are specified in XML and descriptions are published by local or remote repositories. Domain ontologies are used for reusable component retrieval and OQL (Object Query Language) queries are used for discovering the appropriate component.

A component specification can be also generated automatically against its implementation either dynamically, by running the component, or statically by examining the program source. Dynamic approaches are simpler to implement and are rarely blocked by inadequacies of the analysis, but they slow down the program and check only finitely many runs (Ernst, 2000).

Statically Generated Description

There are some tools available in literature and I want to explain some of them (Henninger, 1997) presents a re-engineering tool, called PEEL (Parse and Extract Emacs Lisp), that translates Emacs

Lisp files into individual, reusable, components in a frame-based knowledge representation language named Kandor (Devanbu et al., 1991). Kandor representations can be viewed as a set of attribute/value slots which contain information about a given component.

In (Strunk et al., 2005), the specification extraction is made from SPARK annotations (Barnes, 2003) to a PVS specification (Rust 1998). A function is extracted from each subprogram in SPARK ADA. Type restrictions over input types are extracted from precondition annotations, and PVS function bodies are extracted from postcondition annotations. SPARK is based on a subset of Ada, and adds information-flow analysis. SPARK checks simple dependencies within procedures. PVS specifications are grouped in "theories". These are namespaces which contain type definitions, value definitions (which include values of higher logical types, and which can use an axiomatic or an applicative style), and theorems which are expected to be provable from the axioms.

Johannes and Amer (Henkel & Diwan, 2003) develop a tool which discovers algebraic specifications from Java classes. Algebraic specifications can describe what Java classes implement without revealing implementation details. In this approach they start by extracting the classes signatures automatically using the *Java reflection API*. They use the signatures to automatically generate a large number of terms, using heuristics to guide term generation. Each term corresponds to a legal sequence of method invocations on an instance of the class. The terms are then evaluated and compared with their outcomes. These comparisons yield equations between terms. Finally, equations are generalized to axioms and term rewriting is used to eliminate redundant axioms.

The work of (Corbett et al., 2000) proposes an integrated collection and transformation components, called Bandera which can extract the Java code source into finite-state models. Each state represents an abstraction of the state of the program's and each transition represents the execution of one or more statements transforming this state.

The paper (Evans et al., 1994) describes LCLint, a tool that accepts programs as input (written in ANSI C) and various levels of formal specification. It is intended to be used in developing new code and in helping to understand, to document, and to re-engineer legacy code.

Inscape (Perry 1989) uses a specification language that can specify pre-conditions and post-conditions of a procedure, as well as obligations on the caller following return from the call (such as closing a returned file).

Dynamically Generated Descriptions

Three generation methods are distinguished: the trace assertion method, the invariant detection method and the introspection.

Trace Assertion Method Detection Techniques
The trace assertion method is initially defined by D.L. Parnas (Bartussek & Parnas, 1978). It is a formal state machine-based method for specifying module interfaces. It considers a module as a black-box, identifying all module access programs, and describing their externally visible effects (Janicki & Sekerinski, 2001).

Traces describe the visible behavior of objects. A trace contains all events affecting the object. It is described as a sequence of events. The trace assertion method is based on the following postulates (Janicki & Sekerinski, 2001):

- Information hiding (black box) is fundamental for any specification.
- Sequences are natural and powerful tools for specifying abstract objects.
- Explicit equations are preferable over implicit equations. Implicit equations might provide shorter and more abstract specification, but are much less readable and more difficult to derive than the explicit ones.

- -State machines are powerful formal tools for specifying systems. For many applications they are easier to use than process algebras, and logic-based techniques.

Whaley et al (Whaley et al., 2002) employs dynamic techniques to discover the component interfaces. It proposes using multiple FSM submodels to model the class interface. Each submodel contains a subset of methods. A state-modifying method is represented as state in the FSM, and allowable pairs of consecutive methods are represented as transitions of the FSMs. In addition, state-preserving methods are constrained to execute only under certain states.

The work of (Stotts & Purtilo, 1994) suggests another technique called IDTS (Interactive Derivation of Trace Specs) (Parnas & Wang, 1989), for deriving Parnas' trace specifications from existing code modules. The algebraic specification is also used to automatically generate a specification from modules. It can be seen as a complementary approach for the trace assertion method. The main difference between the two techniques is the use of implicit equations in algebraic specifications, and explicit equations only in trace assertions.

Invariant Detection

Dynamic invariant detection methods discover specifications by learning general properties of a program execution from a set of program runs.

Invariants provide valuable documentation of a program's operation and data structures which help developers to discover the appropriate component in a given repository.

The approach presented in (Ernst, 2000) describes a tool which detects dynamic invariants by starting with a specific space of possible program invariants. It executes the program on a large set of test inputs, and infers likely invariants by ruling out those which are not violated during any of the program runs. Unlike static specification, this approach has the advantage of being automatic

and pervasive, but it is limited by the fixed set of invariants considered as hypothesis.

The paper of (Hangal & Lam, 2002) introduces DIDUCE, a tool which helps developers to specify the behavior of programs by observing its executions. DIDUCE dynamically formulates the developer's invariants hypothesis. It supposes the strictest invariants at the beginning, and gradually relaxes the hypothesis when violations are detected in order to allow new behavior.

Considerable research has addressed static checking of formal specifications (Naumovich et al., 1997), (Leino & Nelson, 1998). This work could be used to verify likely invariants discovered dynamically. For example Jeffords and Heitmeyer (Jeffords & Heitmeyer, 1998) generate state invariants from requirement specifications, by finding a fixed point of equations specifying events causing mode transitions. Compared to code analyzing, this approach permits operation at a high level of abstraction and detection of errors early in the software life cycle.

Introspection

Introspection is the ability of a program to look inside itself and return information for its management.

Introspection is provided for Java programs. It describes the capacity of Java components to provide information about their own interfaces.

Introspection is implemented for Java components. Introspection determines the properties, the events, and the methods exported by a component. The introspection mechanism is implemented by the java.beans.Introspector class; it relies on both the java.lang.reflect reflection mechanism and a number of JavaBeans naming conventions. Introspector can determine the list of properties supported by a component, for example, if a component has a "getColor" method and a "setColor" method, the environment can assume you have a property named "Color" and take action appropriately. Bean developers can also override introspection and explicitly tell the development environment which properties are available.

The introspection mechanism does not rely on the reflection capabilities of Java alone, however any bean can define an auxiliary BeanInfo class that provides additional information about the component and its properties, its events, and its methods. The Introspector automatically attempts to locate and load the Bean-Info class of a Bean. The introspection mechanism is used for many component models and in many approaches. For example all JViews components advertise their aspects using a set of AspectInfo class specializations, similar to BeanInfo introspection classes and COM type libraries. The work presented in (Seacord et al., 1998) describes a search engine for the retrieval of reusable code components. The introspection is used by Agora system and (Varadarajan et al., 2002) respectively for registering code components, through its interface and for discovering the syntactic interface of a component at run-time.

COMPONENT CLASSIFICATION IN REPOSITORY

During the development process, the developer faces handling a significant number of component types. The use of a component repository, having a clear structure, is crucial for the effectiveness of the CBD approach. This allows the developer to easily search and select the component which perfectly meets his/her needs. Several approaches tried to improve software components classification by developing methods to represent the classification of components based on their description.

In existing work, two types of classification are distinguished: The attribute-based classification and the method-based classification.

Attribute-Based Classification

This classification is based on components attributes. It has two forms: an elaborated form, which uses the components attributes to make a relation between components, and a basic form, which uses the attribute types to organize the repository.

The Basic Attribute-Based Classification

The basic attribute-based classification uses the component attributes to classify components. In the basic representation we distinguish three methods: The semantical characteristic-based method, the behavior-based method and the facet-based method.

The Semantical Characteristic-Based Method
The semantic description is trying to use formal methods to model, or, at least, use natural language to describe, the behaviors and features of the elements the semantic description of the components is essential. The components cannot be looked up by identifiers or simple properties. A rich and semantic description is necessary to provide a powerful query mechanism. In literature component semantic characteristic is represented by a pair (attribute, value). The identification of these characteristics and the classification procedure are fixed and verified by an expert of the domain. The similarity between two components is measured based on the number of common characteristics. The search process is based on a syntactic comparison of the set of characteristics.

In (Penix & Alexander, 1999) the retrieval is achieved using feature-based classification scheme. When applying feature-based classification by hand, repository components are assigned a set of features by a domain expert. To retrieve a set of potentially useful components, the designer classifies the problem requirements into sets of features and the corresponding class of components is retrieved from repositories. Queries can be generalized by relaxing how the feature sets are compared.

The Behavior-Based Method

This classification method is based on the exploitation of results provided by the execution of the component. These results are collections of answers which represent the dynamic behavior of the component. A relation of a behavioral nature must be used to classify software components.

In (Pozewaunig & Mittermeir, 2000) this technique is applied to functions. To facilitate the search process, the repository is divided into segments. Each segment contains all the functions having the same types of input and output parameters. For example, a segment contains all the functions having an input and output parameter of type integer. The developer request is presented in the form of a program which calls systematically each function of the concerned segment and collects the output of each function to compare it with the required value. Only the functions which check the value indicated in the request are provided.

In (Podgurski & Pierce, 1992; Atkinson & Duke, 1995) components are identified by classes. The behavior is defined as the response of the objects to sequences of external messages. The comparison is made between the expected and the provided results.

In (Atkinson & Duke, 1995), the selected behavior may come from a class or from a union of two classes.

The Facet-Based Method

Facet classification approaches (Damiani et al., 1999; Vitharana et al., 2003) represent the type of information to describe software components. Each facet has a name which identifies it and a collection of well-controlled terms known as vocabulary to describe its aspects. For example, the facet *componenttype* can have the following values: COM, ActiveX, Javabean, etc. In the search procedure, the user query is specified by

selecting a term for each facet. The set of the selected terms represents the task to be executed by the component.

(Ferreira and Lucena 2001) uses the component external description to organize the repository. Different facets are defined, such as the applicability, the specialization domain and the hardware platform. This approach handles several technologies of components: EJB and CORBA components. (Zhang et al. 2000) distinguishes three granularity levels for a component in a Metacase environment:

- Project level component: like projects for developing information systems.
- Graph level component: like use case diagrams.
- Unit level component: like class, state and transition diagrams.

A facet formed by a n-tuple is designed for each type of component. A hierarchical relation between the three types of facets is considered. The component description is limited to the type of the component, its properties and the name of its superior.

The approach presented in (Franch et al., 1999) is the only one which introduces non-functional constraints. The components are ADA packages. Each facet includes the name of the non-functional constraints, a list of values and constraints called Nfconstraints. An interface can have several implementations (components): the interface which minimizes the number of connections between components can be implemented using several methods like hashing, AVL trees, etc. The comparison

distance is approximate since the developer chooses the component to which he/she applies the correction necessary to adapt it to his/her needs. In this approach, there is no specification phase since the facets are introduced in the implementation level as ADA package.

The Elaborated Classification

The elaborated classification uses the component properties (attributes and/or methods) to form a relation. This relation can have a graph representation or a hierarchical form and is restricted by constraints.

This type of representation is essentially used in the lattice method. The concept of lattice was initially defined by R. Wille (Wille, 1982). This concept is the representation of a relation, R, between a collection of objects G (Gegentande) and a collection of attributes M (Merkmale). The triplet (G, M, R) is called concept. The artificial intelligence is the first discipline which uses this technique for representation and acquisition of knowledge. Wille (Wille, 1982) considers each element of lattice as a formal concept and the graph (Hasse diagram) as a relation of generalisation/specialisation. The lattice is seen as a hierarchy of concepts. Each concept is seen as a pair (E, I) where E is a sub-set of the application instance and I is the intention representing the properties shared by the instances.

Granter and Wille (Granter & Wille, 1996), and Davet and Priesly (Davey & Priesly, 1990) apply the technique of lattice to establish the relation between objects and their attributes. This idea was applied by (Fischer, 2000) and (Davey & Priesly, 1990) to classify software components. The relation R is represented with a tree whose leaves are the components and the nodes are the joint attributes. In the search phase, the user chooses one or more attributes, according to his/her needs. The system notifies the associated components.

Method-Based Classification

This classification is handled using ontologies. For each component method this approach defines its relation with its synonyms, its Hyperonymes and its Hyponymes.

Ontology is defined by Gruber as an explicit specification of a conceptualization or a formal explicit description of concept (denoting sometimes a class) in a speech domain (Natalya & Deborah, 2001). The properties of each concept describe the characteristics and the attributes, also called slots or roles. The restrictions apply to the slots and are called facets. The objects of classes constitute the knowledge base. Several disciplines developed and standardized their own ontology with a well-structured vocabulary as in e-commerce (Fensel et al., 2001) and in medicine (Humphreys & Lindberg, 1993).

In software engineering and particularly in the specification and the searchrelated domains for software components, ontology is also used. This type of description can facilitate organization, browsing, parametric search, and in general provides, more intelligent access to components.

(Braga et al., 2001) uses ODL notations as a tool for the component external specification. Term, ontology term and component are among the used concepts. Term contains the slots names and descriptions. For each term, it defines its relation with its synonyms, its Hyperonymes and its Hyponymes in the concept ontology term. In the class component, a slot called type is defined. The comparison distance in this approach is exact.

The software components organization in (Paez & Straeten, 2002) is based on a multidimensional classification. A dimension is defined by a set of facets. Each facet describes an aspect of the component. The dimension implementation, for example, contains the following facets: programming language, the execution platform, etc. In dimension re-use, the facets are: the history of the use of the component, protocol, environment and components frequently used by the component. Another dimension like ScrabbleGU, contains facets in which are defined the signatures of the methods. The notation used for the specification is Q-SHIQ.

Classification Techniques

The successfulness of the reuse is important and depends on the organization of the reusable components in order to easily retrieving them from existing repositories are among objectives of reuse systems design (Mili et al. 1995). In literature, we distinguish two classification levels. The lower level hierarchy and the higher level hierarchy. The first is created by a subsumption test algorithm (Napoli, 1992) that determines whether one component is more general than another; this level facilitates the application of logical reasoning techniques for a fine-grained, exact determination of reusable candidates. The higher level hierarchy provides a coarse-grained determination of reusable candidates and is constructed by applying the clustering approach to the most general components from the lower-level hierarchy.

Classification by clustering techniques has been used in many areas of research, including image processing and information retrieval. Applying a clustering algorithm to the most general components of the lower-level hierarchy leads to the generation of the higher-level hierarchy of the component library.

Many methods are employed to classify the components by clustering. Such methods include fuzzy subtractive clustering algorithm (Chiu, 1996), neural network techniques, decision tree algorithm and fusion algorithm.

The work of (Nakkrasae et al., 2004) employs Fuzzy Subtractive Clustering (FSC) which is a fast one-pass algorithm for estimating the number of clusters and their centers in a set of data to preprocess the software components. Once the software component groups are formed, classification process can proceed in order to build a repository containing cluster groups of similar components. The center of each cluster will be used to construct the coarse-grained classification indexing structure. Three levels of component description are used: behavior, method and protocol specification. An approximate comparison query and components is employed.

In similar domain, Zhang et al. proposes a fusion algorithm (Jian Zhang & Wang, 2001) which clusters the components in different result sets. Clusters that have high overlap with clusters in other result sets are judged to be more relevant. The components that belong to such clusters are assigned the highest score. The new score is used to combine all the result sets into a single set.

A heuristically approach is used by (Willet, 1988), (Carpineto & Romano, 2000) and (Daudjee & Toptsis, 1994) to cluster the set of components. In (Willet 1988) components are used to implement documents and heuristical decisions are used not only to cluster the component set but also to compute a similarity between individual component clusters and a query. As a result, hierarchical clustering-based ranking may easily fail to discriminate between documents that have manifestly different degrees of relevance for a certain query. Carpineto et al. applies in (Carpineto & Romano, 2000) the same approach to a web page. (Daudjee & Toptsis, 1994) uses heuristical clustering scheme. The scheme clusters software components also contains functional descriptions of software modules. It is automatic and classifies components that have been represented using a knowledge representation-based language. The facet method is used for representing the classification. This representation takes the form of verb-noun pairs where the verb is the action or operation performed and the noun is the object upon which the operation is performed.

The work of (Pozewaunig & Mittermeir, 2000) adopts decision trees to classify and to cluster the repository into partitions with respect to the signatures of all reusable components. In the traditional approach, a partition contains assets which conform with the signature only. However, to allow a higher level of recall, this approach uses generalized signatures by extending the approaches of (Novak, 1997).

The component description is limited to the specification of component methods.

The thesaurus is also used to organize the components into a repository. It provides knowledge about the relationships between index terms; it adds conceptual meaning to simple keyword matching. Similarity between the query posed by the user and the candidate searched for is computed by a model in which similarity between facets gives a measure of conceptual closeness (or distance). After computing the conceptual distances, the result is multiplied with facet weight (which is user-assigned).

Liao et al. (Liao et al., 1997) develop a Software Reuse Framework (SRF) which is based on a built-in hierarchical thesaurus. Its classification process may be made semi-automatic. SRF is a domain-independent framework that can be adapted to various repositories and also provides four search levels to assist users with different levels of familiarity with repositories.

Llorens et al. (Llorens et al., 1996) implements "Software Thesaurus" (ST), a tool whose objective is to develop software while reusing objects produced previously in other software projects. This tool is defined by a new repository metamodel which supports the classification and retrieval of essential software objects defined by current object oriented methodologies using GUI.

In other similar works (Carpineto & Romano, 1996), (Carpineto & Romano, 1994), the thesaurus is integrated into a concept lattice either by explicitly expanding the original context with the implied terms or by taking into account the thesaurus ordering relation during the construction of the lattice.

COMPONENT DISCOVERY

To improve component discovery, we must well classify the component repository as mentioned in previous section. This classification facilitates the discovery process and decrease the search time.

In this section, we study the component discovery related works that include: comparison distance, search style, discovery techniques, interface type and discovery algorithm.

The comparison distance between the specified query and the component description can be approximate or exact. We distinguish also three kinds of search: directed search, automatically indexed search and manually indexed search. We divide the discovery techniques into probabilistic and the learning techniques and we show that the majority of discovery algorithms are based on the decision tree and the unification of component descriptions.

Comparison Distance and Search Style

The search procedure of software components is a delicate task especially when it handles a repository containing a significant number of software components. Indeed, the search procedure explores the structure of the repository to discover the desired component. In literature, we distinguish two kinds of search (Figure 2): directed search and indexed search. The indexed search can be automatically or manually. In the direct search, the developer negotiates directly the component repository. In the indexed technique, the search process is conducted manually (Fischer, 2000) or automatically (Seacord et al., 1998) according to a pre-defined process. CodeFinder (Henninger, 1997) and CodeBroker (Yunwen & Fischer, 2001) use automatic indexing. In CodeFinder, the indices are terms and sentences, whereas in CodeBroker, the indices are comments. The access to the repository is automatically managed by an agent.

The indexed search style is the mostly used in many discovery algorithms such as Decision tree algorithm. In this algorithm the repository is indexed by a decision tree, which is a tree data structure consisting of decision nodes and leaves. A leaf contains a class value and the node specifies a test over one of the attributes.

Figure 2.

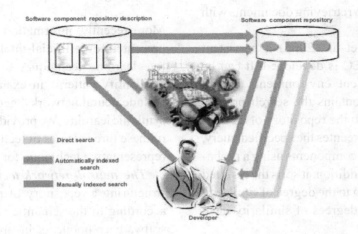

Software component repository description

Software component repository

Direct search

Automatically indexed search

Manually indexed search

Developer

The definition and the use of a comparison distance make it possible to quantify the result of the comparison between the query requirements (Q) and the component properties. This distance is represented by a Vector Space Models in (Li 1998), several evaluation functions in (Cheng & Jeng, 1997) and a probabilistic calculation in (Yunwen & Fischer, 2001). Hence, search can provide an "exact" ($P = 1$) or approximate ($P < 1$) result, where P is the probabilistic calculation. In the first case, the developer can re-use the component as such in the application. In the second case, the developer has to adapt the component to the task specified in the query.

The approximate comparison is used in many discovery techniques such as probabilistic and learning techniques.

The Discovery Techniques

Existing software repositories that provide search facilities adopt different retrieval methods. Based on a variety of technologies, they can be divided into probabilistic and learning techniques.

Probabilistic Techniques

In probabilistic techniques, components indexation and selection can be seen as information retrieval problem. The goal is to estimate the relevance probability of a given component description to a user with respect to a given query. Probabilistic assumptions about the distribution of elements in the representations within relevant and irrelevant documents are required.

The CodeBroker agent (Yunwen & Fischer, 2001) uses both free-text information retrieval techniques and signature matching to retrieve task relevant components. It uses the probability-based information retrieval technique defined in (Robertson & Walker, 1994), in order to compute the concept similarity between queries extracted from doc comments of emacs programs and documents of components in the repository.

In (Callan et al., 1992) the probabilistic retrieval model is a type of Bayesian network. They consist of two component networks; the first for documents and the second for queries. The links in the documents networks are weighed by conditional probabilities defining the probability that the document is related to the concept. Queries are related to different concepts by the user interface. Document selection is achieved using recursive inference to propagate belief values through the inference net, and then retrieving documents with the highest rank.

In (Khemakhem et al., 2006) a persistent component, called SEC is developed. It can be loaded in development environments during project creation. It contains the search process and manages access to the repository of component descriptions. It executes the specified query, retrieves and presents components using a probabilistic technique. In addition, it sorts the resulted components according to the degree of similarity with the query. Four degrees of similarity have been considered:

- **Exact:** If component C and query Q are equivalent concepts, this is the Exact match; denoted, $C \equiv R$. It means that for each couple of the request and the description, there is identity of types.
- **PlugIn:** If query Q is sub-concept of component C, this is the PlugIn match; denoted, $Q \subseteq C$. It means that for each element of the query there is a similar element in component description
- Subsume: If query Q is super-concept of component C, this is the Subsume match ; denoted, $C \subseteq Q$.
- **Disjoint:** The last case is the Disjoint match; for which, $C \cap Q \subseteq \bot$. It means that there is no element of the component description that corresponds to an element of the query.
- Similarly Fuhr and Pfeifer use in (Fuhr & Pfeifer, 1994) a probabilistic technique based on three concepts: abstraction, reductive learning and probabilistic assumptions for information retrieval. The three concepts may relate to: documents, queries, and terms.

Learning Techniques

More recently, information science researchers presented new artificial-intelligence based inductive learning techniques to extract knowledge or identify patterns in examples or data. They include neural networks, genetic algorithms and symbolic learning. We provide below an overview of these three classes of techniques, along with a representative technique for each one.

The neural network technology is used for structuring a repository of reusable component according to the semantic similarities of stored software components in order to facilitate the search and to optimize the retrieval of similar repetitive queries. Neural networks are considered as content-addressable or associative memories in some approach in support of imprecise querying.

The work of Clifton and Wen-Syan (Clifton and Wen-Syan 1995) can be considered as instances of information retrieval methods. In this approach, conventional abstractions are used to describe software. Clifton and Wen-Syan use design information as abstraction and propose neural network technology to accomplish the match.

The approach of (Eichmann & Srinivas, 1992) uses neural network to extend and to improve the traditional methods. They develop an approach based upon neural networks which avoid requiring the repository administrators to define a conceptual closeness graph for the classification vocabulary. The motivations behind using neural networks are to use relaxation, retrieving component based on approximate/best matches, to optimize the retrieval of similar repetitive queries and to retrieve component from large repository, using the fast associative techniques that are natural and inherent in this tools.

Zhiyuan (Zhiyuan, 2000) proposes a neural associative memory and bayesian inference technology to locate components in a repository. For each component, there are ten facets (type, domain, local identifier, etc.). The neural associative memory memorizes the relationship between components and facet values. During the search, the described component representation is mapped to facets. The value of each facet is fed into its dedicated associative memory to recall the components that have the same value for this facet. After one processing step, all the components having this value will be recalled. In this approach, the comparison distance is exact and the information type is functional.

(Nakkrasae et al., 2004) proposes two computational approaches to classify software components for effective archival and retrieval purposes, namely, fuzzy subtractive clustering algorithm and neural network technique. This approach uses a formal specification to describe three properties of components: structural, functional, and behavioral properties. Components specification is represented in a matrix form to support classification in the component repository. Subsequent retrieval of the desired component uses the same matrix to search the appropriate matching. The specification level in this approach is behavioral, the information type is functional and the comparison distance is approximate.

Genetic algorithms are based on the principle of genetics (Michalewicz, 1992). In such algorithms a population of individuals (a component repository) undergoes a sequence of unary (mutation) and higher order (crossover) transformations. These individuals strive for survival: a selection (reproduction) scheme, biased towards selecting fitter individuals, produces the individuals for the next generation. After a number of generations, the program converges - the best individual represents the optimum solution (Chen 1995). In our case the individual represents the component and the best individual is the desired one.

The approach (Xie et al., 2004) uses facet presentation to model query and component. Genetic algorithm, which is based on facet weight self-learning algorithm, can modify dynamically the weight of the facet in order to improve retrieval accuracy. This algorithm is integrated into FWRM's that contains three main implementation parts:

Facet-Weight optimization system, component retrieve system and resource.

In (Chen & Kim, 1995), Chen and Kim developed a hybrid system, called GANNET for information retrieval. The system performs concept optimization for user selected documents using genetic algorithms. They use the optimized concepts to perform concept exploration in a large network of related concepts through the Hopfield net parallel relaxation procedure.

Symbolic learning is represented in the form of symbolic descriptions of the learned concepts, e.g., production rules or concept hierarchies. It is used essentially for information retrieval. The problem of component retrieval can be converted into information retrieval; the information represents the component description.

In literature, several symbolic learning algorithms have been developed. Quinlan's ID3 decision tree building algorithm and its descendants (Quinlan, 1986) are popular algorithms for inductive learning. ID3 takes objects of a known class, specified in terms of properties or attributes, and produces a decision tree containing these attributes that correctly classifies all the given objects. To minimize the number of tests, necessary to classify an object, it uses an information-economics approach. Its output can be summarized in terms of IF-THEN rules.

In (Chen & She, 1994), Chen and She adopted ID3 and the incremental ID5R (Utgoff, 1989) algorithm for information retrieval. Both algorithms were able to use user-supplied samples of desired documents to construct decision trees of important keywords which could represent the user queries.

For large-scale real-life applications, neural networks and, to some extent, genetic algorithms have some limitations. In fact, they suffer from requiring extensive computation time and lack of interpretable results. Symbolic learning, on the other hand, efficiently produces simple production rules or decision tree representations. The effects of the representations on the cognition of searchers in the real-life retrieval environments (e.g., users' acceptance of the analytical results provided by an intelligent system) remain to be determined (Chen, 1995). The importance of sample size has been stressed heavily in the probabilistic techniques (Fuhr & Pfeifer, 1994).

Discovery Algorithm

Well organized repositories can be queried by developers according to a search process. To perform process and to deliver the component that meets the developer's need many algorithms have been proposed. Most of them are based on decision trees and unification of component descriptions. We distinguish two forms of unification: string unification and graph unification. This unification make easy the selection of the appropriate component by using one of the discovery techniques mentioned above.

Unification Based Discovery

We distinguish two forms of unification: string unification and graph unification. This unification make easy the selection of the appropriate component by using one of the discovery techniques mentioned above.

String unification can be used to order components and hence to organize repositories hierarchically. Theses hierarchies can then be exploited to optimize the search process or to compute a navigation structure. The unification in (Cheng & Jeng, 1997) is a unification of logic expressions. It uses the order-sorted predicate logic (OSPL) to specify components. The relationship between two components is based on the sort information and a logical subsumption test applied to the specification body. The search process assesses the equivalence class for each of the predicates and functions and develops a unified hierarchy of components.

The discovery algorithm based on graph unification consists in transforming the query and the component specification into graph representa-

tion. After this step a discovery technique is used to compare between the resulted graphs. AIRS (AI-based Reuse System) (Ostertag et al., 1992) represents a component using a set of (feature; term) pairs. Each feature has a feature graph that the system traverses in search of conceptually close features with respect to the user query. This represents the distance (and thus the user effort) required to modify the retrieved candidate to meet the user's needs. The number of features used to represent all components is fixed.

Manuel el al. (Manuel et al., 2000) use conceptual graphs for the representation of the component(document) and the query. A conceptual graph is a network of concepts and relation nodes. The concept nodes represent entities, attributes, or events (actions). The relation nodes identify the kind of relationship between two concept nodes. The retrieval mechanism consists in comparing two conceptual graph representations. It is composed of two main parts:

1. Find the intersection of the two (sets of) graphs,
2. Measure the similarity between the two (sets of) graphs

The work of (Yao & Etzkorn, 2004) uses conceptual graphs to describe a component. In the retrieval process the query is translated into a conceptual graph in order to enhance both retrieval precision and recall by deploying the same representation technique on both sides: user query side and component side.

Decision Tree-Based Discovery

Decision tree is a classifier in the form of a tree structure, where each node is either:

- **A leaf node** - indicates the value of the target attribute (class) of examples, or
- **A decision node** - specifies some test to be carried out on a single attribute-value, with

one branch and sub-tree for each possible outcome of the test.

A decision tree can be used to classify an example by starting at the root of the tree and moving through it until a leaf node, which provides the classification of the instance.

The literature contains several decision tree algorithms. The survey (Lim et al., 2000) compares twenty-two decision tree algorithms, nine classical and modern statically algorithms, and two neural networks algorithms. These algorithms are compared with respect to the classification accuracy, the training time, and the number of leaves.

In software engineering several approaches use the decision tree to classify and discover web services (Vasiliu et al., 2004), (Chirala, 2004), software components (Fox et al., 1998) and objects (Olaru & Wehenkel, 2003).

Interface Type

As a supporting tool for reusable component selection, a reuse repository system has three constituents: a component repository, a discovery process, and an interface for software developers to interact with. Most of repositories have a conversational interface which is implemented either as in command line interpreter or as in graphical user interface (GUI). To find a reusable component, developers either type command lines or use direct manipulation to search or browse component repositories.

The Agora system is a web-based search approach that searches only on component interfaces, covering solely the component connectiveness problem. Agora query interface supports basic operators, + and -, as well as advanced search capabilities with boolean operators. Users can search for and retrieve components through a web interface.

In (Mori et al., 2001) the user issues a search request with a requirement specification through a web browser. Then the trader passes this information to the inference engine (called PigNose). PigNose responds with a list of views if signature match is successful. The trader receives the result and displays it on the user's web browser.

In (Ferreira & Lucena, 2001), Ferreira and Lucena propose a GUI for component selection. The selection is based on the desired application domain name and its respective specialization, the automation task to be fulfilled, and the position of the desired functionality in the automation hierarchy.

As defined in (Group, 2006),"browse" means reading superficially or at random. It consists in inspecting candidate components for possible extraction, but without a predefined criterion.

In general, people who search an information prefer browsing to searching because they do not need to commit resources at first and can incrementally develop their requirements after evaluating the information along the way (Thompson & Croft, 1989). (Mili et al., 1999) claim that browsing is the main pattern of component repository usage because many software developers often cannot clearly formulate queries.

However, browsing is not scalable; for large repositories, following the right link in a browsing interface requires developers to have a good understanding of the whole system, which is hard for less experienced developers.

The work in (Pozewaunig & Mittermeir, 2000) interests on fine grained search. The principal is to exploit test cases as initial knowledge source for representing component functionalities. Augmented test cases (data points) are then classified using a decision tree algorithm. The resulting hierarchical indexing structure supports interactive browsing without the need for extensive user training.

(Yunwen & Fischer, 2001) proposes an agent called code broker that locates software components in a given component repository: context-aware browsing. Without any explicit input from software developers, this approach automatically

Table 1. Comparison of the main approaches techniques and methods

Methods	Search style			Inf. aspect		Comp. dist.		Specification level				
	C1	C2	C3	C4	C5	C6	C7	C8	C9	C10	C11	C12
Behavior	×			×		×			×		×	
Semantic characteristic		×		×		×		×	×			
Lattice		×		×		×			×			
Ontology		×		×		×		×				
Facet		×		×		×		×	×			

locates and presents a list of software components that could be used in the current work.

SYNTHESIS

In this section, we will summarize the comparison of the main approaches, techniques and methods (see Table 1). We will use a tabular like notation. In the first column we present the different methods of component classification representation.

For each method we point out the search style in the second column, the information aspect in third column, the comparison distance in the fourth column and the component specification level in the fifth column.

For the search styles:

- C1 denotes the direct search,
- C2 denotes the manually indexed search,
- C3 denotes the automatically indexed search.

For the information aspects:

- C4 denotes the functional aspect,
- C5 denotes the non functional aspect.

For the comparison distance:

- C6 denotes exact comparison,
- C7 denotes approximate comparison.

For the specification level:

- -C8 denotes the external specification,

Regarding the search style, the majority of approaches, within each method, use a manually indexed search. Although this method is slow, it has advantages for developers and especially for beginners. It allows them to understand the repository structure and to learn about its content. The search interfaces could provide meaningful messages to explain search and support progressive refinement (Shneiderman, 1997).

The description of the non-functional aspects is, generally, neglected. Both functional and non-functional aspects should be considered during the specification, the design, the implementation, the maintenance and the re-use. In the phase of re-use, and if the search is based only on the functional aspects, the selected component may not satisfy the non-functional constraints of the environment. In several cases, the non-functional constraints play a decisive role in the choice of the most powerful component (Rosa et al., 2001).

The exact distance comparison is the most used to compare the component specified using a query with the discovered components. This type of comparison decreases the re-use of the software components. An approximate comparison not only makes it possible to understand the component functionalities by developers but also to adapt it to the application.

In the classification representation methods, there are few approaches that specify the software components with more than two levels. This allows users to understand many details, and to have higher probability to find the component matching exactly the desired functionalities. The specification details complicate the formulation of the research query. There is a tradeoff between the specification details of the component and the difficulty of query formulation.

DISCUSSION

In summary, we notice a similarity between the facet technique and the semantic characteristics technique. However the classification with facets uses a fixed number of facets per domain and is more flexible. Moreover, one facet can be modified without affecting the others. The facet technique has also the following advantages:

- The maintenance of classification by facet is not complicated. It is achieved by updating the list of the facets,
- It has a high level of description,
- The list of terms for each facet provides a common standard vocabulary for the repository administrator and the user.

However, the developer can face problems at the time of the query formulation and in the classification. Contrarily to the behavior-based technique, it is difficult to specify the query and to combine the good terms to describe the task in the facet technique. This technique requires the repository structure understanding, the terms, and the significance of each facet (Curtis, 1989). Software components classification problems can appear when the component has many states. Component behavior depends on its current state, which multiplies the possibilities of its classification.

These problems are not presented in the ontology-based technique. Ontology facilitates the fusion of the repositories having the same ontology (Fensel et al., 2001), as well as the component insertion. This is not the case for the facet technique where the fusion of two repositories is done manually by adding component per component from one repository to another. Moreover, the ontology-based technique needs a heavy and painful process. Even if the two repositories would use the same terminologies (for example the same facets and same terms), the user must interpret each facet and each term while making the "mapping" in the concepts of the other repository.

The comparison in the behavior-based technique is done between the specified behavior and the behaviors of each component. The search procedure becomes very slow for a repository having a significant number of components.

CONCLUSION

Many different standards have been proposed and various approaches have been taken to create a widely accepted and usable software components

Figure 3.

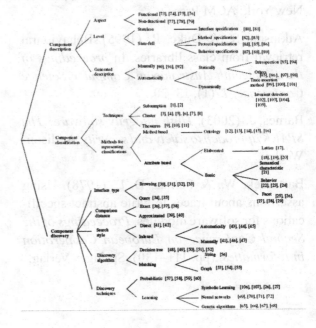

for description, classification and discovery components.

A comparison between the approaches was developed. The comparison is based on search style, information type, comparison distance and specification level. We highlighted the interest of the non-functional constraints in component description, the advantage of the approximate comparison and the tradeoff to be achieved between the level of specification detail and the degree of difficulty to formulate a query.

We can conclude that to have a good search result, one must consider a tradeoff between the component specification detail and the degree of difficulties to formulate a query. It is also important to consider the non-functional aspect into component description, to use an approximate comparison and to follow a manually indexed search.

REFERENCES

Ammons, G., Bodik, R., & Larus, R. J. (2002). Mining specifications. In *proceedings of the 29th ACM SIGPLAN-SIGACT symposium on Principles of programming languages*, (pp.4-16). New York: ACM Press.

Atkinson, S., & Duke, R. (1995). Behavioural retrieval from class libraries. In *proceedings of the Eighteenth Australasian Computer Science Conference, 17*(1), 13–20.

Barnes, J. (2003). *High integrity software: The SPARK approach to safety and security.* Addison-Wesley.

Bartussek, W., & Parnas, D. L. (1978). Using assertions about traces to write abstract specifications for software modules. *Proceedings of the Second Conference on European Cooperation in Informatics,* (pp. 111–130). Springer-Verlag.

Bastide, R., Sy, O., & Palanque, P. (1999). Formal specification and prototyping of corba systems. *ECOOP '99,* (pp. 474–494). Springer-Verlag.

Braga, R., Mattoso, M. & Werner, C. (2001). The use of mediation and ontology technologies for software component information retrieval. *Proceedings of the International Symposium on Software Reusability,* Toronto, Ontario, Canada.

Callan, J. P., Croft, W. B., & Harding, S. M. (1992). The INQUERY retrieval system. In *Proceedings of the Third International Conference on Database and Expert Systems Applications,* (pp. 78-83). New York: Springer-Verlag.

Canal, C., Fuentes, L., Troya, J.M. & Vallecillo, A. (2000). Extending corba interfaces with p-calculus for protocol compatibility. TOOLS'00. *IEEE Press, 19*(2), 292–333.

Carpineto, C., & Romano, G. (1994). Dynamically bounding browsable retrieval spaces: An application to galois lattices. In *Proceedings of RIAO 94: Intelligent Multimedia Information Retrieval Systems and Management.*

Carpineto, C., & Romano, G. (1996). A lattice conceptual clustering system and its application to browsing retrieval. *Machine Learning, 24*(2), 128. doi:10.1007/BF00058654

Carpineto, C., & Romano, G. (2000). Order-theoretical ranking. *Journal of the American Society for Information Science American Society for Information Science, 51*(7), 587–601. doi:10.1002/(SICI)1097-4571(2000)51:7<587::AID-ASI2>3.0.CO;2-L

Chen, H. (1995). Machine learning for information retrieval: Neural networks, symbolic learning and genetic algorithms. [JASIS]. *Journal of the American Society for Information Science American Society for Information Science, 46*(3), 194–216. doi:10.1002/(SICI)1097-4571(199504)46:3<194::AID-ASI4>3.0.CO;2-S

Chen, H., & Kim, J. (1995). GANNET: A machine learning approach to document retrieval. *Journal of Management Information Systems, 11*(3), 7–41.

Chen, H., & She, L. (1994). Inductive query by examples (IQBE): A machine learning approach. In *Proceedings of the 27th Annual Hawaii International Conference on System Sciences (HICSS-27), Information Sharing and Knowledge Discovery Track.*

Cheng, B., & Jeng, J. (1997). Reusing analogous components. *IEEE Transactions on Knowledge and Data Engineering, 9*(2), 341–349. doi:10.1109/69.591458

Chirala, R. C. (2004). *Thesis*. Ph.D. thesis, Department of Computer Science and Engineering, Arizona State University.

Chiu, S. (1996). Method and software for extracting fuzzy classification rules by subtractive clustering. *Proceedings Fuzzy Information Proc. Society, Biennial Conference of the North American,* 461–465.

Cicalese, C. D. T., & Rotenstreich, S. (1999). *Behavioral specification of distributed software component interfaces.* IEEE Computer.

Clifton, C., & Wen-Syan, L. (1995). Classifying software components using design characteristics. *Proceedings the 10th Knowledge-Based Software Engineering Conference,* 139–146.

Corbett, J. C., Dwyer, M. B., Hatcliff, J., Laubach, S., Pasareanu, C. S., Zheng, H., et al. (2000). Bandera: Extracting finite-state models from java source code. *In proceedings of the International Conference on Software Engineering,* 263–276.

Curtis, B. (1989). *Cognitive issues in reusing software artifacts, software reusability.* New York: ACM Press.

Damiani, E. G., Fugini, M., & Bellettini, C. (1999). A hierarchy-aware approach to faceted classification of objected-oriented components. *ACM Transactions on Software Engineering and Methodology, 8*(3), 215–262. doi:10.1145/310663.310665

Daudjee, K. S., & Toptsis, A. A. (1994). A technique for automatically organizing software libraries for software reuse. In *Proceedings of the 1994 conference of the Centre for Advanced Studies on Collaborative research,* (p. 12). IBM Press.

Davey, B. A., & Priesly, H. A. (1990). *Introduction to lattices and order* (2nd ed.). Cambridge, UK: Cambridge University Press.

Devanbu, P., Brachman, R. J., Ballard, B. W., & Selfridge, P. G. (1991). Lassie: A knowledge-based software information system. *Communications of the ACM, 34*(5), 34–49. doi:10.1145/103167.103172

Eichmann, D., & Srinivas, K. (1992). Neural network-based retrieval from software reuse repositories. In *Neural networks and pattern recognition in human-computer interaction.* (pp. 215–228).

Erdur, R., & Dikenelli, O. (2002). *A multi-agent system infrastructure for software component market-place: An ontological perspective* (pp. 55–60). ACM SIGMOD.

Evans, D., Guttag, J., Horning, J., & Tan, Y. M. (1994). Lclint: A tool for using specifications to check code. In *Proceedings of the ACM SIGSOFT Symposium on the Foundations of Software Engineering.*

Faras, A., & Guhneuc, Y. (2003). On the coherence of component protocols. *Proceedings of the ETAPS Workshop on Software Composition.*

Fensel, D., McGuiness, D., Schulten, E., Keong, W., Lim, G., & Yan, G. (2001). Ontologies and electronic commerce. *Intelligent Systems, 16,* 8–14. doi:10.1109/MIS.2001.1183337

Ferreira, V., & Lucena, J. (2001). *Facet-based classification scheme for industrial automation software components.* Paper presented at the 6th International Workshop on Component-Oriented Programming.

Fetike, P., & Loos, P. (2003). Specifying business components in virtual engineering communities. *Proceedings of the Ninth Americas Conference on Information Systems*, (pp. 1937–1947). Tampa, FL.

Fischer, B. (2000). Specification-based browsing of software component libraries. *Automated Software Engineering*, 7(2), 179–200. doi:10.1023/A:1008766409590

Fox, G. C., Furmanski, W., & Pulikal, T. (1998). Evaluating new transparent persistence commodity models: JDBC, Corba PPS, and OLEDB for HPC T and E databases. *Proceedings of the International Test and Evaluation Association (ITEA) Workshop on High Performance Computing for Test and Evaluation*, 13–16.

Franch, X., Pinyol, J., & Vancells, J. (1999). Browsing a component library using nonfunctional information. *Proceedings of the International Conference on Reliable Software Technologies - Ada Europe '99*, (pp. 332–343). Santander, Spain.

Fuhr, N., & Pfeifer, U. (1994). Probabilistic information retrieval as a combination of abstraction, inductive learning, and probabilistic assumptions. *ACM Transactions on Information Systems*, 12(1), 92–115. doi:10.1145/174608.174612

Granter, B., & Wille, R. (1996). *Formale begriffsanalyse. Mathematische grundlagen.* Berlin: Springer.

Group, L. P. Hangal, S. & Lam, M.S. (2002). Tracking down software bugs using automatic anomaly detection. In *Proceedings of the International Conference on Software Engineering*.

Henkel, J., & Diwan, A. (2003). *Discovering algebraic specifications from Java classes.* Paper presented at the 15th European conference on objectoriented programming (ECOOP 2003).

Henninger, S. (1997). An evolutionary approach to constructing effective software reuse repositories. *ACM Transactions on Software Engineering Methodology*.

Humphreys, B., & Lindberg, D. (1993). The UMLS project: Making the conceptual connection between users and the information they need. *Bulletin of the Medical Library Association, 81*(2).

Janicki, R., & Sekerinski, E. (2001). Foundations of the trace assertion method of module interface specification. *IEEE Transactions on Software Engineering*, 27(7), 577–598. doi:10.1109/32.935852

Jeffords, R., & Heitmeyer, C. (1998). Automatic generation of state invariants from requirements specifications. In *Proceedings of the 6th ACM SIGSOFT international symposium on Foundations of software engineering*, (pp. 56–69). New York: ACM Press.

Khemakhem, S., Drira, K., & Jmaiel, M. (2006). Sec: A search engine for component based software development. In *Proceedings of the 21st ACM Symposium on Applied Computing*.

Khemakhem, S., Jmaiel, M., Hamadou, A. B., & Drira, K. (2002). Un environnement de recherche et d'int'egration de composant logiciel. In *Proceedings of the Seventh Conference On computer Sciences*, Annaba.

Leino, K., & Nelson, G. (1998). An extended static checker for modula-3. *Proceedings of the Seventh Int'l Conference of Compiler Construction*, 302–305.

Li, Y. (1998). Toward a qualitative search engine. *Internet Computing, IEEE, 2*, 24–29. doi:10.1109/4236.707687

Liao, H.-C., Chen, M.-F., Wang, F.-J., & Dai, J.-C. (1997). Using a hierarchical thesaurus for classifying and searching software libraries. In *Proceedings of the 21st International Computer Software and Applications Conference*, (pp. 210–216). IEEE Computer Society, Washington, DC.

Lim, T.-S., Loh, W.-Y., & Shih, Y.-S. (2000). A comparison of prediction accuracy, complexity, and training time of thirty-three old and new classification algorithms. *Machine Learning, 40*(3), 203–228. doi:10.1023/A:1007608224229

Llorens, J., Amescua, A., & Velasco, M. (1996). Software thesaurus: A tool for reusing software objects. *Proceedings of the Fourth International Symposium on Assessment of Software Tools (SAST '96)*, (p. 99).

Manuel, M., Aurelio, L., & Alexander, G. (2000). Information retrieval with conceptual graph matching. *Proceedings of the 11th International Conference and Workshop on Database and Expert Systems Applications*, (pp. 4–8).

Meling, R., Montgomery, E., Ponnusamy, P. S., Wong, E., & Mehandjiska, D. (2000). Storing and retrieving software components: A component description manager. In *Proceedings of the 2000 Australian Software Engineering Conference*, (pp. 107-117). Canberra, Australia.

Michalewicz, Z. (1992). *Genetic algorithms + data structures = evolution programs*. Berlin, Heidelberg: Springer-Verlag.

Mili, A. (1999). Toward an engineering discipline of software reuse. *IEEE Software, 16*(5), 22–31. doi:10.1109/52.795098

Mili, H., Mili, F., & Mili, A. (1995). Reuse software: Issues and research directions. *IEEE Transactions on Software Engineering, 21*(6), 528–562. doi:10.1109/32.391379

Mori, A., Futatsugi, T. S. K., Seo, A., & Ishiguro, M. (2001). Software component search based on behavioral specification. *Proceedings of International Symposium on Future Software Technology*.

Nakajima, S., & Tamai, T. (2001). Behavioural analysis of the enterprise Javabeans component architecture. *Proceedings of the 8th International SPIN Workshop*, (163–182). Toronto. Springer.

Nakkrasae, S., Sophatsathit, P., & Edwards, W. (2004). Fuzzy subtractive clustering based indexing approach for software components classification. *International Journal of Computer and Information Science, 5*(1), 63–72.

Napoli, A. (1992). Subsumption and classification-based reasoning in object-based representations. In *Proceedings of the 10th European conference on Artificial intelligence*. (pp. 425-429). New York: John Wiley & Sons, Inc.

Natalya, F., & Deborah, L. M. (2001). *Ontology development 101: A guide to creating your first ontology*. Stanford University.

Naumovich, G., Clarke, L., Osterweil, L., & Dwyer, M. (1997). Verification of concurrent software with flavers. *Proceedings of the 19th Int'l Conf. Software Eng*, 594–595.

Novak, J. G. S. (1997). Software reuse by specialization of generic procedures through views. *IEEE Transactions on Software Engineering, 23*(7), 401–417. doi:10.1109/32.605759

Olaru, C., & Wehenkel, L. (2003). A complete fuzzy decision tree technique. *Fuzzy Sets and Systems, 138*(2), 221–254. doi:10.1016/S0165-0114(03)00089-7

ONeil, J. & Schildt, H. (1998). *Java beans programming from the ground up*. Osborne McGraw-Hill.

Ostertag, E., Hendler, J., Prieto-Diaz, R., & Braun, C. (1992). Computing similarity in a reuse library system, an AI-based approach. *ACM Transactions on Software Engineering and Methodology*, •••, 205–228. doi:10.1145/131736.131739

Paez, M. C., & Straeten, R. V. D. (2002). Modelling component libraries for reuse and evolution. In the *Proceedings of the First Workshop on Model-based Reuse*.

Parnas, D. L., & Wang, Y. (1989). *The trace assertion method of module interface specification*. (Tech. Rep. 89-261). Queen's University, Kingston, Ontario.

Penix, J., & Alexander, P. (1999). Efficient specification-based component retrieval. *Automated Software Engineering*, 6(2), 139–170. doi:10.1023/A:1008766530096

Perkins, J. H., & Ernst, M. D. (2004). Efficient incremental algorithms for dynamic detection of likely invariants. *SIGSOFT Software Engineering Notes*, 29(6), 23–32. doi:10.1145/1041685.1029901

Perry, D. E. (1989). The logic of propagation in the inscape environment. In *Proceedings of the ACM SIGSOFT 89 Third Symposium on Software Testing, Analysis, and Verification (TAV3)*.

Podgurski, A., & Pierce, L. (1992). Behaviour sampling: A technique for automated retrieval of reusable components. In *Proceedings of the 14th International Conference on Software Engineering*, 349–360.

Pozewaunig, H., & Mittermeir, T. (2000). *Self classifying reusable components generating decision trees from test cases*. Paper presented at the International Conference on Software Engineering and Knowledge Engineering.

Quinlan, R. (1986). Induction of decision trees. *Machine Learning*, 1, 81–106. doi:10.1007/BF00116251

Robertson, S. E., & Walker, S. (1994). Some simple effective approximations to the 2-poisson model for probabilistic weighted retrieval. In *Proceedings of the 17th annual international ACM SIGIR conference on Research and development in information retrieval*, (pp. 232-241). New York: Springer-Verlag.

Rosa, N. S., Alves, C. F., Cunha, P. R. F., Castro, J. F. B., & Justo, G. R. R. (2001). Using non-functional requirements to select components: A formal approach. In *Proceedings Fourth Workshop Ibero-American on Software Engineering and Software Environment*, San Jose, Costa Rica.

Ruggieri, S. (2004). Yadt: Yet another decision tree builder. *ICTAI*, 260–265.

Rust, H. (1998). A PVS specification of an invoicing system. *Proceedings of an International Workshop on Specification Techniques and Formal Methods*, (pp. 51–65).

Ryl, I., Clerbout, M., & Bailly, A. (2001). A component oriented notation for behavioral specification and validation. *Proceedings of the OOPSLA Workshop on Specification and Verification on Component Based Systems*.

Seacord, R., Hissam, S., & Wallnau, K. (1998). Agora: A search engine for software components. *IEEE Internet Computing*, 62–70. doi:10.1109/4236.735988

Sessions, R. (1998). *COM and DCOM: Microsoft's vision for distributed objects*. John Wiley and Sons.

Shneiderman, B. (1997). A framework for search interfaces. *Software IEEE*, 14, 18–20. doi:10.1109/52.582969

Stotts, P. D., & Purtilo, J. (1994). Virtual environment architectures: Interoperability through software interconnection technology. In *Proceedings of the Third Workshop on Enabling Technologies (WETICE '94): Infrastructure for Collaborative Enterprises*, (pp. 211-224). IEEE Computer Society Press.

Strunk, E. A., Yin, X., & Knight, J. C. (2005). Echo: A practical approach to formal verification. In *Proceedings of the 10th international Workshop on Formal Methods For industrial Critical Systems. FMICS '05*, (pp. 44-53). New York: ACM Press.

Sun, C. (2003). *Qos composition and decomposition in Uniframe*. Unpublished doctoral thesis, Department of Computer and Information Science, Indiana University Purdue University.

Thompson, R., & Croft, W. (1989). Support for browsing in an intelligent text retrieval system. *International Journal of Man-Machine Studies, 30*(6), 639–668. doi:10.1016/S0020-7373(89)80014-8

Utgoff, P. E. (1989). Incremental induction of decision trees. *Machine Learning, 4*, 161–186. doi:10.1023/A:1022699900025

Varadarajan, S., Kumar, A., Deepak, G. & Pankaj, J. (2002). Component exchange: An exchange for software components. *ICWI*, 62–72.

Vasiliu, L., Zaremba, M., Moran, M., & Bussler, C. (2004). Web-service semantic enabled implementation of machine vs. machine business negotiation. *Proceedings of the IEEE International Conference on Web Services (ICWS'04)*, San Diego: IEEE Computer Society.

Vitharana, P., Zahedi, F. M., & Jain, H. (2003). Knowledge-based repository scheme for storing and retrieving business components: A theoretical design and an empirical analysis. *IEEE Transactions on Software Engineering, 29*(7), 649–664. doi:10.1109/TSE.2003.1214328

Whaley, J., Martin, M. C., & Lam, M. S. (2002). Automatic extraction of object-oriented component interfaces. *SIGSOFT Software Engineering Notes, 27*(4), 218–228. doi:10.1145/566171.566212

Wille, R. (1982). Restructing lattice theory: An approach based on hierarchies of concepts . In Rival, I. (Ed.), *Ordered sets* (pp. 445–470).

Willet, P. (1988). Recent trends in hierarchic document clustering: A critical review. *Information Processing & Management, 24*(5), 577–597. doi:10.1016/0306-4573(88)90027-1

Xie, X., Tang, J., Li, J.-Z., & Wang, K. (2004). *A component retrieval method based on facet-weight self-learning* (pp. 437–448). AWCC.

Yao, H., & Etzkorn, L. (2004). Towards a semantic-based approach for software reusable component classification and retrieval. In *ACM-SE 42: Proceedings of the 42nd annual Southeast regional conference*, (pp. 110-115). New York: ACM Press.

Yellin, D. M., & Strom, R. E. (1997). Protocol specifications and component adaptors. *ACM Transactions on Programming Languages and Systems, 19*(2), 292–333. doi:10.1145/244795.244801

Yunwen, Y., & Fischer, G. (2001). Context-aware browsing of large component repositories. *Proceedings of 16th International Conference on Automated Software Engineering (ASE'01)*, (pp. 99-106). Coronado Island, CA.

Zaremski, A. M., & Wing, J. M. (1995). Specification matching of software components. In *Proceedings of the Third Symposium on the Foundations of Software Engineering (FSE3)*, (pp. 1-17). ACM SIGSOFT.

Zhang, J., Gao, J., Zhou, M., & Wang, J. (2001). *Improving the effectiveness of information retrieval with clustering and fusion*. Computational Linguistics and Chinese Language.

Zhang, Z., Svensson, L., Snis, U., Srensen, C., Fgerlind, H., Lindroth, T., et al. (2000). Enhancing component reuse using search techniques. *Proceedings of IRIS 23*.

Zhiyuan, W. (2000). *Component-based software engineering*. Unpublished doctoral thesis, New Jersey Institute of technology.

Section 4
Software Estimation and Metrics

Chapter 9
Methods for Statistical and Visual Comparison of Imputation Methods for Missing Data in Software Cost Estimation

Lefteris Angelis
Aristotle University of Thessaloniki, Greece

Panagiotis Sentas
Aristotle University of Thessaloniki, Greece

Nikolaos Mittas
Aristotle University of Thessaloniki, Greece

Panagiota Chatzipetrou
Aristotle University of Thessaloniki, Greece

ABSTRACT

Software Cost Estimation is a critical phase in the development of a software project, and over the years has become an emerging research area. A common problem in building software cost models is that the available datasets contain projects with lots of missing categorical data. The purpose of this chapter is to show how a combination of modern statistical and computational techniques can be used to compare the effect of missing data techniques on the accuracy of cost estimation. Specifically, a recently proposed missing data technique, the multinomial logistic regression, is evaluated and compared with four older methods: listwise deletion, mean imputation, expectation maximization and regression imputation with respect to their effect on the prediction accuracy of a least squares regression cost model. The evaluation is based on various expressions of the prediction error and the comparisons are conducted using statistical tests, resampling techniques and a visualization tool, the regression error characteristic curves.

DOI: 10.4018/978-1-60960-215-4.ch009

INTRODUCTION

Software has become the key element of any computer-based system and product. The complicated structure of software and the continuously increasing demand for quality products justify the high importance of software engineering in today's world as it offers a systematic framework for development and maintenance of software. One of the most important activities in the initial project phases is Software Cost Estimation (SCE). During this stage a software project manager attempts to estimate the effort and time required for the development of a software product. For complete discussions on the importance of software engineering and the role of cost estimation in software project planning we refer to Pressman (2005). Cost estimations may be performed before, during or even after the development of software.

The complicated nature of a software project and therefore the difficult problems involved in the SCE procedures emerged a whole area of research within the wider field of software engineering. A substantial part of the research on SCE concerns the construction of software cost estimation models. These models are built by applying statistical methodologies to historical datasets which contain attributes of finished software projects. The scope of cost estimation models is twofold: first, they can provide a theoretical framework for describing and interpreting the dependencies of cost with the characteristics of the project and second they can be utilized to produce efficient cost predictions. Although the second utility is the most important for practical purposes, the first utility is equally significant, since it provides a basis for thorough studies of how the various project attributes interact and affect the cost. Therefore, the cost models are valuable not only to practitioners but also to researchers whose work is to analyse and interpret.

In the process of constructing cost models, a major problem arises from the fact that missing values are often encountered in some historical datasets. Very often missing data are responsible for the misleading results regarding the accuracy of the cost models and may reduce their explanatory and prediction ability. The aforementioned problem is very important in the area of software project management because most of the software databases suffer from missing values and this can happen for several reasons.

A common reason is the cost and the difficulties that some companies face in the collection of the data. In some cases, the cost of money and time needed to collect certain information is forbidding for a company or an organization. In other cases, the collection of data is very difficult because it demands consistence, experience, time and methodology for a company. An additional source of incomplete values is the fact that data are often collected with a different purpose in mind, or that the measurement categories are generic and thus not applicable to all projects. This seems especially likely when data are collected from a number of companies. So, for researchers whose purpose is to study projects from different companies and build cost models on them, the handling of missing data is an essential preliminary step (Chen, Boehm, Menzies & Port, 2005).

Many techniques deal with missing data. The most common and straightforward one is *Listwise Deletion* (LD), which simply ignores the projects with missing values. The major advantage of the method is its simplicity and the ability to do statistical calculations on a common sample base of cases. The disadvantages of the method are the dramatic loss of information in cases with high percentages of missing values and possible bias in the data. These problems can occur when there is some type of pattern in the missing data, i.e. when the distribution of missing values in some variables is depended on certain valid observations of other variables in the data.

Other techniques estimate or "impute" the missing values. The resulting complete data can then be analyzed and modelled by standard methods (for example regression analysis). These methods are called *imputation methods*. The problem is that most of the imputation methods produce continuous estimates, which are not realistic replacements of the missing values when the variables are categorical. Since the majority of the variables in the software datasets are categorical with many missing values, it is reasonable to use an imputation method producing categorical values in order to fill the incomplete dataset and then to use it for constructing a prediction model.

From the above discussion we can identify the components of the complex problem, which we address in this chapter. In general, we assume that there is an available dataset with cost data from historical projects. Each project is characterized by several categorical variables (attributes or features), while a number of values of these variables are missing. The purpose is to build a cost model (usually by least squares regression) using this incomplete dataset. The question is therefore how to handle the missing data in order to build a model with as much accuracy as possible. It is clear that this is a decision-making problem in the sense that we need to compare and decide on which is the "most accurate" (or equivalently the "least inaccurate") method among a number of alternatives.

The goal of this chapter is to present a combination of advanced statistical and computational approaches which can be used in the aforementioned decision-making procedure. The methodologies described are generic, in the sense that can be applied to: (a) any incomplete dataset, (b) any cost estimation model and (c) the comparison of any missing data techniques.

In order to illustrate the overall methodology framework, we chose to present the work with: (a) a specific dataset, i.e. a subset of the ISBSG software project repository (http://www.isbsg.org/) (b) a least squares regression cost model and (c) five specific missing data techniques; a recently proposed one, namely the multinomial logistic regression and four older, namely listwise deletion, mean imputation, expectation maximization and regression imputation. The reason for

these choices was our familiarity with the imputation methods and the dataset, resulting from our previous research experience. The combination of methods we apply for the comparisons is also based on our previous research in different context. Specifically, we use different error measures, nonparametric statistical tests, resampling techniques and a graphical method, recently introduced in cost estimation.

The structure of the chapter is the following: First we outline related work in the area, then we describe the different mechanisms creating missing data and the most common techniques for handling them. In the following section, we present the dataset used in the analysis and the statistical methods. Then, we give the results of the statistical analysis and finally we conclude by discussing the findings along with possible future research directions.

BACKGROUND

Although the problem of handling missing data has been treated adequately in the statistical literature and in various real-world datasets, there are relatively sparse published works concerning software cost missing data. Emam & Birk (2000) used multiple imputation in order to induce missing values in their analysis of software process data performance.

Strike, Emam, & Madhavji (2001) compared LD, MI and eight different types of hot-deck imputation for dealing with missing data in the context of software cost modeling. Three missing data mechanisms were evaluated (MCAR, MAR and NI) and two patterns of missing data were simulated (univariate and monotone) in order to induce missing values on a complete large software engineering dataset. The results showed that all the missing data techniques performed well and therefore the simplest technique, LD, is a reasonable choice. However, best performance was obtained by using hot-deck imputation with Euclidean distance and a z-score standardization.

Myrtveit, Stensrud & Olsson (2001) analyzed datasets with missing data and LD, MI, similar response pattern imputation (SRPI) and full information maximum likelihood (FIML) were evaluated on an enterprise resource planning (ERP) dataset with real missing values. The results indicated that FIML is appropriate when data are not missing completely at random. LD, MI and SRPI resulted in biased prediction models unless the data is MCAR. Also, MI and SRPI, compared to LD, were suitable only if the dataset after applying LD was very small in order to construct a meaningful prediction model.

Cartwright, Shepperd, & Song (2003) examined sample mean imputation (SMI) and k-NN on two industrial datasets with real missing data. They found that both methods improved the model fit but k-NN gave better results than SMI.

Song, Shepperd & Cartwright (2005) used two imputation methods in their research. Class mean imputation (CMI) and k-nearest neighbors (k-NN) were considered with respect to two mechanisms of creating missing data: missing completely at random (MCAR) and missing at random (MAR).

In a previous work by two of the authors (Sentas & Angelis, 2005), a statistical methodology known as *"Multinomial Logistic Regression"* (MLR) was suggested for the estimation and the imputation of categorical missing values. Specifically, MLR was applied on a complete (i.e. with no missing values) dataset from the International Software Benchmarking Standards Group (ISBSG) data base. The missing values were created artificially by simulating three different mechanisms: *missing completely at random* (MCAR), *missing at random* (MAR) and *non-ignorable missingness* (NI). The study was designed to involve three percentages of incomplete data (10%, 20% and 30%) and MLR method was compared with four other missing data techniques: *listwise deletion* (LD), *mean imputation* (MI), *expectation maximization* (EM) and *regression imputation* (RI).

The experimentation was designed to explore the effects of imputation on the prediction error produced by a regression model and showed the efficiency of MLR as an imputation method.

Twala, Cartwright & Shepperd (2006) compared seven missing data techniques (listwise deletion (LD), expectation maximization single imputation (EMSI), k-nearest neighbour single imputation (kNNSI), mean or mode single imputation (MMSI), expectation maximization multiple imputation (EMMI), fractional cases (FC) and surrogate variable splitting (SVS) using eight industrial datasets. The results reveal that listwise deletion (LD) is the least effective technique for handling incomplete data while multiple imputation achieves the highest accuracy rates. Furthermore, they proposed and showed how a combination of MDTs by randomizing a decision tree building algorithm leads to a significant improvement in prediction performance for missing values up to 50%.

Wong, Zhao, Chan & Victor (2006) applied a statistical methodology in order to optimize and simplify software metric models with missing data. In order to deal with missing data, they used a modified k-nearest neighbors (k-NN) imputation method. The results indicate that their methodology can be useful in trimming redundant predictor metrics and identifying unnecessary categories assumed for a categorical predictor metric in the model.

Van Hulse & Khoshgoftaar (2008) presented a comprehensive experimental analysis of five commonly used imputation techniques (mean imputation (MI), regression imputation (RI), Bayesian multiple imputation (BMI), REPTree imputation (RTI) and instance-based learning imputation (IBLI). The authors concluded that Bayesian multiple imputation and regression imputation are the most effective techniques, while mean imputation performs extremely poorly. Also, the authors took under consideration three different mechanisms (MCAR, MAR and NI) governing the distribution of missing values in a dataset, and examined the impact of noise on the imputation process.

Regression analysis plays an important role in SCE. Although there are several forms of regression models, the ordinary least squares regression seems to be one of the most popular techniques. It is used for fitting a linear parametric model for the cost variable by minimizing the sum of squared residuals. This means that a linear equation is first assumed between the dependent variable and the predictors and next its parameters, the regression coefficients, are estimated by the least squares method. The role of regression in SCE is thoroughly discussed in the systematic reviews by Mair & Shepperd (2005) and Jorgensen & Shepperd (2007).

Although least squares regression is an easily implemented and straightforward method, there are certain assumptions to consider when fitting a model. The most important ones are: (a) the relationship between the predictor variables and the dependent variable is linear and (b) the residuals are normally distributed and uncorrelated with the predictors. These two assumptions are usually addressed in the case of software project data by using the logarithmic transformations of the cost (dependent) variable and the size (independent) variable (Kitchenham & Mendes 2004; Mendes & Lokan 2008). In our application, we followed the same practice.

The issue of data quality is critical in SCE. In the recent paper by Liebchen & Shepperd (2008), the researchers discuss the problem of data quality, reporting their concerns about the quality of some of the datasets that are used to learn, evaluate and compare prediction models. In our application which will be described later, we took into account the importance of data quality by removing from the ISBSG dataset the projects which are of low quality (rated with C and D) and from the remaining (rated with A and B) we used only those projects measured by the same sizing method.

Another issue related to the reliability of the specific ISBSG dataset, is whether a multi-organizational dataset can be used to build efficient models in comparison to models built on data from a single company. Several studies address this problem, often with contradictory results. See for example the papers by Jeffery, Ruhe & Wieczorek, (2000 and 2001) and by Mendes, Lokan, Harrison & Triggs (2005). Unfortunately, the lack of a widely acceptable and reliable dataset which can be used to test any statistical model and method does not allow us to draw general conclusions. However, our purpose is to present specific statistical methodologies which can be applied to any dataset, either multi-organizational or from a single company.

Regarding the comparison of different models, there is a large amount of papers suggesting various measures of prediction error (Kitchenham, Pickard, MacDonell & Shepperd 2001, Foss, Stensurd, Kitchenham, & Myrtveit 2003) and statistical procedures (Stensrud & Myrtveit, 1998, Kitchenham & Mendes, 2009). The most common tests for comparing error measures on the same data are the *parametric paired sample t-test* and the *non-parametric Wilcoxon signed rank test* (Kitchenham & Mendes 2004, Mittas & Angelis, 2008a, Mendes & Lokan 2008).

A common problem encountered in the comparisons with statistical tests is that the prediction error measures are skewed with outliers, so it is not easy to assume a theoretical distribution, especially the Gaussian. In a previous study (Mittas & Angelis, 2008a), we proposed a statistical simulation method, the *permutation tests,* in order to test the significance of differences between software cost estimation models. This method is based on resampling, i.e. on drawing a large number of samples from the original sample in order to "reconstruct" the underlying theoretical distribution and for this reason the hypothesis test is carried out without worrying about the distribution of the variables.

Although statistical procedures are critical for comparisons, there is always the need for a visual inspection and comparison of the whole distributions of error measures. In two recent studies (Mittas & Angelis 2008b & 2010), we introduced the *Regression Error Characteristic* (REC) analysis as a class of visualization techniques for the evaluation of the predictive power and comparison of different models.

From the above summary, it is clear that in the present chapter we extend and combine our previous research results in the following directions: (a) by comparing the newer MLR imputation method with the four older missing data techniques (LD, MI, EM, RI) using a dataset with real (not simulated) missing values, (b) by evaluating the effect of the missing data techniques on the prediction error of a regression model, measuring three different aspects of prediction performance, namely *accuracy*, *bias* and *spread* and (c) by using for statistical comparisons of the imputation methods the permutation tests and the REC curves.

MISSING DATA MECHANISMS AND MISSING DATA TECHNIQUES

Missing Data Mechanism

The methods of handling missing data are directly related to the mechanisms that caused the incompleteness. Generally, these mechanisms fall into three classes according to Little & Rubin (2002):

1. **Missing Completely at Random (MCAR):** The missing values in a variable are unrelated to the values of any other variables, whether missing or valid.
2. **Non-Ignorable missingness (NI):** NI can be considered as the opposite of MCAR in the sense that the probability of having missing values in a variable depends on the variable itself (for example a question regarding skills

may be not answered when the skills are in fact low).
3. **Missing at Random (MAR):** MAR can be considered as an intermediate situation between MCAR and NI. The probability of having missing values does not depend on the variable itself but on the values of some other variable.

Unfortunately, it is very difficult to recognize if the mechanism is MCAR, MAR or NI in a dataset with real missing values, which is the case of this chapter. Comparisons under the assumption of specific mechanisms have been considered in Sentas & Angelis (2005) where we used artificial missing data in order to simulate the distribution of missing values. In the present work, no such assumption is made, since the data contain real missing values and their underlying mechanism is unknown.

Missing Data Techniques (MDTs)

In order to handle the missing data, we used the following techniques according to Little & Rubin (2002):

1. **Listwise Deletion (LD):** It is a typical method that belongs to a broader class, namely the deletion methods. According to LD, cases with missing values for any of the variables are omitted from the analysis.
2. **Mean imputation (MI):** This method replaces the missing observations of a certain variable with the mean of the observed values in that variable. It is a simple method that generally performs well, especially when valid data are normally distributed. In our study, the categorical variables with missing values have been preprocessed and transformed using ANOVA (ANOVA is analyzed in the next part of the chapter), with respect to their effect on the effort, so the resulting variables used in the cost model

were finally ordinal. Since the ordinal values are essentially rankings, we decided to use the mean ranking as an imputed value for the missing values. This is consistent to the statistical theory which frequently uses the mean ranking in non-parametric statistical tests.

3. **Regression Imputation (RI):** The missing values are estimated through the application of multiple regression where the variable with missing data is considered as the dependent one and all other variables as predictors.

4. **Expectation Maximization (EM):** The EM algorithm is an iterative two step procedure obtaining the maximum likelihood estimates of a model starting from an initial guess. Each iteration consists of two steps: the Expectation (E) step that finds the distribution for the missing data based on the known values for the observed variables and the current estimate of the parameters and the Maximization (M) step that replaces the missing data with the expected value.

5. **Multinomial Logistic Regression (MLR):** is used to model the relationship between a polytomous (its values are more than two categories) dependent variable and a set of k predictor variables which are either categorical (factors) or numerical. MLR can be used for imputation by considering as dependent the categorical variable with the missing values and as predictors all the others. A similar method has already been used for prediction of productivity by Sentas, Angelis, Stamelos & Bleris (2004), while MLR has already been applied and proposed in Sentas & Angelis (2005), as we already mentioned. Hosmer & Lemeshow (1989) have proposed more detailed descriptions on models with categorical data.

The above techniques are chosen for reasons of consistency with our previous work in Sentas & Angelis (2005). As MLR is a recently proposed method, it is reasonable to compare it with the other four methods which are well known, have been extensively used and they are implemented in statistical software. We must also emphasize the fact that there are other effective non-imputation techniques, such as the Full Information Maximum Likelihood (FIML) method analyzed by Myrtveit, Stensrud & Olsson (2001), which can fit a model without imputing the missing values. However, the basic assumption of this method is that the data are continuous and come from a multivariate normal distribution, which is not true in our case where the data contain categorical variables. Also, the chapter focuses mainly on the methods of comparisons which can be applied in any other imputation method.

RESEARCH METHODOLOGY

The method for comparing MLR with the other four MDTs was based on measuring the impact of each of the MDTs on the predictive accuracy of a cost estimation model. Below we describe the dataset we used, the accuracy measures employed for the comparisons and finally a general design of the study.

Selection of the Dataset

The dataset we used for our application contains 152 projects derived from the International Software Benchmarking Standards Group (ISBSG) project repository (http://www.isbsg.org/). The dataset was formed according to the recommendation of ISBSG, i.e. we chose only projects with quality rating A and B, their size was measured only by the IFPUG method while they all had as 'Recording Method', the staff hours (recorded). Finally, we decided to keep only the categories '1 only', '1+2' and 'TOTAL only' from 'Resource Level'. In Table 1 we can see the original variables of the dataset.

Table 1. Variables in the dataset of ISBSG with real missing values

Variable	Full Name
fpoints	Function Points
Develp	Development type
Platfr	Development platform
Lang	Language type
Primar	Primary Programming Language
implem (year)	Implementation Date
Orgtype	Organisation Type
Bartype	Business Area Type
Apltype	Application Type
Pacost	Package Costomaziation
Dbms	DBMS Used
Usdmet	Used Methodology

Variables of the Cost Model

The cost models built on the data under different MDTs were all linear least squares regression models, constructed by considering as dependent variable the logarithm of work effort (*lneffort*). Only two of the predictor variables are numerical, i.e. the year of implementation (*year*) and the logarithm of function points (*lnfpoints*). The logarithmic transformations for effort and function points were applied since they satisfy the normality assumptions of the linear regression model and improve their efficiency (Maxwell, 2002). Since the rest of the predictor variables are categorical with a large number of categories each, we conducted a preliminary study in order to merge the original categories into homogeneous groups and therefore to work with only a few categories for each factor.

This was achieved first by analysis of variance (ANOVA), in order to identify the most important factors and next by concatenation of the categories with similar mean effort values. The categories of each factor were represented by ordinal values according to their impact on the mean effort. The

categorical variables resulted from this study are given in Table 2.

Two of the categorical predictor variables have real missing observations. These are: 'DBMS used' (*dbms*) and 'Business Area Type' (*bartype*), with 41 and 16 missing observations in each one respectively.

Validation Procedure and Accuracy Measures

The prediction accuracy for each of the comparative models was evaluated through the hold-out procedure. Primarily, we split the dataset into two subsets: a training set with 120 projects and a test set with 32 projects with no missing values. Using the five known MDTs, we replaced the missing observations with predictions, simultaneously to both categorical predictor variables '*dbms*' and '*bartype*' of the training set. So, five complete datasets resulted, one for each MDT. A cost regression model was built on each of the above datasets and its accuracy was evaluated on the test dataset.

Based on the actual value Y_A and the estimated value Y_E, various error functions for the evaluation of the predictive power of the models have been proposed in the SCE literature (Foss, Stensurd, Kitchenham, & Myrtveit, 2003) describing different aspects of their performances. Although the thorough debate concerning the appropriateness of the evaluation measures (Kitchenham, Pickard, MacDonell, & Shepperd, 2001), there has been noted a lack of convergence about which accuracy indicators are suitable for the comparison procedure. Having in mind the abovementioned disagreement, we decided to utilize three measures of local error in order to obtain a more representative view of the predictive performances of the comparative models:

The absolute error (AE),

$$AE_i = \left| Y_{A_i} - Y_{E_i} \right| \tag{1}$$

Table 2. The categorical predictor variables used for the cost models

Variable	Description & Levels
develp	Left out from the analysis
platfr	Development platform. Levels: 1=MainFrame or MF, 2=Mid Range or MR, 3=PC
lang	Language type. Levels: 1=3GL, 2=4GL, 3=Application Generator or ApG
primar_4	Primary Programming Language. Levels (after merging): 1={access, natural, pl/i}, 2={easytrieve, oracle, power builder, sql, telon, visual basic, ideal}, 3={ C, C++, cobol, other 4gl, other apg, }, 4={ C/VB, cobol II, coolgen}
orgtype_4	Organisation Type. Levels (after merging): 1={ computers, consultancy, energy, medical and health care, professional services}, 2={communication, community services, electricity/gas/water, electronics, financial, property & business services, insurance, manufacturing, public administration}, 3={ aerospace/automotive, banking, construction, distribution, government, transport & storage}, 4 ={consumer goods, defense, occupational health and safety, wholesale & retail trade}
bartype_4	Business Area Type. Levels (after merging): 1={ accounting, activity tracking, claims processing-product pays claim, engineering, environment, fine enforcement, generate & distribute electricity, research & development, sales & marketing, telecommunications}, 2={banking, financial (excluding banking), inventory, architectural, project management & job control, provide computer services and IT consultation}, 3={insurance, legal, manufacturing, pension funds managements, personnel, procurement, public administration}, 4={ transport/shipping, blood bank, chartered flight operation, energy generation, logistics}
apltype	Left out from the analysis
pacost	Left out from the analysis
dbms_4	DBMS Used. Levels (after merging): 1={ACCESS, ADABAS, MS SQL Server, ORACLE, RDB, WATCOM}, 2={DB2/2, IMS, Other, SYBASE, WATCOM SQL}, 3={IDMS, DB2, DATA COM, ADABAS V5, RDB 6.0, RDMS}, 4={CA-IDMS, FOXPRO, GUPTA SQL BASIC, INTERACTIVE, RDB 4-2-1, ORACLE V7}
usdmet	Left out from the analysis

The error ratio (z),

$$z_i = \frac{Y_{Ei}}{Y_{Ai}} \qquad (2)$$

The magnitude of relative error (MRE),

$$MRE_i = \frac{\left| Y_{Ai} - Y_{Ei} \right|}{Y_{Ai}} \qquad (3)$$

As we have already mentioned, these error functions measure different aspects of the prediction performance. More precisely, *absolute errors* are used in order to measure the *accuracy* whereas Kitchenham, Pickard, MacDonell & Shepperd (2001), propose the utilization of the error ratio *z*

which is clearly related to the distribution of the residuals, as a measure of *bias* for the predictions obtained by a model. Ideally, an optimum estimation is equal to the actual value (*z*=1), whereas z-values greater or less than 1 show overestimation or underestimation, respectively. On the other hand, the most commonly used measure is the magnitude of relative error (MMRE), but Foss, Stensurd, Kitchenham,& Myrtveit (2003) demonstrate that it does not always select the "best" model. On the other hand, Kitchenham, Pickard, MacDonell, & Shepperd (2001) suggest that *magnitude of relative error* measures the *spread* of the variable z.

These local measures can be the basis for the evaluation of the overall prediction performance of the comparative models by computing a statistic (usually the mean or median) for them. The most commonly used measures in SCE are the followings:

$$MdAE = median\left\{AE_i\right\} \tag{4}$$

$$Medianz = median\{z_i\} \tag{5}$$

$$MdMRE = median\left\{MRE_i\right\} \tag{6}$$

Formal Statistical Comparisons

Except from the overall prediction performance computed from the error functions ((1), (2) and (3)), these samples of errors can be used in order to draw conclusions concerning the differences of the comparative models. The statistical significance of the difference can be tested through traditional and simulation techniques (Mittas & Angelis 2008a).

Due to the fact that the AEs are usually non-normally distributed, we decided to use the traditional non-parametric Wilcoxon sign rank test for matched pairs (Kitchenham & Mendes 2004, Mittas & Angelis 2008a, Mendes & Lokan 2008). The Wilcoxon method tests whether two related (paired) samples have the same median. In our case we considered as the first of the paired samples the AEs derived by MLR and as the second sample, the AE sample derived by each of the other methods (LD, RI, EM and MI). In all tests we consider as statistically significant a difference with p-value (significance) smaller than 0.05. All the tests conducted are one-tailed (directional) in the sense that the alternative hypothesis is that a certain statistic of the AEs derived from the MLR is smaller than that of a comparative model (LD, RI, EM and MI).

The problem with the software projects cost data is that the samples are quite small and skewed,

so it is not easy to make assumptions regarding the distribution of the prediction errors resulting from a certain process or a model and from which the accuracy measures are calculated. For such small-sized type of data it is known from the statistical literature that a certain class of simulation methods may be proved quite beneficial (Mittas & Angelis 2008a)

More specifically, *permutation tests* are utilized in order to investigate the error reduction obtained by the MLR method. Permutation tests are resampling techniques which "reconstruct" the underlying theoretical distribution, based on rearrangements of the data. The method generates a large number of paired samples (for (1), (2) and (3)) where each pair is permuted randomly. The statistic under consideration is computed for each generated paired sample and its sampling distribution is used for testing any hypothesis (for further details see Mittas & Angelis 2008a)

As we have already mentioned, the accuracy of a prediction model can be evaluated through the AEs. For this reason we follow a similar approach presented above for the case of Wilcoxon test, whereas the statistic under consideration is the median of AEs. The algorithm for the evaluation of the permutation test can be described by the following steps:

1. The paired data are randomly permuted as we already described.
2. The difference of the statistic under consideration (median of AEs) is computed.
3. Steps 1 and 2 are repeated a large number of times.
4. The statistic from the original sample is computed and is located in the sampling distribution of all values obtained from Steps 1-3 in order to estimate the significance of the hypothesis (p - value).

Graphical Comparison through Regression Error Characteristic Curve

As we have already mentioned, despite the wide variety of accuracy measures appeared so far in SCE literature, the presentation of overall accuracy tables does not provide any information about the distributions of errors. Furthermore, the tests presented in the previous section make inference about a parameter of the comparative distributions of errors (mean or median) and do not provide any further information for the performances of the comparative models at any other point of their distributions. All of the issues discussed above led us to suggest a graphical tool (Mittas & Angelis, 2010) that can be utilized for comparison purposes in order to reinforce the results of accuracy measures and statistical hypothesis tests through an easily interpretable manner.

Regression Error Characteristic (REC) curve is a recently proposed visualization technique that can also be incorporated in the comparison procedure of alternative prediction models. REC curves, proposed by Bi and Bennett (2003), are a generalization of Receiver Operating Characteristic (ROC) curves that are often utilized in classification problems. A REC curve is a two-dimensional graph where the horizontal axis (or x-axis) represents the *error tolerance* (i.e. all possible values of error for a model) of a predefined accuracy measure and the vertical axis (or y-axis) represents the *accuracy* of a prediction model. Accuracy is defined as the percentage of projects that are predicted within the error tolerance e.

$$accuracy \ (e) = \frac{\#(\text{projects with error} \leq e)}{\#(\text{projects})}$$

(7)

REC curves have been introduced in the SCE area in Mittas & Angelis (2008b, 2010), where it was suggested that their utilization can be proved quite beneficial since they reinforce the knowledge of project managers obtained either by single accuracy indicators or by comparisons through formal statistical tests. They demonstrate that the most important feature is the ability to present easily accuracy results to non-experts and support the decision-making. In addition, REC curves are very informative since they take into account the whole error distribution and not just a single indicator of the errors providing a graphical tool that can guide the modelling process (identification of extreme points) by the inspection of their shapes. Further details of their advantages, interesting characteristics and also the algorithm for their construction can be found in Mittas & Angelis, (2008b, 2010).

In Figure 1, we present the REC curves of three hypothetical comparative models. Generally, a prediction model performs well if the REC curve climbs rapidly towards the upper left corner. It is obvious that Model A outperforms both Model B and Model C since its REC curve is always above the corresponding curves of the comparative models. Considering the curves of Model B and Model C, no conclusion can be derived for the overall prediction performances. On the other hand, valuable information for their performances on different ranges of errors can be derived by the inspection of their relative positions. Their REC

Figure 1. An example of REC curves

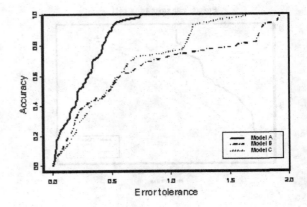

curves reveal that Model B seems to be the "best" choice for small values of errors but the opposite is the case as the error tolerance becomes higher (higher than 0.5).

Although the utilization of statistical comparisons should be always carried out in order to verify the differences between comparative prediction models, specific limitations (i.e. difficulties to the interpretation of the statistical results, heavily-skewed distributions etc) render this hardly applicable. REC curves give the opportunity to a practitioner to draw significant findings by an alternative visualization technique for the whole distribution of error functions. Moreover, there are cases in which a project manager requires further information for the prediction power of alternative models on very specific ranges of the actual cost variable (i.e. effort or productivity). This is due to the fact that the cost of a forthcoming project is not uniform and may have different impact for the earnings of an organization. More precisely, a project manager wishes to get a better insight for projects with high actual cost since an inaccurate prediction can lead to high overruns. On the other hand, a practitioner is also interested in projects with small actual cost in order to bid other contracts and increase the profits of the organization.

The abovementioned analysis can be carried out through partial REC curves proposed by Torgo (2005), whereas in our previous study (Mittas & Angelis, 2010) we present the application of partial REC curves in SCE in a more systematic fashion by detailing the basic principles, properties and the algorithm for constructing them. In general, a partial REC curve can be constructed in the same way as the REC curves by simply estimating the distribution of the prediction errors only for those cases falling within the range of particular interest (i.e. projects with small or high actual cost).

In Figure 2 (a) and (b), we present an illustrative example of the partial REC curves. The critical question we posed is which model presents the best prediction power for projects with small or high actual cost. So, after the estimation of errors obtained by the three hypothetical models, we have to partition our dataset into two subsets containing projects with small and high actual cost. The partial REC curves for small (Figure 2(a)) and high (Figure 2(b)) costs suggest that Model A outperforms both Model B and Model C everywhere, since its curves are always above the corresponding curves of Model B and Model C. On the other hand, Model B seems to outperform Model C for projects with low cost (Figure 2 (a)) but the opposite holds for the projects with high cost (Figure 2 (b)). Now, let us just ignore for the

Figure 2. An example of partial REC curves (a) for small actual costs and (b) for high actual costs

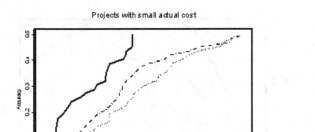

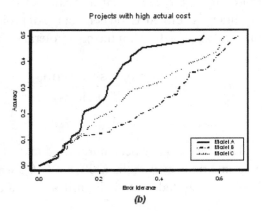

Table 3. Overall prediction measures from the five MDT

MDT	MAE	MdAE	Meanz	Medianz	MMRE	MdMRE
MLR	**2153.04**	**890.44**	**1.16**	**0.91**	**62.45**	**42.86**
LD	2445.92	1240.74	1.17	1.14	65.76	55.62
RI	2538.96	1386.64	1.31	1.20	73.20	50.22
EM	2712.19	1550.29	1.32	1.11	73.78	56.25
MI	4293.78	1649.70	1.55	1.35	96.68	64.05

needs of the example Model A which is the best overall. After a rough estimation of the project's cost level (low or high) we would choose Model B for low cost forthcoming projects and Model C for high cost projects, combining in this way the predictions derived from the two comparative models.

EXPERIMENTATION-RESULTS

In order to fit an effort prediction model in each of the above datasets, we used ordinary least squares (OLS) regression. For each of the five models, the independent variables were always the same. This was done on purpose, in order to preserve the balance of the experimental design and to have a common base for the comparisons. Indeed, removing or adding variables would cause additional sources of variation on accuracy measures and would therefore complicate the analysis and the interpretation of the results. As independent variables of the models we consider the numerical variable '*lnfpoints*' and the two categorical variables '*dbms_4*' and '*barthype_4*' which are the variables with real missing values.

In Table 3, we summarise the results of the comparison of the five missing data techniques in the dataset of ISBSG with real missing values. In general, the above results are in agreement with the results in Sentas & Angelis (2005), but the comparisons in this study extend the prior knowledge due to the evaluation of different error functions. The MLR method appears the

best performance in terms of accuracy, bias and spread since the corresponding indicators have the lowest mean and median values. On the other hand, MI gives the worst performance in all the measures. A closer examination of the indicators reveals a large divergence between the mean and medians of the local measures of errors. This fact may be due to the existence of extreme outlying points and further investigation is needed through REC curves. Moreover, the presence of outliers justifies the utilization of more robust statistical comparisons such as the non-parametric Wilcoxon procedure and permutation tests.

The non-parametric Wilcoxon tests between the AEs of the MLR and the AEs derived by each of the other methods (LD, RI, EM and MI) are presented in Table 4. Since all the values are less than 0.05, there is a statistically significant difference between the performance of MLR and each of the other methods. As the samples of AEs are small-sized, permutation tests should also be carried out in order to have a more realistic aspect of the abovementioned results. As we can see in Table 4, the findings are also verified by the p-

Table 4. Significance of all paired samples tests

Comparison	Wilcoxon Test	Permutation Test
MLR-LD	0.018/Sig.	0.043/Sig.
MLR-RI	0.030/Sig.	0.021/Sig.
MLR-EM	0.037/Sig.	0.012/Sig.
MLR-MI	0.012/Sig.	0.018/Sig.

values of permutation tests and we can infer that MLR seems to be a good choice.

The graphical comparisons through REC curves also indicate the error reduction caused by MLR. More precisely, in Figure 3 (a) and (b) the AEs REC curves for all the comparative models are presented. In order to obtain a more clear inspection of the error distributions, we decided to compare MLR with LD and RI (Figure 3 (a)) and MLR with EM and MI (Figure 3 (b)), separately based on the rankings of their performances. The horizontal dashed reference line from 0.5 intersects each REC curve at a point which corresponds to the median value of the AEs. In this manner, we can geometrically evaluate the overall MdAE for each one of the comparative models. The AE REC curve for MLR is always above the corresponding curves of the rest models verifying the results derived from formal statistical comparisons and overall prediction measures. Moreover, LD seems to have a slightly better accuracy performance than RI whereas MI the worst in all the ranges of possible AE values. An interesting characteristic of all the REC curves is that they are flat for high values of AEs and they do not reach the value of 1 until the error tolerance becomes high. This fact signifies the presence of extreme outlying points which are also responsible for the large variability between the mean and median values of AE presented in Table 3.

Concerning the bias of the models, the mean values of the error z ratio indicate that all methods are prone to overestimation since all values are higher than 1. Due to the fact that the mean statistic is affected by the presence of extreme outliers and the data is highly skewed, we should examine the median as a more robust measure of central tendency for the z distributions. Using the medians, it is clear that only MLR favours underestimates, whereas the other models are susceptible to overestimates.

In Figures 3 (c) and (d) we constructed the REC curves representing the error ratio z for each comparative model. This graph has interesting

characteristics since the curve of the better model has to be under the curve of the comparative one for values smaller than 1 (optimum value) and above the curve of the comparative one for values higher than 1. For better illustration, we present with a vertical dashed reference line the critical value of 1 that signifies the under- or overestimations. Furthermore, we can also assess whether a model favours under or over-estimation by the examination of error tolerance at accuracy 0.50 (that is the median). The median z statistic of MLR is the closest to the optimum value of 1 and appears to be the least biased model whereas MI the most biased model (Figure 3 (d)). On the other hand, LD outperforms MLR for error tolerance higher than 1.6. So, there are a few high outlying points of z values produced by MLR which also affect the mean statistic of the error sample.

As far as the spread of z error ratio concerns, the distributions of MREs (Figures 3 (e) and (f)) show that MLR outperforms the other models and has the lowest median value. In addition, the comparison of MLR and LD models signifies that MLR has bad performance for high values of MREs (higher than 70%) indicating again the existence of outliers.

In our previous analysis, we presented in detail how REC curves can lead a project manager to select the "best" imputation technique. Although this is one of the most crucial issues that have to be addressed for the best management of a new software project, the aforementioned analysis concerns the overall prediction performances of comparative models. As we have already pointed out, partial REC curves offer a specialized analysis and valuable information about the performances of the comparative imputation techniques on specific ranges of interest.

Let us suppose that a practitioner has to investigate how the prediction models perform separately for small and for large values of the dependent variable (effort). In the first step of the partial REC analysis, we have to define the range of interest. For this reason, we calculated the median of the

Figure 3. (a) AE REC curves for MLR, LD, RI, (b) AE REC curves for MLR, EM, MI, (c) z REC curves for MLR, LD, RI, (d) z REC curves for MLR, EM, MI, (e) MRE REC curves for MLR, LD, RI, (f) MRE REC curves for MLR, EM, MI

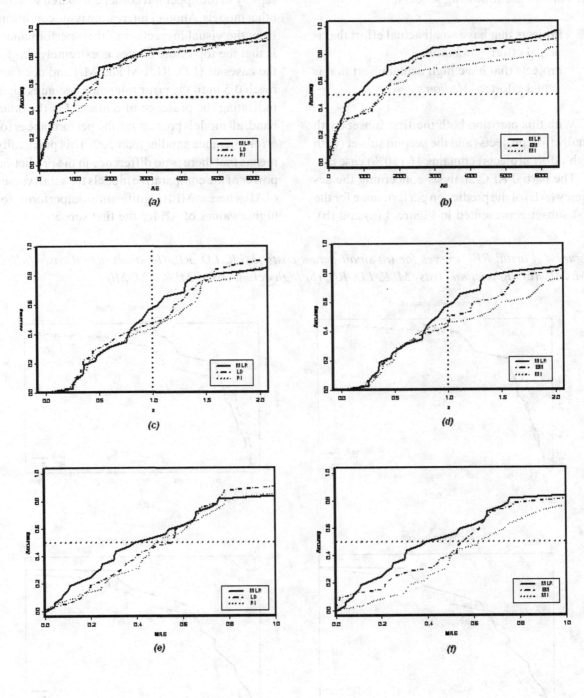

empirical distribution of the dependent variable and we constructed the partial REC curves for each one of the following subsets:

- Projects that have small actual effort that is actual effort $\leq Median$.
- Projects that have high actual effort that is actual effort $> Median$.

With this partition both the first subset (with small effort projects) and the second subset (with high effort projects) contains 16 (50%) cases.

The partial REC analysis concerning the accuracy (AE) of the prediction performance for the first subset is presented in Figure 4 (a) and (b).

Regarding the accuracy of the imputation techniques, we can observe that MLR climbs more rapidly to the upper left corner compared with the other models. Another interesting issue coming up from the visual inspection of their performances is that the top of the curves is extremely flat for the cases of (LD, RI, EM and MI) and does not reach 0.5 until the error tolerance becomes high, indicating the presence of outliers. On the other hand, all models present similar performances for error tolerance smaller than 500. This practically means that there is no difference in the prediction power of the comparative models for small values of AE whereas MLR significantly outperforms for higher values of AE for the first subset.

Figure 4. Partial REC curves for (a) small actual costs (MLR, LD, RI), (b) small actual costs (MLR, EM, MI), (c) high actual costs (MLR, LD, RI), (b) high actual costs (MLR, EM, MI)

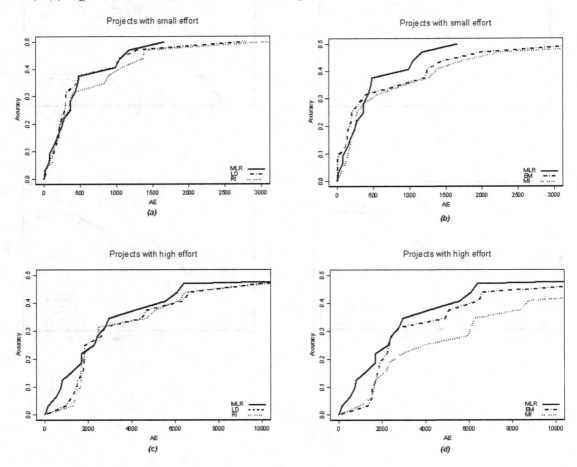

The partial REC analysis is also conducted for the second subset of large effort projects (Figure 4 (c) and (d)). Contrary to the first subset, the partial REC curve of MLR reveals that this imputation method appears the "best" performance for the whole range of error tolerance since its curve outperforms the corresponding curves of the comparative imputation techniques. Now, ignoring for the needs of the analysis MLR which is the best overall, we can point out that LD and RI present similar partial REC curves and for this reason they can be considered as the second "best" imputation techniques for projects with high actual costs.

In summary, the combination of the statistical and computational methods which we applied for the comparisons between MLR and the other missing data techniques managed to reveal the superiority of MLR not only for the whole distribution of errors but also over specific ranges of the actual effort, especially for projects with high actual effort.

CONCLUSION AND DIRECTIONS FOR FUTURE RESEARCH

This chapter presents a combination of statistical and computational methods for handling missing data and for the comparison of missing data techniques applied in software cost datasets for the construction of prediction models. These methods have been introduced in previous works of the authors (Sentas & Angelis (2005), Mittas & Angelis (2008a, 2008b and 2010)), and in the present work are presented as a comprehensive framework which can help a researcher or a practitioner to decide and choose the most suitable missing data technique. The proposed methodology is described as a case study using a dataset with real missing values and specific methods for: (a) building the prediction model, (b) handling the missing data and (c) comparing the missing data techniques by statistical and graphical methods.

More specifically: (a) we used a very popular cost prediction method in SCE, the least squares regression, (b) we applied five missing data techniques: multinomial logistic regression (MLR), Listwise Deletion (LD), Mean Imputation (MI), Expectation Maximization (EM) and Regression Imputation (RI) and (c) we used functions of the prediction error, non-parametric and resampling statistical tests and also a graphical tool, the Regression Error Characteristic (REC) curves in order to compare the performance of MLR with the other four well-known and older methods. The rationale for these comparisons was our previous experience, when we suggested the use of MLR as efficient method for imputing categorical data and compared it with the same missing data techniques. However, our previous work was based on simulated missing data and the comparisons were purely statistical. For the present case study we used a software project dataset with real missing observations and also a comprehensive framework for comparisons.

It is important to note that the missing data techniques were evaluated for their effect on the cost prediction model. That is why we used the results of regression under the application of different missing data approaches in order to make inferences. In general, the results confirmed our previous beliefs for the efficiency of MLR. The combination of the methods used in the present work, showed that MLR gives better results than the other methods in this specific dataset with real missing data.

A very important point of concern is whether an imputation technique produces a new dataset that can be further used for purposes other than cost estimation. In this regard, we have to emphasize that the methods discussed in this chapter, have a specific role: to provide a dataset as a basis for building a cost estimation model. Under this perspective it is clear that the imputation procedure is essentially a method producing artificial data which will be used for a specific reason. These data cannot be used in a straightforward manner for other inferential purposes. So, the result of a comparison between missing data techniques using a cost estimation criterion does not mean that the "best" method under this criterion is necessarily a representative dataset as a whole.

In summary, the conclusions derived from the case study were: First, the comparison of MLR with the compared MTD's revealed high efficiency of the method in terms of accuracy, bias and spread. More specifically, MLR gave significantly better results than the comparative techniques in terms of accuracy that was evaluated through the AE indicators. Second, MLR was the only method that produced the least biased estimates. Moreover, the central location statistics and the inspections of REC curves for MRE measuring the spread of the distributions reflected the very good performance of MLR, compared to the other methods. On the other hand, MI technique appeared to have the "worst" performance in all the aspects of error. The comparisons indicated also that LD showed quite good performance. The comparison of MLR and LD signified that the latter had better performance for high values of error tolerance in terms of bias and spread. The good performance of the LD method may be a consequence of the fact that possibly the missing values in both the categorical variables of our dataset are unrelated to the values of any other variables, whether missing or valid (MCAR mechanism). The aforementioned interpretation is based on our results in Sentas & Angelis (2005), where LD performed well in the case of low percentage of missing values (10%) and MCAR mechanism of missing data.

It is obvious that the above results cannot be generalized for all datasets. The purpose of this study was not to show the superiority of MLR in any dataset and with respect to any other method, but rather to illustrate how the complex problem of missing data can be manipulated by a combination of different methods. The ideas discussed here can be applied to any dataset for the comparison of any other missing data techniques. A general conclusion from the experimentations is that the problems encountered in cost estimation require a variety of advanced methods for efficient decision making and modeling.

The research questions and therefore the directions for future research are several. There are many more MDTs in the literature which deserve thorough comparative studies on various datasets. It would be also interesting to study the effect of missing data techniques on other prediction models and methods, for example on estimation by analogy. Other measures, especially designed for missing data of software projects, could be used or invented so as to evaluate the imputation methods with the highest precision. Furthermore, it would be interesting to include in the analysis, multiple additional performance criteria based on project attributes other than the cost (e.g. bug count estimation). In this manner, although the model will be constructed and compared with respect to the cost attribute, the effectiveness of the imputed values can be tested towards other dimensions. Another issue is the combination of other advanced methods for the comparisons. Finally, the application of the proposed techniques can go beyond software cost estimation, for example in the estimation of other attributes (defects, quality, etc) of more general classes of products.

REFERENCES

Bi, J., & Bennet, K. P. (2003). Regression error characteristics curves. *Proceedings of the 20th International Conference on Machine Learning (ICML-2003)*, (pp. 43-50). Washington DC.

Cartwright, M. H., Shepperd, M. J., & Song, Q. (2003). Dealing with missing software project data. *Proceedings of the 9th IEEE International Metrics Symposium (METRICS'03)*, (pp. 154-165).

Chen, Z., Boehm, B., Menzies, T., & Port, D. (2005). Finding the right data for cost modeling. *IEEE Software, 22*(6), 38–46. doi:10.1109/MS.2005.151

Emam, K. E., & Birk, A. (2000). Validating the ISO/IEC 15504 measure of software requirements analysis process capability. *IEEE Transactions on Software Engineering, 26*(6), 541–566. doi:10.1109/32.852742

Foss, T., Stensurd, E., Kitchenham, B., & Myrtveit, I. (2003). A simulation study of the model evaluation criterion MMRE. *IEEE Transactions on Software Engineering, 29*(11), 985–995. doi:10.1109/TSE.2003.1245300

Hosmer, D. W., & Lemeshow, S. (1989). *Applied logistic regression*. New York: John Willey & Sons.

Jeffery, R., Ruhe, M., & Wieczorek, I. (2000). A comparative study of two software development cost modelling techniques using multi-organizational and company-specific data. *Information and Software Technology, 42*, 1009–1016. doi:10.1016/S0950-5849(00)00153-1

Jeffery, R., Ruhe, M., & Wieczorek, I. (2001). Using public domain metrics to estimate software development effort. *Proceedings of the 7th IEEE International Metrics Symposium (METRICS'01),* (pp. 16-27).

Jorgensen, M., & Shepperd, M. (2007). A systematic review of software development cost estimation studies. *IEEE Transactions on Software Engineering, 33*(1), 33–53. doi:10.1109/TSE.2007.256943

Kitchenham, B., & Mendes, E. (2004) A comparison of cross-company and within-company effort estimation models for web applications. *Proceedings of the 8th International Conference on Empirical Assessment in Software Engineering (EASE 2004),* (pp. 47-55).

Kitchenham, B., & Mendes, E. (2009). Why comparative effort prediction studies may be invalid. *Proceedings of the 5th ACM International Conference on Predictor Models in Software Engineering.*

Kitchenham, B., Pickard, L., MacDonell, S., & Shepperd, M. (2001). What accuracy statistics really measure. *IEE Proceedings. Software, 148*(3), 81–85. doi:10.1049/ip-sen:20010506

Liebchen, G., & Shepperd, M. (2008) Data sets and data quality in software engineering. *Proceedings of the 4th ACM International Workshop on Predictor Models in Software Engineering,* (pp. 39-44).

Little, R. J. A., & Rubin, D. B. (2002). *Statistical analysis with missing data*. New Jersey: John Wiley & Sons.

Mair, C., & Shepperd, M. (2005). The consistency of empirical comparisons of regression and analogy-based software project cost prediction. *Proceedings of the International Symposium on Empirical Software Engineering,* (pp. 509-518).

Maxwell, K. (2002). *Applied statistics for software managers*. New Jersey: Prentice-Hall.

Mendes, E., & Lokan, C. (2008). Replicating studies on cross- vs. single-company effort models using the ISBSG database. *Empirical Software Engineering, 13*(1), 3–37. doi:10.1007/s10664-007-9045-5

Mendes, E., Lokan, C., Harrison, R., & Triggs, C. (2005). A replicated comparison of cross-company and within-company effort estimation models using the ISBSG database. *Proceedings of the 11th IEEE International Software Metrics Symposium (METRICS'05),* (pp.36-45).

Mittas, N., & Angelis, L. (2008a). Comparing cost prediction models by resampling techniques. *Journal of Systems and Software, 81*(5), 616–632. doi:10.1016/j.jss.2007.07.039

Mittas, N., & Angelis, L. (2008b). Comparing software cost prediction models by a visualization tool. *Proceedings of the 34th Euromicro Conference on Software Engineering and Advanced Applications (SEAA'08)*, (pp. 433-440).

Mittas, N., & Angelis, L. (2010). Visual comparison of software cost estimation models by regression error characteristic analysis. *Journal of Systems and Software, 83*, 621–637. doi:10.1016/j. jss.2009.10.044

Myrtveit, I., Stensrud, E., & Olsson, U. (2001). Analyzing data sets with missing data: An empirical evaluation of imputation methods and likelihood-based methods. *IEEE Transactions on Software Engineering, 27*(11), 999–1013. doi:10.1109/32.965340

Pressman, R. S. (2005). *Software engineering: A practitioner's approach.* New York: McGraw-Hill.

Sentas, P., & Angelis, L. (2005). Categorical missing data imputation for software cost estimation by multinomial logistic regression. *Journal of Systems and Software, 79*, 404–414. doi:10.1016/j. jss.2005.02.026

Sentas, P., Angelis, L., Stamelos, I., & Bleris, G. (2004). Software productivity and effort prediction with ordinal regression. *Information and Software Technology, 47*, 17–29. doi:10.1016/j. infsof.2004.05.001

Song, Q., Shepperd, M. J., & Cartwright, M. (2005). A short note on safest default missingness mechanism assumptions. *Empirical Software Engineering, 10*(2), 235–243. doi:10.1007/ s10664-004-6193-8

Stensrud, E., & Myrtveit, I. (1998). Human performance estimating with analogy and regression models: An empirical validation. *Proceedings of the 5th IEEE International Software Metrics Symposium (METRICS'98)*, (pp. 205–213).

Strike, K., Emam, K. E., & Madhavji, N. (2001). Software cost estimation with incomplete data. *IEEE Transactions on Software Engineering, 27*(10), 890–908. doi:10.1109/32.962560

Torgo, L. (2005). Regression error characteristic surfaces. *Proceedings of the 11th ACM SIGKDD International Conference on Knowledge Discovery and Data Mining (KDD '05)*, (pp. 697-702).

Twala, B., Cartwright, M., & Shepperd, M. (2006). Ensemble of missing data techniques to improve software prediction accuracy. *Proceedings of the 28th International Conference on Software Engineering*, (pp. 909 – 912).

Van Hulse, J., & Khoshgoftaar, T. (2008). A comprehensive empirical evaluation of missing value imputation in noisy software measurement data. *Journal of Systems and Software, 81*, 691–708.

Wong, W.E., Zhao, J. & Chan, Victor K.Y. (2006). Applying statistical methodology to optimize and simplify software metric models with missing data. *Proceedings of the 2006 ACM symposium on Applied Computing*, (pp. 1728-1733).

KEY TERMS AND DEFINITIONS

Imputation: Imputation is the estimation of missing values by statistical techniques. The missing values are filled in and the resultant completed dataset can be analysed by standard methods.

Missing Data Techniques: These are sstatistical methods that have been developed in order to deal with the problem of missing data. These methods involve deletion of cases or variables and imputation methods.

Missing Values: A Missing value occurs when no data value is stored for the variable in the current observation.

Regression Error Characteristic (REC) Curves: A REC curve is a two-dimensional graph for visualization of the prediction error of a model.

The horizontal axis represents the error tolerance and the vertical axis represents the accuracy. Accuracy is defined as the percentage of cases that are predicted within the error tolerance.

Resampling Methods: These are statistical methods based on drawing new samples from an original sample of data in order to reconstruct the distribution of the initial population where the sample came from. They are used for various procedures, for example for computing confidence intervals and for making statistical tests. Common resampling techniques include bootstrap, jackknife and permutation tests.

Software Cost Estimation: The process of predicting the cost, in terms of effort or time, required to develop or maintain a software product. Software cost estimation is usually based on incomplete and noisy data, requiring statistical analysis and modeling.

Statistical Tests: Methods for making decisions using empirical data. Statistical tests are based on probability theory and especially on probability distributions in order to make an inference on whether a specific result is significant, in the sense that it is unlikely to have occurred by chance.

Chapter 10
Formalization Studies in Functional Size Measurement

Barış Özkan
Middle East Technical University, Turkey

Onur Demirörs
Middle East Technical University, Turkey

ABSTRACT

Functional size has been favored as a software size attribute that can be measured early in the software development cycles. Its characteristics of being independent of implementation language, technique and technology promoted the use in software cost estimation and other project management practices. It has been about three decades since Albrecht introduced the concept of functional size and a variety of measurement methods have been developed, some of which have been published by International Organization for Standardization (ISO). Although the concept is recognized in the software community, and there is a growing interest in Functional Size Measurement (FSM), the applications in software organizations have not been common as expected. The problems with FSM method structures and practices have been discussed to be the major factors to explain this situation. This chapter reviews the research papers that propose solutions to the problems with FSM via formalizations in FSM practices or related concept definitions. The associations of the formalization ideas to the abstract software models that represent the view of functionality for FSM methods are of particular interest of the chapter.

INTRODUCTION

Software project managers require knowledge on software product for effective management. Size is one of the key software product attributes and

DOI: 10.4018/978-1-60960-215-4.ch010

size measurement supports project management processes in various ways. In scope management, the quantified product size can be set as the baseline and the changes in scope can be measured via measuring change in size. In cost management, software effort and time estimates for a software product can be quantitatively figured out following a productivity model based on size attributes. In contract management, the acquisitions terms of bids, delivery, progress payments and reimbursements can be based on size. The uses can be extended to other project management knowledge areas such as performance, quality and risk measurement (Ozkan, Turetken & Demirors, 2008). When the Service Level Agreements (SLAs) are based on size measurements, then it can be thought that the potentials for uses of size measurements are not limited to project management but can extend to organizational processes like IT demand management. The applicability and uses of such the measures increase as the measure is independent from implementation language, tool, measurer and the organization.

Functional size is a measure of software functional requirements and It has been recognized as one size attribute that shows these characteristics in software research and community. It has been almost three decades since the introduction of the concept and there have been various functional size measurement method and technique developments. Nevertheless, FSM has not been without problems and today, FSM has not been as widely practiced in software community as expected, when its promises are concerned (Symons, 2001). This indicates that there is still work to be done in FSM concept definitions, method structures and the identification of the uses in today's software paradigms.

Some of the problems of FSM have been responded by proposals that introduce formalism into FSM methods and practices. The studies mainly have the common motivations of facilitating a better understanding of FSM methods and their structures and automating the measurements. In this chapter, our primary objective is to give the reader an insight into the challenges in formalizing the FSM methods and an evaluation of the uses of the formalization proposals in FSM. In section two, we familiarize the reader with the concepts of functional size measurement independent from any FSM method. In section three, we give the

results of our analysis from a secondary research study, a review of the formalization studies in FSM. We discuss their applicability such that we explore where and how they can help. In the final section, we conclude and investigate the future work opportunities in FSM through formalizations.

BACKGROUND ON FUNCTIONAL SIZE AND FUNCTIONAL SIZE MEASUREMENT

Software size has been associated with several attributes of software artifacts, documents and deliverables and software development practitioners have measured size using a wide range of metrics and methods. Fenton and Pfleeger (1996), defines software size as a multi attribute and describes it in terms of length, functionality and complexity. Among the various approaches developed to software size measurement, the measures and methods on quantifying the 'functionality' attribute have been widely accepted in practice. Software functional size measures the amount of functionality provided to the users. Functional Size Measurement (FSM) methods are mostly utilized in effort and cost estimation for software development and maintenance projects. Estimation errors are reported to be essential causes of poor management (Glass, 2002; Hughes, 2000) and the need for well established estimation models is so imperative that the relation between FSM and software cost, effort and time estimation can easily cause the misinterpretation of FSM methods as estimation models. Although Albrecht (1979) proposed the original idea as an approach to software estimation, the common approach in FSM methods and software community today is to separate FSM and software estimation as related but different concepts. Detailed explanation of size based cost estimation models and techniques can be found in (Matson, 1994; Abran, 2003; Boehm, 2003).

Albrecht introduced "Function Points" (FP) metric and Function Points Analysis (FPA) method

Table 1. Methods measuring the functionality attribute (Gencel, C. & Demirors, O., 2008)

Year	Method
1979	Albrecht FPA / IFPUG FPA
1982	DeMarco's Bans Metrics
1986	Feature Points
1988	Mk II FPA
1990	NESMA FPA
1990	ASSET- R
1992	3-D FP
1994	Object Points
1994	FP by Matson. Barret and Mellichamp
1997	Full Function Points (FFP)
1997	Early FPA (EFPA)
1998	Object Oriented Function Points
1999	Predictive Object Points
1999	COSMIC FFP
2000	Early&Quick COSMIC FFP
2001	Object Oriented Method FP
2000	Kammelar's Component Object Points.
2004	FiSMA FSM

for measuring software size. After that, variants of the method were developed. During the 1980s and 1990s, several authors suggested new counting techniques that intended to improve the original FPA or extend its domain of application (Symons, 2001). The results from a literature survey (Gencel and Demirors, 2004) on the methods which measure functionality size attribute are presented in Table 1.

Evolution of these methods in time resulted in ambiguities and conceptual inconsistencies among the methods. In 1996, International Organization for Standardization (ISO) established the common principles of Functional Size Measurement (FSM) methods and published ISO/IEC 14143 standard set, in order to promote the consistent interpretation of FSM principles (IEEE Std. 14143.1,2000; ISO/IEC 14143-1,1998; ISO/IEC 14143-2,2002; ISO/IEC 14143-3, 2003; ISO/

IEC 14143-4,2002; ISO/IEC 14143-5,2004; ISO/IEC 14143-6,2005). As of today, COSMIC FSM, IFPUG, FiSMA, MARK II and NESMA FSM methods have been published as ISO standards (ISO/IEC 19761, 2003; ISO/IEC 20926, 2009; ISO/IEC 20968, 2002; ISO/IEC 24570, 2005; ISO/IEC 29881, 2008).

FSM methods derive functional size from functional user requirements (FURs). In practice, FUR may exist in the form of a requirements specification document, or they have to be derived from other software artifacts such as architecture, design documents or even from the components installed on software platforms. Each FSM method measure different things and a FSM method may be suitable for an application domain, purpose or organization where another FSM method may not be appropriate. Although FSM methods have differences, they also have similarities in their application process and structure. One significant similarity is that all FSM have an abstract software model of its own that comprises concepts that are relevant to software functionality. In common, FSM methods include two essential steps of abstraction (Fetcke, 1999). In the first step, the specified software is abstracted into the software model of the selected FSM, following a set of rules. In the second step, numbers are assigned to the identified instances of the concepts. Despite the fact that FSM methods have fundamental differences in what they measure, hence their approach to measuring software functionality, it should not be forgotten that almost all methods have been influenced by the original FPA and the differences came out as the result of the evolution in FSM. The studies in (Fetcke, 2001), (Symons, 2001), (Gencel & Demirors, 2007) and the ISO 14143 standard are our recommendations to the readers to find more about the similarities, differences and evolution of FSM methods.

IFPUG and COSMIC FSM Explained

IFPUG is the most popular FSM method and has the largest community. Besides, it is the dominant FSM method used in sizing projects in project benchmark databases like ISBSG (2007). Another ISO standard, COSMIC method, which has fundamental differences when compared to IFPUG, is attracting FSM community's attention and measurements with COSMIC have been reported to be performed in different countries in different continents with a concentration in Europe. These two methods were selected because of their international characteristics. Moreover, their differences contribute to a wider view of FSM concepts.

The purpose of this section is to familiarize the reader with FSM concepts and the measurement results, such that a basis for the information and discussions about formalizations in FSM will be given. A list of core concepts for COSMIC and IFPUG methods is given to provide the reader with a more complete view of FSM software abstractions and give a simple measurement example with a focus on the software models that depict how software functionality is perceived for each method. A full measurement example and the explanation of a measurement process are beyond the aim of this chapter.

Abstract Software Models of IFPUG and COSMIC Methods

Both methods have an abstract representation of software; hence, the measurements are based on software models that comprise the constituent parts of software functionality. In the method manuals (IFPUG, 2005) (COSMIC, 2009), the definitions of these concepts are given along with rules to identify and validate the instances of the concepts in a set of functional user requirements. The numbers are assigned to a sub-set of these concepts, which are referred as Base Functional Components (BFCs) of a FSM method by standard ISO/IEC 14143-1(1998). The BFCs may have different types that are named and defined as the BFC Types by the standard. Methods determine the number assignment rules and the numbers to assign to a BFC with respect to its BFC Type.

In order to identify and validate the BFCs correctly, it is essential that all the concepts represented in the model should be properly identified from the FURs. This implies that FURs should be prepared at level of detail that is sufficient for accurate identification of model elements. Figure 1 illustrates the abstract software models of COSMIC and IFPUG methods. Following the figure, the core concept definitions from the method manuals are listed in Table 2. The reader is suggested to read the detailed definitions of the listed concepts from the method manuals.

A Measurement Example

Assume the following as a software system description:

"A manufacturing company needs a small application to get orders from all sales offices distributed across the country. Using the application, the company will maintain information about sales offices, products and orders. The company needs to size the system functionality in order to evaluate the proposals from software vendors and the software development costs."

Assume the following functional requirements are taken from the software specification for this system and they are included in the measurement scope of our example.

"At the end of each day the sales offices submit the customer orders. To support this operation,

1. The system shall enable the entry of a multi-item order into a database which already has data about sales offices and products, where
   - the multi-item orders have attributes as follows:

Figure 1. IFPUG and COSMIC FSM software models

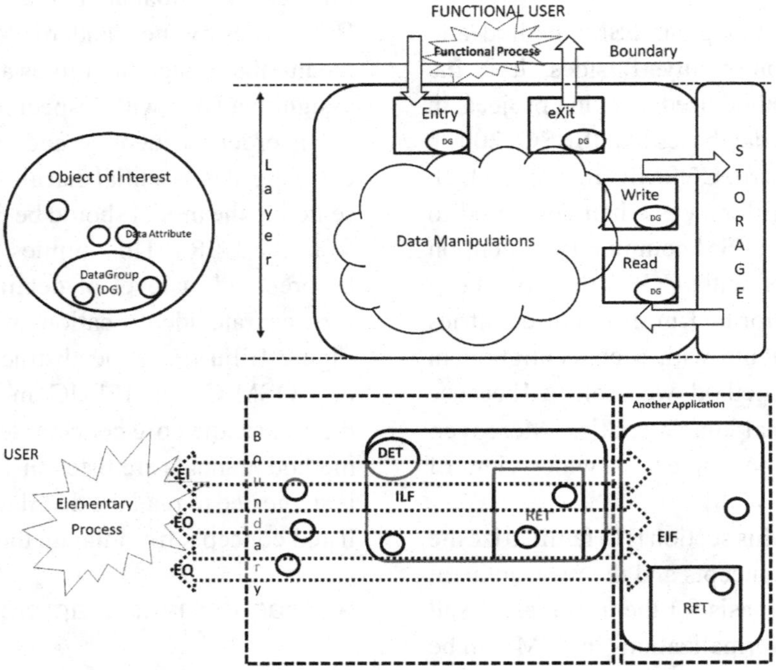

- Order header (Order ID, salesOfficeID, delivery date, delivery address)
- Order item (Order ID, product ID, order quantity, notes)
  - the salesOfficeID and the product ID must be validated on entry, and
    - validation result shall be displayed to the user"

2. The system shall enable the entry of product information.
   - Product information have product Id and categoryName attributes.
   - After the entry error or success message shall be displayed
3. The system shall enable the entry of sales office information.

Table 2. Model elements of COSMIC FSM and IFPUG methods

COSMIC FSM Core Definitions	IFPUG FSM Core Definitions
• Layer • Functional User • Triggering Event • Functional Process • Boundary • Data Manipulation • Data Movement (Types: Enter, Read, Write, Exit) • Object of Interest • Data Group • Data Attribute • Persistent storage	• Elementary Process • Data Element Type • Record Entity Type • File Type Referenced • User • Application Boundary • Control Information • Elementary process (Types: external input, external output, external inquiry) • Logical File (Types: Internal Logical File, External Interface File)

- ◦ A sales office information has salesoficeID, manager name, phoneNumber and cityName attributes.
- ◦ After the entry error or success message shall be displayed

Measurement Results

When the concept definitions are followed and the identification rules are run against the FURs the concepts in Table 3 are identified as the output of the measurement process for COSMIC and IFPUG methods.

FORMALIZATION STUDIES IN FSM

In order to achieve purposive, effective and accurate measurements, a FSM practioner may raise concerns about FSM methods and measurements and may question the possibilities for verification of the measurement results and the automation of measurements. The measurer may want to know about the repeatability, objectivity of the measurement results. He will wonder if the results will be different if the FURs are given in different forms other than the natural language such as Unified Modeling Language, Entity Relationship-diagrams or a formal specification language. He will need guidance in selection of a suitable FSM method and will need to know the differences between the methods and their structures, hence will want to understand whether the results from measurements using different methods are comparable and convertible. These are all valid concerns that a solid metric and the measurement method or tool should have an answer for.

One significant endeavor to answer similar questions was the publication of the ISO standard family, which is a joint-work of the people from communities of several FSM methods. It contains parts that establish a technique for verification and the evaluation of the objectivity, repeatability of the measurements using a selected FSM method. It brings definitions to common concepts in order to decrease inconsistencies among the methods. These expectations, qualifications have also been discussed and evaluated as problems of FSM in various FSM research studies (Kitchenham, 1997; Lother & Dumke, 2001). Among these, the proposals that add formalism into FSM methods and FSM practices were particularly of our interest since a formal approach will enable concrete FSM method concept and rule definitions, verification of measurements and will leave less space for interpretations and promote automation. The formalism here should be referred to as the formal presentations of FSM method concepts, counting rules and measurements.

In this section we give the results of our review on the research studies on FSM that add formalism into FSM methods and FSM practices (Ozkan & Demirors, 2009). The purpose of the review was understanding the particular problems addressed by the proposals, the responses to the problems and their extend.

REVIEW METHOD

The main criterion for including a paper in our review was that the paper should describe research on software functional size measurement and it should follow a formalization approach in the proposals to FSM problems. We limited the extent of the formalization approach in FSM research to defining models, notations or semantics for describing FSM methods and measurements. We included academic publications including, journals, books, conference proceedings, technical reports and MSc and PhD thesis. The proposals in the papers were expected to conform to FSM method definitions and rules without alterations or extensions to the methods. The papers that were a continuation of a previous formalization work were also included in the review. The papers only written in English were included in the review. Some papers in French were understood

Table 3. IFPUG and COSMIC results for the example software system

COSMIC RESULTS		
Layer	Application Layer	
Object of Interests (OOIs)	DataGroups	
• Order header • Order Item • Sales Office • Product • Error/Confirmation	• Order_header_order (OOI: Order header) • Order_Item_details(OOI: Order Item) • Sales_Office_info(OOI: Sales Office) • Product_info(OOI: Product) • Error/Confirmation_Result (OOI: Error/Confirmation)	
Functional Processes	Data Movements	
	DataGroup	Data Movement Type
Enter Customer Order (triggering event: time to enter customer orders for the day has come)	Order_header_order Order_Item_details Sales_Office_info Product_info Order_header_order Order_Item_details Error/Confirmation_Result	Enter (enter order details) Enter (enter order item details) Read (Read for validation) Read (Read for validation) Write (persist order item details) Write (persist order details) Exit (indicate success/error)
Add Sales Office (triggering event: a new sales office has been opened)	Sales_Office_info Sales_Office_info Error/Confirma-tion_Result	Enter (enter office details) Write (persist office details) Exit (indicate success/error)
Add Product (triggering event: company started manu-facturing a new product)	Product_info Product_info Error/Confirmation_Result	Enter (enter office details) Write (persist office details) Exit (indicate success/error)
Total Functional Size	13 cosmic function points(cfps)	
Layer	Application Layer	
Object of Interests	DataGroups	
• Order header • Order Item • Sales Office • Product • Error/Confirmation	• Order_header_order (OOI: Order header) • Order_Item_details(OOI: Order Item) • Sales_Office_info(OOI: Sales Office) • Product_info(OOI: Product) • Error/Confirmation_Result (OOI: Error/Confirmation)	
Functional Processes	Data Movements	
	DataGroup	Data Movement Type
Enter Customer Order (triggering event: time to enter customer orders for the day has come)	Order_header_order Order_Item_details Sales_Office_info Product_info Order_header_order Order_Item_details Error/Confirmation_Result	Enter (enter order details) Enter (enter order item details) Read (Read for validation) Read (Read for validation) Write (persist order item details) Write (persist order details) Exit (indicate success/error)
Add Sales Office (triggering event: a new sales office has been opened)	Sales_Office_info Sales_Office_info Error/Confirma-tion_Result	Enter (enter office details) Write (persist office details) Exit (indicate success/error)
Add Product (triggering event: company started manu-facturing a new product)	Product_info Product_info Error/Confirmation_Result	Enter (enter office details) Write (persist office details) Exit (indicate success/error)
Total Functional Size	13 cosmic function points(cfps)	
IFPUG RESULTS		

Data Functions	RETs	DETs	Complexity*	Contribution

continued on following page

Table 3. Continued

COSMIC RESULTS				
Order Header (ILF)	Order Header Order Item	Order ID, salesOfficeID, delivery date, delivery address, product ID, order quantity, notes	Low	7
Sales Office (ILF)	Sales Office	salesoficeID, manager name, phoneNumber and cityName	Low	7
Product (ILF)	Product	productID, categoryName	Low	7
Transactional Functions		FTR		
Enter Customer Order (EI)		Order Header Sales Office Product	Average	4
Add Sales Office (EI)		Sales Office	Low	3
Add Product (EI)		Product	Low	3
Total Functional Size				31 fps

*Complexity values are calculated from complexity matrices and translation tables given for each BFC in IFPUG manual.

to present relevant work or were referenced by other reviewed papers (Bevo, 2005; Diab, 2003).

Identification of Papers

First, the authors made a search on their paper collection that contains over 400 publications on FSM by reading the paper titles and abstracts. Initially a set of six relevant papers were found to satisfy the inclusion criteria (Diab, Frappier & Denis, 2002), (Diab, Frappier & Denis, 2001), (Fetcke, 1999), (Heričko et al., 2006), (Efe, Demirors & Gencel, 2006), (Demirors & Gencel, 2009). Then, the selected papers were fully read and other research materials that were referenced by the papers were found. When a referenced paper matched the inclusion criteria, it was added to the set of identified papers. The same procedure was repeated on every paper added to the set. Additionally, FSM methods' official websites were checked for other relevant studies. The journal, conference and institutions that published the selected papers were identified and other papers were found through a keyword search in relevant publisher or organization sites and academic

digital libraries. Additionally, candidate papers were found by keyword searches on the academic search and citation search engines. Finally, five journal (Rask, Laamanen & Lyyttinen, 1993; Lamma, Mello & Riguzzi, 2004; Heričko, Rozman & Živkovič, 2006; Diab, Koukane, Frappier & Dennis, 2005; Demirors & Gencel, 2009), nine conference papers (April, Merlo & Abran, 1997; Diab, Frappier & Denis, 2002; Diab, Frappier & Denis, 2001; Miyawaki, Iijimea & Sho, 2008; Fetcke, 1999; Fetcke, 2001; Bevo, Levesque & Meunier, 2004; Bevo, Levesque & Meunier, 2003; Efe, Demiros & Gencel, 2006) and four technical reports (Frappier, 1997; Gramantieri, Lamma, Mello & Riguzzi, 1997; Abran & Paton, 1995; Rask, 2001) were identified to satisfy the inclusion criteria.

Threads to Validity

Publication Bias: As the discussions and their summaries in the selected papers indicate, the research materials that were written in languages other than English were likely to be included and analyzed in this review. However, when the discussions and the summaries of those papers in English are assumed to be representative of the formalization ideas explained therein, they were not evaluated to change the results of our review critically. Formalization in FSM is a subject that can potentially take place in a variety of Software Engineering publications and conferences. The sources to search for related papers were numerous. For this reason, some relevant works may have been overlooked and this may affect the quality of the analysis negatively.

Anachronism: The time span of the papers range from 1991- 2009. In this period, FSM methods were introduced and some have gone through modifications that have been released as method versions. Furthermore, software engineering has been experiencing paradigm shifts in this period. Although the underlying principles of FSM methods have remained almost the same, some formalization suggestions may not be valid or may be obsolete today. Our analysis and observations were based on these principles and core definitions described in of each FSM, which we believe to have been valid in 1990s and today.

Limited Scope: All of the papers we analyzed proposed formalizations in one or more of IFPUG, COSMIC and MARK II FSM methods. The results of our analysis and observations may not be generalized to all FSM methods.

OVERVIEW OF THE PAPERS

The papers were classified into two categories, where the categories were identified by a clear separation of the purposes of suggested formalizations. The first category papers have explained how added formalisms in FSM can contribute to measuring software functionality described in a specific language, notation or model. The category was named as "Formalizations in measurements from formal specifications". The second category papers have proposed formal presentations for FSM method concepts and measurement func-

tions. The second category was named as "Formalizations in FSM foundations".

Although they cannot be perfectly isolated from each other, the motivations for all papers can be given as:

- Resolving ambiguities in FSM method concepts and rules due to abstract or insufficient definitions,
- Decreasing or explaining variability in size of the same set of FURs due to different interpretation of FSM concepts and rules,
- Decreasing measurement errors and
- Exploring the measurement steps for automation possibilities.

Formalizations in Measurements from Formal Specifications

The formal languages describe the desired software functionality in terms of a set of specification elements. FSM methods describe functional aspects of software in terms of the functional components in the software model of a FSM method. As their common characteristics, papers of this category establish correspondences between the functional components of a FSM method software model and the elements of the specification language so that the functional size can be measured directly from the specifications. The correspondences are based on a set of rules that are defined in each specification's context; such that the counting rules and functional components are interpreted, redefined and presented in selected specification notation terms. Thus, the papers propose the automation of this essential step of concept mapping in the FSM process by introducing an automated measurement process for a selected language via formal rules, eliminating the manual work.

One set of studies proposed procedures to measure functional size from requirements in a formal specification language. In (Frappier, 1999) a classification of formal specification languages and an evaluation of the adequacy of language classes by looking at their suitability for formalizations of IFPUG concepts is given. As a continuation of this work, Diab et al.(2002), performed a syntactic analysis of B specification language and the correspondences between IFPUG and B specification concepts and the formal rules for identification of IFPUG functional components for B were given. In the study, IFPUG method completeness was discussed based on the cases that can be specified in B but are not covered in IFPUG. They explained how added formalisms could be used in the structure analysis of the IFPUG method model by showing examples of the concepts that need human judgment for identification and can cause subjective results. Diab et al. (2001) followed the same approach for ROOM (Real-Time Object-Oriented Modeling) specifications and COSMIC-FFP FSM method. They interpreted COSMIC concepts and rules and then defined formal rules in first order logic and set theory to be used in functional component identification. They also found that there is not a corresponding specification concept to map to the layer concept in COSMIC software model. Later in (Diab et al., 2005), they implemented the rules to support automatic measurements from ROOM specifications in a tool to run in a RRRT (Rational Rose RealTime) development environment. In a case study, they compared manual measurement results of a COSMIC expert to the results from the tool obtained automatically and analyzed the sources for variations. Similarly, Miyawaki et al. (2008) proposed a method to measure IFPUG FP from specifications in Vienna Development Method- Specification Language (VDM-ML). They interpreted IFPUG concepts and presented the rules that map the VDM-ML concepts to IFPUG functional components in a mathematical notation. They implemented mapping rules in a tool; they compared manual and automated measurements in a case study and analyzed the sources for variations.

The major motivation of this set of papers is automating functional size measurement from specifications in a state based formal language as classified in (Frappier, 1997). The formal rules added to this automated process are expected to yield consistent results when considered with the concept interpretations that constitute a base for the formalized rules. Commonly, the papers explained the openness of FSM functional component definitions to interpretations and then justified their reasoning in their concept mappings.

Another group of studies defined IFPUG measurement procedures applicable to specifications given in Data Flow Diagrams (DFD) and Entity Relationship(ER) models which are mostly used in structured development environments. In his proposal, Rask (1991) established the conceptual correspondences between the DFD elements and IFPUG concepts. The method included a series of algorithms applied to the specification to identify the IFPUG functional components. The algorithm statements were based on DFD and ER diagram notation elements. Later, he used the algorithms in a simulation study that compares function points with another function metrics (Rask, 1993). Gramantieri et al. (1997), followed the same approach. However, they replaced DFD data stores with E-R entities and ER relations, thus integrated DFD and ER concepts. They translated conditions that are handled by IFPUG rules into formal rules in terms of properties of the ER-DFD graph and then implemented the rules in prolog logical programming language. As a precondition for defining formal rules, a set of assumptions were made to enable consistent interpretations of IFPUG concepts in ER-DFD specifications. Lamma et al. (2004) extended the study with case studies and they obtained close results by automated and manual measurements. Figure 2 shows the ER-DFD graph properties on an example and an ER-DFD instance for a requirement from a series of case study published by IFPUG in (IFPUG, 2001). In the measurement procedure Lamma et al. propose, the software model elements such as elementary processes, ILFs, RETs and DETS are identified in the graph running the interpreted rules. Note that the formalism in our focus was not the specification of the requirements in a formal language but in translating *"the informal counting rules expressed in natural language in the IFPUG manual into rigorous rules expressing properties of the ER-DFD graph* "(Lamma et al., 2004). Once the rules are given in terms of directed arcs, dashed lines, ER multiplicity symbols and other elements, it was possible to automate measurements sticking to the set of assumptions and rule interpretations. For the complete description of the ER-DFD elements and the rules, refer to (Lamma et al., 2004).

Abran and Paton (1995) used a DFD like formal notation in presenting the rules for IFPUG with the motivation of exploring the measurement activities that can be automated in IFPUG. The notation consisted of graphical symbols that represent processes, stored data, data manipulations and software boundary. They used this notation and evaluated all possible patterns for a given process against IFPUG process type (EI, EO, EQ) identification rules. They identified the patterns which require human involvement in determination of the corresponding process type and which

do not. Then they proposed an extended notation to include data files, record types and data fields and defined a measurement procedure for specifications in the given notation. Later, April et.al (1997) extended this notation and represented formal rules that associate IFPUG to computational concepts such as source code, user interfaces, and software modules. They explored the use of these rules in calculating functional size from source code as the part of a reverse engineering technique.

This group of studies show similar characteristics in their formalization approach with the papers that introduces formalizations to measurements from state based formalization languages such that the applicability of the rules depend on assumptions or interpretations on IFPUG counting and identification rule and the specification language. This group of studies suffered fewer difficulties while fitting the software specified in ER and DFD into IFPUG abstract model (Figure 1), since FSM method models are data-oriented and data analysis terminology is used in concept definitions, rules and examples in the IFPUG method manual. Similarly, (IFPUG, 2005) includes a section that guides the identification of ILF, EIF and RET data types via rules given in ER terms; however, the given rules are in terms of different ER properties and IFPUG manual supports identification of only data functions from ER diagrams.

All reviewed papers and many others in FSM literature, consensually agree that in practice FSM methods need interpretations, reasoning that the method concept and rule descriptions given in the manuals and guides are too abstract to be applied directly to software specified in a selected language. Without them, the required transformation of software descriptions in a language to the measurement method software model can potentially result in inaccurate, inconsistent and imprecise measurement results. A variety of FSM research was made to fill this "gap" between software description forms and the FSM software abstract models. They came up with proposals

Figure 2. ER_DFD graph notation and an instance

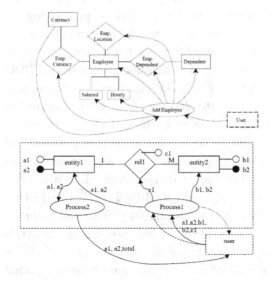

that interpret or specialize the functional concepts and measurement rules of a selected FSM method systematically for a selected software description form (Fetcke, Abran & Nguyen, 1997), (Marin, Pastor & Gaichetti, 2007), (Condori-Fernández, Abrahão & Pastor, 2007), (Uemura, Kusumoto & Inoue, 1999). A recent study reviews the procedure developments for sizing software with COSMIC FSM method (Marin, Pastor & Gaichetti, 2008).

As the FURS can exist in any specification language, the measurer's abstraction approach and interpretation of the functional concepts and rules in a FSM method may lead to different results by different measurers, regardless of the formalism in these interpretations. The formalization studies in the first category proposed partial solutions to this problem by representing the authors' interpretations for a formal language formally. Thus, the interpretations became repeatable and consistent for measurements of the software described in the same language, the consistency in the results is achieved and automations were possible. Nevertheless, the formalizations do not significantly change the nature of the subjective measurements problem due to different interpretations. When the interpretations are different, although they are formally represented, they may still result in different results for the same piece of software. For example, although a DFD process may not always correspond to an IFPUG elementary process, given a set of assumptions and constraints, they may be consistently interpreted to be so through formal rules.

The inherited problems with FSM method definitions and structures, which turned out to be the weaknesses of a formalized measurement process, were clearly identified in the formalization processes of the first category papers. It was not a coincidence that these formalisms' to measurement process studies were for software descriptions in formal state based specification languages (B,ROOM,VDM-SL) or semi-formal ER, DFD presentations. Since their major motivation is automation of FSM, more formal descrip-

tions of software increased the opportunities for automated measurements and delegated the problems from ambiguous requirements in FSM to the requirements engineering domain. The effectiveness of formalizations were tested by few cases where some test or synthetic cases reported by the paper authors' were limited to analyzing case specific variations between manual and automated measurements and few of the studies had industrial software products as the case subjects.. Most of the mappings in this category of papers are based on older method versions, hence may need revisions to adapt to changes.

In summary, the papers of this category provided means and automations to measure functional size for software described in the specification language in their scope and the associated FSM method. However, a functional size measurer should carefully consider the concerns discussed in this section before attempting to use the ideas in practice. Table 4 gives a summary of papers where FSM method concepts and rules were redefined formally to enable automated measurements from a specification language.

Our final observation on the papers of this category is that the analysis of FSM method concepts from a formalization point of view contributes to a more clear identification of the ambiguous points in method definitions and rules. The analysis of the FSM concepts while mapping the specification language elements reveals possible sources for subjective measurements. Moreover, the analysis results address the points that need human intervention in an automated measurement process; thus, they support automation tool design.

Formalizations in FSM Foundations

The papers in this category propose formalizations in representing the functional components defined in FSM method abstract models and the measurement functions. The purposes of the studies are providing formal FSM model definitions in the

Table 4. Summary of formalizations in measurement from different software description styles

Research reference(s)		Specification Language	FSM Method
Original Study	**Continuation Study**		
(Diab et al., 2001)	(Diab et al,, 2005)	ROOM	COSMIC
(Rask, 1991) (Gramantieri et al., 1997)	(Rask et al., 1993) (Lamma et al., 2004)	ER,DFD ER+DFD	IFPUG
(Diab et al., 2002)		B	IFPUG
(Miyawaki et al., 2008)		VDM-SL	IFPUG

solution of problems resulting from ambiguities in FSM method concepts and rules. They also include understanding the differences in FSM method structures, revealing opportunities for method improvements and automated measurement; hence promoting a better understanding of FSM methods.

Fetcke (1999) introduced the idea of defining a generalized structure for IFPUG FPA and MARK II FPA and COSMIC FFP as FPA variants. In the study, two steps of data oriented abstractions in FPA were identified: software requirements are represented in data oriented abstraction (identification of items) and the items in the data oriented representations are mapped into numbers (mapping into numbers). He introduced activity type concept so as to represent the different concepts besides the common concepts in FPA and its variants. Then, the abstractions were formalized in a mathematical model. Using this model, he formally presented and tested dominance and monotonicity empirical assumptions made by Function Point Analysis. In a consequent study, Fetcke (2001) extended the original work and validated the completeness of the generalized presentation against the concept identification rules in different versions of COSMIC FFP, IFPUG and MARK II FSM methods. In this continuation study, he added Control activity type, to enable a better representation of IFPUG and MARK II concepts in the model. Finally, he explored the potential applications of the generalized formal model. The generalized model is shown in Figure

3. In the figure, the abstractions from software documentation to data oriented software model and from model elements to numbers are illustrated. The core concepts of user, application, data and transaction are shown. The definitions of the model are given in Table 5.

Later, Hericko et al. (2006) proposed a measurement process, abbreviated as GASS. The process includes steps of converting any software model into a universal model that is based on Fetcke's generalized representation and then measuring the functional size in any of the three FSM methods. In their study, they presented instances of Fetcke's generalized presentation for the latest versions of the three FSM methods; IFPUG, COSMIC and MARK II FSM. They formally represented measurement functions in the notation Fetcke developed and defined method executions in symbolic code. They showed an execution of the presented measurement process for Object Oriented specifications; they mapped Unified Model Language elements to the universal model elements in symbolic notation and then formally modeled the software functionality in Fetcke's general presentation.

The generalized software abstract model explained and presented in Fetcke's work and used in GASS measurement process was structured to include the relevant information that is deemed relevant to software functional components for all three FSM methods. Nevertheless, the formal model presentations do not include any abstractions for component identification rules which

Figure 3. Generalized data oriented representation for IFPUG, COSMIC and MARK II FSM methods and the definitions

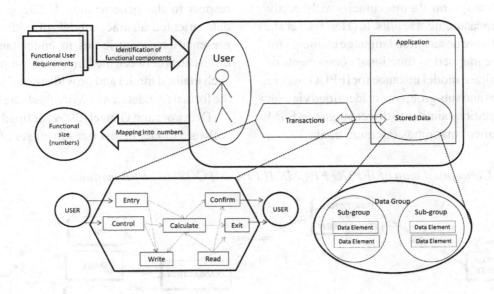

describe the qualifications expected from a valid functional component in the context of a selected FSM method. A data group in IFPUG may not be valid in COSMIC or vice versa. The data group and sub-group concepts in Fetcke's model are also abstract and they become concrete and valid

only in a method's context conforming method definitions and rules. For example, in COSMIC FSM manual (COSMIC, 2009), one data group identification rule is stated as *"Each data group shall be directly related to one object of interest in the software's Functional User Requirements"*.

Table 5.

Definitions:	
Application closure is a vector of τ transaction and types T_i σ data group types F_σ	$H = (T_1,...,T_\tau, F_1,...,F_\sigma)$
Transaction type T_i is a vector of activities	$T_i = (P_{i1},...,P_{in_i})$
Activity P_{ik} is a quadruplet, where θ_{ik} denotes activity class, $\theta_{ik} \in \{$Entry, Exit, Confirm, Read, Write, Calculate$\}$.. r_{ik} denotes data group type referenced, D_{ik} denotes set of data elements handled, C_{ik} set of data elements calculated for Calculate activities.	$P_{ik} = (\theta_{ik}, r_{ik}, D_{ik}, C_{ik})$
FF_{ij} is a set where d_{jk} are data elements, g_{jk} are designate data sub-groups.	$F_j = \{(d_{j1}, g_{j1}),...,(d_{jr_j}, g_{jr_j})\}$

It is obvious that accurate identification of objects of interests is required in order to validate an identified data group; the inaccuracies will directly affect the measurement results. In (Hericzko et al., 2006) software description language elements for UML were mapped to functional components of the generalized model instance for IFPUG, where data groups and sub-groups were identified via a set of interpretations similar to direct language-FSM model element mappings (Uemura et al., 1999).

Hence, the aforementioned gap problem remains to be inherited in performing measurements with respect to the generic model. The generalized data oriented abstract model, providing formal presentations, contributes to understanding the differences between the functional components in each method model and provides a tool to discuss the formal foundations FSM methods are based on.

Demirors and Gencel (2009) defined a unified software model that is a resultant set of IFPUG,

Figure 4. Conceptual map of IFPUG FPA, MK II FPA and COSMIC FFP methods

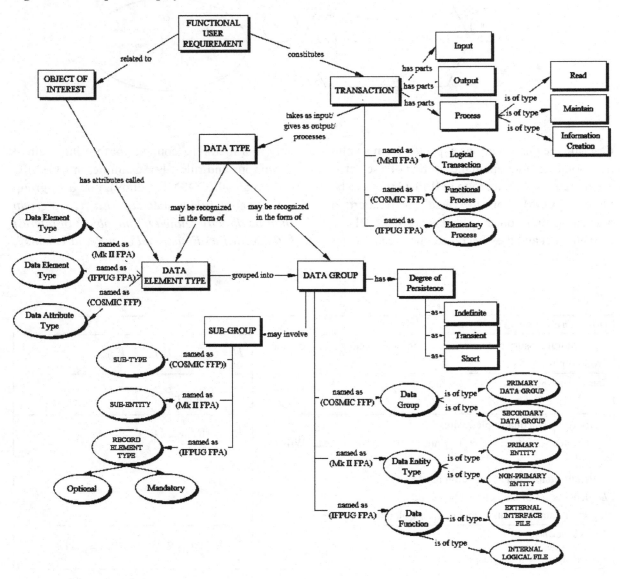

MARK II and COSMIC FSM method software models. In order to construct the model, they first performed a conceptual analysis of each method model and identified the commonalities and the differences between the model concepts and developed a conceptual map of method concepts (Efe et al., 2006) (Figure 4).

Then, they defined the unified model elements, which constitute a superset of all concepts required by each model, and they gave rules that assign model concepts in terms of unified model elements via set and assignment operators. Most uses of the unified model were considered to be in simultaneous measurements and conversion of sizes measured by different methods. The unified model was implemented in an automated measurement tool and it was reported that in several case studies, the measurements in the unified model resulted in the same measurement results by each method. Some rules of unified model rules are shown in Figure 5.

The identification of the components in the unified model requires the knowledge of the concepts and rules of each supported FSM method. For example, following the unified model rules, a measurer may infer that a data group in COSMIC method corresponds to a data group in IFPUG. The example measurement result in the background section of this chapter two separate data groups and object of interests were

Figure 5. Unified model assignment rules

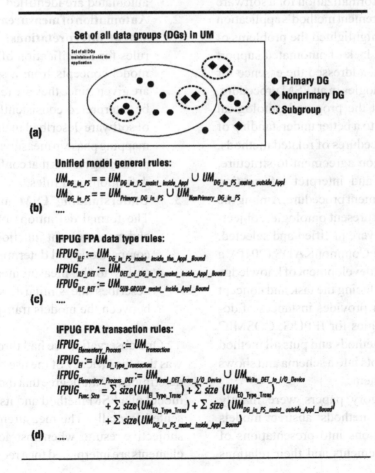

Set of all data groups (DGs) in UM

Set of all DGs maintained inside the application

● Primary DG
◆ Nonprimary DG
◌ Subgroup

(a)

Unified model general rules:

$$UM_{DG\_in\_PS} == UM_{DG\_in\_PS\_maint\_inside\_Appl} \cup UM_{DG\_in\_PS\_maint\_outside\_Appl}$$
$$UM_{DG\_in\_PS} == UM_{Primary\_DG\_in\_PS} \cup UM_{NonPrimary\_DG\_in\_PS}$$

(b) ....

IFPUG FPA data type rules:

$$IFPUG_{ILF} := UM_{DG\_in\_PS\_maint\_inside\_the\_Appl\_Bound}$$
$$IFPUG_{ILF\_DET} := UM_{DET\_of\_DG\_in\_PS\_maint\_inside\_Appl\_Bound}$$
$$IFPUG_{ILF\_RET} := UM_{SUB\-GROUP\_maint\_inside\_Appl\_Bound}$$

(c) ....

IFPUG FPA transaction rules:

$$IFPUG_{Elementary\_Process} := UM_{Transaction}$$
$$IFPUG_{EI} := UM_{EI\_Type\_Transaction}$$
$$IFPUG_{Elementary\_Process\_DET} := UM_{Read\_DET\_from\_I/O\_Device} \cup UM_{Write\_DET\_to\_I/O\_Device}$$
$$IFPUG_{Func.\ Size} = \Sigma\ size(UM_{EI\_Type\_Trans}) + \Sigma\ size(UM_{EO\_Type\_Trans})$$
$$+ \Sigma\ size(UM_{EQ\_Type\_Trans}) + \Sigma\ size(UM_{DG\_in\_PS\_maint\_outside\_Appl\_Bound})$$
$$+ \Sigma\ size(UM_{DG\_in\_PS\_maint\_inside\_Appl\_Bound})$$

(d) ....

identified for the multi-item order data with COSMIC, where,one data group with two sub-groups.(1 ILF,2 RETS) were identified with IF-PUG. This contradicts with the inference of one to one correspondence. The model gives the rules to show associations between method concepts and does not unify the rules which are valid in each method's context. Without knowing each method's details, the exact and complete identification of the concepts in the model is not possible; so the unified model should rather be regarded as a simultaneous measurement method that approximates and unifies the methods with a focus on the similarities in method concepts. Measurement effort can be saved from eliminating the rework for identification and measurement of common concepts

Bevo, Levesque and Meunier (2003,2004) proposed an ontological formalization for a software functional size measurement method's application process. Their work highlighted the problems of technical difficulties, lack of automated support in applying FSM, and addressed the essence for domain and task ontologies in an FSM procedure. It was explained that the proposed ontological formalism contribute to a better understanding of the measurement procedures of related methods, and serve as a common agreement to structure, represent, exchange and interpret information related to the measurement procedure. Among the several formalisms to present ontologies, object-oriented formalisms were justified and selected. He was inspired from CommonKADS (2010), a methodology used for development of knowledge based systems, in producing the task and concept ontologies. The paper provides instances of domain and task ontologies for IFPUG, COSMIC and MARK II FSM methods and puts all method definitions and concepts into a schema and shows the relations among them.

The second category papers were mainly concerned with FSM methods' abstract models and added formalizations into presentations of the models, model elements and their relations

so that the FSM methods and measurement functions are understood better and can be compared and contrasted.

CONCLUSION AND DIRECTIONS FOR FUTURE RESEARCH

After an analysis of the papers we included in our review, we concluded that formalization studies in FSM, help FSM research and measurement practices in three typical ways:

1. **Exploring opportunities for automation:** The measurement steps and concepts that can be formalized are good candidates for automation. The steps that can be fully automated, semi-automated or cannot be automated are identified.

2. **Automation of measurement through consistent interpretations:** When the formal rules for identification of the FSM method model concepts from a specification form are given, since they are repeatable, they can be interpreted consistently for every piece of software described in the same form. The mapping phase in measurement is automated, producing results that conform to the method definitions and rules.

3. **Understanding FSM model structures:** The formal definitions of method models and measurement functions enable method comparisons and determination of the suitability to the measurement purposes, thus describes the similarities and differences between the models transparently.

One observation we had throughout the study was that the efficacy of the use of formalisms was determined by the degree that the abstract software model of a FSM method and its rules can be presented formally. The measurements are open to subjective results, when abstract software model elements are interpreted for a requirement description language. Although consistent interpretations can provide comparable measurements results, it may lead to incomparable software functional sizes for benchmarking purposes. The studies in the first category papers in our review partially eliminated the potential problem getting contributions from FSM method founders or co-founders. Nevertheless, it becomes a problem when FSM method experts and founders are scarce and there exists a variety of software description languages that specify software functionality. One recent approach to software production is model driven development, which adheres to Model-Driven Architecture (MDA) principles. Although the motivation in MDA is achieving platform dependency, the MDA notions of model transformations might be inspiring in describing a FSM software model and a relevant ontology in the sense that the FSM method's abstract software models can qualify a degree of formalism. We believe this need addresses potentials for further formalization studies, in particular, the studies that address the verification and automation of measurements.

FSM method software models are data oriented and the data requirements described by the functional user should be carefully analyzed to measure the software functionality accurately. In IFPUG (2005) Part 2, data modeling concepts were introduced and the mapping of ER concepts to IFPUG Logical File (LF), Record Entity Type (RET) and Data Element Type (DET) was given in a formalism that is represented in Entity-Relationship properties of multiplicity, participation and entity dependency types. Although ER formalism may not be sufficient or suitable to reflect all aspects of data related concepts as perceived by a FSM method, when the method rules are described formally and are based on a formal data model, measurers will be supported in identification of the method data concepts from the FURs where user data is described. For example, COSMIC FSM business application guide COSMIC (2008) explain functional component identification rules referring to ER formalism in order to clarify the ambiguities in the relations between functional

components where the same information can hardly be produced from COSMIC manual.

As the final conclusion, we believe one significant and common contribution of the all formalization studies came from the formalization processes themselves. A set of critical problems with FSM have been discovered, revealed and communicated in concrete terms and the researchers were enabled with tools to be used in evaluating and expressing their method improvement proposals.

REFERENCES

Abran, A., Ndiaye, I., & Bourque, P. (2003). *Contribution of software size in effort estimation*. École de Technologie Supérieure, Canada: Research Lab. in Software Engineering.

Abran, A., & Paton, K. (1995). *A formal notation for the rules of function point analysis*. Research Report 247. Retrieved from http://publicationslist.org/data/a.abran/ref-1995/43.pdf

Albrecht, A. J. (1979). Measuring application development productivity. *In Proceedings of Joint SHARE, GUIDE, and IBM Application Development Symposium*, (pp. 83-92). Monterey, CA.

April, A., Merlo, E., & Abran, A. (1997). *A reverse engineering approach to evaluate function point rules*, (pp. 236-246). Paper presented at the Working Conference on Reverse Engineering.

Bevo, V. (2005). *Analyse et formalisation ontologiques des mesures associées aux méthodes de mesure de la taille fonctionnelle des logiciels: de nouvelles perspectives pour la mesure*. Unpublished doctoral thesis in Cognitive Informatics, University of Quebec in Montreal, Canada.

Bevo, V., Lévesque, G., & Meunier, J.-G. (2004). Toward an ontological formalisation for a software functional size measurement method's application process: The FPA case. In *Proceedings IEEE-RIVF International Conference on Computing and Telecommunication Technologies*, (pp 113-118).

Boehm, B., & Abts, C. (2000). Software development Cost estimation approaches-a survey. *Annals of Software Engineering, 10*(1-4), 77–205.

Comman, K. A. D. S. (2010). *CommanKADS*. Retrieved from http://www.commonkads.uva.nl/frameset-commonkads.html.

Condori-Fernández, N., Abrahão, S., & Pastor, O. (2007). On the estimation of the functional size of software from requirements specifications. *Journal of Computer Science and Technology, 22*, 358–370. doi:10.1007/s11390-007-9050-6

COSMIC. (2008). *The COSMIC business application guideline (v1.1). The Common Software Measurement International Consortium*. COSMIC.

COSMIC. (2009). *COSMIC method measurement manual, (ver. 3.0.1). The Common Software Measurement International Consortium*. COSMIC.

Demirors, O., & Gencel, C. (2010). Conceptual association of functional size measurement methods. *IEEE Software, 26*(3), 71–78. doi:10.1109/MS.2009.60

Diab, H. (2003). *Formalisation et automatisation de la mesure des points de fonction*. Unpublished doctoral Thesis, Department of Informatics Faculté Des Sciences, Université de Sherbrooke, Quebec, Canada.

Diab, H., Frappier, M., & St.-Denis, R. (2001). Formalizing COSMIC-FFP using ROOM. *Proceedings of International Conference on Computer Systems and Applications*, (pp. 312-318).

Diab, H., Frappier, M., & St.-Denis, R. (2002). A formal definition of function points for automated measurement of B specifications. *Proceedings of International Conference on Formal Engineering Methods: Formal Methods and Software Engineering*, (pp. 483-494).

Diab, H., Koukane, F., Frappier, M., & St-Denis, R. (2005). µCROSE: Automated Measurement of COSMIC-FFP for rational rose real time. *Information and Software Technology, 47*(3), 151–166. doi:10.1016/j.infsof.2004.06.007

Efe, P., Demirors, O., & Gencel, C. (2006). A unified model for functional size measurement methods. In *Proceedings of the International Workshop on Software Measurement*, (pp. 343–358).

Fenton, N. E., & Pfleeger, S. L. (1996). *Software metrics: A rigorous and practical approach* (2nd ed.). Boston: International Thomson Computer Press.

Fetcke, T. (1999). A generalized structure for function point analysis. *Proceedings of International Workshop on Software Measurement*, (pp. 143-153).

Fetcke, T. (2001). A generalized representation for selected functional size measurement methods. *Proceedings of the International Workshop on Software Measurement*, (pp. 1-25).

Fetcke, T., Abran, A., & Nguyen, T.-H. (Eds.). (1997). *Mapping the OO-Jacobson approach into Function Point Analysis* (pp. 192–202). Proceedings of Technology of Object-Oriented Languages and Systems.

Frappier, M. (1999). *An overview of formal specification languages and their adequacy for formalizing the definition of function points. Technical Report, Department of D'epartement de math'ematiques et d'informatique*. Quebec, Canada: Universit'e de Sherbrooke.

Gencel, C., & Demirors, O. (2007). Conceptual differences among functional size measurement methods. In *Proceedings of International Symposium on Empirical Software Engineering and Measurement*, (pp. 305-313).

Gencel, C., & Demirors, O. (2008). Functional size measurement revisited. *ACM Transactions on Software Engineering and Methodology, 17*(3), 1–36. doi:10.1145/1363102.1363106

Glass, R. L. (2002). *Facts and fallacies of software engineering*. United States: Addison Wesley.

Gramantieri, F., Lamma, E., Mello, P., & Riguzzi, F. (Eds.). (1997). *A system for measuring function points from specifications. Research report DEIS-LIA-97-006*. Italy: Università di Bologna.

Heričko, M., Rozman, I., & Živkovič, A. (2006). A formal representation of functional size measurement methods. *Journal of Systems and Software*, *79*, 1341–1358. doi:10.1016/j.jss.2005.11.568

Hughes, B. (2000). *Practical software measurement*. Maidenhead: McGraw-Hill.

IFPUG. (2001). *Function point counting practices: Case studies, case study 2. International function points user group*. NJ: Princeton Junction.

IFPUG. (2005). *Function point counting practices manual. International Function Point Users Group*. Princeton Junction, NJ: IFPUG.

ISBSG. (2007). *ISBSG data, release 10.0*. The International Software Benchmarking Standards Group.

ISO/IEC 14143-1. (1998). *Information Technology-software measurement, functional size measurement, part 1: Definition of concepts*.

ISO/IEC 14143-2. (2002). Information Technology-software measurement, functional size measurement, part 2: Conformity evaluation of software size measurement methods to ISO/IEC 14143-1:1998.

ISO/IEC 14143-6. (2005). *Guide for the use of ISO/IEC 14143 and related international standards*.

ISO/IEC 19761. (2003). *Software engineering-COSMIC-FFP-a functional size measurement method*.

ISO/IEC 20926. (2009). Software and systems engineering-software measurement-IFPUG functional size measurement method, 2009.

ISO/IEC 20968. (2002). *Software engineering-Mk 2 function point analysis-counting practices manual*.

ISO/IEC 24570. (2005). Software engineering-NESMA functional size measurement method version 2.1-definitions and counting guidelines for the application of function point analysis.

ISO/IEC 29881. (2008). Information Technology-software and systems engineering-FiSMA 1.1 functional size measurement method.

ISO/IEC TR 14143-3. (2003). Information Technology-software measurement-functional size measurement-part 3: verification of functional size measurement methods.

ISO/IEC TR 14143-4. (2002). *Information Technology-software measurement-functional size measurement-part 4: Reference model*.

ISO/IEC TR 14143-5. (2004). Information Technology-software measurement-functional size measurement-part 5: Determination of functional domains for use with functional size measurement.

Kitchenham, B. (1997). The problem with function points. *IEEE Software*, *14*(2), 29–31. doi:10.1109/MS.1997.582972

Lamma, E., Mello, P., & Riguzzi, F. (2004). A system for measuring function points from an ER-DFD specification. *The Computer Journal*, *47*, 358–372. doi:10.1093/comjnl/47.3.358

Lother, M., & Dumke, R. (2001). Points metrics-comparison and analysis. In *Proceedings of International Workshop on Software Measurement*, (pp. 155-172).

Marín, B., Giachetti, G., & Pastor, O. (2008). Measurement of functional size in conceptual models: A survey of measurement procedures based on COSMIC. In *Proceedings of International Workshop on Software Measurement*, (pp. 170-183).

Marín, B., Pastor, O., & Giachetti, G. (2008). Automating the measurement of functional size of conceptual models in an MDA environment. In *Proceedings of the International Conference on Product-Focused Software Process Improvement*, (pp. 215-229).

Matson, J. E., Barrett, B. E., & Mellichamp, J. M. (1994). Software development cost estimation using function points. *IEEE Transactions on Software Engineering*, *20*(4), 275–287. doi:10.1109/32.277575

Miyawaki, T., Iijima, J., & Ho, S. (2008). Measuring function points from VDM-SL specifications. In *Proceedings of International Conference on Service Systems and Service Management*, (pp. 1-6).

Ozkan, B., & Demirors, O. (2009). Formalization studies in functional size measurement: How do they help? In *Proceedings of International Workshop on Software Measurement*, (pp. 197-211).

Ozkan, B., Turetken, O., & Demirors, O. (2008). Software functional size: For cost estimation and more. In *Proceedings of the European Software Process Improvement Conference*, (pp. 59-69).

Rask, R. (1991). *Algorithms for counting unadjusted function points from dataflow diagrams. Research report A-1991-1*. Finland: University of Joensuu.

Rask, R., Laamanen, P., & Lyyttinen, K. (1993). Simulation and comparison of Albrecht's function point and DeMarco's function bang metrics in a CASE environment. *IEEE Transactions on Software Engineering*, *19*, 661–671. doi:10.1109/32.238567

IEEE Std. 14143.1. (2000). *Information Technology-software measurement-functional size measurement-Part 1: Definition of concepts*. Implementation note for IEEE adoption of ISO/IEC 14143-1:1998.

Symons, C. (2001). Come back function point analysis-all is forgiven! In *Proceedings of the European Conference on Software Measurement and ICT Control*, (pp. 413-426).

Uemura, T., Kusumoto, S., & Inoue, K. (1999). Function point measurement tool for UML design specification. In *Proceedings of International Symposium on Software Metrics*, (p. 62).

KEY TERMS AND DEFINITIONS

Abstract Software Model of a FSM method: An abstraction of software by the method which comprises the conceptual components of software that are related to software functionality.

Base Functional Component: An elementary unit of Functional Requirements defined by and used by an FSM method for measurement purposes.

Functional Size Measurement Method: A specific implementation of functional size measurement defined by a set of principles and rules.

Functional Size: A size of the software derived by quantifying the Functional User Requirements.

Requirements Specification: A precise definition of the client's requirements written in some notation. A notation is formal if it has a formal syntax and formal semantics. A notation is said to be semi-formal if it only has a formal syntax.

Chapter 11
Cognitive Complexity Measures:
An Analysis

Sanjay Misra
Federal University of Technology, Nigeria

ABSTRACT

Cognitive informatics (CI), a multidisciplinary area of research tries to solve the common problems in the field of informatics, computer science, software engineering, mathematics, cognitive science, neurobiology, psychology, and physiology. Measurement in software engineering is also a core issue which is still striving for its standardization process. In recent years, several cognitive complexity measures based on CI have been proposed. However, each of them has their own advantages and disadvantages. This chapter presents a critical review on existing cognitive complexity measures. Furthermore, a comparative study based on some selected attributes has been presented.

INTRODUCTION

Software metrics play an important role in the software development process, since; they assist the software developer in assuring the software quality. Developers use these metrics in the entire life cycle of software development to better understand and assess the quality of engineered products or systems that they built. On the other hand, it

is a common observation that it is not possible to develop the absolute measure (Fenton, 1994). Instead, software engineers attempt to derive a set of indirect measures that lead to metrics that provide an indication of quality of some representation of software. The quality objectives may be listed as performance, reliability, availability and maintainability (Somerville, 2001) and are closely related to software complexity.

IEEE (1990) defines software complexity as "the degree to which a system or component has

DOI: 10.4018/978-1-60960-215-4.ch011

a design or implementation that is difficult to understand and verify". Further, there are two categories of software complexities: computational and psychological (Fenton, 1997). Computational complexity is related to algorithm complexity and evaluates time and memory needed to execute a program. The second is psychological complexity also called as cognitive complexity is concerned to evaluate the human effort needed to perform a software task. This definition is also related to understandability of the software and task and evaluates the difficulty experienced in comprehending and/or performing such a task. Further, there are several definitions of the cognitive complexity. Henderson-Sellers (1996) define the cognitive complexity as 'The cognitive complexity of software refers to those characteristics of software that affect the level of resources used by a person performing a given task on it.' Fenton (1997) defines cognitive complexity as it measures the effort required to understand the software. Zuse (1998) definition of complexity also represents the notion of cognitive complexity, which states that software complexity is the difficulty to maintain, change and understand software. Here, it is worth mentioning that metrics and measures are often used as synonyms terms in software engineering. It is because of the fact that both terms have approximately similar definitions. Pressman (2001) explains the measure in software engineering context as 'a measure provides a quantitative indication of the extent, amount, dimension, capacity, or size of some attributes of a product or process'. A metric is defined by IEEE as 'a quantitative measure of the degree to which a system, component, or process possesses a given attribute".

Cognitive informatics (CI), a multidisciplinary area of research is emerging. It includes the researches in the field of informatics, computer science, software engineering, mathematics, cognitive science, neurobiology, psychology, and physiology (Wang, 2002, 2004, 2005, 2006, 2007, 2009). The importance of the researches in CI is due to the fact that, it tries to solve the common problems of two related area in a bi-directional and multidisciplinary approach (Wang, 2004). CI uses the computing technique to solve the problem of cognitive science, neurobiology, psychology, and physiology and on the other hand the theories of cognitive science, neurobiology, psychology, and physiology are used to investigate the issues and their solution in informatics, computing, and software engineering. For examples, the measurement in software engineering is a major issue which is still not mature and needs a lot of efforts to standardize it (i.e. the measurement techniques for software engineering). In last few years numbers of researchers have tried to solve these problems by combining the principles of cognitive science and (measurement in) software engineering. The numbers of proposals of cognitive complexity measures (Shao & Wang, 2003; Misra, 2006, 2007, 2010; Kushvaha & Misra, 2006; Auprasert & Limpiyakorn, 2008, 2009) are the results of these efforts.

Cognitive Complexity refers to the human effort needed to perform a task or the difficulty experienced in understanding the code or the information packed in it (Misra & Kushvaha, 2006). Understandability of the code is known as program comprehension and is a cognitive process and related to cognitive complexity. In other words, the cognitive complexity is the mental burden on the user who deals with the code, for example the developer, tester and maintenance staff. Cognitive complexity provides valuable information for the design of systems. High cognitive complexity indicates poor design, which sometimes can be unmanageable (Briand, Bunse & Daly, 2001). In such cases, the maintenance effort increases drastically. In this respect, cognitive complexities are important in evaluating the performance of the system; they refer to those characteristics of software which affect the level of resources used by a person performing a given task on it (Zuse, 1998). The system with reduced cognitive complexity will not only improve the quality of the code but also reduce the future comprehension and therefore maintenance efforts. In 2003, Shao & Wang (2003) have proposed the first cognitive complexity measure based on the principles of cognitive informatics which states that the nature of software is characterized by its informatics, behavioural, mathematical, and cognitive properties. Further, the complexity of software is the function of input, output and cognitive weights. Following this approach, several proposals (Misra 2006, 2007, 2010; Kushvaha & Misra, 2006; Auprasert & Limpiyakorn 2008, 2009) for cognitive complexity measures have appeared. Apart from these measures (based on cognitive informatics), some other proposals (Rauterberg, 1992; Klemola, 2003) for estimating cognitive complexity can be found in literature. However, they are neither sufficient nor they cover other aspects of the complexity, like internal architecture, operational complexity etc (Wang, 2007,2009). There is one more way to calculate the complexity of code only by using cognitive weights (Misra 2009). However, it does not include the other factors (operators, and operands) and provide their relation with the BCSs. This is the reason we have not included this measure in our comparison.

The objective of the present paper is to review and compare all the available cognitive complexity metrics that are based on cognitive informatics. These metrics include: Cognitive functional size (CFS) (Shao & Wang, 2003), Modified cognitive complexity measure (MCCM) (Misra, 2006), Cognitive information complexity measure (CICM) (Kushvaha and Misra, 2006), Cognitive program complexity measure (CPCM) (Misra, 2007), Structured cognitive information measurement: (SCIM) (Auprasert & Limpiyakorn, 2009), Unified complexity measure (Misra & Akman, 2010). It is worth mentioning that all the above mentioned measures uses cognitive weight proposed by Shao & Wang (2003) in his cognitive functional size (CFS) measure. In the following sections, first we discuss the features of all complexity measures and then evaluate each complexity metrics based

on different criteria and attributes. These criteria and attributes are selected based on the standard evaluation methodology for software complexity measures. For example, we check that are all these proposals evaluated and validated through proper theoretical, practical and empirical validation process? Finally we compare all of them based on their pros and cons. This comparative study provides the useful information regarding these measures which will be useful for future work as well as for selecting appropriate metric.

This chapter is organized in the following way. In the next section, we are providing the background of the cognitive complexity metrics, and their relation to cognitive informatics. Later we discuss the available cognitive complexity metrics. Advantages and limitations of Cognitive Complexity Measures are discussed in forthcoming section. We evaluate and compare cognitive complexity metrics in later section. A brief discussion on the observations and conclusion drawn are in last section of this chapter.

BACKGROUND OF COGNITIVE COMPLEXITY MEASURES

In cognitive informatics, it is found that the functional complexity of software in design and comprehension depends on three fundamental factors: internal processing and its input and output (Shao & Wang, 2003). Initially three basic control structures (BCS), sequence, branch and iteration were identified (Hore, 1987). Later, Shao & Wang (2003) modified these BSC's and introduced ten BCS's which are summarized in the Table 1. These BCS's are the basic logic building blocks of software. The cognitive weight of software is the extent of difficulty or relative time and effort for comprehending given software modeled by a number of BCS's.

There are two different architectures for calculating Wbcs: either all the BCS's are in a linear layout or some BCS's are embedded in others.

Table 1. Basic control structures and their cognitive weight

Category	BCS	Weight
Sequence	Sequence (SEQ)	1
Branch	If-Then-Else (ITE)	2
	Case	3
Iteration	For-do	3
	Repeat-until	3
	While-do	3
Embedded Component	Function Call (FC)	2
	Recursion (REC)	3
Concurrency	Parallel (PAR)	4
	Interrupt (INT)	4

For the former case, sum of the weights of all n BCS's; are added and for the latter, cognitive weights of inner BCS's are multiplied with the weights of external BCS's. The cognitive weights for different Basic Control Structures are as given in Table 1. Actually, these weights are assigned on the classification of cognitive phenomenon as discussed by He proved and assigned the weights according to the complexity of the functions. For example, weight for lowest cognitive function is assigned as 1 for sequence structure of the program and weights for concurrency and interrupts are assigned as 4, the most complex structure of the programs. These weights also show the structure of the program and can be easily represented by the graph. We refer authors to read Shao & Wang (2003) paper for the details of the cognitive weights.

EXISTING COGNITIVE COMPLEXITY MEASURE

Cognitive complexity based on cognitive informatics is an emerging field of research. In this section we are providing all existing cognitive complexity measures based on cognitive informat-ics. The computation of each measure is shown in appendix 1, by an example program.

COGNITIVE FUNCTIONAL SIZE COMPLEXITY MEASURE

Shao & Wang (2003) have proposed a complexity measure to calculate Cognitive Functional Size (CFS) of a program. His proposal is based on following definitions:

Definition 1. The cognitive weight of software is the degree of difficulty or relative time and effort required for comprehending a given piece of software modeled by a number of BCSs. The categories of BCSs described in Table 1, are profound architectural attributes of software systems. These BCSs and corresponding cognitive weights (W_i) of each BCS for determining a component's functionality and complexity are defined based on empirical studies in cognitive informatics (Wang 2002).

Definition 2. The total cognitive weight of a software component, W_c, is defined as the sum of the cognitive weights of its q linear blocks composed of individual BCSs. Since each block may consist of m layers of nesting BCSs, and each layer of n linear BCSs, the total cognitive weight, W_c, can be calculated by;

$$W_c = \left\{ \sum_{j=1}^{q} \left[\sum_{k=1}^{m} \sum_{i=1}^{n} W_c(j,k,i) \right] \right\}$$

If there is no embedded BCS in any of the m components, i.e., m=1, then the equation can be simplified as:

$$W_c = \sum_{j=1}^{q} \sum_{i=1}^{n} W_c(j,k,i)$$

Definition 3. The unit of cognitive weight (CWU) of software, Sfo, is defined as the cognitive weight of the simplest software component with only a single I/O and a linear structured BCS.

```
Sfo  =  f(Ni/o, Wbcs)
     =  (Ni  + No) Wi
     = 1*1
     = 1 CWU
```

Definition 4. The cognitive functional size of a basic software component that only consists of one method, S_f, is defined as a product of the sum of inputs and outputs ($N_{i/o}$) and the total cognitive weight, i.e.,

```
Sfo  =  Ni/o * Wc
           =  (Ni+No)
```

$$\{\sum_{j=1}^{q}[\sum_{k=1}^{m} \sum_{i=1}^{n}W_{c}(j,k,i)]\}$$

Further, the cognitive functional size of a complex component, Sf(c), can be derived as follows:

$$Sf(c) = \sum_{c=1}^{n}S_{f}(c)$$

Where Sf(c) is the CFS of the cth method that can be directly measured.

Modified Cognitive Complexity Measure (MCCM)

Misra(2006) proposed modified cognitive complexity measure (MCCM), which depends upon the following factors:

1. The total number of occurrence of operators and operands. Therefore, the complexity measure due to operators and operands can be calculated as,

```
SOO= Ni1 +Ni2
```

Where, Ni1: The total number of occurrences of operators.

Ni2: The total number of occurrences of operands.

SOO: Total number of operators and operands.

2. The cognitive weights of basic control structures (Wc). For example, if in a simple program without any loop, the weights assigned to such code is one.

Using the above considerations, Misra (2006) has suggested a formula for modified cognitive complexity measure:

Modified Cognitive complexity Measure (MCCM) = Soo*Wc.

In this formulation, the Soo values are multiplied by Wc values because of the possible higher structure value. The authors explained that for a simple program having only basic control structure the "sequence", Wc will not have any additional contribution to complexity. Therefore, for those programs the complexities are only due to Soo.

Cognitive Information Complexity Measure (CICM)

Kushvaha and Misra (2006) developed CICM based on the Shao & Wang (2003). They have argued that, the amount of information contained in the software is a function of the identifiers that hold the information and the operators that perform the operations on the information.

Information = f (Identifiers, Operators)

Where identifiers are variable names, defined constants and other labels in software. Further, the authors have proposed the following definitions:

Definition 1. Information contained in one line of code is the number of all operators and operands in that line of code. Thus in kth line of code the Information contained is:

```
Ik = (Identifiers + Operands)k
   = (IDk  +  OPk) IU
```

Where ID = Total number of identifiers in the kth LOC of software,

```
   OP  = Total number of operators
in the kth LOC of  software,
```

Definition 2. Total Information contained in software (ICS) is the sum of information contained in each line of code i.e.

```
       LOCS
 ICS  =  Σ  Ik
     k=1
```

Where Ik = Information contained in kth line of code,

```
   LOCS = Total lines of code in
the software.
```

Definition 3. The Weighted Information Count of a line of code (WICL) of software is a function of identifiers, operands and LOC and is defined as:

```
WICLk = ICSk  / [LOCS - k]
```

Where WICk = Weighted Information Count for the kth line,

```
    ICSk    = Information contained
in a software for the  kth line.
```

Therefore the Weighted Information Count of the Software (WICS) is defined as:

```
   LOCS
WICS  =   Σ      WICLk
   k  = 1
```

Definition 4. Cognitive Information Complexity Measure (CICM) is defined as the product of the weighted information count (WIC) and cognitive weight (Wc) of the BCS in the software i.e.

CICM = WICS * Wc

The authors claimed that their complexity measure encompasses all the major parameters that have a bearing on the difficulty in comprehending software or the cognitive complexity of the software, which clearly establishes a relationship between difficulty in understanding software and its cognitive complexity.

Definition 5. Information Coding Efficiency (EI) of software is defined as

(EI) = ICS / LOCS.

The cognitive information complexity is higher for the programs which have higher information coding efficiency.

COGNITIVE PROGRAM COMPLEXITY MEASURE (CPCM)

Further Misra has proposed cognitive program complexity measure (CPCM) (Misra 2007), which follows the rules of cognitive informatics and depends on total occurrences of inputs, outputs and cognitive weights. Accordingly, they have proposed the following definition for CPCM;

$$= Soo+ Wc. \qquad (3)$$

Where Soo is the sum of the total occurrences of input and output variables. The difference between CPCM and MCCM is only that, MCCM depends on operators and operands both while CPCM only depends on operands (inputs and outputs). Also instead of multiplying, as taken in the formulation of MCCM, the addition of the number of inputs and outputs are considered in the formulation of CPCM. This way of computation reduces the complexity values.

STRUCTURED COGNITIVE INFORMATION MEASURE (SCIM) WITH GRANULAR COMPUTING STRATEGIES

Benjapol, Auprasert & Yachai(2009) have applied the principles, strategies of granular computing and combined the approach proposed by Wang, to measure the complexity of the program. They proposed the following definitions to evaluate the cognitive complexity of the program.

Definition 1. At the beginning of the program, the Informatics Complexity Number (ICN) of every variable is zero. When a variable is assigned the value in the program, its ICN increases by I, and if that assignment statement contains operators, ICN of the variable that is assigned the value also further increases by the number of operators in that statement.

Definition 2. For variable 'V' appearing in leaf node granule 'L ', ICNmox(V,L) is the highest ICN of v 's occurrences in L.

Definition 3. Information contained in leaf node granule 'L' (I(L)) is defined as the sum of ICNmox(V,L) of every variable V exists in L.

Definition 4. SCIM is defined as the total sum of the products of corresponding cognitive weights and information contained in leaf node granule (I(L)). Since software may consist of q linear blocks composed in individual BCS 's, and each block may consist of 'm ' layers of nesting BCS's, and each layer with 'n ' linear BCS 's, then

$$SCIM = \{\sum_{j=1}^{q} \prod_{k=1}^{m} [W_c(j,k) \sum_{i=1}^{n} (j,k,i)]\}$$

where weights Wc (j.k) of BCS's are cognitive weights of BCS's presented in (Wang, 2003), and I(j,k,i) are information contained in a leaf BCS granule as defined in Definition 3.

In the proposal of SCIM, The authors claim that that SCIM evaluates the complexity by taking into account the dependencies of variables and their position in the BCS's structure.

UNIFIED COMPLEXITY MEASURE

Misra and Akman (2010) have proposed a Unified Complexity Measure(UCM) which is actually a unified version of existing approches. According to their approach, when a program code is inspected it is found that that number of lines (size), total occurrence of operators and operands (size), numbers of control structures (control flow structuredness), function calls (coupling) are the factors which directly affect the complexity. Accordingly, the complexity of software depends upon on the following factors:

Complexity of program depends on the size of the code. We suggest that the size of the code can be measured by total occurrence of operators and operands. Therefore, the complexity due to ith line of the code can be calculated as

$$SOO_i = N_{i1} + N_{i2} \qquad \text{Where}$$

Ni1: The total number of occurrences of operators at line i,

Ni2: The total number of occurrences of operands at line i,

2. Complexity of the program is directly proportional to the cognitive weights of Basic Control Structures (BSC).

Based on above considerations, a model to establish a proper relationship among internal attributes of software is given by;

$$Unified Complexity Measure (UCM)$$
$$= \sum_{i=1}^{n} \sum_{j=1}^{m_i} (SOO_{ij} * CW_{ij})$$

where complexity measure of the software code *UCM*(Unified Complexity Measure) is defined as the sum of complexity of its n modules and module *i* consists of m*i* line of code. In the context of formula, the concept of cognitive weights is used as an integer multiplier. Therefore, the unit of the *UCM*: unified complexity unit- *UCU* is always a positive integer number. This implies achievement of scale compatibility of *SOO* and *CW*.

The authors further claim that in the above formula:

- Number of lines (mi), number of operators and operands correspond to size of software,
- Total occurrence of basic control structures, operators and operands (SOOij) is related to algorithm complexity,
- Basic control structures (CWij) are related to control flow structuredness, therefore corresponds to structural complexity,
- CWij also corresponds to cognitive complexity.
- Number of modules (n) is related to modularity,
- Function calls in terms of basic control structures are related to coupling between modules(in terms of CWij's).

These are the major factors which are responsible for the program comprehension, therefore complexity of the software system.

ADVANTAGES AND LIMITATIONS OF COGNITIVE COMPLEXITY MEASURES

In the previous section, we have shown the formulation of the different cognitive complexity measures based on cognitive informatics. In this section, (in Table 2), we are providing the specific features and the limitation of the each measure under considerations.

EVALUATION OF COGNITIVE COMPLEXITY MEASURES AND COMPARATIVE STUDY

In the previous section we have demonstrated the features and limitation of all existing complexity measures. In this section we are evaluating and comparing each measure based on different attributes. We include all those attributes for evaluation and comparison purpose which are commonly used by researchers in software engineering community.

Theoretical Validation

- Measurement theory
- Representation Condition
- Scale measurement
- Extensive Structure
- Weyuker's properties
- Briand Properties for Complexity measures

Practical Validation

- GQM approach (Basili, Caldiera & Rombach(1994))
- Caner's Framework
- Any other Criteria

Empirical Validation

- Small examples
- Case study
- Big projects from the web
- Real projects from the Industry

Theoretical validation: It is very easy to find numbers of theoretical evaluation criteria in the literature. However, evaluation through measurement theory (Briand, Emam & Morasca, 1996; Briand, Morasca & Basili, 1996) and Weyuker's(1986) properties is more common and used for evaluating complexity measures. If we analyze all the cognitive complexity measures, we found that all measures are evaluated against Weyuker's properties. CFS, MCCM and CPCM and UCM satisfy seven Weyuker's properties. CICM and SCIM satisfy all nine Weyuker's properties. However, we are not agreeing with the claim of the developer of CICM and SCIM i.e. their measures are satisfied by all Weyuker's properties. Actually, there are some misunderstandings amongst the developers of a complexity measures that a measure should satisfy all Weyuker's properties. However, it is not the case. If a measure is a sensible measure, it should not satisfy all the Weyuker's properties (Cherniavsky, & Smith, 1991) otherwise it may violate the rules of measurement theory. It is because of, some of Weyuker's properties contradict to each other (e.g. Weyuker's property 5 and 6). In this chapter, our aim is not to check

Table 2. Features and limitations of existing cognitive complexity measures

Measure	Features and Advantages	Limitations
1.CFS(2003)	Based on principles of cognitive informatics. Becomes a breakthrough in software complexity measurements. The formulation of CFS is based on the cognitive weights, which reflects the effort required to comprehend a given peace of software. Cognitive weights represents the architecture of the basic control structure of a software code, therefore CFS is capable of evaluating complexity from both architectural and cognitive points of view. Cognitive weight becomes benchmarks for several new measures.	Consider only distinct number of input and output in the formulation. Only compared with lines of code measures. No practical evaluation Till date no knowledge for the application to the industry. No automated tool is available for computing CFS.
2.MCCM(2006)	Modified version of cognitive functional size. Measuring Complexity due to operators, operands and basic control structures. Straightforward and simple calculation only by counting total number of operators, operands and weights of BCSs. Similar trends with CFS values in the outputs of sample programs that proves that it really represents the modified version of CFS, by including the contribution due to operators and operands.	Providing complexity values high in number. Do not follow the principles of cognitive informatics. No tool is developed by the author.
3.CICM(2006)	Based on the concept that the information contained in the software is a function of identifiers and operators. Counting operators and operands of each line of code. A good attempt to modify the CFS approach. This work encouraged to the community to include the complexity due to operators in the computation of cognitive complexity.	It includes the complexity due to operators and operands and therefore do not follow the principles of cognitive informatics. Operators are run time attributes and therefore can not be treated as information contents. Complexity calculation for CICM is complex. No tool is developed by authors to compute the CICM. And therefore, for a big program it is not very easy to compute the complexity by human.
4.CPCM(2007)	Based on principles of cognitive informatics. It is also the modified version of CFS. It computes complexity of code due to basic control structures and total occurrences of operands, instead a distinct number of input and output as computed in CFS. Simple calculation of metric. Trends of metric values for CPCM are very close to CFS.	Complexity due to operators is not included in the formulation. No dependencies between variables and their position are considered (Benjapol & Yachi 2009).

continued on following page

Table 2. Continued

5.SCIM (2009)	An integrating approach of Granular Computing and other available measures. Intended to measure the complexity of BCS not only due to its weight but at the same time counting the variables and operators. The whole program is divided into granules. Granules are the basic control structures. Similar approach to MCCM, integrating operator's operands and basic control structures. In MCCM operators and operands are accumulated for the whole program and then multiplied to BCSs however in SCIM, operator and operators are summed and multiplied to BCS for each granule (i.e. basic control structures). Computation of SCIM is simple.	No any software tool is available. Similar to the CICM, Information of the program is considered in the form of operators and operands. However, Operators cannot be considered as a part of information. It includes the complexity due to operators; therefore do not follow the basic principles of cognitive informatics, which states that cognitive complexity depends on inputs/outputs and basic control structures. The trends of the output of programs are similar to CFS and MCCM.
6. UCM (2010)	It is a unified approach and includes all possible features which are responsible for increasing cognitive complexity. Line is treated as a basic unit. It considers the complexity due to operators, operands and structure of each line in terms of cognitive weights. It doesn't consider the irrelevant line for example; comment lines and a line which does not include any operators and operands. On the other hand, it considers the dependencies between variables and their positions. It is capable of measuring several internal and external attributes. Although UCM computes complexity of each line of code, its calculation is easy in comparison to CICM and SCIM.	Similar to MCCM, UCM provides high complexity values. No tool is available to compute UCM.

the applicability of Weyuker's properties on these measures. In this respect, their claims that their measures are satisfied by all Weyuker's properties are not appropriate. CFS, MCCM and UCM have also been evaluated through the representation condition and satisfy this condition. However other measures have not been evaluated against the principles of measurement theory.

Scale of a new measure can only be evaluated after application of representation condition or extensive structure. Except CFS, MCCM and UCM none of the measures have been evaluated for scale measurement. Most of them are on ratio or weak ratio scale. The developers of SCIM and CPCM claim that their metrics are on ratio scale but no proof is given in support.

Practical Evaluation: Kaner's (2004) framework is a more appropriate choice for most devel-

opers of cognitive complexity measures. Kaner has proposed a set of definitions/questions, which evaluates the practical utility of the proposed measures. All complexity measures except CICM have been evaluated against the Caner's framework. In general their (all cognitive complexity measures) purpose, aim, scope, attributes, and all the required definitions are almost same. For example: The scope of SCIM as mentioned in the original paper 'SCIM is categorized as a technical metric applicable after coding. Its scope of usage is for software development and maintenance groups' is the same with all earlier proposed metrics. It is due to the fact that they are developed for same purpose (i.e. for cognitive complexity) and their background (i.e. cognitive weight and cognitive informatics) are also same. It is important to note that Caner's framework only evaluates the practical utility from theoretical point of view; however, it is possible that even after satisfying these conditions a measure will not fit or be appropriate in real life applications.

Empirical validation: It is the real evaluation of any complexity measure. It evaluates the practical applicability of any new measure in real life applications. In other words, a new metric must be applied to the software industry to evaluate its practical applicability. However, the conditions of empirical validations for measurement models /metrics are not very good. To the best of our knowledge, none of the cognitive complexity metrics are applied to industry till date. All the proposed metrics including the base metric CFS (proposal of Wang's) have used programs either from the book or from internet. The applicability of measures/metrics on these programs only proves the partial empirical validation. In other words, all the cognitive complexity metrics are not evaluated or tested for their practical implementations in real life, i.e. in industry. It is the task for future work. In fact, there is a practical problem behind this. Most of the metrics are developed by academicians and it is very difficult for them to apply their new model of metric to the industry, if they are not associated with industry. Further, most of the medium and small scale software industries do not care for quality aspects and particularly the use of software metrics in these organizations is very limited. Of course, there are several constraints in small and medium scale companies like budget, time pressure and less number of software developers. For big and established companies, it is very difficult for the developer of a new metric to promote the benefits of his measure. As a result, most of the proposed metrics lack in their real empirical validation. In fact this is the major problem for developer of a new measure. To implement the new metric in industry, the academicians should try for collaborative work / program with industry. In this way they can solve the problem of real empirical validation.

DISCUSSION

All the cognitive complexity measures under consideration are based on the concept of cognitive weight. They all used cognitive weight as a basic unit and added other terms for better representation of cognitive complexity. The way of interaction for other terms with cognitive weighs are different in different measures. For example in the original proposal of CFS, only distinct number of inputs and outputs are taken into consideration. However, total numbers of occurrences of input and outputs are equally important as the total occurrences of BCS's (Misra 2007). In cognitive informatics the functional complexity of software depend on input, output and internal architecture and therefore total occurrences of inputs and outputs is considered in the formulation of CPCM, i.e. CFS has modified by taking consideration of cognitive weights and total occurrences of inputs and outputs. Further, by considering the importance of operators in design construction, in MCCM, it is proposed that the cognitive complexity also depends on total occurrences of operators and operands instead of only input and output. Total occurrences of operators directly affect the internal architecture as well as cognitive complexity of software. In CICM, information contained in software is assumed to be a function of operators and operands. However, the Misra (2006) does not agree with this claim of Kushwaha and Misra (2006). He has argued that operators are run time attributes and cannot be taken as information contained in the software. SCIM is based on granular computing and has similar approach as MCCM. The difference between MCCM is at the level of interaction of operators and operands with cognitive weight. However, both MCCM and SCIM are using operators in their formulation and therefore do not follow the rules of cognitive informatics. Further, the developers of SCIM agree that operators are not the function of information but they used operators in their formulation.

A unified approach of all these complexity measure is the UCM. In the formulation of UCM each line is treated as a granular and the weight of line depends on the number of operators, operands and structure of line. Weight of each line of code is assumed to one for simplest structural line, on the other hand irrelevant lines, comment lines and lines without any operator and operand do not provide any value. The only disadvantage of this measure is that it provides normally high vales for large programs.

In software engineering and especially in software development process, maintenance of the software takes a lot of efforts and money. In maintenance process, the comprehension of the software is the major factor which increases the maintenances cost. Further, comprehension of the code is cognitive process, which is related to cognitive complexity. In summary, if the code will be complex, it will be hard to comprehend and as a result its maintenance increases. To reduce the maintenance we must have to control the complexity. Cognitive complexity measurers are one of the way through which we can control the complexity of the code. Six different types of cognitive complexity measurers are discussed in this chapter. However, again a question arises which one is better and how can we select the best? Our suggestion is that first we have to see what we want to measure. If anybody is interested to find overall code complexity, UCM is the better option, because it includes all the factors which are responsible for complexity. Further, if anybody is specifically interested in computing cognitive complexity based on rules of cognitive informatics then he can choose CFS, CPCM, CICM or SCIM. However, in particular each one of them has their own advantages and disadvantages as summarised in the previous sections. UCM, MCCM provides very high values, CFS is moderate but it does not consider all the required factors, responsible for complexity. Further, the limitation of all the considered measures in this chapter is that they are not appropriate for those languages where

the relation between inputs, outputs, operators and basic control structures cannot be easily defined. If we want to use these measures for large software projects, developed in object oriented environment, we have to make changes in these measures according to the required property under estimation. For example, none of the complexity measure under considerations is capable to evaluate complexity due to inheritance. In general, in object oriented environment, we can apply cognitive weight (Misra, 2009) or any enhanced version (Misra, & Akman, 2008) of this measure, to compute the complexity of methods, classes or any specific feature.

CONCLUSION

Cognitive complexity metrics based on cognitive informatics are analysed and compared. Cognitive complexity metrics play a crucial role in maintaining the quality of software, which is one of the most important issues in any type of software systems. Cognitive complexity metrics can be applied at the design level to reduce the complexity and can be further used for evaluating programs during software review and testing phase. We have analysed all the available cognitive complexity metrics in terms of their features. For comparison, we have selected some significant and common attributes, to find a comparative view of all available cognitive complexity measures. These all metrics are based on the concept of cognitive weight. Furthermore, these all metrics uses cognitive weights, operators and/or operands in different way, i.e. the way of interaction between them are different in these metrics. If we closely observe all the papers in which these metrics are proposed, we can easily observe that their trends in graphs (when apply on different examples) are similar. This is an advantageous point in these measures and therefore the organisations have flexibility to adopt them as per availability of tool.

REFERENCES

Basili, V. R., Caldiera, G., & Rombach, H. D. (1994). The goal question metric paradigm. In Marciniak, J. J. (Ed.), *Encyclopedia of Software Engineering* (pp. 578–583). John Wiley.

Benjapol, A., & Limpiyakorn, Y. (2008). Underlying cognitive complexity measure computation with combinatorial. *World Academy of Science. Engineering and Technology, 45*, 431–436.

Benjapol, A., & Limpiyakorn, Y. (2009). Towards structured software cognitive complexity measurement with granular computing strategies. In *Proceedings of the 8th IEEE International Conference on Cognitive Informatics, 365-370*.

Briand, L., El Emam, K., & Morasca, S. (1996). On the application of measurement theory in software engineering. *Journal of Empirical Software Engineering, 1*(1), 61–88. doi:10.1007/BF00125812

Briand, L. C., Bunse, C., & Daly, J. W. (2001). A controlled experiment for evaluating quality guidelines on the maintainability of object-oriented design. *IEEE Transactions on Software Engineering, 27*, 513–530. doi:10.1109/32.926174

Briand, L. C., Morasca, S., & Basili, V. R. (1996). Property based software engineering measurement. *IEEE Transactions on Software Engineering, 22*(1), 68–86. doi:10.1109/32.481535

Cherniavsky, J. C., & Smith, C. H. (1991). On Weyuker's axioms for software complexity measures. *IEEE Transactions on Software Engineering, 17*, 636–638. doi:10.1109/32.87287

Fenton, N. (1994). Software measurement: A necessary scientific basis. *IEEE Transactions on Software Engineering, 20*(3), 199–206. doi:10.1109/32.268921

Fenton, N. (1997). *Software metrics: A rigorous and practical approach*. Boston: PWS Publishing Company.

Henderson-Sellers, B. (1996). *Object-Oriented metrics: Measures of complexity*. Prentice-Hall.

Hoare, C. A. R., Hayes, I. J., He, J., Morgan, C. C., Roscoe, A. W., & Sanders, J. W. (1987). Laws of programming. *Communications of the ACM, 30*(8), 672–686. doi:10.1145/27651.27653

IEEE Computer Society. (1990). IEEE standard glossary of software engineering terminology.

Kaner, C. (2004). Software engineering metrics: What do they measure and how do we know? In *Proceedings of the International Software Metrics Symposium*. (pp. 1-10).

Klemola, T., & Rilling, J. (2003). A cognitive complexity metric based on category learning. In *Proceedings of IEEE (ICCI'03)*, (pp. 103-108).

Kushwaha, D. S., & Misra, A. K. (2005). A modified cognitive information complexity measure of software. In *Proceedings of the 7th International Conference on Cognitive Systems (ICCS'05)*.

Misra, S. (2006). *Modified cognitive complexity measure*. (pp. 1050-1059). (LNCS 4263).

Misra, S. (2007). Cognitive program complexity measure. In *Proceedings of IEEE (ICCI'07)*, (pp. 120-125).

Misra, S. (2009). A metric for global software development environments. *Proceedings of the Indian National Science Academy, 75*(4), 1–14.

Misra, S., & Akman, I. (2008). Weighted class complexity: A measure of complexity for Object Oriented systems. *Journal of Information Science and Engineering, 24*, 1689–1708.

Misra, S., & Akman, I. (2010). Unified complexity measure: A measure of complexity. *Proceedings of the National Academy of Sciences of the United States of America, 80*.

Pressman, R. S. (2001). *Software engineering: A practitioner's approach* (5th ed.). McGraw Hill.

Rauterberg, M. (1992). *A method of a quantitative measurement of cognitive complexity, Human-Computer Interaction: task and organization* (pp. 295–307). Roma: CUD Publishing.

Sommerville, I. (2001). *Software engineering* (6th ed.). Addison-Wesley.

Wang, Y. (2002). On cognitive informatics: Keynote lecture. In *Proceedings of the 1st IEEE Int. Conf. Cognitive Informatics (ICCI'02)*, (pp. 34–42).

Wang, Y. (2004). On the cognitive informatics foundation of software engineering. In *Proceedings of the 3rd IEEE International Conference of Cognitive Informatics (ICCI'04)*, (pp. 1-10).

Wang, Y. (2005), Keynote: Psychological experiments on the cognitive complexities of fundamental control structures of software systems. In *Proceedings of the 4th IEEE International Conference on Cognitive Informatics (ICCI'05)*, (pp. 4-5).

Wang, Y. (2006). On the informatics laws and deductive semantics of software. *IEEE Transactions on Systems, Man, and Cybernetics*, *36*(2), 161–171. doi:10.1109/TSMCC.2006.871138

Wang, Y. (2007). The theoretical framework of cognitive informatics. *International Journal of Cognitive Informatics and Natural Intelligence*, *1*(1), 1–27.

Wang, Y., & Shao, J. (2003). A new measure of software complexity based on cognitive weights. *Canadian Journal of Electrical and Computer Engineering*, 69–74.

Wang, Y., & Shao, J. (2009). On the cognitive complexity of software and its quantification and formal methods. *International Journal of Software Science and Computational Intelligence*, *1*(2), 31–53.

Zuse, H. A. (1998). *Framework of software measurement*. Berlin: Walter de Gruyter.

APPENDIX 1.

Example: An algorithm to calculate the average of a set of numbers

```
# define N   10
main()
{
int count;
float sum, average, number;
sum = 0;
count = 0;
while (count < N)
{
        scanf("%f", &number);
        sum = sum + number;
        count = count + 1;
}
average = sum/N;
Printf("N=%d sum = %f"',N,sum);
Printf("average = %f"'average);
}
```

a.   The CFS of this program can be calculated as:


```
Ni(distinct number of inputs) =3
No(no of output)=1
BCS (sequence) W1 = 1
BCS (iteration) W2 = 3
CFS= (Ni+No)*Wc
            = (3+1)*4= 16
```

b.   We illustrate the MCCM to calculate the complexity of the above program as under:


```
Total number of operands =18
Total number of operators = 4
Soo= 18+4= 22
BCS (sequence) W1 = 1
BCS (iteration) W2 =  3
 Wc = W1+W2=1+3      = 4
MCCM   =   Soo* Wc
       =   22 *   4
       =    88
```

c.   We illustrate the CPCM to calculate the complexity of the above program, as under:

```
Total no. of inputs and outputs = 18
Soo= 18
BCS (sequence) W1 = 1
BCS (iteration) W2 = 3
Wc = W1+W2=1+3        = 4
CPCM = Soo+ Wc       =  18 +    4
                     =    22
```

d.   We illustrate the CICM to calculate the complexity of the above program as under:

```
Total number of operands =18
Total number of operators = 4
BCS(sequence)       W1    = 1
BCS(while)                W2    = 3
Wc = W1 + W2 = 1+3 = 4
WIC S= [ 1/16 + 1/13 + 3/12 + 1/11 + 1/10 + 3/9 + 1/7 + 4/6 + 3/5 + 4/3]
 = 3.63
CICM =  WICS * Wc
                    = 3.63 * 4
                    = 14.53
```

The cognitive information complexity of the algorithm above is 14.53 CICU (Cognitive Information Complexity unit).

e.   The SCIM can be estimated as follows:

The whole program is divided in three granular say G1, G2, G3. All are sequential.

```
# define N 10
main()
{
int count;
float sum, average, number;
sum = 0;
```

G1= 6*1= 6

```
while (count < N)
{
        scanf("%f", &number);
```

```
        sum = sum + number;
      count = count + 1;
}
```

G2= 3*7= 21

```
{
average = sum/N;
Printf("N=%d sum = %f"',N,sum);
Printf("average = %f"'average);
}
```

G3= 1*9= 9

The CSCM

$$= \{\sum_{j=1}^{q}\prod_{k=1}^{m}[W_c(j,k)\sum_{i=1}^{n}(j,k,i)]\}$$

=6+21+9=36

f.   The UCM of the program can be calculated as follows

	Soo	CWi	UCM
# define N 10	1	0	0
main()	0	1	0
{	1	1	1
int count;	2	1	2
float sum, average, number;	4	1	4
sum = 0;	4	1	4
count = 0;	4	1	4
while (count < N)	3	3	9
{	1	1	1
scanf("%f", &number);	3	1	3
sum = sum + number;	6	1	6
count = count + 1;	6	1	6
average = sum/N;	6	1	6
Printf("N=%d sum = %f"',N,sum);	3	1	3
Printf("average = %f"'average);	3	1	3
}	1	1	1
Total UCM			53 UCU

Section 5
Software Process Improvement and Design Tools

Chapter 12
Introducing Agility into Plan–Based Assessments

Minna Pikkarainen
University of Limerick, Ireland & VTT Technical Research Centre of Finland, Finland

Fergal McCaffery
Dundalk Institute of Technology, Ireland

ABSTRACT

Agile or Plan-driven approaches to software process improvement (such as the Capability Maturity Model Integration (CMMI) and the ISO/IEC 15504 standard) claim to provide companies with improved processes, higher quality software and faster software development. Assessment is an important component of any software process improvement programme, as in order for an organisation to commence an improvement programme, they must first be aware of the current state of their software development practices. Therefore, in the case of small companies such assessments need also to be cost effective and focused only on the most relevant process areas.

INTRODUCTION

In this chapter we will address the question of how to integrate agile practices into traditional software process assessments. We will begin by presenting a background section that will detail traditional

software process assessment and agile software development. We then will illustrate research we performed to develop and implement a low resource hybrid approach (AHAA) (McCaffery et al. 2008) for software process assessment and improvement that integrates CMMI (CMMI, 2006), Automotive SPICE™ (Automotive S, 2007) and agile practices together. We will also discuss the

DOI: 10.4018/978-1-60960-215-4.ch012

applicability of combining agile and plan-driven software development approaches for different types of domains e.g. financial, safety-critical. Next, we provide an empirical examination, based on assessments that were performed in two Small to Medium Sized Enterprises (SMEs) using the AHAA method. Finally, we discuss the empirical findings from both assessments, the evolvement of the AHAA method and provide conclusions and recommendations for researchers and practitioners wishing to combine traditional and agile software development practices.

BACKGROUND

This section describes SPI, software process assessment and agile development.

Software Process Improvement

Continuous SPI can assist companies to satisfy customers through providing high quality deliverables in an efficient and repeatable manner. This may be particularly beneficial to SMEs that have to satisfy increasingly demanding customers using a limited pool of resources. In fact, SMEs often lack maturity in their software development processes. In many cases, SMEs have chaotic models of operation that impact the success of the entire organisation (Batista & Figueiredo, 2000). However, just as the standards world has recognised that software engineering standards should not only apply to large high maturity organisations but also to low capability level organisations and this has lead to the development of an International standard for Very Small Enterprises (Laporte et al. 2008), there also is a need for SPI models and assessment methods for such organisations. A software process assessment may be used to determine weaknesses in an organisation's software development processes and consequently be used to initiate SPI work within an organisation (Humphrey, Snyder et al. 1991). In SMEs, such assessments need to

be cost effective (Batista & Figueiredo, 2000) and focused on specific and important process areas (Richardson, 2001). Agile approaches constituting a set of principles, methods and practices have become popular within software companies (Hansson et al. 2006). The reasons for this adoption are obvious in that companies need to be agile in order to survive in dynamic business environments (Kettunen, 2009). An agile approach can also provide a systematic mechanism to manage projects (Sutherland, Viktorov et al. 2007). Although it has been argued that: "Both agile and planned approaches have situation-dependent shortcomings that, if left unaddressed, can lead to project failures" (Boehm & Turner, 2003) and that companies should integrate best practices from both agile and traditional software development, there has been very little input from the research community or practitioners on how to increase agility through performing software process assessments.

Agile methods promise companies improved software productivity and quality (Holström, Fitzgerald et al. 2006). Such improvements have previously been achieved through adopting traditional SPI models and assessment methods (Galin & Avrahami, 2006; Niazi et al., 2006). It has been shown, for instance, that CMMI based SPI programmes have resulted in companies obtaining between 28–53% improvements in lead time and between 70 to 74% improvement in terms of quality (measured by the amount of defects) (Galin & Avrahami, 2006). To obtain benefits from traditional and agile methods, both approaches must however be deployed. Yet, agile researchers have known for some time that there are fundamental differences between traditional (e.g. CMMI) and agile methods that may cause difficulties when integrating these approaches. For example, whilst agile methods emphasise face to face discussions and reduced documentation, CMMI improvements can led to a situation in which the developers have implemented more documentation than software code (Boehm & Turner, 2003).

There are some case studies that suggest using a lightweight software process assessment may be used as a starting point for agile deployment (Pikkarainen and Passoja 2005; Pikkarainen et al. 2005; Svensson and Höst 2005; McCaffery et al. 2008). These examples provide the following basic insight: the company should understand what may be improved through adopting a combination of traditional and agile improvement practices. While these studies prove that it is possible to integrate agile practices into traditional software process assessments, there is a lack of an empirical evaluation for this hybrid improvement approach. Such an evaluation is really important, particularly in relation to SMEs where assessment costs are a critical issue.

Plan Driven SPI – CMMI and ISO/IEC 15504 (SPICE)

The two main reference models for plan-driven SPI are CMMI and ISO/IEC 15504 (SPICE). The following sections describe both of these models.

Overview of CMMI

The US Department of Defence recognised a key risk in software projects with respect to increased software costs and quality issues. Therefore, in the early 1980's they established the Software Engineering Institute (SEI), located in Carnegie Mellon University. The SEI then developed a formal software process improvement (SPI) model for software engineering in August 1991 released the initial version of the Capability Maturity Model for Software (CMM 1991). In 1997, efforts in the CMM model halted in preference for the more comprehensive Capability Maturity Model Integration (CMMI). Version 1.1 of the CMMI® (CMMI 2002a, CMMI 2002b) was released in 2002 by the SEI CMMI Product Team with v1.2 following in August 2006. A key change in the CMMI® for Development v1.2 (CMMI 2006) is that one document describes both the continuous and staged models. In Version 1.1 the continuous and staged representations were detailed in separate documents.

The primary difference between the continuous and staged representations of CMMI is as follows. In selecting the continuous representation, an organisation may choose to focus on either a single or multiple related process areas with the goal of improving capability within those process areas. Different process areas may be progressed at different rates, thereby providing the organisation with maximum flexibility to focus upon areas they view to be critical. In implementing the staged representation of CMMI, organisations must progress through the model one stage at a time in a prescribed fashion. The process areas within the model are associated with maturity levels. The organisation may only progress to the next maturity level of the model once they have demonstrated capability for all process areas within their current maturity level. This method of progression through the model ensures that an adequate foundation has been laid at each maturity stage before tackling the more advanced process areas of the subsequent stages.

The CMMI® model comprises 22 key process areas. A process area as defined by CMMI is "a cluster of related practices in an area that, when performed collectively, satisfy a set of goals considered important for making significant improvement in that area" (CMMI 2006). A process area typically comprises 1 to 4 specific goals. The specific goals are further divided into practices that are specific to that process area. In addition, the model contains generic goals and practices that are common across all of the process areas. Within the continuous representation of the CMMI® model capability levels are used to measure performance with respect to the specific and generic practices. The levels include: Level 0 - Incomplete, Level 1 - Initial, Level 2 - Repeatable, Level 3 - Defined, Level 4 – Managed and Level 5 – Optimised.

Overview of ISO/IEC 15504 (SPICE)

ISO/IEC 15504, also known as SPICE™ (Software Process Improvement and Capability Determination) is an international standard for software process assessment. It was developed by the Joint Technical Subcommittee between ISO and IEC. It was developed after CMMI®, it uses many of the ideas of CMMI.

SPICE™ is used in defining and assessing an organisation's capability in the areas of management and the definition of their process structures. The model is therefore broken into a process and capability dimension. The key process categories include: customer-supplier, engineering, supporting, management and organisation. Similar to CMMI®, the capability level for the process areas broken into six levels, 0 – 5 as follows: measured as follows: Level 0 - Incomplete process, Level 1 - Performed process, Level 2 - Managed process, Level 3 - Established process, Level 4 - Predictable process and Level 5 - Optimised process.

Assessment Types

Assessments facilitate improvements in an organisation's software development and management processes (Humphrey, Snyder et al. 1991): "An organization characterizes the current state of its software process and provides findings and recommendations to facilitate improvement." (Humphrey, Snyder et al. 1991). Empirical studies have proven that assessments, integrated with the successful implementation of a change, can enable organizations to improve the speed and reduce the cost of the software development (Niazi, Wilson et al. 2003; Galin & Avrahami, 2006). Software process assessments have been used, with all of the existing SPI models (IDEAL (McFeeley, 1996), QIP (Basili, 1989), and plan-do-check-act-cycle (Deming, 1990)), as a mechanism to identify the strengths and weaknesses in software development projects and this information is used for improvement purposes (Humphrey, Snyder et al.

1991). The assessments are often supported by standards (e.g. ISO standards e.g. 15504 (2006) or paradigms (e.g. capability maturity model (CMM) (Curtis et al. 2001) (Agrawal & Chari 2007), more recently CMMI (2006)). These 'standards' (Niazi et al. 2003; Agarwal and Chari 2007) define how to achieve managed, defined and optimized software development (Boehm & Turner, 2003). The most important ISO standards applicable to software development are ISO/IEC 12207:1995 and its replacement ISO/IEC 15288:2002, (both referring to the Software life cycle processes), ISO/IEC 12207:1995 standard, ISO/IEC 15939:2002 (Software measurement process) and ISO/IEC 14143 (Software measurement - Functional size measurement). There are few reports available discussing the use of ISO standards in assessments combined with agile development. The focus of ISO 12207:1995 is in software development, which motivates and provides guidelines for implementing the standard in an agile context. According to Theunissen et al. (2003) implementation guidelines are proposed that will ensure that an agile-based project conforms to ISO 12207:1995. These guidelines are derived from both an analysis of the standard and an analysis of the characteristics of the agile methodologies. The task of implementing an agile methodology in such a way that it conforms to ISO 12207:1995 can first tailor the project to meet the requirements of the ISO standard and then to map it to the development methods and processes that are used.

In some cases, a reference model such as CMMI is also perceived as too 'heavy' and too bureaucratic (Nawrocki et al. 2002). For example, Anderson (2005) points out that CMMI suggests that as many as 400 document types and 1000 artefacts are required to facilitate an appraisal. This is the main reason, why many of the CMMI adopters have argued that the use of CMMI itself actually results in increased cost for companies (Boehm & Turner, 2003). This is a critical issue especially in the SMEs. As a response to the critique of heavy and time consuming assessments, tailored 'lightweight' assessment techniques have been provided in several studies (Kautz, 1998; Batista & Figueiredo, 2000; Horvat, 2000; Richardson, 2001; Wilkie & et al., 2005). They have been developed in order to offer techniques for implementing assessments rapidly, but only in small companies that have high dependencies on a low number of individuals and projects. CMMI is often used in the context of lightweight assessments (Batista & Figueiredo, 2000; Horvat, 2000; Wilkie et. al, 2005). For example, Batista and Figueiredo (2000) argue that a more pragmatic application of CMM and a simplification of the assessment method are key factors for assessments in small teams. There are three different types of CMMI assessment:

- **SCAMPI class A:** a rigorous and heavy-weight assessment that is used to provide an official certification rating;
- **Class B:** a somewhat lighter assessment that is used to prepare an organisation for an official class A assessment;
- **Class C:** the most lightweight of the three assessments.

The pragmatic application of CMMI in both class B and C assessments in a lightweight assessment approach means that the improvement initiatives are defined based on the improvements that are most relevant for the assessed organization.

Lightweight assessment methods have been developed in order to offer techniques for implementing assessments rapidly based on the needs of SMEs that have high dependencies on a small number of individuals and projects (Kautz, 1998; Batista & Figueiredo, 2000; Horvat, 2000; Richardson, 2001; Wilkie et al., 2005). Lightweight assessments typically follow the class C-type assessment type. Although SMEs have a need for high software product quality and fast software production, high overhead assessments present issues for them (Batista & Figueiredo, 2000).

Thus, lightweight assessment approaches should focus on key process areas such as requirements management, project planning, configuration management, and project monitoring and control (Richardson, 2001; Wilkie et al., 2005) and keep the assessment process as simple as possible (Kautz, 1998; Horvat, 2000) to avoid high costs and effort used in the SPI (Richardson, 2001).

Although, lightweight assessment approaches appear attractive solutions the current literature lacks studies in which lightweight reference model based assessment approaches have been mediated with agile practices.

Agile Development

Agile methods have been increasingly used in software development organisations. For example, F-Secure1 reported that using agile methods such as short cycles, continuous planning and daily meetings has resulted in 50% improvements in software quality (Agile Newsletter, 2005). The results of the current agile research includes numerous definitions of agility (Conboy & Fitzgerald, 2004). Among the well established generalizations are:

1. Agile methods are lightweight approaches for software development. They are used to minimise waste and complexity
2. Agile methods make use of face to face communication as opposed to documentation
3. Agile methods encourage continuous planning and integration

In agile software development the problem of the rigidity of a plan-driven software development process is solved with a 'planning driven' approach in which the planning has been made constant, frequent and fluid to enable the team to respond to changes quickly (Wang et al. 2008). In parallel with frequent planning the agile approaches also bring people regularly together for face to face communication. This should improve software development if we understand software development to be as Cockburn (2002) states: "Software development is a group game in which the team should cooperate together to achieve the defined goals" (Cockburn, 2002). The game is co-operative because all the team members are able to help each other reach the set goals. Most agile research is either pure eXtreme Programming (XP), or Scrum based, or a mixture of both (Fitzgerald et al. 2006). Related studies are primarily concerned with understanding the use of agile methods.

XP is an agile method originally presented by Kent Beck (2000). It is a 'lightweight' methodology with four key values: communication, simplicity, feedback and courage (Beck, 2000). Scrum has been pioneered by Schwaber and Beedle (Schwaber & Beedle, 2002). It is a simple process mainly focused on the project management of software development (Fitzgerald, Hartnett et al., 2006). Scrum was originally influenced by Boehm's 'spiral' model, but it was developed based on industrial experiences to simplify the complexity of the project and requirements management in software organizations (Schwaber, 2003). Scrum describes practices in an iterative, incremental time boxed process skeleton. At the beginning of the iteration, the team has a sprint planning meeting in which they decide what the team will do during the following iteration. At the end of the iteration, the team presents the results to all the stakeholders in the sprint review meetings to gain feedback on their work. Iteration is the heart of Scrum, with self-organizing teams building software based on the goals and plans defined in a sprint planning meeting (Schwaber, 2003). Both XP and Scrum define practices for the software development process. Beck (1999) identifies 12 key practices for the software development process, which mostly focus on software engineering. Beck (Beck, 2000) argues that the XP practices are situation dependent, which means that the application of the practices is a

choice which can be made based on the current development context.

During the 2000s, interest in agile methods has increased dramatically (Lindvall et al., 2004). These methods have been adopted in different types of software projects and in wide-ranging application domains (Karlström, 2002). It has been shown that the use of agile methods can be beneficial for product manageability, visibility and team communication (Larman, 2003) as well as ensuring frequent feedback from the customer (Rising & Janoff, 2000). In Motorola, on the other hand a selected set of XP practices was used also in the field of safety critical systems (Grenning, 2001). In that case, the use of XP practices was reported to have improved the software development quality by 53% compared to the plan-driven software development project.

ISSUES IN INTEGRATING AGILE AND PLAN DRIVEN ASSESSMENT APPROACHES

Is it Really Possible to Integrate both Approaches?

Integrating plan-driven and agile software development approaches has been referred to as a fundamental challenge that is almost "like oil and water" (Turner & Jain, 2002). The most important ISO standards applicable to software development are ISO/IEC 12207:1995 and its replacement ISO/IEC 15288:2002, (both referring to the Software life cycle processes), ISO/IEC 12207:1995 standard, ISO/IEC 15939:2002 (Software measurement process) and ISO/IEC 14143 (Software measurement - Functional size measurement). There are few reports available discussing the use of ISO standards in assessments combined with agile development. The focus of ISO 12207:1995 is in software development, which motivates and provides guidelines for implementing the standard in an agile context. According to Theunissen et al.

(2003) implementation guidelines are proposed that will ensure that an agile-based project conforms to ISO 12207:1995. These guidelines are derived from both an analysis of the standard and an analysis of the characteristics of the agile methodologies. The task of implementing an agile methodology in such a way that it conforms to ISO 12207:1995 can first tailor the project to meet the requirements of the ISO standard and then to map it to the development methods and processes that are used. From a CMMI perspective, it is assumed that CMMI compliant processes tend to be heavyweight, bureaucratic and slow-moving (Andersson, 2005). The common belief has been that to follow a CMMI SPI programme teams must document requirements, decisions, meetings, risks, plans and the effort spent on software development in order to develop high quality software. Alternatively, when an agile approach is used teams can achieve quality software using informal, lightweight documentation (Boehm & Turner, 2003).

Agile principles suggest that a team needs to reflect regularly on how to become more productive and more efficient (Beck, Beedle et al., 2001). Agile software development companies typically respond to this problem by adopting the practice of iteration retrospectives, in which teams continuously collect and evaluate their strengths and improvement needs in a face to face manner (Salo & Abrahamsson, 2007). The problem with an iteration retrospective approach is that it does not provide a way for sharing information between teams or communicating the strengths and improvement needs of teams at an organizational level (Salo & Abrahamsson, 2007). However, traditional software process assessments can provide some answers to this gap by describing well established processes for collecting and sharing improvement information that is required at an organizational level. When an agile approach is used teams can achieve high quality software through adopting informal, lightweight documentation (Boehm & Turner, 2003). Heavy and time-consuming assess-

ments may however not suit an organization that uses "working software" as its primary measure of progress. Therefore such assessments need to be implemented in the lightest way possible (i.e. not taking too much of the organisation's time) (Wilkie et al., 2005; McCaffery et al., 2006).

There are some case studies available that describe how CMMI and agile practices have successfully been used together to formulate the so called combined improvement approach (Paulk, 2001; Morkel et al., 2003; Paetch et al., 2003; Vriens, 2003; Fritzsche & Keil, 2007; Sutherland et al., 2007). Compliance with reference models usually entails the generation of documentation, which may not be obtained through adopting the agile principle of "working software over comprehensive documentation" (Morkel, Kourie et al. 2003). Although a lack of documented evidence can present a problem in achieving the goals of the CMMI process areas using agile practices. For example, the CMMI description of *Requirements Management* does not explicitly state that requirements must be documented (Nawrocki, Jasinski et al., 2002). In an agile context, this means that requirements can exist but are documented in some other form than in plan-driven development projects, e.g. with user story cards or a user story database (Nawrocki, Jasinski et al. 2002).

Applicability of Combining these Approaches for Different Types of Domains

The relationship between CMMI and the software development process in which agile practices have been used has been discussed in several empirical reports, but only in a few research journals (Glazer, 2001; Paulk, 2001; Boehm, 2002; Highsmith, 2002; Cohen, Lindvall et al., 2004). Many have criticized the use of CMMI based assessments in the software development process in which agile practices have been used. For example, Boehm (2002) argues that agile methods are a reaction against traditional methodologies, also known as plan-driven methodologies. Turner and Jain (2002) indicate that companies using agile methods face a risk of emphasizing too much tacit knowledge, and informal communication across teams. One reason for the concern is that tacit, informal communication is often dependent on an individual's experience of sharing information (Turner & Jain, 2002). However, the software development process in which agile practices are used includes more than informal communication. For example, source code, test cases, and a minimum, essential amount of documentation is also used in the agile software development process, but in a much lighter way than in the plan-driven software development process (Turner & Jain, 2002).

SUGGESTED SOLUTION: THE AHAA METHOD

AHAA is an agile, hybrid assessment method for the automotive industry (AHAA). It combines two plan-driven software process models (CMMI, Automotive SPICE™) with agile development practices.

Why include CMMI?

CMMI (2006) was included in the AHAA method for a number of reasons. First, CMMI based assessments integrated with other assessments are a widely-used approach for evaluating software processes within a company (Trudel et al. 2006) and indicating weaknesses for immediate attention and improvement (Daskalantona, 1994). Secondly, beneficial experiences of CMM and CMMI programmes have been reported as a part of many studies during the past decades (Stelzer & Mellis, 1998; Niazi et al. 2003; Galin & Avrahami, 2006). For example, 400 projects reported improvements in productivity and development speeds in software development due to CMM/CMMI programmes (Stelzer and Mellis

1998; Galin and Avrahami 2006). Based on the results of the analysis, they reported 26 to 187% improvements in productivity, 28–53% improvements in cycle time and 120–650% return in investment due to the use of CMMI programmes (Galin & Avrahami, 2006).

Why include Automotive SPICE?

In the automotive sector, a challenge that faced the Hersteller Initiative Software (HIS) process assessment working group was that each manufacturer had a different approach to evaluating suppliers' capability/maturity (Hersteller, 2007). Based on the different requirements for a common assessment method, ISO/IEC 15504-5 (ISO, 2006) was adopted for supplier assessment within the HIS. From 2001 to 2006, HIS members executed some 200 ISO/IEC 15504 assessments (Hersteller, 2007). According to (Automotive, 2007) *"the focus on software capability assessment provided significant business benefits for its use, but at the same time has highlighted the scale of the potential problem, particularly with suppliers of safety-critical embedded software system components"*.

Automotive SPICE™ was an initiative of the Automotive Special Interest Group (SIG), which is a joint special interest group of The SPICE User Group, and the Procurement Forum together with major automotive manufacturers (Automotive, 2007). Automotive SPICE™ consists of a Process Assessment Model (PAM) and a Process Reference Model (PRM) (Automotive, 2007). The Automotive SPICE™ Process Assessment Model is based on the ISO/IEC 15504-5 (ISO 2006). Thirty-one of the processes from ISO/IEC 15504-5 were selected for inclusion in Automotive SPICE™. Since 2007, all HIS members perform and accept only Automotive SPICE™ assessments. Therefore automotive assessments based on ISO/IEC 15504 have been replaced by Automotive SPICE™. Therefore, for organisations wanting to supply software to the automotive industry it is important that coverage of Automotive SPICE™ is provided.

Why Include Agile Development?

Agile approaches such as eXtreme Programming (Beck & Andres, 2005) and Scrum (Schwaber & Beedle, 2002) have been increasingly used in companies as a way of addressing key problems in software development such as: "software takes too long to develop, costs too much and has quality issues upon delivery" (Cohn & Ford, 2003). Although, agile software development practices have benefited some companies producing safety-critical software (Drobka et al., 2004; Wils et al., 2006), Boehm and Turner (2003) have argued that plan-driven approaches are better suited to these situations. However, the way forward may be to combine suitable agile practices as part of a company's current plan-driven software development activities (Boehm & Turner, 2003; Pikkarainen & Passoja, 2005). Although assessments are often characterized as a plan-driven technique for SPI and are rarely used within agile practices, Paulk (2001) argues that "Adopting two methods (plan-driven and agile) can create synergy, particularly in conjunction with other good engineering and management practices."

The first step in engaging in SPI is to assess the current state of the software development practices. An SPI path may be developed based upon a combination of this starting point and the business goals of the organization (McCaffery, Richardson et al., 2006). Processes in SMEs must be catered for in a different manner than within large companies (Richardson, 2001) as existing SPI assessment methods are very heavyweight and are not suited to the needs of SMEs. Furthermore, they do not consider both plan-driven and agile practices. Small companies need specialized assessment methods because they do not have the same ability to invest in SPI as the bigger enterprises.

Aims of AHAA

The initial aim of the AHAA was to improve the software processes of software organisations that wanted to become automotive software suppliers. However, upon usage we discovered that the method provides an ideal opportunity to educate software SMEs in terms of generic SPI. Therefore, the assessment also provides significant benefits for companies not wishing to become automotive software suppliers. Consequently, AHAA provides both automotive specific and non-automotive specific recommendations. Assessed companies are supplied with feedback in relation to CMMI®, Automotive SPICE™ and agile practices which enables them to decide whether they wish to follow a CMMI, Automotive SPICE™ or agile SPI path.

AHAA was designed to adhere to 8 of the 10 criteria outlined by Anacleto et al. (2004), for the development of lightweight assessment methods:

1. Low cost;
2. Detailed description of the assessment process;
3. Guidance for process selection;
4. Detailed definition of the assessment model;
5. Support for identification of risks and improvement suggestions;
6. Conformity with ISO/IEC 15504;
7. No specific software engineering knowledge required from companies' representatives;
8. Tool support is provided.

The two exceptions to the criteria outlined in Anacleto et al. 2004, are that no support is provided for high-level process modelling and only the authors currently have access to the method. AHAA also shares the following requirements with the lightweight Adept method that was previously developed by one of the authors (McCaffery et. al 2006):

1. Improvement is more important than certification;

2. A rating is not required;
3. Preparation time required by the company is minimised;
4. Assessment time is minimized;
5. Companies should be enabled to select assessment in process areas that are most relevant to their business goals.

Additionally, AHAA recommends agile based improvement solutions for companies coping with high quality complex software development. AHAA provides the assessed company with a findings document presented in terms of CMMI®, Automotive SPICE™ processes and agile practices.

AHAA Development

The development of the AHAA method is explained in detail in a paper by the authors (Mc Caffery et al., 2008). In summary, the AHAA method was developed through selecting four process areas from the CMMI® model that previous research found to provide a significant level of benefit to software development organisations (Reichlmayr, 2003; Blowers and Richardson, 2005) (Meehan and Richardson, 2002; Coleman 2005). The four CMMI® process areas selected were Requirements Management, Project Planning, Project Monitoring and Control, and Configuration Management. By recommending focus upon these 4 process areas we are not stating that there is no advantage from focusing on other process areas but based upon previous research that has been performed into which process areas bring the most significant benefit to low maturity organisations these process areas are deemed to have a higher perceived value than other process areas (Wilkie et al. 2005).

These process areas were then integrated with associated processes from Automotive SPICE™ and agile practices.

Selection was as follows:

*   Serially scan the chosen CMMI® process areas against the following list of 15 HIS process areas and select related Automotive SPICETM processes:
    *   System requirements analysis; System architectural design; Software requirements analysis; Software design; Software construction; Software integration; Software testing; System integration; Software testing; System integration; System testing; Quality assurance; Configuration management; Problem resolution management; Change request management; Project management; Supplier monitoring.
*   Map relevant agile practices against the process area

As a result of performing these steps AHAA will provide coverage of 4 CMMI® process areas, 5 Automotive SPICE processes and several agile practices.

The CMMI® Requirements Management process area was integrated with two processes from Automotive SPICE™ (Software requirements management, Change request management) and 5 Agile practices (Stories, Planning game, Daily meetings, On-site customer, Self-organising teams).

The CMMI® process areas of Project Management and Project Monitoring and Control were integrated with two processes from the Automotive SPICE™ (Project management, Problem resolution management) and 5 Agile practices (Retrospective user stories, Planning game, Small releases, Daily stand-up meetings retrospective, Task estimations).

The CMMI® configuration management process area was integrated with the configuration management process from Automotive SPICE™ and the agile practice of continuous integration.

Questions were added to enable coverage of relevant processes and agile practices. Even though each assessment process adopts a CMMI® process area name, it also contains questions providing coverage of Automotive SPICE™ and agile practices.

We restricted the duration of the on-site interviewing to one day (Paulk, 2001) thus minimising the time and cost associated with the assessment and encourage uptake.

AHAA makes use of scripted questions. When developing the interview questions we examined the base practices, checking the relevant interview questions to ensure coverage of their counterparts in agile and Automotive SPICE™. This resulted in 80 scripted questions being developed for the Project Planning interviews, 53 scripted questions being developed for the Project Monitoring and Control interviews, 60 scripted questions being developed for the Requirements Management interviews, and 35 scripted questions being developed for the Configuration Management interviews. Therefore a total of 228 scripted questions will be asked during the 4 interviews. However, additional non-scripted questions may also be asked during each interview. Table 1, illustrates

Table 1. AHAA questions for managing requirements changes

1) Question	2) CMMI	3) Automotive SPICE	4) Agile
5) How are you communicating the CRs between the customer and development team?	6)	7)	8) Yes
9) In which phases of development are changes analysed?	10)	11)	12) Yes
13) How do you agree upon the implementation of CRs?	14)	15)	16) Yes
17) How do you manage requirements and changes to agreed requirements? E.g. Do you have a strategy- How are they captured and communicated to appropriate staff, then analysed, their impact evaluated and reported? Are any tools used? What types of activities are included?	18) Yes	19) Yes	20)
21) How do you ensure that all changes are handled consistently?	22)	23) Yes	24)
25) How do you identify CRs?	26)	27) Yes	28)
29) Explain how you track CRs?	30)	31) Yes	32)
33) How do you record the status of CRs?	34)	35) Yes	36)
37) How do you evaluate the impact of changes to requirements?	38) Yes	39) Yes	40) Yes
41) Who are the key actors in these requirements/CRs impacts evaluation? How is the information of the CRs communicated between these actors?	42)	43)	44) Yes
45) How are you dividing the bigger CRs in the smaller pieces (e.g. features, tasks)? What is the size of these pieces?	46)	47)	48) Yes
49) Do you evaluate the impact of such changes in terms of - cost, schedule + technical impact	50)	51) Yes	52)
53) How do you prioritise CRs?	54)	55) Yes	56) Yes
57) How do you approve changes ?	58)	59) Yes	60)
61) Who are the key customers of your product? (external, internal =product manager in many cases)?	62)	63)	64) Yes
65) How often are you delivering your products versions for the customers?	66)	67)	68) Yes
69) How does the customer check the product, and what kind of feedback do you get?	70)	71)	72) Yes
73) How do you identify validation and verification activities for each change	74)	75) Yes	76)
77) How do you schedule an approved CR?	78)	79) Yes	80)
81) What activities have to occur in order for a CR to be closed?	82)	83) Yes	84)
85) Do you update the requirements specification ?	86)	87) Yes	88)
89) Do you record and monitor the rate and sources of change requests?	90) Yes	91)	92)

the scripted questions in relation to managing requirements changes.

RECOMMENDATION: IMPLEMENTATION OF AHAA IN TWO SMES

In this section we describe how the AHAA assessments were conducted in two SMEs in Ireland. We also provide a comparison of the strengths, issues and improvement suggestions produced from the assessment of the two case companies using the AHAA method.

The Assessment Organisations

The first AHAA assessment was implemented in an Irish software development SME called AutoSoft

(a pseudonym). At the time of the first assessment, AutoSoft had ten software development staff, six of them focusing on software and two of them focusing on hardware development, and 2 managers, working on three ongoing projects. The release had delivered to the customer in one project and was still under development in the two projects. In AutoSoft there were 2 junior developers having a few years experience and six senior developers with several years of expertise of the automotive domain. Also two managers (site manager and project manager) participated in the coding work and they had considerable experience in relation to system development. AutoSoft works closely with its larger parent company in Denmark (founded 1992)) in order to develop solutions and services for the automotive industry. (see Table 2). The goal of the AutoSoft is to deliver embedded systems with high customer satisfaction. Additionally,

Table 2. Characteristics of the SMEs

Characteristics	AutoSoft	GeniSoft
Employees	10	8
Amount of people implementing Software	6	4
Amount of people implementing Hardware	2	4
Amount of Projects ongoing	1 six months release done, 2 under construction	4 software development projects
Status of the company	The Irish site of the company started 6 months ago, the parent company 18 years ago	The company started 5 years ago
Status of the ongoing projects	Requirements specified by the parent company, 1 release done for a product 1, In 2 other products first releases were under construction	4 software development projects, first version software the products delivered. Additionally 3 system development products delivered. 4 additional product development projects were under negotiation with potential customers
Previous efforts improving the process	Ad hock processes, processes important due to the safety critical domain	ad hock process, situation possible to manage now but in the future when the company is growing the more systematic process approach is needed
Level of expertise/ developers (Junior developer 1-3 years of expertise); (senior developer 3- of years experience)	2 junior developers: 6 senior developers several years, 2 managers with senior development expertise involving in development	1 junior developer, 6 senior developers, 1 senior manager involving in the development
Subcontractors	seven subcontractor to deal with	No subcontractors
Technologies	UML 2.0, SysML, AADL, Simulink, SCADE, formal methods, DO-178B, ECSS-E-ST-40C, Hazop analysis, FTA, FMECA	Win32 C++, C#, ASP.NET, T-SQL, V, Web Technologies (HTML, CSS, DOM, Javascript...)

one of the company's goals was to focus upon reliability due to the safety criticality demands of the developed software systems.

The second AHAA assessment was implemented in an Irish SME which was focused on general application software development. The SME is called GeniSoft (a pseudonym) (founded 2005). At the time of the assessment they had eight employees, four working on hardware development and four working on software development. In GeniSoft the company had one manager who performed software development but was also responsible for marketing and customer communication. At the time of the assessment GeniSoft had delivered software development products to the four key customers. (Table 2). In addition, they had several new customer product contracts under negotiation. Like AutoSoft, GeniSoft also had both senior (7 – including the manager) and junior (1) developers. The goal of the GeniSoft is similar to the AutoSoft, since they aimed to achieve high customer satisfaction and on time delivery. This is particularly important as they both delivered fixed price projects. They has also a clear goal to grow as a system provider which presented challenges that needed to be taken into account when planning future process activities.

Performing the Assessment

Each assessment started with an overview briefing and a discussion with the management of the assessed organisation in relation to the schedule, management expectations and the responsibilities of the participants during the assessment. In both cases, management felt that "the assessment needed to be implemented in as light a manner as possible" (i.e. not taking up too much of the organisation's limited resources). The continuous representation of CMMI was used in both assessment cases. This was because the goal of both of the evaluated companies was to achieve business goals through the improvement of selected software development processes.

The assessment was implemented in both companies using the same procedure. The goals of the companies were clarified in the initial meeting with management. The interviews lasted approximately 1.5 hours for each of the 4 process areas (in each organisation). The same process areas were assessed in each organisation. Typically, 3-5 people (managers and developers) from the assessed organisation participated in each interview. Due to the size of the organisations the same staff participated in each of the interviews. After the interviews were completed the assessment team spent one day reviewing the responses to the scripted questions that were asked in each of the process area interviews. Based upon this review the assessment team (of 2 assessors) generated a report of the assessment results. The results of the assessments were then presented and discussed in a findings report workshop with each of the interview representatives. The findings report consists of a set of strengths, issues and suggested actions to address the issues. The assessment team and the senior management from the organisation then work together to prioritise the recommendations based upon the organisations business goals. It is important that such recommendations are prioritised as due to the limited resources available to SMEs it is important that they focus upon the highest value suggestions and use these as the basis for their SPI programme (Pettersson et al. 2008). After a period of 6 months had elapsed the assessors revisited both organisations to evaluate the level of improvement that had been obtained within each process area. This also enabled the organisations to provide feedback and to identify any additional issues that required improvement.

Comparison of the Assessment Findings in the SMEs

Although AutoSoft and GeniSoft were both working in a different domains (AutoSoft: automotive and GeniSoft: generic software applications), their requirements management strengths were surprisingly similar. In fact five strengths were identified in AutoSoft context whereas four strengths appeared from GeniSoft assessment.

As illustrated in Figure 1, GeniSoft had a larger number of strengths in the areas of project planning and project monitoring and control. However, both companies were equally strong in terms of configuration management and requirements management. Also, both organisations had considerable issues in terms of project planning.

Requirements Management

In both companies, requirements were collected from a single source and linked to a single point of contact. Since both companies were relatively small requirements communication occurred in

an informal daily manner. In AutoSoft, it was possible to link the requirements back to their original sources, whereas this was not possible in GeniSoft.

The assessment team discovered five strengths, 14 issues and seven improvement suggestions for the AutoSoft requirements management process area. In GeniSoft there were four strengths, 16 issues and 13 improvement suggestions. Both companies had a lot in common in relation to requirements management with both organisations sharing four of the same strengths, nine of the same issues and seven improvement suggestions. However, some of the issues were quite different. Both of the companies had a problem with customer interface management. However, in AutoSoft the customer requirements are de-

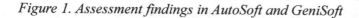

Figure 1. Assessment findings in AutoSoft and GeniSoft

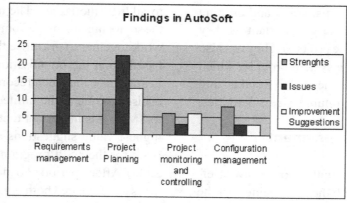

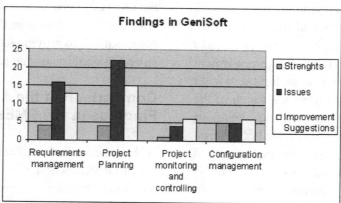

fined by the parent company and are delivered to AutoSoft in the form of a requirements document plus informal, ad hoc communications between the parent company and AutoSoft (see Figure 2).

Table 3, summarises the requirements management findings for both AutoSoft and GeniSoft. Even though, projects were generally well planned. in AutoSoft, the requirements were often at a high level and were not prioritized. The developers could neither effect requirements identification or obtain feedback from the customers in relation to the implemented product. This causes a significant risk, as any misconception may not be highlighted until the customer provides feedback six months later, at which time six months may have been wasted developing the "wrong" product.

In GeniSoft requirements identification was mainly the responsibility of one person who developed the requirements definition as part of a fixed price contract. The requirements definition and prioritization was based on good collaboration

Figure 2. Customer interface management in AutoSoft and GeniSoft

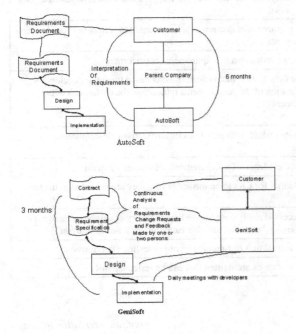

between the actual customer and the developers. In fact, the manager stated: "*the customer prioritises our requirements*". In GeniSoft, the major problems were focused in the area of requirements validity, consistency and testing. In fact, the company lacked criteria for checking requirements consistency, performed little requirements traceability or impact analysis, and had no practices in place for performing unit testing. Thus, in GeniSoft, there was a risk to the quality of the end products.

Project Planning

Table 4, summarises the project planning findings for both AutoSoft and GeniSoft. In terms of project planning, the AutoSoft assessment revealed 10 strengths, 22 issues and 13 suggested actions. Whereas, the GeniSoft assessment revealed four strengths, 22 issues and 15 suggested actions. Both companies had a lot in common in relation to project planning i.e. sharing four common strengths, 18 common issues, and 13 common suggested actions. For example, in terms of the strengths both companies made use of high level planning, had good informal communication channels, provided some evidence of the reuse and also made use of 3rd party components. In AutoSoft, projects were divided into suitable tasks. This was performed jointly by managers and developers. As product safety was identified as a significant requirement especially in the automotive system development domain, the company representatives in AutoSoft emphasised activities related to risk management. Risks were taken into consideration in the planning phase and identified on the critical path of the development. In contrast, little emphasis was placed upon risk management in GeniSoft. However, in both cases risk management could be improved through the development of a risk management strategy. In GeniSoft, the lack of risk management is a major risk to the company, and the company had already encountered long, difficult working hours on projects as a result of

Table 3. AHAA requirements management findings

AutoSoft Strengths	GeniSoft Strengths
1. Requirements come from a single source	1. Requirements come from a single source and are linked to single point of contact
2. Good (Informal) communication	2. Good informal communication in relation to Time/Materials
3. Some evidence of traceability E.g. product requirements – architect design –test cases	
4. Requirements are documented by the parent company	3. Requirements are documented (Proposal with customer)
5. CRs are well controlled	4. Once CRs are captured they are well controlled
AutoSoft Issues	**GeniSoft Issues**
1. There is not a direct link to the customer	1. Little communication with the customer in relation to Fixed Price projects
2. Requirements totally dependant upon the accuracy and clarity of the requirements captured by the parent company	
3. Have to go through a communication chain in order to clarify questions –This can cause delays	
4. Little feedback from the customer	
5. Little visibility of parent company's requirements in Doors	
	2. Little analysis of the impact of changes upon existing requirements
6. Traceability is a manual process	3. Little traceability – only possible as a manual process based upon experience and no tool used for requirements management
7. No documented procedure for CR closure	4. No documented procedure for CR handling
8. No monitoring of the rate and source of CRs	5. No monitoring of the rate and source of CRs – what areas are CRs being requested in?
9. No mapping of requirements to future releases	6. Little evidence of mapping CRs to future releases
10. No procedure for uniquely identifying CRs –Little evidence of a requirements acceptance criteria	
11. Currently requirements may be accepted that cannot be tested against	7. Currently requirements may be accepted that cannot be tested against
12. The project plan is not updated to reflect new or changing requirements	8. The requirements document is not updated to reflect new or changing requirements
13. Requirements are not prioritized	9. Little prioritisation of requirements is performed
14. The absence of a first-hand requirements specification means testing may be carried out against development's interpretation of requirements rather than the customer's actual requirements.	10. The only testing that is performed is based upon the developer's interpretation of the requirements rather than the customer's actual requirements.
	11. No Procedure or Template to Ensure Consistent Requirements Capture
	12. Little evidence of a requirements acceptance criteria
	13. Potential for CRs to be missed before they are recorded in the tool (SVR)
	14. Success is really based upon having a very experienced designer who knows what to test and this cannot always be relied upon
	15. No formal unit testing or integration testing is performed
	16. No test cases are written that can be tested against

continued on following page

Table 3. continued

AutoSoft Actions	GeniSoft Actions	Plan-driven or Agile
1. Continuous requirements and change request analysis in sprint planning meetings (links to the issues 1, 2, 3, 4, 5, 14)	1. Continuous requirements and change request analysis in sprint planning meetings (fixed price but changing content) (!)	Agile
2. Consider using product and sprint backlogs in requirements management (2, 4, 7, 8, 13, 14)	2. Consider using product and sprint backlogs in requirements management (2, 9)	Agile
3. Consider adopting a Requirements Management tool such as Doors (as used by the parent company) to assist with automated traceability (5, 6)	3. Consider adopting a Requirements Management tool to assist with automated traceability (3)	Plan
4. Develop a requirements capture template, including (11): • A comprehensive list of possible interfaces that should be considered; • A list of what constitutes an acceptable requirement; • A point of contact for requirements within each project	4. Develop a lightweight requirements capture template, including: • A list of possible interfaces that should be considered;	Plan
5. Develop a procedure for CRs, including: • Closure (7, 8, 10, 9) • How to monitor the rate and source of CRs • Mapping large CRs (really new requirements to releases) • Use Jira to uniquely identify CRs	5. Develop a procedure for CRs, including (11, 12, 13, 4, 5, 6): • Closure • How to monitor the rate and source of CRs • Mapping large CRs possibly to new releases	Plan
6. Project plans should reflect up-to-date requirements (12)	6. Requirements document should reflect up-to-date requirements (8)	Plan
7. Consider consulting technical staff before agreeing to requirements	7. Involve the development team more in the requirements process (14)	Plan
	8. List what constitutes an acceptable requirement (12): • Checklists for completeness, verifiability, can it be validated, doesn't contradict other requirements	Plan
	9. Schedule regular meetings with project customers to receive feedback in relation to the direction of the project – deadlines etc. (10)	Agile
	10. Projects could contain well defined less risky core deliverables on a Fixed Price basis. Then additional more risky elements should be agreed on a time/materials basis (1)	Agile
	11. Customer satisfaction could be measured (1)	Plan
	12. Consider introducing a lightweight requirements traceability matrix that could be used to assist with development of similar future projects, Links from Reqs – Design – Test – Code (3)	Plan
	13. Consider a new approach to agreeing project requirements (15, 16, 7)	Plan

not having a risk management and mitigation strategy in place.

The issues found in both organisations were almost identical. For example, both companies had problems with estimation, and both companies had exposure to fixed price projects so there was no flexibility for planning. Additionally, both companies had to resource projects through reaction as opposed to prior planning based upon skills and resources. In GeniSoft such issues were more significant as the company had plans to expand in the near future. Whereas, in AutoSoft no such plans existed.

Table 4. AHAA project planning findings

AutoSoft Strengths	GeniSoft Strengths
1. Evidence of high-level planning	1. Evidence of high-level planning
2. Project is decomposed into suitable tasks –"Splitting tasks into daily units"	
3. Involvement of development staff in developing project plans	
4. Known resources are allocated into the project plan	
5. Risk is considered during the planning phase	
6. Risks are identified on the critical path	
7. Good informal communication channels	2. Good informal communication
8. Understanding of interfaces and boundaries	
9. Efficient use of 3rd Party Components	3. Some use of 3rd Party Components - Realisation of the benefits
10. Some evidence of component reuse	4. Some evidence of component reuse
AutoSoft Issues	**GeniSoft Issues**
1. No evidence of requirements in the Project Plan	
2. Little evidence of the Project Plan being updated e.g. to include change requests as the project progresses, scope etc.	1. Little evidence of the Project Plan being updated
3. Limited evidence of formal estimation approaches	2. Limited evidence of formal estimation approaches
4. Historical data is not used	3. Historical data is not used
5. Estimates based solely on knowledge/familiarity of system components	4. Estimates based solely on knowledge/familiarity of system components
6. Insufficient linkage between project budget and estimates	5. Insufficient linkage between project budget and estimates
7. No usage of short iterations and milestones	6. Length of iteration vary
8. The initial project plan does not contain the full set of resources required	7. The initial project plan does not contain the full set of resources required
9. Requirements are not always defined in the initial set of resources	8. Requirements are not always defined in the initial set of resources
10. No use of continuous integration approaches	9. No use of continuous integration approach
11. Fixed price projects – so no flexibility for planning – not based on any estimates	10. Fixed price project – so no flexibility for planning
12. No systematic way of managing risk	11. No systematic way of managing risk
13. No common risk list	12. No common risk list
14. Little evidence of mitigation at the planning stage	13. Little evidence of mitigation at the planning stage
15. Little evidence of formal communication channels	14. No formal communication channel to ensure that everyone has the "up-to-date" information that they require
16. Staff utilization load not properly understood e.g. how realistic is it to plan for a 7.5 hr day?	15. Staff utilisation load not properly understood
17. Knowledge and skills are not recorded and managed	16. Knowledge and skills are not recorded and managed
18. Due to resourcing issues external skills are sought rather than providing training	
19. Reactive rather than planned approach to resourcing	17. Reactive rather than planned approach to resourcing
20. Resources not always costed into the project plan	18. Resources not always costed into the project plan
21. Resources tend not to be allocated in a timely manner	19. Resources tend not to be allocated in a timely manner
22. There is no strategy for component reuse	20. There is no strategy for component reuse

continued on following page

Table 4. Continued

	21. Overall picture of the project is not documented		
	22. Insufficient time allocated to QA activity, Meetings, Documentation		
AutoSoft Actions	**GeniSoft Actions**	**Plan-driven or Agile**	
1. Consider the use of historical data as input into the estimation process (4, 5, 6)	1. Consider the use of historical data as input into the estimation process (2, 3, 4)	Plan	
2. Consider the use of daily estimation procedures e.g. Make use of useful metrics (3)	2. Consider the use of daily estimation procedures e.g. Make use of useful metrics (2)	Plan	
3. Plan on the basis of a shorter – more realistic (actual working time) day e.g. set aside time for "skilling up" etc ().	3. Plan on the basis of a shorter – more realistic (actual working time) day e.g. set aside time for "skilling up" etc. (5)	Plan	
4. Consider using incremental release delivery (7)	4. Consider using incremental release delivery (6)	Agile	
5. Perhaps use a senior member as an internal customer (1)	5. Perhaps use a senior member as an internal customer (14)	Agile	
6. Update the project plan iteratively (2)	6. Update the project plan iteratively (1)	Agile	
7. Link requirements to the project plan (1)	7. Link requirements to the project plan (14)	Plan	
8. Perhaps use Scrum product Backlog, sprint backlog and Sprint Planning e.g. Scrum would also assist with formalising communication procedures (1)	8. Perhaps use Scrum product Backlog, sprint backlog and Sprint Planning (14)	Agile	
9. Consider the development of a risk management strategy e.g. include a common risk list and mitigations for risk items (12)	9. Consider the development of a risk management strategy e.g. include a common risk list and mitigations for risk items (11,12)	Plan	
10. Consider developing a skills database (17, 18, 19, 20)	10. Consider keeping an up-to-date record of resource commitments (8, 7, 8, 9) • Plan for skills that will be needed to grow the company	Plan	
11. Provide training opportunities for staff to skill-up (17, 18, 19)	11. Provide training opportunities for staff to skill-up (7)	Plan	
12. Consider resources at the planning stage (20, 21)	12. Consider resources at the planning stage (7)	Plan	
13. Consider strategy for the reuse of standard components (22)	13. Consider strategy for the reuse of standard components (20)	Plan	
	14. Lightweight template for creating a project plan so that project plans are consistent across different projects – giving the overall picture (21)	Plan	
	15. Plan on the basis of a shorter – more realistic (actual working time) day (22)	Plan	

Project Monitoring and Control

Table 5, summarises the project monitoring and control findings for both AutoSoft and GeniSoft. As a result of performing the AHAA method in both organisations we discovered that AutoSoft were stronger in the area of project monitoring and control and this was reflected by the fact that they exhibited 6 strengths for this area, whereas GeniSoft only demonstrated two strengths for this area. Both companies provided evidence that they monitor their commitments throughout the life of a project. For example, in the case of AutoSoft, project members felt that project tracking within the local team was efficient. However, they also believed that the customer, the parent company and the subcontractors were not fully focused upon what actually happens during the development of the project. Due to the gap in communication between AutoSoft, their parent company, their subcontractors and their custom-ers, the developers felt it was difficult to fully understand the project requirements. AutoSoft received the project scope and requirements in the form of a large requirements specification that had not been produced by them but rather by the parent company and therefore they were not able to directly interact with the customer to clarify ambiguous requirements. This then created an issue when development tasks had to be planned

Table 5. AHAA project monitoring & control findings

AutoSoft Strengths	GeniSoft Strengths	
1. Some evidence that commitments are monitored	1. Some evidence that commitments are monitored	
2. Good involvement from all stakeholders		
3. Evidence that project reviews and status reporting occur		
4. Actionable outcomes are minuted and reviewed at the next meeting		
5. Corrective actions are taken as appropriate		
6. Close monitoring of sub-contractors		
	2. Good informal awareness of project status	
AutoSoft Issues	**GeniSoft Issues**	
1. No formalized structure for review meetings	1. No formalised structure for review meetings	
2. Actual effort is not effectively tracked against planned effort		
3. No formal record is kept of deviations from the project plan	2. No formal record is kept of deviations from the project plan	
	3. Little evidence that internal project reviews and status reporting occur	
AutoSoft Actions	**GeniSoft Actions**	**Plan-driven or Agile**
1. Consider using daily stand-up team meetings to (2): • Monitor task estimations • Analyse risk	1. Consider using daily stand-up team meetings (1, 3) • Monitoring task estimations • Analyse risk • Project tasks could be arranged on the wall	Agile
2. The use of burn-down charts to measure velocity. These can graphically demonstrate estimated performance against actual performance. With experience, estimated and actual performance will become similar. Project tasks could be arranged on the wall (2)	2. The use of burn-down charts to measure velocity (3) • These can graphically demonstrate estimated performance against actual performance • With experience, Estimated and Actual performance will become similar	Agile
3. Track actual effort against planned effort and highlight any deviations (2)	3. Track actual effort against planned effort and highlight any deviations (2)	Plan
4. Maintain a documented record of any deviations from the project plan to enable proper traceability and for use in future project estimating (3)	4. Maintain a documented record of any deviations from the project plan to enable proper traceability and for use in future project estimating (2)	Plan
5. It may be worth considering how information should be distributed and controlled (e.g. security) if the company expands (1)	5. It may be worth considering how information should be distributed and controlled (e.g. security) if the company expands (1)	Plan
6. Develop a structure and a schedule for meetings (1)	6. Develop a structure and a schedule for meetings (1)	Plan

based upon ambiguous requirements, Therefore, making the link between the requirements and the development tasks became somewhat blurred during project planning.

In GeniSoft, project monitoring and control was dependent upon two persons. The developers did not feel that they had an opportunity to be involved in the project monitoring and control activities. However, the developers in GeniSoft were interested and willing to be in contact with GeniSoft's customers in relation to requirements gathering and obtaining feedback on the implementation.

Three issues were discovered within both organisations, with both organisations having no formal structure for review meetings and neither keeping a formal record of deviations from the project plan. As the issues were similar for both

Table 6. AHAA configuration management findings

AutoSoft Strengths	GeniSoft Strengths	
1. A Configuration Management System has been successfully implemented	1. A Configuration Management System has been successfully implemented	
2. Code is stored in CVS		
3. Manual system for storing documentation		
4. Documentation and source code are version controlled	2. Documentation and source code are version controlled	
5. Everything is unit tested before submission to the CMS		
6. A change log may be obtained via CVS		
7. Approach for creating baselines - Though informal	3. Approach for creating baselines	
8. Only items stored in the CMS are included in baselines 9. –CRs are recorded, reviewed, tracked and prioritized		
	4. Some evidence of code reviewing	
	5. Software is integrated on a daily basis, Code generation	
AutoSoft Issues	**GeniSoft Issues**	
1. CRs are closed after unit testing but without integration testing	1. Little evidence of unit testing and integration testing before CRs are closed	
2. Problems analysing the impact of change requests	2. Problems analysing the impact of change requests	
3. No auditing of the use of either CM or the CM tool.	3. No auditing of the use of either CM or the CM tool.	
	4. No evidence of automated unit testing	
	5. No evidence of integration testing	
AutoSoft Actions	**GeniSoft Actions**	**Plan-driven or Agile**
1. Apply Scrum to analyse CRs in either the Sprint planning or the daily stand-up meeting (2)	1. Apply Scrum to analyse CRs in either the Sprint planning or the daily stand-up meeting (2)	Agile
2. Consider introducing continuous integration (1, 2)	2. Consider checking that the CR comments are meaningful (2)	Agile
3. CM and the usage of the CM tool to be audited by an appropriate party on a regular basis (3)	3. CM and the usage of the CM tool to be audited by an appropriate party on a regular basis (3)	Plan
	4. Perform Unit testing before submitting to CM (1, 4)	Plan
	5. Perform Integration testing (1, 5)	Plan
	6. Consider using SubVersion to generate reports (2)	Plan

companies the same six recommendations were provided to each organisation.

Configuration Management

Table 6, summarises the configuration management findings for both AutoSoft and GeniSoft. Configuration management was generally a well applied process in AutoSoft. All work products were managed and controlled, although manually. The configuration process area was stronger in AutoSoft (8 strengths) than in GeniSoft (5 strengths). However, both organisations share three common strengths - a configuration management tool was used to support version management of the developed products, both documentation and code are placed under version control, and practices were in place for creating baselines. Even though GeniSoft has fewer strengths in relation to configuration management than Auto-Soft they do perform code reviews and integrate their software on a daily basis – both of which are not performed in AutoSoft. However, some worrying risks appeared in GeniSoft, as no unit and integration testing were performed and this could have very negative future impacts on the developed systems. Whereas, AutoSoft performed more thorough testing practices on a regular basis. However, a problem that emerged in relation to AutoSoft's testing practices was that unit testing was not always performed before closing the change requests.

Summary of the Findings

In the both companies, the assessment team made suggestions that combined agile and plan based improvements related to project planning, project monitoring and control, configuration management and requirements management. Both companies were asked to move towards more regular and scheduled customer communication and to adopt a more incremental planning driven development approach. However, in AutoSoft, the

improvement suggestions were more related to communication with the parent company (Figure 3). The suggestion made by the assessment team was to use incremental planning and to incorporate feedback and continuous requirements analysis meetings between the increments as a way to communicate between the Irish site, the parent company in Denmark, and the customers. We found integration testing, unit testing and resource allocation in the QA activities much stronger in AutoSoft than in GeniSoft.

In GeniSoft, the assessment team wanted to involve the developers more in incremental development and development planning. The assessment suggestion for GeniSoft was to encourage shorter increments. In this new approach, the release planning and feature list will be re-prioritized by the customer for the each upcoming release. Another suggestion was to demonstrate the results of each increment to the project customers in a meeting that included both developers and management. The aim of this approach is to

Figure 3. Agile-based improvement suggestions

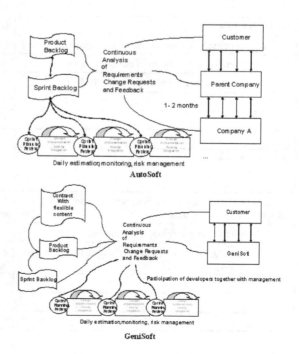

create more regular and improved customer communication and to improve the level of developer involvement in relation to the requirements analysis work. From a development perspective, the idea is to use daily meetings to facilitate regular task status updating and revision of estimates.

Reaction of the Assessed Companies after the Findings Report had been Delivered

During the findings presentations in both companies, the company representatives agreed that the highlighted strengths and issues were an accurate reflection of company's software development practices. Managers from both companies acknowledged that the AHAA recommendations were achievable and if implemented they will be beneficial.

According to the GeniSoft senior manager the AHAA assessment was very useful especially as the company had plans to expand in the near future which meant that in order to grow successfully the company needed to adopt more systematic practices for requirements management, project planning, project monitoring and control and configuration management.

Senior management from AutoSoft commented that the suggested movement towards incremental software development (encompassed regular iteration planning, daily team meetings and iteration reviews) will enable the company to respond better to change requests from the customer and the parent company. Additionally, AutoSoft's future success depends upon being able to correctly estimate future projects. Adopting an incremental development approach combined with suggested plan-driven practices for sizing the effort of project tasks could enable the company to develop a capability for providing realistic estimates for future projects.

What Happened in the Organisations as a Result of the Assessment?

The links between the problems and improvements has been now added to the book chapter. Over the six months time AutoSoft completed 4 requirements management, 7 project planning, 2 project monitoring and controlling and 3 configuration management identified. In GeniSoft, the improvement progressed more slowly with only 2 requirements management, 4 project planning and 1 project monitoring and controlling and no configuration management identified actions being performed six months after the initial assessment (See Appendix 1).

The improvements in GeniSoft had focused on some specific improvement areas. The manager felt that as a result of the AHAA assessment findings they now have adopted a more flexible management solution and achieved better customer satisfaction. The next step for them is to improve the testing activities in order to assure better quality of the customized products. In the areas of project planning and monitoring and control, the biggest change was moving from fixed price only projects to the adoption of fixed price projects for standard development parts of projects and time and materials priced elements for the more innovative parts of projects. The company management recognised the benefit of having both fixed price and changing content projects. The use of this new approach reduced the company's exposure to running over on fixed price projects that contain unknown and potentially time-consuming elements. This has also enabled the company representatives to be more in touch with their customers than before. Although the customer meetings were still not organized regularly communication between the company and their customers was significantly improved. According to the management, this had already decreased conflicts and has lead to increased customer satisfaction.

One improvement suggestion in the assessment was that the company should, instead of relying too much on one person's expertise that they should instead try to involve the development team more in the requirement gathering process. According to the GeniSoft manager, the company was slowly moving in that direction. However, the suggested agile approach had not been adopted in GeniSoft yet because there are currently only two developers on the project. "Scrum will come into play when we have a bigger team or if we have more changes, now the requirements are the same all the time, and when we have only two people in the project there is no point in having Scrum as a communication mechanism". Manager - GeniSoft. Since the company have a goal to grow in the near future, the manager's opinion was that the agile approach will definitely be adopted as soon as this change happens. Improvements had also commenced in the area of unit testing. However, test automation was still identified as a problem for the company representatives.

In AutoSoft, the Irish based team have adopted a more agile based approach with shorter increments, and introduced daily meetings and continuous integration into their software development processes. In this new development approach the requirements and change requests are regularly discussed between the development team and management. This has, according to developers improved communication in relation to project plans and requirements.

During the six months after the assessment, the team have also moved to the shorter increments that are continuously checked by the internal customer. However, the communication issues highlighted in the initial assessment between the parent company and Irish company have not been significantly improved over this period. Iteration planning meetings have been planned to improve this issue.

OBSERVATIONS ON THE USE OF THE AHAA METHOD

The initial discussion with management of the assessed organization about the schedule, management expectations and the responsibilities of the participants should happen at least one week prior to the assessment to enable the appropriate staff to be available for the assessment.

All staff that will be involved in the assessment interviews should attend the overview briefing which will provide staff with information as to their responsibilities throughout the assessment. It should also be stressed that all information provided will be treated in an anonymous nature and if possible management should be encouraged not to participate in the interviews as this tends to affect the responses provided by staff. It is also important that knowledgeable people that are performing the actual tasks on a daily basis are present within the interviews.

In order to make the assessment as attractive as possible the overview briefing should be conducted on the same day as the assessment so that only 1 day is required for the overview briefing and the 4 process interviews. Therefore, the overview briefing should be restricted to a maximum time of 1 hr and the interviews to 1.5 hrs as otherwise the assessment day becomes too long and as a result of this the interviewees and assessors become tired thereby negatively impacting the final process interview.

The power of the method is in having two assessors. During each of the interview sessions, one of the team led the questioning while the other made notes. The person leading the session had a PC based tool which enabled them to make snap judgements about the answers being given by judging on a discrete set of values – Red (not practiced), Amber (partially practiced), Yellow (largely practiced) and Green (fully practiced). In this way, the opinions of the questioner could also be recorded for subsequent review.

After the interviews both assessors discuss the findings and the spreadsheets used to record initial judgements are reviewed along with notes taken by the 2nd assessor. When both appraisers are happy, the tool produced histograms which prove very useful in judging performance against the process goals.

It is also important that everyone that participated in the interviews should be present at the findings report workshop so that they may endorse or object to the contents of the findings report. In order to ensure that the company embarks upon the SPI suggestions provided within the findings report a date should be scheduled for a follow-up assessment.

The AHAA method relies heavily on information obtained from interviewing company personnel and performs limited cross-referencing checks (due to the limited time available for data collection and analysis). Consequently, this approach depends on the willingness of the company to engage in SPI. It is important that the company encourages it's employees to answer interview questions in a truthful and helpful manner so that the resultant findings report will provide an accurate an reflection of the company's strengths and weaknesses within each of the appraised process areas. The findings report contains a list of recommendations which each company must prioritise into an action plan based upon their goals and aspirations.

RELIABILITY AND VALIDITY OF THE RESEARCH

Validity of research is often discussed through construct and external validity. There are three tactics for addressing construct validity: (1) drawing on multiple sources of evidence, (2) establishing a chain of evidence, and (3) member-checking the research results with key informants (Yin 2004). Reliability is related to the repeatability of the research. In order to address the question of our research reliability we firstly provided a description of the assessment process. Secondly, we created an assessment tool, framework which was used in a similar way in the both SMEs. By doing this, we actually provided overall, traceable, documented justification of the process by which research conclusions were reached (Guba, 1981).

The way we conducted the research in the SMEs can be considered as case studies in which we used multiple data collection modes including recorded and transcripted group interviews, document reviews and notes made in the meetings with case company representatives. Since the information in case studies are typically snapshots of some specific situation, results are not really generalizable in the traditional sense, we prepared an interview protocol based on a CMMI, Automotive SPICE and agile practices framework to guide the interview process. We performed the evaluation in both companies in order to avoid the problem of the snapshot cases.

The interview process was deliberately flexible so as to allow for discussions that stimulate new awareness and interest in particular issues which could then require additional probing in the case companies. In order to address reliability, we used the same data analysis approach in both companies. In our analysis approach, we categorized all the strengths, issues and actions based on the process areas. As a part of the member checking, all the analysis interpretations were discussed by both assessors who both had considerable expertise from performing assessment based upon CMMI, Automotive SPICE and agile methodologies. Additionally, all the findings were presented and discussed with the interviewed developers and project managers from the case companies.

External validity relates to the extent to which the research results apply in other real-world settings. The fact that our research took place in the two companies itself supports external validity. Additionally, the fact that we used well accepted standards and paradigms to build our assessment framework also supports the external validity and the possibility to generalize the results. New research from other companies, however, is needed in order to support the generalization of the results. Additionally, quantitative measurement data could be collected from both SMEs to support and assure the validity of the presented results.

FUTURE RESEARCH DIRECTION

The AHAA method currently consists of a small subset of CMMI process areas (4 process areas out of a possible 22 process areas) integrated with associated Automotive SPICE™ processes and relevant agile practices. This research has demonstrated that it is possible to integrate agile and plan driven software development practices successfully within two SMEs. However, in the future, this work should be expanded in a number of different ways so that the following research questions may be answered:

- Will integrating the remaining CMMI process areas with associated Automotive SPICE™ processes and relevant agile practices be as successful or will the remaining process areas be less suited to such integration?

- If the AHAA method was extended to include the full suite of CMMI/Automotive Spice™ processes and agile practices would SMEs still only wish to adopt the initial 4 process areas already included in the AHAA method, as through previous research it has been shown that these processes are the most beneficial to small organisations? (Our plan would be still to restrict the scope of an individual AHAA to 4 processes but if a company desired assessment in different processes than the 4 that we have originally provided then this would be possible – additionally if an organisation wanted to be assessed in more than 4 processes they would have to em-

bark on multiple AHAAs as the method is only designed to assess 4 processes at a time.)

- Will the AHAA method be useful for larger organisations?

We intend to develop a more generic version of the AHAA method through replacing Automotive SPICE™ with ISO/IEC 15504 so that the assessment does not include practices that are specific to the automotive software development industry. However, the original AHAA method will still be available for automotive organisations.

At the moment, there is also an IEEE project management standard under development covering the aspects of agile development (http://standards.ieee.org/announcements/pr_1490p1648.html). In the future, this standard will need to be taken into account when further developing the introduced assessment approach. Additionally, we intend to integrate Lean manufacturing practices into the AHAA model so that any waste practices may be removed and to then determine the extent of any efficiencies gained or lost from this integration. It will also be important that the findings of additional AHAA assessments (in different types and sizes of software development organisations) are analysed to fully understand the benefits that may be gained through combining plan-driven and agile based software development practices for different sizes and types of software development organisations. Additionally, the authors plan for the assessment model to be integrated with Medi SPICE (McCaffery and Dorling, 2009) as opposed to Automotive SPICE and for the method to then be validated within the medical device industry. This would be particularly interesting, as due to the regulatory and safety-critical nature of the medical device industry it tends to rely almost completely upon plan-driven software development practices.

From this research we have found that:

- Agile practices are particularly suited in relation to requirements gathering, obtaining regular customer interaction and feedback, continuous integration and for small frequent deliveries;
- Plan driven practices are particularly suited for the development of software that requires significant documentation and traceability to comply with standards;
- A future research challenge is to be able to combine the advantages of both in a usable manner for the efficient development of safety-critical software that has to obtain regulatory compliance.

CONCLUSION

The relationship between CMMI and the software development process in which agile practices have been used has been discussed in several empirical reports (Glazer, 2001; Paulk, 2001; Boehm, 2002; Highsmith, 2002; Cohen et al., 2004). For example, Boehm (2002) argues that agile methods are a reaction against traditional methodologies, also known as plan-driven methodologies. Turner and Jain (2002) indicate that the companies using agile methods face a risk of emphasizing too much tacit knowledge and too less formal communication across the team. It seems that organizations that are accustomed to improving their process capability utilizing standards (such as ISO/IEC 15504) and models (such as CMMI) seem to have limited agility in their specific software development processes (Boehm & Turner, 2003). This is especially the situation in SMEs where assessments need to be cost effective and to provide practical improvement suggestions for only the most relevant processes.

AHAA, Agile Hybrid Assessment Method for Automotive industry was developed by the authors of this chapter in a response to this issue. This lightweight assessment method was developed to enable SMEs to combine CMMI, agile practices and Automotive SPICE™ approaches together. In this chapter we addressed the question of how to integrate agile practices into traditional software process assessments via the AHAA method. The AHAA method was implemented and validated in two SMEs in Ireland (GeniSoft and AutoSoft). Furthermore, we also provided a comparison of the AHAA assessment results in the two companies for the process areas of project planning, project monitoring and control, requirements management and configuration management.

ACKNOWLEDGMENT

This research has been supported by the SFI Stokes Lectureship Programme, grant number 07/SK/I1299, the SFI Principal Investigator Programme, grant number 08/IN.1/I2030, and Lero - the Irish Software Engineering Research Centre (http://www.lero.ie)

Part of the work was done in the ITEA project called Flexi funded by TEKES and Nokia Foundation in Finland as a part of VTT, Technical Research Centre of Finland

REFERENCES

Agarwal, R., & Chari, K. (2007). Software effort, quality and cycle time: A study of CMM level 5 projects. *IEEE Transactions on Software Engineering, 33*(3), 145–155. doi:10.1109/TSE.2007.29

Agile. (2005). Agile Newsletter. Retrieved from http://www.agile-itea.org

Anacleto, A., von Wangenheim, C. G., Salviano, C. F., & Savi, R. (2004). *Experiences gained from applying ISO/IEC 15504 to small software companies in Brazil*. Paper presented at the 4th International SPICE Conference on Process Assessment and Improvement, Lisbon, Portugal, (pp.33-37).

Andersson, D. J. (2005). *Stretching agile to fit CMMI level 3*. Denver: Agile Development.

Automotive, S. (2007). *The SPICE user group, Automotive SPICETM process reference model*. Retrieved from http://www.automotivespice.com

Basili, V. R. (1989). *Software development: A paradigm for the future*. Paper presented at COMPSAC '89, Orlando, FL.

Batista, J., & Figueiredo, A. D. (2000). SPI in a very small team: A case with CMMI. *Software Process Improvement and Practice, 5*(4), 243–250. doi:10.1002/1099-1670(200012)5:4<243::AID-SPIP126>3.0.CO;2-0

Beck, K. (1999). Embracing change with extreme programming. *IEEE Computer, 32*(10), 70–77.

Beck, K. (2000). *Extreme programming explained: Embrace change*. Addison Wesley Longman, Inc.

Beck, K., & Andres, C. (2005). *Extreme programming explained*. Addison-Wesley Professional.

Beck, K., Beedle, M., et al. (2001). *Manifesto for agile software development*. 2008.

Blowers, R., & Richardson, I. (2005). *The capability maturity model (SW and Integrated) tailored in small indigenous software industries*. Paper presented at the International Research Workshop for Process Improvement in Small Settings, Software Engineering Institute, Pittsburgh, PA.

Boehm, B. (2002). Get ready for the agile methods, with care. *Computer, 35*(1), 64–69. doi:10.1109/2.976920

Boehm, B., & Turner, R. (2003). *Balancing agility and discipline-a guide for the perplexed* (p. 304). Addison Wesley.

CMM1. *(2002a). Capability Maturity Model Integration (CMMI) for software engineering, version 1.1, continuous representation (CMMI-SW, V1.1, continuous)*. Carnegie Mellon University Software Engineering Institute. (Tech. Rep. CMU/SEI-2002-TR-028). Retrieved on February 25, 2008, from http://www.sei.cmu.edu/publications/documents/02.reports/02tr028.html

CMM1. *(2002b). Capability Maturity Model Integration (CMMI) for software engineering, version 1.1, staged representation (CMMI-SW, V1.1, staged)*. Carnegie Mellon University Software Engineering Institute. (Tech. Rep. CMU/SEI-2002-TR-029). Retrieved on March 7, 2008 from http://www.sei.cmu.edu/publications/documents/02.reports/02tr029.html, Accessed on 07th March, 2008.

CMM. (1991). Capability Maturity Model for software (CMM). *Carnegie Mellon University Software Engineering Institute. Retrieved on February25, 2008, from* http://www.sei.cmu.edu/cmm/

CMMI. (2006). *Capability Maturity Model® Integration for development, version 1.2*. (Tech. Rep. CMU/SEI-2006-TR-008). Retrieved from http://www.sei.cmu.edu/publications/documents/06.reports/06tr008.html

Cockburn, A. (2002). *Agile software development*. Boston: Addison-Wesley.

Cohen, D., & Lindvall, M. (2004). *An introduction to agile methods*. Elsevier Academic Press.

Cohn, M., & Ford, D. (2003). Introducing an agile process to an organization. *IEEE Computer, 36*(6), 74–78.

Coleman, G. (2005). An empirical study of software process in practice. *Proceedings of the 38th Annual Hawaiian International Conference on System Sciences, Big Island, HI*, (p. 315).

Conboy, K., & Fitzgerald, B. (2004). *Toward a conceptual framework of agile methods: A study of agility in different disciplines.* ACM Workshop on Interdisciplinary Software Engineering Research. New York: ACM Press.

Curtis, P., Phillips, D. M., & Weszka, J. (2001). CMMI–the evolution continues. *Systems Engineering*, 7–18.

Daskalantona, M. K. (1994). Achieving higher SEI levels. *IEEE Software, 11*(4), 17–24. doi:10.1109/52.300079

Deming, W. E. (1990). *Out of the crisis.* Massachusetts Institute of Technology, Center of Advanced Engineering Study.

Drobka, J., & Noftz, D. (2004). Piloting XP on four mission critical projects. *IEEE Software, 21*(6), 70–75. doi:10.1109/MS.2004.47

Fitzgerald, B., & Hartnett, G. (2006). Customising agile methods to software practices at Intel Shannon. *European Journal of Information Systems, 15*(2), 200–213. doi:10.1057/palgrave.ejis.3000605

Fritzsche, M., & Keil, P. (2007). Agile methods and CMMI: Compatibility or conflict? *Software Engineering Journal, 1*(1), 9–26.

Galin, D., & Avrahami, M. (2006). Are CMM program investment beneficial? Analysing Past Studies. *IEEE Software, 23*(6), 81–87. doi:10.1109/MS.2006.149

Glazer, H. (2001). Dispelling the process myth: Having a process does not mean sacrificing agility or creativity. *CrossTalk, The Journal of Defense Software Engineering*, 27-30.

Grenning, J. (2001). *Using XP in a big process company: A report from the field.* Raleigh, NC: XP Universe.

Guba, E. (1981). Criteria for assessing the trustworthiness of naturalistic inquiries. *Educational Communication and Technology, 29*, 75–92.

Hansson, C., & Dittrich, Y. (2006). How agile are industrial software development practices? *Journal of Systems and Software, 79*, 1295–1311. doi:10.1016/j.jss.2005.12.020

Hersteller. (2007). *Initiative software (OEM software).* Retrieved from http://www.automotivehis.de/download/HIS_Praesentation_2007.pdf.

Highsmith, J. (2002). What is agile software development? *Crosstalk*, 4-9.

Holström, H., & Fitzgerald, B. (2006). Agile practices reduce distance in global software development. *Information Systems Management, 23*(3), 7–18. doi:10.1201/1078.10580530/46108.23.3.20060601/93703.2

Horvat, R. V., & Rozman, I. (2000). Managing the complexity of SPI in small companies. *Software Process Improvement and Practice, 5*(1), 45–54. doi:10.1002/(SICI)1099-1670(200003)5:1<45::AID-SPIP110>3.0.CO;2-2

Humphrey, W. S., & Snyder, T. R. (1991). Software process improvement at Hughes Aircraft. *IEEE Software, 8*(4), 11–23. doi:10.1109/52.300031

ISO. (2006). *ISO TR 15504, part 5: Information Technology-software process assessment.* Geneva: International Organisation of Standardisation.

Karlström, D. (2002). *Introducing extreme programming-an experience report. XP 2002, Alghero.* Sardinia, Italy: Springer-Verlag.

Kautz, K. (1998). Software process improvement in very small enterprises: Does it pay off? *Software Process Improvement and Practice, 4*(4), 209–226. doi:10.1002/(SICI)1099-1670(199812)4:4<209::AID-SPIP105>3.0.CO;2-8

Kettunen, P. (2009). Adopting key lessons from agile manufacturing to agile software and product development-a comparative study. *Technovation, 29*, 408–422. doi:10.1016/j.technovation.2008.10.003

Laporte, C. Y., Alexandre, S., & Renault, A. (2008). Developing international standards for very small enterprises. *Computer, 41*(3), 98–101. doi:10.1109/MC.2008.86

Larman, C. (2003). *Agile & iterative software development*. Boston: Addison Wesley.

Lindvall, M., & Muthig, D. (2004). Agile software development in large organizations. *Computing Practices, 37*(12), 38–46.

McCaffery, F., & Dorling, A. (2009). *Medi SPICE development*. Software Process Improvement and Practice Journal.

McCaffery, F., Pikkarainen, M., & Richardson, I. (2008). *AHAA -Agile, hybrid assessment method for automotive, safety critical SMEs*. ICSE 2008, Leipzig, Germany.

McCaffery, F., Richardson, I., & Coleman, G. (2006). *Adept-a software process appraisal method for small to medium-sized Irish software development organisations. EuroSPI06*. Finland: Joensuu.

McFeeley, B. (1996). *A users guide for software process improvement*. Pittsburgh: Carnegie Mellon University.

Meehan, B., & Richardson, I. (2002). Identification of software process knowledge management. *Process: Improvement and Practice, 7*(2), 47–56. doi:10.1002/spip.154

Morkel, W.H., Kourie, D.G., et al. (2003). *Standards and agile software development*. SAICSIT 2003.

Nawrocki, J., Jasinski, M., et al. (2002). *Extreme programming modified: Embrace requirements engineering practices*. Paper presented at the International Conference of Requirements Engineering, Essen, Germany.

Niazi, M., & Wilson, D. (2003). A maturity model for the implementation of software process improvement: An empirical study. *Journal of Systems and Software*, 1–18.

Niazi, M., & Wilson, D. (2006). Critical success factors for software process improvement implementation: An empirical study. *Software Process Improvement and Practice, 11*, 193–211. doi:10.1002/spip.261

Paetch, F., Eberlein, A., et al. (2003). *Requirements engineering and agile software development*. 12th IEEE international workshop on Enabing Technologies: Insfrastructure for Collaborative Enterprises, Computer Society.

Paulk, M. C. (2001). Extreme programming from a CMM perspective. *Software, 18*(6), 19–26. doi:10.1109/52.965798

Pettersson, F., Ivarsson, M., Gorschek, T., & Öhman, P. (2008). A practitioner's guide to light weight software process assessment and improvement planning. *Journal of Systems and Software, 81*(6), 972–995. doi:10.1016/j.jss.2007.08.032

Pikkarainen, M., & Mäntyniemi, A. (2006). *An approach for using CMMI in agile software development assessments: Experiences of three case studies. SPICE 2006*. Luxemburg.

Pikkarainen, M., & Passoja, U. (2005). *An approach for assessing suitability of agile solutions: A case study*. The Sixth International Conference on Extreme Programming and Agile Processes in Software Engineering, Sheffield University, UK.

Pikkarainen, M., Salo, O., et al. (2005). Deploying agile practices in organizations: A case study. In *European Software Process Improvement and Innovation*. Budapest: EuroSPI.

Reichlmayr, T. (2003). *The agile approach in an undergraduate software engineering course project* (pp. 13–18).

Richardson, I. (2001). Software process matrix: A small company SPI model. *Software Process Improvement and Practice*, *6*(3), 157–165. doi:10.1002/spip.144

Rising, L., & Janoff, N. S. (2000). The scrum software development process for small teams. *IEEE Software*, *17*(4), 26–32. doi:10.1109/52.854065

Salo, O., & Abrahamsson, P. (2007). An iterative improvement approach for agile development: Implications from multiple case studies. *Software Process Improvement and Practice*, *12*(1), 81–100. doi:10.1002/spip.305

Schwaber, K. (2003). *Agile project management with Scrum*. Washington, DC: Microsoft Press.

Schwaber, K., & Beedle, M. (2002). *Agile software development with Scrum*. Upper Saddle River, NJ: Prentice-Hall.

Stelzer, D., & Mellis, W. (1998). Success factors of organizational change in software process improvement. *Software Process Improvement and Practice*, *4*(4), 227–250. doi:10.1002/(SICI)1099-1670(199812)4:4<227::AID-SPIP106>3.0.CO;2-1

Sutherland, J., Jakobsen, C. R., et al. (2007). *Scrum and CMMI level 5: The magic potion for code warriors*. Agile 2007, Washington D.C.

Sutherland, J., Viktorov, A., et al. (2007). *Distributed Scrum: Agile project management with outsourced development teams*. Paper presented at the 40th Hawaii International Conference on System Sciences, Hawaii.

Svensson, H., & Höst, M. (2005). *Introducing an agile process in a software maintenance and evolution organization*. Paper presented at the 9th European Conference of Maintenance and Reengineering, Manchester, UK.

Theunissen, W. Kourie, D.G. Watson, B.W. (2003). Standards and agile software development. *Proceedings of SAICSIT* 2003, (p. 1–11).

Trudel, S., & Lavoie, J. M. (2006). The small company-dedicated software process quality evaluation method combining CMMI and ISO/IEC 14598. *Software Quality Journal*, *14*(3).

Turner, R., & Jain, A. (2002). *Agile meets CMMI: Culture clash or common cause*. Paper presented at the 1st Agile Universe Conference, Chicago.

Vriens, C. (2003). *Certifying for CMM level 2 and ISO9001 with XP@Scrum*. Agile Development Conference, Salt Lake City, Utah. EEE Computer Society.

Wang, X., Oconchuir, E., & Vidgen, R. (2008). A paradoxical perspective on contradictions in agile software development. In *proceedings from European Conference of Information Systems (ECIS)* 2008. Galway, Ireland.

Wilkie, F. G., McFall, D., & McCaffery, F. (2005). Evaluation of CMMI process areas for small to medium-sized software development organizations. *Software Process Improvement and Practice*, *10*(2), 189–202. doi:10.1002/spip.223

Wils, A., Baelen, S., et al. (2006). *Agility in the avionics software world*. XP 2006, Oulu.

Yin, R. (1994). *Case study research: Design and methods* (2nd ed.). Thousand Oaks, CA: Sage Publications.

APPENDIX 1.

Actions done and ongoing after the six months period from the first assessment.

Requirements Management

AutoSoft Actions	Done (D) Ongoing (O)	GeniSoft Actions	Done (D), Ongoing (O)
8. Continuous requirements and change request analysis in sprint planning meetings	D	14. Continuous requirements and change request analysis in sprint planning meetings (fixed price but changing content)	O
9. Consider using product and sprint backlogs in requirements management	D	15. Consider using product and sprint backlogs in requirements management	O
10. Consider adopting a Requirements Management tool such as Doors (as used by the parent company) to assist with automated traceability	O	16. Consider adopting a Requirements Management tool to assist with automated traceability	O
11. Develop a requirements capture template, including: • A comprehensive list of possible interfaces that should be considered; • A list of what constitutes an acceptable requirement; • A point of contact for requirements within each project	O	17. Develop a lightweight requirements capture template, including: • A list of possible interfaces that should be considered;	O
12. Develop a procedure for CRs, including: • Closure • How to monitor the rate and source of CRs • Mapping large CRs (really new requirements to releases) • Use Jira to uniquely identify CRs	O	18. Develop a procedure for CRs, including: • Closure • How to monitor the rate and source of CRs • Mapping large CRs possibly to new releases	O
13. Project plans should reflect up-to-date requirements	D	19. Requirements document should reflect up-to-date requirements	O
14. Consider consulting technical staff before agreeing to requirements	D	20. Involve the development team more in the requirements process	O
		21. List what constitutes an acceptable requirement: • Checklists for completeness, verifiability, can it be validated, doesn't contradict other requirements	D
		22. Schedule regular meetings with project customers to receive feedback in relation to the direction of the project – deadlines etc.	D
		23. Projects could contain well defined less risky core deliverables on a Fixed Price basis. Then additional more risky elements should be agreed on a time/materials basis	O
		24. Customer satisfaction could be measured	O
		25. Consider introducing a lightweight requirements traceability matrix that could be used to assist with development of similar future projects, Links from Reqs – Design – Test – Code	O
		26. Consider a new approach to agreeing project requirements	O

Project Planning

AutoSoft Actions	Done (D) Ongo-ing (O)	GeniSoft Actions	Done (D) Ongo-ing (O)
14. Consider the use of historical data as input into the estimation process	O	16. Consider the use of historical data as input into the estimation process	O
15. Consider the use of daily estimation procedures e.g. Make use of useful metrics	O	17. Consider the use of daily estimation procedures e.g. Make use of useful metrics	O
16. Plan on the basis of a shorter – more realistic (actual working time) day e.g. set aside time for "skilling up" etc.	D	18. Plan on the basis of a shorter – more realistic (actual working time) day e.g. set aside time for "skilling up" etc.	O
17. Consider using incremental release delivery	D	19. Consider using incremental release delivery	O
18. Perhaps use a senior member as an internal customer	D	20. Perhaps use a senior member as an internal customer	O
19. Update the project plan iteratively	D	21. Update the project plan iteratively	O
20. Link requirements to the project plan	D	22. Link requirements to the project plan	O
21. Perhaps use Scrum product Backlog, sprint backlog and Sprint Planning e.g. Scrum would also assist with formalising communication procedures	D	23. Perhaps use Scrum product Backlog, sprint backlog and Sprint Planning	O
22. Consider the development of a risk management strategy e.g. include a common risk list and mitigations for risk items	O	24. Consider the development of a risk management strategy e.g. include a common risk list and mitigations for risk items	O
23. Consider developing a skills database	O	25. Consider keeping an up-to-date record of resource commitments • Plan for skills that will be needed to grow the company	D
24. Provide training opportunities for staff to skill-up	O	26. Provide training opportunities for staff to skill-up	O
25. Consider resources at the planning stage	O	27. Consider resources at the planning stage	D
26. Consider strategy for the reuse of standard components	D	28. Consider strategy for the reuse of standard components	O
		29. Lightweight template for creating a project plan so that project plans are consistent across different projects – giving the overall picture	D
		30. Plan on the basis of a shorter – more realistic (actual working time) day	D

Project Monitoring and Controlling

AutoSoft Actions	Done (D) Ongoing (O)	GeniSoft Actions	Done (D) Ongoing (O)
7. Consider using daily stand-up team meetings to: • Monitor task estimations • Analyse risk	D	7. Consider using daily stand-up team meetings • Monitoring task estimations • Analyse risk • Project tasks could be arranged on the wall	O
8. The use of burn-down charts to measure velocity. These can graphically demonstrate estimated performance against actual performance. With experience, estimated and actual performance will become similar. Project tasks could be arranged on the wall	O	8. The use of burn-down charts to measure velocity • These can graphically demonstrate estimated performance against actual performance • With experience, Estimated and Actual performance will become similar	O
9. Track actual effort against planned effort and highlight any deviations	O	9. Track actual effort against planned effort and highlight any deviations	D
10. Maintain a documented record of any deviations from the project plan to enable proper traceability and for use in future project estimating	O	10. Maintain a documented record of any deviations from the project plan to enable proper traceability and for use in future project estimating	O
11. It may be worth considering how information should be distributed and controlled (e.g. security) if the company expands	O	11. It may be worth considering how information should be distributed and controlled (e.g. security) if the company expands	O
12. Develop a structure and a schedule for meetings	D	12. Develop a structure and a schedule for meetings	O

Configuration Management

AutoSoft Actions	Done (D) Ongoing (O)	GeniSoft Actions	Done (D) Ongoing (O)
4. Apply Scrum to analyse CRs in either the Sprint planning or the daily stand-up meeting	D	7. Apply Scrum to analyse CRs in either the Sprint planning or the daily stand-up meeting	O
5. Consider introducing continuous integration	D	8. Consider checking that the CR comments are meaningful	O
6. CM and the usage of the CM tool to be audited by an appropriate party on a regular basis	D	9. CM and the usage of the CM tool to be audited by an appropriate party on a regular basis	O
		10. Perform Unit testing before submitting to CM	O
		11. Perform Integration testing	O
		12. Consider using SubVersion to generate reports	O

Chapter 13
Software Development Governance:
A Case Study for Tools Integration

Nagehan Pala Er
ASELSAN Microelectronics, Guidance and Electro-Optics Division, Turkey

Cengiz Erbaş
ASELSAN Microelectronics, Guidance and Electro-Optics Division, Turkey

Bahar Çelikkol Erbaş
TOBB University of Economics and Technology, Turkey

ABSTRACT

Software development governance can be defined as the application of "governance" in software engineering in order to increase the probability of success in the level of individual projects as well as in the level of the organization comprising many interrelated projects. The topic deserves an interdisciplinary perspective, as the general subject of governance has been analyzed quite extensively under the field of Transaction Cost Economics. This interdisciplinary approach enabled the identification of three main modes of governance for software engineering, namely: top-down governance, bottom-up governance and reuse governance, each having unique transaction cost characteristics. To be cost effective, (1) the organizations should adapt the right governance structure for their projects based on their characteristics, and (2) the software development tools should support and be in alignment with the underlying governance structure. In this chapter, we briefly overview the first premise and then outline an approach to address the second premise, specifically tackling the issue of tools integration, for software modeling and configuration management tools. We use Dependency Structure Matrix (DSM) to represent the mapping between governance structures and software modules, propose a configuration management approach for each mode of software governance, and demonstrate a successful integration using Lattix LDM, IBM Rational ClearCase and IBM Rational Rhapsody, three broadly available tools in the software industry.

DOI: 10.4018/978-1-60960-215-4.ch013

INTRODUCTION

Business success or failure for a software development organization is determined by its competitiveness in the marketplace in recognizing and fulfilling the customer needs. Independent of the characteristics of the underlying business, the success or failure is influenced by the organization's ability to accomplish not only individual projects - given particular cost, duration and quality constraints; but also an undetermined number of existing and future projects given their collective performance targets under uncertainty. The amount of uncertainty varies based on the maturity of the domain and the technologies involved. Software development governance, a new field which applies the economics intuition from an interdisciplinary literature, is promising to better understand the issues involved in business success in software engineering.

In essence, the objective of software development governance is to guide the software engineering organization so that it produces value that aligns with the needs of the underlying business (Kofman, Yaeli, Klinger, & Tarr, 2009). Software development governance intends to establish and maintain efficient and effective operations and workable arrangements among the parties involved in software development. It provides an integrated view, as opposed to the dominant functional and structural perspectives for managing the management of this particular domain (Bannerman, 2009; Ambler, 2009; Cataldo & Herbsleb, 2009; Anderson & Carney, 2009). Given these broad objectives, it is not unexpected that the field is building on an interdisciplinary foundation, benefitting primarily from the prior work on the general topic of "governance" in the Transaction Cost Economics (TCE) literature (Erbas & Erbas, 2005).

TCE states that efficient governance structure depends on the characteristics of the transaction, and places a central role to bounded rationality and opportunism when analyzing which governance structure should be preferred for a given situation. Considering the wicked nature of large-scale software development, it is evident that bounded rationality and opportunism play a central role also in software development. Applying this TCE perspective, three primary categories of approaches for governance were identified: one based on top-down (planned), another based on bottom-up (adaptive) processes, and another based on software reuse (Erbas & Erbas, 2009). It was demonstrated that in order to minimize transaction costs for a particular project, software organizations should select the governance structure based on certain project characteristics, such as asset specificity, uncertainty and frequency. It was further suggested that the software development and management tools should support and be in alignment with the selected governance structure.

Software projects in an organizational setting may have interdependencies for many reasons, such as due to shared functionality, delivery schedule, personnel availability, leveraged technology, underlying platforms and/or utilized tools. Among the sources of such interdependencies, uncertainties over module and interface specifications, as well as their impact on the development and reuse of shared functionality and resources, are critical subjects from the software development governance perspective. A successful implementation of governance in software development requires a governance framework with an integrated tools support at many different levels, including requirements management, role assignment, software modeling/code generation, configuration management and policy enforcement. Even though, there is some work performed related to tools integration, such as Kofman, Yaeli, Klinger, and Tarr (2009) for automated role assignment, this is an area unexplored for the most part (Cheng, Jansen, & Remmers, 2009; Lehto & Rautiainen, 2009; Talby & Dubinsky, 2009).

In this chapter, we first provide a brief overview of the prior work in software development governance from (Erbas & Erbas, 2009), and then outline an approach to partially address the challenges associated with tools integration, in particular for software modeling/development and configuration management tools. Our approach leverages DSMs as an operational representation and a bridge between governance structures and software modules. Then, we explore if the existing configuration management tools and patterns can be leveraged to provide support for the implementation of the proposed governance mechanisms. Finally, we perform a case study illustrating how the proposed configuration management strategy can be used in a model-driven environment for a real-world industrial project, and whether it can be integrated with the other software development tools. This study is based on Lattix LDM, IBM Rational ClearCase and IBM Rational Rhapsody tools.

A TRANSACTION COST ECONOMICS APPROACH

Transaction Costs in Business

A transaction, in business, is defined as an exchange of products or services between a supplier and a client. The total costs in an exchange consist of production costs, which are the costs of developing and distributing the products and services, and transaction costs, which are the costs of coordinating the work and the costs associated with creating and enforcing agreements. Transaction costs may take different forms, such as: research costs to determine the availability and pricing of the products and services; bargaining costs to reach to an acceptable agreement and to design a contract acceptable to both parties; enforcement costs to ensure that the terms of the contract are followed and to take appropriate action if this is not the case.

Transactions can take place under various forms of governance structures. On one end, we have markets, where basic goods and services are traded by unspecified clients and suppliers. On the other end, we have vertically integrated organizations, where both the client and the supplier are under joint control, and the transactions can be altered by managerial decision. Between the two, we have contracts with varying degrees of complexity and duration, where the client and the supplier are bound together for a specified period (Kreps 1990; Pint & Baldwin 1997).

The governance structure impacts the transaction costs. From a manager's perspective, for example, purchasing a good from the market involves different types of transaction costs compared to producing that good within her organization. The governance structure for a particular transaction should be selected to maximize value after deducting both development and transaction costs. TCE states that efficient governance structure for a given transaction depends on the characteristics of that transaction, including asset-specificity, uncertainty and frequency (Erbas & Erbas, 2009). Asset specificity can take a variety of forms, such as, investing in specialized tools for a particular client; and developing technology specific to the client-supplier relationship. Every governance structure, accordingly, has distinctive strengths and weaknesses as follows:

- Markets provide incentive to the suppliers to maximize the net value from development costs, as the supplier obtains the full benefits and assumes the full costs of his activities. However, since the parties can abort spot market transactions, markets provide no protection against opportunism when either party invests in transaction-specific assets.
- Contracts provide some protection for transaction-specific assets, since the client and the supplier are, for a period of time, legally joined to work together. However, bounded rationality prevents comprehensive ex ante contracting that specifies contingencies for all possible circumstances.

This, in turn, provides ground for opportunistic behavior.

- Organizations reduce the contracting problems by internalizing the value of transaction-specific assets. Vertical integration provides flexibility for reallocation of assets when the business environment changes. However, bounded rationality may hinder effective management, and may not able to control the costs as well as the others.

Transaction Costs in Software Development

TCE places a central role, as we have seen in the previous section, to bounded rationality and opportunism when analyzing which governance structure should be favored for a given transaction. Due to the wicked nature of software development, we know that bounded rationality and opportunism also play a fundamental role in large-scale software development projects. Due to bounded rationality, module and interface specifications and design do almost never capture all the contingencies, and hence leave room for parties to benefit from opportunistic behavior. The governance structure for a software development project, as a result, should be chosen by taking into consideration the transaction costs involved (Erbas & Erbas, 2009).

A transaction, in the context of software engineering, is an exchange of requirements and corresponding software between two parties. The client provides a set of requirements to the supplier, and in return the supplier develops a software module that satisfies these requirements in accordance to time, budget and quality constraints. Without loss of generality, we will refer to the client as the manager, and the supplier as the developer. With a well-working interface, these exchanges can operate seamlessly. However, as in business transactions, various factors - as a result of bounded rationality and opportunism, come into play: Do the parties operate agreeably, or are there frequent misunderstandings and conflicts that lead to delays and breakdowns? Transaction cost analysis supersede the usual production costs by examining comparative costs of planning, adapting, and monitoring task completion under alternative development processes (Erbas & Erbas 2009).

As in business, the total costs of software engineering projects can be broken into two parts, development costs and transaction costs. The transaction costs include research costs - to determine the availability of software modules; bargaining costs – to reach to an agreement with the other party over the specification of modules and interfaces; and enforcement costs – to verify that the modules are developed based on the specifications, and to take appropriate action, if this is not the case. As long as, there is enough continuity or frequency of a transaction to raise concern for the efficient use of resources, two characteristics of transactions, asset specificity and uncertainty, determine which governance structure is the most efficient (Erbas & Erbas, 2009).

- Asset specificity increases as the parties become more dependent on each other. The parties developing a software module have a choice between special-purpose and general purpose technology. Assuming that the module is completed as intended, the former will often permit cost savings. However, special-purpose technology also increases the risks in that specialized modules cannot be redeployed without losing value if the development should be interrupted or prematurely terminated. General purpose reusable technologies do not pose the same difficulties. A tradeoff thus needs to be evaluated.
- Uncertainty in software development may have two sources. The primary uncertainty arises from random acts of nature and unpredictable changes in customer's preferences, while secondary uncertainty arises

from lack of communication, that is from one module developer having no way of finding out the concurrent decisions and plans made by others. A process which can handle uncertainty better, may not handle stability as well.

Transactions in software engineering also take place under various governance structures. Reuse is one way of fulfilling the requirements, where an existing module is reused to satisfy the requirements. Conversely, both client and the supplier may be collaborating under a bottom-up process. In this case, both parties work under joint control, open to cooperative adaptation, where, the transactions can be altered quickly according to the evolving needs. Or else, the client and the supplier may be interacting under a top-down process, where the interfaces between the client and the supplier are specified up-front very much like writing a contract.

By now, the correspondence between software development and business transactions should be obvious. We can see that the top-down and bottom-up processes and the software reuse map quite straightforward to the governance structures in business transactions, as follows:

- Software reuse has the same transaction cost characteristics as markets. Reusing an existing module provides strong incentives as it eliminates the development costs for the required functionality. In fact it should be the most cost effective method for developing standard components. However, due to asset specificity, it may be applicable only for relatively generic functions, as reusable modules may not exist or costly to locate for application-specific functionality.

- Top-down decomposition is built on mechanisms resembling contracting, since decomposing a system requires specifying the behavior of each subsystem similar to writing a contract. Once the system is decomposed into modules and the interfaces are specified, then the development of each module can be done independent from each other. However, bounded rationality prevents comprehensive ex-ante specification covering all possible contingencies.

- Bottom-up construction has identical transaction cost characteristics as vertical integration, as it allows flexible deployment of resources. Rather than specifying all contingencies up-front, bottom-up processes allow deferring design decisions, while enforcing the parties to be open to cooperative adaptation throughout. However, it may open the door for free riding and as a result may not be able to control costs as well as top-down process.

A Governance Framework

When we apply the results from (Williamson, 2002), we obtain Figure 1, which illustrates a heuristic model of the transaction cost characteristics of reuse R, top-down D, and bottom-up C governance with respect to asset specificity k. At k=0, the administrative overhead of bottom-up governance place it at a disadvantage compared to top-down governance and reuse governance,

Figure 1. Transaction costs versus asset specificity (Erbas & Erbas, 2009)

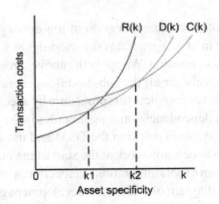

319

which minimizes the costs. When uncertainty is kept constant at a moderate level, however, while asset specificity rises, the cost disparity between decomposition D(k) and construction C(k) narrows and reverses as the need for cooperative adaptation exceeds a threshold k2.

This transaction-cost analysis suggests that the governance structure for a particular project should be selected by taking into consideration the asset specificity and uncertainty associated with the project. Since, asset specificity and uncertainty varies on different parts of large scale projects, than it may be more effective to adapt different development processes on different parts of the project. The uncertainty also changes, typically improves, over time in project life-cycle. Therefore, it may also be more effective to change the development process over time. These observations lead us to propose a governance framework as follows:

- **Step 1:** Identify generic functionality for which reusable modules may exist and locatable. Apply reuse governance for these modules.
- **Step 2:** Identify functionality for which the interfaces may be relatively simple and specifiable. Apply top-down governance for these modules.
- **Step 3:** The asset specificity and uncertainty over the remaining functionality is considered high. Apply bottom-up governance.

Note that the application of top-down governance in Step 2 generates sub-modules as a result of decomposition. We apply the above three steps recursively for all the sub-modules generated in Step 2. We complete this procedure by specifying all the dependencies among modules in the DSM form. We then partition the DSM and use as the governance framework at the start of the project.

From a tools integration perspective, a general block diagram of a software development gover-nance framework is illustrated in Figure 2. The framework integrates many software development and management tools. The particular case study presented in this chapter includes the integration of one software architecture tool (Lattix LDM), a modeling and development tool (Rational Rhapsody), and a configuration management tool (Rational ClearCase).

CONFIGURATION MANAGEMENT PATTERNS

Software configuration management (SCM) is the discipline of managing change in large and complex software systems (Estublier et al., 2005). Each organization should specify its own SCM processes which deal with many SCM concerns such as branching, change control, baseline management, etc. There are proposed SCM patterns which address the most common SCM concerns. These patterns can be integrated into organizational SCM processes in order to overcome some of the known issues.

One of the most important issues is branching (Walrad & Strom, 2002). Adopting the right branching model facilitates parallel and rapid

Figure 2. Software development governance framework

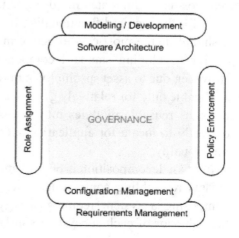

development. If a component is developed by parallel projects, adopted branching model should allow developing the shared component in parallel. In this section, we review three different SCM patterns about branching models. A preliminary work is presented in (Pala & Erbas, 2010).

We use IBM Rational ClearCase to demonstrate the implementation of the proposed patterns. ClearCase is a widely used configuration management tool in the software industry. The basic terminology used in this chapter is explained briefly, for further detail refer to ClearCase Introduction Guide. A *Versioned Object Base* (VOB) is a repository which stores versions of the configuration items. A *Project VOB* (PVOB) is a project repository which holds objects associated with a project environment, such as components, Unified Change Management (UCM) projects, and baselines. A *component* is composed of a set of semantically related functions and corresponds to a set of configuration items that should be controlled and versioned as a single unit. A *UCM project* consists of one or more components, and defines the policies used on that project. A version of a component is called a *baseline.*

Producer Project: Consumer Project(s) Pattern

According to Producer Project – Consumer Project(s) pattern, there exists only one producer

project that has the modification rights on the shared component. Shared component is developed by the producer project. There can be one or more consumer projects which use the shared component as read-only, so they cannot modify the shared component. In that case, shared component cannot be changed at the same time by different projects, so there is no need to merge the configuration items when deliver and rebase operations take progress (Bellagio & Milligan, 2005).

The baseline tree of a component which is developed by Producer Project – Consumer Project(s) pattern is given in Figure 3. The integration stream of the producer project is named as *Producer_Project_Int*. There are two consumer projects; *Consumer_Project_1* and *Consumer_Project_2*. When a new baseline is released, it can be used by the consumer projects, so the arrows always start from the integration stream of the producer project and end at the integration stream of the consumer projects.

Parallel Projects Development: Mainline Project Pattern

According to mainline project pattern, there are multiple parallel projects sharing some of their components. Shared components can be modified by any one of the projects. In this situation, the projects can change the same parts of the software at the same time, so deliver and rebase operations

Figure 3. Baseline tree of producer project - consumer project(s) pattern

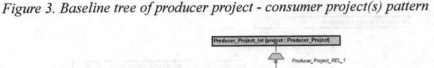
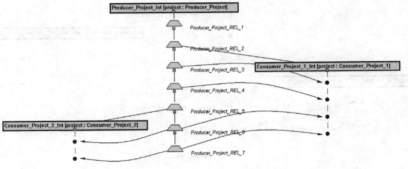

will require merging configuration items. If the shared components are changed without coordination, this will lead to merge problems. The projects try to adapt the changes. If the adaptation cannot be achieved for some of the projects, the changes may be reverted. This means the waste of the resources. The coordination problems between projects must be solved before making changes on the shared components. Mainline project pattern is suggested to make the coordination easier. In this section, we explain the mainline project pattern and its application with ClearCase tool.

Original Usage of Mainline Project Pattern

A software configuration can be managed by a series of successive baselines. When a new version of the software is developed, a new *follow-on project* is created. The new follow-on project is based on the previous version (baseline) of the software and is used to develop the new version of the software. As long as the previous versions of the software are supported, it is possible to make changes for a bug fix. The changes made in the previous follow-on projects must be propagated to the subsequent follow-on projects. Changes are propagated between projects by deliver operations. On the other hand, the changes made in the subsequent versions should not be transferred

to the previous versions. So, deliver operations must be under control. The control mechanism can be accomplished by a *mainline project* (Bellagio & Milligan, 2005). Changes made by the follow-on projects are integrated in the mainline project. New follow-on projects are created from the mainline project.

Figure 4 shows a mainline project and two follow-on projects. The first version of the project is developed in *Followon_Project_1* and delivered to the mainline project. Then, *Followon_Project_2* is started from the recommended baseline of the mainline project in order to develop the second version of the project. While the software development continues in *Followon_Project_2*, assume that some bugs are found in the first release and they are fixed by *Followon_Project_1*. After the changes are delivered from *Followon_Project_1* to the mainline project, *Followon_Project_2* is rebased in order to get the changes.

Adopting Mainline Project Pattern for Shared Software Component Development

The purpose of using a mainline project is to control and integrate old and new releases of a software project as explained in the previous section. Mainline project pattern can be adopted in order to control and integrate the releases of a

Figure 4. Baseline tree of mainline project pattern

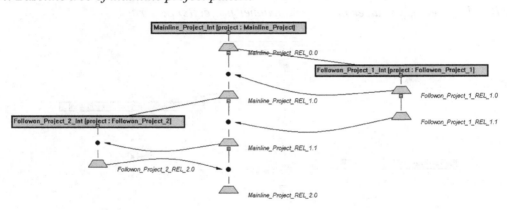

software component when the software component is developed by different parallel software development projects (Pala & Erbas, 2006). In this section, we explain how mainline project pattern is adopted for shared component development between different projects.

A mainline UCM project is created for each shared component which contains the shared software between parallel projects. Shared components are added to the parallel UCM projects as modifiable components. Changes made by a parallel project are delivered to the mainline UCM project created for the related shared component. New baselines are provided by the mainline project when new changes are integrated. The parallel projects are rebased from the newly recommended baseline in order to get the newly integrated changes.

Figure 5 shows how mainline project pattern is adopted for shared component development. According to the figure:

- The shared component is *Comp_Shared*,
- The mainline project is *Prj_Mainline*,

- The parallel projects which develop the shared component are *Prj_1* and *Prj_2*,
- The components which are not shared between projects are *Comp_1* and *Comp_2*,
- *Prj_1* develops two components; *Comp_1* and *Comp_Shared*,
- *Prj_2* develops two components; *Comp_2*, *Comp_Shared*.

Comp_Shared is developed by the two parallel projects. The first arrow between Prj_1 and the mainline project represents the deliver operation which transfers the changes made by Prj_1 to the mainline project. Then, a new baseline is created and recommended by the mainline project. The first arrow between the mainline project and Prj_2 shows the rebase operation which transfers the changes from the mainline project to Prj_2. After these steps are completed, Prj_2 has the changes made by Prj_1. In order to get the changes made by Prj_2 to Prj_1, similar operations are performed. The changes made by Prj_2 are delivered to the mainline project and a new baseline is created by the mainline project. Then, Prj_1 is rebased from the newly created baseline.

Figure 5. Shared component development using mainline project pattern

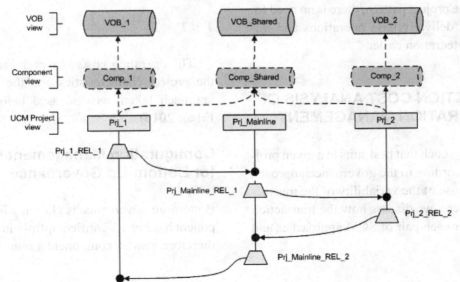

Figure 6. Baseline tree of single-line project pattern

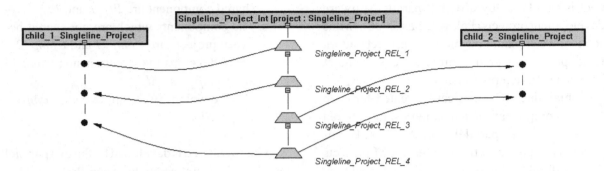

Single-Line Project Pattern

According to single-line project pattern, all development is done under one UCM project. Figure 6 represents the baseline tree of a component which is developed by single-line project pattern. *Singleline_Project_Int* is the integration stream of the single-line UCM project. *child_1_Singleline_Project* and *child_2_Singleline_Project* streams are the child streams of the integration stream. A child stream is created for each developer and developers make changes in their specific child streams. The changes made in the child streams are delivered to the integration stream of the project in order to integrate the changes made by developers. When a component is developed by single-line project pattern, there is no need for inter-project deliver-rebase operations and this makes the integration easier.

TRANSACTION COST ANALYSIS OF CONFIGURATION MANAGEMENT

The SCM approach that best suits to a given project varies according to the governance approach chosen, because of the variability of the transaction costs. Here, we discuss how the transaction costs vary for each pair of SCM approaches and

governance structures. We consider two different types of costs:

1. **Set-up costs:** The effort spent to set up an SCM infrastructure,
2. **Operating costs:** The effort spent to operate and maintain an SCM approach.

Set-up cost of an SCM approach includes the efforts spent to create VOBs, PVOBs, UCM projects and components. Baseline, deliver, rebase and merge operations are included in the operating costs. Independent of the governance approach taken, the relationship between the setup costs for single-line (T_s), producer/consumer (T_p), and mainline (T_m) patterns are:

$$T_s < T_p < T_m$$

The operating costs however vary based on the project characteristics and the governance approach taken, as discussed below (Pala & Erbas, 2010).

Configuration Management Costs for Bottom-Up Governance

Bottom-up governance is chosen when no component has been identified upfront in the project, therefore shared component usage will not be required. Therefore, we do not gain any benefit from using a configuration management method that supports componentization. Actually, early componentization in the SCM setup may increase the transaction costs, if the initial set of components change during implementation. Further, since $T_s < T_p < T_m$, the transaction costs for mainline pattern (T_{mb}) and producer–consumer pattern (T_{pb}) with respect to single-line pattern (T_{sb}) for bottom-up governance are as follows:

$$T_s + T_{sb} < T_m + T_{mb} \text{ and } T_s + T_{sb} < T_p + T_{pb}$$

Therefore, Single-line pattern should be the most cost effective for bottom-up governance.

Configuration Management Costs for Top-Down Governance

Top-down governance is chosen when the software can be decomposed into components whose interfaces can be specified upfront fairly well. Single-line pattern (T_{st}) does not support developing components that can be easily identified and used for future projects. This implies that, if we start with single-line pattern, we will have to perform the componentization in the CM system at the end, with net result of increasing the transaction costs tremendously. Producer-consumer pattern (T_{pt}) provides support for developing components, however if the development is from scratch or based on reuse with major modifications, then this requires many delivery operations through baselines, especially if the component is also used by other projects. This significantly increases the transaction costs of this approach. Mainline pattern helps to coordinate the development efforts for shared components, which implies that:

$$T_m + T_{mt} < T_s + T_{st} \text{ and } T_m + T_{mt} < T_p + T_{pt}$$

Therefore, mainline pattern which makes coordination easier should be the most cost effective for Top-Down Decomposition based development.

Configuration Management Costs for Reuse Governance

Reuse governance is chosen when there are existing components that can be reused for the current project. Mainline pattern (T_{mr}) coordinates most cost-effectively the complex merge operations. However, software reuse may require only minor modifications which should not cause complex merges. Therefore, there is no reason to incur the cost of setting up a mainline pattern environment. Single-line pattern (T_{sr}) for a project whose development process is Software Reuse will require the reusable component to be merged in the Single-line Project CM environment. This internalizes a component which has to be kept external. If the component is to be kept as reusable at the end, then it requires splitting the component, which will increase the transaction costs tremendously. This implies that:

$$T_p + T_{pr} < T_s + T_{sr} \text{ and } T_p + T_{pr} < T_m + T_{mr}$$

Therefore, producer-consumer pattern (T_{pr}), which handles minor modifications most cost-effectively, should be the most cost effective for reuse governance.

Mapping from Configuration Management to Governance

Based on the discussion above, the transaction cost characteristics for these three configuration management approaches, and their applicability for the software governance mechanisms can be summarized as in Table 1.

A CASE STUDY FOR TOOLS INTEGRATION

A case study is developed in order to demonstrate how the identified SCM patterns are used in a model-driven development environment which

Table 1. Mapping from governance structures to SCM approaches

Governance	SCM Pattern	Relationship
Reuse	Producer / Consumer	Cost effective implementation of one way dependencies to generic components.
Top-Down	Mainline	Minimizes the merge operations for implementing application-specific components.
Bottom-Up	Single line	Handles best the uncertainty and unidentified interdependencies.

integrates IBM Rational ClearCase and IBM Rational Rhapsody. Two aircraft computer management systems will be developed in the case study. These systems are called as Aircraft-1 and Aircraft-2. Top-down decomposition development process is applied to the systems initially in order to identify high level components. The identified components of each aircraft are showed in Table 2.

According to Table 2, Aircraft-1 has seven components and Aircraft-2 has six components. Each aircraft has its own Engine Control (EC1 and EC2) and User Interface Management (UIM1 and UIM2) components. Automatic Flight Control (AFC) component will be developed by only Aircraft-1 project. Both of the projects need to develop Navigation System and Communication System components so these two components will be developed by both of them. Assume that Databus Management and Redundancy Management components are developed previously so they are re-used by Aircraft-1 and Aircraft-2 projects.

Figure 7 shows the DSM generated using Lattix LDM for this application. DSM gives information about the dependencies between components. According to this DSM, UIM 1 uses EC 1, AFC, Communication, Navigation, Databus Management and Redundancy Management components. UIM 2 uses EC 2, Communication, Navigation, Databus Management and Redundancy Management components.

Creating ClearCase UCM Projects

In this section, we explain the establishment of ClearCase environment. For each component, the recommended SCM pattern is given in Table 2.

- We recommend using Databus Management and Redundancy Management components with producer-consumer pattern because these two components are developed previously and may require only minor modi-

Table 2. Aircraft components and CM patterns

Components	Aircraft-1	Aircraft-2	CM Pattern
User Interface 1	X		Single-line
Engine Control 1	X		Single-line
Automatic Flight Control	X		Single-line
User Interface 2		X	Single-line
Engine Control 2		X	Single-line
Databus Management	X	X	Producer-Consumer
Redundancy Management	X	X	Producer-Consumer
Navigation System	X	X	Mainline
Communication System	X	X	Mainline

Figure 7. DSM of Aircraft-1 and Aircraft-2

$root			1	2	3	4	5	6	7	8	9
UIM 1	1		·								
UIM 2	2			·							
EC 1	3		1		·						
AFC	4		1		1	·					
EC 2	5			1			·				
Communication	6		1	1				·			
Navigation	7		1	1					·		
Databus Management	8		1	1	1	1	1	1	1	·	
Redundancy Management	9		1	1	1	1	1	1	1		·

fications. According to our cost analysis, producer-consumer pattern is the most cost effective pattern when previously developed components are re-used.

- We recommend developing UIM 1, UIM 2, EC 1, EC 2 and AFC components with single-line pattern because these components will be developed by only one aircraft system. A component can have sub-components but these sub-components and their interfaces cannot be identified by top-down process initially. So, each component

will be developed by bottom-up process. According to our cost analysis, single-line is the most cost effective pattern when a system is developed using bottom-up process by only one project.

- We recommend developing Communication and Navigation components with mainline pattern because these two components are developed by both of the projects. These two components will be developed from scratch so many merge operations will be required. According to our cost analysis,

Figure 8. ClearCase infrastructure for the case study

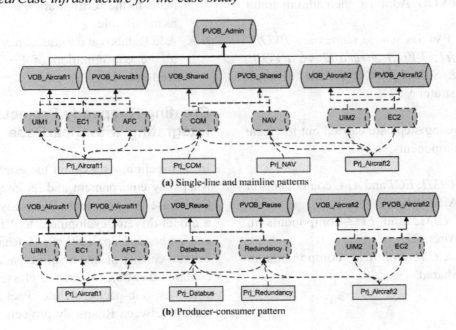

(a) Single-line and mainline patterns

(b) Producer-consumer pattern

mainline pattern is the most cost effective pattern when a system is developed from scratch by more than one project.

Figure 8(a) shows ClearCase infrastructure established to develop UIM 1, UIM 2, EC 1, EC 2, AFC, Communication and Navigation components. UIM1, EC1 and AFC components are developed by Prj_Aircraft1. UIM2 and EC2 are developed by Prj_Aircraft2. COM and NAV components are developed by both Prj_Aircraft1 and Prj_Aircraft2. Figure 8(b) shows ClearCase infrastructure established to re-use Databus and Redundancy components. Databus component is developed by Prj_Databus producer project. Redundancy component is developed by Prj_Redundancy producer project. Databus and Redundancy components are used by Prj_Aircraft1 and Prj_Aircraft2 consumer projects.

The following steps are implemented to create ClearCase VOBs and PVOBs.

1.   Create administrator PVOB whose name is *PVOB_Admin,*
2.   Create VOBs whose names are *VOB_Aircraft1*, *VOB_Aircraft2* and *VOB_Shared*. Select PVOB_Admin as their administrator VOB.
3.   Create PVOBs whose names are *PVOB_Aircraft1*, *PVOB_Aircraft2* ve *PVOB_Shared*. Select PVOB_Admin as their administrator VOB.

The following steps are carried out to create ClearCase components:

1.   Create *UIM1*, *EC1* and *AFC* components in VOB_Aircraft1,
2.   Create *UIM2* and *EC2* components in VOB_Aircraft2,
3.   Create *COM* and *NAV* components in VOB_Shared.

The following steps are implemented to create Mainline UCM projects:

1.   Create a UCM project in PVOB_Shared and name it as *Prj_COM.*
2.   Add COM component to the configuration of Prj_COM as modifiable.
3.   Create a UCM project in PVOB_Shared and name it *Prj_NAV*.
4.   Add NAV component to the configuration of Prj_NAV as modifiable.

The following steps are carried out to create single-line UCM projects:

1.   Create a UCM project in PVOB_Aircraft1 and name it as *Prj_Aircraft1*.
2.   Add UIM1, EC1, AFC, COM and NAV components to the configuration of Prj_Aircraft1 as modifiable.
3.   Add Databus and Redundancy components to the configuration of Prj_Aircraft1 as read-only.
4.   Create another UCM project in PVOB_2 and name it as *Prj_Aircraft2*.
5.   Add UIM2, EC2, COM and NAV components to the configuration of Prj_Aircraft2 as modifiable.
6.   Add Databus and Redundancy components to the configuration of Prj_Aircraft2 as read-only.

Creating Rhapsody Projects and Integrating with ClearCase

In this section, we explain the establishment of Rhapsody environment and its integration with ClearCase environment. Rhapsody is used as a model-driven development tool for real time and embedded applications. A Rhapsody project can consist of one or more packages which contain other objects, such as classes, functions, variables, sub-packages, etc. Packages can be shared between Rhapsody projects. Each package has only one owner Rhapsody project which modifies the package. Other Rhapsody projects can add the package as *reference* in order to use it. The referenced packages are read-only so they cannot be modified.

Before sharing a package with other Rhapsody projects, owner Rhapsody project should make the package a unit which can be added to the source control and becomes a configuration item. The sub-packages created within the shared package can also be made unit or maintained in the shared package.

Rhapsody projects are placed in the configuration management structure. The following steps are carried out to create Rhapsody projects which will own the shared packages:

1. Create a Rhapsody project in COM component from a view created on the integration stream of Prj_COM UCM project and name it as *COM_Prj*.
2. Create a package in COM_Prj and name it as *COM_Pkg*.
3. Make COM_Pkg package a unit in order to use it from other Rhapsody projects.
4. Create a baseline from Prj_COM UCM project. Prj_Aircraft1 and Prj_Aircraft2 UCM projects are rebased with the new baseline.
5. Create a Rhapsody project in NAV component from a view created on the integration

stream of Prj_NAV UCM project and name it *NAV_Prj*.
6. Create a package in NAV_Prj and name it as *NAV_Pkg*.
7. Make NAV_Pkg package a unit in order to use it from other Rhapsody projects.
8. Create a baseline from Prj_NAV UCM project. Prj_Aircraft1 and Prj_Aircraft2 UCM projects are rebased with the new baseline.

Figure 9 shows the Rhapsody projects and their shared packages created in the shared components.

The following steps are implemented to create the Rhapsody projects which use the shared packages as reference:

1. Create a Rhapsody project in UIM1 component from a view created on the integration stream of Prj_Aircraft1 and name it as *UIM1_Prj*.
2. Add COM_Pkg and NAV_Pkg packages as reference to UIM1_Prj.
3. Create a Rhapsody project in UIM2 component from a view created on the integration stream of Prj_Aircraft2 and name it as *UIM2_Prj*.
4. Add COM_Pkg and NAV_Pkg packages as reference to UIM2_Prj.

Figure 9. Creating shared packages

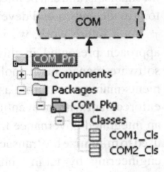
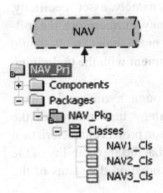

Figure 10. Using shared packages

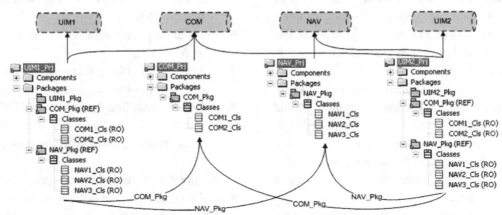

Figure 10 shows the integrated Rhapsody and ClearCase environment. UIM1_Prj and UIM2_Prj share COM_Pkg and NAV_Pkg packages.

CONCLUSION

Software development governance is a nascent area of research in software engineering. It provides an interdisciplinary perspective primarily from TCE perspective, and promises to better understand the issues involved in business success for software engineering organizations. We reviewed the existing literature, which identified three primary modes of governance for software development, each having distinct transaction cost characteristics. To be cost effective, the software engineering organizations should adapt the right governance structure based on their project characteristics, namely, asset specificity, uncertainty and frequency. Furthermore, the software development and management tools should support and be in alignment with the underlying governance structure.

We developed through a transaction cost analysis an SCM strategy that minimizes the transaction costs based on project characteristics. Our analysis revealed that the applicability of the SCM approaches depended on the status of the component under consideration. The producer/consumer pattern can be used as part of reuse governance for the existing components. These components can be added to the project without any modification or with minor modifications. The mainline pattern can be used in conjunction with top-down governance for the components which do not exist and their interface can be specified. Single-line pattern can be used as part of bottom-up governance for the components whose interface cannot be specified, as the development of these components requires frequent integrations. We then tackled the challenges for tools integration, from a practical implementability perspective, using Lattix LDM, IBM Rational ClearCase and IBM Rational Rhapsody tools three widely available tools in industry. We demonstrated that ClearCase can be leveraged to provide support for the implementation of the proposed governance mechanisms, and can be integrated with Rhapsody to provide end-to-end development support.

As a future work, we intend to enhance the approach presented in this chapter with other software management tools, including requirements management, role assignment and policy enforcement with an eventual goal of developing an integrated governance framework that can be used to minimize the transaction costs in software engineering by taking into consideration the project characteristics. On a complementary line of research, we are also in the process of extending the three governance structures mentioned in this chapter with "service governance" targeting systems of systems development projects.

REFERENCES

Ambler, S. W. (2009). *Scaling agile software development through lean governance*. Paper presented at the Software Development Governance Workshop, Vancouver, Canada.

Anderson, W., & Carney, D. (2009). *Distributed Project Governance Assessment (DPGA): Contextual, hands-on analysis for project governance across sovereign boundaries*. Paper presented at the Software Development Governance Workshop, Vancouver, Canada.

Bannerman, P. (2009). *Software development governance: A meta-management perspective*. Paper presented at the Software Development Governance Workshop, Vancouver, Canada.

Bellagio, D. E., & Milligan, T. J. (2005). *Software configuration management strategies and IBM® Rational® ClearCase®, a practical introduction* (6th ed.). NJ: Addison Wesley Professional.

Cataldo, M., & Herbsleb, J. D. (2009). *End-to-end features as meta-entities for enabling coordination in geographically distributed software development*. Paper presented at the Software Development Governance Workshop, Vancouver, Canada.

Cheng, T. H., Jansen, S., & Remmers, M. (2009). *Controlling and monitoring agile software development in three Dutch product software companies*. Paper presented at the Software Development Governance Workshop, Vancouver, Canada.

Erbas, B. C., & Erbas, C. (2005). *A transaction cost economics approach to software development and acquisition*. Paper presented at the Integrated Design and Process Technology Conference, San Diego, California.

Erbas, C., & Erbas, B. C. (2009). *Software development under bounded rationality and opportunism*. Paper presented at the Software Development Governance Workshop, Vancouver, Canada.

Estublier, J., Leblang, D., Hoek, A., Conradi, R., Clemm, G., & Tichy, W. (2005). Impact of software engineering research on the practice of software configuration management. *ACM Transactions on Software Engineering and Methodology, 14*, 1–48. doi:10.1145/1101815.1101817

IBM. (2008). *IBM Rational Rhapsody*. Retrieved May 01, 2010, from http://www.ibm.com/developerworks/rational/products/rhapsody/?S_TACT=105AGX15

IBM. (2009). *IBM Rational ClearCase introduction*. Retrieved May 01, 2010, from http://www-01.ibm.com/support/docview.wss?rs=984&uid=pub1gi11636000

Kofman, A., Yaeli, A., Klinger, T., & Tarr, P. (2009). *Roles, rights and responsibilities: Better governance through decision rights automation*. Paper presented at the Software Development Governance Workshop, Vancouver, Canada.

Kreps, D. M. (1990). *A Course in microeconomic theory*. New Jersey: Princeton University Press.

Lehto, I., & Rautiainen, K. (2009). *Software development governance challenges of a middle-sized company in agile transition*. Paper presented at the Software Development Governance Workshop, Vancouver, Canada.

Pala, N., & Erbas, C. (2006). *Supporting reusability through ClearCase UCM* (Tech. Rep. No. TR-06-0001). Ankara, Turkey: ASELSAN, MGEO.

Pala, N., & Erbas, C. (2010). *Aligning software configuration management with governance structures*. Paper presented at the Software Development Governance Workshop, Cape Town, South Africa.

Pint, E. M., & Baldwin, L. H. (1997). *Strategic sourcing: Theory and evidence from economics and business management.* (Tech. Rep. No. MR-865-AF). RAND Monograph Report.

Talby, D., & Dubinsky, Y. (2009). *Governance of an agile software project.* Paper presented at the Software Development Governance Workshop, Vancouver, Canada.

Walrad, C., & Strom, D. (2002). The importance of branching models in SCM. *IEEE Computer, 35,* 31–38.

Williamson, O. E. (2002). The theory of the firm as governance structure: From choice to contract. *The Journal of Economic Perspectives, 16,* 171–195. doi:10.1257/089533002760278776

KEY TERMS AND DEFINITIONS

Reusability: The likelihood of using previously developed software in a new software project.

SCM Pattern: A general reusable solution to a commonly occurring issue in SCM.

Software Configuration Management: The discipline of managing change in large and complex software systems.

Software Development Governance: The application of "governance" in software engineering in order to increase the probability of success in the level of individual projects as well in the level of the organization comprising many inter-related projects.

Transaction (in Business): An exchange of products or services between a supplier and a client.

Transaction (in Software Engineering): An exchange of requirements and corresponding software between a manager and a developer.

Transaction Cost Economics: The economic theory that inspects the characteristics of transactions.

Transaction Costs: The costs of coordinating work and the costs associated with creating and enforcing agreements.

Chapter 14

A Software Cost Model to Assess Productivity Impact of a Model-Driven Technique in Developing Domain-Specific Design Tools

Achilleas Achilleos
University of Cyprus, Cyprus

Nektarios Georgalas
British Telecom (BT) Innovate, UK

Kun Yang
University of Essex, UK

George A. Papadopoulos
University of Cyprus, Cyprus

ABSTRACT

Programming languages have evolved through the course of research from machine dependent to high-level "platform-independent" languages. This shift towards abstraction aims to reduce the effort and time required by developers to create software services. It is also a strong indicator of reduced development costs and a direct measure of a positive impact on software productivity. Current trends in software engineering attempt to raise further the abstraction level by introducing modelling languages as the key components of the development process. In particular, modelling languages support the design of software services in the form of domain models. These models become the main development artefacts, which are then transformed using code generators to the required implementation. The major predicament with model-driven techniques is the complexity imposed when manually developing the domain-specific design tools used to define models. Another issue is the difficulty faced in integrating these design tools with

DOI: 10.4018/978-1-60960-215-4.ch014

model validation tools and code generators. In this chapter a model-driven technique and its supporting model-driven environment are presented, both of which are imperative in automating the development of design tools and achieving tools integration to improve software productivity. A formal parametric model is also proposed that allows evaluating the productivity impact in generating and rapidly integrating design tools. The evaluation is performed on the basis of a prototype domain-specific design tool.

INTRODUCTION

The escalating and rapidly changing user requirements contribute towards increased complexity in the software development process. Furthermore, the advancements and diversity in technologies currently present escalate further the complexity introduced to the process. Consequently, the software engineering community seeks innovative and abstract techniques that provide the capability to scale down the complexity problem, in order to simplify and expedite the development of domain-specific software services. The objective is to provide "platform-independent" techniques that support the creation of software services at an abstract level steering the developer away from platform-specific implementation complexities.

During the early years of *Software Engineering* the difficulties and pitfalls of designing complex software services were identified and a quest for improved software development methodologies and tools began (Wirth, 2008). The first steps towards this goal introduced formal notations, known as programming languages, used mainly for performing mathematical analysis computing tasks. Examples of such numerical programming languages are *FORTRAN, Algol and COBOL.* Since then demand for more powerful software applications that perform complex computational tasks, rather than simple mathematical tasks, has largely grown. Therefore, it was acknowledged that more competent programming languages, software tools and automation capabilities were

required to successfully implement these complex computing tasks (Wirth, 2008).

The software engineering discipline concentrated on the development of high-level programming languages, which simplify the development of software applications. A minor setback in the inclination towards programming abstraction was the machine dependent *C language*. As Wirth (2008, p. 33) clearly states:

"From the point of view of software engineering, the rapid spread of C therefore represented a great leap backward....... It revealed that the community at large had hardly grasped the true meaning of the term "high-level language", which became a poorly understood buzzword. What, if anything, was to be "high level" now?"

Although the *C language* provides efficiency in creating simple hardware-dependent software services, it proved scarce and complex in developing, testing and maintaining large and versatile software applications (Wirth, 2008). The lessons learned from using the *C language* guided though software engineers to devise abstract and disciplined software techniques, like the predominant *Object-Oriented (OO)* programming model (Chonacky, 2009). On the basis of this model different 3GLs were developed such as Smalltalk, C++, Java and C#. These languages aimed to raise the level abstraction in software engineering and facilitate the definition of disciplined, systematic and object-oriented techniques for software development. 3GLs allow building advanced software services that feature visual objects (e.g. buttons, labels) with distinct state and behaviour.

The continuous development of programming languages can be considered as a sign of healthy evolution (Chonacky, 2009), which stems from the necessity to overcome complexities imposed by the software development process. In particular, this pragmatic progress leaded to the creation of many Domain-specific Languages (DSLs) that tackle software development at a higher abstraction level (Deursen et. al., 2000; Graff et. al., 2007; Iscoe et. al., 1991) and introduce a shift from code-centric to model-centric development (Staron, 2006; Afonso et. al., 2006). This category of languages can be divided into two closely related subcategories: (i) text-based DSLs and (ii) model-based DSLs. Examples of such DSLs are *Matlab, Simulink* and *SolidWorks*, which describe and/or combine text-based and modelling software capabilities. These languages are proven to be highly competent in terms of their targeted problem domain rather than being all-around General-Purpose Languages (GPLs). Therefore, the semantics of these languages can be interpreted precisely to a platform-specific implementation since they are very precise and leave no room for miscellaneous interpretations (Evermann et. al., 2005; Clark et. al., 2004). The well-acknowledged success of DSLs comes as an outcome of the following: (i) satisfying the domain's requirements, (ii) using proficient software tools to support them and (iii) restricting user input to properties of the target domain while providing easy access to artefacts (Sprinkle et. al., 2009). Moreover, they provide modelling and coding simplicity and aim for platform-independence (Chonacky, 2009).

Domain-specific Modelling (DSM) refers to the activity that allows developing and using graphical DSLs. It is a software engineering paradigm that raises the level of abstraction by introducing models as the prime entities of the development process. Although DSM is currently at its peeks, it is rather a revived and improved concept that shifts the focus to narrower applica-

tion domains of increased abstraction (Sprinkle et. al., 2009). In particular, early programming languages such as FORTRAN and COBOL can be also regarded as DSLs, which embrace though the much broader domains of scientific and business computing. As aforesaid the added-value of DSLs lies in their focused expressive power and not their broad applicability (Freudenthal, 2009). Therefore, the success of DSLs lies in addressing smaller domains and defining concepts restricted to these problem-specific domains. In addition, tools have evolved significantly in terms of providing the software capabilities that allow defining DSLs, validating and transforming models and automatically generating the implementation from models.

In this chapter we introduce a model-driven technique and a supporting environment, which allow automatically generating concrete, customisable, extensible and bug-free domain-specific design tools. Our focus is to provide a quantitative evaluation method that considers a large number of parameters to assess the impact of the proposed model-driven technique and its supporting environment on software productivity. In particular, the evaluation method should provide the capability to assess the productivity impact in generating and rapidly integrating design tools into a unified environment. The evaluation is based on a well-documented and widely accepted formal model (i.e. COCOMO II.2000 - Post-Architecture model), which allows estimating the effort, time and cost related to software development (Boehm et. al., 2000; Chen et. al., 2005). In particular, due to the nature of the model-driven technique the evaluation method takes into consideration an extension of the Use of Software Tools (TOOLS) parameter defined in the model. Using this extension the critical role of software tools is heavily considered in the estimation of the impact on software productivity. Finally, the evaluation takes into consideration the following requirements, which should be satisfied to efficiently accomplish design tools generation. Figure 1 illustrates

Figure 1. The necessary artefacts for defining a domain-specific modelling language

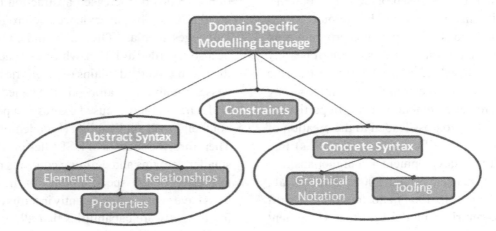

explicitly these requirements (i.e. artefacts), which are imperative for developing a DSL and its supporting design tool.

R1. *A standardised language is required that provides rich syntax, semantics and a supporting tool for defining the abstract syntax of DSLs.*

R2. *The capability to define constraints should be provided using a software tool that conforms to a standardised language and allows defining rules that restrict the abstract syntax of the DSL.*

R3. *A widely-used modelling language and a supporting tool is required that allows defining the concrete syntax of DSLs.*

R4. *The capability to merge the abstract syntax, constraints and concrete syntax into a common representation (i.e. a model) that allows generating automatically the modelling tools of DSLs.*

The chapter is structured as follows: Section 2 presents background information on Model-Driven Development (MDD) environments, which target explicitly the generation of domain-specific design tools. Moreover, Section 3 introduces related work that uses MDD environments for auto-

mating the development of domain-specific design tools. In Section 4 we present the model-driven technique with particular focus in *automating the generation of DSLs and their supporting modelling tools*. Section 5 presents the *architectural design of the proposed model-driven environment*. Following, Section 6 showcases the automatic generation of a prototype design tool used in the *Product Lifecycle Management process*. A quantitative evaluation is then performed on the basis of the above requirements and the selected software cost estimation model. Finally, Section 7 summarises, concludes and proposes directions for future research work.

BACKGROUND

The progress of research work on MDD acknowledges that practising domain-specific modelling in conjunction with the Model Driven Architecture (MDA) paradigm (Frankel, 2003; Kleppe, 2005; OMG MDA, 2003) can increase software productivity (Kelly & Pohjonen, 2009; Balasubramanian et. al., 2005). These research efforts recognize also the main issue with domain-specific modelling, which is the necessity to rapidly develop the modelling tools that support the DSLs. The growth of MDD environments and the capabilities they currently provide allow overcoming this issue to a great extend. Most of these environments provide automation in developing domain-specific languages and their supporting modelling tools. However, deficiencies still exist due to the failure to adopt a common, systematic model-driven technique and align fully with the MDA standards. In this section we present the most competent and widely-used environments, which are capable of providing proprietary or standardised support to the proposed model-driven technique, to identify possible limitations.

The Generic Modelling Environment (GME) is a research environment that practises Model Integrated Computing (MIC). MIC is actually a methodology developed to steer the GME in the development of embedded software systems. The tool stemmed from earlier research on domain-specific visual programming environments to become a highly competent domain-specific modelling environment (Molnár et. al., 2007). In particular, it can be adapted and configured at the meta-level to obtain a domain-specific modelling tool that is tailored to an explicit engineering domain. The GME defines a proprietary metamodelling language that includes the concepts built-in to the tool. Therefore, a DSL can be defined using a UML-like Class Diagram (i.e. metamodel) that describes the concepts of the engineering domain. Furthermore, it provides additional tools for defining domain rules using the Object Constraint Language (OCL) (OMG OCL, 2005) and GME-specific configurable model visualization properties. Although MetaGME is conceptually similar to the Meta-Object Facility (MOF) specification (OMG MOF, 2005) it is still not MOF-based. Hence, model-to-model transformations need to be defined to translate between the two languages (Emerson & Sztipanovits, 2004). Essentially, the requirement for compliance to MDA standards and the common interest on metamodelling motivated the GME research community to bridge

with the Eclipse modelling community into a joined initiative.

AndroMDA is an extensible generator environment that utilises UML tools to define models that can be transformed to a platform-specific implementation. In particular, the environment adheres to the MDA paradigm by utilising UML profiling rather than focusing on metamodelling. The environment is bound mainly to the notion of a "cartridge", which allows processing model elements with specific stereotypes using the template files defined within the cartridge. Templates describe how the models are transformed to deployable components that target well-known platforms such as J2EE, Spring,. NET. Consequently, the environment does not provide any inherent support for metamodelling and domain-specific modelling, since it is largely based on UML. In a latest snapshot release (i.e. AndroMDA 4.0-M1) the environment shifts its focus towards metamodelling using Eclipse-based modelling implementations and the concept of domain-specific modelling.

The XMF-Mosaic is a model-driven environment, which is based on the concept of metamodelling and provides support for domain-specific modelling. In particular, the metamodelling environment provides advanced capabilities for defining and generating DSLs and their supporting modelling tools. Furthermore, the software tools provided by the model-driven environment are largely aligned with the MDA specifications defined by the Object Management Group (OMG). Although the XMF-Mosaic is a powerful open-source model-driven environment built on top of the Eclipse platform, its development was terminated. In its latest version the tool interoperates closely with the Eclipse modelling implementations. This is basically due to the wide-acceptance of these implementations by the larger modelling community. Finally, the environment is to become part of the Eclipse Generative Modelling Technologies (GMT) project, which sole purpose is to produce a set of prototypes in the area of Model Driven Engineering.

Microsoft DSL Tools is a powerful model-driven environment that supports model-driven development with particular focus on domain-specific modelling. The software factory comprises a bundle of proprietary software tools developed on top of the Visual Studio development platform. In particular, DSL Tools facilitate explicitly the definition of the abstract syntax and the constraints that govern the DSL, which provides the capability to validate the designed models. Furthermore, the capability is provided to define the concrete syntax of the modelling language, in order to facilitate the generation of the required modelling tools for the language. The only predicament with the DSL factory is the necessity to learn how to use the proprietary languages and tools since the factory does not conform to the OMG specifications. Microsoft Corporation recently joined the OMG in an attempt to meet the standards so as to fulfil their strategy and assist in taking modelling into mainstream industry use.

Borland Together is the final model-driven environment examined in this chapter that provides the necessary tools to support the definition of DSLs and the generation of the accompanying modelling tools. First, the environment allows defining the abstract syntax and constraints that govern domain models. Moreover, the concrete syntax can be defined to provide a graphical notation for the artefacts of the DSL and the necessary tooling for the generated modelling tool. The environment is composed mainly by open-source Eclipse modelling implementations, which are customised to improve user experience and aid designers and developers to perform efficiently the required modelling and implementation tasks. The Eclipse implementations composing the environment are highly compliant to the OMG standards and are widespread and widely-known to an extensive group of designers and developers. Borland Together, like Microsoft DSL tools, is a commercial product that is not freely avail-

able and as a result does not allow designers and developers to extend it or customise it to satisfy their explicit requirements.

Most of these Eclipse implementations were introduced as new software capabilities in Borland Together 2008. These implementations are equivalent to the ones composing the model-driven environment initially proposed in (Achilleos et. al., 2007) and evaluated in this chapter. To the author's best knowledge when the environment was initially designed the existing literature and documentation (Borland, 2006) did not disclose such software capabilities. This does not abolish the fact that analogous attempts were made by Borland during that period to develop and deliver a unified model-driven environment with analogous software capabilities. Regardless of that fact, the objective of this chapter is not to perform a comparison of existing model-driven environments but rather to propose an evaluation method that can be applied for each environment to assess their impact on software productivity. In particular, the objective is to evaluate the capability of the environment to support a model-driven technique for automatically generating domain-specific modelling languages.

RELATED WORK

Different MDA approaches have been proposed in the literature that attempt to automate the development of DSLs, so as to simplify MDD. An approach that differentiates from mainstream DSL development (Santos et. al., 2008) proposes the extension of generic frameworks with an additional layer that encodes a DSL. The approach is solely based on a generic language workbench that allows extracting DSL concepts (i.e. DSL metamodel) from the DSM layer and transforming model instances into code that conforms to that particular DSM layer. Thus, developers are able to define DSL models like if they were using a conventional modelling tool. Moreover, the generic language workbench allows processing domain models for generating code, rather than developing individual code generators for each DSL. The main shortcoming is that the definition of a concrete syntax for the DSL is not addressed by the approach but it is regarded as a separate issue that is handled independently from the abstract syntax. We argue though that the definition of a DSL should involve also the specification of its concrete syntax.

As aforesaid, GME is a metamodelling environment that enables the creation of domain-specific modelling environments from metamodels (Lédeczi et. al, 2001). It uses the MetaGME metamodelling language that allows defining domain concepts in a proprietary form, which is similar to a UML class diagram. Consequently, since the metamodel is proprietary, it can only be used within the GME environment and cannot be imported in different modelling tools; e.g. UML tools. This limits the applicability of the domain-specific modelling language to designers and developers that are acquainted with GME. In addition, designers and developers are not familiar with the domain concepts described in such a proprietary metamodel and cannot comprehend and transform as a result the domain models. Finally, the flexibility of DSL definition is restricted to the semantics of MetaGME and does not conform to a widely used metamodelling language (e.g. MOF) that provides a richer set of semantics.

A comparable approach (Zbib et. al., 2006), which follows the conventional DSL development process proposes the automatic generation of domain-specific modelling editors directly from metamodels. In particular, the metamodel is defined as an extension of the UML metamodel that captures domain modelling concepts. This can be described as the notion of UML profiling where each stereotype of the DSL extends an artefact of the UML metamodel; e.g. class, package, attribute. The benefit of using such an approach is that the metamodel can be imported and used in many UML tools. However, no standard way is

defined to access model stereotypes in these UML tools, so as to enforce constraints and develop the necessary code generators. In addition, as admitted also in (Zbib et. al., 2006), there is greater flexibility in defining the DSL using MOF constructs; rather than being bounded by the UML semantics. Hence, we argue in this work that an approach that adheres to the MOF specification (i.e. EMF) and utilises an open-source MDD environment is largely beneficial and preferred. Furthermore, this work proposes an evaluation method that allows determining the efficiency and applicability of the MDA approach. This is an important point that is not addressed by existing work.

AUTOMATING THE DEVELOPMENT OF DOMAIN-SPECIFIC MODELLING LANGUAGES

As aforementioned, the principal issue that hinders the application of MDD is the difficulty faced with the development of domain-specific modelling languages (DSMLs). Note that we refer to the development of a DSML, rather than its definition, since it involves both the definition of the DSML and the implementation of its necessary supporting modelling tool. In particular, each DSML requires a supporting modelling tool that allows designing models that conform to the syntax, semantics and constraints of the DSML. Developing a DSML from scratch involves a time-consuming and error-prone process that necessitates high development effort; especially the implementation of the modelling tool (Nytun et. al., 2006). Consequently, the following questions arise that necessitate effective solutions for rapidly developing a DSML:

i. How to define the abstract syntax and constraints of the modelling language?
ii. How to define the concrete syntax of the modelling language?

iii.   How to develop a supporting software modelling tool for the language?

In this chapter we argue that explicit focus should be given to software tools in order to improve automation in domain-specific modelling tools generation. In particular, the capabilities of model-driven development tools should be fully exploited to automate the definition of DSMLs and the generation of offspring domain-specific design tools. The idea put-forward in this chapter is to utilise common, standardised and widely-used specifications to automate the development of DSMLs. Therefore, since existing MDA specifications do not provide the necessary tooling, we need to identify and/or develop software tools with high conformance to the standards. Furthermore, a disciplined and systematic model-driven technique is required that automates the development of DSMLs by utilising the capabilities of the selected software tools.

Figure 2 presents such a model-driven technique that refers to the primary phase of the methodology introduced by Achilleos et. al. (2008). This technique illustrates the tasks undertaken to accomplish the generation of DSMLs. Irrespective of the model-driven environment used, these tasks should form the baseline in order to effectively achieve increased automation in DSMLs generation. The primary task involves a requirements analysis, which helps to identify domain concepts and formulate the *Abstract Syntax* of the modelling language. In particular, the elements, properties and relationships are identified that symbolize the concepts of the domain. These concepts are then represented using a graphical notation that defines the *Abstract Syntax* of the modelling language.

The next task involves restricting the design of models to non-erroneous instances by imposing the necessary rules onto the *Abstract Syntax* of the language. This enables the execution of the third task because it allows extracting the *Concrete Syntax* of the language from its *Abstract Syntax* using model-to-model transformations. The *Concrete Syntax* of the language maps the language's domain concepts to a suitable graphical representation. For instance, an element of the language maybe mapped to a rectangle figure while a property of the language maybe mapped to a label figure. Furthermore, Task 5 illustrates the capability to customise the graphical representation of the language for human structuring purposes; i.e. improve understanding of the designed models. The next task involves merging the *Abstract* and *Concrete Syntax* of the language into a common representation that includes all the required arte-

Figure 2. Model-driven technique for automating DSMLs generation

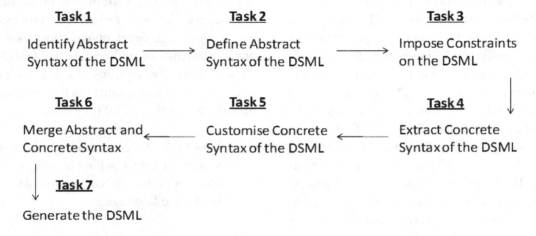

facts of the modelling language to facilitate its tool generation (i.e. Task 7). The execution of the final task is based on the capability to translate the common representation of the modelling language to the required implementation using an existing code generator. The resulting code implements a domain-specific modelling tool that conforms to the abstract syntax, constraints and concrete syntax of the defined modelling language.

The technique provides a set of unambiguous tasks that steer the development of DSMLs. In addition the nature of the tasks allows using model-driven software tools that provide the capability to support and automate their execution. The next section describes an architectural design and proposes an environment composed by a set of Eclipse modelling implementations to support and automate the development of DSMLs.

ARCHITECTURAL DESIGN OF THE MODEL-DRIVEN ENVIRONMENT

Architectural design refers to the composition of the necessary components of a system into a coherent unit that follows a methodology for accomplishing explicit tasks in an efficient manner. The architectural design described in this subsection is based on the plug-in architecture of the Eclipse platform. Eclipse is a software platform designed for building Integrated Development Environments (IDEs) and arbitrary tools (IBMC, 2009). Hence, in accordance to the Eclipse architecture each developed software tool can be installed directly as a plug-in of the platform. The only requirement is to export the deployable plug-in (i.e. a packaged JAR file) into the "plugins" directory of the Eclipse platform. This is a dedicated directory for loading software tools or capabilities during start-up, which can be used as necessary by the designer or developer. Keeping in line with the architecture of the Eclipse platform allows satisfying the main prerequisite, which refers to the automatic generation and rapid deployment of domain-specific design tools. Furthermore, the Eclipse platform provides an extensive library of software tools many of which are dedicated to modelling and adhere to the MDA specifications.

In principle the architectural design of the environment comprises of core software tools, which support the generation of offspring domain-specific design tools. The generated design tools can be integrated directly into the model-driven environment to compose a domain-specific software service creation environment. Figure 3 illustrates the architectural design of the environment; composed by four core modelling components (i.e. software tools) developed by the Eclipse

Figure 3. Architectural design of the model-driven environment

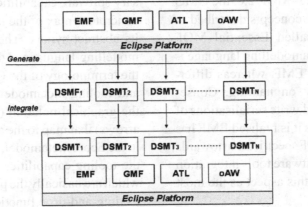

modelling community and associated alliances. Note that the selection of these four components is not an arbitrary one but it is decided on the basis of the requirements proposed and examined by Achilleos et. al. (2007). The rationale behind the components' selection can be summarised into three key points: (i) the components should provide the necessary software capabilities to support the generation of domain-specific modelling tools (DSMTs), (ii) the components should conform to the MDA standards and (iii) the components should provide the required capabilities for transforming and generating code from models. Figure 1 illustrates the components that are namely, the Eclipse Modelling Framework (EMF), Graphical Modelling Framework (GMF), Atlas Transformation Language (ATL) and openArchitectureWare (oAW).

The root component is the EMF that started initially as an implementation of the Meta-Object Facility formal specification (OMG MOF, 2005). Both describe (meta-) modelling languages that facilitate the definition of domain-specific modelling languages. As a matter of fact they are conceptually similar and express comparable metamodelling concepts (Gerber & Raymond, 2003; Mohamed et. al., 2007). In principle EMF emphasises on the development of the essential tooling for defining metamodelling concepts, while the MOF specification provides more rigorous and expressive meta-modelling concepts for defining modelling languages; i.e. metamodels. In its current version, that is MOF 2.0, the OMG introduces a subset of the concepts described in the full specification, called Essential MOF (EMOF). The EMOF metamodelling language is conceptually identical to EMF, whereas differences are predominantly on naming. Consequently, EMF can read and write serialisations of the EMOF metamodel. As it is realised EMF has influenced heavily the MOF specification towards the critical direction of software tools integration and can be considered in this aspect as the most

suitable candidate to drive the vision of model-driven development.

As aforesaid, the EMF is the heart of the environment that allows defining DSMLs using its *Ecore metamodelling language*. In particular, it allows defining the abstract syntax and semantics of the modelling language in the form of a domain metamodel. Furthermore, it provides a code generation capability that is based on Java Emitter Templates (JET) engine. This software capability enables the transformation of the metamodel into EMF-based Java implementation code, which is delivered as deployable plug-ins. The model plug-in provides the Java interfaces and implementation classes that represent the artefacts of the modelling language and the adapter plug-in provides the implementation classes that adapt the domain metamodel classes for editing and display. The final generated editor plug-in provides the classes that implement a modelling editor that conforms to the tree-based representation of the EMF. This editor supports the definition of domain models that conform to the modelling language in the form of abstract trees that include parent nodes and children as leafs.

The GMF is another important component of the environment that complements the functionality of the EMF. A modelling language requires apart from its abstract syntax and a concrete syntax that defines the graphical notation and the palette of a visual modelling tool. This is where the GMF comes in place since it provides the necessary software capabilities that allow deriving the concrete syntax of the modelling language from its abstract syntax. The concrete syntax of the modelling language is defined, in accordance to the terminology of the GMF, using the graphical and tooling metamodels. The former describes the graphical notation (e.g. rectangles, ellipses, arrows) that map to the abstract concepts defined in the Ecore metamodel, while the latter describes the tooling capabilities of the modelling editor, which are basically the palette buttons that enable its drag-and-drop functionality.

Having at hand the domain, graphical and tooling metamodels we can combine them using additional software capabilities of the GMF into a mapping metamodel to generate the visual editor plug-in. The plug-in includes the implementation classes that contribute the functionality of a structured GMF-based editor. Therefore, the set of generated plug-ins composes a fully-fledged domain-specific modelling tool, which is integrated into the original environment to deliver a software service development environment. Note that, a problem domain can be described by a single or multiple complementary modelling languages. Hence, multiple design tools might be generated and integrated into a unified environment for software service development; as illustrated in Figure 3. Examples of our work reveal that dividing the problem domain into smaller complementary sub-domains aids in terms of reducing models complexity and improve understanding (Achilleos et. al., 2008, Georgalas et. al., 2007). Finally, apart from the components that deal with the development of DSLs, the environment comprises of two supplementary frameworks that aid the transformation of models and the generation of implementation code from domain models. In this chapter, the focus is basically on the automation of the development of DSMLs and their accompanying tools. Consequently, it is out of the scope of this chapter to provide details on the operation of these frameworks.

A PROTOTYPE DESIGN TOOL FOR PRODUCT LIFECYCLE MANAGEMENT

The rapid development of large volumes of industrial software products and services is generally based on automated Product Lifecycle Management (PLM) systems (Georgalas et. al., 2009). This type of systems merge together all engineering disciplines involved and aid organisations to manage the complexity of the software development process. Telecommunication providers have recently began adopting such systems (i.e. PLM systems) because technologies such as 3G and IP are currently common practice also in the communications field. Furthermore, companies that are not inherently associated to the telecommunications field have entered the market and competition became incredibly fierce. Another factor that contributed in the adoption of PLM systems is the complexity involved in developing new software products and services. Mainly the requirement to assemble diverse components and services developed by different vendors introduces immense complexity that needs to be effectively managed. Therefore, telecommunication providers decided to adopt and adapt the PLM process, whose success is acknowledged in other industrial fields, so as to expedite and increase the efficiency in developing, deploying and offering software product and services (Georgalas et. al., 2009).

Developing a Product Lifecycle Management Design Tool

This subsection presents an industrial-based case study that involves the development of a prototype domain-specific design tool. The developed and adopted product design tool allows designers to unambiguously model products, share product specifications with other stakeholders and exchange product data amongst different Operational/ Business Support Systems (OSS/BSS) in different formats. The objective is to tackle the deficiencies introduced to the PLM process by the current techniques and tooling, used to develop software products and services. In particular, Georgalas et. al. (2009) identify the following issues with the PLM process:

1. Current practice does not automatically drive the process from the formulation of the concept all the way through to the deployment of the product in the OSS.

2. It does not minimize the effort spend by the iterative interactions amongst the managers, designers and developers involved.

3. It does not provide and maintain an enterprise-wide understanding of the software product, mainly due to the method high-level product information is disseminated; i.e. enormous MS Word documents.

In this chapter we utilize the proposed model-driven technique and the accompanying environment to develop a domain-specific design tool that steers efficiently the PLM process. It should be noted that in this PLM case study we have used both the proposed environment and Borland Together 2008 to perform a preliminary comparison during the evaluation phase. The design tool is based on the abstract syntax, constraints and concrete syntax of the product modelling language used to

generate it. The language is actually derived from a corresponding information model that defines the necessary concepts, which allow a designer to specify information regarding a software product in the form of a domain model; i.e. product specification. The information model describes concepts such as product offering, product specification, pricing information and domain rules. In particular, the information model used for the definition of the product modelling language is the Common Capability Model (CCM) defined by the British Telecom (BT) Group. The CCM describes common capabilities of BT's Matrix architecture and its portfolio package is a Unified Modelling Language (UML) Class Diagram that defines product specification concepts (Georgalas et. al., 2009).

The product-specific design tool is developed by following the tasks defined by the model-driven

Figure 4. Defining the product modelling language in the model-driven environment

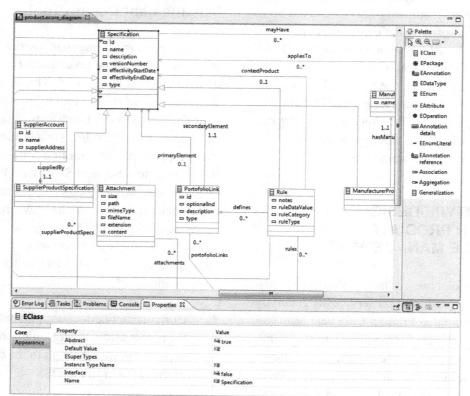

technique introduced in this chapter. Initially, product modelling concepts are derived directly from the existing UML Class Diagram of the CCM information model. Therefore, the primary task of requirement analysis is not executed since the concepts described in the product information model are taken for granted. The second task involves adapting the concepts of the CCM model to meet the expectations of the Ecore metamodelling language. This is straightforward since the artefacts defined within class diagrams are reasonably similar to metamodel artefacts. Therefore, the elements, relationships and properties of the product specification language are captured in the form of an Ecore metamodel. Figure 4 presents the product metamodel defined using the proposed model-driven environment, which defines the *Abstract Syntax* of the modelling language. The following task involves determining the rules that govern the product specification language and imposing, as illustrated in Figure 5, the required constraints onto the abstract syntax of the modelling language. This provides the capability to limit the designer input so as to avoid the definition of erroneous product models.

The definition of the abstract syntax and constraints is followed by the automated extraction of the concrete syntax of the modelling language. A suitable wizard allows the designer to select

the product metamodel as the input model and fine-tune the model-to-model transformation by choosing the desired graphical notation for each metamodel artefact. The result obtained is an output model, called a *graphical metamodel*, which represents graphical objects such as rectangles, ellipses and connectors. In particular, the GMF component of the model-driven environment includes a visual library of objects from which the designer is able to select the desired ones in order to fine-tune the output graphical metamodel. Consequently, the graphical metamodel defines a mapping of the concepts of the modelling language to visual objects that allow representing the language concepts in a diagram.

Figure 5 illustrates that apart from the graphical notation, the *Concrete Syntax* of the modelling language includes also the necessary software tooling; *i.e. tooling metamodel*. The software tooling is obtained via an analogous wizard that allows mapping each metamodel artefact to the corresponding palette tooling of the product design tool to be generated. This step allows organising the concepts of the product specification language in separate groups of software tooling (i.e. buttons) on a palette. The palette is made available in the generated design tool and enables the drag-and-drop functionality, which allows designing the product model in the drawing canvas. Figure 4 illustrates

Figure 5. Developing the product design tool using the model-driven technique

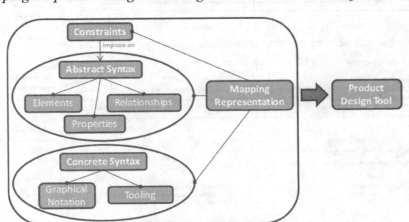

an analogous palette on the right hand-side of the figure, which refers to the software tooling of the Ecore metamodelling language. The generated product design tool resembles an equivalent modelling editor to the one illustrated in Figure 4, with the only difference that it incorporates the concepts of the product modelling language.

The subsequent task is optional since it allows customising the graphical and tooling metamodels in order to improve the presentation characteristics of the design tool. This is possible using the tree-based GMF editors that provide the capability to add, for instance, stereotypes (i.e. *labels*) to the visual objects that represent the language's concepts. Also the capability is provided to load icons for an artefact of the language instead of using graphical figures included within the GMF pool of visual objects. Further customisation ca-

pabilities are also provided in accordance to the requirements of the designer.

Having customised the concrete syntax of the language the software capability is provided that allows associating the artefacts of the product, graphical and tooling metamodels into a common *mapping representation*; i.e. *mapping metamodel*. For instance, an association describes how a metamodel concept (e.g. *"Specification" inFigure 4*) is mapped to the corresponding visual object (e.g. *rectangle figure*) and the respective palette tooling (i.e. *design tool palette button*). Therefore, the mapping defines all the necessary artefacts so as to facilitate the generation of the product design tool. This final task is actually an automated one since existing code generators are used to translate the mapping metamodel into an EMF-based Java implementation. As aforementioned the implementation of the design

Figure 6. Definition of the "BTEverywhere" software product using the product design tool

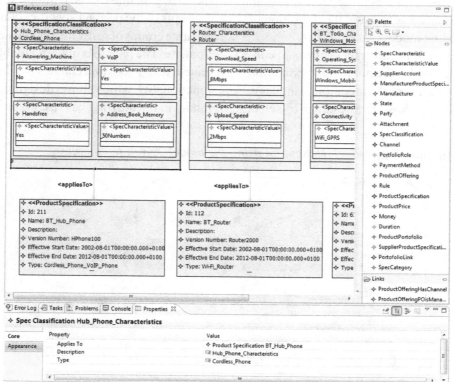

tool is delivered as Eclipse plug-ins, which are immediately integrateable and deployable as new capabilities of the environment.

The result is a product modelling tool (as illustrated in Figure 6) strictly dedicated to the abstract syntax, constraints, concrete syntax and semantics of the product modelling language. Figure 6 showcases an example domain model designed using the modelling tool that represents a software product called *"BTEverywhere"*, which provides the user with telephony, VoIP and broadband services. The software product actually offers the capability to shift seamlessly from the conventional telephony service while away from home to the VoIP service offered via broadband when located at home. This concludes the domain-specific modelling language development phase that delivers a fully-fledged product modelling tool to satisfy the designers and developers requirements. Hence, the proposed technique provides solutions to the aforementioned issues of the PLM process. It provides an enterprise-wide understanding of the software product, minimising the time and effort spend for interaction and product iterations amongst stakeholders and automates the process from concept inception all the way to product deployment.

Although the focus is on the development of design tools, we touch briefly how the product model is actually transformed into a fully-fledged deployable software product, so as to exemplify the end-to-end PLM-based development process. More details, on the transformation and the actual mapping can be found in (Georgalas et. al., 2009). Figure 7 illustrates at the top of the chain the *Toolsmiths* that are responsible to utilise the proposed *Model-Driven Environment* to generate the necessary *Product Design Tool*. *Product Designers* engage then with the definition of product models, which are subsequently transformed to *Product Master Data*. These data are captured in a specific format defined by an accepted enterprise-wide data model of the Master Data Management Platform (MDMP). Therefore, using the capabilities of the ATL and oAW frameworks of the model-driven environment the necessary data transformation scripts are defined that facilitate the transformation of product models to Product Master Data that populate respectively the MDMP repository. The generated product data captured in an XML format drive the configuration of OSS and BSS, so as to support the deployment of the new software product. Consequently, existing XML-based access interfaces defined in the form of adapters allow communicating Product Master Data to the OSS and BSS by transforming them to the system's native format as it flows to and from the MDMP. MDMP is the foundation for SOA capabilities across BT's Matrix architecture that makes OSS and BSS platforms data-driven

Figure 7. Master data management and PLM tooling driving OSS/BSS platforms (Georgalas et. al., 2009)

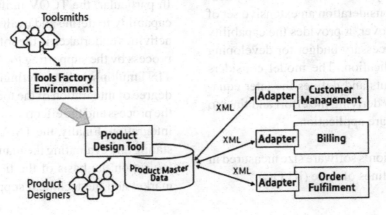

(Georgalas et. al., 2009). This removes laborious hard-coding tasks and maximizes data reuse in the PLM process.

Quantitative Evaluation using a Software Cost Estimation Model

This section examines the model-driven technique and environment introduced in this chapter and assesses their impact on software productivity. In particular, the capability to automate the development of domain-specific design tools is evaluated so as to determine the impact on software productivity. The evaluation examines the effect of the model-driven technique on the time, effort and cost required to develop the prototype product design tool using the following approaches:

1. Developing the product design tool using the proposed model-driven technique and its supporting intergrated Model Driven Environment (iMDE).
2. Developing the product design tool using the proposed model-driven technique and Borland Together 2008.
3. Manually implementing the product design tool from scratch without following any explicitly stated development process.

The evaluation is performed using the Post-Architecture model of COCOMO.II that allows estimating the *Effort in Person-Months (PM)* and the *Time to Develop (TDEV)* a software application taking into consideration an extensive set of parameters. Moreover, it provides the capability to estimate the necessary budget for developing the software application. The model considers the following inputs and defines the later equations, which allow deriving the effort and time to develop the software application.

1. The application's software size measured in thousand of lines of code (KLOC).

2. Five Scale Factors (SFs) that affect the development of the software application.

Seventeen Effort Multipliers (EMs) from which the TOOLS multiplier is divided and calibrated into three complementary (sub-) multipliers.

$$PM = A \times (KLOC)^E \times \prod_{i=1}^{17} EM_i, \text{ where } E = B +$$

$$(0.01 \times \sum_{j=1}^{5} SF_j),$$

$$A = 2.94 \text{ and } B = 0.91 \ (COCOMOII.2000)$$

$$(1)$$

$$TDEV = C \times (PM)^F, \text{ where } F = D + 0.2 \times (E - B),$$

$$C = 3.67 \text{ and } D = 0.28 \ (COCOMOII.2000)$$

$$(2)$$

Due to the importance of software tools in automating the development of design tools an extension of the model is considered (Baik et. al., 2002). The extension calibrates and divides the TOOLS multiplier into three complementary (sub-) multipliers, which are namely the completeness of Tool COVerage (TCOV), the degree of Tool INTegration (TINT) and the Tool MATurity (TMAT). These (sub-) multipliers are very important in the case of the model-driven technique since they describe important features of the model-driven environment that affect software productivity. In particular, the TCOV multiplier provides the capability to define and evaluate the coverage of activities undertaken in the software development process by the supporting tools. Furthermore, the TINT multiplier allows defining and evaluating the degree of integration of the tools used throughout the process and the effectiveness in achieving this integration. Finally, the TMAT multiplier allows stating and evaluating the maturity of the adopted toolset on the basis of the time it is used in the market and the technical support provided. This

Table 1. Satisfying the requirements for automating design tools development

	R1 - Abstract Syntax Definition	R2 – Imposing Constraints	R3 - Concrete Syntax Definition	R4 – Design Tools Generation
iMDE	MOF (EMF)	OCL	GMF	EMF, GMF
Borland Together 2008	MOF (EMF)	OCL	GMF	EMF, GMF

extension provides a more comprehensive estimate of the TOOL effort multiplier by calibrating the above (sub-) multipliers using the following equation (Baik et. al., 2002).

$$TOOL = 0.51 \times TCOV + 0.27 \times TINT + 0.22 \times TMAT \quad (3)$$

Prior to performing the calculations using the formal model, we assess the technique in a subjective manner against the requirements introduced in Section 1. Table 1 presents the software capabilities of the iMDE and Borland Together 2008, which satisfy the four necessary requirements for automating the development of design tools. The interesting point is that the same set of software capabilities is supplied by both environments for generating modelling tools. Firstly, the EMF provides a metamodelling language that conforms to the MOF standard and provides the capability to unambiguously define the abstract syntax of the modelling language. Secondly, the OCL specification is used as a common capability to impose the necessary rules that restrict the design

of domain models. In addition, GMF facilitates the definition of the concrete syntax of the language and in conjunction with the EMF support the generation of design tools. It is important to point out that we have developed the prototype design tool using both environments in order to identify the differences in the development process. The dissimilarities identified are limited and have to do mainly with the enhanced graphical user interfaces provided by Borland Together, which eases to some extent the model-driven development tasks. Both environments provide though widely-used software capabilities that conform to the standards and support precisely the necessary development tasks.

Complementing the above subjective evaluation, we have utilised the software cost estimation model to carry out a quantitative assessment of the impact of the model-driven technique on software productivity. Note that the assessment is based on the assumption that developing the product design tool by manual coding, involves writing the same lines of code as in the case of the code generated for the design tool using the

Table 2. Rating scales for completeness of tool coverage

	TCOV
Very Low (1.17)	Text-Based Editor, Basic 3GL Compiler, etc.
Low (1.09)	Graphical Interactive Editor, Simple Design Language, etc.
Nominal (1.00)	Local Syntax Checking Editor, Standard Template Support, Document Generator, Simple Design Tools, etc.
High (0.9)	Local Semantics Checking Editor, Automatic Document Generator, Extended Design Tools, etc.
Very High (0.78)	Global Semantics Checking Editor, Tailorable Automatic Document Generator, Requirement Specification Aids and Analyser with Tracking Capability, etc.
Extra High (N/A)	Groupware Systems, Distributed Asynchronous Requirement Negotiation and Trade-off Tools, etc.

iMDE. Table 2 presents the ratings scales (Baik et. al., 2002) used to derive the TCOV multiplier, which serves as an example of how the rest of the ratings used in the calculations are derived. First, when the design tool is developed using the iMDE the TCOV rating is derived as *"HIGH"* (i.e. TCOV = 0.9) since the core components of the environment support most of the properties defined in this rating scale. For instance, automatic document generation is provided by the EMF component, extended design tools are also provided using the EMF and GMF components and local syntax checking by the GMF component.

By applying the same reasoning the TINT and TMAT sub-multiplier ratings are derived from the corresponding rating scales defined in (Baik et. al., 2002) and applied to Eq.3 to derive the TOOLS effort multiplier. For the iMDE the TINT rating is estimated as *"VERY HIGH"* (i.e. TINT = 0.78) due to the high degree of software tools integration, which is essentially provided by the plug-in architecture of the Eclipse platform. Finally, the TMAT rating is defined as *"VERY HIGH"* (i.e. TMAT = 0.78) due to the maturity of the environment's software tools (i.e. available in the market for more than three years) and the strong, large and experienced modelling community developing and/or using these modelling tools. Consequently, applying these individual sub-ratings in Eq. 3 the calibrated TOOLS rating for the case of using the iMDE is calculated as follows.

$$TOOL_{iMDE} = 0.51 \times 0.9 + 0.27 \times 0.78 + 0.22 \times 0.78 \Rightarrow TOOL_{iMDE} = 0.8412$$

$$TOOL_{Borland} = 0.51 \times 0.78 + 0.27 \times 0.78 + 0.22 \times 0.78 \Rightarrow TOOL_{Borland} = 0.78$$

$$TOOL_{Coding} = 0.51 \times 1.17 + 0.27 \times 1 + 0.22 \times 0.78 \Rightarrow TOOL_{Coding} = 1.0383$$

Using an analogous approach the individual sub-ratings and the calibrated TOOLS rating are calculated (as shown above) for the cases of using Borland Together 2008 and manual coding. For the case of Borland the individual sub-ratings are estimated as *TCOV=0.78, TINT=0.78* and *TMAT=0.78*. The only disparity has to do with the TCOV rating, which is estimated as *"VERY HIGH"*, mainly because of the enhanced front-end of the software tools provided by Borland that simplify the MDD tasks. Finally, in the case of manual coding the individual sub-ratings are estimated as *TCOV=1.17, TINT=1* and *TMAT=0.78*. The TCOV rating is estimated as *"VERY LOW"*, because text-based coding editors are used with basic 3GLs compilers, libraries and debuggers for creating manually the modelling tool; see Table 2. Furthermore, the integration of these software tools is relatively *"HIGH"* in development environments such as Netbeans and Eclipse and the maturity and competence of these software tools is *"VERY HIGH"*, since they are widely-used in the market for many years. Also a strong development and support group exists that evolves the capabilities of these software tools on a constant basis.

Apart from the TOOLS ratings, the ratings for the Scale Factors and the remaining Effort Multipliers included in COCOMO II are derived on the basis of the rating scales provided in (Boehm et. al., 2000). In this chapter, due to space limitations, we only discuss how one example multiplier is derived; i.e. SITE effort multiplier. This multiplier refers to multisite development (as defined by Boehm et. al., 2000) and determines if the members of the development team are collocated and if their communication is highly interactive or not. In the case of BT's development team the multiplier is rated as *"EXTRA HIGH"* (*i.e. SITE=0.80*). This is because the members of the team are collocated and their communication is highly interactive, since email, voice, video conferencing and other communication capabilities are provided. By applying analogous reasoning all individual ratings of the COCOMO II model are derived and applied to equations 1 and 2 to calculate the nominal effort and the time for developing the product design tool. Therefore, using all the estimated ratings the calculations illustrated next are performed for the three individual cases described in this chapter.

(1) – MDD with Borland 2008

$E = 0.91 + [0.01 \times (3.72 + 2.03 + 4.24 + 1.1 + 1.56)] \Rightarrow E = 1.0365$

$PM_{Borland} = 2.94 \times (97.049)^{1.0365} \times [1 \times 0.9 \times (1 \times 1 \times 0.87 \times 1.17 \times 1.34) \times 1 \times 1.07 \ 1 \times 1 \times 0.87 \times 0.85 \times 0.88 \times 0.9 \times 1 \times 0.91 \times 0.91 \times 0.78 \times 0.8 \times 1] \Rightarrow PM_{Borland} = 2.94 \times 114.69 \times 0.4 \Rightarrow$

$PM_{Borland} = 134.88$ Person-Months

$F = 0.28 + 0.2 \times (1.0365 - 0.91) \Rightarrow F = 0.28 + 0.2 \times 0.1265 \Rightarrow F = 0.3053$

$TDEV_{Borland} = 3.67 \times (134.8)^{0.3053} \Rightarrow TDEV_{Borland} = 16.4$ Months

(2) – MDD with the iMDE

$E = 0.91 + [0.01 \times (3.72 + 2.03 + 4.24 + 1.1 + 1.56)] \Rightarrow E = 1.0365$

$PM_{iMDE} = 2.94 \times (97.548)^{1.0365} \times [1 \times 0.9 \times (1 \times 1 \times 0.87 \times 1.17 \times 1.34) \times 1 \times 1.07 \ 1 \times 1 \times 0.87 \times 0.85 \times 0.88 \times 0.9 \times 1 \times 0.91 \times 0.91 \times 0.8412 \times 0.8 \times 1] \Rightarrow PM_{iMDE} = 2.94 \times 115.29 \times 0.427 \Rightarrow$

$PM_{iMDE} = 144.73$ Person-Months

$F = 0.28 + 0.2 \times (1.0365 - 0.91) \Rightarrow F = 0.28 + 0.2 \times 0.1265 \Rightarrow F = 0.3053$

$TDEV_{iMDE} = 3.67 \times (144.73)^{0.3053} \Rightarrow TDEV_{iMDE} = 16.77$ Months

(3) – Manual Coding with IDEs

$E = 0.91 + [0.01 \times (3.72 + 2.03 + 4.24 + 1.1 + 1.56)] \Rightarrow E = 1.0365$

$PM_{Coding} = 2.94 \times (97.548)^{1.0365} \times [1 \times 0.9 \times (1 \times 1 \times 0.87 \times 1.17 \times 1.34) \times 1 \times 1.07 \ 1 \times 1 \times 0.87 \times 0.85 \times 0.88 \times 0.9 \times 1 \times 0.91 \times 0.91 \times 1.0383 \times 0.8 \times 1] \Rightarrow PM_{Coding} = 2.94 \times 115.29 \times 0.53 \Rightarrow$

$PM_{Coding} = 179.65$ Person-Months

$F = 0.28 + 0.2 \times (1.0365 - 0.91) \Rightarrow F = 0.28 + 0.2 \times 0.1265 \Rightarrow F = 0.3053$

$TDEV_{Coding} = 3.67 \times (179.65)^{0.3053} \Rightarrow TDEV_{Coding} = 17.9$ Months

The above calculations illustrate that both the effort and time for developing the prototype design tool are decreased when highly competent model-driven environments are used. In contrast, implementing manually the product design tool increases noticeably the development effort and time. Consequently, this increase in effort and time results in a corresponding increase of the development costs. For instance, if we assume that the Average Monthly Work Rate (AMWR) is $1k then the development cost can be calculated for the individual cases using the following equation:

$$Cost = PM * AMWR \qquad (4)$$

Therefore, the development of the product design tool using the iMDE and Borland Together 2008 incurs costs of $144.73k and $134.88k. On the contrary, higher costs are involved (i.e. $179.65k) when the design tool is implemented manually from scratch. The results depict clearly that the use of a competent model-driven environment that conveys to a systematic model-driven technique benefits the creation of design tools by reducing the development effort, time and cost.

Although the Post-Architecture model is widely-used and calibrated through data obtained from miscellaneous software projects, it still involves a degree of uncertainty and risk mainly due to its parametric inputs. In order to cope with these issues the evaluation introduces a complementary computational method that is based on the model. This is known as the Monte Carlo Simulation method that provides the capability to cope with the uncertainty and lack of knowledge involved when modelling phenomena such as the calculation of the effort, time and cost for the development of software design tools. The simulation is described as a method that computes samples within an input range and generates output data. These data define the probabilities that indicate if a software tool can be developed within a specific time frame and with a corresponding effort and budget involved. In particular, the application of the Monte Carlo Simulation method involves initially the definition of an estimated input range for each Scale Factor and Effort Multiplier using the Microsoft Excel Software Cost Analysis Tool (Lum & Monson 2003). These input ranges are also derived objectively on the basis of the rating scales presented in (Boehm et. al., 2000, Baik et. al., 2002). Hence, with the defined parameter ranges and the software size of the design tool as inputs the Analysis Tool executes a deterministic computation (i.e. using a mathematical formula). This generates a set of output data, which are aggregated into Cumulative Distribution Functions (CDFs) that represent respectively the effort and cost to develop the prototype design tool.

Figure 8 illustrates the CDF graphs generated by the Monte Carlo Simulation method that represent the corresponding effort and cost for developing the prototype design tool using the distinct development environments. The effort CDFs indicate clearly that for the set of computed probabilities the effort devoted to the development of the prototype is less when model-driven environments (i.e. iMDE, Borland Together 2008) are used. Furthermore, the costs CDFs illustrate that the development costs are correspondingly increased when the prototype design tool was manually developed from scratch using code-driven IDEs. In particular, for both CDFs the probable

mean values computed are higher when manually developing the product design tool from scratch.

CONCLUSION

In this chapter we propose a model-driven technique and a supporting environment that demonstrate the benefits of employing MDD for automatically generating competent domain-specific design tools. The actual benefits are determined by a software cost estimation model that allows deriving the positive impact of the model-driven approach on software productivity. A prototype design tool is developed that forms the basis for assessing the impact of the approach with regards to the development effort, time and cost. Apart from the proposed model-driven environment (i.e.

Figure 8. Prototype design tool effort and cost cumulative distribution graphs

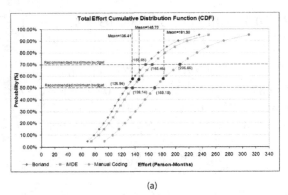

(a)

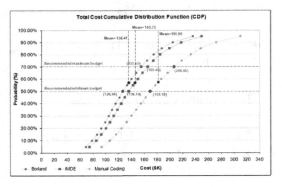

(b)

iMDE), an analogous environment (i.e. Borland Together 2008) is used to develop the prototype design tool. This reveals the necessity of using competent model-driven environments that adhere to a systematic model-driven technique for automating the development of domain-specific design tools. Furthermore, the environments conformance to the MDA specifications is established as another fundamental requirement that enables better understanding of the defined modelling languages and facilitates rapid adoption of the developed domain-specific design tools.

The development of the product design tool using the iMDE and/or Borland Together showcased a reduction in development overheads; i.e. effort, time and cost. In particular, the use of these environments provided an increased automation in software generation, reducing the overheads to a greater extent than what the software cost analysis results indicate; i.e. expected effort is reduced by 19.88%. Nevertheless, the estimated analysis results are suggestive of the positive impact of advanced model-driven tools in rapidly and unambiguously developing domain-specific design tools. For instance, the Figure 8 illustrates that the mean nominal effort is equal to *PM=181.90 Person-Months* and the mean cost is equal to *Cost=$181.90k* when manually implementing the product design tool. In contrast, the nominal effort and cost are significantly reduced when developing the design tool using the iMDE or Borland Together as illustrated also clearly in Figure 8.

As part of future work the extension and/or calibration of the software cost estimation model, so as to address parameters (i.e. Effort Multipliers) that are closely correlated to model-driven software development, will enable the optimisation of the quantitative evaluation method introduced in this chapter. For example, the TOOLS effort multiplier can be extended to include *Code Generation* as a sub-multiplier that affects significantly the estimation on software productivity for model-driven techniques.

REFERENCES

Achilleos, A., Georgalas, N., & Yang, K. (2007). *An open source domain-specific tools framework to support model driven development of OSS*. In ECMDA-FA, (LNCS 4530), (pp. 1 – 16).

Achilleos, A., Yang, K., & Georgalas, N. (2008). A model-driven approach to generate service creation environments. In *Proceedings of the IEEE Globecom, Global Telecommunications Conference,* (pp. 1–6).

Achilleos, A., Yang, K., Georgalas, N., & Azmoodeh, M. (2008). Pervasive dervice vreation using a model driven Petri Net based approach. In *Proceedings of the IEEE International Wireless Communications and Mobile Computing Conference (IWCMC)*, (pp. 309-314).

Afonso, M., Vogel, R., & Texeira, J. (2006). From code centric to model centric software engineering: Practical case study of MDD infusion in a systems integration company. In *Proceedings of the Workshop on Model-Based Development of Computer-Based Systems and International Workshop on Model-Based Methodologies for Pervasive and Embedded Software,* (pp.125-134).

Baik, J., Boehm, B., & Stecee, B. M. (2002). Disaggregating and calibrating the CASE tool variable in COCOMO 2. *IEEE Transactions on Software Engineering, 28*(11), 1009–1022. doi:10.1109/TSE.2002.1049401

Balasubramanian, K., Gokhale, A., Karsai, G., Sztipanovits, J., & Neema, S. (2006). *Developing applications using model-driven design environments. IEEE Computer.* Vanderbilt University.

Boehm, B., Abts, C., Clark, B., Devnani-Chulani, S., Horowitz, E., & Madachy, R. (2000). *COCOMO 2 model definition manual, version 2.1.* Center for Systems and Software Engineering, University of Southern California.

Borland Together Integrated and Agile Design Solutions. (2006). Getting started guide for Borland Together 2006 for Eclipse. Retrieved from http://techpubs.borland.com/together/tec2006/en/GettingStarted.pdf

Chen, Z., Boehm, B., Menzies, T., & Port, D. (2005). Finding the right data for software cost modelling. *IEEE Software, 22*(6), 38–46. doi:10.1109/MS.2005.151

Chonacky, N. (2009). A modern Tower of Babel. *Computing in Science & Engineering, 11*(3), 80. doi:10.1109/MCSE.2009.45

Clark, T., Evans, A., Sammut, P., & Willans, J. (2004). An eXecutable metamodelling facility for domain-specific language design. In *Proceedings of the Object-Oriented Programming, Systems, Languages, and Applications Workshop on Domain-Specific Modelling.*

Deursen, A. V., Klint, P., & Visser, J. (2000). Domain-specific anguages: An annotated bibliography. *ACM SIGPLAN Notices, 35*(6), 26–36.

Emerson, J. M., & Sztipanovits, J. (2004). Implementing a MOF-based metamodelling environment using graph transformations. In *Proceedings of the 4th OOPSLA Workshop on Domain-Specific Modeling.* Retrieved from http://www.dsmforum.org/events/DSM04/emerson.pdf

Evermann, J., & Wand, Y. (2005). Toward formalizing domain modelling semantics in language syntax. *IEEE Transactions on Software Engineering, 31*(1), 21–37. doi:10.1109/TSE.2005.15

Frankel, D. S. (2003). *Model driven architecture: Applying MDA to enterprise computing.* Indianapolis: Wiley Publishing Inc.

Freudenthal, M. (2009). Domain-specific languages in a customs Information System. *IEEE Software, 99*(1), 1–17.

Georgalas, N., Achilleos, A., Freskos, V., & Economou, D. (2009). Agile product lifecycle management for service delivery frameworks: History, architecture and tools. *BT Technology Journal, 26*(2).

Georgalas, N., Ou, S., Azmoodeh, M., & Yang, K. (2007). Towards a model-driven approach for ontology-based context-aware application development: A case study. In *Proceedings of the IEEE 4th International Workshop on Model-based Methodologies for Pervasive and Embedded Software (MOMPES),* (pp. 21-32).

Gerber, A., & Raymond, K. (2003). MOF to EMF: There and back again. In *Proceedings of the OOPSLA Workshop on Eclipse Technology eXchange,* (pp. 60 – 64).

Graaf, B., & Deursen, A. V. (2007). Visualisation of domain-specific modelling languages using UML. In *Proceedings of the Annual IEEE International Conference and Workshops on the Engineering of Computer-Based Systems,* (pp. 586-595).

IBM. (2009). *Eclipse platform technical overview.* Retrieved from http://www.eclipse.org/whitepapers/eclipse-overview.pdf

Iscoe, N., Williams, G. B., & Arango, G. (1991). Domain modelling for software engineering. In *Proceedings of the IEEE International Conference on Software Engineering,* (pp. 340-343).

Kelly, S., & Pohjonen, R. (2009). Worst practices for domain-specific modelling. *IEEE Software, 26*(4), 22–29. doi:10.1109/MS.2009.109

Kleppe, A., Warmer, J., & Bast, W. (2005). *MDA explained: The model driven architecture, practice and promise.* Boston: Addison-Wesley.

Ledeczi, A., Bakay, A., Maroti, M., Volgyesi, P., Nordstrom, G., & Springle, J. (2001). Composing domain-specific design environments. *IEEE Computer, 34*(11), 44–51.

Lum, K., & Monson, E. (2003). *Software cost analysis tool user document*. California: NASA-Jet Propulsion Laboratory Pasadena.

Mohamed, M., Romdhani, M., & Ghedira, K. (2007). EMF-MOF alignment. In *Proceedings of the 3rd International Conference on Autonomic and Autonomous Systems*, (pp. 1 – 6).

Molnár, Z., Balasubramanian, D., & Lédeczi, A. (2007). *An introduction to the generic modelling environment*. Model-driven development tool implementers forum. Retrieved from http://www.dsmforum.org/events/MDD-TIF07/GME.2.pdf

Nytun, J. P., Prinz, A., & Tveit, M. S. (2006). Automatic generation of modelling tools. *In Proceedings of the European Conference on Model-Driven Architecture, Foundations and Applications (ECMDA-FA)* (LNCS 4066), (pp. 268-283).

OMG. (2003). *Model Driven Architecture (MDA) specification guide v1.0.1*. Retrieved from http://www.omg.org/docs/omg/03-06-01.pdf

OMG. (2005). *Meta Object Facility (MOF) core specification v2.0*. Retrieved from http://www.omg.org/docs/formal/06-01-01.pdf.

OMG. (2005). Object Constraint Language (OCL) specification v2.0. Retrieved from http://www.omg.org/docs/formal/06-05-01.pdf

Santos, L. A., Koskimies, K., & Lopes, A. (2008). Automated domain-specific modeling languages for generating framework-based applications. In *Proceedings of the 12th International Conference on Software Product Lines*, (pp. 149-158).

Sprinkle, J., Mernik, M., Tolvanen, J.-P., & Spinellis, D. (2009). What kinds of nails need a domain-specific hammer? *IEEE Software*, *26*(4), 15–18. doi:10.1109/MS.2009.92

Staron, M. (2006). Adopting model driven software development in industry-a case study at two companies. In *Proceedings of the International Conference on Model Driven Engineering Languages and Systems*, (LNCS 4199), (pp. 57-72).

Wirth, N. (2008). A brief history of software engineering. *IEEE Annals of the History of Computing*, *30*(3), 32–39. doi:10.1109/MAHC.2008.33

Zbib, R., Jain, A., Bassu, D., & Agrawal, H. (2006). Generating domain-specific graphical modelling editors from metamodels. In *Proceedings of the Annual IEEE Computer Software and Applications Conference*, (pp. 129-138).

KEY TERMS AND DEFINITIONS

Domain Specific Language(s): A modelling/specification or programming language(s) that describes a specific problem domain and can be used to design domain specific models.

Domain Specific Modelling: Describes a process that raises the level of abstraction by introducing domain models as the prime entities in software development.

Metamodelling: The process that guides the definition of a metamodel, which describes the elements, properties and relationships of a particular modelling domain; i.e. domain specific language.

Model-Driven Development: A software development methodology that focuses on the design and implementation of software applications at an abstract platform-independent level.

Software Cost Model: A mathematical model that provides the capability to estimate/calculate the required time, effort and cost to develop software applications.

Software Productivity: Defines the measure of efficiency, which can be described in terms of time, effort and cost required for the development of software applications.

Software Service Creation: Describes a software development process that deals with the analysis, design, validation and implementation of software services.

Section 6
Parallel Applications and Multicore Software Engineering

Chapter 15
Model–Driven Development of Multi–Core Embedded Software

Shang-Wei Lin
National Chung Cheng University, Taiwan

Chao-Sheng Lin
National Chung Cheng University, Taiwan

Chun-Hsien Lu
National Chung Cheng University, Taiwan

Yean-Ru Chen
National Taiwan University, Taiwan

Pao-Ann Hsiung
National Chung Cheng University, Taiwan

ABSTRACT

Multi-core processors are becoming prevalent rapidly in personal computing and embedded systems. Nevertheless, the programming environment for multi-core processor based systems is still quite immature and lacks efficient tools. This chapter will propose a new framework called VERTAF/Multi-Core (VMC) and show how software code can be automatically generated from high-level SysML models of multi-core embedded systems. It will also illustrate how model-driven design based on SysML can be seamlessly integrated with Intel's Threading Building Blocks (TBB) and Quantum Platform (QP) middleware. Finally, this chapter will use a digital video recording (DVR) system to illustrate the benefits of the proposed VMC framework.

INTRODUCTION

With the proliferation of multi-core architectures (Akhter, 2006) for embedded processors, multi-

DOI: 10.4018/978-1-60960-215-4.ch015

core programming for embedded systems is no longer a luxury. We need embedded software engineers to be adept in programming such processors; however, the reality is that very few engineers know how to program them. The current state-of-the-art technology in multi-core programming is based on the use of language extensions such as OpenMP ("OpenMP," 2008), multi-core Java (Robert Eckstein, 2008) or libraries such as Intel Threading Building Blocks (TBB) (Reinders, 2007), Microsoft® Task Parallel Library (TPL)/ Parallel LINQ (PLINQ) ("Introduction to PLINQ"), (Daan Leijen & Judd Hall, 2007).

OpenMP, multi-core Java, TBB, and TPL/PLINQ are all very useful when programmers are already experts in multithreading and multi-core programming; however, there still exists a tremendous challenge in this urgent transition from unicore systems to multi-core systems. To aid embedded software designers in a smoother transition, we propose a framework that integrates software engineering techniques such as software component reuse, formal software synthesis techniques such as scheduling and code generation, formal verification techniques such as model checking, and multi-core programming technique such as TBB.

Several issues are encountered in the development of the integrated design framework. First and foremost, we need to decide upon an architecture for the framework. Since our goal is to integrate reuse, synthesis, and verification, we need to have greater control on how the final generated application will be structured, thus we have chosen to implement it as an object-oriented application framework (Fayad & Schmidt, 1997), which is a "semi-complete" application, where users fill in application specific objects and functionalities. A major feature is "inversion of control", that is the framework decides on the control flow of the generated application, rather than the designer. Other issues encountered in architecting an application framework for multi-core embedded software are as follows.

1. To allow software component reuse, how do we define the syntax and semantics of a reusable component? How can a designer uniformly and guidedly specify the requirements of a system to be designed? How can

the existing reusable components with the user-specified components be integrated into a feasible working system?

2. What is the control-data flow of the automatic design and verification process? When do we verify and when do we schedule?

3. What kinds of model can be used for each design phase, such as scheduling and verification?

4. What method is to be used for verification? How do we automate the process? What kinds of abstraction are to be employed when system complexity is beyond our handling capabilities?

5. How do we generate portable code that not only crosses operating systems but also hardware platforms. What is the structure of the generated code?

6. How much and what kinds of explicit parallelism must be specified by a software engineer through system modeling? How can we automatically and correctly realize the user-specified models into multi-core embedded software code?

Briefly, our solutions to the above issues can be summarized as follows.

1. **Software Component Reuse and Integration:** A subset of the Systems Modeling Language (SysML) is used with minimal restrictions for automatic design and analysis. Precise syntax and formal semantics are associated with each kind of SysML diagram. Guidelines are provided so that requirement specifications are more error-free and synthesizable.

2. **Control Flow:** A specific control flow is embedded within the framework, where scheduling is first performed and then verification because the complexity of verification can be greatly reduced after scheduling (Hsiung, 2000).

3. **System Models:** For scheduling, we use conventional thread models and TBB task models and for verification, we use Extended Timed Automata (ETA) (Liao & Hsiung, 2003), both of which are automatically generated from user-specified SysML models that follow our restrictions and guidelines.

4. **Design Automation:** For verification, we employ symbolic model checking (Clarke & Emerson, 1981), (Clarke, Grumberg, & Peled, 1999), (Queille & Sifakis, 1982), which generates a counterexample in the original user-specified UML models whenever verification fails for a system under design. The whole design process is automated through the automatic generation of respective input models, invocation of appropriate scheduling and verification kernels, and generating reports or useful diagnostics. For handling complexity, abstraction is inevitable, thus we apply model-based, architecture-based, and function-based abstractions during verification.

5. **Portable Efficient Multi-Layered Code:** For portability, a multi-layered approach is adopted in code generation. To account for performance degradation due to multiple layers, system-specific optimization and flattening are then applied to the portable code. System dependent and independent parts of the code are distinctly segregated for this purpose.

6. **Parallelism:** We take SysML models as input, which contain user specified model-level explicit parallelism, and generate corresponding multi-core embedded software code in C++, which are scheduled and tested for a particular platform such as ARM 11MPCore and Linux OS. The code architecture consists of an OS, the TBB library, the Quantum Platform (QP) for executing concurrent state machines, and the application code.

In summary, this work illustrates how an application framework may integrate all the above proposed design and verification solutions for multi-core embedded software. Our implementation has resulted in a Verifiable Embedded Real-Time Application Framework for Multi-Core Systems (VERTAF/Multi-Core, VMC for short) whose features include formal modeling of real-time embedded systems through well-defined SysML semantics, formal verification that checks if a system satisfies user-given properties or system-defined generic properties, and code generation that produces multi-core embedded software code.

The chapter is organized as follows. Section PREVIOUS WORK describes existing related work. Section VERTAF/MULTI-CORE (VMC) FRAMEWORK describes the proposed VERTAF/Multi-Core (VMC) framework. Section MULTI-CORE CODE GENERATION describes the code generation process in VMC. Section CASE STUDY uses a digital video recording system example to illustrate how VMC achieves automatic multi-core programming using TBB and QP. Finally, section CONCLUSIONS AND FUTURE WORK gives the conclusions with some future work.

PREVIOUS WORK

Though object-oriented technology has been applied to the design of real-time systems in several areas, such as language design (Achauer, 1996), (Bollella, Gosling, Brosgol, Dibble, Furr, & Turnbull, 2000), (Grimshaw, Silberman, & Liu, 1989), (Ishikawa, Tokuda, & Mercer, 1990), verification and analysis (Browne, 1996), (Gergeleit, Kaiser, & Streich, 1996), distributed system design (Hammer, Welch, & Roosmalen, 1996), (Kim, 2000), (Schmidt, 1997), (Selic, 1993), (Selic, 1996), (Selic, Gullekan, & Ward, 1994), and embedded system design (Samek, 2002), (Welch, 1996), there has been very little work on the development of application frameworks for real-time application design. Two known frameworks are Object-Oriented Real-Time System Framework (OORTSF), (Kuan, See, & Chen, 1995), (See & Chen 2000) and SESAG (Hsiung, 1998), which are simple frameworks that have been applied to avionics software development. In these frameworks, some design patterns related to real-time application design were proposed and code automatically is generated. Nevertheless, there are still some scheduling and real-time synchronization issues not addressed such as asynchronous event handling and protocol interfacing. VERTAF (Hsiung, Lin, Tseng, Lee, Fu, & See, 2004) is an enhanced version of SESAG, incorporating software component technology, synthesis, formal verification, and standards such as UML.

Other related toolsets for the design and verification of systems include the B-toolkit ("B-toolkit, B-core (UK) Ltd," 2002), SCR toolset (Heitmeyer, Kirby, Labaw, & Bharadwaj, 1998), NIMBUS (Thompson, Heimdahl, & Miller, 1999), and SCADE Suite ("Esterel Technologies," 2003). The B-toolkit takes abstract machines as system models and applies theorem proving for proof-obligation generation and verification. The SCR toolset uses the SPIN model checker, PVS-based TAME theorem prover, a property checker, and an invariant generator for the formal verification of a real-time embedded system specified using the SCR tabular notation. It supports the generation of test cases through the TVEC toolset. NIMBUS is a specification-based prototyping framework for embedded safety-critical systems. It allows execution of software requirements expressed in RSML with various models of the environment such as physical hardware, RSML models or user input scripts. NIMBUS supports model checking through a variety of model checkers and a framework based on Tame by SCR, as well as theorem proving using PVS. Lustre-based (Halbwachs, Caspi, Raymond, & Pilaud, 1991) SCADE Suite from Esterel Technologies uses Safe State Machines (SSM) for requirement specification

and automatically generates DO-178B Level A ("DO-178B," 1992) compliant and verified C/Ada code for avionics systems. Nondeterminism is not allowed by SSM in SCADE.

Worldwide research projects targeting embedded real-time embedded software design include the MoBIES project ("Intel Core2TM Duo Processors," 2008), (Niz & Rajkumar, 2003), (Wang, Kodase, & Shin, 2002) supported by USA DARPA, the HUGO project (Knapp, Merz, & Rauh, 2002) by Germany's Ludwig-Maximilians-Universität München, the DESS project (Lavazza, 2001) supported by Europe's EUREKA-ITEA, and the TIMES project (Amnell, Fersman, Mokrushin, Petterson, & Wang, 2003) by the Uppsala University of Sweden. In the DARPA supported MoBIES (Model-Based Integration of Embedded Systems) project, there are several subprojects that cover varied parts of the embedded software design process. For example, Kodase et al. (2003) and Wang et al. (2002) proposed AIRES (Automatic Integration of Reusable Embedded Software), which focuses on automatically generating a runtime model from a structural model through several metamodels: software architecture, platform, runtime, and performance metamodels. AIRES has been effectively applied to avionics and automotive applications. Further, de Niz and Rajkumar proposed Time Weaver (Niz & Rajkumar, 2003), which is a software-through-models framework that focuses on capturing para-functional properties into models of different semantic dimensions such as event flow, deployment, timing, fault tolerance, modality, and concurrency.

Knapp et al. have been developing HUGO (Knapp et al., 2002) that focuses on model checking statecharts against collaborations. Code generation is also possible by HUGO, but scheduling is not performed and, thus, the generated code might not satisfy user-specified temporal constraints. The DESS project by EUREKA-ITEA (Lavazza, 2001) is another effort at defining a methodology for the design of real-time and embedded systems, which provides guidelines for incorporating various kinds of tools into the design process and how formal methods may be exploited. Neither real implementation of the concepts nor any toolset is provided by DESS. Lastly, TIMES (Amnell et al., 2003) is a set of tools for the symbolic schedulability analysis and code synthesis of predictable real-time systems. No features of embedded systems are considered in TIMES and the input model is a set of timed automata and not the engineer-friendly UML model.

VERTAF/Multi-Core (VMC) is an extension of VERTAF (Hsiung et al., 2004), which is a UML-based application framework for embedded real-time software design and verification. VERTAF is an integration of software component-based reuse, formal synthesis, and formal verification. It takes three types of extended UML models (Rumbaugh, Booch, & Jacobson, 1999), namely Class Diagrams with deployments, timed statecharts, and extended sequence diagrams. The sequence diagrams are translated into Power-Aware Real-Time Petri Nets and then scheduled for low power design along with satisfaction of memory constraints. The timed statecharts are translated into Extended Timed Automata (ETA) and model checked using the SGM (State Graph Manipulators) model checker. The class diagram and the statecharts are used for code generation.

VERTAF differs from academic research-oriented project application frameworks and from commercial code generating frameworks mainly in the following aspects.

1. **System Models:** In contrast to the use of ad hoc system models, VERTAF uses standard models such as UML with stereotype extensions for design specification, Petri nets for synthesis, and extended timed automata for verification, which allow compatibility with other tools.

2. **Formal Synthesis:** Synthesis consists of two phases: scheduling and code generation. Commercial and academic application frameworks either rely on manual refine-ments or automatically generate embedded software code without guarantee on satisfaction of temporal or spatial constraints, whereas VERTAF tries to find a schedule that satisfies user-defined timing constraints. If no feasible schedule exists, VERTAF illustrates the location of constraint violations in the original user-specified UML diagrams.

3. **Formal Verification:** Commercial tools due to product marketing strategies and academic application frameworks due to lack of interdiscipline expertise normally leave the verification of generated embedded code to the user who invokes another tool for verification. The problem is that there is a gap between design and verification and this causes problems when some design errors are detected in verification, but cannot be easily illustrated in the original design models. Consequently, VERTAF has a built-in model checker to solve the problems aforementioned.

The Unified Modeling Language (UML) (Rumbaugh et al., 1999) is an industry de-facto standard language used for designing software from various application domains, including embedded systems. UML allows software designers to visualize, and document models of their software. In order to analyze, design, and verify complex systems, an extension of UML called the OMG System Modeling Language (SysML) ("SysML. (n.d.)") was recently proposed. SysML reuses several components from UML and extends the system requirements model by supporting more diagrams, such as requirement and parametric diagrams where the former is used for requirements engineering and the latter is used for performance analysis and quantitative analysis. Thus, in this work, instead of using UML as in VERTAF, we have started to adopt SysML as our modeling language in VMC.

In VERTAF, formal ETA models are generated automatically from user-specified SysML models by a flattening scheme that transforms each state machine into a set of one or more ETA. The three types of states in state machine are mapped into ETA entities as follows: Each basic state is mapped to an ETA state. An OR-state is mapped to the set of ETA states corresponding to the states within the OR-state and additional ETA transitions are added to account for state machine transitions that cross hierarchy levels. An AND-state is mapped to two or more concurrent ETA corresponding to the parallelism in the AND-state. Labels are used for synchronizing the concurrent ETA. Details on the hierarchy flattening scheme can be found in (Knapp et al., 2002), (Lavazza, 2001). Clock variables and constraints appearing in state machine can be directly copied to ETA. For a time-out value of *TO* on a transition *t* of a state machine, a temporary clock variable x is used to represent a corresponding timer. Variable x is reset on all incoming ETA transitions to the mapped source state of *t*. A time invariant $x \leq TO$ is added to the mapped source state of *t*. A triggering condition $x = TO$ is added to the ETA transition that corresponds to *t*.

VERTAF uses the Quantum Platform (QP) (Quantum Leaps, 2010) for embedded software code generation because QP provides programmers designing well-structured embedded applications which are a set of concurrency executing hierarchical state machines. QP also helps to rapidly implement software in an object-oriented fashion. A SysML state machine can be implemented by a QP Active Object. Based on the programming principles and APIs provided by QP, VERTAF translates a system modeled by a user with UML state machines into C/C++ embedded software code. The generated code based on QP framework is lightweight and easily portable across different embedded software platforms.

TBB is a library, expressing parallelism in a C++ program, which helps us to leverage multi-core processor performance without having to be a threading expert. It represents a higher-level, task-based parallelism that abstracts platform details and threading mechanisms for performance and scalability. TBB realizes the concept of scalability in writing efficient scalable programs, i.e. a program can benefit from the increasing number of processor cores. Nevertheless, it requires expertise in parallel programming before a software engineer can correctly apply the different parallel programming interfaces provided by TBB. TBB tasks are the basic logical units of computation. The library provides a task scheduler, which is the engine that drives the algorithm templates. The scheduler maps the TBB tasks onto TBB threads. The scheduler tries to trade off between memory demands and cross-thread communication by evaluating the task graph which is a directed graph. The node in the task graph represents task, and the edge from the node points to the task's parent task waiting for its completion or NULL task. The scheduler processes the tasks in a task graph in two ways, including the depth-first and breadth-first executions, which can be seen as sequential execution and concurrent execution, respectively. The breadth-first scheduling consumes more memory than the depth-first scheduling. The scheduler also performs task stealing when a thread's task queue is empty. The task stealing strategy achieves better load balancing among cores.

Multi-core architectures are becoming more and more pervasive such as ARM's Cortex-A9 MPCore ("ARM Cortex-A9 MPCore," 2008), Intel's Core™ 2 Duo E4300, T7500, T7400, L7500, L7400, U7500, Quad-Core Intel Xeon Processor E5300 series ("Intel Quad-Core Xeon Processor 5300 Series," 2008). This makes multi-core programming more and more important. The current state-of-the-art technologies in multicore programming are OpenMP, multi-core Java, Intel *Threading Building Blocks* (TBB), and TPL/PLINQ.

VERTAF/MULTI-CORE (VMC) FRAMEWORK

Software synthesis in VMC is defined as a two-phase process: a machine-independent software

Figure 1. VMC overall flow

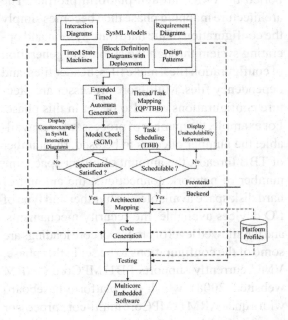

construction phase and a machine-dependent software implementation phase. This separation helps us plug-in different target languages, middleware, real-time operating systems, and hardware device configurations. We call the two phases as front-end and backend phases as illustrated in Figure 1. The front-end phase is further divided into three sub-phases, namely SysML modeling phase, multi-core embedded software scheduling phase, and formal verification phase. There are three sub-phases in the back-end phase, namely architecture mapping, code generation, and testing. We describe these sub-phases in detail in this section.

SysML Modeling

The Systems Modeling Language (SysML) is a general-purpose modeling language for systems engineering applications. It is defined as an extension of a subset of the Unified Modeling Language (UML). After scrutiny of all diagrams in SysML, we have chosen four diagrams for a user to input as system specification models, namely requirement diagram, extended interaction diagram, block definition diagram, and timed state machine. The four diagrams are restricted, as well as, enhanced for modeling multi-core embedded software.

1. **Requirement Diagram:** For multi-core embedded systems, a designer can specify the functional or non-functional requirements of his/her system such as the encoding or streaming rates in terms of the number of video frames per second for a multimedia system.
2. **Extended Interaction Diagram:** Interaction diagrams are mapped to formal Petri net models for scheduling.
3. **Block Definition Diagram with Hardware Deployment:** On a block definition diagram a deployment relation is used for specifying the deployment of a software object on a hardware object.
4. **Timed State Machine:** State machines are extended with real-time clocks that can be reset and values checked for state transition triggering.

Parallel design patterns can be modeled by the four SysML models. In VMC, some predefined parallel design patterns such as parallel pipeline, parallel tasks, and parallel loops are provided such that system designers can use them to model parallelism in his/her system.

Thread/Task Mapping and Scheduling

Each state machine is mapped to an active object in QP. Design patterns for multi-core programming are mapped to parallel tasks and task graphs in the TBB terminology. The QP active objects and TBB tasks are all executed by user-level pthreads, which are then mapped one-to-one to the Linux OS kernel threads. The threads associated to QP active objects are scheduled by the POSIX library, and the TBB threads are scheduled by the TBB library along with thread migration among different cores for load balancing.

Formal Verification

VERTAF employs the popular model checking paradigm for formal verification of multi-core embedded software. In VMC, formal ETA models are generated automatically from user-specified SysML models by a flattening scheme that transforms each state machine into a set of one or more ETA, which are merged, along with the scheduler ETA generated in the scheduling phase, into a state-graph. The verification kernel used in VMC is adapted from State Graph Manipulators (SGM) (Wang & Hsiung, 2002), which is a high-level model checker for real-time systems that operate on state-graph representations of system behavior through manipulators, including a state-graph merger, several state-space reduction techniques, a dead state checker, and a CTL model checker.

We have also modeled real-time task scheduling, task migration between processor cores, and several load balancing policies into the SGM model checker, which is used in VMC to formally verify the automata models by combining simulation and model checking techniques to evaluate the system performance. The methodology is proposed in (Tsao, 2008).

Architecture Mapping

Hardware classes specified in the deployments of the SysML block definition diagram are sup-ported by VMC through platform profiles. The architecture mapping phase then becomes simply the configuration of the hardware system and operating system through the automatic generation of configuration files, make files, header files, and dependency files. Multi-core processor architecture configurations can also be set in this phase. For example, the number of processor cores available, the number of cores to be used, the number of TBB threads, the amount of buffer space, the number of network connections, the amount of hard disk space available, the number and type of I/O devices available, the security mechanisms, and the allowed level of processor core loadings are some of the configurations to be set in this phase. VMC currently supports PB11MPCore ("ARM website," 2008), which is a platform baseboard with a quad ARM11MPCore multi-core processor running the Linux OS.

Code Generation

As shown in Figure 2, we adopt a multi-tier approach for code generation: an application layer, a middleware layer (Quantum Platform), a multi-core threading library layer (TBB), an operating system layer, and a multi-core platform layer. Since both QP and TBB are very small in size and very efficient in performance, they are quite suitable for real-time embedded system software implementation. Later in this section, we will discuss the TBB

Figure 2. VMC code architecture

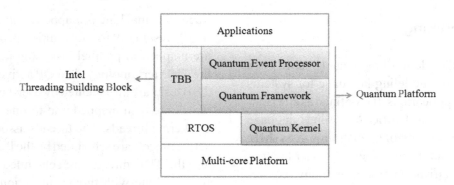

task model and how we mapped it into VMC. In the operating system layer, we adopt Linux as our target operating system. VMC currently supports PB11MPCore and Intel's processor architecture running the Linux OS.

Testing

After the multi-core embedded software code is generated, the code needs to be tested for several purposes, such as functional validation, non-functional evaluation, and race condition detection. A remote debugging environment is used to perform testing, monitoring test results, and checking if the cross-compiled code running on the target system works as expected and satisfies all the user-specified requirements. Of course the code instrumentation is required after the code generation, and the information required by testing is transmitted from network socket interface or debugging port, such as UART, in terms of the target platform's architecture.

MULTI-CORE CODE GENERATION

A typical embedded system consists of input units such as sensors or devices, computation units such as encoders, transformers, or decoders, and output units such as actuators or network devices. Multi-core embedded systems are typically computation and/or communication intensive, because otherwise there is no need for powerful multi-core processors. In VMC, a multi-core embedded system application is specified by a set of SysML models. To alleviate the burden of application designers, VMC supports model-driven development in two ways. First, VMC provides abstract architecture models of multi-core computing along with real-time task scheduling such as rate monotonic first and earliest deadline first (Liu & Layland, 1973) and load balancing mechanisms such as task migration among cores. Second, VMC also supports parallel design patterns such as parallel pipeline to

hide latency, parallel loop to reduce latency, and parallel tasks to increase throughput. These design patterns correspond exactly to the three real-world concurrency issues (Cantrill & Bonwick, 2008), including reducing latency, hiding latency, and increasing throughput. By concurrent execution of a unit of work, the systems can reduce latency. Systems can hide latency by continue doing work when there is a long-latency operation. As to increasing throughput, we can make the systems doing more works concurrently.

Task and Thread Models

In the operating system terminology, the terms task and thread have been used interchangeably. For example, the basic unit of computation in the Linux OS is task, while it is a thread in the Windows OS. However, in VMC, we adopt the TBB terminology, that is, a task is a computation job that obeys the run-to-completion semantics, while a thread is a basic unit of computation that can be assigned a task to execute.

In TBB, an application is represented by a task graph. The tasks that are ready are assigned by a task scheduler for execution by threads from a thread pool. The scheduler performs breadth first execution to increase parallelism and depth first execution to reduce resource usage. TBB thus hides the complexity of native threads by addressing common performance issues of parallel programming such as load balancing and task migration.

The task and thread models of TBB are quite generic and are suitable for general-purpose computing. However, for embedded systems we need to satisfy real-time constraints, thus we need to have threads that are devoted for specific tasks such as the input sensing, the computation, and the actuator outputs. The task/thread model in VMC consists of the following three parts:

1. **User-Level Pthreads:** The POSIX threads are devoted threads, that is, unlike TBB threads, they are never reused for execut-

ing other tasks. There are two uses of such Pthreads in VMC as follows:

a. To execute the user-specified state machines (represented by QP active objects)

b. To execute conventional legacy parallel tasks such as the tasks forked by a concurrent TCP server.

The Pthreads are scheduled by the POSIX thread library scheduler using default scheduling algorithms such as FIFO or round robin or user-defined scheduling algorithms.

2. **User-Level TBB threads:** These are the threads maintained by the TBB scheduler. They can be reused and migrated across different cores. The TBB threads are scheduled by the TBB threading library using a nonpreemptive unfair scheduling approach that trades-off between depth first execution and breadth first execution of tasks on the task graph, which are ready for execution.

3. **Kernel-Level OS threads:** Each of the above user-level threads, including POSIX and TBB, is mapped to a kernel thread of the underlying OS such as Linux in VMC. The kernel threads are scheduled by the OS scheduler using a preemptive priority-based scheduling algorithm.

Model and Code-Level Parallelism

As introduced at the beginning of Section MULTI-CORE CODE GENERATION, the three real-world concurrency issues include latency hiding, latency reduction, and throughput increasing. The corresponding solutions are parallel pipeline, parallel loop, and parallel tasks, respectively. TBB supports all of these solutions with certain restrictions such as the parallel loop is supported only in four forms, namely parallel_for, parallel_reduce, parallel_scan, and parallel_while. Since VMC generates code based on the QP and

TBB APIs, all of the three corresponding solutions are supported at the code level. However, the main issue to be addressed here is how and what kinds of parallelism to allow application designers to specify at the model level.

The following approach is adopted in VMC. VMC provides a UML profile to support parallel design patterns such that users can apply stereotype tags to SysML models. Currently, VMC users can apply the following sets of stereotype tags:

1. <<pipeline>> to a transition in the state machine model

2. <<serial_filter>>, <<parallel_filter>> to a function invocation on a state transition, where a filter is the TBB terminology for a pipeline stage

3. <<parallel_for>>, <<parallel_reduce>>, <<parallel_scan>>, <<parallel_while>> to a method or a part of a method

4. <<parallel_tasks>> to a method, and <<task>> to a part of a method

Using this parallel design pattern profile, VMC thus bridges the gap between model-level and code-level parallelism. Application designers are required to explicitly specify parallelism at the model level because the designers know best what to parallelize and what not to. VMC alleviates the burden of parallel programming through automatic code generation. Designers have to only tag the models with the above stereotypes and VMC takes care of the rest.

Code Generation

VMC generates multi-core embedded software code automatically from the user-specified SysML state machine models. As introduced in Section VERTAF/MULTI-CORE (VMC) FRAMEWORK, the code leverages two existing open-source software code, including the Quantum Platform (QP) and the Intel Threading Building Blocks (TBB) library. QP is a set of application programming interfaces implemented in C++ for executing hierarchical state machines. TBB is a user-level thread library that helps programmers avoid the tedious job of thread management across multiple processor cores. QP has a very small footprint and TBB is a very lightweight library, thus they are both quite suitable for embedded systems that have constrained physical resources such as memory space and computation power.

VMC realizes each SysML state machine as a QP active object by generating code that invokes the QP APIs for states, transitions, and communication events. Each active object is executed by a user-level Pthread that maps to a kernel thread in the Linux OS. Within an active object, each do method that is executed in a state, is encapsulated as a TBB task or a TBB task graph depending on the complexity of the method and its ability to be parallelized. Thus, there are basically two sets of user-level threads, namely Pthreads and TBB threads.

The distinction between these two sets of threads is mainly due to the requirement of UML state machines to satisfy the run-to-completion (RTC) semantics. The RTC semantics is required by both the do methods in a QP active object and a TBB task. A QP active object cannot be modeled as a TBB task because the active object never terminates execution and thus will violate the RTC semantics if it is a TBB task. Hence, a devoted user-level Pthread is used instead.

Another effect of the RTC semantics is that whenever there is an indefinite polling of some I/O devices such as a remote controller, that is, the polling task never terminates, then the polling task can neither be a QP do_method nor a TBB task because otherwise the RTC semantics will be violated. VMC addresses this issue by modeling such polling tasks as an independent state machine with a single state, a self-looping transition, and a single triggering event such as data input. Since the specific state machine need not do anything else, it waits on the single event and thus there is no need to follow the RTC semantics, which

is required only if there is more than one type of event incoming to a state machine.

In Section CASE STUDY, we will use a real-world application example to illustrate the various strategies employed in VMC as described in this section.

CASE STUDY: DIGITAL VIDEO RECORDING (DVR) SYSTEM

We use a real-world example called Digital Video Recording (DVR) system to illustrate how VMC works and the benefits of applying VMC to multi-core embedded software development. DVR is a real-time multimedia system that is typically used in concurrent remote monitoring of multiple sites. The DVR server can perform both real-time and on-demand streaming of videos to multiple clients simultaneously. Several digital video cameras provide the input for real-time video streaming and previously recorded videos are stored for on-demand streaming. We chose DVR as an illustration example because there is not only task parallelism, but also data parallelism and data flow parallelism in the system.

The overall architecture of DVR is illustrated in Figure 3, which shows that DVR has two subsystems, namely Parallel Video Encoder (PVE) and Video Streaming Server (VSS). PVE is responsible for collecting videos from multiple cameras and encoding them into more compressed data format such as MPEG. VSS is responsible for allowing connections from multiple Remote Monitor Clients (RMC), servicing the clients with status information, real-time video streams, on-demand video streams, and storing the encoded video streams in large video databases.

In the rest of this section, we will describe how task parallelism, data parallelism, and data flow parallelism, i.e., parallel pipeline, are automatically realized in the embedded software code generated from user-specified models of the PVE. We will also describe how conventional thread

Figure 3. Architecture of digital video recording (DVR) system

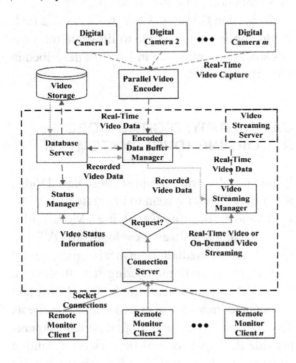

Figure 4. Encoding flow of parallel video encoder (PVE)

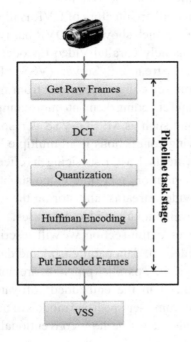

parallelism is integrated into the embedded software code generated from user-specified models of the VSS. Finally, we will summarize on the amount of software components generated by VMC for the DVR system.

Parallel Video Encoder (PVE)

The PVE subsystem has three functions including the capturing of raw video data from all digital cameras, the encoding of the raw video from each camera into more compressed data format for efficient network transmission and for smaller storage space requirement, and the transmission of the encoded video data to the buffer manager in the VSS subsystem. Figure 5 illustrates the state machine model for PVE, which consists of two state machines. Two separate state machines are used because of the need to satisfy RTC semantics. Camera polling is an infinite loop which violates the RTC semantics introduced in Section MULTI-CORE CODE GENERATION. Thus, an independent single-state state machine called Video Capture is used to model the infinite loop in PVE.

We now use an example to illustrate the mapping between model and code via several snippets

Figure 5. State machines of the parallel video encoder (PVE)

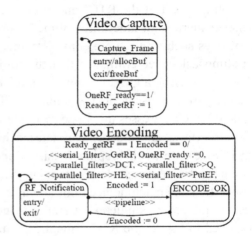

of code that are generated according to the state machine model of SysML. As illustrated in Figure 5, the PVE subsystem model consisting of two state machines, namely Video Capture and Video Encoding. Video Capture model has only one state, namely *Capture_Frame*. The state machine keeps polling the I/O of digital camera devices and stores the raw video frame in a buffer, and then notifies the state machine, Video Encoding, to process the raw video frame. The Video Encoding state machine has two states, namely *RF_Notification* and *ENCODE_OK*. The code generated by VMC using QP API is as follows for the Video Encoding state machine.

```
class Video_Encoding: public QActive
{
public:
PVEEncoding();
~PVEEncoding();
protected:
void initial(QEvent const *e);
QSTATE RF_Notification(QEvent const
*e);
QSTATE ENCODE_OK (QEvent const *e);
private:
/*member functions and data are de-
clared here*/
};
```

The class, *Video_Encoding*, inherits the *QActive* class from the QP library and can be used to realize the state machine. The two states, *RF_Notification* and *ENCODE_OK*, are realized by the QP class, *QSTATE*. PVE is a very good illustration example for all the three issues of real-world concurrency as described in the rest of this section.

Task Parallelism

Capturing and processing video from each camera is an independent task. However, due to the requirement of RTC semantics in UML and QP, as described in Section MULTI-CORE CODE GENERATION, we need to segregate the capture and the processing of the video into two different state machines as illustrated in Figure 5. The video capture state machine is devoted to capturing video from a camera, while the video encoding state machine performs the real-time encoding of video. Thus, for a set of n cameras, there are $2n$ QP active objects that are executed by $2n$ Pthreads.

Data Parallelism

Since video data is composed of a large number of frames and the encoding process is iteratively applied to a data block of 8×8 pixels in a frame, there is a high degree of data parallelism in video encoding. Further, since the color model of the video in DVR is RGB, with 8-bits per pixel color, the encoding process can be parallelized into a multiple of 3, that is, one set of threads for each of the three colors. For example, a frame size of 640×480 pixels consists of $80 \times 60 \times 3 = 14400$ data blocks of 8×8 pixels. Thus, the maximum data parallelism in encoding this video will be 14, 400. However, this might consume too much system resources and cause more timing overhead than the time saved through parallelization (latency reduction). The minimum data parallelism could be 3 for this video as one thread can be used for each color. A tradeoff between parallelism and resource usage is required to achieve high system efficiency.

In the method for encoding, the stereotypes *<<parallel_for>>*, *<<parallel_while>>*, *<<parallel_task>>*, *<<task>>* can all be used for parallelizing the video encoding method.

Data Flow Parallelism

Besides the task parallelism for multiple camera video inputs and the data parallelism for multiple data blocks within each frame, we can also apply data flow parallelism to PVE because the video encoding process applied to each data block is

Figure 6. Class diagram for the TBB pipeline in PVE

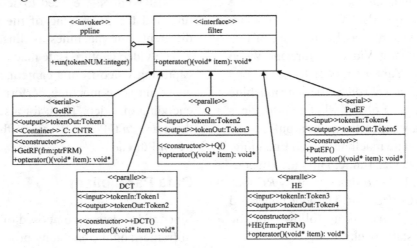

itself a sequence of functions. For most multimedia standards such as MPEG, the sequence of functions consists of Discrete Cosine Transform (DCT), Quantization (Q), and Huffman Encoding (HE) as shown in Figure 6, which results in lossy compression of data. This sequence of functions can be parallelized as a pipeline to hide latency such that more than one data block is processed at any time instant.

In Figure 5, note how data flow parallelism is specified by a designer through the three stereotypes: <<pipeline>>, <<serial filter>>, and <<parallel filter>>. The encoding pipeline in PVE has two serial filters, namely GetRF that gets and decomposes a raw frame for parallel processing by the parallel filters and PutEF that collects all encoded data blocks and composes an encoded frame for transmission to the video buffer. The other three parallel filters in PVE pipeline are responsible for computing in parallel the functions: DCT, quantization, and Huffman encoding. For each pipeline stereotype, users need to specify a class diagram as illustrated in Figure 6 that includes information for all filters, while the sequence of the filters is specified by the sequence of stereotypes appearing on a state machine transition. A template is provided through a design pattern for

the pipeline. Users instantiate the pipeline class which consists of two or more filter classes.

The code generated for the pipeline is as follows:

```
tbb::task_scheduler_init init; /*
initialize TBB libraries*/
tbb::pipeline ppline;          /* in-
stantiate pipeline class*/
_GetRF __GetRF(&container);    /*
instantiate __GetRF filter*/
_DCT __DCT();                  /*
instantiate __DCT filter*/
_Q __Q();                      /* in-
stantiate __Q filter*/
_HE __HE();                    /*
instantiate __HE filter*/
_PutEF __PutEF();              /*
instantiate __PutEF filter*/
ppline.add_filter(__GetRF);    /* Add
filters to pipeline*/
ppline.add_filter(__DCT);
ppline.add_filter(__Q);
ppline.add_filter(__HE);
ppline.add_filter(__PutEF);
ppline.run(numToken);          /* run
pipeline*/
ppline.clear();                /*
```

```
clear pipleline resources*/
```

Firstly, the code generator initializes the TBB environment for the pipeline and then instantiates the pipeline. Subsequently, the code generator instantiates and initializes the filters that are specified in the state machine, including the __GetRF, __DCT, __Q, __HE, and __PutEF filters, and then adds these filters to the pipeline.

The code for the GetRF filter is as follows.

```
class _GetRF:public tbb::filter{
Token1 tokenOut;
CNTR          C;
public:
_GetRF(usertype*
ptrBuffer):filter(serial){
C = ptrBuffer;
}
void* GetRF(void* item){//user manual
code};
void* operator(void* itme){
Token1* tokenOut =
<static_case>(Token1*)GetRF(null);
return tokenOut;
}
};
```

The class, *_GetRF*, inherits the *filter* class provided by TBB, with the keyword serial used in the constructor for initialization. Users have to write the code in the member function *Operator()* to process data according to their objectives for the filter. For the parallel filter, the argument of parent constructor is the keyword parallel.

VIDEO STREAMING SERVER (VSS)

We use the Video Streaming Server (VSS) subsystem as a typical example of how conventional or legacy multithreaded software can be integrated into the VMC framework such that the integration between the threads in legacy multi-threaded soft-

ware, the POSIX threads for executing QP active objects, and the TBB threads work together seamlessly. The main functions of the (VSS) include (a) accepting multiple connections from remote clients, (b) streaming multiple real-time videos and/or on-demand videos to the remote clients, (c) providing requested server status information to the remote clients, and (d) recording the encoded videos into storage devices. The architecture of the VSS subsystem is shown in Figure 7 and the functionalities of each component in VSS are described as follows.

Task Parallelism

Legacy threads are simply multiple threads that exist in legacy software. This is illustrated in the Connection Server (CS) and the Video Streaming Server (VSM).

The connection server is responsible for handling connections and invoking services corresponding to multiple client requests. Traditionally,

Figure 7. Architecture of video streaming server (VSS)

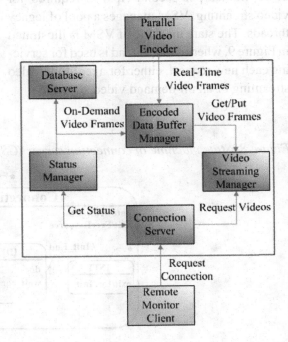

this has almost always been implemented as an iterative or concurrent TCP server using either the select or the fork mechanism. The state machine for the connection server is shown in Figure 8. In the DISPATCH state, the server simply forks a new thread for servicing a new request from a client. The threads that are forked from the concurrent TCP server are what we call legacy threads. It is simply unreasonable to forsake well-established proven concurrent artifacts such as a concurrent TCP server. This example shows that the VMC framework does not force one to model everything for TBB or QP. Another reason for not applying the TBB principle here is that the parallelism is explicitly designed into the system and it is required for providing real-time services to the clients.

The video streaming manager (VSM) is also a typical concurrent manager that creates new streams at run-time to serve client requests. Due to quality-of-service (QoS) requirements, the manager simply forks new threads to serve new requests. A thread pool is managed for efficiency so that thread creation and destruction are avoided at run time. In DVR, because a minimum QoS of 15 frames per second (fps) is required for video streaming, VSM manages a pool of legacy threads. The state machine of VSM is illustrated in Figure 9, where a new thread is used for servicing each new request, either for a real-time video streaming or an on-demand video streaming.

TBB Tasks/Threads

The VMC framework uses TBB tasks mainly for two reasons as follows: (a) A job is parallelizable, but there are no real-time constraints, or (b) A job is parallelizable, but the underlying hardware device is not. The first case is illustrated by the Status Manager (SM) and the second case by the Database Server (DS) and the Encoded Data Buffer Manager (EDBM). Note that the EDBM also utilizes multiple QP threads for executing concurrent states.

The status manager retrieves the list of recorded video files and the list of on-line digital video cameras from the database server and passes the

Figure 9. State machine of video streaming manager (VSM)

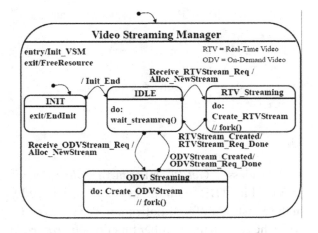

Figure 8. State machine of connection server (CS)

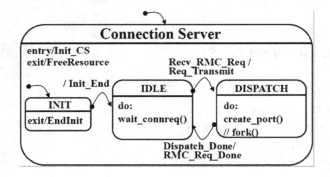

information to remote clients. Though there are multiple incoming requests, there are no real-time constraints and the workload is very light, thus there is no need for devoted threads, instead, VMC realizes these jobs as TBB tasks which can be executed by the TBB scheduler using a set of TBB threads. The stereotype <<parallel_task>> is used to specify request servicing as a set of parallel TBB tasks.

The database server provides recorded video files to VSM upon client requests and allows storing of real-time video data from EDBM. Multiple clients request and multiple camera video inputs require the database server to be a concurrent one. However, since DVR considers a single hard-disk for database storage, allowing multiple devoted threads for each read and write request is unnecessary because ultimately all the requests must be serialized by the OS disk scheduler. Instead, VMC maps such read and write jobs as TBB tasks. Parallelism is still needed so that the disk accesses can be made efficient through the OS disk scheduler.

The encoded data buffer manager (EDBM) is responsible for buffering the video streams including both the real-time ones from the PVE and the stored ones from the database server. In the case of real-time videos, EDBM buffers the video data, sends them to the database for storage and future retrieval, and also sends them to the remote clients through VSM. Since the EDBM buffers are physically located in the main memory which usually has a single access port, all memory accesses are, in fact, serialized at the lowest level. Thus, similar to the database server, multiple devoted threads are also unnecessary and VMC realizes these memory accesses as TBB tasks with TBB synchronization mechanisms. However, unlike the single QP thread for the database server, EDBM has a concurrent state, as shown in Figure 10, and thus two QP threads are required: one for sending the real-time videos to the database and another for sending buffered videos to VSM.

REMOTE MONITOR CLIENT (RMC)

The remote monitor client (RMC) allows users to interact with the DVR server through a graphical user interface in the following ways: (a) acquiring the status information of the DRV server, (b) real-time video streaming, (c) on-demand video

Figure 10. State machine of encoded data buffer manager (EDBM)

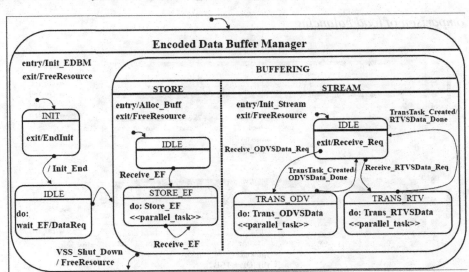

streaming, and (d) debugging and testing. The RMC can also used to gather the server performance statistics for improving the video streaming QoS guarantees.

EXPERIMENT RESULT

Due to issues in porting the TBB library to the PB11MPCore platform, we have currently implemented the DVR system on an Intel machine with a Core2 Quad Q6600 2.4 GHz CPU and 2GB RAM. Performance and load-balancing are evaluated in this experiment. Two different versions of DVR implementation are compared. One version is implemented using QP only, and the other version is implemented using both TBB and QP. Several parameters are also used to configure our experiments, which are the number of cores, the number of connections for real-time video streaming, the number of digital cameras, and the capture rate of raw videos.

Before going into the experiments, we first introduce you the environment setup and some limitations of our applications. The Intel machine has totally 4 cores, and a Linux OS is installed on it. The DVR systems can support at most 2 digital cameras for concurrent video encoding and

at most 4 network connections for current video streaming. The digital cameras are USB video class (UVC) compliant. We also observed at the following important measurement when testing and evaluating our system, consisting of core utilization, raw video capture rate, video encoding rate, encoding buffer usage, and video streaming rate. We store the information in the Linux file system. A monitor and code instrumentation help to gather the information from the target machine. Of course most of embedded systems does not have file systems, but these information can still be transmitted from debug port, such as URT, or network socket infteraces.

In the first experiment, we focus on load-balancing of processor cores. We compared the two implementation versions with a configuration of 4 cores, 1 real-time streaming, 2 cameras, and 16~20 frame per second (fps) capture rate. As shown in Figure 11, in the QP+TBB version, load balancing among processor cores is achieved through the random stealing in TBB.

In the second experiment, we measured the performance of DVR in terms of the frame encoding rate in frames per second (fps). The configuration of this experiment is the same as in the first experiment. As illustrated in Figure 12, the average encoding rate of QP only version is 12 fps,

Figure 11. Comparison of load balancing

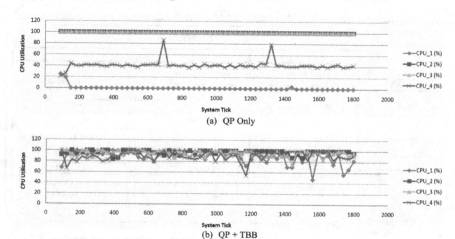

(a) QP Only

(b) QP + TBB

Figure 12. Performance of encoding rate

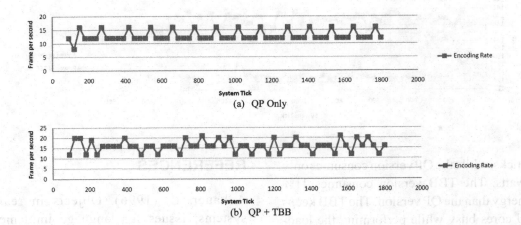

(a) QP Only

(b) QP + TBB

while the average encoding rate in the TBB version is about 16 fps. The performance of TBB version is 1.33 faster than the QP only version. The superior performance in the TBB version is due to the TBB parallel pipeline code generated by VMC into the TBB version of DVR after the designer associated a pipeline stereotype to the PVE state machine. In the TBB pipeline concurrent tasks are used to process (encode) more than one block of a raw frame at the same time. Thus, TBB pipeline reduces the time for encoding each raw image frame.

We then experimented with different comparisons of the second experiment such as reducing the number of cores from four to two and three. We realized this by limiting all the QP and TBB threads to use only two or three cores through the Linux system call, that is sched_setaffinity. With three cores, the average encoding rate of the QP version was still 12 fps, but that of the TBB version dropped to 6.13 fps. With two cores, the encoding rate of the QP version dropped to 9.78 fps, and that of the TBB version was 6.58 fps. We can observe that the less the number of cores used, the worse is the performance provided by TBB, due to TBB introduces the overhead of splitting and merging parallel tasks. The phenomenon is more obvious when the number of cores is reduced. As for the streaming rate all experiments, the streaming rate was consistent with the encoding rate, because the streaming tasks are I/O bound.

The third experiment shows the power consumption of the QP and TBB versions. We evaluated the power consumption according to the core utilization. We adopted the power model proposed by Lien et.al. (2007), and represented by the following equation

$$P = D + (M - D) \cdot \alpha \cdot U^{\beta}$$

where P represents the average power consumption in Watts, and D represents the base power consumption in Watts when core is idle, M represents the full-load power consumption in Watts, U is for the core utilization, and α and β are platform-specific parameters set to be 1 and 0.5, respectively. We also set D to 69 Watts and M to 142 Watts according to the power measurement of our target platform. The configuration of this experiment is the same to the first one with 4 core, 1 real-time streaming, 2 cameras, and capture rate of 16 to 20 fps.

As shown in Figure 13, the TBB version consumes totally 8076 Watts during a period of 1800

Figure 13. Power consumption

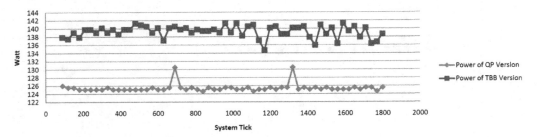

system ticks, while the QP version consumes only 7274 Watts. The TBB version consumes 11% more energy than the QP version. The TBB keeps all CPU cores busy while performing the load-balancing, thus it also consumes more energy than the QP version. Nevertheless, the performance is also enhanced as shown in the first experiment.

CONCLUSION AND FUTURE WORK

VERTAF/Multi-Core (VMC) is an application framework for developing multi-core embedded software. It adopts a model-driven approach with automatic code generation from SysML models. The code generated by VMC uses the Quantum Platform (QP) APIs and the Intel's Threading Building Blocks (TBB) library along with an operating system that supports multi-core processors such as Linux. VMC shows how easy it is to develop embedded software for multi-core processors. We used a real-world example, namely a digital video recording (DVR) system, to illustrate how VMC solves several of the issues related to model-driven development for multi-core embedded systems.

VMC currently supports homogenous multi-core platform. We want to extend VMC to support heterogeneous multi-core platforms consisting of general-purpose multi-core processors and digital signal processors.

REFERENCES

Achauer, B. (1996). Objects in real-time systems: Issues for language implementers. *ACM SIGPLAN OOPS Messenger*, 7, 21–27. doi:10.1145/227986.227991

Akhter, S. (2006). *Multi-core programming: Increasing performance through software multi-threading*. Intel Press.

Amnell, T., Fersman, E., Mokrushin, L., Petterson, P., & Wang, Y. (2003). TIMES: A tool for schedulability analysis and code generation of real-time systems. *Proceedings of the 1st Workshop on Formal Modeling and Analysis of Timed Systems (FORMATS)*, (pp. 60-72). Berlin / Heidelberg: Springer.

ARM. (2010). Cortex-A9 MPCore. Retrieved May 10, 2010, from http://www.arm.com/products/CPUs/ARMCortex-A9_MPCore.html

ARM. (2010). *Hardware platforms*. Retrieved May 10, 2010, from http://www.arm.com/products/DevTools/PB11MPCore.html

B-toolkit. (2002). *B-core (UK) Ltd*. Retrieved from http://www.b-core.com/

Bollella, G., Gosling, J., Brosgol, B., Dibble, P., Furr, S., & Turnbull, M. (2000). *The real-time specification for Java*. Addison Wesley.

Browne, J. (1996). Object-Oriented Development of real-time systems: Verification of functionality and performance. *ACM OOPS Messenger*, 7, 59–62. doi:10.1145/227986.227996

Cantrill, B., & Bonwick, J. (2008). Real-world concurrency. *ACM Queue; Tomorrow's Computing Today*, 6(5), 16–25. doi:10.1145/1454456.1454462

Clarke, E. M., & Emerson, E. A. (1981). Design and synthesis of synchronization skeletons using branching time temporal logic. *Proceedings of the Logics of Programs Workshop*, (pp. 52-71). Springer Verlag.

Clarke, E. M., Grumberg, O., & Peled, D. A. (1999). *Model Checking*. MIT Press.

DO-178B. (1992). *Software considerations in airborne systems and equipment certification*. RTCA Inc.

Eckstein, R. (2008). *Working with Java technology in a multicore world*. Paper presented at the JavaOne Conference. Retrieved May 10, 2010, from http://java.sun.com/javaone/sf/2008/articles/concurrency.jsp

Esterel Technologies. (2003). Retrieved May 10, 2010, from http://www.esterel-technologies.com/

Fayad, M., & Schmidt, D. (1997). Object-Oriented application framework. *Communications of the ACM*, 40(10). doi:10.1145/262793.262798

Gergeleit, M., Kaiser, J., & Streich, H. (1996). Checking timing constraints in distributed Object-Oriented programs. *ACM OOPS Messenger*, 7, 51–58. doi:10.1145/227986.227995

Grimshaw, A., Silberman, A., & Liu, J. (1989). Real-time Mentat, a data-driven, Object-Oriented system. Proceedings of the IEEE Globecom Conference, (pp. 141-147).

Halbwachs, N., Caspi, P., Raymond, P., & Pilaud, D. (1991). The synchronous dataflow programming language lustre. *Proceedings of the IEEE*, 79(9), 1305–1320. doi:10.1109/5.97300

Hammer, D., Welch, L., & Roosmalen, O. V. (1996). A taxonomy for distributed Object-Oriented real-time systems. *ACM OOPS Messenger*, 7, 78–85. doi:10.1145/227986.227999

Heitmeyer, C. L., Kirby, J., Labaw, B., & Bharadwaj, R. (1998). SCR: A toolset for specifying and analyzing software requirements. Proceedings of 10th International Conference in Computer-Aided Verification, (pp. 526-531).

Hsiung, P. A. (1998). RTFrame: An Object-Oriented application framework for real-time applications. Proceedings of 27th International Conference in Technology of Object-Oriented Languages and Systems, (pp. 138-147).

Hsiung, P. A. (2000). Embedded software verification in hardware-software codesign. *Journal of Systems Architecture*, 46(15), 1435–1450. doi:10.1016/S1383-7621(00)00034-5

Hsiung, P. A., Lin, S. W., Tseng, C. H., Lee, T. Y., Fu, J. M., & See, W. B. (2004). VERTAF: An application framework for the design and verification of embedded real-time software. *IEEE Transactions on Software Engineering*, 30(10), 656–674. doi:10.1109/TSE.2004.68

Intel. (2008). *Core2TM duo processors*. Retrieved from http://www.intel.com/design/intarch/core2duo/index.htm?iid=ipp_embed+proc_core2duo

Intel. (2008). *Quad-Core Xeon Processor 5300 Series*. Retrieved from http://www.intel.com/design/intarch/quadcorexeon/5300/index.htm

Ishikawa, Y., Tokuda, H., & Mercer, C. W. (1990). Object-Oriented real-time language design: Constructs for timing constraints. ACM SIGPLAN Notices, Proceedings of ECOOP/OOPSL Conference, (pp. 289-298).

Kim, K. H. (2000). APIs for real-time distributed object programming. *Computer*, 33(6), 72–80. doi:10.1109/2.846321

Knapp, A., Merz, S., & Rauh, C. (2002). Model checking timed UML state machines and collaboration. Proceedings of the 7th International Symposium in Formal Techniques in Real-Time and Fault-Tolerant Systems, (pp. 395-414). Berlin / Heidelberg: Springer.

Kodase, S., Wang, S., & Shin, K. G. (2003). Transforming structural model to runtime model of embedded real-time systems. Proceedings of the Design Automation and Test in Europe Conference, (pp. 170-175).

Kuan, T., See, W. B., & Chen, S. J. (1995). An Object-Oriented real-time framework and development environment. Proceedings of OOPSLA Conference Workshop, (p.18).

Lavazza, L. (2001). *A methodology for formalizing concepts underlying the DESS notation*. Retrieved from http://www.dess-itea.org

Leijen, D., & Hall, J. (2007). Optimize managed code for multi-core cachines. Retrieved May 10, 2010, from http://msdn.microsoft.com/en-us/magazine/cc163340.aspx#S1

Liao, W. S., & Hsiung, P. A. (2003). FVP: A Formal Verification Platform for SoC. *Proceedings of the* 16th IEEE International SoC Conference, (pp. 21-24).

Lien, C. H., Bai, Y. W., & Lin, M. B. (2007). Estimation by software for the power consumption of streaming-media servers. *IEEE Transactions on Instrumentation and Measurement, 56*(5), 1859–1870. doi:10.1109/TIM.2007.904554

Liu, C. L., & Layland, J. (1973). Scheduling algorithms for multiprogramming in a hard-real time environment. *Journal of the Association for Computing Machinery, 20*, 46–61.

MSDN. (2010). *Introduction to PLINQ*. Retrieved from http://msdn.microsoft.com/en-us/library/dd997425(v=VS.100).aspx

Niz, D. d., & Rajkumar, R. (2003). Time Weaver: A software-through-models framework for embedded real-time systems. Proceedings of the Internation Workshop on Languages, Embedded Systems, (pp. 133-143).

Open, M. P. (2008). *Home information*. Retrieved from http://www.openmp.org

Quantum Leaps. (2010). *What is QP™?* Quantum Leaps®, LLC. Retrieved May 10, 2010, from http://www.state-machine.com/products/

Queille, J. P., & Sifakis, J. (1982). Specification and verification of concurrent systems in CESAR. Proceedings of the International Symposium on Programming, (pp. 337-351). Berlin / Heidelberg: Springer.

Reinders, J. (2007). *Intel threading building blocks: Outfitting C++ for multi-core processor parallelism.* O'Reilly Media, Inc.

Rumbaugh, J., Booch, G., & Jacobson, I. (1999). *The UML Reference Guide.* Addison Wesley Longman.

Samek, M. (2002). *Practical StateCharts in C/C.* CMP.

Schmidt, D. (1997). Applying design patterns and frameworks to develop Object-Oriented communication software. In Handbook of Programming Languages.

See, W. B., & Chen, S. J. (2000). Object-Oriented real-time system framework. In *Domain-specific* application frameworks. (pp. 327-338).

Selic, B. (1993). An efficient Object-Oriented variation of the statecharts formalism for distributed real-time systems. Proceedings of the IFIP Conference in Hardware Description Languages and Their Applications. (pp. 335-344). Amsterdam: North-Holland Publishing Co.

Selic, B. (1996). Modeling real-time distributed software systems. *Proceedings of 4th International* Workshop in Parallel and Distributed Real-Time Systems, (pp. 11-18).

Selic, B., Gullekan, G., & Ward, P. T. (1994). *Real-time Object Oriented modeling.* John Wiley and Sons.

Sys, M. L. (2010). *Homepage information*. Retrieved May 10, 2010, from http://www.sysml.org/

Thompson, J. M., Heimdahl, M. P., & Miller, S. P. (1999). Specification-based prototyping for embedded systems. *Proceedings of 7th ACM SIGSOFT Symposium in Foundations of Software Engineering*, (pp. 163-179).

Tsao, C. C. (2008). *An efficient collaborative verification methodology for multiprocessor SoC with run-time task migration*. Master Thesis, Department of Computer Science and Information Engineering, National Chung Cheng University, Taiwan.

Wang, F., & Hsiung, P. A. (2002). Efficient and user-friendly verification. *IEEE Transactions on Computers*, *51*(1), 61–83. doi:10.1109/12.980017

Wang, S., Kodase, S., & Shin, K. G. (2002). Automating embedded software construction and analysis with design models. *Proceedings of the International Conference of Euro-uRapid*.

Welch, L. R. (1996). A metrics-driven approach for utilizing concurrency in Object-Oriented real-time systems. *ACM OOPS Messenger*, *7*, 70–77. doi:10.1145/227986.227998

KEY TERMS AND DEFINITIONS

Multi-Core Processor: A processor integrates more than one central processing unit (CPU) in a single physical package.

Thread: In computer science, a thread of execution results from a fork of a computer program into two or more concurrently running tasks. (Reference: http://en.wikipedia.org/wiki/Thread_%28computer_science%29. 2010, July)

Multithreading: Computers have hardware support to efficiently execute multiple threads. (Reference: http://en.wikipedia.org/wiki/Multithreading. 2010, July)

Model-Driven Development: A methodology in software engineering that is also known as model-driven architecture (MDA). OMG's Model Driven Architecture® (MDA®) starts with the well-known and long established idea of separating the specification of the operation of a system from the details of the way that system uses the capabilities of its platform. MDA provides an approach for, and enables tools to be provided for: (1) specifying a system independently of the platform that supports it; (2) specifying platforms; (3) choosing a particular platform for the system, and (4) transforming the system specification into one for a particular platform. The three primary goals of MDA are portability, interoperability and reusability through architectural separation of concerns. (Reference: Joaquin Miller, & Jishnu Mukerji. (2003). MDA Guide Version 1.0.1. Object Management Group. From http://www.omg.org/cgi-bin/doc?omg/03-06-01. 2010, July)

Framework (Software Framework): In the perspective of VMC, the framework is a structural methodology in computer programming that wraps and simplifies complex operations among objects or functions to support and reuse model-driven design.

Middleware: In computer programming, the middleware is the software that is used to bridge the gap of the software or applications.

Formal Verification: The use of mathematical techniques to ensure that a design conforms to some precisely expressed notion of functional correctness (Reference: Per Bjesse. (2005). What is formal verification? ACM SIGDA Newsletter, Vol 35, Issue 24, Page 1.)

Chapter 16
Analyzing Concurrent Programs Title for Potential Programming Errors

Qichang Chen
University of Wyoming, USA

Liqiang Wang
University of Wyoming, USA

Ping Guo
University of Wyoming, USA

He Huang
University of Wyoming, USA

ABSTRACT

Today, multi-core/multi-processor hardware has become ubiquitous, leading to a fundamental turning point on software development. However, developing concurrent programs is difficult. Concurrency introduces the possibility of errors that do not exist in sequential programs. This chapter introduces the major concurrent programming models including multithreaded programming on shared memory and message passing programming on distributed memory. Then, the state-of-the-art research achievements on detecting concurrency errors such as deadlock, race condition, and atomicity violation are reviewed. Finally, the chapter surveys the widely used tools for testing and debugging concurrent programs.

DOI: 10.4018/978-1-60960-215-4.ch016

INTRODUCTION

The development in the computing chip industry has been roughly following Moore's law in the past four decades. As a result, most classes of applications have enjoyed regular performance gains even without real improvement on the applications themselves, because the CPU manufacturers have reliably enabled ever-faster computer systems. However, the chip industry is now facing a number of engineering challenges associated with power consumption, power dissipation, slower clock-frequency growth, processor-memory performance gap, etc. Instead of driving clock speeds and straight-line instruction throughput ever higher, the CPU manufacturers are instead turning to multi-core architectures.

With the prevalence of multi-core hardware on the market, the software community is witnessing a dramatic shift from the traditional sequential computing paradigm to the parallel computing world. Parallel computing exploits the inherent data and task parallelism and utilizes multiple working processes or threads at the same time to improve the overall performance and speed up many scientific discoveries. Although threads have certain similarities to processes, they have fundamental differences. In particular, processes are fully isolated from each other; threads share heap memory and files with other threads running in the same process. The major benefits of multithreading include faster inter-thread communication and more economical creation and context switch.

Here, we use "concurrent" and "parallel" interchangeably, although there is a little difference between them. Usually, "parallel programming" refers to a set of tasks working at the same time physically, whereas "concurrent programming" has a broader meaning, *i.e.*, the tasks can work at the same time physically or logically.

Although for the past decade we have witnessed increasingly more concurrent programs, most applications today are still single-threaded and can no longer benefit from the hardware improvement without significant redesign. In order for software applications to benefit from the continued exponential throughput advances in new processors, the applications will need to be well-written concurrent software programs.

However, developing concurrent programs is difficult. Concurrency introduces many new errors that are not present in traditional sequential programs. Recent events range from failing robots on Mars to the year 2003 blackout in northeastern United States, which were both caused by a kind of concurrency error called race condition. Debugging concurrent programs is also difficult. Concurrent programs may behave differently from one run to another because parallelism cannot be well determined and predicted beforehand. Existing debugging techniques that are well adopted for sequential programs are inadequate for concurrent programs. Specialized techniques are needed to ensure that concurrent programs do not have concurrency-related errors. Detecting concurrency errors effectively and efficiently has become a research focus of software engineering in recent years.

In the rest of the chapter, we review the state-of-the-art research achievements on detecting concurrency errors as well as the corresponding parallel programming models. Major debugging tools are also introduced and compared with regard to their usability and capability.

PARALLEL COMPUTING PLATFORMS

Advances on Architecture: Multi-Core Processor

Due to the physical limitations of the technology, keeping up with Moore's Law by increasing the number of transistors on the limited chip area has been becoming a more difficult challenge for the CPU industry. In the past decade, we have witnessed an increasing number of hardware architectures that shift towards parallelism instead of clock speed. The industry has gradually turned to parallelism in computational architectures with the hope of living up to Moore's law in terms of GFLOPS (1 GFLOPS = 109 floating-point-operations per second) performance growth per chip area instead of transistors growth per chip area. The prominent CPU vendors (namely, Intel and AMD) are packing two or more cores into each processor unit while the clock speed no longer grows at the rate of as Moore law dictates the transistor density growth. The multi-core processor architecture has become an industrial standard and is gradually changing the way people write programs.

In essence, a multi-core processor is a single chip containing more than one microprocessor core, which multiplies the potential performance with the number of cores. Some components, such as the bus interface and second level cache, are shared between cores. Because the cores are physically very close, they communicate at much higher bandwidth and speed compared to conventional discrete multiprocessor systems, which significantly reduces the communication overhead and improves overall system performance.

In order to fully utilize the multi-core capability, the programmers need to explicitly migrate their sequential code into parallel version. This opens the door to introduce many subtle concurrent programming errors that could be very difficult to detect and uncover. Those concurrent programming errors are introduced in details in Section 4.

Advances on Architecture: Accelerator for General Purpose Computing

As the scale of computing increases dramatically, coprocessor is becoming a popular attracting technique to accelerate general purpose computing. At this point, there are two types of widely used accelerators, i.e., GPU (Graphic Processing Unit) and Cell Broadband Engine (BE).

GPU is specifically designed to provide high throughput on parallel computation using many-core chips. Unlike conventional CPU that supports a much larger set of general instructions, GPU supports only graphics-related computations, which can be adopted for general-purpose scientific computations. More specifically, unlike a conventional CPU, in a GPU, much more transistors are devoted to data processing rather than data caching and flow control, which is especially well suited to address problems that can be expressed as data-parallel computations, where the same program is executed on many data elements in parallel with high arithmetic intensity. Because the same program is executed for multiple data elements, there is a lower requirement for sophisticated flow control; and because it is executed on many data elements and has high arithmetic intensity, the memory access latency can be hidden with calculations instead of big data caches.

Due to its high arithmetic computation power, GPU is becoming an attractive co-processor option for general-purpose computing. A typical GPU (e.g., NVIDIA GeForce GTX 295) can reach a peak processing rate of 1788 GFLOPS and a peak memory bandwidth of 224 GB/s, which are not possible to be achieved on a typical current-generation CPU.

As another type of well-known accelerator, Cell BE is a hybrid processor between conventional desktop processors (e.g., Intel Core 2) and more specialized high-performance processors (e.g., GPU). A Cell BE chip consists of a main processor called Power Processor Element (PPE), which can run general operating systems (e.g., Linux) and functions, and eight Synergistic Processor Elements (SPE), which are designed to accelerate data-parallel computing. The latest Cell BE, PowerXCell 8i, supports a peak performance of 102 GFLOPS double-precision calculations. Cell BE accelerators have been deployed on the supercomputer Roadrunner designed by IBM at the Los Alamos National Laboratory, which is the world's first petaflops system.

Super, Cluster, Grid, and Cloud Computing

Supercomputers are specialized computers that rely on innovative and throughput-oriented design in order to obtain high-performance and high-throughput computing gain over conventional computers. For example, the memory hierarchy in supercomputer is carefully designed to minimize the idle time of processors. The I/O systems are designed to support large-scale parallel I/O operations with high bandwidth. Many CPUs with specific tuned instructions set (*e.g.*, Complex Instruction Set Computer/ CISC) and advanced pipeline mechanisms have been invented for the purpose of high-throughput computing. Vector processor, or array processor, is such a CPU design where the instructions can perform mathematical operations on multiple data elements simultaneously. Supercomputers are usually specialized for certain types of computation, such as numerical calculations.

As the most popular parallel computing platform, a computing cluster is a collection of computers that are located physically in a small area and are linked through very fast local area network. Clusters are usually deployed for higher performance and availability, while typically being much more cost-effective than supercomputers with the comparable speed or availability. Cluster computing typically incorporates fault tolerance, data redundancy, load balancing and other features to ensure the high availability and reliability.

Grid computing is an extension of cluster computing. Computers in grid can be geographically dispersed and do not fully trust each other. Hence, the communication in grid may suffer much higher latency than cluster. A grid combines various compute resources from multiple domains to solve a common scientific problem that requires a lot of compute processing cycles

and large amount of data. It is a form of distributed computing in practice.

As an emerging parallel computing platform, cloud computing has recently gained wide attention. A cloud encompasses the cluster of machines as well as the system and application software that work together to provide some kind of service. Cloud computing is more scalable than the classical cluster, and can typically offer higher data availability and throughput as well as virtualized services. These services are broadly divided into three categories: Infrastructure-as-a-Service (IaaS), Platform-as-a-Service (PaaS), and Software-as-a-Service (SaaS). Amazon Web Services is such an example of IaaS, where virtual server instances are provided according to the capacity that users purchase. Google Apps is an example of PaaS, where users can create their own applications based on the provider's platform over the Internet. In the SaaS cloud model, services can be very broad, ranging from Web-based email to database processing. This type of cloud computing delivers a client-side application through the Internet browser to thousands of customers with much lower maintenance cost. In addition, cloud computing is more reliable and scalable than cluster and grid computing as it allows redundancy and can easily incorporate more machines, more processors, and more storage space to improve the overall performance without affecting the end users. All traditional and new concurrent programming models ranging from MPI, OpenMP, to CUDA might be adopted on cloud computing. Specifically, cloud computing is extremely amenable to the MapReduce concurrent programming model as most applications running on the cloud are data-parallel.

PARALLEL PROGRAMMING MODELS

In order to fully utilize the power of underlying parallel computing platforms, various parallel programming models have been developed. Most parallel programming models are derived from the traditional sequential programming. The sequential programming is embodied through an imperative or functional program that executes on a single processor. The behavior of the sequential program is predictable and the outcome is expectable every time it runs. In order to improve the performance of sequential programs, people resort to the processor clock frequency and other hardware optimization improvements which have grown relatively slowly recently. Concurrent programming models allow parts of the sequential program to run in parallel on multiple processors or concurrently on a single processor. The current widely used concurrent programming models include multithreaded programming on shared memory and message passing programming on distributed memory.

In multithreaded programming, multiple threads share the memory. Synchronization among threads is mainly enforced through lock (mutex), semaphore, spinlock (spinmutex), and monitor. A semaphore is an object that carries a value and uses a blocking mechanism to enforce the mutual exclusion among multiple threads. A lock or mutex is a special case of semaphore (i.e., binary semaphore) whose values can be only true or false. A spinlock or spinmutex is also a mutually exclusive object that instead uses a non-blocking mechanism to enforce the mutual exclusive property. Spinlock differs from the usual lock in that it utilizes busy waiting/checking without enforcing context switches. A monitor is a mutually exclusive code region that can be executed by one thread at a time. It is achieved through the acquisition and release of the lock or spinlock immediately before the entrance and after the exit of the code region. The major multithreaded programming paradigms include Java/C# Threads, Pthreads, Windows threads, OpenMP, TBB (Intel Threading Building Block), as well as CUDA and openCL for GPU computing.

On distributed memory, each compute node has its own private memory. Communication and synchronization among processes are carried out by sending and receiving messages. The main message passing programming model is MPI (Message Passing Interface).

Some hybrid parallel programming models exists. UPC is such a model which combines the programmability advantages of the shared memory programming paradigm and the control over data layout of the **message passing programming paradigm**.

This section introduces the major parallel programming models for shared memory and distributed memory, with focusing on comparing their synchronization mechanisms.

Multithreaded Programming on Shared Memory Model

The traditional parallel programming model on shared memory is multiprocessing, where multiple processes share the same memory. Compared to forking or spawning new processes, threads require less overhead because the system does not initialize a new system virtual memory space and environment for the process. In addition, the overhead of context switch on threads is also much less than on processes. In contrast to parallel programming paradigms such as MPI in a distributed computing environment, threads are usually limited to a single computer system. All threads within a process share the same address space.

Java Threads

Multithreaded execution is an essential feature of Java platform. Multithreaded Java programs start with the main thread, which then spawns additional threads. The conventional synchronization mechanisms supported by Java include *monitor, wait/notify, semaphore,* and *barrier*.

A *monitor* is an object implementation where at most one thread can simultaneously execute

Algorithm 1.

synchronized(this){
this.balance += depositAmount;
}
	synchronized(this){
	this.balance -= withdrawAmount;
	}

any of its methods (*i.e.*, *critical sections*). If one thread is inside the monitor (*i.e.*, holding the lock associated to the monitor), the other threads must wait for that thread to exit the monitor (*i.e.*, release the lock) before they can enter the monitor. The lock of monitor in Java is reentrant, which means that a thread holding a lock can request it again. To use monitor, programmer can explicitly label an entire method or a well-defined code block inside a method as critical sections using the keyword "synchronized". As "synchronized" enforces paired lock acquire and lock release, the "Lock" class in Java allows more flexible structuring by providing Lock.lock() and Lock. unlock(). Algorithm 1 shows that two threads use "synchronized" to keep the integrity of the "balance" for a bank account.

A thread can hang itself and wait for another thread by calling "wait", which will release the corresponding lock if in critical section. When the other thread invokes "notify" to wake up the suspended thread, it will acquire the lock and resume its execution. Algorithm 2 shows how to enforce the deposit/withdraw order using wait/ notify. In this case, a deposit should always occur before a withdraw can take place.

In addition, Java introduces a few specialized synchronization mechanisms. Java supports the keyword "volatile", which is used on variables that may be modified concurrently by multiple threads. Compiler will enforce fetching fresh volatile variables each time, rather than caching them in registers. Note that volatile does not guarantee atomic access, *e.g.*, i++. Java provides a series of classes (such as AtomicInteger and AtomicIntegerArray) to support atomic operations. When a thread performs an atomic operation, the other threads see it as a single operation. The advantage of atomic operations is that they are relatively quick compared to locks, and do not suffer from deadlock. The disadvantage is that they support only a limited set of operations, and are often not enough to synthesize complex operations efficiently.

In addition, Java JDK also contains a set of collection classes (*e.g.*, HashTable, Vector) to support safe concurrent modification. They may run slightly slower than their counterparts (*e.g.*, HashMap, ArrayList) that may throw exceptions or have incorrect results when performing concurrent operations.

C# Threads

Threads in C# behave similarly to Java threads. However, instead of using "synchronized", C# provides its own synchronization keywords. To enforce critical sections, Monitor class can be used to acquire a lock at the beginning of the code section by calling Monitor.Enter(object). Any other

Algorithm 2.

synchronized(this){
this.wait();
this.balance -= withdrawAmount;
}
	synchronized(this){
	this.balance += depositAmount;
	this.notify();
	}

Algorithm 3.

```
bool acquiredLock = false;              bool acquiredLock = false;
try{                                    try{
Monitor.Enter(lockObject,               Monitor.Enter(lockObject,
ref acquiredLock);                      ref acquiredLock);
this.balance -= withdrawAmount;         this.balance += depositAmount;
}    finally {                          }    finally {
if (acquiredLock)                       if (acquiredLock)
Monitor.Exit(lockObject);               Monitor.Exit(lockObject);
}                                       }
```

thread wanting to execute the same code would need to acquire the same lock and will be paused until the first thread releases the lock by calling Monitor.Exit(object). Algorithm 3 illustrates the usage of Monitor to protect the integrity of the field "balance".

C# also provides a keyword "lock", a syntactic shortcut for a paired call to the methods Monitor.Enter and Monitor.Exit, which is converse compared to Java Synchronized and Lock. Algorithm 4 illustrates the similar use of lock in C# as "synchronized" in Java.

The mutual exclusion enforced by lock and monitor in C# is only among threads inside a process. To enforce mutual exclusion across multiple processes, Mutex can be used, which works in the same way as lock inside a process. Besides Monitor, Lock, and Mutex, C# also supports Semaphore, Barrier, Volatile, and atomic operations (by calling System.Threading.Interlocked), whose meanings and usages are similar to these in Java.

Pthreads

Pthreads stands for POSIX Threads libraries for C/C++. Thread operations provided by Pthreads include thread creation, termination, synchronization, scheduling, data management, and process interaction. Threads in the same process share process instructions, most data, open files (descriptors), signals and signal handlers, current working directory, user and group identifies. However, each thread has its own thread ID, set of registers, stack pointer, stack for local variables, return addresses, signal mask priority, and return value.

Pthreads provides three synchronization mechanisms: *join, mutex,* and *condition variables.* After a thread has been spawned, programmers can perform join operation by calling pthread_join. The calling thread will suspend its execution until the thread to be joined has finished its execution. This allows certain cooperation between different tasks, for example, one thread is waiting for the results from other threads for further execution.

Mutex is mainly used to protect memory access thus prevent data races. A mutex variable is declared by "pthread_mutex_t mutex = PTHREAD_MUTEX_INITIALIZER". After a mutex variable is created, acquiring and releasing locks can be performed by calling pthread_mutex_lock(&mutex) and pthread_mutex_unlock(&mutex), respectively.

Algorithm 4.

```
lock(this){                             lock(this){
this.balance -= withdrawAmount;         this.balance += depositAmount;
}                                       }
```

Algorithm 5.

pthread_mutex_lock(&mutex);
while (!cond)
thread_cond_wait(&cond,&mutex);
do_something();
pthread_mutex_unlock(&mutex);
	pthread_mutex_lock(&mutex);
	… //make condition TRUE
	if (cond)
	pthread_cond_signal(&cond);
	pthread_mutex_unlock(&mutex);

A condition variable is a variable in the type of pthread_cond_t and offers a more flexible way for threads to suspend/resume execution than the "join" mechanism. A condition variable should be protected with a mutex in order to avoid race conditions. Without mutex, the signaling thread and the waiting thread may access the condition variable as well as other shared variables simultaneously, which results in race conditions. Algorithm 5 shows how to use condition variable and mutex together.

To force the current thread to wait on a condition variable, pthread_cond_wait is called. At the same time, the mutex currently held is also released. pthread_cond_timedwait works similarly except for waiting for a specific time period then resuming that thread's execution. Other threads can wake up a waiting thread by calling pthread_cond_signal or pthread_cond_broadcast (which wakes up all waiting threads). After receiving waking up signal, the waiting thread will acquire mutex again and resume its execution.

OpenMP

OpenMP (Open Multi-Processing) is another multithreaded programming model that supports C, C++, and Fortran on many platforms including Linux and Microsoft Windows. It is composed of a set of compiler directives, library routines, and environment variables that influence program's run-time behavior.

The OpenMP compiler directives are manually inserted into programs and indicate how to execute the code sections in parallel. For example, consider the following loop to sum the elements

of two arrays, the directive indicates that the iterations of the loop can be executed in parallel, *i.e.*, a few concurrent threads will be spawned at runtime and each thread handles some iterations.

```
#pragma omp parallel for
for (i=0; i<n; i++){
    c[i] = a[i] + b[i];
}
```

In order to be parallelized, the loop must obey certain patterns. OpenMP does not detect dependencies between loop iterations, which may incur race conditions. A way to avoid such race conditions is to use critical introduced below.

Other widely-used OpenMP directives include "master", "critical" and work-sharing "for" and "section directives.

The "master" directive specifies a region that is to be executed only by the master thread of the thread group. All other threads on the group skip this section of code. The example below allows only the master thread to initialize the counter and other threads to skip the initialization.

```
#pragma omp master
int counter = 0;
```

The "critical" directive specifies a region of code that must be executed by only one thread at a time. The following example shows how to allow multiple threads to update the variable "balance" in a concurrent way without incurring race conditions.

```
#pragma omp critical
balance += depositAccount;
```

The work-sharing "for" directive specifies that the iterations of the for-loop are executed in parallel. The granularity of the parallelism can be decided statically using a keyword "static" or run time using the keyword "dynamic". Optionally one can provide a chunk size if she/he wants to assign more than one iteration to a thread. This following example shows an example to assign iterations evenly among the threads in compile time (statically).

```
#pragma omp for schedule static
for (i=0; i<n; i++){
    c[i] = a[i] + b[i];
}
```

The work-sharing "sections" directive allows multiple threads to execute different code blocks only once. In the example below, three threads will execute the first, second, third block labeled with "#pragma omp section" independently once.

```
#pragma omp sections
{
    #pragma omp section
    { int a = 0; }
    #pragma omp section
    { int b = 0; }
    #pragma omp section
    { int c = 0; }
}
```

In principle, one of advantages for the compiler directive strategy is that the code can run as ordinary sequential code if the directives are ignored. Unfortunately, some of the OpenMP directives, such as these managing memory consistency and local copies of variables, affect the semantics of the sequential code, compromising this desirable property unless the code avoids these directives.

Intel TBB

Intel TBB (Threading Building Block) is a runtime-based parallel programming paradigm. It is a C++ template library that consists of data structures and algorithms aiming to reduce the complexity arising from the use of the more primitive threading packages such as Pthread and Windows threads. Like the high-level concurrency objects in Java, TBB library simplifies thread-level parallelism further into task-level. Programmers only need to specify the intended parallel code as tasks and do not need to explicitly control the underling scheduling and synchronization technicalities. The library's runtime engine will take care of the rest which prevents programmers from making potential concurrency errors. This offers an alternative way for developers to leverage multi-core processors without being an expert on multithreading. However, this might limit the type of applications that can be ported to TBB since many tightly-coupled programs require more fine-grained synchronization between threads.

Intel TBB provides mutual exclusion and atomic operations for synchronization among different threading blocks. TBB has several kinds of mutex objects (spin_mutex, queuing_mutex, spin_rw_mutex, queuing_rw_mutex, mutex) for different performance, fairness, and reentrant, *etc*. For example, a thread trying to acquire a lock on spin_mutex is in busy wait till acquiring the lock. A spin_mutex is appropriate when the lock is held for a short time (*e.g.* a few instructions). However incorrect uses may incur huge performance penalty. As a cheaper alternative to mutex, atomic operations can be used. The Class atomic<T> implements atomic operations. It supports three popular atomic non-blocking operations: fetch_and_store, fetch_and_add, and compare_and_swap.

CUDA and OpenCL

GPU software development tools have evolved rapidly with the dramatic advances of GPU hardware. In the early stage, people struggled with the implementation of scientific computing using graphics primitives. Then several high-level abstractions for streaming programming, such as BrookGPU (Buck, et al., 2004) and Sh (McCool, et al., 2004), were designed to hide the graphics-specific details of GPU programming. Recently, commercially supported GPU program toolkits, in particularly CUDA (Cuda), RapidMind (Rapid-Mind), and OpenCL (Open Computing Language (OpenCL)), dramatically promote general computing on GPU and help leverage GPU capabilities and manage data parallel computations on high-level programming languages, such as C/C++.

NVIDIA's CUDA is the leader of programming interfaces for GPU computing. The CUDA software stack is composed of several layers including a hardware driver, an application programming interface (API) and its runtime environment, as well as high-level mathematical libraries. The main synchronization mechanism in CUDA is barrier (through calling "__syncthreads()"). CUDA also provides atomic operations that are performed without interference from any other threads in order to prevent race conditions. The following example (NCSA-CUDA) shows how to use CUDA to conduct addition operations on two vectors. The keyword label "__global__" declares a function to be a kernel function which is executed on CUDA device and called from the host only. In this case, the kernel code computes the sum of two float vectors in parallel on the CUDA device. The host code (the rest code in the example) allocates the device memory and provides some essential parameters such as the grid dimension, number of blocks, number of thread per block when calling the kernel function. In this case, the host code first calls CUDA memory functions to allocate the device memory for the two input vectors A and B and the sum vector C and then specifies the number of block to be 1 and the number of threads per block to be 10 when calling the CUDA kernel function "vecAdd". At the end of the program, the host code calls CUDA memory functions to release the allocated memory.

```
__global__ void vecAdd(float* A,
float* B, float* C) {
    int i = threadIdx.x;
    A[i]=0;
    B[i]=i;
    C[i] = A[i] + B[i];
}
int main() {
    int N=10, SIZE=10;
    float A[SIZE], B[SIZE],
C[SIZE];
    // Kernel invocation

    float *devPtrA;
    float *devPtrB;
    float *devPtrC;
    int memsize= SIZE *
sizeof(float);

    cudaMalloc((void**)&devPtrA,
memsize);
    cudaMalloc((void**)&devPtrB,
memsize);
    cudaMalloc((void**)&devPtrC,
memsize);
    cudaMemcpy(devPtrA, A, memsize,
cudaMemcpyHostToDevice);
    cudaMemcpy(devPtrB, B, memsize,
cudaMemcpyHostToDevice);
    vecAdd<<<1, N>>>(devPtrA, devP-
trB, devPtrC);
    cudaMemcpy(C, devPtrC, memsize,
cudaMemcpyDeviceToHost);

    for (int i=0; i<SIZE; i++)
        printf("C[%d]=%f\n",i,C[i]);

    cudaFree(devPtrA);
```

```
    cudaFree(devPtrA);
    cudaFree(devPtrA);
}
```

Another open GPGPU program interface is OpenCL (OpenCL) which is similar to CUDA in many aspects. OpenCL programs are a mixed form of host code and device code. It uses keyword labeling to express data parallelism for device code and the host code. The execution of an OpenCL program involves simultaneous execution of multiple instances of a kernel on the OpenCL devices as they are queued and controlled by the host application. Each instance of a kernel is referred to as a work-item. The data parallelism lies in that each work item executes the same code on different portions of the data. Each work-item runs independently on a single core of OpenCL device.

OpenCL supports two forms of synchronization between work-items in the same workgroup: barriers and memory fences. The barrier operation barrier() allows the work-items in the same group to have the same progress before starting the next stage. The fence operation mem_fence() forces all outstanding loads and stores on the OpenCL device memory to be completed before execution proceeds, and disallows the compiler and runtime system from reordering any loads and stores. This can be used to ensure that all data produced in a work-group are flushed to global OpenCL device memory before proceeding, which prevents other work-groups from reading premature results.

Parallel Programming on Distributed Memory Model: MPI

MPI (Message Passing Interface) is currently the *de facto* standard programming model for high-performance scientific computing. MPI defines the syntax and semantics of a core of library routines for writing portable message-passing programs. Besides supporting distributed memory, MPI can also utilize the shared memory for faster data communication between processes on the same node. MPI supports many popular languages such as C, C++, Fortran, Python, and Java. There are several open source implementations of MPI like MPICH, LAM MPI, and OpenMPI, and commercial implementations from Portland Group, HP, Intel, Sun, IBM, and Microsoft.

Unlike multithreading, message passing is a form of distributed memory programming paradigm based on the sending and receiving messages. In message passing, multiple processes coordinate their progress and communicate their immediate results by sending messages to one or more designated receivers and receiving messages from one or more designated senders. A send/receive can be a blocking or non-blocking operation. A blocking operation blocks the process from executing next instruction until it completes. A non-blocking operation does not need to wait for the finish of designated events, the process will continue without suspending. For example, in MPI, mpi_send() is a blocking send and mpi_isend() is a non-blocking one. The blocking operations are unsafe operations as improper use of them would lead to deadlock and other type of concurrency errors. The nonblocking ones can be safe but more difficult for coding.

A send/receive can target at a specific group of processes by specifying a communicator. A communicator designates a group of processes for sending/receiving message. For example, in MPI, the macro MPI_COMM_WORLD is the initially defined universe intracommunicator for all processes to conduct various communications. A send/receive can also use a message tag to indicate what kind of message it expects to send/receive. Tags are used to distinguish different message types a process might send/receive.

There are a number of message passing patterns that are commonly used in MPI programs. *Point-to-point* is the most basic communication pattern in MPI. One process uses MPI_Send() or its variant to send a message to a designated receiving process which uses MPI_Recv() or its variant to receive the message. A *collective communication* is a communication pattern that involves all the processes in a communicator. Consequently, a collective communication is usually associated with more than two processes. *Barrier* is a program point where all processes in the same communicator should reach before proceeding.

Most MPI routines also enforce some kind of synchronization. For example, MPI_Bcast() broadcasts a message to the whole communication group; a node will not continue until it receives the message. In addition, MPI explicitly provides barrier operation to synchronize the progress of different processes. A process that calls MPI_Barrier() will block itself until all processes in the same

Algorithm 6.

```
#include "mpi.h"
#include <stdio.h>
#include <math.h>
int main(int argc, char *argv[]){
int n, myid, numprocs, i;
double PI25DT = 3.141592653589793238462643;
double mypi, pi, h, sum, x;
MPI_Init(&argc,&argv);
MPI_Comm_size(MPI_COMM_WORLD,&numprocs);
MPI_Comm_rank(MPI_COMM_WORLD,&myid);
while (1) {
if (myid == 0) {
printf("Enter the number of intervals: (0 quits) ");
scanf("%d",&n);
}
MPI_Bcast(&n, 1, MPI_INT, 0, MPI_COMM_WORLD);
    if (n == 0)
    break;
else {
h = 1.0 / (double) n;
sum = 0.0;
for (i = myid + 1; i <= n; i += numprocs) {
x = h * ((double)i - 0.5);
sum += (4.0 / (1.0 + x*x));
}
mypi = h * sum;
MPI_Reduce(&mypi, &pi, 1, MPI_DOUBLE, MPI_SUM, 0,
MPI_COMM_WORLD);
if (myid == 0)
printf("pi is approximately %.16f, Error is
%.16f\n",pi, fabs(pi - PI25DT));
}
}
MPI_Finalize();
return 0;
}
```

group have reach the barrier point. The following example taken from (ANL MPI) shows how to use MPI to calculate π on parallel machines. Every process on each machine will execute the same code except they use "myid" to distinguish from each other. MPI_Comm_size stores the total number of processes in the variable "numprocs" for further use. Since MPI programs can be started with any number of processes using the option "-np", it is very useful to take into account the total number of processes in the computation as the number may vary each time. In this program, it asks user to provide the number of intervals (steps) for computing π which is broadcasted to each process from the root process. Later, each process except the root process (process with rank 0) does its own computation and calls MPI_Reduce to sum up their results. Finally, the root process prints out the computed pi against a 25-digit π.

MapReduce

MapReduce (Dean 2008) is a loosely-coupled parallel computation model that designs to handle data-intensive computations. MapReduce derives its name from the map and reduce combinators from the functional programming languages. In functional programming languages, a *map* takes a function and a sequence of values as input. It then applies the function to each value in the sequence. A *reduce* combines all the elements of a sequence using a binary operation. One example of MapReduce is that Map takes a function which breaks the input string into characters and Reduce uses a 'count' function to count the total number of characters in the sequence. This model is specifically suitable for many data-intensive applications because those applications usually only apply simple operations on large data which can be easily split into multiple chunks for independent processing. **(Hadoop) is a prominent open source MapReduce implementation that has been adopted for many data-intensive computations.**

UPC

Unified Parallel C (UPC) extends C programming language with a few additional structs to enable Single Program Multiple Data (SPMD) parallel computing model on large-scale machines. The language provides a uniform and integrated programming model for both shared and distributed memory hardware.

UPC provides the following synchronization mechanisms: *barrier, wait/notify, lock, fence,* and *spinlock*. Among them, barrier, wait/notify, and lock work similarly to other multithreaded programming paradigms. The *fence* struct (*i.e.,* upc_fence) in UPC ensures that all the shared references issued ahead of the fence are complete. *Spinlock* is a non-blocking alternative to lock, which is designed for relatively fast operations on shared variables with less performance penalty.

CONCURRENCY ERRORS

With the introduction of the above concurrent programming models, there also come concurrency errors, such as deadlock, race condition, and atomicity violation, that are not present in traditional sequential programming. Like most traditional programming errors such as memory leak, buffer overrun, null pointer dereferencing, *etc.* Preventing and/detecting concurrency errors may suffer performance loss. For example, data race can be prevented using a lock to guard every shared variable's access. This inevitably brings down the performance of concurrent program as too many lock contentions will affect the performance dramatically.

Deadlock

Deadlock is perhaps the most common concurrency error that might occur in almost all parallel programming paradigms including both shared-memory and distributed memory. A *deadlock* occurs when a chain of processes/threads are involved in a cycle in which each process is waiting for resources/locks that are held by some other processes. When a deadlock happens, none of the processes/threads can proceed, which in turn causes the whole or part of the program to halt.

In shared-memory programming models, such as Java threads and Pthreads, when programmers use multiple locks to coordinate the accesses to shared variables from multiple threads, it may result in deadlock if two locks are acquired in different orders in multiple threads. Hence, to avoid such deadlock, successive locks should be locked in the same order. An example of deadlock in Java is shown in Algorithm 7.

Another kind of deadlock may occur in Pthreads is that a thread tries to reacquire a lock that it already owns, as shown in Algorithm 8.

Such kind of deadlock will not happen in Java threads because both "synchronized" and "lock" support reentrant locking. However, it is recommended that locking and unlocking are performed in the same scope. Otherwise, we should use try-finally or try-catch to ensure that unlocking is conducted finally, as shown below.

```
Lock.lock();
try {
    ...
} finally {
    Lock.unlock();
}
```

Message passing programs can also be victims of deadlock. The features of MPI (such as blocking communication and non-deterministic scheduling) and different implementations of MPI would potentially lead to deadlock. For example, an intuitive deadlock scenario is that some processes are awaiting messages, but these messages may never be sent out because the sending processes are blocked or unable to send. This scenario causes part of processes or even the whole MPI program to be blocked forever.

Algorithm 7.

thread-1:	thread-2:

synchronized(lock1){
synchronized(lock2){}
}
	synchronized(lock2){
	synchronized(lock1){}
	}

Algorithm 8.

| g() {
pthread_mutex_lock (&mutex);
...
pthread_mutex_unlock(&mutex);
} | f() {
pthread_mutex_lock (&mutex);
g();
pthread_mutex_unlock(&mutex);
} |

Figure 1, which is taken from (Hilbrich et al. 2009), shows three kinds of MPI deadlocks. As shown in the example of Figure 1(a), an MPI deadlock would occur when two blocking receives wait for each other, the program cannot continue.

Another example is shown in Figure 1(b). Point-to-point blocking routines may incur deadlock when their executions do not succeed. Point-to-point blocking routines, such as MPI_Send() and MPI_Recv(), do not return to the program until the message data have been safely stored (in message storage or buffer). However, if some problems arise in message storage (*e.g.*, it is full), this may cause some processes to infinitely wait for messages or responses from other processes, although such kind of MPI deadlock happens very rarely.

Point-to-point non-blocking routines can also lead to deadlock, although functions like MPI_Irecv() and MPI_Isend() can return to the program immediately without waiting the messages copying into buffers. But programmers often have to associate a request to a non-blocking routine and later invoke MPI_Wait(), which is also a blocking point-to-point routine.

Many collective MPI routines, such as MPI_Bcast() and MPI_Barrier(), can also cause deadlock if not used correctly. For example, programmers sometimes make mistakes like incomplete barrier operations, which means that not all the processes in the same communicator

Figure 1. Deadlock scenario for MPI programs

process 0	process 1
Recv:(from 1)	Recv:(from 0)
Send:(to 1)	Send:(to 0)

(a). Simple deadlock scenario

process 0	process 1
Send:(to 1)	Send:(to 0)
Recv:(from 1)	Recv:(from 0)

(b). Another possible deadlock scenario

process 0	process 1	process 2
SSend:(to 1)	Recv:(from ANY)	SSend:(to 1)
SSend:(to 2)	Recv:(from 2)	Recv:(from 0)

(c). Possible deadlock scenario involving 3 processes

invoke MPI_Barrier() which leads to a deadlock situation where the whole program can not proceed if the "barrier" point has not been reached by all processes in the same communicator group.

Incorrect use of wildcard receive is another scenario leading to deadlock. As an example shown in Figure 1(c), the labels MPI_ANY_SOURCE and MPI_ANY_TAG allow a process to receive any message from any source or any tag, respectively, but only the first incoming message is matched. If there is any subsequent MPI_Recv() on a specific process whose MPI_Send() is just matched by the previous wild card receive, then the process is blocked.

Data Race

Data race (also called race condition) is present only in the parallel programming models based on shared memory. *Data race* happens when two or more accesses from different threads access the same shared variable without proper synchronization and at least one of the accesses is a write to the variable.

Data race may or may not affect the correctness of the executing program depending on the context in which it occurs. That is, there are two types of data races: *harmful* and *benign*. For example, if thread 1 and thread 2 execute "x=1; y=x+1" and "x=2" (where x is a shared variable by both threads), respectively, a harmful data race may occur because the value of y depends on which statement of "x=1" and "x=2" runs first. A benign data race is shown below, where a boolean variable "flag" controls the ordering of thread 1 and thread 2. When thread 2 is done

with its task, it notifies thread 1 by setting "flag" to be true. Thread 1 is constantly checking "flag" to wait for thread 2. In this situation, the data race on the variable "flag" is benign.

Similar to data race in multithreaded programs, message race may occur on programs that utilize message passing mechanisms such as MPI. *Message race* occurs when a process receives messages from other processes at a non-deterministic order. Due to various process schedulings and communication latencies, messages may reach a process at various orders, and thus incur different schedulings and results. In the following example, the process P2 receives its message from process P1 and process P3. There is a message race in the first wildcard receive of P2. Depending on the order, P2 might receive the message from P1 with the value 1 or receive the message from P3 with the value of 0.

Atomicity Violation

Atomicity violation, which is caused when concurrent execution unexpectedly violates the atomicity of a code segment, is another kind of common concurrency errors. Atomicity is well known in the context of transaction processing, where it is sometimes called *serializability*. An *atomicity violation* occurs when an interleaved execution of a set of code blocks (expected to be atomic) by multiple threads is not equivalent to any serial execution of the same code blocks. Figure 2 illustrates two examples in Java from (Chen et al. 2009), where Program 1 contains obvious data races on the shared variable "bal", and Program 2 eliminates the data races in Program 1

Algorithm 9.

Thread 1	Thread 2
…	…
while(!flag){	flag = true;
…	…
}	

Algorithm 10.

Process 1(P1) MPI_Isend(P2, data = 1);	Process 2(P2) MPI_Irecv(*, x);	Process 3(P3) MPI_Isend(P2, data = 0);

by adding a lock o. However, it is still incorrect. In this example, the deposit method is expected to be atomic otherwise it would cause the bank account balance to be inconsistent. An atomicity violation would occur when the two synchronization blocks in Thread 2 execute between the two synchronization blocks in Thread 1. From this example, we can observe that the occurrence of atomicity violation depends on thread scheduling.

Other Concurrency-Related Programming Errors

Starvation describes a situation where a thread is unable to gain regular access to shared resources and is unable to make progress. It occurs when shared resources are made unavailable for long periods by other "greedy" and higher priority threads.

Livelock occurs when two or more processes/threads are busy in responding to each other's request while none of them can make further progress. Same as deadlock, it causes the whole or part of program to block indefinitely.

Lost Wait-Notify is another kind of common concurrency error. In multithreaded programming such as Java threads, two or more threads can use the "wait/notify/notifyAll" methods to synchronize between each other. In Pthreads, "pthread_cond_wait/pthread_cond_signal" are used instead, which work similarly. If a notifying thread calls "notify()" before the thread to be notified calls "wait()", the signal will be missed by the waiting thread. This may not be a problem if there are subsequent calls to "notify()". But if no thread calls "notify()" again, the waiting thread may wait forever because the waking up signal will never be received. Such kind of error highly depends on the thread scheduling and may not repeat in subsequent executions.

DETECTING CONCURRENCY ERRORS

In this section, we introduce the state-of-the-art research progress on detecting various concurrency errors including deadlock, data race, and atomicity violation. Most techniques for detecting concurrency errors fall into some categories of program analysis: dynamic analysis, static analysis, hybrid analysis, or model checking. We first introduce these four kinds of program analysis,

Figure 2. Examples in Java demonstrating data races and atomicity violations

```
                  Program 1
Thread 1                Thread 2
deposit(int val){       deposit(int val){
  int tmp = bal;          int tmp = bal;
  tmp = tmp + val;        tmp = tmp + val;
  bal = tmp;              bal = tmp;
}                       }
```

```
                  Program 2
Thread 1                Thread 2
deposit(int val){       deposit(int val){
  synchronized(o){        synchronized(o){
    int tmp = bal;          int tmp = bal;
    tmp = tmp + val;        tmp = tmp + val;
  }                       }
  synchronized(o){        synchronized(o){
    bal = tmp;              bal = tmp;
  }                       }
}                       }
```

then survey the detection approaches for deadlock, race condition, and atomicity violation.

Overview of Program Analysis

Dynamic Analysis

Dynamic analysis reasons about behavior of a program through observing its executions. It is usually performed by instrumenting source code (like (Wang and Stoller 2006b), bytecode (like (O'Callahan and Choi 2003)), or binary code (like (Savage et al. 1997)), and monitoring the programs' executions. The observed events can be analyzed on-line (*i.e.*, during executions) or off-line (*i.e.*, after executions terminate). To detect concurrency errors, dynamic analysis extends the traditional testing techniques. It tries to look for potential concurrency errors by searching specific patterns based on the current observed events, even the errors do not show up in the current execution paths. For example, to detect deadlock, the approaches in (Havelund 2000, Bensalem and Havelund 2005, Agarwal et al. 2005b)) search all lock acquires and releases for a potential cyclic chain. To detect data races, the approaches in (Savage et al. 1997) keep track of common locks for each shared variable, and a warning is issued when the common lock becomes empty. To improve the accuracy, the approaches in (O'Callahan and Choi 2003, Yu et al. 2005, Ratanaworabhan et al. 2009, Flanagan and Freund 2009) integrate the associated lock-set with happen-before relationships for events. The approaches to detect race condition on OpenMP (Kang et al. 2009] and CUDA (Hou et al. 2009, Boyer et al. 2008)) are very similar to the previous approach. To detect atomicity violations, the approaches in (Flanagan and Freund 2004a, Xu et al. 2005, Wang and Stoller 2006b, Wang and Stoller 2006a, Lu et al. 2006, Flanagan et al. 2008, Chen et al. 2008) search all events related with shared variable accesses and synchronization for specified violation patterns. Randomized dynamic program analysis (Sen 2008, Park and Sen 2008, Joshi et al. 2009) use two stages to detect and confirm real deadlocks, races, and atomicity violations: in the first stage, it uses an imprecise dynamic analysis to find potential errors; in the second stage, it controls a random thread scheduler to create these potential errors with high probability.

In addition, the monitoring overhead is another problem of dynamic analysis, which usually slows down the speed of programs by a factor of 2 to 100. One approach to reduce overhead is to use random sampling (Liblit et al. 2003). This approach works only when a large set of sample executions are available. Another approach is to perform selective monitoring on program region, avoid remonitoring the same code region under the same context. However, checking the equivalence of program context is also expensive. The work in (Fei and Midkiff 2006) takes approximation for variables and pointers.

Static Analysis

Static analysis makes predictions about a program's runtime behavior based on analyzing its source code. Static analysis tools like Codesurfer (Anderson et al. 2003), PREfix and PRE-fast (Bush et al.2000), ESP (Das et al. 2002), ESC/Java (Detlefs et al. 1998), and LockSmith (Pratikakis et al. 2006) aim to detect potential errors by analyzing the source code (or byte/binary code) without actually executing the programs. Type systems are proposed to avoid deadlocks (Boyapati et al. 2002, Agarwal et al. 2005b), data races (Flanagan and Freund 2000, Boyapati and Rinard 2001, Boyapati et al. 2002, Flanagan and Freund 2004b, Agarwal et al. 2005a, Sasturkar et al. 2005, Naik and Aiken 2007), and atomicity violations (Flanagan and Qadeer 2003, Agarwal et al. 2005a, Sasturkar et al. 2005, Flanagan et al. 2005, Wang and Stoller 2005). A type system is a system of programmer added types that express some correctness requirement on the variables or functions that can be involved in concurrent error. For example, the deadlock types express a partial order on the locks, and the type rules ensure that whenever a thread holds multiple locks, the thread acquires the locks in a descending order (Boyapati et al. 2002, Agarwal et al. 2005b). However, it is a big burden for programmers to manually annotate programs with extra type information. Moreover, even the very expressive type systems may report many false positives. Inter-procedural static analysis is also used to detect potential concurrency errors (Choi et al. 2002, Engler and Ashcraft 2003). Compared to type systems, these inter-procedural analyses do not need annotations for types, but still produce numerous false positives. Static analysis can be sound, but it sacrifices accuracy and reports many false positives.

Hybrid Analysis

Static and dynamic analyses can be combined in various ways. Static analysis can be used to reduce the overhead of dynamic analysis. For example, static analysis can show that some statements are not involved in any data races or atomicity violations and hence do not need to be instrumented; this can significantly reduce the overhead of dynamic analysis by up to a factor of 20 (von Praun and Gross 2001, Choi et al. 2002, Agarwal et al. 2005a, Sasturkar et al. 2005, Agarwal et al. 2005b, Elmas et al. 2007). Dynamic analysis can help static analysis by providing more accurate runtime information. Daikon (Ernst et al. 2001) examines program executions to determine invariants to assist static analysis such as theorem proving. Static analysis and dynamic analysis can be performed interactively. Synergy (Gulavani et al. 2006) combines testing (*i.e.*, dynamic analysis) and verification (*i.e.*, static analysis) to simultaneously search for bugs and proofs. Concolic testing (Godefroid et al. 2005, Cadar et al. 2006, Majumdar and Sen 2007) runs symbolic execution simultaneously with concrete executions to generate new test inputs for better path coverage.

(Chen et al. 2009) designs a hybrid approach that integrates static and dynamic analyses to attack this problem. It first performs static analysis to obtain summaries of synchronizations and accesses to shared variables. The static summaries are then instantiated with runtime values during dynamic executions to speculatively approximate the behaviors of branches that are not taken. Compared to dynamic analysis, the hybrid approach is able to detect atomicity violations in unexecuted parts of the code.

Model Checking

Model checking is a formal method for proving that a finite-state model satisfies a temporal logic property. Explicit state model checkers, such as SPIN (Holzmann 2003), enumerate the reachable states explicitly. They also utilize additional techniques such as partial order reduction (Holzmann and Peled 1994). Symbolic model checking (McMillan 1994) avoids an explicit enumeration of the state space using symbolic representations of sets of states and transitions based on Binary Decision Diagrams (BDDs) or Boolean Satisfiability Solving. Model checking can also be applied to real programs. CHESS (Musuvathi and Qadeer 2008), Java PathFinder (Visser et al. 2003), Bogor (Dwyer et al. 2005) and VeriSoft (Godefroid 1997) are such tools. Although the most rigorous automatic method to verify software, model checking faces a combinatorial blow up of the state space, commonly known as the state explosion problem. Hence it cannot handle large-scale software systems.

Approaches to Detect Deadlock

Detecting deadlock has been a decades-long problem. Recall that a deadlock occurs when all threads are blocked, each waiting for some action by one of the other threads. Thus dependences among threads and resources can be modeled by a resource allocation graph, where nodes denote threads and exclusive resources, and edges denote allocation or wait-for relations between threads and resources. A common way to detect deadlock is to check whether the resource allocation graph contains a cycle (Silberschatz et al. 2008). Most approaches are based on it by checking against cycles, just in different ways. However, detecting deadlock thoroughly is very expensive. Large-scale software systems such as operating systems take an ostrich way, *i.e.*, assume that deadlock will not happen, hence never detect or prevent it in order to keep the performance to be efficient.

Detect Deadlocks in Multithreaded Programs

To introduce how to detect potential deadlocks in multithreaded programs, we use the GoodLock algorithm (Havelund 2000) as a typical algorithm. The GoodLock algorithm assumes that all locks are acquired and released in nested pairs, like "synchronized" in Java threads. It records a run-time lock tree for each thread as shown in Figure 3. A lock tree is a tree that represents the lock acquire order and relation for each thread as the control flows in each thread. An edge from a parent node to a child node in the lock tree indicates that the thread is currently holding a lock represented by the parent node when acquiring another lock denoted by the child node. The lock

tree for a thread represents the nested pattern in which locks are acquired by the thread. Each node of the lock tree is labeled with a lock. If a thread re-acquires a lock that it already holds, its run-time lock tree does not contain a node representing the re-acquire. At the end of the execution of the program, if there exist threads $t1$ and $t2$ and locks $l1$ and $l2$ such that $t1$ acquires $l2$ while holding $l1$, and $t2$ acquires $l1$ while holding $l2$, then a warning of potential deadlock is issued, unless there is a common lock, called a *gate lock*, that is held by both threads when they acquire $l1$ and $l2$; the gate lock prevents the acquires of $l1$ and $l2$ from being interleaved in a way that leads to deadlock. For example, in Figure 3, the left branches in thread 1 and thread 2 denote two lock acquiring sequences, where *L2* and *L3* are acquired in the reverse order. However, there is no deadlock in this example because of the gate lock *L1*.

The GoodLock algorithm was extended in (Agarwal and Stoller 2006), which presents a runtime detection approach for potential deadlocks in Java programs that involves locks, semaphore, and condition variables. They extended the runtime lock tree in the GoodLock algorithm into a directed graph $G = (V;E)$, where V contains all the nodes of all the run-time lock trees, and the set E of directed edges contains (1) tree edges, which are the directed (from parent to child) edges in each of the lock trees, and (2) inter edges, which

Figure 3. A lock tree example. The small superscript numbers identify each unique lock acquire event.

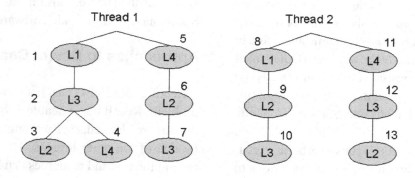

are the bidirectional edges between nodes labeled with the same lock in different run-time lock trees. In order to detect potential deadlocks, they use a modified DFS (Depth First Search) to traverse the graph to look for cycles. To check deadlocks involving semaphore and condition variables, they check possible permutations of the program execution trace and report if any feasible permutation would result in a deadlock.

However, most deadlock approaches suffer from false positives which might baffle the programmers from distinguishing real bugs from false alarms. To improve the quality of deadlock checking, (Agarwal et al.) proposes more extensions that help eliminate possible false positives or label them as low severity deadlocks in the lock graph generated by static or dynamic analysis. In addition, they present a technique that effectively combines information from multiple runs of the program into a single lock graph. Such a technique may help find deadlock potentials that might not be revealed by one arbitrary run of the program because of nondeterministic scheduling. Finally they describe the use of static analysis to automatically reduce the overhead of dynamic checking for deadlock potentials.

There are many other approaches to detect deadlock. For example, (Li et al.2005) implements a tool that is integrated with operating systems and dynamically detects various types of deadlocks in application programs. Their tool runs as a system daemon and periodically scans the system for processes that have been blocked for a long time. To determine if these processes are deadlocked, the tool speculatively executes them ahead to discover their dependences. Based on this information, it constructs a general resource graph and detects deadlock by checking whether the graph contains cycles. (Williams et al. 2005) applies a flow-sensitive, context-sensitive inter-procedural static analysis on detecting deadlock in Java libraries. Their analysis builds a single lock-order graph that captures locking information

for an entire Java library source code and checks for cycles in the graph.

Detecting Deadlock in MPI Programs

The simplest way to detect deadlock in MPI program is to use timer when MPI program is running. If the blocking time of some process exceeds the pre-defined threshold, those processes are announced to be in deadlock. Timer approach is easy to implement and does not impose too much overhead, but is difficult to set and adjust the threshold, and it may potentially report many false positives.

Dependency graph is one of the major approaches to detect deadlocks in MPI programs. It is usually implemented as a dynamic approach. In (Hilbrich et al. 2009), based on the concept of AND model, OR model and the combination of AND-OR model, dependency graph expresses the waiting relation between various processes at specific time. If part of the dependency graph satisfies the pre-defined deadlock conditions such as a circle or some kind of knot, then that part of the dependency graph is considered in a deadlock. This approach can only find deadlock happening during execution for specific schedules, but will not report all potential deadlock for all schedules.

(Luecke et al. 2002) uses a dynamic hand-shaking approach to detect potential and actual deadlocks. Handshaking code (handshake_send and handshake_recv) is statically instrumented before each MPI send/receive call in the source program and when the instrumented program is compiled and run, the dynamic monitor tracks the handshaking code to match a send and a receive. A handshake is a matching pair of instrumented handshake method calls for a send event and a receive event. If a handshake is not observed for each send or receive call after a user-defined time, then it reports a potential or actual deadlock warning for that send or receive call depending on the scenarios. They summarize a collection of situations where a actual deadlock will occur

Algorithm 11.

```
Let held(t) be the set of locks held by thread t.
For each v, initialize C(v) to the set of all locks.
On each access to v by thread t,
  C(v):= C(v) ∩ locks_held(t);
  if C(v) == { }, then issue a warning.
```

and a set of possible deadlock situations if the handshake is not observed. In (Vo et al. 2008), a dynamic formal verification approach is proposed to detect potential deadlocks in MPI programs. In the proposed approach, the execution of MPI program is under control of an interleaving scheduler where nondeterministic constructs are explored for all possible interleavings.

Approaches to Detect Race Condition

Detecting Race Condition in Multithreaded Programs

Many static and dynamic approaches have been proposed to detect race conditions in multithreaded programs. They are based on either lockset analysis or happen-before order. However, detecting race conditions is not an easy problem, which has been proved to be NP-hard (Netzer and Miller 1992).

We use the Eraser algorithm (Savage et al. 1997) shown above as a typical algorithm of lockset analysis. As a dynamic approach, Eraser checks all shared-memory accesses against a simple locking policy, *i.e.*, all accesses to a shared variable should be protected by a common lock. As shown above, for each shared variable v, Eraser maintains a set $C(v)$ of candidate locks for v. This set contains those common locks that have protected v in the execution so far. That is, a lock l is in $C(v)$ if, in the execution up to that point, every thread that has accessed v was holding l at the moment of the access. When v is initialized, its candidate set $C(v)$ is considered to hold all possible locks. Whenever the variable is accessed,

Eraser updates $C(v)$ with the intersection of $C(v)$ and the set of locks held by the current thread. This process, called lockset refinement, ensures that any lock consistently protecting v is contained in $C(v)$. If some lock l consistently protects v, it will remain in $C(v)$ during the refinement. If $C(v)$ becomes empty, which indicates that there is no lock consistently protecting v, Eraser will report a warning of race condition on v.

Figure 4 illustrates how the Eraser algorithm is applied to detect potential data races. The left two columns contain two threads. Thread 2 runs after thread 1. The third and forth column reflect the corresponding locks held by the current thread and the set of candidate locks $C(v)$, respectively. This example has two locks, so $C(v)$ starts containing both of them. When v is accessed by thread 1 while holding lock $o1$, $C(v)$ is refined to contain that lock. Later, v is accessed again by thread 2 while holding only $o2$. The intersection of the singleton sets $\{o1\}$ and $\{o2\}$ is the empty set, which indicates that no lock protects v. Hence, a race condition is reported on v.

However, the simple locking discipline may report many false positives. More improvements are designed for better accuracy. The extended Eraser algorithm proposed in (Savage et al. 1997) distinguishes states such as variable initialization (*i.e.*, *Exclusive*), initialized then read-only (*i.e.*, *Shared*), and read/write by multiple threads (*i.e.*, *Shared-Modified*). The state transitions are shown in Figure 5. When a variable is first allocated, it will be in the *Virgin* state, which implies that the variable is not shared among multiple threads yet. Once it has been accessed by the first thread, it enters the *Exclusive* state. Any following reads and writes from the same thread do not change the variable's state and do not update $C(v)$. With a read access from a different thread, the state is changed to *Shared* from *Exclusive*. In the *Shared* state, $C(v)$ is updated, but no data race will be reported because this is a read-shared situation. Alternatively, a write access from a different thread changes the state from *Exclusive* or *Shared* to the

Figure 4. An example illustrating the Eraser algorithm

Thread 1	Thread 2	Locks held	C(v)
			{o1, o2}
lock(o1);		{}	{o1, o2}
v:= v + 1;		{o1}	{o1}
unlock(o1);		{}	{o1}
	lock(o2);	{}	{o1}
	v:= v -1;	{o2}	{}
	unlock(o2);	{}	{}

Shared-Modified state, in which *C(v)* is updated and races are reported as the original Eraser algorithm would.

To improve accuracy and achieve lower run-time overhead of dynamic analysis, (Choi et al. 2002) proposes an efficient and precise dynamic detection approach on multithreaded programs. They take into account a *weaker-than* relationship that allows dynamic analysis to consider only portion of memory accesses rather than monitor all memory accesses. Given two memory access events e_i and e_j, if for every subsequent access e_k, isRace(e_j, e_k) implies isRace(e_i, e_k), then e_i is more *weakly protected* from data race than e_j, or in another word, e_i is weaker than e_j. With the weaker-than relation, they only need to store information about the weaker one of two events, which reduces both space and time overhead. In addition, caching technique is used to detect and remove redundant accesses thus further reduce space overhead. Before running the dynamic analysis, a static analysis is performed to identify all possible statements involving data races. Thus, the dynamic analysis will not need to monitor the irrelevant statements. The static analysis uses inter-thread control flow graph, points-to analysis, and extended escape analysis to help identify data races more accurately.

The hybrid approach in (O'Callahan and Choi 2003) further extends the Eraser algorithm (Savage et al. 1997) and the work in (Choi et al. 2002) with happens-before order relationship to reduce false positives. "Hybrid" means that the approach integrates the lockset-based analysis and the happen-before order relationship. The happens-before relationship was originally defined by

Figure 5. State transition of the extended Eraser algorithm

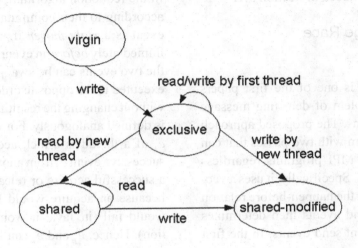

Lamport as a partial order on events occurring in a distributed system (Lamport1978). Informally, a pair of events (e_i, e_j) has happen-before relationship if (1) e_i and e_j are events in the same thread, and e_i occurs before e_j; or (2) If e_i is the sender of a message and e_j is the receiver of the message; or (3) e_i and e_j have transitive happen-before order. The hybrid race detection helps reduce many false positives reported by the Eraser algorithm alone.

Based on the lockset analysis and happen-before orders, there are many other approaches to detect race conditions. (Engler and Ashcraft 2003) proposes a static technique that uses flow-sensitive, inter-procedural static analysis to check race conditions and deadlocks. One of the contributions is to rank all warnings using various criteria such as simple checking, simple statistical measure, and precise statistical measure. (Yu et al. 2005) proposes an adaptive tracking scheme that can reduce the runtime monitoring overhead to at most 3x slowdown of the original program. In addition, a post-processing step is performed to rank race warnings with the most likely ones on top. Their implementation on Microsoft.NET platform exploits the benefits of Common Language Runtime so that the instrumentation happens on the virtual machine level and no modification on the original programs is needed. They track the happen-before order through the vector clock attached to each memory access. Many other related work have been introduced in Section 5.1.

Detecting Message Race in MPI Programs

(Netzer et al. 1996) is one of the first papers that explore the problem of detecting message races in MPI programs. The proposed approach is a dynamic algorithm with two passes that can handle long running MPI programs regardless their execution length. Specifically, it uses a vector timestamp to track the happen-before relation between different send events then determines the possible concurrent send events. In the first

pass, for each send event that has been matched by a receive event in the real execution, it tries to find out all possible send events that could be matched by that receive event. The second pass uses the information reported by the first pass to validate the message races.

(Park et al., 2007) detects all potential race conditions by checking concurrent communication between processes. It uses vector timestamps to determine possible concurrency between send/receive events in MPI programs. To capture all points-to-points MPI function calls, it replaces all the original calls with the profiling calls defined by MPI profiling interface.

Approaches to Detect Atomicity Violation

The approaches to detect atomicity violations root in the detection of serializability in database systems. The algorithms can be classified into two main categories: the approaches based on Lipton's reduction theorem (Lipton 1975), and the approaches based on detecting unserializable patterns.

The approach in (Flanagan and Qadeer 2003) is a typical algorithm based on Lipton reduction theorem for analyzing atomicity in multithreaded programs. The theory of reduction is based on the notion of right-mover and left-mover actions. In the reduction algorithm, events are classified according to their commutativity properties. An event is a *right-mover* if, whenever it appears immediately *before* an event of a different thread, the two events can be swapped (*i.e.*, they can be executed in the opposite order without blocking) without changing the resulting state. A *left-mover* is defined analogously. For example, if an event e_1 of a thread is a lock acquire, its immediate successive event e_2 from another thread cannot be a successful acquire or release of the same lock because an acquire would block and a release would fail (in Java, it would throw an exception). Hence, e_1 and e_2 can be swapped without affecting the result, so e_1 is a right-mover. Lock release events are left-movers for similar reasons. An event is a *both-mover* if it is both a left-mover and a right-mover. For example, if there are only read events (no write) on a given variable, the read events commute in both directions with all events, so these read events are both-movers. Events not known to be left or right movers are non-movers. For Java programs, a classification of events can be conveniently obtained based on synchronization operations. Lock acquire events are right-movers. Lock release events are left-movers. Race-free reads and race-free writes are both-movers. An execution path is considered to be atomic if it contains sequence of right-movers, followed by at most one non-mover action and then a sequence of left-movers.

The approach in (Wang and Stoller 2006b) is a typical algorithm based on detecting unserializable patterns. The algorithm checks atomicity violations by permuting the order of events that are consistent with the synchronization events. Explicitly enumerating these permutations would be prohibitively expensive. Instead, they look for unserializable patterns of operations from these events. An unserializable pattern is a sequence in which operations from different threads are interleaved in an unserializable way. As an example, the following table shows four unserializable patterns when multiple threads share exactly one variable. The more complex cases, such as multiple shared variables, are introduced in (Wang and Stoller 2006b).

From top left to bottom right, these four patterns shown in Algorithm 12 are described below.

- A read in one transaction occurs between two writes in another transaction.
- A write in one transaction occurs between two reads in another transaction.
- A write in one transaction occurs between a write and a subsequent read in another transaction.
- The final write in one transaction occurs between a read and a subsequent write in another transaction.

Many other approaches have been proposed to check atomicity violations. (Vaziri et al. 2006) takes a similar approach to check atomicity problems by searching non-serializable interleaving scenarios. In addition, they present a language extension called *atomic set of locations* to allow programmers to specify existence of properties between fields in objects. They use an inter-procedural static analysis technique that automatically infers those points where synchronization is missing. (Xu et al. 2005) proposes a tool to detect serializability violation (*i.e.*, atomicity violation). It can automatically infer atomic regions where serializability criterion must be met. (Lu et al. 2006) proposes an approach to detect atomicity violations based on access interleaving invariants that are observed in multiple runs of the concurrent program. The access interleaving invariants imply the programmers' assumptions about the atomicity of certain code regions. (Farzan and Madhusudan 2008) proposes a space-efficient monitoring algorithm for checking atomicity violations. The algorithm builds a conflict-graph through dynamic monitoring the program and then reduces the conflict graph into a summarized conflict graph to check atomicity problem. (Chen et al. 2009) presents a hybrid approach that complements dynamic analysis with static speculation to detect potential atomicity violations in concurrent Java programs. Their approach first performs static analysis to obtain summaries of synchronizations

Algorithm 12.

W(x) R(x) W(x)	R(x) W(x) R(x)
W(x) W(x) R(x)	R(x) FW(x) W(x)

and accesses to shared variables. The static summaries are then instantiated with runtime values during dynamic executions to speculatively approximate the behaviors of branches that are not taken. Compared to dynamic analysis, the hybrid approach is able to detect atomicity violations in unexecuted parts of the code. Compared to static analysis, the hybrid approach produces fewer false alarms. More approaches about checking atomicity violations appear in Section 5.1.

TOOLS TO DETECT CONCURRENCY ERRORS

There are many methods and tools that have been developed for ensuring the correctness of multithreaded and MPI programs. Here we give a brief overview of the widely used or well-known tools. The commercial debugging tools include PGI Tools, TotalView, Intel Message Checker, Allinea Distributed Debugging Tool (DDT), and Nvidia Nexus and CUDA GDB. The open source community offers Eclipse Parallel Tools Platform (PTP), MPI-CHECK, Umpire, MARMOT, ISP, MPI-Spin, and MS CHESS.

Commercial Debugging Tools

PGDBG (pgi2009) is developed by the Portland Group, Inc. (PGI) as a symbolic debugger for Fortran, C/C++, and assembly language programs. It provides most typical debugger features such as breakpoint setting, single instruction stepping, visualization of application variables, memory locations, and registers. It supports debugging parallel applications using Pthreads or Windows threads, OpenMP and MPI, as well as hybrid programming paradigms that combine two or more of aforementioned parallel programming interfaces.

Intel Message Checker (DeSouza et al. 2005) is an MPI correctness tool that helps ensure the correctness of MPI programs. It can detect many MPI errors such as mismatched arguments and buffers (size and type), race conditions, resources leaking, overlapped read/write to the same message buffers, message checksum errors, and potential deadlocks. It comes with a user-friendly graphical user interface. However, the trace files generated by Intel Message Checker can be very large thus it may be inefficient to analyze the trace files.

Intel Thread Checker (inta) is a data race and deadlock detection tool for 32-bit and 64-bit multithreaded and OpenMP applications in Windows and Linux. However, its overhead could be as high as 200x of the original program's performance which makes it hard to be adopted on long-running server programs (Sack et al. 2006).

Intel Trace Analyzer and Collector (intb) contains an MPI correctness checking library that can dynamically detect many communication errors including deadlocks, data corruption, or errors regards to MPI parameters, data types, buffers, communicators, point-to-point messages, and collective operations. The tool supports setting debugger breakpoints to greatly help the analysis. It can also instrument the original source code of MPI programs to monitor data types and MPI calls with their wrapper calls and compile the instrumented programs with their checking library. It can scale to large systems with many processes running concurrently.

TotalView (Kingsbury 2007) is a commercial MPI tool providing industrial level of debugging support. It can debug one or many processes and/or threads with complete control over program execution. In addition, it has the capability of reproducing programs crashes. It can visualize the state of the running program for efficient debugging of memory errors and leaking and diagnosing subtle problems like deadlocks and race conditions. It works with C, C++, and FORTRAN applications. Its latest extension supports debugging CUDA programs.

Allinea Distributed Debugging Tool (DDT) (DDT) is another commercial debugging tool with graphical user interface that supports both centralized and distributed debugging. It supports

C/C++, FORTRAN, OpenMP, MPI, Pthreads, Windows threads, and CUDA. DDT supports fine-grained control over the target program to examine the program states in more effective ways during execution. In addition, with the support of controlling individual threads and/or processes separately or collectively, it allows programmer to examine data across threads/processes. The programmable STL Wizard that comes with DDT enables the programmers to view C++ Standard Template Library structures such as lists, maps, sets, pairs, and strings.

Nvidia introduces **Nexus** (NVIDIA Nexus, 2009) in October, 2009, which is a tool integrated into Microsoft Visual Studio 2008 to debug, profile, and analyze CUDA programs. **CUDA-GDB** (CUDA-GDB) is an extension of the GNU Project Debugger (GDB) to debug CUDA programs on both 32-bit and 64-bit Linux. CUDA-GDB supports debugging both host and GPU code. CUDA-GDB runs only on CUDA-capable GPUs with the compute capability later than 1.1.

Open-source Debugging Tools

Eclipse Parallel Tools Platform (PTP) (Watson et al. 2006) is a plug-in to Eclipse IDE and contains many productivity tools to help programmers launch, control, monitor, and debug MPI programs. It is also a framework for developers to integrate external tools so that they can take advantage of the user interface components and services provided by both PTP and Eclipse. The latest version is 4.0 published at the end of June, 2010.

PTP manages MPI source programs as projects. With PTP, programmers can utilize all the productivity features in Eclipse to develop their programs such as syntax highlighting, static code checking, automatic build, and error location. PTP uses the resource manager to manage and control the resources required for launching a parallel job. For example, given a cluster with Open MPI installed, the Open MPI runtime system would be considered the resource manager. Once the pro-

grammers configure the resource manager, they can launch, monitor, and control their programs on the target resource regardless whether the target resource is remote or local. Programmers can also launch a MPI program in debug mode of PTP. In the debug mode, PTP switches Eclipse to Parallel Debug View which allows programmers to suspend processes, and visualize the detailed information about the suspended processes such as stack frame content and local variables values. Parallel break point is another feature supported in PTP. Programmers can either set global breakpoints in the source program that apply to all processes in any job or set local breakpoints that apply only to a specific set of processes (which can include the root set) for a single job. The difference is that a global breakpoint remains in effect between job launches while local breakpoints are removed when the job completes.

MARMOT (Krammer et al. 2004) is a runtime detection tool that samples the MPI-calls invoked in the runtime and subsequently checks the correct usage of these calls and their arguments. It can be used in conjunction with traditional sequential debuggers such as GDB to help the programmers pinpoint the bugs. It supports both C and FORTRAN languages. After the runtime monitoring, it generates a human-readable log file which can be analyzed for reporting the violations of MPI specification. It can also check the call stack trace for potential deadlocks based on a time-out mechanism. However, the deadlock detection could report false positives since some calls would take longer than expected due to physical network problems or other reasons.

UMPIRE (Vetter and de Supinski 2000) is another dynamic tool to analyze MPI programming errors using a profiling interface like MARMOT. It can detect deadlocks by combining time-out mechanism and dependency graphs together.

ISP (Vo et al. 2008) is a tool that dynamically verifies MPI programs. It consists of three parts: profiler, scheduler, and checker. The profiler wraps the MPI-related function calls inside their wrapper functions and intercepts these MPI function call events for later processing. The scheduler carries out all possible schedulings while using POE (Partial Order Reduction) to remove the redundant states and minimize the state space. The scheduler explicitly considers and handles MPI-specific properties including wildcard receives, barriers, which are important to scheduling. The checker checks each permuted ordering for possible violations of properties such as deadlocks and resource leaking.

MPI-Spin (Siegel 2007) is an extension to the popular model checker Spin (Holzmann 2003). It adds to Spin's input language a number of functions, types, and constants for modeling MPI programs. By default, MPI-Spin checks a number of generic correctness properties in MPI programs. These properties include (1) the program cannot deadlock, (2) there are never two incomplete requests whose buffers intersect non-trivially, (3) the total number of outstanding requests never exceeds a specified bound, (4) when MPI_Finalize is called, there are no request objects allocated for and there are no buffered messages destined for the calling process, and (5) the size of an incoming message is never greater than the size of the receive buffer. In addition, MPI-Spin can check application-specific user-written properties that are formulated in temporal logic. It provides extensive support for symbolic execution, making it possible to verify that a program behaves correctly on all possible inputs.

MPI-CHECK (Luecke et al. 2003) is an open-source tool developed for checking MPI programs in FORTRAN and C/C++ languages. It provides both compile-time and runtime checks on the target MPI programs. With macro and the wrappers for MPI routines, compiler can invoke MPI-CHECK to statically check the data type of each argument, the intent of each argument, and the number of arguments in the routines. For the runtime checking, MPI-CHECK first instruments the original source program and links it with their modules to produce an instrumented executable.

When the resulting executable runs, instrumented code emits events to MPI-CHECK and possible error/warning messages are reported if found. MPI-CHECK run-time checker checks all MPI-1 and MPI-2 routines for problems such as buffer data type inconsistency, buffer out of bounds, improper placement of MPI_INIT, illegal message length, and invalid MPI rank. However, MPI-CHECK places significant performance overhead for the target programs under test which could prevent it from being deployed to large scale real-world programs.

Library-Based MPI Debugging Tools

Some level of debugging support is also provided in many MPI implementations such as OpenMPI (Graham et al. 2005), LAM-MPI (Burns et al. 1994) and MPICH (Worringen et al.2002). They either provide additional compile-time flags for checking MPI function calls, or come with a separate profiler/monitor for runtime testing. OpenMPI provides several compiler flags for statically checking some properties of function calls such as null parameter passing, checking potential resource leaking, displaying runtime configuration such as MCA parameters and their values during MPI_INIT call, and printing stack trace when MPI_ABORT() is invoked. LAM-MPI implementation has a GUI-based tool called XMPI that allows programmers to debug and visualize the running MPI programs. It can take snapshots of runtime synchronization events and retrieve detailed information about MPI events such as communicator, data type, tag, and message content and length. MPICH provides support for external debuggers such as TotalView and DDT.

Summary and Comparison of Tools

To summarize the differences and commonality between these tools, we present a comparison in Table 1.

Table 1. Comparison of MPI error prevention and detection tools. **S** *denotes using static analysis;* **D** *denotes using dynamic analysis which includes both online analysis and offline trace-based analysis;* **H** *denotes using both Static and Dynamic; × denotes Not Available. The column "MPI-specific problems" include resource leak, mismatched buffer size and type, null parameter passing etc. None of the tools is able to support detecting atomicity violations so far.*

	Deadlock Detection	MPI-specific problems	Message Race Detection	Data Race Detection	Runtime Debugging Support
Allinea Distributed Debugging Tool (DDT)	×	×	×	×	Pthreads Windows Threads OpenMP MPI in C MPI in Fortran CUDA
Intel Message Checker	×	MPI in C: **D** MPI in Fortran: **D**	MPI in C: **D** MPI in Fortran: **D**	×	×
Intel Thread Checker	OpenMP: **D** Pthreads: **D**	×	×	OpenMP: **D** Pthreads: **D**	×
Intel Trace Analyzer and Collector	MPI in C: **D** MPI in Fortran: **D**	MPI in C: **D** MPI in Fortran: **D**	MPI in C: **D** MPI in Fortran: **D**	×	MPI in C MPI in Fortran
ISP	MPI in C: **D**	MPI in C: **D**	×	×	×
MARMOT	MPI in C: **D** MPI in Fortran: **D**	MPI in C: **D** MPI in Fortran: **D**	×	×	×
MPI-CHECK	MPI in C: **D** MPI in Fortran: **D**	MPI in C: **H** MPI in Fortran: **H**	×	×	×
MPI-Spin	MPI in C: **S**	MPI in C: **S**	×	×	×
Nvidia Nexus	×	×	×	×	CUDA
PGDBG	×	×	×	×	Pthreads Windows Threads OpenMP MPI in C MPI in Fortran
Eclipse Parallel Tools Platform (PTP)	×	×	×	×	OpenMP MPI in C MPI in Fortran
TotalView	×	×	×	×	Pthreads WindowsThreads OpenMP MPI in C MPI in Fortran
UMPIRE	MPI in C: **D** MPI in Fortran: **D**	×	×	×	×
LAM-MPI	×	×	×	×	MPI in C MPI in Fortran
MPICH	×	×	×	×	×
Open MPI	×	MPI in C: **S** MPI in Fortran: **S**	×	×	×

As we can see from this Table 1, most current tools are using dynamic analysis to find out and correct potential errors. This could be partly attributed to the precision of dynamic analysis which leads to much fewer false positives. However, due to the nature of dynamic analysis, users might find difficulty in adopting them on many large programs.

CONCLUSION

We give a comprehensive introduction to multithreaded and message passing programming, including the approaches to detect deadlock, race condition, and atomicity violation, as well as the widely used tools to debug concurrent programs. With the prevalence of multi-core CPU and many-core co-processor, concurrent programming is becoming more popular and bringing significant effect on the practice and research of software engineering. The research on detecting concurrency errors is attracting more and more attentions. With the effort of industry and academia, we expect that the next generation of concurrent programming will be easier for coding and debugging.

REFERENCES

Agarwal, R., Bensalem, S., Farchi, E., Havelund, K., Nir-Buchbinder, Y., & Stoller, S. D. (in press). Detection of deadlock potentials in multi-threaded programs. *IBM Journal of Research and Development*.

Agarwal, R., Sasturkar, A., Wang, L., & Stoller, S. D. (2005a). Optimized run-time race detection and atomicity checking using partial discovered types. In *Proceedings of the 20th IEEE/ACM International Conference on Automated Software Engineering (ASE)*. ACM Press.

Agarwal, R., Wang, L., & Stoller, S. D. (2005b). Detecting potential deadlocks with static analysis and runtime monitoring. *In Proceedings of the Parallel and Distributed Systems: Testing and Debugging (PADTAD)*. Springer-Verlag.

Anderson, P., Reps, T., Teitelbaum, T., & Zarins, M. (2003). Tool support for fine-grained software inspection. *IEEE Software, 20*(4), 42–50.

ANL MPI Using MPI in Simple Programs http://www.mcs.anl.gov/research/projects/mpi/usingmpi/examples/simplempi/main.htm

Bensalem, S., & Havelund, K. (2005). Scalable deadlock analysis of multi-threaded programs. In S. Ur (Ed.), *IBM Verification Conference*, (LCNS 3875), Haifa, Israel. Springer.

Borthakur, D. (2007). *The Hadoop Distributed File System: Architecture and design*. The Apache Software Foundation.

Boyapati, C., Lee, R., & Rinard, M. (2002). Ownership types for safe programming: Preventing data races and deadlocks. In *Proceedings of the 17th ACM Conference on Object-Oriented Programming, Systems, Languages and Applications (OOPSLA)*, (pp. 211–230). ACM Press.

Boyapati, C., & Rinard, M. C. (2001). A parameterized type system for race-free Java programs. In *Proceedings of ACM Conference on Object-Oriented Programming, Systems, Languages, and Applications (OOPSLA)*, (pp. 56–69). ACM Press.

Boyer, M., Skadron, K., & Weimer, W. (2008). Automated dynamic analysis of CUDA programs. In *Proceedings of the Third Workshop on Software Tools for Multi-Core Systems*.

Buck, I., Foley, T., Horn, D., Sugerman, J., Fatahalian, K., & Houston, M. (2004). Brook for GPUs: Stream computing on graphics hardware. *ACM Transactions on Graphics, 23*(3), 777–786.

Burns, G., Daoud, R., & Vaigl, J. (1994). LAM: An open cluster environment for MPI. In *Proceedings of Supercomputing Symposium*, (pp. 379–386).

Bush, W., Pincus, J. D., & Sielaff, D. J. (2000). A static analyzer for finding dynamic programming errors. *Software, Practice & Experience, 30*(7), 775–802.

Cadar, C., Ganesh, V., Pawlowski, P. M., Dill, D. L., & Engler, D. R. (2006). EXE: Automatically generating inputs of death. In *Proceedings of the 13th ACM conference on Computer and communications security (CCS)*. ACM Press.

Chen, F., Serbanuta, T. F., & Rosu, G. (2008). jPredictor: A predictive runtime analysis tool for Java. In *Proceedings of the 30th international conference on Software engineering (ICSE '08)*, pages 221–230. ACM.

Chen, Q., Wang, L., Yang, Z., & Stoller, S. D. (2009). HAVE: Integrated dynamic and static analysis for atomicity violations. *In Proceedings of International Conference on Fundamental Approaches to Software Engineering (FASE)*, (LNCS 5503), (pp. 425–439). Springer.

Choi, J.-D., Lee, K., Loginov, A., O'Callahan, R., Sarkar, V., & Sridharan, M. (2002). Efficient and precise datarace detection for multi-threaded object-oriented programs. In *Proceedings of the ACM SIGPLAN Conference on Programming Language Design and Implementation (PLDI)*, (pp. 258–269). ACM Press.

Cuda, N. V. I. D. I. A. *CUDA Compute Unified Device Architecture Programming Guide*. http://www.nvidia.com/object/cuda_home.html

CUDA-GDB. CUDA-GDB: The NVIDIA CUDA Debugger. http://developer.download.nvidia.com/compute/cuda/2_1/cudagdb/CUDA_GDB_User_Manual.pdf

Das, M., Lerner, S., & Seigle, M. (2002). Esp: Path-sensitive program verification in polynomial time. In *proceedings of the ACM SIGPLAN Conference on Programming Language Design and Implementation (PLDI)*.

DDT Allinea Software, Allinea DDT The Distributed Debugging Tool. http://www.allinea.com/index.php?page=48.

Dean, J., & Ghemawat, S. (2008). MapReduce: Simplified data processing on large clusters. *Communications of the ACM, 51*(1), 107–113.

DeSouza, J., Kuhn, B., de Supinski, B. R., Samofalov, V., Zheltov, S., & Bratanov, S. (2005). Automated scalable debugging of MPI programs with Intel message checker. In *Proceedings of the Second International Workshop on Software Engineering for High Performance Computing System Applications*, (pp. 78–82). New York: ACM.

Detlefs, D. L., Leino, K. R. M., Nelson, G., & Saxe, J. B. (1998). Extended static checking. Research Report 159, Compaq SRC. Retrieved from http://www.research.compaq.com/SRC/esc/

Dwyer, M., Hatcliff, J., Hoosier, M. & Robby (2005). *Building your own software model checker using the Bogor extensible model checking framework*. Computer Aided Verification (CAV).

Elmas, T., Qadeer, S., & Tasiran, S. (2007). Goldilocks: A race and transaction-aware Java runtime. In *Proceedings of the ACM SIGPLAN Conference on Programming Language Design and Implementation (PLDI)*. ACM Press.

Engler, D., & Ashcraft, K. (2003). RacerX: Effective, static detection of race conditions and deadlocks. In *Proceedings of ACM SIGOPS Symposium on Operating Systems Principles (SOSP)*. ACM Press.

Ernst, M. D., Cockrell, J., Griswold, W. G., & Notkin, D. (2001). Dynamically discovering likely program invariants to support program evolution. *IEEE Transactions on Software Engineering, 27*(2), 99–123.

Fei, L., & Midkiff, S. P. (2006). Artemis: Practical run-time monitoring of applications for execution anomalies. In *Proceedings of the ACM SIGPLAN Conference on Programming Language Design and Implementation (PLDI)*, (pp. 84–95). ACM Press.

Flanagan, C., & Freund, S. (2000). Type-based race detection for Java. In *Proceedings of the ACM SIGPLAN Conference on Programming Language Design and Implementation (PLDI)*, (pp. 219–232). ACM Press.

Flanagan, C., & Freund, S. N. (2004a). Atomizer: A dynamic Atomicity checker for multithreaded programs. *In Proceedings of the ACM Symposium on Principles of Programming Languages (POPL)*, (pp 256–267). ACM Press.

Flanagan, C., & Freund, S. N. (2004b). *Type inference against races.* In Static Analysis Symposium, (LNCS 3148). Springer-Verlag.

Flanagan, C., & Freund, S. N. (2009). FastTrack: Efficient and precise dynamic race detection. In *Proceedings of the ACM SIGPLAN Conference on Programming Language Design and Implementation (PLDI)*, (pp. 121–133). ACM Press.

Flanagan, C., Freund, S. N., & Qadeer, S. (2005). Exploiting purity for Atomicity. *IEEE Transactions on Software Engineering, 31*(4).

Flanagan, C., Freund, S. N., & Yi, J. (2008). Velodrome: A sound and complete dynamic Atomicity checker for multithreaded programs. In *Proceedings of the ACM SIGPLAN Conference on Programming Language Design and Implementation (PLDI)*, (pp. 293–303), New York: ACM.

Flanagan, C., & Qadeer, S. (2003). A type and effect system for Atomicity. In *Proceedings of the ACM SIGPLAN Conference on Programming Language Design and Implementation (PLDI)*. ACM Press.

Godefroid, P. (1997). Model checking for programming languages using Verisoft. In *Proceedings of the ACM Symposium on Principles of Programming Languages (POPL)*. ACM Press.

Godefroid, P., Klarlund, N., & Sen, K. (2005). DART: Directed Automated Random Testing. In *Proceedings of the ACM SIGPLAN Conference on Programming Language Design and Implementation (PLDI)*. ACM Press.

Graham, R. L., Woodall, T. S., & Squyres, J. M. (2005). Open MPI: A flexible high performance MPI. In *Proceedings, 6th Annual International Conference on Parallel Processing and Applied Mathematics*, Poznan, Poland.

Gulavani, B. S., Henzinger, T. A., Kannan, Y., Nori, A. V., & Rajamani, S. K. (2006). Synergy: A new algorithm for property checking. In *Proceedings of the 14th ACM SIGSOFT International Symposium on Foundations of Software Engineering (SIGSOFT '06/FSE-14)*. ACM Press.

Hadoop Hadoop Open Source MapReduce Platform. http://lucene.apache.org/hadoop/

Havelund, K. (2000). Using runtime analysis to guide model checking of Java programs. In *Proceedings of the 7th Int'l. SPIN Workshop on Model Checking of Software*, (LNCS 1885), (pp. 245–264). Springer-Verlag.

Hilbrich, T., de Supinski, B. R., Schulz, M., & Müller, M. S. 2009. A graph based approach for MPI deadlock detection. In *Proceedings of the 23rd International Conference on Supercomputing*, Yorktown Heights, NY, (pp. 296-305). New York: ACM.

Holzmann, G. J. (2003). *The SPIN model checker*. Addison-Wesley.

Holzmann, G. J., & Peled, D. (1994). An improvement in formal verification. In *Proceedings of International Conference on Formal Description Techniques (FORTE'94), volume 6 of IFIP Conference Proceedings*, (pp. 197–211). Chapman & Hall.

Hou, Q., Zhou, K., & Guo, B. (2009). Debugging GPU stream programs through automatic dataflow recording and visualization. In *ACM SIGGRAPH papers* (pp. 1–11). New York: ACM.

inta Intel Thread Checker. http://software.intel.com/en-us/intel-thread-checker

intb Intel Trace Analyzer. http://software.intel.com/en-us/intel-trace-analyzer

Joshi, P., Park, C.-S., Sen, K., & Naik, M. (2009). A randomized dynamic program analysis technique for detecting real deadlocks. In *Proceedings of the 2009 ACM SIGPLAN conference on Programming Language Design and Implementation (PLDI)*, (pp. 110–120). ACM Press.

Kang, M.-H., Ha, O.-K., Jun, S.-W., & Jun, Y.-K. (2009). A tool for detecting first races in OpenMP programs. In *Proceedings from the 10th International Conference Parallel Computing Technologies*, (pp. 299–303).

Kingsbury, B. (2007). Organizing processes and threads for debugging. In *Proceedings of the 2007 ACM Workshop on Parallel and Distributed Systems: Testing and Debugging*, (pp. 21–26), New York: ACM.

Krammer, B., Muller, M. S., & Resch, M. M. (2004). MPI application development using the analysis tool MARMOT. In *Proceedings from the International Conference on Computational Science*, (pp 464–471).

Liblit, B., Aiken, A., Zheng, A., & Jordan, M. I. (2003). Bug isolation via remote program sampling. In *Proceedings of the ACM SIGPLAN Conference on Programming Language Design and Implementation (PLDI)*, (pp. 141–154). ACM Press.

Lu, S., Tucek, J., Qin, F., & Zhou, Y. (2006). AVIO: Detecting Atomicity violations via access interleaving invariants. In *Proceedings of the Twelfth International Conference on Architectural Support for Programming Languages and Operating Systems (ASPLOS)*. ACM Press.

Luecke, G., Chen, H., Coyle, J., Hoekstra, J., Kraeva, M., & Zou, Y. (2003). MPI-CHECK: A tool for checking FORTRAN 90 MPI programs. *Concurrency and Computation, 15*(2), 93–100.

Luecke, G., Zou, Y., Coyle, J., Hoekstra, J., & Kraeva, M. (2002). Deadlock detection in MPI programs. [John Wiley & Sons.]. *Concurrency and Computation, 14*(11), 911–932.

Majumdar, R., & Sen, K. (2007). Hybrid concolic testing. In *Proceedings of the 29th International Conference on Software Engineering (ICSE)*. IEEE Press.

McCool, M., Du Toit, S., Popa, T., Chan, B., & Moule, K. (2004). Shader algebra. *ACM Transactions on Graphics, 23*(3), 787–795.

McMillan, K. L. (1994). *Symbolic model checking*. Boston: Kluwer Academic Publishers.

Musuvathi, M., & Qadeer, S. (2008). Fair stateless model checking. In *Proceedings of the ACM SIGPLAN Conference on Programming Language Design and Implementation (PLDI)*, (pp. 362–371). ACM Press.

Naik, M., & Aiken, A. (2007). Conditional must not aliasing for static race detection. In *Proceedings of the 34th annual ACM SIGPLAN-SIGACT Symposium on Principles of Programming Languages (POPL)*. ACM Press.

NCSA-CUDA NCSA CUDA Tutorial. http://www.ncsa.illinois.edu/UserInfo/Training/Workshops/CUDA/presentations/tutorial-CUDA.html

Netzer, R. H. B., Brennan, T. W., & Damodaran-Kamal, S. K. (1996). Debugging race conditions in message-passing programs. In *Proceedings of the SIGMETRICS Symposium on Parallel and Distributed Tools*, (pp. 31–40). New York: ACM.

Nexus, N. V. I. D. I. A. 2009 - Visual Studio-based GPU Development, http://developer.nvidia.com/object/nexus.html

O'Callahan, R., & Choi, J.-D. (2003). Hybrid dynamic data race detection. In *Proceedings of ACM SIGPLAN 2003 Symposium on Principles and Practice of Parallel Programming (PPoPP)*, (pp. 167–178). ACM.

OpenCL Open Computing Language (OpenCL). http://www.khronos.org/opencl/.

Park, C.-S., & Sen, K. (2008). Randomized active Atomicity violation detection in concurrent programs. In *Proceedings of the 16th ACM SIGSOFT International Symposium on Foundations of Software Engineering (FSE'08)*, (pp. 135–145). New York: ACM.

pgi2009 (2009). PGI Tools Guide. http://www.pgroup.com/doc/pgitools.pdf

Pratikakis, P., Foster, J. S., & Hicks, M. (2006). Locksmith: Context-sensitive correlation analysis for race detection. In *Proceedings of the ACM SIGPLAN Conference on Programming Language Design and Implementation (PLDI)*, (pp. 320–331). ACM.

RapidMind RapidMind. http://www.rapidmind.com/.

Ratanaworabhan, P., Burtscher, M., Kirovski, D., Zorn, B., Nagpal, R., & Pattabiraman, K. (2009). Detecting and tolerating asymmetric races. In *Proceedings of the 14th ACM SIGPLAN symposium on Principles and Practice of Parallel Programming (PPoPP)*, (pp. 173–184). ACM Press.

Sack, P., Bliss, B. E., Ma, Z., Petersen, P., & Torrellas, J. (2006). Accurate and efficient filtering for the Intel thread checker race detector. In *Proceedings of the 1st Workshop on Architectural and System Support for Improving Software Dependability*, (pp. 34–41) New York: ACM.

Sasturkar, A., Agarwal, R., Wang, L., & Stoller, S. D. (2005). Automated type-based analysis of data races and Atomicity. In *Proceedings of the ACM SIGPLAN 2005 Symposium on Principles and Practice of Parallel Programming (PPoPP)*. ACM Press. Savage, S., Burrows, M., Nelson, G., Sobalvarro, P. & Anderson, T.E. (1997). Eraser: A dynamic data race detector for multithreaded programs. *ACM Transactions on Computer Systems*, *15*(4), 391–411.

Sen, K. (2008). Race directed random testing of concurrent programs. In *Proceedings of the ACM SIGPLAN Conference on Programming Language Design and Implementation (PLDI)*, (pp. 11–21). ACM Press.

Siegel, S. F. (2007). Verifying parallel programs with MPI-SPIN. In *Proceedings of the 14th European PVM/MPI User's Group Meeting on Recent Advances in Parallel Virtual Machine and Message Passing Interface*, (pp. 13–14). Berlin/Heidelberg: Springer-Verlag.

Silberschatz, A., Galvin, P. B., & Gagne, G. (Eds.). (2008). *Operating system concepts* (8th ed.). John Wiley & Sons.

UPC UPC. UPC language specifications. http://upc.gwu.edu/docs/upc_spec_1.1.1.pdf

Vetter, J. S., & de Supinski, B. R. (2000). Dynamic software testing of MPI applications with UMPIRE. In *Proceedings of the 2000 ACM/IEEE Conference on Supercomputing (CDROM)*, (p. 51). Washington, DC: IEEE Computer Society.

Visser, W., Havelund, K., Brat, G., Park, S., & Lerda, F. (2003). Model checking programs. *Automated Software Engineering*, *10*(2), 203–232.

Vo, A., Vakkalanka, S., DeLisi, M., Gopalakrishnan, G., Kirby, R. M., & Thakur, R. (2008). Formal verification of practical MPI programs. In *Proceedings of the 14th ACM SIGPLAN Symposium on Principles and Practice of Parallel Programming*, (pp. 261–270). New York: ACM.

von Praun, C., & Gross, T. R. (2001). Object race detection. In *Proceedings of the ACM Conference on Object-Oriented Programming, Systems, Languages, and Applications (OOPSLA)*, (pp. 70–82). ACM Press.

Wang, L., & Stoller, S. D. (2005). Static analysis of Atomicity for programs with non-blocking synchronization. In *Proceedings of the ACM SIGPLAN 2005 Symposium on Principles and Practice of Parallel Programming (PPoPP)*. ACM Press.

Wang, L., & Stoller, S. D. (2006a). Accurate and efficient runtime detection of Atomicity errors in concurrent programs. In *Proceedings of the ACM SIGPLAN 2006 Symposium on Principles and Practice of Parallel Programming (PPoPP)*. ACM Press.

Wang, L., & Stoller, S. D. (2006b). Runtime analysis of Atomicity for multi-threaded programs. *IEEE Transactions on Software Engineering, 32*(2), 93–110.

Watson, G., Rasmussen, C., & Tibbitts, B. (2006). Application development using eclipse and the parallel tools platform. In *Proceedings of the 2006 ACM/IEEE Conference on Supercomputing*, (p. 204). New York: ACM.

Worringen, J., Scholtyssik, K., Dr, P. & Bemmerl, T. (2002). *MP-MPICH: User documentation technical notes*.

Xu, M., Bodik, R., & Hill, M. D. (2005). A serializability volation detector for shared-memory server programs. In *Proceedings of the ACM SIGPLAN Conference on Programming Language Design and Implementation (PLDI)*. ACM Press.

Yu, Y., Rodeheffer, T., & Chen, W. (2005). RaceTrack: Efficient detection of data race conditions via adaptive tracking. In *Proceedings of the Symposium on Operating Systems Principles (SOSP)*. ACM Press.

ADDITIONAL READING

Chen., et al. 2008 Chen, F., Serbanuta, T. F., and Rosu, G. (2008). jPredictor: A Predictive Runtime Analysis Tool for Java. In Proceedings of the 30th international conference on Software engineering (ICSE '08), pages 221–230. ACM.

Chen., et al. 2009 Chen, Q., Wang, L., Yang, Z., and Stoller, S. D. (2009). HAVE: Integrated Dynamic and Static Analysis for Atomicity Violations. In Proceedings of International Conference on Fundamental Approaches to Software Engineering (FASE), volume 5503 of LNCS, pages 425–439. Springer.

Choi., et al. 2002 Choi, J.-D., Lee, K., Loginov, A., O'Callahan, R., Sarkar, V. and Sridharan, M. (2002). Efficient and Precise Datarace Detection for Multi-threaded object-oriented programs. In Proc. ACM SIGPLAN Conference on Programming Language Design and Implementation (PLDI), pages 258–269. ACM Press.

Engler and Ashcraft 2003 Engler, D. and Ashcraft, K. (2003). RacerX: Effective, Static Detection of Race Conditions and Deadlocks. In Proceedings of ACM SIGOPS Symposium on Operating Systems Principles (SOSP). ACM Press.

Ernst, (2001). Ernst, M. D., Cockrell, J., Griswold, W. G., and Notkin, D. (2001). Dynamically Discovering Likely Program Invariants to Support Program Evolution. *IEEE Transactions on Software Engineering, 27*(2), 99–123.

Fei and Midkiff 2006 Fei, L. and Midkiff, S. P. (2006). Artemis: Practical Run-time Monitoring of Applications for Execution Anomalies. In Proc. ACM SIGPLAN Conference on Programming Language Design and Implementation (PLDI), pages 84–95. ACM Press.

Flanagan, (2005). Flanagan, C., Freund, S. N., and Qadeer, S. (2005). Exploiting Purity for Atomicity. *IEEE Transactions on Software Engineering*, *31*(4).

Flanagan., et al. 2008 Flanagan, C., Freund, S. N., and Yi, J. (2008). Velodrome: A Sound and Complete Dynamic Atomicity Checker for Multithreaded Programs. In Proceedings of the ACM SIGPLAN Conference on Programming Language Design and Implementation (PLDI), pages 293–303, New York, NY, USA. ACM.

Flanagan and Freund 2000 Flanagan, C. and Freund, S. (2000). Type-based Race Detection for Java. In Proc. ACM SIGPLAN Conference on Programming Language Design and Implementation (PLDI), pages 219–232. ACM Press.

Flanagan and Freund 2004a Flanagan, C. and Freund, S. N. (2004a). Atomizer: A Dynamic Atomicity Checker for Multithreaded Programs. In Proc. ACM Symposium on Principles of Programming Languages (POPL), pages 256–267. ACM Press.

Flanagan and Freund 2004b Flanagan, C. and Freund, S. N. (2004b). Type Inference Against Races. In Static Analysis Symposium (SAS), volume 3148 of LNCS. Springer-Verlag.

Flanagan and Freund 2009 Flanagan, C. and Freund, S. N. (2009). FastTrack: Ffficient and Precise Dynamic Race Detection. In Proc. ACM SIGPLAN Conference on Programming Language Design and Implementation (PLDI), pages 121–133. ACM Press.

Flanagan and Qadeer 2003 Flanagan, C. and Qadeer, S. (2003). A Type and Effect System for Atomicity. In Proc. ACM SIGPLAN Conference on Programming Language Design and Implementation (PLDI). ACM Press.

Godefroid 1997 Godefroid, P. (1997). Model Checking for Programming Languages Using Verisoft. In Proc. ACM Symposium on Principles of Programming Languages (POPL). ACM Press.

Graham., et al. 2005 Graham, R. L., Woodall, T. S., and Squyres, J. M. (2005). Open MPI: A flexible high performance MPI. In Proceedings, 6th Annual International Conference on Parallel Processing and Applied Mathematics, Poznan, Poland.

O'Callahan and Choi 2003 O'Callahan, R. and Choi, J.-D. (2003). Hybrid Dynamic Data Race Detection. In Proc. ACM SIGPLAN 2003 Symposium on Principles and Practice of Parallel Programming (PPoPP), pages 167–178. ACM.

Park and Sen 2008 Park, C.-S. and Sen, K. (2008). Randomized Active Atomicity Violation Detection in Concurrent Programs. In Proceedings of the 16th ACM SIGSOFT International Symposium on Foundations of Software Engineering (FSE'08), pages 135–145, New York, NY, USA. ACM.

Wang and Stoller 2005 Wang, L. and Stoller, S. D. (2005). Static Analysis of Atomicity for Programs with Non-blocking Synchronization. In Proc. ACM SIGPLAN 2005 Symposium on Principles and Practice of Parallel Programming (PPoPP). ACM Press.

Wang and Stoller 2006a Wang, L. and Stoller, S. D. (2006a). Accurate and Efficient Runtime Detection of Atomicity Errors in Concurrent Programs. In Proc. ACM SIGPLAN 2006 Symposium on Principles and Practice of Parallel Programming (PPoPP). ACM Press.

Wang and Stoller 2006b Wang, L. and Stoller, S. D. (2006b). Runtime Analysis of Atomicity for Multi-threaded Programs. IEEE Transactions on Software Engineering, 32(2):93–110.

Xu., et al. 2005 Xu, M., Bodik, R., and Hill, M. D. (2005). A Serializability Volation Detector for Shared-memory Server Programs. In Proc. ACM SIGPLAN Conference on Programming Language Design and Implementation (PLDI). ACM Press.

Yu., et al. 2005 Yu, Y., Rodeheffer, T., and Chen, W. (2005). RaceTrack: Efficient Detection of Data Race Conditions via Adaptive Tracking. In Symposium on Operating Systems Principles (SOSP). ACM Press.

KEY TERMS AND DEFINITIONS

Atomicity Violation: An atomicity violation refers to a program error that an interleaved execution of a set of code blocks (expected to be atomic) by multiple threads is not equivalent to any serial execution of the same code blocks.

Benign Warning: A benign warning is a false warning about some code that actually does not affect the correctness of the program but matches the definition of a specific bug. Examples include the benign data race on the busy-wait and compare-and-swap flag.

Concurrent Programs: Concurrent programs are programs that contain portion of code that can run concurrently on a machine or a collection of machines.

Data Race: A data race refers to a scenario that two concurrent threads perform conflicting accesses (*i.e.*, accesses to the same shared variable and at least one access is a write) and the threads use no explicit mechanism to prevent the accesses from being simultaneous.

Deadlock: A deadlock occurs when a chain of processes/threads are involved in a cycle in which each process is waiting for resources/locks that are held by some other processes.

Dynamic Analysis: Dynamic analysis is a program analysis technique that observes and analyzes the actual behaviors of a program by executing it.

False Positive: A false positive is a false bug warning that has been erroneously reported by the bug detection tool due to the imperfect or inaccurate algorithm or approach that is used by the tool.

Hybrid Analysis: Hybrid analysis refers to a hybrid program analysis technique that combines both dynamic and static analysis to analyze the program.

Static Analysis: Static analysis is a program analysis methodology that examines the program source code without running the program.

Compilation of References

Abadi, M., & Lamport, L. (1989). Composing specifications. In de Bakker, J. W., de Roever, W.-P., & Rozenberg, G. (Eds.), *Stepwise refinement of distributed systems-models, formalisms, correctness* (*Vol. 430*, pp. 1–41). Berlin: Springer-Verlag.

Abran, A., Ndiaye, I., & Bourque, P. (2003). *Contribution of software size in effort estimation*. École de Technologie Supérieure, Canada: Research Lab. in Software Engineering.

Abran, A., & Paton, K. (1995). *A formal notation for the rules of function point analysis*. Research Report 247. Retrieved from http://publicationslist.org/data/a.abran/ref-1995/43.pdf

Achauer, B. (1996). Objects in real-time systems: Issues for language implementers. *ACM SIGPLAN OOPS Messenger, 7*, 21–27. doi:10.1145/227986.227991

Achilleos, A., Georgalas, N., & Yang, K. (2007). *An open source domain-specific tools framework to support model driven development of OSS*. In ECMDA-FA, (LNCS 4530), (pp. 1 – 16).

Achilleos, A., Yang, K., & Georgalas, N. (2008). A model-driven approach to generate service creation environments. In *Proceedings of the IEEE Globecom, Global Telecommunications Conference*, (pp. 1–6).

Achilleos, A., Yang, K., Georgalas, N., & Azmoodeh, M. (2008). Pervasive dervice vreation using a model driven Petri Net based approach. In *Proceedings of the IEEE International Wireless Communications and Mobile Computing Conference (IWCMC)*, (pp. 309-314).

Afonso, M., Vogel, R., & Texeira, J. (2006). From code centric to model centric software engineering: Practical case study of MDD infusion in a systems integration company. In *Proceedings of the Workshop on Model-Based Development of Computer-Based Systems and International Workshop on Model-Based Methodologies for Pervasive and Embedded Software*, (pp.125-134).

Agarwal, R., & Chari, K. (2007). Software effort, quality and cycle time: A study of CMM level 5 projects. *IEEE Transactions on Software Engineering, 33*(3), 145–155. doi:10.1109/TSE.2007.29

Agarwal, R., Bensalem, S., Farchi, E., Havelund, K., Nir-Buchbinder, Y., & Stoller, S. D. (in press). Detection of deadlock potentials in multi-threaded programs. *IBM Journal of Research and Development*.

Agarwal, R., Sasturkar, A., Wang, L., & Stoller, S. D. (2005a). Optimized run-time race detection and atomicity checking using partial discovered types. In *Proceedings of the 20th IEEE/ACM International Conference on Automated Software Engineering (ASE)*. ACM Press.

Agarwal, R., Wang, L., & Stoller, S. D. (2005b). Detecting potential deadlocks with static analysis and runtime monitoring. *In Proceedings of the Parallel and Distributed Systems: Testing and Debugging (PADTAD)*. Springer-Verlag.

AgenaRisk. (2006). *Bayesian network and simulation software for risk analysis and decision support*. Retrieved May 25, 2010, from http://www.Agenarisk.Com/

Agile. (2005). Agile Newsletter. Retrieved from http://www.agile-itea.org

Akhter, S. (2006). *Multi-core programming: Increasing performance through software multi-threading*. Intel Press.

Akkermans, H., Baida, Z., Gordijn, J., Pena, N., Altuna, A., & Laresgoiti, I. (2004). Using ontologies to bundle real world services. *IEEE Intelligent Systems*, *19*, 57–66. doi:10.1109/MIS.2004.35

Albrecht, A. J. (1979). Measuring application development productivity. *In Proceedings of Joint SHARE, GUIDE, and IBM Application Development Symposium*, (pp. 83-92). Monterey, CA.

Aldrich, J. Chambers, C. & Notkin, D. (2002). Archjava: Connecting software architecture to implementation. In *International Conference on Software Engineering*, Orlando, FL.

Alexander, C., Ishikawa, S., Silverstein, M., Jacobson, M., Fiksdahl-King, I., & Angel, S. (1977). *A pattern language: Towns, buildings, construction*. New York: Oxford University Press.

Allen, R. J. (1997). *A formal approach to software architecture*. Unpublished doctoral thesis.

Alter, S. (2008). Service system fundamentals: Work system, value chain, and life cycle. *IBM Systems Journal*, *47*, 71–85. doi:10.1147/sj.471.0071

Alves, A., Arkin, A., Askary, S., Barreto, C., Bloch, B., Curbera, F., et al. (2007). *Web services business process execution language, version 2.0 (OASIS Standard)*. WS-BPEL TC OASIS. Retrieved from http://docs.oasis-open.org/wsbpel/2.0/wsbpel-v2.0.html

Ambler, S. W. (2009). *Scaling agile software development through lean governance*. Paper presented at the Software Development Governance Workshop, Vancouver, Canada.

Ammons, G., Bodik, R., & Larus, R. J. (2002). Mining specifications. In *proceedings of the 29th ACM SIGPLAN-SIGACT symposium on Principles of programming languages*, (pp.4-16). New York: ACM Press.

Amnell, T., Fersman, E., Mokrushin, L., Petterson, P., & Wang, Y. (2003). TIMES: A tool for schedulability analysis and code generation of real-time systems. *Proceedings of the 1st Workshop on Formal Modeling and Analysis of Timed Systems (FORMATS)*, (pp. 60-72). Berlin / Heidelberg: Springer.

Anacleto, A., von Wangenheim, C. G., Salviano, C. F., & Savi, R. (2004). *Experiences gained from applying ISO/IEC 15504 to small software companies in Brazil*. Paper presented at the 4th International SPICE Conference on Process Assessment and Improvement, Lisbon, Portugal, (pp.33-37).

Andersen, B., & Fagerhaug, T. (2000). *Root cause analysis: Simplified tools and techniques*. Milwaukee: ASQ Quality.

Anderson, D. (2003). *Agile management for software engineering: Applying the theory of constraints for business results*. Prentice Hall.

Anderson, P., Reps, T., Teitelbaum, T., & Zarins, M. (2003). Tool support for fine-grained software inspection. *IEEE Software*, *20*(4), 42–50.

Anderson, W., & Carney, D. (2009). *Distributed Project Governance Assessment (DPGA): Contextual, hands-on analysis for project governance across sovereign boundaries*. Paper presented at the Software Development Governance Workshop, Vancouver, Canada.

Andersson, D. J. (2005). *Stretching agile to fit CMMI level 3*. Denver: Agile Development.

Ankolekar, A., Hobbs, J. R., Lassila, O., Martin, D. L., McIlraith, S. A., Narayanan, S., et al. (2001). DAML-S: semantic markup for Web services. *In proceedings of the first Semantic Web Working Symposium (SWWS)*, (p. 4). Stanford University.

ANL MPI Using MPI in Simple Programs http://www.mcs.anl.gov/research/projects/mpi/usingmpi/examples/simplempi/main.htm

April, A., Merlo, E., & Abran, A. (1997). *A reverse engineering approach to evaluate function point rules*, (pp. 236-246). Paper presented at the Working Conference on Reverse Engineering.

ARM. (2010). Cortex-A9 MPCore. Retrieved May 10, 2010, from http://www.arm.com/products/CPUs/ARMCortex-A9_MPCore.html

ARM. (2010). *Hardware platforms*. Retrieved May 10, 2010, from http://www.arm.com/products/DevTools/PB11MPCore.html

Arrango, G. (1994). Domain analysis methods. In Schäfer, R., Prieto-Díaz, R., & Matsumoto, M. (Eds.), *Software reusability*. Ellis Horwood.

Aspect, J. Project. (2004). AspectJ project. Retrieved from http://eclipse.org/aspectj/

AT&T. (2006). *SRE toolkit*. Retrieved May 25, 2010, from http://www.Cse.Cuhk.Edu.hk/~lyu/book/reliability/sretools.Html

Atkinson, S., & Duke, R. (1995). Behavioural retrieval from class libraries. In *proceedings of the Eighteenth Australasian Computer Science Conference, 17*(1), 13–20.

Automotive, S. (2007). *The SPICE user group, Automotive SPICETM process reference model*. Retrieved from http://www.automotivespice.com

Baader, F., Knechtel, M., & Penaloza, R. (2009). *A generic approach for large-scale ontological reasoning in the presence of access restrictions to the ontology axioms* (p. 49).

Baber, R.L. (1997). Comparison of electrical engineering of Heaviside's times and software engineering of our times. *IEEE Annals of the History of Computing archive, 19*(4), 5-17.

Bachmann, F., Bass, L., Chastek, G., Donohoe, P., & Peruzzi, F. (2000). *The architecture-based design method*. Unpublished Technical Report 2000-TR-001, CMU/SEI.

Baida, Z., Gordijn, J. & Omelayenko, B. (2004). A shared service terminology for online service provisioning.

Baida, Z., Gordijn, J. & Akkermans, H. (2001). *Service ontology*. OBELIX Deliverable 6.1 / Free University Amsterdam–Forschungsbericht.

Baik, J., Boehm, B., & Stecee, B. M. (2002). Disaggregating and calibrating the CASE tool variable in COCOMO 2. *IEEE Transactions on Software Engineering, 28*(11), 1009–1022. doi:10.1109/TSE.2002.1049401

Balasubramanian, K., Gokhale, A., Karsai, G., Sztipanovits, J., & Neema, S. (2006). *Developing applications using model-driven design environments. IEEE Computer*. Vanderbilt University.

Bannerman, P. (2009). *Software development governance: A meta-management perspective*. Paper presented at the Software Development Governance Workshop, Vancouver, Canada.

Barbier, F., Eveillard, S., Youbi, K., Guitton, O., Perrier, A., & Cariou, E. (2010). Model-driven reverse engineering of COBOL-based applications. In Ulrich, W. M., & Newcomb, P. H. (Eds.), *Information Systems transformation: Architecture-driven modernization case studies* (pp. 283–299). Burlington, MA: Morgan Kauffman.

Barnes, J. (2003). *High integrity software: The SPARK approach to safety and security*. Addison-Wesley.

Barrett, M., Davidson, E., Middleton, C., & De-Gross, J. I. (2008). *Information Technology in the service economy: Challenges and possibilities for the 21st Century*. Springer Publishing Company. doi:10.1007/978-0-387-09768-8

Barros, A., & Dumas, M. (2006). The rise of Web service ecosystems. *IT Professional, 8*, 31–37. doi:10.1109/MITP.2006.123

Barros, A., Dumas, M. & Bruza, P. (2005). *The move to Web service ecosystems*. BPTrends.

Barry, D. K. (2003). *Web services and service-oriented architectures: The savvy manager's guide*. San Francisco: Morgan Kaufmann Publishers.

Bartussek, W., & Parnas, D. L. (1978). Using assertions about traces to write abstract specifications for software modules. *Proceedings of the Second Conference on European Cooperation in Informatics,* (pp. 111–130). Springer-Verlag.

Basili, V. R., Caldiera, G., & Rombach, H. D. (1994). The goal question metric paradigm. In Marciniak, J. J. (Ed.), *Encyclopedia of Software Engineering* (pp. 578–583). John Wiley.

Basili, V. R. (1989). *Software development: A paradigm for the future*. Paper presented at COMPSAC '89, Orlando, FL.

Basole, R. C., & Rouse, W. B. (2008). Complexity of service value networks: Conceptualization and empirical investigation. *IBM Systems Journal, 47*(1), 31–37. doi:10.1147/sj.471.0053

Bass, L., Clements, P., & Kazman, R. (1998). *Software architecture in practice*. Boston: Addison-Wesley.

Bastide, R., Sy, O., & Palanque, P. (1999). Formal specification and prototyping of corba systems. *ECOOP '99*, (pp. 474–494). Springer-Verlag. Braga, R., Mattoso, M. & Werner, C. (2001). The use of mediation and ontology technologies for software component information retrieval. *Proceedings of the International Symposium on Software Reusability*, Toronto, Ontario, Canada.

Batista, J., & Figueiredo, A. D. (2000). SPI in a very small team: A case with CMMI. *Software Process Improvement and Practice*, 5(4), 243–250. doi:10.1002/1099-1670(200012)5:4<243::AID-SPIP126>3.0.CO;2-0

Beck, K. (2000). *Extreme Programming explained: Embrace change*. Reading, MA: Addison-Wesley.

Beck, K. (2003). *Test-driven development: By example*. Boston: Addison-Wesley.

Beck, K. (2004). *JUnit pocket guide*. Sebastopol, CA: O'Reilly.

Beck, K. (1999). Embracing change with extreme programming. *IEEE Computer*, 32(10), 70–77.

Beck, K. (2000). *Extreme programming explained: Embrace change*. Addison Wesley Longman, Inc.

Beck, K., & Andres, C. (2005). *Extreme programming explained*. Addison-Wesley Professional.

Beck, K., Beedle, M., et al. (2001). *Manifesto for agile software development*. 2008.

Beck, K., et al. (2001). *Manifesto for agile software development*. Retrieved from http://agilemanifesto.org

Beecham, S., Baddoo, N., Hall, T., Robinson, H., & Sharp, H. (2008). Motivation in software engineering: A systematic literature review. *Information and Software Technology*, 50(9-10), 860–878. doi:10.1016/j.infsof.2007.09.004

Belhaouari, H., & Peschanski, F. (2008). A lightweight container architecture for runtime verification. In *proceedings of 8th international runtime verification workshop*, LNCS 5289. (pp. 173–187). Springer-Verlag.

Bellagio, D. E., & Milligan, T. J. (2005). *Software configuration management strategies and IBM® Rational® ClearCase®, a practical introduction* (6th ed.). NJ: Addison Wesley Professional.

Bellwood, T., Clement, L., Ehnebuske, D., Hately, A., Hondo, M., & Husband, Y. L. (2002). *UDDI Version 3.0. Published specification*. Oasis.

Bendaoud, R., Toussaint, Y., & Napoli, A. (2008). PACTOLE: A methodology and a system for semi-automatically enriching an ontology from a collection of texts. In *proceedings ICCS 2008*.

Bengtsson, P. O., & Bosch, J. (1998). Scenario-based architecture reengineering. *Proceedings Fifth International Conference on Software Reuse (ICSR 5)*. (pp. 308).

Bengtsson, P. O., & Bosch, J. (1999). Architecture level prediction of software maintenance. *Third European Conference on Software Maintenance and Reengineering*, (pp. 139-147).

Benjapol, A., & Limpiyakorn, Y. (2008). Underlying cognitive complexity measure computation with combinatorial. *World Academy of Science. Engineering and Technology*, 45, 431–436.

Benjapol, A., & Limpiyakorn, Y. (2009). Towards structured software cognitive complexity measurement with granular computing strategies. In *Proceedings of the 8th IEEE International Conference on Cognitive Informatics*, 365-370.

Bennett, K. H., & Rajlich, V. T. (2000). Software maintenance and evolution: A roadmap. *Proceedings of the Conference on The Future of Software Engineering*. Limerick, Ireland: ACM.

Bensalem, S., & Havelund, K. (2005). Scalable deadlock analysis of multi-threaded programs. In S. Ur (Ed.), *IBM Verification Conference*, (LCNS 3875), Haifa, Israel. Springer.

Berbner, R. (2007). *Dienstgüteunterstützung für Service-orientierte Workows*, Technischen Universität Darmstadt, Diss., Berre, A.J. (2008). UPMS-UML Pro-le and metamodel for services–an emerging standard. In *Proceedings of the 12th international IEEE Enterprise Distributed Object Computing Conference*.

Bergin, T. J., & Gibson, R. G. (Eds.). (1996). *History of programming languages*. Addison-Wesley.

Bevo, V. (2005). *Analyse et formalisation ontologiques des mesures associées aux méthodes de mesure de la taille fonctionnelle des logiciels: de nouvelles perspectives pour la mesure.* Unpublished doctoral thesis in Cognitive Informatics, University of Quebec in Montreal, Canada.

Bevo, V., Lévesque, G., & Meunier, J.-G. (2004). Toward an ontological formalisation for a software functional size measurement method's application process: The FPA case. In *Proceedings IEEE-RIVF International Conference on Computing and Telecommunication Technologies,* (pp 113-118).

Bhatti, N., & Weber, S. H. (2009). Semantic visualization to support knowledge discovery in multi-relational service communities. In Cruz-Cunha, M. M., de Oliveira, E. F., Tavares, A. J. V., & Ferreira, L. G. (Eds.), *Handbook of research on social dimensions of semantic technologies and Web services.* Hershey, PA: IGI Global. doi:10.4018/9781605666501.ch014

Bhatti, N. (2008). Web-based semantic visualization to explore knowledge spaces-an approach for learning by exploring. In J. Luca & Weippl, E.R. (Eds.), *Association for the Advancement of Computing in Education (AACE): Proceedings of ED-Media 2008 World Conference on Educational Multimedia, Hypermedia & Telecommunications,* (pp. 312-317).

Bi, J., & Bennet, K. P. (2003). Regression error characteristics curves. *Proceedings of the 20th International Conference on Machine Learning (ICML-2003),* (pp. 43-50). Washington DC.

Bianchi, A., Caivano, D., Marengo, V., & Visaggio, G. (2003). Iterative reengineering of legacy systems. *IEEE Transactions on Software Engineering, 29*(3), 225–241. doi:10.1109/TSE.2003.1183932

Biegler, L. T., Grossmann, I. E., & Westerberg, A. W. (1997). *Systematic methods of chemical process design.* Prentice Hall.

Biffl, S., & Aurum, B. B. A. (2005). *Value-based software engineering.* New York: Springer.

Biggerstaff, T., Mitbander, B., & Webster, D. (1993). The concept assignment problem in program understanding. In *Proceedings of the 15th International Conference on Software Engineering.*

Billington, J., Christensen, S., et al. (2003). The Petri Net Markup Language: Concepts, technology, and tools. In *Proceedings of the 24th International Conference on Applications and Theory of Petri Nets (ICATPN 2003),* LNCS 2679, (pp. 483–505). Springer-Verlag.

Bitsaki, M., Danylevych, O., & Heuvel, W. van d., Koutras, G., Leymann, F., Mancioppi, M., et al. (2008). An architecture for managing the lifecycle of business goals for partners in a service network. In *LNCS: An architecture for managing the lifecycle of business goals for partners in a service network.*

Blau, B., Kramer, J., Conte, T., & van Dinther, C. (2009). Service value networks. *Proceedings of the 11th IEEE Conference on Commerce and Enterprise Computing.*

Blowers, R., & Richardson, I. (2005). *The capability maturity model (SW and Integrated) tailored in small indigenous software industries.* Paper presented at the International Research Workshop for Process Improvement in Small Settings, Software Engineering Institute, Pittsburgh, PA.

BLU AGE. (2010). *BLU AGE - agile model transformation.* Netfective Technology S.A.

Boehm, B., & Turner, R. (2003). *Balancing agility and discipline.* Addison-Wesley.

Boehm, B., & Abts, C. (2000). Software development Cost estimation approaches-a survey. *Annals of Software Engineering, 10*(1-4), 77–205.

Boehm, B. (2002). Get ready for the agile methods, with care. *Computer, 35*(1), 64–69. doi:10.1109/2.976920

Boehm, B., & Turner, R. (2003). *Balancing agility and discipline-a guide for the perplexed* (p. 304). Addison Wesley.

Boehm, B., Abts, C., Clark, B., Devnani-Chulani, S., Horowitz, E., & Madachy, R. (2000). *COCOMO 2 model definition manual, version 2.1.* Center for Systems and Software Engineering, University of Southern California.

Boer, R. C. D., Lago, P., Telea, R., & Vliet, H. V. (2009). *Ontology-driven visualization of architectural design decisions* (pp. 51–60). Cambridge, UK: WICSA/ECSA.

Bollella, G., Gosling, J., Brosgol, B., Dibble, P., Furr, S., & Turnbull, M. (2000). *The real-time specification for Java*. Addison Wesley.

Booch, G. (1991). *Object-oriented analysis and design, with applications*. Redwood City, CA: The Benjamin/Cummins Publishing Company.

Booth, D., Haas, H., McCabe, F., Newcomer, E., Champion, M., Ferris, C., et al. (2004). Web Services Architecture. *W3C Working Group Note, 11*(1).

Borland Together Integrated and Agile Design Solutions. (2006). Getting started guide for Borland Together 2006 for Eclipse. Retrieved from http://techpubs.borland.com/together/tec2006/en/GettingStarted.pdf

Borthakur, D. (2007). *The Hadoop Distributed File System: Architecture and design*. The Apache Software Foundation.

Bosch, J. (2000). *Design & use of software architectures-adopting and evolving a product line approach*. Addison-Wesley.

Bourque, P., Dupuis, R., & Abran, A. (1999). The guide to the software engineering body of knowledge. *IEEE Software, 16*(6), 35–44. doi:10.1109/52.805471

Boyapati, C., & Rinard, M. C. (2001). A parameterized type system for race-free Java programs. In *Proceedings of ACM Conference on Object-Oriented Programming, Systems, Languages, and Applications (OOPSLA)*, (pp. 56–69). ACM Press.

Boyapati, C., Lee, R., & Rinard, M. (2002). Ownership types for safe programming: Preventing data races and deadlocks. In *Proceedings of the 17th ACM Conference on Object-Oriented Programming, Systems, Languages and Applications (OOPSLA)*, (pp. 211–230). ACM Press.

Boyer, M., Skadron, K., & Weimer, W. (2008). Automated dynamic analysis of CUDA programs. In *Proceedings of the Third Workshop on Software Tools for Multi-Core Systems*.

Braha, D., & Maimon, O. (1997). The design process: Properties, paradigms, and structure. *IEEE Transactions on Systems, Man, and Cybernetics, 27*(2).

Brambilla, M., Celino, I., Ceri, S., Cerizza, D., Valle, E. V., & Facca, F. M. (2006). A software engineering approach to design and development of semantic Web service applications. In the *proceedings of the 5th International Semantic Web Conference, ISWC 2006*, Athens, Georgia.

Briand, L., El Emam, K., & Morasca, S. (1996). On the application of measurement theory in software engineering. *Journal of Empirical Software Engineering, 1*(1), 61–88. doi:10.1007/BF00125812

Briand, L. C., Bunse, C., & Daly, J. W. (2001). A controlled experiment for evaluating quality guidelines on the maintainability of object-oriented design. *IEEE Transactions on Software Engineering, 27*, 513–530. doi:10.1109/32.926174

Briand, L. C., Morasca, S., & Basili, V. R. (1996). Property based software engineering measurement. *IEEE Transactions on Software Engineering, 22*(1), 68–86. doi:10.1109/32.481535

Briscoe, G., & De Wilde, P. (2006). Digital ecosystems: Evolving service-orientated architectures. In *Bio-inspired models of network, information and computing systems*, (pp. 1-6).

Brooks, F. (1975). *The mythical man-month*. Reading, MA: Addison-Wesley.

Browne, J. (1996). Object-Oriented Development of real-time systems: Verification of functionality and performance. *ACM OOPS Messenger, 7*, 59–62. doi:10.1145/227986.227996

Bryant, R. E. (1986). Graph-based algorithms for Boolean function manipulation. *IEEE Transactions on Computers, C-35*(8), 677–691. doi:10.1109/TC.1986.1676819

B-toolkit. (2002). *B-core (UK) Ltd*. Retrieved from http://www.b-core.com/

Buck, I., Foley, T., Horn, D., Sugerman, J., Fatahalian, K., & Houston, M. (2004). Brook for GPUs: Stream computing on graphics hardware. *ACM Transactions on Graphics, 23*(3), 777–786.

Budgen, D. (2003). *Software design* (2nd ed.). Addison-Wesley.

Bullinger, H. (2003). Service engineering–methodical development of new service products. *International Journal of Production Economics*, 275–287. doi:10.1016/S0925-5273(03)00116-6

Burch, J. R., Clarke, E. M., McMillan, K. L., Dill, D. L., & Hwang, L. J. (1990). Symbolic model checking: 10^{20} states and beyond. In *Proceedings of the Fifth Annual IEEE Symposium on Logic in Computer Science*, (pp.1–33). Washington, D.C.: IEEE Computer Society Press.

Burkhardt, J., Henn, H., & Hepper, S. Rintdorff, K. & Sch"ack, T. (2002). *Pervasive computing–technology and architecture of mobile internet applications*. Addison-Wesley.

Burns, G., Daoud, R., & Vaigl, J. (1994). LAM: An open cluster environment for MPI. In *Proceedings of Supercomputing Symposium*, (pp. 379–386).

Buschmann, F., Meunier, R., Rohnert, H., Sommerlad, P., & Stal, M. (1996). *Pattern-oriented software architecture: A system of patterns*. New York: Wiley.

Bush, W., Pincus, J. D., & Sielaff, D. J. (2000). A static analyzer for finding dynamic programming errors. *Software, Practice & Experience*, 30(7), 775–802.

Cadar, C., Ganesh, V., Pawlowski, P. M., Dill, D. L., & Engler, D. R. (2006). EXE: Automatically generating inputs of death. In *Proceedings of the 13th ACM conference on Computer and communications security (CCS)*. ACM Press.

Callan, J. P., Croft, W. B., & Harding, S. M. (1992). The INQUERY retrieval system. In *Proceedings of the Third International Conference on Database and Expert Systems Applications*, (pp. 78-83). New York: Springer-Verlag.

Canal, C., Fuentes, L., Troya, J.M. & Vallecillo, A. (2000). Extending corba interfaces with p-calculus for protocol compatibility. TOOLS'00. *IEEE Press, 19*(2), 292–333.

Canfora, G., & Penta, M. D. (2007). *New frontiers of reverse engineering. 2007 Future of Software Engineering*. IEEE Computer Society.

Cantrill, B., & Bonwick, J. (2008). Real-world concurrency. *ACM Queue; Tomorrow's Computing Today*, 6(5), 16–25. doi:10.1145/1454456.1454462

Card, S., Mackinlay, J. D., & Shneiderman, B. (1999). *Readings in information visualization: Using vision to think. San Fransisco*. Morgan Kaufmann Publishers, Inc.

Cardoso, J., & Sheth, A. (2003). Semantic e-workflow composition. *Journal of Intelligent Information Systems*, 21, 191–225. doi:10.1023/A:1025542915514

Cardoso, J., Voigt, K., & Winkler, M. (2009). *Service engineering for the Internet of Services* (pp. 15–27). Berlin, Heidelberg: Springer.

Cardoso, J., Winkler, M., & Voigt, K. (2009). A service description language for the Internet of Services. *Proceedings First International Symposium on Services Science (ISSS'2009)*. Berlin: Logos Verlag.

Carpineto, C., & Romano, G. (1996). A lattice conceptual clustering system and its application to browsing retrieval. *Machine Learning*, 24(2), 128. doi:10.1007/BF00058654

Carpineto, C., & Romano, G. (2000). Order-theoretical ranking. *Journal of the American Society for Information Science American Society for Information Science*, 51(7), 587–601. doi:10.1002/(SICI)1097-4571(2000)51:7<587::AID-ASI2>3.0.CO;2-L

Carpineto, C., & Romano, G. (1994). Dynamically bounding browsable retrieval spaces: An application to galois lattices. In *Proceedings of RIAO 94: Intelligent Multimedia Information Retrieval Systems and Management*.

Cartwright, M. H., Shepperd, M. J., & Song, Q. (2003). Dealing with missing software project data. *Proceedings of the 9th IEEE International Metrics Symposium (METRICS'03)*, (pp. 154-165).

Cataldo, M., & Herbsleb, J. D. (2009). *End-to-end features as meta-entities for enabling coordination in geographically distributed software development*. Paper presented at the Software Development Governance Workshop, Vancouver, Canada.

Chan, W., Anderson, R. J., Beame, P., Burns, S., Modugno, F., & Notkin, D. (1998). Model checking large software specification. *IEEE Transactions on Software Engineering*, 24(7), 498–520. doi:10.1109/32.708566

Chang, E., & West, M. (2006). Digital ecosystems a next generation of the collaborative environment. *Proceedings from the Eight International Conference on Information Integration and Web-Based Applications & Services*, (pp. 3-24).

Chen, W. F. (1998). *The civil engineering handbook.* CRC Press.

Chen, H. (1995). Machine learning for information retrieval: Neural networks, symbolic learning and genetic algorithms. [JASIS]. *Journal of the American Society for Information Science American Society for Information Science, 46*(3), 194–216. doi:10.1002/(SICI)1097-4571(199504)46:3<194::AID-ASI4>3.0.CO;2-S

Chen, H., & Kim, J. (1995). GANNET: A machine learning approach to document retrieval. *Journal of Management Information Systems, 11*(3), 7–41.

Chen, Z., Boehm, B., Menzies, T., & Port, D. (2005). Finding the right data for software cost modelling. *IEEE Software, 22*(6), 38–46. doi:10.1109/MS.2005.151

Chen, F., Serbanuta, T. F., & Rosu, G. (2008). jPredictor: A predictive runtime analysis tool for Java. In *Proceedings of the 30th international conference on Software engineering (ICSE '08)*, pages 221–230. ACM.

Chen, H., & She, L. (1994). Inductive query by examples (IQBE): A machine learning approach. In *Proceedings of the 27th Annual Hawaii International Conference on System Sciences (HICSS-27), Information Sharing and Knowledge Discovery Track*.

Chen, Q., Wang, L., Yang, Z., & Stoller, S. D. (2009). HAVE: Integrated dynamic and static analysis for atomicity violations. *In Proceedings of International Conference on Fundamental Approaches to Software Engineering (FASE)*, (LNCS 5503), (pp. 425–439). Springer.

Cheng, B., & Jeng, J. (1997). Reusing analogous components. *IEEE Transactions on Knowledge and Data Engineering, 9*(2), 341–349. doi:10.1109/69.591458

Cheng, T. H., Jansen, S., & Remmers, M. (2009). *Controlling and monitoring agile software development in three Dutch product software companies.* Paper presented at the Software Development Governance Workshop, Vancouver, Canada.

Cherniavsky, J. C., & Smith, C. H. (1991). On Weyuker's axioms for software complexity measures. *IEEE Transactions on Software Engineering, 17*, 636–638. doi:10.1109/32.87287

Cheung, R. C. (1980). A user-oriented software reliability model. *IEEE Transactions on Software Engineering, 6*(2), 118–125. doi:10.1109/TSE.1980.234477

Chikofsky, E. J. (1989). *Computer-Aided Software Engineering (CASE)*. Washington, D.C.: IEEE Computer Society.

Chikofsky, E. J., & Cross, J. H. (1990). Reverse engineering and design recovery: A taxonomy. *IEEE Software, 7*(1), 13–17. doi:10.1109/52.43044

Chirala, R. C. (2004). *Thesis.* Ph.D. thesis, Department of Computer Science and Engineering, Arizona State University.

Chiu, S. (1996). Method and software for extracting fuzzy classification rules by subtractive clustering. *Proceedings Fuzzy Information Proc. Society, Biennial Conference of the North American*, 461–465.

Choi, J.-D., Lee, K., Loginov, A., O'Callahan, R., Sarkar, V., & Sridharan, M. (2002). Efficient and precise datarace detection for multi-threaded object-oriented programs. In *Proceedings of the ACM SIGPLAN Conference on Programming Language Design and Implementation (PLDI)*, (pp. 258–269). ACM Press.

Chomsky, N. (1965). *Aspects of the theory of syntax.* MIT Press.

Chonacky, N. (2009). A modern Tower of Babel. *Computing in Science & Engineering, 11*(3), 80. doi:10.1109/MCSE.2009.45

Christensen, E., Curbera, F., Meredith, G., & Weerawarana, S. (2001). *Web Services Description Language (WSDL)*. Retrieved October 10, 2009, from http://www.w3.org/TR/wsdl

Chung, L., Nixon, B. A., Yu, E., & Mylopoulos, J. (2000). *Non-functional requirements in software engineering.* Kluwer Academic Publishing.

Cicalese, C. D. T., & Rotenstreich, S. (1999). *Behavioral specification of distributed software component interfaces.* IEEE Computer.

Cimiano, P., Hothos, A., & Staab, S. (2005). Learning concept hierarchies from text corpora using formal concept analysis. *Journal of Artificial Intelligence Research, 24,* 305–339.

Cimiano, P., Hotho, A., Stumme, G., & Tane, J. (2004). *Conceptual knowledge processing with formal concept analysis and ontologies.* Berlin/Heidelberg: Springer. Retrieved from http://www.springerlink.com/content/4r62l72l3baayxdu/?p=d23d0d6442a244d8a6872c1f38 13e8b2&pi=0.

Clark, T., Evans, A., Sammut, P., & Willans, J. (2004). An eXecutable metamodelling facility for domain-specific language design. In *Proceedings of the Object-Oriented Programming, Systems, Languages, and Applications Workshop on Domain-Specific Modelling.*

Clarke, E. M., Grumberg, O., & Peled, D. A. (1999). *Model Checking.* MIT Press.

Clarke, E. M., & Emerson, E. A. (1981). Design and synthesis of synchronization skeletons using branching time temporal logic. *Proceedings of the Logics of Programs Workshop,* (pp. 52-71). Springer Verlag.

Clarke, O. G. E., & Long, D. (1994). Verification tools for finite-state concurrent systems. In *Proceedings of In A Decade of Concurrency–Reflections and Perspectives,* LNCS 803.

Clavel, P. L. M., Eker, S., & Meseguer, J. (1996). Principles of Maude. Vol. 4. *Electronic Notes in Theoretical Computer Science.* Elsevier Science Publishers.

Clements, P., & Northrop, L. (2002). *Software product lines: Practices and patterns.* Addison-Wesley.

Clifton, C., & Wen-Syan, L. (1995). Classifying software components using design characteristics. *Proceedings the 10th Knowledge-Based Software Engineering Conference,* 139–146.

CMM. (1991). Capability Maturity Model for software (CMM). *Carnegie Mellon University Software Engineering Institute. Retrieved on February 25, 2008, from* http://www.sei.cmu.edu/cmm/

CMM1. *(2002a). Capability Maturity Model Integration (CMMI) for software engineering, version 1.1, continuous representation (CMMI-SW, V1.1, continuous).* Carnegie Mellon University Software Engineering Institute. (Tech. Rep. CMU/SEI-2002-TR-028). Retrieved on February 25, 2008, from http://www.sei.cmu.edu/publications/documents/02.reports/02tr028.html

CMM1. *(2002b). Capability Maturity Model Integration (CMMI) for software engineering, version 1.1, staged representation (CMMI-SW, V1.1, staged).* Carnegie Mellon University Software Engineering Institute. (Tech. Rep. CMU/SEI-2002-TR-029). Retrieved on March 7, 2008 from http://www.sei.cmu.edu/publications/documents/02.reports/02tr029.html, Accessed on 07th March, 2008.

CMMI. (2006). *Capability Maturity Model® Integration for development, version 1.2.* (Tech. Rep. CMU/SEI-2006-TR-008). Retrieved from http://www.sei.cmu.edu/publications/documents/06.reports/06tr008.html

Coad, P., & Yourdon, E. (1991). *Object-oriented design.* Yourdon Press.

Cockburn, A. (2002). *Agile software development.* Boston: Addison-Wesley.

Cohen, D., & Lindvall, M. (2004). *An introduction to agile methods.* Elsevier Academic Press.

Cohn, M., & Ford, D. (2003). Introducing an agile process to an organization. *IEEE Computer, 36*(6), 74–78.

Colburn, T. R. (2000). Philosophy of computer science, part 3. In *Philosophy and Computer Science* (pp. 127–210). Armonk, USA: M.E. Sharpe.

Coleman, G. (2005). An empirical study of software process in practice. *Proceedings of the 38th Annual Hawaiian International Conference on System Sciences, Big Island, HI,* (p. 315).

Comman, K. A. D. S. (2010). *CommanKADS.* Retrieved from http://www.commonkads.uva.nl/frameset-commonkads.html.

Conboy, K., & Fitzgerald, B. (2004). *Toward a conceptual framework of agile methods: A study of agility in different disciplines.* ACM Workshop on Interdisciplinary Software Engineering Research. New York: ACM Press.

Condori-Fernández, N., Abrahão, S., & Pastor, O. (2007). On the estimation of the functional size of software from requirements specifications. *Journal of Computer Science and Technology*, 22, 358–370. doi:10.1007/s11390-007-9050-6

Connolly, D., Harmelen, F., Horrocks, I., McGuiness, D., Patel-Schneider, P. F., & Stein, L. A. (2001). *Annotated DAML+OIL ontology markup*. Retrieved October 10, 2009, from http://www.w3.org/TR/daml+oil-walkthru/#1

Corbett, J. C., Dwyer, M. B., Hatcliff, J., Laubach, S., Pasareanu, C. S., Zheng, H., et al. (2000). Bandera: Extracting finite-state models from java source code. *In proceedings of the International Conference on Software Engineering*, 263–276.

Cortellessa, V., Singh, H., & Cukic, B. (2002). *Early reliability assessment of UML-based software models*. Paper presented at the Third International Workshop on Software and Performance, (pp. 302-309).

COSMIC. (2008). *The COSMIC business application guideline (v1.1). The Common Software Measurement International Consortium*. COSMIC.

COSMIC. (2009). *COSMIC method measurement manual, (ver. 3.0.1). The Common Software Measurement International Consortium*. COSMIC.

Coyne, R. D., Rosenman, M. A., Radford, A. D., Balachandran, M., & Gero, J. S. (1990). *Knowledge-based design systems*. Addison-Wesley.

Cross, N. (1989). *Engineering design methods*. Wiley & Sons.

Cuda, N. V. I. D. I. A. *CUDA Compute Unified Device Architecture Programming Guide*. http://www.nvidia.com/object/cuda_home.html

CUDA-GDB. CUDA-GDB: The NVIDIA CUDA Debugger. http://developer.download.nvidia.com/compute/cuda/2_1/cudagdb/CUDA_GDB_User_Manual.pdf

Curtis, B. (1989). *Cognitive issues in reusing software artifacts, software reusability*. New York: ACM Press.

Curtis, P., Phillips, D. M., & Weszka, J. (2001). CMMI–the evolution continues. *Systems Engineering*, 7–18.

Czarnecki, K., & Helsen, S. (2006). Feature-based survey of model transformation approaches. *IBM Systems Journal*, 45(3). doi:10.1147/sj.453.0621

Dali. (2006). The Dali workbench. Retrieved May 25, 2010, from http://www.Cs.Cmu.edu/afs/cs/project/tinker-rch/www/html/1998/Lectures/25.RevEng/base.007.Html

Damiani, E. G., Fugini, M., & Bellettini, C. (1999). A hierarchy-aware approach to faceted classification of objected-oriented components. *ACM Transactions on Software Engineering and Methodology*, 8(3), 215–262. doi:10.1145/310663.310665

Das, M., Lerner, S., & Seigle, M. (2002). Esp: Path-sensitive program verification in polynomial time. In *proceedings of the ACM SIGPLAN Conference on Programming Language Design and Implementation (PLDI)*.

Daskalantona, M. K. (1994). Achieving higher SEI levels. *IEEE Software*, 11(4), 17–24. doi:10.1109/52.300079

Daudjee, K. S., & Toptsis, A. A. (1994). A technique for automatically organizing software libraries for software reuse. In *Proceedings of the 1994 conference of the Centre for Advanced Studies on Collaborative research*, (p. 12). IBM Press.

Davey, B. A., & Priesly, H. A. (1990). *Introduction to lattices and order* (2nd ed.). Cambridge, UK: Cambridge University Press.

DDT Allinea Software, Allinea DDT The Distributed Debugging Tool. http://www.allinea.com/index.php?page=48.

De Kinderen, S., & Gordijn, J. (2008a). e3Service-a model-based approach for generating needs-driven e-service bundles in a networked enterprise. In: *Proceedings of 16th European Conference on Information Systems*.

De Kinderen, S., & Gordijn, J. (2008b). e3Service-an ontological approach for deriving multi-supplier IT-service bundles from consumer needs. In: *Proceedings of the 41st Annual Hawaii International Conference on System Sciences*.

de la Peyronnie, J., Newcomb, P. H., Morillo, V., Trimech, F., Nguyen, L., & Purtill, M. (2010). Modernization of the Eurocat Air Traffic Management System (EATMS). In Ulrich, W. M., & Newcomb, P. H. (Eds.), *Information Systems Transformation: Architecture driven modernization case studies* (pp. 91–131). Burlington, MA: Morgan Kauffman.

Dean, J., & Ghemawat, S. (2008). MapReduce: Simplified data processing on large clusters. *Communications of the ACM, 51*(1), 107–113.

Deek, F. P., Turoff, M., & McHugh, J. A. (1999). A common model for problem solving and program development. *IEEE Transactions on Education, 4*, 331–336. doi:10.1109/13.804541

Delamaro, M., Maldonado, J., & Mathur, A. P. (1996). *Integration testing using interface mutations.* Paper presented at The Seventh International Symposium on Software Reliability Engineering (ISSRE'96), (pp. 112–121).

DeMarco, T. (1978). *Structured analysis and system specification.* Yourdon Inc.

DeMarco, T., & Lister, T. (1999). *Peopleware: Productive projects and teams.* New York: Dorset House Publishing.

Deming, W. E. (1990). *Out of the crisis.* Massachusetts Institute of Technology, Center of Advanced Engineering Study.

Demirors, O., & Gencel, C. (2010). Conceptual association of functional size measurement methods. *IEEE Software, 26*(3), 71–78. doi:10.1109/MS.2009.60

DeSouza, J., Kuhn, B., de Supinski, B. R., Samofalov, V., Zheltov, S., & Bratanov, S. (2005). Automated scalable debugging of MPI programs with Intel message checker. In *Proceedings of the Second International Workshop on Software Engineering for High Performance Computing System Applications*, (pp. 78–82). New York: ACM.

Detlefs, D. L., Leino, K. R. M., Nelson, G., & Saxe, J. B. (1998). Extended static checking. Research Report 159, Compaq SRC. Retrieved from http://www.research.compaq.com/SRC/esc/

Deursen, A. V., Klint, P., & Visser, J. (2000). Domain-specific anguages: An annotated bibliography. *ACM SIGPLAN Notices, 35*(6), 26–36.

Devanbu, P., Brachman, R. J., Ballard, B. W., & Selfridge, P. G. (1991). Lassie: A knowledge-based software information system. *Communications of the ACM, 34*(5), 34–49. doi:10.1145/103167.103172

Diab, H., Koukane, F., Frappier, M., & St-Denis, R. (2005). μCROSE: Automated Measurement of COSMIC-FFP for rational rose real time. *Information and Software Technology, 47*(3), 151–166. doi:10.1016/j.infsof.2004.06.007

Diab, H. (2003). *Formalisation et automatisation de la mesure des points de fonction.* Unpublished doctoral Thesis, Department of Informatics Faculté Des Sciences, Université de Sherbrooke, Quebec, Canada.

Diab, H., Frappier, M., & St.-Denis, R. (2001). Formalizing COSMIC-FFP using ROOM. *Proceedings of International Conference on Computer Systems and Applications*, (pp. 312-318).

Diab, H., Frappier, M., & St.-Denis, R. (2002). A formal definition of function points for automated measurement of B specifications. *Proceedings of International Conference on Formal Engineering Methods: Formal Methods and Software Engineering*, (pp. 483-494).

Diaper, D. (Ed.). (1989). *Knowledge elicitation.* Chichester, UK: Ellis Horwood.

Dijkstra, E. W. (1969). *Structured programming, software engineering techniques.* Brussels: NATO Science Committee.

Ding, Z., & Liu, J. (2009). An improvement of software architecture verification. In *Proceedings of the 2nd International Workshop on Harnessing Theories for Tool Support in Software (TTSS 2008), 243*, 49-67.

Dingel, J. (2003). Computer-assisted assume/guarantee reasoning with Verisoft. In *ICSE '03: Proceedings of the 25th International Conference on Software Engineering*, (pp. 138–148). Washington, DC: IEEE Computer Society.

Dinger, U., Oberhauser, R., & Reichel, C. (2006). SWS-ASE: Leveraging Web service-based software engineering. In the *proceedings of the IEEE International Conference on Software Engineering Advances, ICSEA 06*, Papeete, Tahiti, French Polynesia.

Discussion of the Object Management Architecture. (1997). *OMG Document 00-06-41.*

DO-178B. (1992). *Software considerations in airborne systems and equipment certification.* RTCA Inc.

Dobrica, L., & Niemelä, E. (2002). A survey on software architecture analysis methods. *IEEE Transactions on Software Engineering*, *28*(7), 638–653. doi:10.1109/TSE.2002.1019479

Dogac, A., Kabak, Y., Laleci, G. B., Mattocks, C., Najmi, F., & Pollock, J. (2005). Enhancing ebXML registries to make them OWL aware. *Distributed and Parallel Databases*, *18*, 9–36. doi:10.1007/s10619-005-1072-x

Domik, G. (2010). *Computer-generated visualization, the need for visualization*. Universität Paderborn. Retrieved April 2010, from http://cose.math.bas.bg/SciVisualization/compGenVis/download/chapter1.pdf

Domingue, J., & Zaremba, M. (2007). *Reference ontology for semantic service oriented architectures*. OASIS working draft 0.1. Retrieved April, 2010, from http://www.oasis-open.org

Dorf, R. C. (1997). *The electrical engineering handbook*. New York: Springer Verlag.

Drobka, J., & Noftz, D. (2004). Piloting XP on four mission critical projects. *IEEE Software*, *21*(6), 70–75. doi:10.1109/MS.2004.47

Ducrou, J. (2007). *Design for conceptual knowledge processing: Case studies in applied formal concept analysis*. Unpublished doctoral dissertation, University of Wollongong.

Duenas, J. C., Oliveira, W. L. D., & de la Puente, J. A. (1998). *A software architecture evaluation model*. Paper presented at the Second Int'l ESPRIT ARES Workshop, (pp. 148-157).

Dumez, C., Gaber, J., & Wack, M. (2008). *Model-driven engineering of composite web services using UML-S* (pp. 395–398). ACM.

Dunsheath, P. (1997). *A history of electrical engineering*. London: Faber & Faber.

Dwyer, M., Hatcliff, J., Hoosier, M. & Robby (2005). *Building your own software model checker using the Bogor extensible model checking framework*. Computer Aided Verification (CAV).

Dybå, T., & Dingsøyr, T. (2008). Empirical studies of agile software development: A systematic review. *Information and Software Technology*, *50*(9-10), 833–859. doi:10.1016/j.infsof.2008.01.006

Eckstein, R. (2008). *Working with Java technology in a multicore world*. Paper presented at the JavaOne Conference. Retrieved May 10, 2010, from http://java.sun.com/javaone/sf/2008/articles/concurrency.jsp

Eclipse. (2005). *Home page*. Retrieved May 25, 2010, from http://www.eclipse.org/

Efe, P., Demirors, O., & Gencel, C. (2006). A unified model for functional size measurement methods. In *Proceedings of the International Workshop on Software Measurement*, (pp. 343–358).

Eichmann, D., & Srinivas, K. (1992). Neural network-based retrieval from software reuse repositories. In *Neural networks and pattern recognition in human-computer interaction*. (pp. 215–228).

Eighth Workshop on Runtime Verification (2008). *Lecture Notes in Computer Science, 5289*.

Elmas, T., Qadeer, S., & Tasiran, S. (2007). Goldilocks: A race and transaction-aware Java runtime. In *Proceedings of the ACM SIGPLAN Conference on Programming Language Design and Implementation (PLDI)*. ACM Press.

Elrad, T., Filman, R. E., & Bader, A. (2001). Aspect-oriented programming: Introduction. *Communications of the ACM*, *44*(10), 29–32. doi:10.1145/383845.383853

Emam, K. E., & Birk, A. (2000). Validating the ISO/IEC 15504 measure of software requirements analysis process capability. *IEEE Transactions on Software Engineering*, *26*(6), 541–566. doi:10.1109/32.852742

Emerson, J. M., & Sztipanovits, J. (2004). Implementing a MOF-based metamodelling environment using graph transformations. In *Proceedings of the 4th OOPSLA Workshop on Domain-Specific Modeling*. Retrieved from http://www.dsmforum.org/events/DSM04/emerson.pdf

Emmrich, A. (2005). *Ein Beitrag zur systematischen Entwicklung produktorientierter Dienstleistungen*. Paderborn: University of Paderborn.

Engler, D., & Ashcraft, K. (2003). RacerX: Effective, static detection of race conditions and deadlocks. In *Proceedings of ACM SIGOPS Symposium on Operating Systems Principles (SOSP)*. ACM Press.

Erbas, B. C., & Erbas, C. (2005). *A transaction cost economics approach to software development and acquisition*. Paper presented at the Integrated Design and Process Technology Conference, San Diego, California.

Erbas, C., & Erbas, B. C. (2009). *Software development under bounded rationality and opportunism*. Paper presented at the Software Development Governance Workshop, Vancouver, Canada.

Erdur, R., & Dikenelli, O. (2002). *A multi-agent system infrastructure for software component market-place: An ontological perspective* (pp. 55–60). ACM SIGMOD.

Ernst, M. D., Cockrell, J., Griswold, W. G., & Notkin, D. (2001). Dynamically discovering likely program invariants to support program evolution. *IEEE Transactions on Software Engineering, 27*(2), 99–123.

Ertas, A., & Jones, J. C. (1996). *The engineering design process*. Wiley.

Esterel Technologies. (2003). Retrieved May 10, 2010, from http://www.esterel-technologies.com/

Estublier, J., Leblang, D., Hoek, A., Conradi, R., Clemm, G., & Tichy, W. (2005). Impact of software engineering research on the practice of software configuration management. *ACM Transactions on Software Engineering and Methodology, 14*, 1–48. doi:10.1145/1101815.1101817

Evans, E. (2004). *Domain-driven design: Tackling complexity in the heart of software*. Addison-Wesley.

Evans, D., Guttag, J., Horning, J., & Tan, Y. M. (1994). Lclint: A tool for using specifications to check code. In *Proceedings of the ACM SIGSOFT Symposium on the Foundations of Software Engineering*.

Everett, W. (1999). *Software component reliability analysis*. Paper presented at the Symposium on Application-Specific Systems and Software Engineering Technology (ASSET'99), (pp. 204–211).

Evermann, J., & Wand, Y. (2005). Toward formalizing domain modelling semantics in language syntax. *IEEE Transactions on Software Engineering, 31*(1), 21–37. doi:10.1109/TSE.2005.15

Evesti, A. (2007). *Quality-oriented software architecture development* (p. 79). Espoo: VTT Publications.

Fagan, M. E. (1976). Design and code inspections to reduce errors in program development. *IBM Systems Journal, 15*(3), 182–211. doi:10.1147/sj.153.0182

Faras, A., & Guhneuc, Y. (2003). On the coherence of component protocols. *Proceedings of the ETAPS Workshop on Software Composition*.

Fayad, M., & Schmidt, D. (1997). Object-Oriented application framework. *Communications of the ACM, 40*(10). doi:10.1145/262793.262798

Fei, L., & Midkiff, S. P. (2006). Artemis: Practical run-time monitoring of applications for execution anomalies. In *Proceedings of the ACM SIGPLAN Conference on Programming Language Design and Implementation (PLDI)*, (pp. 84–95). ACM Press.

Fellbaum, C. (1998). *WordNet–an electronic lexical database*. Cambridge, MA/London: MIT Press.

Fensel, D., McGuiness, D., Schulten, E., Keong, W., Lim, G., & Yan, G. (2001). Ontologies and electronic commerce. *Intelligent Systems, 16*, 8–14. doi:10.1109/MIS.2001.1183337

Fenton, N. E., & Pfleeger, S. L. (1996). *Software metrics: A rigorous and practical approach* (2nd ed.). Boston: International Thomson Computer Press.

Fenton, N. (1994). Software measurement: A necessary scientific basis. *IEEE Transactions on Software Engineering, 20*(3), 199–206. doi:10.1109/32.268921

Fenton, N. (1997). *Software metrics: A rigorous and practical approach*. Boston: PWS Publishing Company.

Ferrario, R., Guarino, N. (2008): *Towards an ontological foundation for services science*.

Ferreira, V., & Lucena, J. (2001). *Facet-based classification scheme for industrial automation software components*. Paper presented at the 6th International Workshop on Component-Oriented Programming.

Fetcke, T., Abran, A., & Nguyen, T.-H. (Eds.). (1997). *Mapping the OO-Jacobson approach into Function Point Analysis* (pp. 192–202). Proceedings of Technology of Object-Oriented Languages and Systems.

Fetcke, T. (1999). A generalized structure for function point analysis. *Proceedings of International Workshop on Software Measurement*, (pp. 143-153).

Fetcke, T. (2001). A generalized representation for selected functional size measurement methods. *Proceedings of the International Workshop on Software Measurement*, (pp. 1-25).

Fetike, P., & Loos, P. (2003). Specifying business components in virtual engineering communities. *Proceedings of the Ninth Americas Conference on Information Systems*, (pp. 1937–1947). Tampa, FL.

Fifth Workshop on Runtime Verification (2005). *Electronic Notes in Theoretical Computer Science, 144.*

Filman, R.E. Elrad, T., Clark, S. & Aksit, M. (2004). *Aspect-oriented software development*. Pearson Eduction.

First Joint Workshop on Formal Aspects of Testing and Runtime Verification (2006). *Lecture Notes in Computer Science, 4262.*

First Workshop on Runtime Verification (2001). *Electronic Notes in Theoretical Computer Science, 55*(2).

Fischer, B. (2000). Specification-based browsing of software component libraries. *Automated Software Engineering, 7*(2), 179–200. doi:10.1023/A:1008766409590

Fitzgerald, B., & Hartnett, G. (2006). Customising agile methods to software practices at Intel Shannon. *European Journal of Information Systems, 15*(2), 200–213. doi:10.1057/palgrave.ejis.3000605

Flanagan, C., Freund, S. N., & Qadeer, S. (2005). Exploiting purity for Atomicity. *IEEE Transactions on Software Engineering, 31*(4).

Flanagan, C., & Freund, S. (2000). Type-based race detection for Java. In *Proceedings of the ACM SIGPLAN Conference on Programming Language Design and Implementation (PLDI)*, (pp. 219–232). ACM Press.

Flanagan, C., & Freund, S. N. (2004a). Atomizer: A dynamic Atomicity checker for multithreaded programs. *In Proceedings of the ACM Symposium on Principles of Programming Languages (POPL)*, (pp 256–267). ACM Press.

Flanagan, C., & Freund, S. N. (2004b). *Type inference against races*. In Static Analysis Symposium, (LNCS 3148). Springer-Verlag.

Flanagan, C., & Freund, S. N. (2009). FastTrack: Efficient and precise dynamic race detection. In *Proceedings of the ACM SIGPLAN Conference on Programming Language Design and Implementation (PLDI)*, (pp. 121–133). ACM Press.

Flanagan, C., & Qadeer, S. (2003). A type and effect system for Atomicity. In *Proceedings of the ACM SIG-PLAN Conference on Programming Language Design and Implementation (PLDI)*. ACM Press.

Flanagan, C., Freund, S. N., & Yi, J. (2008). Velodrome: A sound and complete dynamic Atomicity checker for multithreaded programs. In *Proceedings of the ACM SIGPLAN Conference on Programming Language Design and Implementation (PLDI)*, (pp. 293–303), New York: ACM.

Fleischmann, A. (1994). *Distributed systems: Software design and implementation*. Springer.

Foley, J. D., & Ribarsky, W. (1994). Next-generation data visualization tools. In: *Scientific visualization: Advances and challenges*.

Foss, T., Stensurd, E., Kitchenham, B., & Myrtveit, I. (2003). A simulation study of the model evaluation criterion MMRE. *IEEE Transactions on Software Engineering, 29*(11), 985–995. doi:10.1109/TSE.2003.1245300

Fourth Workshop on Runtime Verification (2004). *Electronic Notes in Theoretical Computer Science, 113.*

Fox, G. C., Furmanski, W., & Pulikal, T. (1998). Evaluating new transparent persistence commodity models: JDBC, Corba PPS, and OLEDB for HPC T and E databases. *Proceedings of the International Test and Evaluation Association (ITEA) Workshop on High Performance Computing for Test and Evaluation*, 13–16.

France Telecom R&D. (2008). *SmartQVT: An open source model transformation tool implementing the MOF 2.0 QVT-Operational language.* Retrieved from http://smartqvt.elibel.tm.fr/.

Franch, X., Pinyol, J., & Vancells, J. (1999). Browsing a component library using nonfunctional information. *Proceedings of the International Conference on Reliable Software Technologies - Ada Europe '99*, (pp. 332–343). Santander, Spain.

Frankel, D. S. (2003). *Model driven architecture: Applying MDA to enterprise computing.* Indianapolis: Wiley Publishing Inc.

Frappier, M. (1999). *An overview of formal specification languages and their adequacy for formalizing the definition of function points. Technical Report, Department of D'epartement de math'ematiques et d'informatique.* Quebec, Canada: Universit'e de Sherbrooke.

Fregonese, G. Zorer, A. & Cortese, G. (1999). Architectural framework modeling in telecommunication domain. In *ICSE '99: Proceedings of the 21st international conference on Software engineering*, (pp. 526–534). Los Alamitos, CA: IEEE Computer Society Press.

Freudenthal, M. (2009). Domain-specific languages in a customs Information System. *IEEE Software, 99*(1), 1–17.

Fritzsche, M., & Keil, P. (2007). Agile methods and CMMI: Compatibility or conflict? *Software Engineering Journal, 1*(1), 9–26.

Fu, Y., Dong, Z., & He, X. (2007). A translator of software architecture design from SAM to Java. *International Journal of Software Engineering and Knowledge Engineering, 17*(6), 1–54. doi:10.1142/S0218194007003483

Fu, Y. Dong, Z. & He, X. (2006). A method for realizing software architecture design. In *Proceedings of QSIC06: Sixth International Conference on Quality Software*, Beijing, China, October 26 - 28.

Fu, Y., Dong, Z., Ding, J., & He, X. (2008). *Towards rewriting semantics of a Software Architecture Model.* Paper presented at The 8th International Conference of Quality Software, Oxford UK, Aug 12-13.

Fu, Y., Dong, Z., Ding, J., He, X., & Atluri, V. (2009). A modular analysis of Software Architecture Model. In *Proceedings of The Nineth International Conference on Software Engineering and Research Practice (SERP '09)*, Las Vegas, USA.

Fuger, S., Najmi, F. & Stojanovic, N. (2005). *ebXML registry information model, version 3.0.*

Fuhr, N., & Pfeifer, U. (1994). Probabilistic information retrieval as a combination of abstraction, inductive learning, and probabilistic assumptions. *ACM Transactions on Information Systems, 12*(1), 92–115. doi:10.1145/174608.174612

Galin, D., & Avrahami, M. (2006). Are CMM program investment beneficial? Analysing Past Studies. *IEEE Software, 23*(6), 81–87. doi:10.1109/MS.2006.149

Gamma, E., Helm, R., Johnson, R., & Vlissides, J. (1995). *Design patterns: Elements of reusable object-oriented software.* Boston: Addison Wesley Longman Publishing Co.

Gangemi, A., Guarino, N., Masolo, C., Oltramari, A., & Schneider, L. (2002). Sweetening ontologies with DOLCE. In: *Proceedings of the EKAW.*

Ganter, B., Stumme, G., & Wille, R. (2005). Formal concept analysis–foundations and applications. In *Lecture Notes in Computer Science, Lecture Notes in Artificial Intelligence, 3626.* Heidelberg: Springer Verlag.

Ganter, B., & Wille, R. (1999). *Formal concept analysis, mathematical foundations.* Berlin: Springer Verlag.

Gencel, C., & Demirors, O. (2008). Functional size measurement revisited. *ACM Transactions on Software Engineering and Methodology, 17*(3), 1–36. doi:10.1145/1363102.1363106

Gencel, C., & Demirors, O. (2007). Conceptual differences among functional size measurement methods. In *Proceedings of International Symposium on Empirical Software Engineering and Measurement*, (pp. 305-313).

Gennari, J. H. (2003). The evolution of protégé: An environment for knowledge-based systems development. *International Journal of Human-Computer Studies, 58,* 89–123. doi:10.1016/S1071-5819(02)00127-1

Georgalas, N., Achilleos, A., Freskos, V., & Economou, D. (2009). Agile product lifecycle management for service delivery frameworks: History, architecture and tools. *BT Technology Journal, 26*(2).

Georgalas, N., Ou, S., Azmoodeh, M., & Yang, K. (2007). Towards a model-driven approach for ontology-based context-aware application development: A case study. In *Proceedings of the IEEE 4th International Workshop on Model-based Methodologies for Pervasive and Embedded Software (MOMPES)*, (pp. 21-32).

Gerber, A., & Raymond, K. (2003). MOF to EMF: There and back again. In *Proceedings of the OOPSLA Workshop on Eclipse Technology eXchange*, (pp. 60 – 64).

Gergeleit, M., Kaiser, J., & Streich, H. (1996). Checking timing constraints in distributed Object- Oriented programs. *ACM OOPS Messenger, 7*, 51–58. doi:10.1145/227986.227995

Ghazarian, A. (2009). A case study of source code evolution. In R. Ferenc, J. Knodel and A. Winter (Eds.), *13th European Conference on Software Maintenance and Reengineering (CSMR'09)*. (pp. 159-168). Kaiserslautern, Germany, IEEE Computer Society.

Ghezzi, C., Jazayeri, M., & Mandrioli, D. (2002). *Fundamentals of software engineering*. Prentice-Hall.

Glass, R. L., & Vessey, I. (1995). Contemporary application domain taxonomies. *IEEE Software, 12*(4), 63–76. doi:10.1109/52.391837

Glass, R. L. (2002). *Facts and fallacies of software engineering*. United States: Addison Wesley.

Glazer, H. (2001). Dispelling the process myth: Having a process does not mean sacrificing agility or creativity. *CrossTalk, The Journal of Defense Software Engineering*, 27-30.

GNU. (2006). *The GNU profiler*. Retrieved 25 May, 2010, from http://www.Cs.Utah.edu/dept/old/texinfo/as/gprof_toc.html

Godefroid, P. (1997). Model checking for programming languages using Verisoft. In *Proceedings of the ACM Symposium on Principles of Programming Languages (POPL)*. ACM Press.

Godefroid, P., Klarlund, N., & Sen, K. (2005). DART: Directed Automated Random Testing. In *Proceedings of the ACM SIGPLAN Conference on Programming Language Design and Implementation (PLDI)*. ACM Press.

Godehardt, E. (2009). *Kontextualisierte Visualisierung am Wissenintensiven Arbeitsplatz*. Unpublished doctoral dissertation, Technische Universität Darmstadt.

Gokhale, S., Wong, W. E., Trivedi, K., & Horgan, J. R. (1998). *An analytical approach to architecture based software reliability prediction*. Paper presented at the Third International Computer Performance and Dependability Symposium (IPDS'98), (pp. 13-22).

Goseva-Popstojanova, K., Mathur, A. P., & Trivedi, K. S. (2001). *Comparison of architecture-based software reliability models*. Paper presented at the 12th International Symposium on Software Reliability Engineering, (p. 22).

Graaf, B., & Deursen, A. V. (2007). Visualisation of domain-specific modelling languages using UML. In *Proceedings of the Annual IEEE International Conference and Workshops on the Engineering of Computer-Based Systems*, (pp. 586-595).

Graham, R. L., Woodall, T. S., & Squyres, J. M. (2005). Open MPI: A flexible high performance MPI. In *Proceedings, 6th Annual International Conference on Parallel Processing and Applied Mathematics*, Poznan, Poland.

Gramantieri, F., Lamma, E., Mello, P., & Riguzzi, F. (Eds.). (1997). *A system for measuring function points from specifications. Research report DEIS-LIA-97-006*. Italy: Università di Bologna.

Granter, B., & Wille, R. (1996). *Formale begriffsanalyse. Mathematische grundlagen*. Berlin: Springer.

Greengrass, E. (2000). *Information retrieval: A survey*. Retrieved October 10, 2009, from http://clgiles.ist.psu.edu/IST441/materials/texts/IR.report.120600.book.pdf

Grenning, J. (2001). *Using XP in a big process company: A report from the field*. Raleigh, NC: XP Universe.

Grimshaw, A., Silberman, A., & Liu, J. (1989). Real-time Mentat, a data-driven, Object-Oriented system. Proceedings of the IEEE Globecom Conference, (pp. 141-147).

Griswold, W. G., & Akit, M. (Eds.). (2003). *Proceedings of the 2nd International Conference on Aspect-oriented Doftware Development*. ACM Press.

Grose, T. J., Doney, G. C., & Brodsky, S. A. (2001). *Mastering XMI: Java programming with XMI, XML, and UML*. John Wiley & Sons.

Group, L. P. Hangal, S. & Lam, M.S. (2002). Tracking down software bugs using automatic anomaly detection. In *Proceedings of the International Conference on Software Engineering*.

Guba, E. (1981). Criteria for assessing the trustworthiness of naturalistic inquiries. *Educational Communication and Technology, 29*, 75–92.

Gulavani, B. S., Henzinger, T. A., Kannan, Y., Nori, A. V., & Rajamani, S. K. (2006). Synergy: A new algorithm for property checking. In *Proceedings of the 14th ACM SIGSOFT International Symposium on Foundations of Software Engineering (SIGSOFT '06/FSE-14)*. ACM Press.

Haav, H. M. (2004). A semi-automatic method to ontology design by using FCA. In: *proceedings of the International Workshop on Concept Lattices and their Applications (CLAS)*, (p. 23-24).

Hadoop Hadoop Open Source MapReduce Platform. http://lucene.apache.org/hadoop/

Hainaut, J.-L., Henrard, J., Hick, J.-M., Roland, D., & Englebert, V. (1996). Database design recovery. *Proceedings of the 8th International Conference on Advances Information System Engineering*, (pp. 463-480). Springer-Verlag.

Halbwachs, N., Caspi, P., Raymond, P., & Pilaud, D. (1991). The synchronous dataflow programming language lustre. *Proceedings of the IEEE, 79*(9), 1305–1320. doi:10.1109/5.97300

Hamdy, M., Koenig-Ries, B., & Kuester, U. (2007). Non-functional parameters as first class citizens in service description and matchmaking-an integrated approach. In *Proceeding International Conference on Service Oriented Computing*.

Hammer, D., Welch, L., & Roosmalen, O. V. (1996). A taxonomy for distributed Object-Oriented real-time systems. *ACM OOPS Messenger, 7*, 78–85. doi:10.1145/227986.227999

Hamp, B., & Feldweg, H. (1997). Germanet–a lexical-semantic net for German. In *proceedings of the ACL Workshop on Automatic Information Extraction and Building of Lexical Semantic Resources for NLP Applications*, Madrid.

Hansmann, U., Merk, L., Nicklous, M. S., & Stober, T. (2001). *Pervasive computing handbook*. Springer Verlag.

Hansson, C., & Dittrich, Y. (2006). How agile are industrial software development practices? *Journal of Systems and Software, 79*, 1295–1311. doi:10.1016/j.jss.2005.12.020

Harding, C. (2010). *Service-oriented architecture ontology*. The open group draft 2.0. Retrieved April, 2010, from http://www.opengroup.org/projects/soa-ontology/

Harris, Z. (1968). *Mathematical structures of language*. Wiley.

Havelund, K. (2000). Using runtime analysis to guide model checking of Java programs. In *Proceedings of the 7th Int'l. SPIN Workshop on Model Checking of Software*, (LNCS 1885), (pp. 245–264). Springer-Verlag.

Havre, S., Hetzler, B., & Nowell, L. (2000). Visualizing theme changes over time. In *IEEE Symposium on Information Visualization*.

He, X., Yu, H., Shi, T., Ding, J., & Deng, Y. (2004). Formally analyzing software architectural specifications using SAM. *Journal of Systems and Software, 71*(1-2), 11–29. doi:10.1016/S0164-1212(02)00087-0

He, X., Ding, J., & Deng, Y. (2002). Model checking software architecture specifications in SAM. In *Proceedings of the 14th international conference on Software engineering and knowledge engineering (SEKE'02)*, volume 27 of *ACM International Conference Proceeding Series*, (pp. 271–274). New York: ACM Press.

Heck, E., & Vervest, P. (2007). Smart business networks: How the network wins. *Communications of the ACM, 6*, 28–37. doi:10.1145/1247001.1247002

Heitmeyer, C. L., Kirby, J., Labaw, B., & Bharadwaj, R. (1998). SCR: A toolset for specifying and analyzing software requirements. Proceedings of 10th International Conference in Computer-Aided Verification, (pp. 526-531).

Helm, R., & Maarek, Y. (1991). Integrating information retrieval and domain specific approaches for browsing and retrieval in object-oriented class libraries. In *proceedings of Object-oriented Programming Systems, Languages, and Applications.*

Henderson-Sellers, B. (1996). *Object-Oriented metrics: Measures of complexity.* Prentice-Hall.

Henkel, J., & Diwan, A. (2003). *Discovering algebraic specifications from Java classes.* Paper presented at the 15th European conference on objectoriented programming (ECOOP 2003).

Henninger, S. (1997). An evolutionary approach to constructing effective software reuse repositories. *ACM Transactions on Software Engineering Methodology.*

Heričko, M., Rozman, I., & Živkovič, A. (2006). A formal representation of functional size measurement methods. *Journal of Systems and Software, 79,* 1341–1358. doi:10.1016/j.jss.2005.11.568

Hersteller. (2007). *Initiative software (OEM software).* Retrieved from http://www.automotivehis.de/download/HIS_Praesentation_2007.pdf.

Herzum, P., & Sims, O. (2000). *Business component factory.* New York: John Wiley.

Hess, A., & Kushmerick, N. (2003). Learning to attach semantic metadata to Web Services. In: *Proceedings Second International Semantic Web Conference.*

Hess, A., & Kushmerick, N. (2004). Machine learning for annotating semantic Web Services. In *AAAI Spring Symposium on Semantic Web Services.*

Hess, A., Johnston, E., & Kushmerick, N. (2004). A tool for semi-automatically annotating semantic Web Services. In *Proceeding third International Semantic Web Conference.*

Heuser, L., Alsdorf, C., & Woods, D. (2008). *Proceedings of the International Research Forum 2007.* Evolved Technologists Press.

Highsmith, J. (2002). What is agile software development? *Crosstalk,* 4-9.

Hilbrich, T., de Supinski, B. R., Schulz, M., & Müller, M. S. 2009. A graph based approach for MPI deadlock detection. In *Proceedings of the 23rd International Conference on Supercomputing,* Yorktown Heights, NY, (pp. 296-305). New York: ACM.

Hirsch, M. (2005). Moving from a plan driven culture to agile development. In *proceedings of the 27th International Conference on Software Engineering (ICSE 2005),* (p. 38).

Hoare, C. A. R., Hayes, I. J., He, J., Morgan, C. C., Roscoe, A. W., & Sanders, J. W. (1987). Laws of programming. *Communications of the ACM, 30*(8), 672–686. doi:10.1145/27651.27653

Hofmeister, C., Nord, R., & Soni, D. (2000). *Applied software architecture.* Addison-Wesley.

Holström, H., & Fitzgerald, B. (2006). Agile practices reduce distance in global software development. *Information Systems Management, 23*(3), 7–18. doi:10.1201/1078.10580530/46108.23.3.20060601/93703.2

Holzmann, G. J. (1997). The model checker SPIN. *IEEE Transactions on Software Engineering, 23*(5). doi:10.1109/32.588521

Holzmann, G. J. (2003). *The SPIN model checker.* Addison-Wesley.

Holzmann, G. J., & Peled, D. (1994). An improvement in formal verification. In *Proceedings of International Conference on Formal Description Techniques (FORTE '94), volume 6 of IFIP Conference Proceedings,* (pp. 197–211). Chapman & Hall.

Horgan, J. R., & London, S. (1992). *ATAC: A data flow coverage testing tool for C.* Paper presented at the Second Symposium on Assessment of Quality Software Development Tools, (pp. 2–10).

Horvat, R. V., & Rozman, I. (2000). Managing the complexity of SPI in small companies. *Software Process Improvement and Practice, 5*(1), 45–54. doi:10.1002/(SICI)1099-1670(200003)5:1<45::AID-SPIP110>3.0.CO;2-2

Hosmer, D. W., & Lemeshow, S. (1989). *Applied logistic regression.* New York: John Willey & Sons.

Höst, M., & Regnell, B., och Dag, J. N., Nedstam, J. & Nyberg, C. (2001). Exploring bottlenecks in market-driven requirements management processes with discrete event simulation. *Journal of Systems and Software, 59*(3), 323–332. doi:10.1016/S0164-1212(01)00072-3

Hotho, A., Nürnberger, A., & Paaß, G. (2005). A brief survey of text mining. *GLDV Journal for Computational Linguistics and Language Technology, 20*(1), 19–62.

Hou, Q., Zhou, K., & Guo, B. (2009). Debugging GPU stream programs through automatic dataflow recording and visualization. In *ACM SIGGRAPH papers* (pp. 1–11). New York: ACM.

Hsiung, P. A. (2000). Embedded software verification in hardware-software codesign. *Journal of Systems Architecture, 46*(15), 1435–1450. doi:10.1016/S1383-7621(00)00034-5

Hsiung, P. A., Lin, S. W., Tseng, C. H., Lee, T. Y., Fu, J. M., & See, W. B. (2004). VERTAF: An application framework for the design and verification of embedded real-time software. *IEEE Transactions on Software Engineering, 30*(10), 656–674. doi:10.1109/TSE.2004.68

Hsiung, P. A. (1998). RTFrame: An Object-Oriented application framework for real-time applications. Proceedings of 27th International Conference in Technology of Object-Oriented Languages and Systems, (pp. 138-147).

Hughes, B. (2000). *Practical software measurement.* Maidenhead: McGraw-Hill.

Humphrey, W. S., & Snyder, T. R. (1991). Software process improvement at Hughes Aircraft. *IEEE Software, 8*(4), 11–23. doi:10.1109/52.300031

Humphreys, B., & Lindberg, D. (1993). The UMLS project: Making the conceptual connection between users and the information they need. *Bulletin of the Medical Library Association, 81*(2).

Hunt, A., & Thomas, D. (2002). Software archaeology. *IEEE Software, 19*(2), 20–22. doi:10.1109/52.991327

IBM. (2008). *IBM Rational Rhapsody.* Retrieved May 01, 2010, from http://www.ibm.com/developerworks/rational/products/rhapsody/?S_TACT=105AGX15

IBM. (2009). *Eclipse platform technical overview.* Retrieved from http://www.eclipse.org/whitepapers/eclipse-overview.pdf

IBM. (2009). *IBM Rational ClearCase introduction.* Retrieved May 01, 2010, from http://www-01.ibm.com/support/docview.wss?rs=984&uid=pub1gi11636000

IEEE Computer Society. (1990). IEEE standard glossary of software engineering terminology.

IEEE Std. 14143.1. (2000). *Information Technology-software measurement-functional size measurement-Part 1: Definition of concepts.* Implementation note for IEEE adoption of ISO/IEC 14143-1:1998.

IEEE. (2000). *IEEE recommended practice for architectural description of software-intensive systems.* IEEE Std-1471-2000.

IFPUG. (2001). *Function point counting practices: Case studies, case study 2. International function points user group.* NJ: Princeton Junction.

IFPUG. (2005). *Function point counting practices manual. International Function Point Users Group.* Princeton Junction, NJ: IFPUG.

ikv++. (2008). *Medini QVT.* Retrieved from http://www.ikv.de/index.php?option=com_content&task=view&id=75&Itemid=77, ikv++ technologies

Immonen, A., & Niemelä, E. (2007). Survey of reliability and availability prediction methods from the viewpoint of software architecture. *Software and Systems Modeling, 7*(1), 49–65. doi:10.1007/s10270-006-0040-x

Immonen, A. (2006). A method for predicting reliability and availability at the architectural level. In Kakola, T., & Duenas, J. C. (Eds.), *Research issues in software product-lines-engineering and management* (pp. 373–422). Berlin, Heidelberg: Springer Verlag.

Immonen, A., & Niskanen, A. (2005). *A tool for reliability and availability prediction.* Paper presented at the 31st Euromicro Conference on Software Engineering and Advanced Applications, (p. 416).

INRIA. (2005). *ATL transformation description template, version 0.1.* ATLAS group. Retrieved from http://www.eclipse.org/m2m/atl/doc/ATL_Transformation_Template%5Bv00.01%5D.pdf

inta Intel Thread Checker. http://software.intel.com/en-us/intel-thread-checker

intb Intel Trace Analyzer. http://software.intel.com/en-us/intel-trace-analyzer

Intel. (2008). *Core2TM duo processors*. Retrieved from http://www.intel.com/design/intarch/core2duo/index.htm?iid=ipp_embed+proc_core2duo

Intel. (2008). *Quad-Core Xeon Processor 5300 Series*. Retrieved from http://www.intel.com/design/intarch/quadcorexeon/5300/index.htm

ISBSG. (2007). *ISBSG data, release 10.0*. The International Software Benchmarking Standards Group.

Iscoe, N., Williams, G. B., & Arango, G. (1991). Domain modelling for software engineering. In *Proceedings of the IEEE International Conference on Software Engineering*, (pp. 340-343).

Ishikawa, Y., Tokuda, H., & Mercer, C. W. (1990). Object-Oriented real-time language design: Constructs for timing constraints. ACM SIGPLAN Notices, Proceedings of ECOOP/OOPSL Conference, (pp. 289-298).

ISO. (2006). *ISO TR 15504, part 5: Information Technology-software process assessment*. Geneva: International Organisation of Standardisation.

ISO/IEC 14143-1. (1998). *Information Technology-software measurement, functional size measurement, part 1: Definition of concepts*.

ISO/IEC 14143-2. (2002). Information Technology-software measurement, functional size measurement, part 2: Conformity evaluation of software size measurement methods to ISO/IEC 14143-1:1998.

ISO/IEC 14143-6. (2005). *Guide for the use of ISO/IEC 14143 and related international standards*.

ISO/IEC 19761. (2003). *Software engineering-COSMIC-FFP-a functional size measurement method*.

ISO/IEC 20926. (2009). Software and systems engineering-software measurement-IFPUG functional size measurement method, 2009.

ISO/IEC 20968. (2002). *Software engineering-Mk 2 function point analysis-counting practices manual*.

ISO/IEC 24570. (2005). Software engineering-NESMA functional size measurement method version 2.1-definitions and counting guidelines for the application of function point analysis.

ISO/IEC 29881. (2008). Information Technology-software and systems engineering-FiSMA 1.1 functional size measurement method.

ISO/IEC TR 14143-3. (2003). Information Technology-software measurement-functional size measurement-part 3: verification of functional size measurement methods.

ISO/IEC TR 14143-4. (2002). *Information Technology-software measurement-functional size measurement-part 4: Reference model*.

ISO/IEC TR 14143-5. (2004). Information Technology-software measurement-functional size measurement-part 5: Determination of functional domains for use with functional size measurement.

ISO/IEC. (1992). *ISO/IEC 9075*, Database Language SQL.

ISO/IEC. (1997). *ISO/IEC CD 9126-1: Software quality characteristics and metrics, part 1: Quality characteristics and sub-characteristics*.

ISO/IEC. (2006). *ISO/IEC 14764*, Software engineering-software life cycle processes- Maintenance. ISO/IEC. Retrieved from http://www.iso.org/iso/catalogue_detail.htm?csnumber=39064

ISO/IEC. (2009). *ISO/IEC DIS 19506*, Knowledge Discovery Meta-model (KDM), v1.1. Retrieved from http://www.iso.org/iso/catalogue_detail.htm?csnumber=32625

Jaaksi, A., Aalto, J., Aalto, A., & Vatto, K. (1999). *Tried & true object development, industry-proven approaches with UML*. Cambridge University Press.

Jackson, M. (1975). *Principles of program design*. Academic Press. Jackson, M. (2000). *Problem frames: Analyzing and structuring software development problems*. Addison-Wesley.

Jacobson, I., Booch, G., & Rumbaugh, J. (1999). *The unified software development process*. Addison-Wesley.

Jacobson, I., Christerson, M., Jonsson, P., & Övergaard, G. (1992). *Object-oriented software engineering: A use case driven approach*. Boston: Addison-Wesley.

Janicki, R., & Sekerinski, E. (2001). Foundations of the trace assertion method of module interface specification. *IEEE Transactions on Software Engineering, 27*(7), 577–598. doi:10.1109/32.935852

Janiesch, C., Niemann, M., & Repp, N. (2009). Towards a service governance framework for the Internet of Services. *Proceedings of the 17th European Conference on Information Systems.* Verona, Italy.

Jeffery, R., Ruhe, M., & Wieczorek, I. (2000). A comparative study of two software development cost modelling techniques using multi-organizational and company-specific data. *Information and Software Technology, 42,* 1009–1016. doi:10.1016/S0950-5849(00)00153-1

Jeffery, R., Ruhe, M., & Wieczorek, I. (2001). Using public domain metrics to estimate software development effort. *Proceedings of the 7th IEEE International Metrics Symposium (METRICS'01),* (pp. 16-27).

Jeffords, R., & Heitmeyer, C. (1998). Automatic generation of state invariants from requirements specifications. In *Proceedings of the 6th ACM SIGSOFT international symposium on Foundations of software engineering,* (pp. 56–69). New York: ACM Press.

Jensen, J. B., & Kletzer, L. G. (2005). *Understanding the scope and impact of services outsourcing.* Social Science Research Network.

Jia, H., Newman, J., & Tianfield, H. (2008). A new formal concept analysis-based learning approach to ontology building. In *Metadata and semantics.* US: Springer.

Jones, J. C. (1992). *Design methods: Seeds of human futures.* London: Wiley International.

Jorgensen, M., & Shepperd, M. (2007). A systematic review of software development cost estimation studies. *IEEE Transactions on Software Engineering, 33*(1), 33–53. doi:10.1109/TSE.2007.256943

Joshi, P., Park, C.-S., Sen, K., & Naik, M. (2009). A randomized dynamic program analysis technique for detecting real deadlocks. In *Proceedings of the 2009 ACM SIGPLAN conference on Programming Language Design and Implementation (PLDI),* (pp. 110–120). ACM Press.

Juristo, N., & Moreno, A. M. (2001). *Basics of software engineering experimentation.* Kluwer Academic Publishers.

Kagermann, H., & Österle, H. (2006). *Wie CEOs Unternehmen transformieren.* Frankfurter Allgemeine Buch.

Kaner, C. (2004). Software engineering metrics: What do they measure and how do we know? In *Proceedings of the International Software Metrics Symposium.* (pp. 1-10).

Kang, M.-H., Ha, O.-K., Jun, S.-W., & Jun, Y.-K. (2009). A tool for detecting first races in OpenMP programs. In *Proceedings from the 10th International Conference Parallel Computing Technologies,* (pp. 299–303).

Kanoun, K., & Sabourin, T. (1987). Software dependability of a telephone switching system. Paper presented at the 17th International Symposium on Fault-Tolerant Computing (FTCS'17), (pp. 236–241).

Kanoun, K., Kaaniche, M., Laprie, J., & Metge, S. (1993). *SoRel: A tool for reliability growth analysis and prediction from statistical failure data.* Paper presented at The Twenty-Third International Symposium on Fault-Tolerant Computing, (p. 654).

Kantorovitch, J., & Niemelä, E. (2008). Service description ontologies. *Encyclopedia of information science and technology, second edition,* (pp. 3445-3451).

Karlsson, C., & Ahlström, P. (2009). The difficult path to lean product development. *Journal of Product Innovation Management, 13*(4), 283–295. doi:10.1016/S0737-6782(96)00033-1

Karlström, D. (2002). *Introducing extreme programming-an experience report. XP 2002, Alghero.* Sardinia, Italy: Springer-Verlag.

Katifori, A., Halatsis, C., Lepouras, G., Vassilakis, E., & Giannopoulou, E. (2007). Ontology visualization methods-a survey. In *ACM Computational survey.* New York: ACM.

Katz, S., & Peled, D. (1989). An efficient verification method for parallel and distributed programs. In *Linear time, branching time and partial order in logics and models for concurrency, school/workshop* (pp. 489–507). London: Springer-Verlag. doi:10.1007/BFb0013032

Kautz, K. (1998). Software process improvement in very small enterprises: Does it pay off? *Software Process Improvement and Practice, 4*(4), 209–226. doi:10.1002/(SICI)1099-1670(199812)4:4<209::AID-SPIP105>3.0.CO;2-8

Kazman, R., Abowd, G., Bass, L., & Clements, P. (1996). Scenario-based analysis of software architecture. *IEEE Software, 13*(6), 47–55. doi:10.1109/52.542294

Kazman, R., Klein, M., Barbacci, M., Lipson, H., Longstaff, T., & Carriere, S. J. (1998). *The architecture tradeoff analysis method.* Paper presented at the Fourth International Conference Eng. of Complex Computer Systems (ICECCS '98).

Kazman, R., Woods, S. G., & Carrière, S. J. (1998). Requirements for integrating software architecture and reengineering models: CORUM 2. *Proceedings of the Working Conference on Reverse Engineering (WCRE'98),* (pp. 154-163). IEEE Computer Society.

KDMAnalytics. (2008). *Knowledge Discovery Metamodel (KDM) software development kit 2.0 eclipse plugin.* Retrieved from http://www.kdmanalytics.com/kdmsdk/ KDMSDK_brochure.pdf, Hatha Systems.

Keim, D., Andrienko, G., Fekete, J. D., Görg, C., Kohlhammer, J., & Melancon, G. (2008). Visual analytics: Definition, process, and challenges. In *Journal Information Visualization.* Springer Verlag. doi:10.1007/978-3-540-70956-5_7

Keller, A., & Ludwig, H. (2002). The WSLA framework: Specifying and monitoring of service level agreements for web services. *Journal of Network and Systems Management, 11*(1), 57–81. doi:10.1023/A:1022445108617

Kelly, S., & Pohjonen, R. (2009). Worst practices for domain-specific modelling. *IEEE Software, 26*(4), 22–29. doi:10.1109/MS.2009.109

Kerievsky, J. (2005). *Refactoring to patterns.* Boston: Addison-Wesley.

Kerrigan, M. (2005). *Web Service Modeling Toolkit (WSMT).* Techreport.

Kett, H., Voigt, K., Scheithauer, G. & Cardoso, J. (2009). *Service engineering for business service ecosystems.*

Kettunen, P. (2009). Adopting key lessons from agile manufacturing to agile software and product development-a comparative study. *Technovation, 29,* 408–422. doi:10.1016/j.technovation.2008.10.003

Khemakhem, S., Drira, K., & Jmaiel, M. (2006). Sec: A search engine for component based software development. In *Proceedings of the 21st ACM Symposium on Applied Computing.*

Khemakhem, S., Jmaiel, M., Hamadou, A. B., & Drira, K. (2002). Un environnement de recherche et d'int'egration de composant logiciel. In *Proceedings of the Seventh Conference On computer Sciences,* Annaba.

Khusidman, V. (2008). *ADM transformation White Paper. DRAFT V.1.* Retrieved from http://www.omg.org/docs/ admtf/08-06-10.pdf

Khusidman, V., & Ulrich, W. (2007). *Architecture-driven modernization: Transforming the enterprise. DRAFT V.5.* Retrieved from http://www.omg.org/docs/ admtf/07-12-01.pdf

Kim, K. H. (2000). APIs for real-time distributed object programming. *Computer, 33*(6), 72–80. doi:10.1109/2.846321

Kingsbury, B. (2007). Organizing processes and threads for debugging. In *Proceedings of the 2007 ACM Workshop on Parallel and Distributed Systems: Testing and Debugging,* (pp. 21–26), New York: ACM.

Kitchenham, B., Pickard, L., MacDonell, S., & Shepperd, M. (2001). What accuracy statistics really measure. *IEE Proceedings. Software, 148*(3), 81–85. doi:10.1049/ip-sen:20010506

Kitchenham, B. (1997). The problem with function points. *IEEE Software, 14*(2), 29–31. doi:10.1109/ MS.1997.582972

Kitchenham, B., & Mendes, E. (2004) A comparison of cross-company and within-company effort estimation models for web applications. *Proceedings of the 8th International Conference on Empirical Assessment in Software Engineering (EASE 2004),* (pp. 47-55).

Kitchenham, B., & Mendes, E. (2009). Why comparative effort prediction studies may be invalid. *Proceedings of the 5th ACM International Conference on Predictor Models in Software Engineering.*

Klemola, T., & Rilling, J. (2003). A cognitive complexity metric based on category learning. In *Proceedings of IEEE (ICCI'03),* (pp. 103-108).

Kleppe, A., Warmer, J., & Bast, W. (2005). *MDA explained: The model driven architecture, practice and promise.* Boston: Addison-Wesley.

Knapp, A., Merz, S., & Rauh, C. (2002). Model checking timed UML state machines and collaboration. Proceedings of the 7th International Symposium in Formal Techniques in Real-Time and Fault-Tolerant Systems, (pp. 395-414). Berlin / Heidelberg: Springer.

Knuth, D. (1967). *The art of computer programming.* Addison-Wesley.

Knuth, D. (1974). Computer programming as an art. *Communications of the ACM, 17*(12), 667-673. Transcript of the 1974 Turing Award lecture.

Koch, A. S. (2005). *Agile software development: Evaluating the methods for your organization.* Boston: Artech House.

Kodase, S., Wang, S., & Shin, K. G. (2003). Transforming structural model to runtime model of embedded real-time systems. Proceedings of the Design Automation and Test in Europe Conference, (pp. 170-175).

Kofman, A., Yaeli, A., Klinger, T., & Tarr, P. (2009). *Roles, rights and responsibilities: Better governance through decision rights automation.* Paper presented at the Software Development Governance Workshop, Vancouver, Canada.

Kopecky, J., Vitvar, T., Bournez, C., & Farrell, J. (2007). SAWSDL: Semantic annotations for WSDL and XML schema. *IEEE Internet Computing, 11,* 60–67. doi:10.1109/MIC.2007.134

Koskinen, J., Ahonen, J., Lintinen, H., Sivula, H., & Tilus, T. (2004). *Estimation of the business value of software modernizations.* Information Technology Research Institute, University of Jyväskylä.

Koskinen, J., Ahonen, J. J., Sivula, H., Tilus, T., Lintinen, H., & Kankaanpää, I. (2005). Software modernization decision criteria: An empirical study. *European Conference on Software Maintenance and Reengineering,* (pp. 324-331). IEEE Computer Society.

Krammer, B., Muller, M. S., & Resch, M. M. (2004). MPI application development using the analysis tool MARMOT. In *Proceedings from the International Conference on Computational Science,* (pp 464–471).

Kreps, D. M. (1990). *A Course in microeconomic theory.* New Jersey: Princeton University Press.

Krishnamurthy, S., & Mathur, A. P. (1997). On the estimation of reliability of a software system using reliabilities of its components. *Proceedings of the Eighth International Symposium on Software Reliability Engineering,* (pp. 146-155).

Kruchten, P. B. (1995). The 4+1 view model of architecture. *IEEE Software, 12*(6), 42–50. doi:10.1109/52.469759

Kuan, T., See, W. B., & Chen, S. J. (1995). An Object-Oriented real-time framework and development environment. Proceedings of OOPSLA Conference Workshop, (p.18).

Kubat, P. (1989). Assessing reliability of modular software. *Operations Research Letters, 8*(1), 35–41. doi:10.1016/0167-6377(89)90031-X

Kurshan, R. P. (1994). *Computer-aided verification of coordinating processes: The automata-theoretic approach.* Princeton, NJ: Princeton University Press.

Kurshan, R. P. (1987). *Reducibility in analysis of coordination.* (pp. 19–39). LNCS 103.

Kushwaha, D. S., & Misra, A. K. (2005). A modified cognitive information complexity measure of software. In *Proceedings of the 7th International Conference on Cognitive Systems(ICCS'05).*

Lahteenmaki, J., Leppanen, J., & Kaijanranta, H. (2007). *Document-based service architecture for communication between health and wellness service providers and customers.* (pp. 275-278). ICHIT2007.

Lamma, E., Mello, P., & Riguzzi, F. (2004). A system for measuring function points from an ER-DFD specification. *The Computer Journal, 47,* 358–372. doi:10.1093/comjnl/47.3.358

Laporte, C. Y., Alexandre, S., & Renault, A. (2008). Developing international standards for very small enterprises. *Computer, 41*(3), 98–101. doi:10.1109/MC.2008.86

Laprie, J. C. (1984). Dependability evaluation of software systems in operation. *IEEE Transactions on Software Engineering, 10*(6), 701–714. doi:10.1109/TSE.1984.5010299

Larman, C. (2004). *Agile and iterative development: A manager's guide.* Boston: Addison-Wesley.

Larman, C. (2003). *Agile & iterative software development*. Boston: Addison Wesley.

Lassing, N., Rijsenbrij, D., & Vliet, H. v. (1999). *On software architecture analysis of flexibility, complexity of changes: Size isn't everything.* Paper presented at the Second Nordic Software Architecture Workshop (NOSA '99), (pp. 1103-1581).

Lavazza, L. (2001). *A methodology for formalizing concepts underlying the DESS notation.* Retrieved from http://www.dess-itea.org

Ledeczi, A., Bakay, A., Maroti, M., Volgyesi, P., Nordstrom, G., & Springle, J. (2001). Composing domain-specific design environments. *IEEE Computer, 34*(11), 44–51.

Ledoux, J. (1999). Availability modeling of modular software. *IEEE Transactions on Reliability, 48*(2), 159–168. doi:10.1109/24.784274

Lehman, M. M., Perry, D. E., & Ramil, J. F. (1998). Implications of evolution metrics on software maintenance. *Proceedings of the International Conference on Software Maintenance*, (pp. 208-217). IEEE Computer Society.

Lehmann, S., & Buxmann, P. (2009). Pricing strategies of software vendors. *Journal of Business and Information Systems Engineering, 6,* 1–10.

Lehto, I., & Rautiainen, K. (2009). *Software development governance challenges of a middle-sized company in agile transition.* Paper presented at the Software Development Governance Workshop, Vancouver, Canada.

Leijen, D., & Hall, J. (2007). Optimize managed code for multi-core cachines. Retrieved May 10, 2010, from http://msdn.microsoft.com/en-us/magazine/cc163340.aspx#S1

Leino, K., & Nelson, G. (1998). An extended static checker for modula-3. *Proceedings of the Seventh Int'l Conference of Compiler Construction,* 302–305.

Leon, A. (2005). *Software configuration management handbook.* Boston: Artech House.

Li, Y. (1998). Toward a qualitative search engine. *Internet Computing, IEEE, 2,* 24–29. doi:10.1109/4236.707687

Liao, H.-C., Chen, M.-F., Wang, F.-J., & Dai, J.-C. (1997). Using a hierarchical thesaurus for classifying and searching software libraries. In *Proceedings of the 21st International Computer Software and Applications Conference,* (pp. 210–216). IEEE Computer Society, Washington, DC.

Liao, W. S., & Hsiung, P. A. (2003). FVP: A Formal Verification Platform for SoC. *Proceedings of the* 16th IEEE International SoC Conference, (pp. 21-24).

Liblit, B., Aiken, A., Zheng, A., & Jordan, M. I. (2003). Bug isolation via remote program sampling. In *Proceedings of the ACM SIGPLAN Conference on Programming Language Design and Implementation (PLDI),* (pp. 141–154). ACM Press.

Liebchen, G., & Shepperd, M. (2008) Data sets and data quality in software engineering. *Proceedings of the 4th ACM International Workshop on Predictor Models in Software Engineering,* (pp. 39-44).

Lien, C. H., Bai, Y. W., & Lin, M. B. (2007). Estimation by software for the power consumption of streaming-media servers. *IEEE Transactions on Instrumentation and Measurement, 56*(5), 1859–1870. doi:10.1109/TIM.2007.904554

Lim, T.-S., Loh, W.-Y., & Shih, Y.-S. (2000). A comparison of prediction accuracy, complexity, and training time of thirty-three old and new classification algorithms. *Machine Learning, 40*(3), 203–228. doi:10.1023/A:1007608224229

Lindvall, M., & Muthig, D. (2004). Agile software development in large organizations. *Computing Practices, 37*(12), 38–46.

Little, R. J. A., & Rubin, D. B. (2002). *Statistical analysis with missing data.* New Jersey: John Wiley & Sons.

Littlewood, B. (1979). Software reliability model for modular program structure. *IEEE Transactions on Reliability, 28*(3), 241–246. doi:10.1109/TR.1979.5220576

Liu, C. L., & Layland, J. (1973). Scheduling algorithms for multiprogramming in a hard-real time environment. *Journal of the Association for Computing Machinery, 20,* 46–61.

Llorens, J., Amescua, A., & Velasco, M. (1996). Software thesaurus: A tool for reusing software objects. *Proceedings of the Fourth International Symposium on Assessment of Software Tools (SAST '96)*, (p. 99).

Lopez-Sanz, M., Acuna, C. J., Cuesta, C. E., & Marcos, E. (2008). *Defining service-oriented software architecture models for a MDA-based development process at the PIM level* (pp. 309–312). IEEE Computer Society.

Lother, M., & Dumke, R. (2001). Points metrics-comparison and analysis. In *Proceedings of International Workshop on Software Measurement*, (pp. 155-172).

Lu, L., Li, X., Xiong, Y., & Zhou, X. (2002). Xm-adl: An extensible markup architecture description language. In *IEEE*, (pp. 63–67). IEEE Press.

Lu, S., Tucek, J., Qin, F., & Zhou, Y. (2006). AVIO: Detecting Atomicity violations via access interleaving invariants. In *Proceedings of the Twelfth International Conference on Architectural Support for Programming Languages and Operating Systems (ASPLOS)*. ACM Press.

Luckham, D., Kenney, J. J., Augustin, L. M., Vera, J., Bryan, D., & Mann, W. (1995). Specification and analysis of system architecture using Rapide. *IEEE Transactions on Software Engineering, 21*(4), 336–353. doi:10.1109/32.385971

Luckham, D., & Kenney, J. L.A., et al (1995). Specification and analysis of system architecture using Rapide. In *IEEE Transactions on Software Engineering, 21*, 336–355.

Luecke, G., Chen, H., Coyle, J., Hoekstra, J., Kraeva, M., & Zou, Y. (2003). MPI-CHECK: A tool for checking FORTRAN 90 MPI programs. *Concurrency and Computation, 15*(2), 93–100.

Luecke, G., Zou, Y., Coyle, J., Hoekstra, J., & Kraeva, M. (2002). Deadlock detection in MPI programs. [John Wiley & Sons.]. *Concurrency and Computation, 14*(11), 911–932.

Lum, K., & Monson, E. (2003). *Software cost analysis tool user document*. California: NASA- Jet Propulsion Laboratory Pasadena.

Lung, C., Bot, S., Kalaichelvan, K., & Kazman, R. (1997). An approach to software architecture analysis for evolution and reusability. *Proceedings of CASCON '97*, (pp.15).

Lyu, M. R. (1995). *Handbook of software reliability engineering*. McGraw-Hill.

Lyu, M. R., & Nikora, A. (1992). *CASRE: A computer-aided software reliability estimation tool*. Paper presented at the Fifth International Workshop on Computer-Aided Software Engineering, (pp. 264-275).

Maarek, Y., Berry, D., & Kaiser, G. (1991). An information retrieval approach for automatically constructing software libraries. *IEEE Transactions on Software Engineering, 17*(8), 800–813. doi:10.1109/32.83915

Maedche, A. (2002). *Ontology learning for the Semantic Web*. Boston: Kluwer Academic Publishers.

Maedche, A., & Staab, S. (2001). Ontology learning for the Semantic Web. *IEEE Intelligent Systems, 16*(2), 72–79. doi:10.1109/5254.920602

Maimon, O., & Braha, D. (1996). On the complexity of the design synthesis problem. *IEEE Transactions on Systems, Man, and Cybernetics, 26*(1).

Mair, C., & Shepperd, M. (2005). The consistency of empirical comparisons of regression and analogy-based software project cost prediction. *Proceedings of the International Symposium on Empirical Software Engineering*, (pp. 509-518).

Majumdar, R., & Sen, K. (2007). Hybrid concolic testing. In *Proceedings of the 29th International Conference on Software Engineering (ICSE)*. IEEE Press.

Manna, Z., & Pnueli, A. (1992). *Temporal logic of reactive and concurrent systems*. Springer.

Manuel, M., Aurelio, L., & Alexander, G. (2000). Information retrieval with conceptual graph matching. *Proceedings of the 11th International Conference and Workshop on Database and Expert Systems Applications*, (pp. 4–8).

Marín, B., Giachetti, G., & Pastor, O. (2008). Measurement of functional size in conceptual models: A survey of measurement procedures based on COSMIC. In *Proceedings of International Workshop on Software Measurement*, (pp. 170-183).

Marín, B., Pastor, O., & Giachetti, G. (2008). Automating the measurement of functional size of conceptual models in an MDA environment. In *Proceedings of the International Conference on Product-Focused Software Process Improvement*, (pp. 215-229).

Marks, L. S. (1987). *Marks' standard handbook for mechanical engineers*. McGraw-Hill.

Marks, E., & Michael, B. (2006). *Service oriented architecture: A planning and implementation guide for business and technology*. Hoboken, NJ: John Wiley & Sons.

Matinlassi, M. (2006). *Quality driven software architecture model transformation towards automation*. Espoo, Finland: VTT Publications.

Matinlassi, M., Niemelä, E., & Dobrica, L. (2002). *Quality-driven architecture design and quality analysis method: A revolutionary initiation approach to a product line architecture*. Espoo, Finland: VTT Publications.

Matson, J. E., Barrett, B. E., & Mellichamp, J. M. (1994). Software development cost estimation using function points. *IEEE Transactions on Software Engineering, 20*(4), 275–287. doi:10.1109/32.277575

Maxwell, K. (2002). *Applied statistics for software managers*. New Jersey: Prentice-Hall.

May, T., & Kohlhammer, J. (2008). Towards closing the analysis gap: Visual generation of decision supporting schemes from raw data. *Computer Graphics Forum, 27*, 911–918. doi:10.1111/j.1467-8659.2008.01224.x

McCaffery, F., & Dorling, A. (2009). *MediSPICE development*. Software Process Improvement and Practice Journal.

McCaffery, F., Richardson, I., & Coleman, G. (2006). *Adept-a software process appraisal method for small to medium-sized Irish software development organisations*. EuroSPI06. Finland: Joensuu.

McCaffery, F., Pikkarainen, M., & Richardson, I. (2008). *AHAA -Agile, hybrid assessment method for automotive, safety critical SMEs*. ICSE 2008, Leipzig, Germany.

McConnell, S. (2003). *Professional software development: Shorter schedules, better projects, superior products, enhanced careers*. Boston: Addison-Wesley.

McCool, M., Du Toit, S., Popa, T., Chan, B., & Moule, K. (2004). Shader algebra. *ACM Transactions on Graphics, 23*(3), 787–795.

McFeeley, B. (1996). *A users guide for software process improvement*. Pittsburgh: Carnegie Mellon University.

McGuinness, D., & van Harmelen, F. (2004). *OWL web ontology language overview*. W3C recommendation. Retrieved February 10, 2004, from http://www.w3.org/TR/owl-features/

McIlraith, S., Son, T. C., & Zeng, H. (2001). Semantic-Web services. *IEEE Intell. Syst. Special Issue Semantic Web, 16*(2), 46–53.

McMillan, K. L. (1994). *Symbolic model checking*. Boston: Kluwer Academic Publishers.

McMillan, K. L. (1992). *Symbolic model checking: An approach to the state explosion problem*. Unpublished doctoral thesis, Carnegie Mellon University.

Medvidovic, N., Dashofy, E. M., & Taylor, R. N. (2007). Moving architectural description from under the technology lamppost. *Information and Software Technology, 49*(1), 12–31. doi:10.1016/j.infsof.2006.08.006

Medvidovic, N., & Jakobac, V. (2006). Using software evolution to focus architectural recovery. *Automated Software Engineering, 13*(2), 225–256. doi:10.1007/s10515-006-7737-5

Medvidovic, N., & Taylor, R. N. (2000). A classification and comparison framework for software architecture description languages. *Software Engineering, 26*(1), 70–93. doi:10.1109/32.825767

Medvidovic, N., Malek, S., & Mikic-Rakic, M. (2003). Software architectures and embedded systems. In *Proceedings of the Monterey Workshop on Software Engineering for Embedded Systems (SEES 2003)*, (pp. 65–71).

Medvidovic, N., Oreizy, P., et al. (1996). Using object-oriented typing to support architectural design in the C2 style. In *Proceedings of the 4th ACM SIGSOFT Symposium on Foundations of Software Engineering*, (pp 24–32).

Meehan, B., & Richardson, I. (2002). Identification of software process knowledge management. *Process: Improvement and Practice, 7*(2), 47–56. doi:10.1002/spip.154

Meling, R., Montgomery, E., Ponnusamy, P. S., Wong, E., & Mehandjiska, D. (2000). Storing and retrieving software components: A component description manager. In *Proceedings of the 2000 Australian Software Engineering Conference*, (pp.107-117). Canberra, Australia.

Melton, J., & Simon, A. R. (1993). *Understanding the new SQL: A complete guide*. USA: Morgan Kaufmann Publishers, Inc.

Mendes, E., & Lokan, C. (2008). Replicating studies on cross- vs. single-company effort models using the ISBSG database. *Empirical Software Engineering, 13*(1), 3–37. doi:10.1007/s10664-007-9045-5

Mendes, E., Lokan, C., Harrison, R., & Triggs, C. (2005). A replicated comparison of cross-company and within-company effort estimation models using the ISBSG database. *Proceedings of the 11th IEEE International Software Metrics Symposium (METRICS'05)*, (pp.36-45).

Mens, T., & Demeyer, S. (2008). *Software Evolution*. Berlin, Heidelberg: Springer-Verlag.

Merilinna, J., & Niemelä, E. (2005). A stylebase as a tool for modelling of quality-driven software architecture. *Proceedings of the Estonia Academy of Sciences Engineering, Special Issue on Programming Languages and Software Tools, 11*(4), 296-312.

Michalewicz, Z. (1992). *Genetic algorithms + data structures = evolution programs*. Berlin, Heidelberg: Springer-Verlag.

Micro Focus. (2009). *Modernization Workbench™*. Retrieved from http://www.microfocus.com/products/modernizationworkbench/

Mili, A., Mili, R., & Mittermeir, R. (1998). A survey of software reuse libraries. *Annals of Software Engineering, 5*, 349–414. doi:10.1023/A:1018964121953

Mili, A. (1999). Toward an engineering discipline of software reuse. *IEEE Software, 16*(5), 22–31. doi:10.1109/52.795098

Mili, H., Mili, F., & Mili, A. (1995). Reuse software: Issues and research directions. *IEEE Transactions on Software Engineering, 21*(6), 528–562. doi:10.1109/32.391379

Mili, H., Ah-Ki, E., Godin, R., & Mcheick, H. (1997). Another nail to the coffin of faceted controlled-vocabulary component classification and retrieval. In *SIGSOFT Software Engineering Notes, 22*, 89 – 98.

Miller, J., & Mukerji, J. (2003). *MDA Guide Version 1.0.1*. Retrieved from www.omg.org/docs/omg/03-06-01.pdf

Milner, R. (1995). *Communication and concurrency*. Prentice Hall PTR.

Misra, S. (2009). A metric for global software development environments. *Proceedings of the Indian National Science Academy, 75*(4), 1–14.

Misra, S., & Akman, I. (2008). Weighted class complexity: A measure of complexity for Object Oriented systems. *Journal of Information Science and Engineering, 24*, 1689–1708.

Misra, S., & Akman, I. (2010). Unified complexity measure: A measure of complexity. *Proceedings of the National Academy of Sciences of the United States of America, 80*.

Misra, S. (2006). *Modified cognitive complexity measure*. (pp. 1050-1059). (LNCS 4263).

Misra, S. (2007). Cognitive program complexity measure. In *Proceedings of IEEE (ICCI'07)*, (pp. 120-125).

Mittas, N., & Angelis, L. (2008a). Comparing cost prediction models by resampling techniques. *Journal of Systems and Software, 81*(5), 616–632. doi:10.1016/j.jss.2007.07.039

Mittas, N., & Angelis, L. (2010). Visual comparison of software cost estimation models by regression error characteristic analysis. *Journal of Systems and Software, 83*, 621–637. doi:10.1016/j.jss.2009.10.044

Mittas, N., & Angelis, L. (2008b). Comparing software cost prediction models by a visualization tool. *Proceedings of the 34th Euromicro Conference on Software Engineering and Advanced Applications (SEAA'08)*, (pp. 433-440).

Miyawaki, T., Iijima, J., & Ho, S. (2008). Measuring function points from VDM-SL specifications. In *Proceedings of International Conference on Service Systems and Service Management*, (pp. 1-6).

ModelWare. (2006). *MODELWARE*. Retrieved August 24, 2009, from http://www.modelware-ist.org/

MoDisco. (2008). *KDM-to-UML2 converter*. Retrieved from http://www.eclipse.org/gmt/modisco/toolBox/KDMtoUML2Converter/

Mohamed, M., Romdhani, M., & Ghedira, K. (2007). EMF-MOF alignment. In *Proceedings of the 3rd International Conference on Autonomic and Autonomous Systems*, (pp. 1 – 6).

Molnár, Z., Balasubramanian, D., & Lédeczi, A. (2007). *An introduction to the generic modelling environment.* Model-driven development tool implementers forum. Retrieved from http://www.dsmforum.org/events/MDD-TIF07/GME.2.pdf

Molter, G. (1999). Integrating SAAM in domain-centric and reuse-based development processes. *Proceedings of the Second Nordic Workshop on Software Architecture (NOSA '99),* (pp. 1103-1581).

MOMOCS. (2008). *MOdel driven MOdernisation of Complex Systems is an EU-Project.* Retrieved from http://www.momocs.org/. 2008, from http://www.momocs.org/

Morgan, J. M., & Liker, J. K. (2006). *The Toyota product development system: Integrating people, process, and technology.* New York: Productivity Press.

Mori, A., Futatsugi, T. S. K., Seo, A., & Ishiguro, M. (2001). Software component search based on behavioral specification. *Proceedings of International Symposium on Future Software Technology.*

Morkel, W.H., Kourie, D.G., et al. (2003). *Standards and agile software development.* SAICSIT 2003.

Moser, O., Rosenberg, F., & Dustdar, S. (2008). Non-intrusive monitoring and service adaptation for WS-BPEL. *Proceedings of the World Wide Web Conference,* (pp. 815-824). New York: ACM.

Moyer, B. (2009). Software archeology: Modernizing old systems. *Embedded Technology Journal, 1,* 1–4.

MSDN. (2010). *Introduction to PLINQ.* Retrieved from http://msdn.microsoft.com/en-us/library/dd997425(v=VS.100).aspx

Müller, H. A., Jahnke, J. H., Smith, D. B., Storey, M.-A., Tilley, S. R., & Wong, K. (2000). Reverse engineering: A roadmap. *Proceedings of the Conference on The Future of Software Engineering.* Limerick, Ireland: ACM.

Murphy, G., & Lieberherr, K. (Eds.). (2004). *Proceedings of the 3rd International Conference on Aspect-oriented Software Development.* ACM Press.

Musa, J. (1998). *Software reliability engineering, more reliable software faster development and testing.* McGraw-Hill.

Musa, J. D., Iannino, A., & Okumoto, K. (1987). *Software reliability: Measurement, prediction, application.* McGraw-Hill.

Musuvathi, M., & Qadeer, S. (2008). Fair stateless model checking. In *Proceedings of the ACM SIGPLAN Conference on Programming Language Design and Implementation (PLDI),* (pp. 362–371). ACM Press.

Myrtveit, I., Stensrud, E., & Olsson, U. (2001). Analyzing data sets with missing data: An empirical evaluation of imputation methods and likelihood-based methods. *IEEE Transactions on Software Engineering, 27*(11), 999–1013. doi:10.1109/32.965340

Nadhan, E. G. (2004). Service-oriented architecture: Implementation challenges. In *Microsoft Architect Journal, 2.*

Naik, M., & Aiken, A. (2007). Conditional must not aliasing for static race detection. In *Proceedings of the 34th annual ACM SIGPLAN-SIGACT Symposium on Principles of Programming Languages (POPL).* ACM Press.

Nakagawa, E. Y., Barbosa, E. F., & Maldonado, J. C. (2009). *Exploring ontologies to support the establishment of reference architectures: An example on software testing* (pp. 249–252). Cambridge, UK: WICSA/ECSA.

Nakajima, S., & Tamai, T. (2001). Behavioural analysis of the enterprise Javabeans component architecture. *Proceedings of the 8th International SPIN Workshop,* (163–182). Toronto. Springer.

Nakkrasae, S., Sophatsathit, P., & Edwards, W. (2004). Fuzzy subtractive clustering based indexing approach for software components classification. *International Journal of Computer and Information Science, 5*(1), 63–72.

Napoli, A. (1992). Subsumption and classification-based reasoning in object-based representations. In *Proceedings of the 10th European conference on Artificial intelligence.* (pp. 425-429). New York: John Wiley & Sons, Inc.

Natalya, F., & Deborah, L. M. (2001). *Ontology development 101: A guide to creating your first ontology.* Stanford University.

Naumovich, G., Clarke, L., Osterweil, L., & Dwyer, M. (1997). Verification of concurrent software with flavers. *Proceedings of the 19th Int'l Conf. Software Eng,* 594–595.

Nawrocki, J., Jasinski, M., et al. (2002). *Extreme programming modified: Embrace requirements engineering practices*. Paper presented at the International Conference of Requirements Engineering, Essen, Germany.

Nazemi, K., Breyer, M., & Hornung, C. (2009). SeMap: A concept for the visualization of semantics as maps. In *HCI International 2009. Proceedings and Posters (DVD-ROM), with 10 further associated conferences*. Berlin, Heidelberg, New York: Springer.

Nazemi, K., Breyer, M., Burkhardt, D., Stab, C., Hofmann, C. & Hornung, C. (2009). *D.CTC.5.7.1: Design und Conceptualization Semantic Visualization*.

NCSA-CUDA NCSA CUDA Tutorial. http://www.ncsa.illinois.edu/UserInfo/Training/Workshops/CUDA/presentations/tutorial-CUDA.html

Netzer, R. H. B., Brennan, T. W., & Damodaran-Kamal, S. K. (1996). Debugging race conditions in message-passing programs. In *Proceedings of the SIGMETRICS Symposium on Parallel and Distributed Tools*, (pp. 31–40). New York: ACM.

Newell, N., & Simon, H. A. (1976). *Human problem solving*. Englewood Cliffs, NJ: Prentice-Hall.

Nexus, N. V. I. D. I. A. 2009 - Visual Studio-based GPU Development, http://developer.nvidia.com/object/nexus.html

Niazi, M., & Wilson, D. (2003). A maturity model for the implementation of software process improvement: An empirical study. *Journal of Systems and Software*, 1–18.

Niazi, M., & Wilson, D. (2006). Critical success factors for software process improvement implementation: An empirical study. *Software Process Improvement and Practice*, *11*, 193–211. doi:10.1002/spip.261

Niemelä, E., & Immonen, A. (2006). Capturing quality requirements of product family architecture. *Information and Software Technology*, *49*(11-12), 1107–1120. doi:10.1016/j.infsof.2006.11.003

Niemelä, E., Kalaoja, J., & Lago, P. (2005). Toward an architectural knowledge base for wireless service engineering. *IEEE Transactions on Software Engineering*, *31*(5), 361–379. doi:10.1109/TSE.2005.60

Ninth Workshop on Runtime Verification (2009). *Lecture Notes in Computer Science, 5779*.

Niz, D. d., & Rajkumar, R. (2003). Time Weaver: A software-through-models framework for embedded real-time systems. Proceedings of the Internation Workshop on Languages, Embedded Systems, (pp. 133-143).

Novak, J. G. S. (1997). Software reuse by specialization of generic procedures through views. *IEEE Transactions on Software Engineering*, *23*(7), 401–417. doi:10.1109/32.605759

Noy, N. F., & McGuinness, D. L. (2006). *Ontology development 101: A guide to creating your first ontology*. Retrieved May 25, 2010, from http://ksl.Stanford.edu/people/dlm/papers/ontology101/ontology101-Noy-Mcguinness.Html

Nytun, J. P., Prinz, A., & Tveit, M. S. (2006). Automatic generation of modelling tools. *In Proceedings of the European Conference on Model-Driven Architecture, Foundations and Applications (ECMDA-FA)* (LNCS 4066), (pp. 268-283).

O'Callahan, R., & Choi, J.-D. (2003). Hybrid dynamic data race detection. In *Proceedings of ACM SIGPLAN 2003 Symposium on Principles and Practice of Parallel Programming (PPoPP)*, (pp. 167–178). ACM.

Obeo. (2007a). *Acceleo™*. Retrieved from http://www.obeo.fr/pages/acceleo/en

Obeo. (2007b). *Agility™*. Retrieved from http://www.obeo.fr/pages/agility/en

Oberle, D., Bhatti, N., Brockmans, S., Niemann, M., & Janiesch, C. (2009). Countering service information challenges in the Internet of Services. *Business and Information Systems Engineering*, *1*, 370–390. doi:10.1007/s12599-009-0069-9

Oberle, D., Lamparter, S., Grimm, S., Vrandecic, D., Staab, S., & Gangemi, A. (2006). *Towards ontologies for formalizing modularization and communication in large software systems*. Applied Ontology.

Oberle, D., Bhatti, N., Brockmans, S., Niemann, M., & Janiesch, C. (2009). Countering service information challenges in the Internet of Services. In *Journal Business & Information Systems Engineering – Special issue Internet of Services*.

Olaru, C., & Wehenkel, L. (2003). A complete fuzzy decision tree technique. *Fuzzy Sets and Systems, 138*(2), 221–254. doi:10.1016/S0165-0114(03)00089-7

Oltramari, A., Gangemi, A., Guarino, N., & Masolo, C. (2002). *Sweetening ontologies with DOLCE.* Springer.

OMG. (2003). *Model Driven Architecture (MDA) specification guide v1.0.1.* Retrieved from http://www.omg.org/docs/omg/03-06-01.pdf

OMG. (2003a). *CWM. Common Warehouse Metamodel, v1.1 Specification.* Retrieved from http://www.omg.org/spec/CWM/1.1/PDF/

OMG. (2003b). *Why do we need standards for the modernization of existing systems?* OMG ADM task force.

OMG. (2005). *Meta Object Facility (MOF) core specification v2.0.* Retrieved from http://www.omg.org/docs/formal/06-01-01.pdf.

OMG. (2005). Object Constraint Language (OCL) specification v2.0. Retrieved from http://www.omg.org/docs/formal/06-05-01.pdf

OMG. (2006a). *ADM Glossary of Definitions and Terms.* Retrieved from http://adm.omg.org/ADM_Glossary_Spreadsheet_pdf.pdf

OMG. (2006b). *Architecture-driven modernization scenarios.* Retrieved November, 2, 2009, from http://adm.omg.org/ADMTF_Scenario_White_Paper%28pdf%29.pdf

OMG. (2007a). *ADM task force by OMG.* Retrieved June 15, 2009, 2008, from http://www.omg.org/

OMG. (2007b). *Unified modeling language: Superstructure, version 2.0.* Retrieved August 16, 2007, from http://www.omg.org/docs/formal/05-07-04.pdf

OMG. (2008a). *Architecture-Driven Modernization (ADM): Knowledge Discovery Meta-Model (KDM), v1.0.* Retrieved from http://www.omg.org/docs/formal/08-01-01.pdf

OMG. (2008b). *QVT. Meta Object Facility (MOF) 2.0 query/vew/transformation specification.* Retrieved from http://www.omg.org/spec/QVT/1.0/PDF

OMG. (2009a). *Architecture-Driven Modernization (ADM): Knowledge Discovery Meta-Model (KDM), v1.1.* Retrieved from http://www.omg.org/spec/KDM/1.1/PDF/

OMG. (2009b). *Architecture-Driven Modernization standards roadmap.* Retrieved October 29, 2009, from http://adm.omg.org/ADMTF%20Roadmap.pdf

OMG. (2009c). *UML (Unified Modeling Language) superstructure specification. Version 2.2.* Retrieved June 24, 2009, from http://www.omg.org/spec/UML/2.2/Superstructure/PDF/

ONeil, J. & Schildt, H. (1998). *Java beans programming from the ground up.* Osborne McGraw-Hill.

Open, M. P. (2008). *Home information.* Retrieved from http://www.openmp.org

OpenCL Open Computing Language (OpenCL). http://www.khronos.org/opencl/.

Oreizy, L. P., Taylor, R. N., Heimbigner, D., Johnson, G., Medvidovic, N., & Quilici, A. (1999). Self-adaptive software: An architecture-based approach. *IEEE Intelligent Systems, 14*(3), 54–62. doi:10.1109/5254.769885

Ossher, H., & Kiczales, G. (Eds.). (2002). *Proceedings of the 1st International Conference on Aspect-oriented Software Development.* ACM Press.

Ostertag, E., Hendler, J., Prieto-Diaz, R., & Braun, C. (1992). Computing similarity in a reuse library system, an AI-based approach. *ACM Transactions on Software Engineering and Methodology, ***, 205–228. doi:10.1145/131736.131739

Ostroff, J. S. (1999). Composition and refinement of discrete realtime systems. *ATSEM, 8*(1), 1–48.

OSullivan, J. (2006). *Towards a precise understanding of service properties.* Queensland University of Technology.

Ovaska, E., Evesti, A., Henttonen, K., Palviainen, M., & Aho, P. (2010). Knowledge based quality-driven architecture design and evaluation. *Information and Software Technology, 52*(6), 577–601. doi:10.1016/j.infsof.2009.11.008

Ozkan, B., & Demirors, O. (2009). Formalization studies in functional size measurement: How do they help? In *Proceedings of International Workshop on Software Measurement*, (pp. 197-211).

Ozkan, B., Turetken, O., & Demirors, O. (2008). Software functional size: For cost estimation and more. In *Proceedings of the European Software Process Improvement Conference*, (pp. 59-69).

Paetch, F., Eberlein, A., et al. (2003). *Requirements engineering and agile software development*. 12th IEEE international workshop on Enabing Technologies: Insfrastructure for Collaborative Enterprises, Computer Society.

Paez, M. C., & Straeten, R. V. D. (2002). Modelling component libraries for reuse and evolution. In the *Proceedings of the First Workshop on Model-based Reuse*.

Pala, N., & Erbas, C. (2006). *Supporting reusability through ClearCase UCM* (Tech. Rep. No. TR-06-0001). Ankara, Turkey: ASELSAN, MGEO.

Pala, N., & Erbas, C. (2010). *Aligning software configuration management with governance structures*. Paper presented at the Software Development Governance Workshop, Cape Town, South Africa.

Pan, T., & Fang, K. (2009). Ontology-based formal concept analysis in radiology report impact by the adoption of PACS. In *proceedings of ICFCA 2009*.

Pandit, B., Popescu, V., & Smith, V. (2010). *SML service modeling language*. Retrieved April, 2010, from http://www.w3.org/TR/sml/. Accessed 2009-06-15

Paolucci, M., & Wagner, M. (2006). *Grounding OWL-S in WSDL-S* (pp. 913–914). IEEE Computer Society.

Papazoglou, M. P., Traverso, P., Dustdar, S., Leymann, F., & Kramer, B. J. (2008). Service-oriented computing: A research roadmap. *International Journal of Cooperative Information Systems*, 17, 223–255. doi:10.1142/S0218843008001816

Papazoglou, M. P. (2003). Service-oriented computing: Concepts, characteristics and directions. In *proceedings of the Web Information Systems Engineering (WISE)*.

Paradauskas, B., & Laurikaitis, A. (2006). Business knowledge extraction from legacy Information Systems. *Journal of Information Technology and Control*, 35(3), 214–221.

Park, C.-S., & Sen, K. (2008). Randomized active Atomicity violation detection in concurrent programs. In *Proceedings of the 16th ACM SIGSOFT International Symposium on Foundations of Software Engineering (FSE'08)*, (pp. 135–145). New York: ACM.

Parnas, D. L. (1972). On the criteria to be used in decomposing systems into modules. *Communications of the ACM*, 15(12). doi:10.1145/361598.361623

Parnas, D. L. (1998). Software engineering programmes are not computer science programmes. *Annals of Software Engineering*, 19–37. doi:10.1023/A:1018949113292

Parnas, D. L., & Wang, Y. (1989). *The trace assertion method of module interface specification*. (Tech. Rep. 89-261). Queen's University, Kingston, Ontario.

Patil, A., Oundhakar, S., Sheth, A., & Verma, K. (2004). METEOR-S Web service annotation framework. In *Proceedings of the 13th International World Wide Web Conference (WWW 04)*.

Paulk, M. C. (2001). Extreme programming from a CMM perspective. *Software*, 18(6), 19–26. doi:10.1109/52.965798

Peneder, M., Kaniovski, S., & Dachs, B. (2003). What follows tertiarisation? Structural change and the role of knowledge-based services. *The Service Industries Journal*, 23, 47–66. doi:10.1080/02642060412331300882

Penix, J., & Alexander, P. (1999). Efficient specification-based component retrieval. *Automated Software Engineering*, 6(2), 139–170. doi:10.1023/A:1008766530096

Perez, A.G.D. & Mancho, D.M. (2003). *A survey of ontology learning methods and techniques*. OntoWeb Delieverable 1.5.

Pérez-Castillo, R., García-Rodríguez de Guzmán, I., Ávila-García, O., & Piattini, M. (2009a). MARBLE: A modernization approach for recovering business processes from legacy systems. *International Workshop on Reverse Engineering Models from Software Artifacts (REM'09)*, Lille, France.

Pérez-Castillo, R., García-Rodríguez de Guzmán, I., Ávila-García, O., & Piattini, M. (2010). Business process patterns for software archeology. *25th Annual ACM Symposium on Applied Computing (SAC'10)*. Sierre, Switzerland: ACM.

Pérez-Castillo, R., García Rodríguez de Guzmán, I., Caballero, I., Polo, M., & Piattini, M. (2009b). PRECISO: A reengineering process and a tool for database modernisation through Web services. *24th Annual ACM Symposium on Applied Computing. Track on Service Oriented Architectures and Programming (SOAP 2009)*, (pp. 2126-2133). Waikiki Beach, Honolulu, Hawaii: ACM.

Perkins, J. H., & Ernst, M. D. (2004). Efficient incremental algorithms for dynamic detection of likely invariants. *SIGSOFT Software Engineering Notes*, 29(6), 23–32. doi:10.1145/1041685.1029901

Perry, R. (1984). *Perry's chemical engineer's handbook*. New York: McGraw-Hill.

Perry, D. E., & Wolf, A. L. (1992). Foundations for the study of software architecture. *ACM SIGSOFT Software Engineering Notes*, 17(4), 40–52. doi:10.1145/141874.141884

Perry, D. E. (1989). The logic of propagation in the inscape environment. In *Proceedings of the ACM SIGSOFT 89 Third Symposium on Software Testing, Analysis, and Verification (TAV3)*.

Petersen, K., & Wohlin, C. (2009). A comparison of issues and advantages in agile and incremental development between state of the art and an industrial case. *Journal of Systems and Software*, 82(9), 1479–1490. doi:10.1016/j.jss.2009.03.036

Petersen, K. & Wohlin, C. (2010). Software process improvement through the lean measurement (SPI-LEAM) method. *Journal of Systems and Software*.

Petersen, K., Wohlin, C., & Baca, D. (2009). The waterfall model in large-scale development. In *proceedings of the International Conference on Product-Focused Software Process Improvement (PROFES 2009)*, (pp 386-400).

Petri Net Markup Language. (2009). *About*. Retrieved from http://www2.informatik.hu-berlin.de/top/pnml/about.html

Petrie, C., Margaria, T., Lausen, H., & Zaremba, M. (2008). *Semantic Web Services challenge: Results from the first year*. Springer Publishing Company.

Petroski, H. (1992). *To engineer is human: The role of failure in successful design*. New York: Vintage Books.

Pettersson, F., Ivarsson, M., Gorschek, T., & Öhman, P. (2008). A practitioner's guide to light weight software process assessment and improvement planning. *Journal of Systems and Software*, 81(6), 972–995. doi:10.1016/j.jss.2007.08.032

pgi2009 (2009). PGI Tools Guide. http://www.pgroup.com/doc/pgitools.pdf

Pikkarainen, M., & Mäntyniemi, A. (2006). *An approach for using CMMI in agile software development assessments: Experiences of three case studies. SPICE 2006*. Luxemburg.

Pikkarainen, M., & Passoja, U. (2005). *An approach for assessing suitability of agile solutions: A case study*. The Sixth International Conference on Extreme Programming and Agile Processes in Software Engineering, Sheffield University, UK.

Pikkarainen, M., Salo, O., et al. (2005). Deploying agile practices in organizations: A case study. In *European Software Process Improvement and Innovation*. Budapest: EuroSPI.

Pint, E. M., & Baldwin, L. H. (1997). *Strategic sourcing: Theory and evidence from economics and business management*. (Tech. Rep. No. MR-865-AF). RAND Monograph Report.

Pnueli, A. (1985). *In transition from global to modular temporal reasoning about programs* (pp. 123–144).

Podgurski, A., & Pierce, L. (1992). Behaviour sampling: A technique for automated retrieval of reusable components. In *Proceedings of the 14th International Conference on Software Engineering*, 349–360.

Polo, M., Piattini, M., & Ruiz, F. (2003). *Advances in software maintenance management: Technologies and solutions*. Hershey, PA: Idea Group Publishing.

Poppendieck, M., & Poppendieck, T. (2003). *Lean software development: An agile toolkit*. Boston: Addison-Wesley.

Poppendieck, M., & Poppendieck, T. (2007). *Implementing lean software development: From concept to cash*. Boston: Addison-Wesley.

Poppendieck, M., & Poppendieck, T. (2009). *Leading lean software development*. Boston: Addison-Wesley.

Popper, K. (2001). *All life is problem solving*. Routledge.

Popstojanova, K. G., & Trivedi, K. S. (2001). Architecture-based approach to reliability assessment of software systems. *Performance Evaluation, 45*(2), 179–204. doi:10.1016/S0166-5316(01)00034-7

Pozewaunig, H., & Mittermeir, T. (2000). *Self classifying reusable components generating decision trees from test cases*. Paper presented at the International Conference on Software Engineering and Knowledge Engineering.

Pratikakis, P., Foster, J. S., & Hicks, M. (2006). Locksmith: Context-sensitive correlation analysis for race detection. In *Proceedings of the ACM SIGPLAN Conference on Programming Language Design and Implementation (PLDI)*, (pp. 320–331). ACM.

Preist, C. (2004). *A conceptual architecture for semantic Web services* (pp. 395–409). Springer.

Preist, C. (2004). A conceptual architecture for semantic web services. In *Proceedings Third International Semantic Web Conference.*

Pressman, R. S. (2008). *Software engineering: A practitioner's approach*. McGraw-Hill.

Pressman, R. (2009). *Software engineering: A practitioner's approach* (7th ed.). McGraw-Hill Companies.

Pressman, R. S. (2005). *Software engineering: A practitioner's approach*. New York: McGraw-Hill.

Pressman, R. S. (2001). *Software engineering: A practitioner's approach* (5th ed.). McGraw Hill.

Priss, U. (2006). Formal concept analysis in Information Science. In B. Cronin (Ed.), *Annual Review of Information Science and Technology,* 521-543.

Purhonen, A., Niemelä, E., & Matinlassi, M. (2004). Viewpoints of DSP software and service architectures. *Journal of Systems and Software, 69*(1), 57–73. doi:10.1016/S0164-1212(03)00050-5

Quantum Leaps. (2010). *What is QP™?* Quantum Leaps®, LLC. Retrieved May 10, 2010, from http://www.statemachine.com/products/

Queen's University. NSERC & IBM. (2009). Turing eXtender Language (TXL). Retrieved from http://www.txl.ca/

Queille, J. P., & Sifakis, J. (1982). Specification and verification of concurrent systems in CESAR. Proceedings of the International Symposium on Programming, (pp. 337-351). Berlin / Heidelberg: Springer.

Quinlan, R. (1986). Induction of decision trees. *Machine Learning, 1,* 81–106. doi:10.1007/BF00116251

Rapaport, B. (2006). *Philosophy of computer science: What I think it is, what I teach, & how I teach it. Herbert A. Simon Keynote Address*. NA-CAP Video.

RapidMind RapidMind. http://www.rapidmind.com/.

Rask, R. (1991). *Algorithms for counting unadjusted function points from dataflow diagrams. Research report A-1991-1*. Finland: University of Joensuu.

Rask, R., Laamanen, P., & Lyyttinen, K. (1993). Simulation and comparison of Albrecht's function point and DeMarco's function bang metrics in a CASE environment. *IEEE Transactions on Software Engineering, 19,* 661–671. doi:10.1109/32.238567

Ratanaworabhan, P., Burtscher, M., Kirovski, D., Zorn, B., Nagpal, R., & Pattabiraman, K. (2009). Detecting and tolerating asymmetric races. In *Proceedings of the 14th ACM SIGPLAN symposium on Principles and Practice of Parallel Programming (PPoPP)*, (pp. 173–184). ACM Press.

Ratiu, D. (2009). Reverse engineering domain models from source code. *International Workshop on Reverse Engineering Models from Software Artifacts (REM'09)*. Lille, France.

Rauterberg, M. (1992). *A method of a quantitative measurement of cognitive complexity, Human-Computer Interaction: task and organization* (pp. 295–307). Roma: CUD Publishing.

Reichlmayr, T. (2003). *The agile approach in an undergraduate software engineering course project* (pp. 13–18).

Reinders, J. (2007). *Intel threading building blocks: Outfitting C++ for multi-core processor parallelism*. O'Reilly Media, Inc.

Reussner, R., Schmidt, H., & Poernomo, I. (2003). Reliability prediction for component-based software architectures. *Journal of Systems and Software, 66*(3), 241–252. doi:10.1016/S0164-1212(02)00080-8

Richardson, I. (2001). Software process matrix: A small company SPI model. *Software Process Improvement and Practice, 6*(3), 157–165. doi:10.1002/spip.144

Riedl, C., Bohmann, T., Leimeister, J. M., & Krcmar, H. (2009). A framework for analysing service ecosystem capabilities to innovate. *Proceedings of 17th European Conference on Information Systems.*

Rising, L., & Janoff, N. S. (2000). The scrum software development process for small teams. *IEEE Software, 17*(4), 26–32. doi:10.1109/52.854065

Rittel, H. W., & Webber, M. M. (1984). Planning problems are wicked problems. *Policy Sciences, 4,* 155–169. doi:10.1007/BF01405730

Robertson, S. E., & Walker, S. (1994). Some simple effective approximations to the 2-poisson model for probabilistic weighted retrieval. In *Proceedings of the 17th annual international ACM SIGIR conference on Research and development in information retrieval,* (pp. 232-241). New York: Springer-Verlag.

Rodrigues, G., Rosenblum, D., Uchitel, S., Bt, W., & Rh, S. (2005). *Using scenarios to predict the reliability of concurrent component-based software systems.* FASE 2005 – LNCS 3442, (pp. 111-126).

Roman, D., de Bruijn, J., Mocan, A., Lausen, H., Domingue, J., Bussler, C., et al. (2006). WWW: WSMO, WSML, and WSMX in a nutshell. In *Proceedings of the XIX. International conference of RESER.*

Rosa, N. S., Alves, C. F., Cunha, P. R. F., Castro, J. F. B., & Justo, G. R. R. (2001). Using non-functional requirements to select components: A formal approach. In *Proceedings Fourth Workshop Ibero-American on Software Engineering and Software Environment,* San Jose, Costa Rica.

Roshandel, R., Hoek, A. V. D., Mikic-Rakic, M., & Medvidovic, N. (2004). Mae—a system model and environment for managing architectural evolution. *ACM Transactions on Software Engineering and Methodology, 13*(2), 240–276. doi:10.1145/1018210.1018213

Roshandel, R., & Medvidovic, N. (2004). Toward architecture-based reliability estimation. *Proceedings from The International Conference on Dependable Systems and Networks.*

Rosu, G. & Havelund, K. (2004). Rewriting-based techniques for runtime verification. *Journal of Automated Software Engineering.*

Royce, W. (2009). Managing the development of large software systems: Concepts and techniques. In *Proceedings IEEE WESCOM.* IEEE Computer Society.

Rubinstein, M. F., & Pfeiffer, K. (1980). *Concepts in problem solving.* Englewood Cliffs, NJ: Prentice-Hall.

Ruggieri, S. (2004). Yadt: Yet another decision tree builder. *ICTAI,* 260–265.

Rumbaugh, J., Jacobson, I., & Booch, G. (1998). *The unified modeling language reference manual.* Addision-Wesley.

Rumbaugh, J., Booch, G., & Jacobson, I. (1999). *The UML Reference Guide.* Addison Wesley Longman.

Rust, R. T., & Kannan, P. K. (2003). E-service a new paradigm for business in the electronic environment. *Communications of the ACM, 46*(6), 36–42. doi:10.1145/777313.777336

Rust, H. (1998). A PVS specification of an invoicing system. *Proceedings of an International Workshop on Specification Techniques and Formal Methods,* (pp. 51–65).

Ryl, I., Clerbout, M., & Bailly, A. (2001). A component oriented notation for behavioral specification and validation. *Proceedings of the OOPSLA Workshop on Specification and Verification on Component Based Systems.*

Sabou, M., & Pan, J. (2007). Towards semantically enhanced Web service repositories. In *Web Semantics.* Sci. Services Agents World Wide Web.

Sabou, M., Wroe, C., Goble, C., & Stuckenschmidt, H. (2005). Learning domain ontologies for Semantic Web service descriptions. *Journal of Web Semantics, 3*(4). doi:10.1016/j.websem.2005.09.008

Sabou, M. (2004). From software APIs to Web service ontologies: A semi-automatic extraction method. In the *proceedings of the Third International Semantic Web Conference, ISWC 04,* Hiroshima, Japan.

Sabou, M. (2005). Visual support for ontology learning: An experience report. In the *proceedings of the Ninth International Conference on Information Visualization.*

Sabou, M. (2006). Building Web Service ontologies. Unpublished doctoral dissertation, Dutch Graduate School for Information and Knowledge Systems.

Sabou, M., Wroe, C., Goble, C., & Mishne, G. (2005). Learning domain ontologies for Web service descriptions: An experiment in bioinformatics. In the *proceedings of the 14th International World Wide Web Conference*, Chiba, Japan.

Sack, P., Bliss, B. E., Ma, Z., Petersen, P., & Torrellas, J. (2006). Accurate and efficient filtering for the Intel thread checker race detector. In *Proceedings of the 1st Workshop on Architectural and System Support for Improving Software Dependability*, (pp. 34–41) New York: ACM.

Sadovykh, A., Hahn, C., Panfilenko, D., Shafiq, O., & Limyr, A. (2009). *SOA and SHA tools developed in SHAPE project* (p. 113). University of Twente.

Salo, O., & Abrahamsson, P. (2007). An iterative improvement approach for agile development: Implications from multiple case studies. *Software Process Improvement and Practice*, *12*(1), 81–100. doi:10.1002/spip.305

Samek, M. (2002). *Practical StateCharts in C/C.* CMP.

Sampson, S. & Froehle, C. (2006). Foundations and implications of a proposed unified services theory. *Production and Operations Management.*

Sandia, N. L. (2005). Java expert system shell (JESS). Retrieved May 25, 2010, from http://herzberg.ca.sandia.gov/jess/

Santos, L. A., Koskimies, K., & Lopes, A. (2008). Automated domain-specific modeling languages for generating framework-based applications. In *Proceedings of the 12th International Conference on Software Product Lines*, (pp. 149-158).

Sasturkar, A., Agarwal, R., Wang, L., & Stoller, S. D. (2005). Automated type-based analysis of data races and Atomicity. In *Proceedings of the ACM SIGPLAN 2005 Symposium on Principles and Practice of Parallel Programming (PPoPP)*. ACM Press. Savage, S., Burrows, M., Nelson, G., Sobalvarro, P. & Anderson, T.E. (1997). Eraser: A dynamic data race detector for multithreaded programs. *ACM Transactions on Computer Systems*, *15*(4), 391–411.

Scheithauer, G., Voigt, K., Bicer, V., Heinrich, M., Strunk, A. & Winkler, M. (2009). *Integrated service engineering workbench: Service engineering for digital ecosystems.*

Schmidt, D. (1997). Applying design patterns and frameworks to develop Object-Oriented communication software. In Handbook of Programming Languages.

Schwaber, K. (2003). *Agile project management with Scrum.* Washington, DC: Microsoft Press.

Schwaber, K., & Beedle, M. (2002). *Agile software development with Scrum.* Upper Saddle River, NJ: Prentice-Hall.

Schwaber, K. (2004). *Agile project management with Scrum.* Redmond, WA: Microsoft Press. Mujtaba, S., Feldt, R. & Petersen, K. (2010). Waste and lead time reduction in a software product customization process with value stream maps. *Proceedings of the Australian Software Engineering Conference (ASWEC 2010).*

Seacord, R., Hissam, S., & Wallnau, K. (1998). Agora: A search engine for software components. *IEEE Internet Computing*, •••, 62–70. doi:10.1109/4236.735988

Second Workshop on Runtime Verification (2002). *Electronic Notes in Theoretical Computer Science, 70*(4).

See, W. B., & Chen, S. J. (2000). Object-Oriented real-time system framework. In *Domain-specific* application frameworks. (pp. 327-338).

Selic, B., Gullekan, G., & Ward, P. T. (1994). *Real-time Object Oriented modeling.* John Wiley and Sons.

Selic, B. (1993). An efficient Object-Oriented variation of the statecharts formalism for distributed real-time systems. Proceedings of the IFIP Conference in Hardware Description Languages and Their Applications. (pp. 335-344). Amsterdam: North-Holland Publishing Co.

Selic, B. (1996). Modeling real-time distributed software systems. *Proceedings of 4th International* Workshop in Parallel and Distributed Real-Time Systems, (pp. 11-18).

Sen, K. (2008). Race directed random testing of concurrent programs. In *Proceedings of the ACM SIGPLAN Conference on Programming Language Design and Implementation (PLDI)*, (pp. 11–21). ACM Press.

Sentas, P., & Angelis, L. (2005). Categorical missing data imputation for software cost estimation by multinomial logistic regression. *Journal of Systems and Software, 79*, 404–414. doi:10.1016/j.jss.2005.02.026

Sentas, P., Angelis, L., Stamelos, I., & Bleris, G. (2004). Software productivity and effort prediction with ordinal regression. *Information and Software Technology, 47*, 17–29. doi:10.1016/j.infsof.2004.05.001

Sessions, R. (1998). *COM and DCOM: Microsoft's vision for distributed objects*. John Wiley and Sons.

Seventh Workshop on Runtime Verification (2007). *Lecture Notes in Computer Science, 4839*.

Shannon, B., Hapner, M., Matena, V., Davidson, J., Davidson, J., & Cable, L. (2000). *Java 2 platform, enterprise edition: Platform and component specifications*. Pearson Education.

Shapiro, S. (1997). Splitting the difference: The historical necessity of synthesis in software engineering. *IEEE Annals of the History of Computing, 19*(1), 20–54. doi:10.1109/85.560729

Shaw, M. (1990). Prospects for an engineering discipline of software. *IEEE Software*, 15–24. doi:10.1109/52.60586

Shaw, M., & Garlan, D. (1996). *Software architecture: Perspectives on an emerging discipline*. Prentice Hall.

Shneiderman, B. (1997). A framework for search interfaces. *Software IEEE, 14*, 18–20. doi:10.1109/52.582969

Shooman, M. (1976). Structural models for software reliability prediction, (pp. 268–280). Paper presented at the Second International Conference on Software Engineering.

Siegel, S. F. (2007). Verifying parallel programs with MPI-SPIN. In *Proceedings of the 14th European PVM/MPI User's Group Meeting on Recent Advances in Parallel Virtual Machine and Message Passing Interface*, (pp. 13–14). Berlin/ Heidelberg: Springer-Verlag.

Silberschatz, A., Galvin, P. B., & Gagne, G. (Eds.). (2008). *Operating system concepts* (8th ed.). John Wiley & Sons.

Smith, A. A., Hinton, E., & Lewis, R. W. (1983). *Civil engineering systems analysis and design*. Wiley & Sons.

Smith, G. F., & Browne, G. J. (1993). Conceptual foundations of design problem solving. *IEEE Transactions on Systems, Man, and Cybernetics, 23*(5). doi:10.1109/21.260655

Sneed, H. M. (2005). *Estimating the Costs of a Reengineering Project*. IEEE Computer Society.

Sneed, H. M. (2008). *Migrating to Web services. Emerging Methods, Technologies and Process Management in Software Engineering* (pp. 151–176). Wiley-IEEE Computer Society Pr.

Sommerville, I. (2006). *Software Engineering*. Addison Wesley.

Sommerville, I. (2001). *Software engineering* (6th ed.). Addison-Wesley.

Song, Q., Shepperd, M. J., & Cartwright, M. (2005). A short note on safest default missingness mechanism assumptions. *Empirical Software Engineering, 10*(2), 235–243. doi:10.1007/s10664-004-6193-8

Speiser, S., Blau, B., Lamparter, S., & Tai, S. (2008). Formation of service value networks for decentralized service provisioning. In *proceedings of the 6th International Conference on Service Oriented Computing*.

Sprinkle, J., Mernik, M., Tolvanen, J.-P., & Spinellis, D. (2009). What kinds of nails need a domain-specific hammer? *IEEE Software, 26*(4), 15–18. doi:10.1109/MS.2009.92

Stahl, T., & Völter, M. (2006). *Model-driven software development*. Wiley.

Standard. (1991). *Standard glossary of software engineering terminology*.

Staron, M. (2006). Adopting model driven software development in industry-a case study at two companies. In *Proceedings of the International Conference on Model Driven Engineering Languages and Systems*, (LNCS 4199), (pp. 57-72).

Stelzer, D., & Mellis, W. (1998). Success factors of organizational change in software process improvement. *Software Process Improvement and Practice, 4*(4), 227–250. doi:10.1002/(SICI)1099-1670(199812)4:4<227::AID-SPIP106>3.0.CO;2-1

Stensrud, E., & Myrtveit, I. (1998). Human performance estimating with analogy and regression models: An empirical validation. *Proceedings of the 5th IEEE International Software Metrics Symposium (METRICS '98)*, (pp. 205–213).

Stotts, P. D., & Purtilo, J. (1994). Virtual environment architectures: Interoperability through software interconnection technology. In *Proceedings of the Third Workshop on Enabling Technologies (WETICE '94): Infrastructure for Collaborative Enterprises*, (pp. 211-224). IEEE Computer Society Press.

Strike, K., Emam, K. E., & Madhavji, N. (2001). Software cost estimation with incomplete data. *IEEE Transactions on Software Engineering, 27*(10), 890–908. doi:10.1109/32.962560

Strunk, E. A., Yin, X., & Knight, J. C. (2005). Echo: A practical approach to formal verification. In *Proceedings of the 10th international Workshop on Formal Methods For industrial Critical Systems. FMICS '05*, (pp. 44-53). New York: ACM Press.

Studer, R., Grimm, S., & Abecker, A. (2007). *Semantic Web services: Concepts, technologies, and applications. New York.* Secaucus, NJ: Springer-Verlag Inc.

Sun Microsystems. (1999). *Java code conventions.* Retrieved from http://java.sun.com/docs/codeconv/

Sun, C. (2003). *Qos composition and decomposition in Uniframe.* Unpublished doctoral thesis, Department of Computer and Information Science, Indiana University Purdue University.

Sun, W., Shi, T., Argote-Garcia, G., Deng, Y., & He, X. (2006). Achieving a better middleware design through formal modeling and analysis. In the *proceedings of SEKE '06: The 18th International Conference of Software Engineering and Knowledge Engineering*, San Francisco Bay, July 5–7.

Sutherland, J., Jakobsen, C. R., et al. (2007). *Scrum and CMMI level 5: The magic potion for code warriors.* Agile 2007, Washington D.C.

Sutherland, J., Viktorov, A., et al. (2007). *Distributed Scrum: Agile project management with outsourced development teams.* Paper presented at the 40th Hawaii International Conference on System Sciences, Hawaii.

Svensson, H., & Höst, M. (2005). *Introducing an agile process in a software maintenance and evolution organization.* Paper presented at the 9th European Conference of Maintenance and Reengineering, Manchester, UK.

SWEBOK. (2004). *Guide to the software engineering body of knowledge.*

Symons, C. (2001). Come back function point analysis-all is forgiven! In *Proceedings of the European Conference on Software Measurement and ICT Control*, (pp. 413-426).

Sys, M. L. (2010). *Homepage information.* Retrieved May 10, 2010, from http://www.sysml.org/

Szyperski, C. (1997). *Component software, beyond object-oriented programming.* New York: Addison Wesley Longman Ltd.

Talby, D., & Dubinsky, Y. (2009). *Governance of an agile software project.* Paper presented at the Software Development Governance Workshop, Vancouver, Canada.

Tapscott, D., Ticoll, D., & Lowy, A. (2000). *Digital capital: Harnessing the power of business Webs.* Harvard Business School Press.

Taylor, R. N., Medvidovic, N., Anderson, K. M., Whitehead, E. J. Jr, Robbins, J. E., & Nies, K. A. (1996). A component and message-based architectural style for GUI software. *IEEE Transactions on Software Engineering, 22*(6), 390–406. doi:10.1109/32.508313

Taylor, R. N., Medvidovic, N., & Dashofy, E. M. (2009). *Software architecture: Foundations, theory, and practice.* Wiley.

Teboul, J. (2005). *Service is in front stage.*

Tekinerdoğan, B., & Akşit, M. (2006). Introducing the concept of synthesis in the software architecture design process. *Journal of Integrated Design and Process Science, 10*(1), 45–56.

Tetlow, P., Pan, J. Z., Oberle, D., Wallace, E., Uschold, M., & Kendall, E. (2006). *Ontology driven architectures and potential uses of the Semantic Web in systems and software engineering.* Retrieved August 2009, from http://www.w3.org/2001/sw/BestPractices/SE/ODA/

Theunissen, W. Kourie, D.G. Watson, B.W. (2003). Standards and agile software development. *Proceedings of SAICSIT* 2003, (p. 1–11).

Third Workshop on Runtime Verification (2003). *Electronic Notes in Theoretical Computer Science, 89*(2).

Thomason, M. G., & Whittaker, J. A. (1999). *Rare failure-state in a Markov chain model for software reliability*, (pp. 12-19). Paper presented at the 10th International Symposium on Software Reliability Engineering.

Thompson, R., & Croft, W. (1989). Support for browsing in an intelligent text retrieval system. *International Journal of Man-Machine Studies, 30*(6), 639–668. doi:10.1016/S0020-7373(89)80014-8

Thompson, J. M., Heimdahl, M. P., & Miller, S. P. (1999). Specification-based prototyping for embedded systems. Proceedings of 7th ACM SIGSOFT Symposium in Foundations of Software Engineering, (pp. 163-179).

TOPCASED. (2007). *Home page*. Retrieved May 25, 2010, from http://topcased-mm.Gforge.Enseeiht.fr/website/index.Html

Torgo, L. (2005). Regression error characteristic surfaces. *Proceedings of the 11th ACM SIGKDD International Conference on Knowledge Discovery and Data Mining (KDD '05)*, (pp. 697-702).

Trudel, S., & Lavoie, J. M. (2006). The small company-dedicated software process quality evaluation method combining CMMI and ISO/IEC 14598. *Software Quality Journal, 14*(3).

Tsao, C. C. (2008). An efficient collaborative verification methodology for multiprocessor SoC with run-time task migration. Master Thesis, Department of Computer Science and Information Engineering, National Chung Cheng University, Taiwan.

Turner, R., & Jain, A. (2002). *Agile meets CMMI: Culture clash or common cause*. Paper presented at the 1st Agile Universe Conference, Chicago.

Twala, B., Cartwright, M., & Shepperd, M. (2006). Ensemble of missing data techniques to improve software prediction accuracy. *Proceedings of the 28th International Conference on Software Engineering*, (pp. 909 – 912).

Uemura, T., Kusumoto, S., & Inoue, K. (1999). Function point measurement tool for UML design specification. In *Proceedings of International Symposium on Software Metrics*, (p. 62).

Ulrich, W. M. (2002). *Legacy systems: Transformation strategies*. Prentice Hall.

Ulrich, W. M. (2010). Launching and sustaining modernization initiatives. In Ulrich, W. M., & Newcomb, P. H. (Eds.), *Information Systems Transformation: Architecture driven modernization case studies* (pp. 403–418). Burlington, MA: Morgan Kauffman.

UML2. (2006). *Home page*. Retrieved May 25, 2010, from http://www.Eclipse.org/uml2/

Unified. (2006). *Unified modeling language*. Retrieved May 25, 2010, from http://en.Wikipedia.org/wiki/Unified_Modeling_Language.

UPC UPC. UPC language specifications. http://upc.gwu.edu/docs/upc_spec_1.1.1.pdf

Upton, N. (1975). *An illustrated history of civil engineering*. London: Heinemann.

Utgoff, P. E. (1989). Incremental induction of decision trees. *Machine Learning, 4*, 161–186. doi:10.1023/A:1022699900025

Van Hulse, J., & Khoshgoftaar, T. (2008). A comprehensive empirical evaluation of missing value imputation in noisy software measurement data. *Journal of Systems and Software, 81*, 691–708.

van Wijk, J. J. (2005). The value of visualization. In *IEEE Visualization, 11*.

Varadarajan, S., Kumar, A., Deepak, G. & Pankaj, J. (2002). Component exchange: An exchange for software components. *ICWI*, 62–72.

Vasiliu, L., Zaremba, M., Moran, M., & Bussler, C. (2004). Web-service semantic enabled implementation of machine vs. machine business negotiation. *Proceedings of the IEEE International Conference on Web Services (ICWS '04)*, San Diego: IEEE Computer Society.

Vervest, P. H. M. (2005). *Smart business networks*. Heidelberg, Berlin: Springer. doi:10.1007/b137960

Vestal, S. (1998). *MetaH user's manual*.

Vetter, J. S., & de Supinski, B. R. (2000). Dynamic software testing of MPI applications with UMPIRE. In *Proceedings of the 2000 ACM/IEEE Conference on Supercomputing (CDROM)*, (p. 51). Washington, DC: IEEE Computer Society.

Visaggio, G. (2001). Ageing of a data-intensive legacy system: Symptoms and remedies. *Journal of Software Maintenance*, *13*(5), 281–308. doi:10.1002/smr.234

Visser, W., Havelund, K., Brat, G., Park, S., & Lerda, F. (2003). Model checking programs. *Automated Software Engineering*, *10*(2), 203–232.

Vitharana, P., Zahedi, F. M., & Jain, H. (2003). Knowledge-based repository scheme for storing and retrieving business components: A theoretical design and an empirical analysis. *IEEE Transactions on Software Engineering*, *29*(7), 649–664. doi:10.1109/TSE.2003.1214328

Vo, A., Vakkalanka, S., DeLisi, M., Gopalakrishnan, G., Kirby, R. M., & Thakur, R. (2008). Formal verification of practical MPI programs. In *Proceedings of the 14th ACM SIGPLAN Symposium on Principles and Practice of Parallel Programming*, (pp. 261–270). New York: ACM.

Voas, J. M. (1998). Certifying off-the-shelf software components. *IEEE Comput.*, *31*(6), 53–59.

Voas, J., Charron, F., & Miller, K. (1996). Robust software interfaces: Can COTS-based systems be trusted without them? (pp. 126–135). Paper presented at the 15th International Conference on Computer Safety.

von Foerster, F. (1979). Cybernetics of cybernetics. In Krippendorff, K. (Ed.), *Communication and control in society*. New York: Gordon and Breach.

von Praun, C., & Gross, T. R. (2001). Object race detection. In *Proceedings of the ACM Conference on Object-Oriented Programming, Systems, Languages, and Applications (OOPSLA)*, (pp. 70–82). ACM Press.

Vriens, C. (2003). *Certifying for CMM level 2 and ISO9001 with XP@Scrum*. Agile Development Conference, Salt Lake City, Utah. EEE Computer Society.

W3C. (2007). *WSDL in Web Services description working group*. Retrieved August 1, 2008, from http://www.w3.org/2002/ws/desc/

W3C-WSA. (2004). *Web services architecture*. Retrieved May 25, 2010, from http://www.w3.org/TR/ws-arch/#whatis

Wada, H., & Suzuki, J. (2006). Modeling non-functional aspects in service oriented architecture, (pp. 222-229). Paper presented at the IEEE International Conference on Service Computing.

Walrad, C., & Strom, D. (2002). The importance of branching models in SCM. *IEEE Computer*, *35*, 31–38.

Wang, W., Pan, D., & Chen, M. (2006). Architecture-based software reliability modeling. *Journal of Systems and Software*, *79*(1), 132–146. doi:10.1016/j.jss.2005.09.004

Wang, J., He, X., & Deng, Y. (1999). Introducing software architecture specification and analysis in SAM through an example. *Information and Software Technology*, *41*(7), 451–467. doi:10.1016/S0950-5849(99)00009-9

Wang, Y. (2006). On the informatics laws and deductive semantics of software. *IEEE Transactions on Systems, Man, and Cybernetics*, *36*(2), 161–171. doi:10.1109/TSMCC.2006.871138

Wang, Y. (2007). The theoretical framework of cognitive informatics. *International Journal of Cognitive Informatics and Natural Intelligence*, *1*(1), 1–27.

Wang, Y., & Shao, J. (2003). A new measure of software complexity based on cognitive weights. *Canadian Journal of Electrical and Computer Engineering*, 69–74.

Wang, Y., & Shao, J. (2009). On the cognitive complexity of software and its quantification and formal methods. *International Journal of Software Science and Computational Intelligence*, *1*(2), 31–53.

Wang, F., & Hsiung, P. A. (2002). Efficient and user-friendly verification. *IEEE Transactions on Computers*, *51*(1), 61–83. doi:10.1109/12.980017

Wang, L., & Stoller, S. D. (2006b). Runtime analysis of Atomicity for multi-threaded programs. *IEEE Transactions on Software Engineering*, *32*(2), 93–110.

Wang, L., & Stoller, S. D. (2005). Static analysis of Atomicity for programs with non-blocking synchronization. In *Proceedings of the ACM SIGPLAN 2005 Symposium on Principles and Practice of Parallel Programming (PPoPP)*. ACM Press.

Wang, L., & Stoller, S. D. (2006a). Accurate and efficient runtime detection of Atomicity errors in concurrent programs. In *Proceedings of the ACM SIGPLAN 2006 Symposium on Principles and Practice of Parallel Programming (PPoPP)*. ACM Press.

Wang, S., Kodase, S., & Shin, K. G. (2002). Automating embedded software construction and analysis with design models. Proceedings of the International Conference of Euro-uRapid.

Wang, W., Pan, D., & Chen, M. (1999). An architecture-based software reliability model. *In Proceedings of the Pacific Rim International Symposium on Dependable Computing (PRDC'99)*, (pp. 143-150).

Wang, X., Oconchuir, E., & Vidgen, R. (2008). A paradoxical perspective on contradictions in agile software development. In *proceedings from European Conference of Information Systems (ECIS)* 2008. Galway, Ireland.

Wang, Y. (2002). On cognitive informatics: Keynote lecture. In *Proceedings of the 1st IEEE Int. Conf. Cognitive Informatics (ICCI'02)*, (pp. 34–42).

Wang, Y. (2004). On the cognitive informatics foundation of software engineering. In *Proceedings of the 3rd IEEE International Conference of Cognitive Informatics (ICCI'04)*, (pp. 1-10).

Wang, Y. (2005), Keynote: Psychological experiments on the cognitive complexities of fundamental control structures of software systems. In *Proceedings of the 4th IEEE International Conference on Cognitive Informatics (ICCI'05)*, (pp. 4-5).

Watson, G., Rasmussen, C., & Tibbitts, B. (2006). Application development using eclipse and the parallel tools platform. In *Proceedings of the 2006 ACM/IEEE Conference on Supercomputing*, (p. 204). New York: ACM.

Wei, D., & Wang, T. Wang, J. & Chen, Y. (2008). Extracting semantic constraint from description text for semantic Web services discovery. In *Proceedings 7th International Semantic Web Conference, ISWC 2008*. Karlsruhe, Germany.

Weinberg, G. M. (1999). Egoless programming. *IEEE Software, 16*(1). doi:10.1109/MS.1999.744582

Welch, L. R. (1996). A metrics-driven approach for utilizing concurrency in Object-Oriented real-time systems. *ACM OOPS Messenger, 7,* 70–77. doi:10.1145/227986.227998

Wermter, S., & Hung, C. (2002). Self-organizing classification on the Reuters news corpus. In *Proceedings of the 19th International Conference on Computational Linguistics, 1*. ACM.

Wersig, G. (1985). *Thesaurus-Leitfaden*. Münschen.

Whaley, J., Martin, M. C., & Lam, M. S. (2002). Automatic extraction of object-oriented component interfaces. *SIGSOFT Software Engineering Notes, 27*(4), 218–228. doi:10.1145/566171.566212

White, S.A. (2004). Introduction to BPMN. *IBM Cooperation*, 2008-029.

Wilcox, A. D., Huelsman, L. P., Marshall, S. V., Philips, C. L., Rashid, M. H., & Roden, M. S. (1990). *Engineering design for electrical engineers*. Prentice-Hall.

Wilkie, F. G., McFall, D., & McCaffery, F. (2005). Evaluation of CMMI process areas for small to medium-sized software development organizations. *Software Process Improvement and Practice, 10*(2), 189–202. doi:10.1002/spip.223

Wille, R. (1982). Restructing lattice theory: An approach based on hierarchies of concepts. In Rival, I. (Ed.), *Ordered sets* (pp. 445–470).

Willet, P. (1988). Recent trends in hierarchic document clustering: A critical review. *Information Processing & Management, 24*(5), 577–597. doi:10.1016/0306-4573(88)90027-1

Williams, M. R. (1997). *A history of computing technology*. IEEE Computer Society.

Williams, S., & Kindel, C. (1994). *The component object model: Technical overview*. Dr. Dobbs Journal.

Williamson, O. E. (2002). The theory of the firm as governance structure: From choice to contract. *The Journal of Economic Perspectives, 16*, 171–195. doi:10.1257/089533002760278776

Wils, A., Baelen, S., et al. (2006). *Agility in the avionics software world*. XP 2006, Oulu.

Winkler, M., & Schill, A. (2009). *Towards dependency management in service compositions* (pp. 79–84).

Wirth, N. (1971). Program development by stepwise refinement. *Communications of the ACM, 14*(4), 221–227. doi:10.1145/362575.362577

Wirth, N. (2008). A brief history of software engineering. *IEEE Annals of the History of Computing, 30*(3), 32–39. doi:10.1109/MAHC.2008.33

Womack, J. P. (2007). *The machine that changed the world*. London: Simon & Schuster.

Wong, W.E., Zhao, J. & Chan, Victor K.Y. (2006). Applying statistical methodology to optimize and simplify software metric models with missing data. *Proceedings of the 2006 ACM symposium on Applied Computing,* (pp. 1728-1733).

Wongthongtham, P., Chang, E., & Dillon, T. (2006). Software design process ontology development. In *On the move to meaningful internet systems* (pp. 1806–1813). Berlin, Heidelberg: Springer.

Worringen, J., Scholtyssik, K., Dr, P. & Bemmerl, T. (2002). *MP-MPICH: User documentation technical notes*.

Wright. (2006). The Wright architecture description language. Retrieved May 25, 2010, from http://www.Cs.Cmu.edu/afs/cs/project/able/www/wright/index.Html

Wroe, C., Goble, C., Greenwood, M., Lord, P., Miles, S., & Papay, J. (2004). Automating experiments using semantic data on a bioinformatics grid. *IEEE Intelligent Systems, 19*(1), 48–55. doi:10.1109/MIS.2004.1265885

Xie, X., Tang, J., Li, J.-Z., & Wang, K. (2004). *A component retrieval method based on facet-weight self-learning* (pp. 437–448). AWCC.

Xu, M., Bodik, R., & Hill, M. D. (2005). A serializability volation detector for shared-memory server programs. In *Proceedings of the ACM SIGPLAN Conference on Programming Language Design and Implementation (PLDI)*. ACM Press.

Yacoub, S., Cukic, B., & Ammar, H. (1999). *Scenario-based reliability analysis of component-based software,* (pp. 22-31). Paper presented at the 10th International Symposium on Software Reliability Engineering (ISSRE'99).

Yao, H., & Etzkorn, L. (2004). Towards a semantic-based approach for software reusable component classification and retrieval. In *ACM-SE 42: Proceedings of the 42nd annual Southeast regional conference,* (pp. 110-115). New York: ACM Press.

Yellin, D. M., & Strom, R. E. (1997). Protocol specifications and component adaptors. *ACM Transactions on Programming Languages and Systems, 19*(2), 292–333. doi:10.1145/244795.244801

Yin, R. (1994). *Case study research: Design and methods* (2nd ed.). Thousand Oaks, CA: Sage Publications.

Yourdon, E., & Constantine, L. L. (1979). *Structured design*. Prentice-Hall.

Yu, Y., Rodeheffer, T., & Chen, W. (2005). RaceTrack: Efficient detection of data race conditions via adaptive tracking. In *Proceedings of the Symposium on Operating Systems Principles (SOSP)*. ACM Press.

Yunwen, Y., & Fischer, G. (2001). Context-aware browsing of large component repositories. *Proceedings of 16th International Conference on Automated Software Engineering (ASE'01),* (pp. 99-106). Coronado Island, CA.

Zachman, J. A. (1987). A framework for information systems architecture. *IBM Systems Journal, 26,* 276–292. doi:10.1147/sj.263.0276

Zaremski, A. M., & Wing, J. M. (1995). Specification matching of software components. In *Proceedings of the Third Symposium on the Foundations of Software Engineering (FSE3),* (pp. 1-17). ACM SIGSOFT.

Zbib, R., Jain, A., Bassu, D., & Agrawal, H. (2006). Generating domain-specific graphical modelling editors from metamodels. In *Proceedings of the Annual IEEE Computer Software and Applications Conference,* (pp. 129-138).

Zhang, J., Gao, J., Zhou, M., & Wang, J. (2001). *Improving the effectiveness of information retrieval with clustering and fusion*. Computational Linguistics and Chinese Language.

Zhang, Z., Svensson, L., Snis, U., Srensen, C., Fgerlind, H., Lindroth, T., et al. (2000). Enhancing component reuse using search techniques. *Proceedings of IRIS 23.*

Zhiyuan, W. (2000). *Component-based software engineering*. Unpublished doctoral thesis, New Jersey Institute of technology.

Zhou, J., Niemelä, E., Evesti, A., Immonen, A., & Savolainen, P. (2008). *OntoArch approach for reliability-aware software architecture development* (pp. 1228–1233). Turku, Finland.

Zhou, L. (2007). Ontology learning: State of the art and open issues. In *Springer Science*. Business Media.

Zhou, J., & Dieng, R. (2004). A semantic knowledge management system for knowledge-intensive manufacturing, (pp. 114-122). Paper presented at the 2004 IADIS International Conference of e-Commerce.

Zhou, J., & Niemelä, E. (2006). *Toward semantic QoS-aware web services: Issues, related studies and experience*. Paper presented at the IEEE/WIC/ACM International Conference on Web Intelligence.

Zhou, L., Booker, Q., & Zhang, D. (2002). ROD–towards rapid ontology development for underdeveloped domains. *In proceedings 35th Hawaii International Conference on System Sciences*, Hawaii, USA.

Zuse, H. A. (1998). *Framework of software measurement*. Berlin: Walter de Gruyter.

About the Contributors

Ali H. Doğru is a faculty member in the Department of Computer Engineering at the Middle East Technical University since 1993, where he has founded and directed the MS program in software Engineering. He has also been teaching for University of Texas and Texas Tech University, since 1995, for training and degree programs involving the engineers in the industry. He has actively participated in development projects as a consultant, besides providing training to various organizations. His current research areas are mainly focused on software development approach fundamentals, and practical approaches for Software Product lines, having published his ideas in various papers, books, and book chapters He has received the Engineering Faculty Academic performance award (METU) twice and has served in various committees of many conferences. Dr. Doğru has obtained his PhD degree in Computer Science from the Southern Methodist University, Dallas, Texas, USA, in 1992.

Veli Biçer is a research scientist and PhD candidate at Research Center for Computer Science (FZI – Forschungszentrum Informatik) at Karlsruhe Institute of Technology. He obtained his two B.S. degrees in Computer Engineering and Computer Education and Instructional Technology and his M.S. in Computer Engineering from the Middle East Technical University in Ankara, Turkey. He has several publications at several international conferences, journals, and has co-authored chapters including International Conference on Data Engineering, ACM Sigmod Record Journal, and International Journal on Semantic Web and Information Systems. He also participated in several national and international research and industry projects including German Theseus research program and EU-ICT projects.

* * *

Achilleas Achilleos obtained recently his PhD from the School of Computer Science and Electronic Engineering at the University of Essex, having being awarded a studentship, co-funded by the UK Engineering and Physical Sciences Research Council (EPSRC) and British Telecom (BT). During that time, he was also working as part-time researcher at BT. He received his M.Sc. with distinction from the same department and a B.Sc. with excellence from the Budapest University of Technology and Economics in Hungary. He is currently working as a post-doc researcher at the Department of Computer Science at the University of Cyprus. His research interests include model-driven development, pervasive service creation, mobile and service-oriented computing. He has published his research work in internationally refereed journals and conferences and as book chapters. He served also as a TPC member and referee in various conferences related to his research area. He is a member of the IEEE Computer Society and Cyprus Scientific and Technical Chamber (ETEK).

Erwin Aitenbichler received his MSc in Computer Science from Johannes Kepler University in Linz, Austria and his PhD in Computer Science from Darmstadt University of Technology, Germany. Currently he is a post-doctoral researcher in the Telecooperation Lab at Darmstadt University and head of the area Smart Environments. Erwin is a member of the ACM.

Mehmet Akşit holds an MSc degree from the Eindhoven University of Technology and a PhD degree from the University of Twente. Currently, he is working as a full professor at the Department of Computer Science, University of Twente. He is the head of the Software Engineering chair and the leader of the Twente Research and Education on Software Engineering (TRESE) Group. His research interests include aspect-oriented software development, synthesis based software design, application of fuzzy logic to software design processes, and design algebra for managing large design spaces.

Lefteris Angelis was born in Thessaloniki, Greece. He received his BSc and PhD degree in Mathematics from Aristotle University of Thessaloniki (A.U.Th.). The topic of his Ph.D. dissertation was the study and construction of optimal experimental designs. He is currently an Assistant Professor at the Department of Informatics of A.U.Th. with expertise in statistical methods applied to information systems. He has taught several courses on advanced mathematics, probability and statistics, operations research, and simulation. He has published more than 100 papers on various research topics involving mathematics and statistics in journals and conference proceedings. His research is focused on statistical methods for software engineering, especially software cost estimation, statistical analysis of Web data, computational methods and simulation. He has participated in more than 20 funded programs, he supervised three PhD dissertations and he is reviewer for several journals and conference proceedings.

Nadeem Bhatti studied computer engineering in the technical university of Darmstadt, Germany. He has been at Fraunhofer Institute for Computer Graphics since October 2002. He is responsible for the Visual Semantic Analysis (VSA). The VSA approach combines semantic analysis (ontology learning) and visualization techniques to support semi-automatic modeling of Semantic Service Descriptions. Nadeem Bhatti has worked on different projects in Knowledge Asset Management to assist business consultants in order to assess the knowledge assets of companies (KAM-SYS) and best practices based knowledge management at work (ALF). He is now project manager for the projects THESEUS and THESEUS-TEXO at IGD.

Stephan Borgert is currently doing his PhD in the area of automatic composition for subject oriented business process models at the Technical University of Darmstadt. Before, he studied physics as his major and computer science as his minor subject at the University of Siegen. He wrote his diploma thesis on the automated classification of protein graphs by applying inexact graph matching methods.

Jorge Cardoso joined the Information System Group at the University of Coimbra in 2009. Previously he worked at SAP Research in Germany on the Internet of Services, business processes management, and service specification languages. He previously gave lectures at the University of Madeira (Portugal) and the University of Georgia (USA). Dr. Cardoso was the organizer of several international conferences on Semantic Web and Information Systems. He has published over 100 refereed papers in the areas of service engineering, workflow management systems, semantic Web, and related fields. He has also authored or edited 7 books on distributed systems, business process modeling, semantic Web and Web services. His areas of interest include business process management, compliance and complexity analysis, the Internet of Services, service design, and service engineering. He is currently writing a book on service engineering and service design.

Panagiota Chatzipetrou was born in Thessaloniki, Greece. She received her BSc degree in informatics and her MSc in computer science and business administration from Aristotle University of Thessaloniki (AUTh). She is currently a PhD student in the Department of Informatics, AUTh. The area of her Ph.D. research is statistical methods for quality information systems and her special research interests involve applications of statistical data analysis to software engineering, especially to requirements prioritization and cost estimation. She is also working as a computer science teacher in one of the best private high schools in Northern Greece.

Qichang Chen is currently a PhD student working in the Department of Computer Science at the University of Wyoming. His research mainly focuses on improving the reliability of concurrent software especially for concurrent Java, OpenMP, and MPI programs, using a combination of static and dynamic program analysis techniques. He received his BE from Fuzhou University, China in 2006.

Yean-Ru Chen received the BS degree in Computer Science and Information Engineering from the National Chiao Tung University, Hsinchu, Taiwan, ROC in 2002. From 2002 to 2003, she was employed as an engineer in SoC Technology Center, Industrial Technology Research Institute, Hsinchu, Taiwan, ROC. She received the MS degree in Computer Science and Information Engineering from the National Chung Cheng University, ChiaYi, Taiwan, ROC in 2006. She is currently a PhD candidate in Graduate Institute of Electronics Engineering of National Taiwan University, Taipei, Taiwan, ROC. Her current research interests include model checking, safety-critical systems, Electronic System Level (ESL) Design, and Multi-Core embedded software.

Onur Demirors is an associate professor and the chair of the Software Management Program in the Information Systems Department at Middle East Technical University, as well as the strategy director of Bilgi Grubu. His work focuses on software process improvement, software project management, software measurement, software engineering education, software engineering standards, and organizational change management. He leads the Software Management Research Group (www.ii.metu.edu.tr/research_group/software-management-research-group). Demirors has a PhD in computer science from Southern Methodist University.

Zhijiang Dong received the BS and MS degrees in Huazhong Tech University, and the PhD degree in computer science from Florida International University. He currently is assistant professor at Middle Tennessee University. Dr. Dong's research is mainly in software engineering. Dr. Dong also actively serves as reviewers of several top journals and conferences. He continuously serves as a member of IEEE and ACM.

Khalil Drira received the Engineering and MS (DEA) degrees in Computer Science from ENSEEIHT (INP Toulouse), in June and September 1988 respectively. He obtained the PhD and HDR degrees in Computer Science from UPS, University Paul Sabatier Toulouse, in October 1992, and January 2005 respectively. He has been Chargé de Recherche since 1992, a full-time research position at the French National Center for Scientific Research (CNRS). His research interests include formal design, implementation, testing and provisioning of distributed communicating systems and cooperative networked services. His research activity addresses different topics in this field focusing on model-based analysis and design of correctness properties including testability, robustness, adaptability and reconfiguration. He is involved in several national and international projects in the field of distributed and concurrent communicating systems. He is author of more than 150 regular and invited papers in international conferences and journals. More details are available on his wiki: http://homepages.laas.fr/khalil

Nagehan Pala Er is a senior software engineer at ASELSAN Microelectronics Guidance and Electro-Optics Division, Ankara, Turkey. Her research interests include software engineering, model-driven software development, software configuration management and software product lines. She received her MS degree in Computer Engineering from Bilkent University, Ankara, Turkey and her BS degree in Computer Engineering from Hacettepe University, Ankara, Turkey.

Cengiz Erbaş is the software engineering manager of ASELSAN Microelectronics Guidance and Electro-Optics Division, Ankara, Turkey. His research interests include software engineering, software economics and embedded and real-time systems development. Previously, he worked as engineering manager for Trimble Navigation, Wind River, and TRW in Silicon Valley, California. He received his PhD in Computer Science from Southern Methodist University, Dallas, Texas, with a dissertation titled "A Precedence Graph based Approach for Modeling and Verification of Real-Time Systems".

Bahar Çelikkol Erbaş is an assistant professor in the Department of Economics at TOBB University of Economics and Technology, Ankara, Turkey. Her research interests include applied microeconomics, innovation economics, environmental, natural resource and energy economics, and transfer pricing. Previously, she worked as an industry economist in the U.S. Department of the Treasury in Silicon Valley, California, as a researcher at University of California at Berkeley, and as an economist in the Department of Public Utilities, the Executive Office of Energy and Environmental Affairs, Boston, Massachusetts. She received her PhD degree from Pennsylvania State University, University Park, Pennsylvania and her MS degree in Business Administration from Bilkent University, Ankara, Turkey.

Antti Evesti, of the VTT Technical Research Centre of Finland, finished his M.Sc. degree in computer engineering at the University of Oulu, Finland in 2007. He is working for VTT Technical Research Centre of Finland as a Research Scientist. He has participated both national and international research and customer projects. Currently, he is working towards a doctoral degree. His research is focusing on run-time security management, containing security measurement of software, and security adaptation.

Dieter W. Fellner is the director of the Fraunhofer Institute of Computer Graphics (IGD) in Darmstadt , Germany and a Professor of Computer Science at the University of Technology in Darmstadt with a joint affiliation with the Graz University of Technology, Austria. His research interests include computer graphics, modeling, immersive systems, and 3D objects in digital libraries. He has held academic positions at Universities in Graz, Austria, Denver, Colorado, St.John's, Canada, Bonn, Germany, and Braunschweig, Germany. Dr. Fellner has an MS and a PhD from Graz University of Technology, Austria. He is a member of the ACM, Eurographics, Gesellschaft für Informatik (GI), and IEEE, and is on the editorial board of several international journals.

Yujian Fu received PhD degree in computer science from Florida International University in 2007 under the advisory of Dr. Xudong He. Since then, she joined Department of Computer Science at the Alabama A&M University as tenure track assistant professor. Dr. Yujian Fu conducts research in several areas of software engineering, such as software verification, software quality assurance, runtime verification, and formal methods. Dr. Yujian Fu has many publications of software verification, model checking and runtime checking in prestigious conference proceedings and journals. Dr. Yujian Fu also actively serves as reviewer of several top journals and prestigious conferences. She continuously commits as a member of IEEE, ACM, and ASEE.

Nektarios Georgalas holds a Diploma in Electrical and Computer Engineering from the University of Patras, Greece, an MPhil in Computation from University of Manchester (UMIST) and a PhD in Computer Science from the University of London. He joined British Telecom (BT) in 1998 and is now a principal researcher in the company's Centre for Information and Security Systems Research. During his career with BT, he has participated and managed research projects in areas including active networks, market-driven data management systems, policy-based management, distributed information systems, service-oriented architectures, and web services. His research is currently focused on product lifecycle management, particularly migration planning and concept-to-market, and rapid service assembly. Nektarios has led numerous international collaborations on the application of model-driven architecture and New Generation Operations Systems and Software (NGOSS) standards in telecoms operational support systems and has both led and contributed to the work of the TeleManagement Forum. He holds five patents, has authored more than 30 papers, and has frequently been invited to speak at international conferences.

Ping Guo is currently a PhD student in the Department of Computer Science at the University of Wyoming. She received the MS degree in Computer Science from the University of Kentucky in 2008 and the BS degree in Computer Science from Harbin University of Science and Technology of China in 2005. Her research focuses on designing parallel computing systems.

Ignacio García-Rodriguez de Guzmán is assistant professor at the University of Castilla-La Mancha and belongs to the Alarcos Research Group at the UCLM. He holds the PhD degree in Computer Science from the University of Castilla-La Mancha. His research interests include software maintenance, model-driven development and software modernization. Contact him at Escuela Superior de Informática, Paseo de la Universidad 4, 13071-Ciudad Real, Spain.

Xudong He is a professor of computing and Information Science and director of the Center for Advanced and Distributed System Engineering at Florida International University. Dr. He's research focuses on software engineering. Dr. He also specifically dedicates his time to the formal methods and formal verification of large scale safety critical systems. Dr. He currently has over one hundred publications in prestigious journals and conferences. He has been serving as committee chair and committee member of several distinguish conferences, and editing several journals. Dr. He continuously commits as a member of IEEE and ACM.

Pao-Ann Hsiung, PhD, received his BS in Mathematics and his PhD in Electrical Engineering from the National Taiwan University, Taipei, Taiwan, ROC, in 1991 and 1996, respectively. From 1996 to 2000, he was a post-doctoral researcher at the Institute of Information Science, Academia Sinica, Taipei, Taiwan, ROC. From February 2001 to July 2002, he was an assistant professor and from August 2002 to July 2007 he was an associate professor in the Department of Computer Science and Information Engineering, National Chung Cheng University, Chiayi, Taiwan, ROC. Since August 2007, he has been a full professor. Dr. Hsiung has published more than 190 papers in international journals and conferences. He was the recipient of the 2001 ACM Taipei Chapter Kuo-Ting Li Young Researcher for his significant contributions to design automation of electronic systems. He was also a recipient of the 2004 Young Scholar Research Award given by National Chung Cheng University to five young faculty members per year. He received several advisor awards for Best Master Theses, embedded system competitions, and RFID design competitions. Dr. Hsiung is a senior member of the IEEE, a senior member of the ACM, and a life member of the IICM. He has been included in several professional listings such as Marquis' Who's Who in the World, Marquis' Who's Who in Asia, Outstanding People of the 20th Century by International Biographical Centre, Cambridge, England, Rifacimento International's Admirable Asian Achievers (2006), Afro/Asian Who's Who, and Asia/Pacific Who's Who. Dr. Hsiung is an editorial board member of the International Journal of Embedded Systems (IJES), Inderscience Publishers, USA; the International Journal of Multimedia and Ubiquitous Engineering (IJMUE), Science and Engineering Research Center (SERSC), USA; an associate editor of the Journal of Software Engineering (JSE), Academic Journals, Inc., USA; an editorial board member of the Open Software Engineering Journal (OSE), Bentham Science Publishers, Ltd., USA; an international editorial board member of the International Journal of Patterns (IJOP). Dr. Hsiung has been on the program committee of more than 70 international conferences. He served as session organizer and chair for PDPTA'99, and as workshop organizer and chair for RTC'99, DSVV'2000, PDES'2005, WoRMES'2009, ITNG'2010. He has taken an active part in paper refereeing for international journals and conferences. Dr. Hsiung's main research interests include reconfigurable computing and system design, multi-core programming, cognitive radio architecture, System-on-Chip (SoC) design and verification, embedded software synthesis and verification, real-time system design and verification, hardware-software codesign and coverification, and component-based object-oriented application frameworks for real-time embedded systems.

He Huang is currently a PhD student in the Department of Computer Science at the University of Wyoming. He received a BS in Computer Science from Southeast University, China. His research interest includes data-intensive parallel computing on multi-core CPU and GPU, program analysis of parallel computing program and Cloud computing.

Anne Immonen is a research scientist at VTT Technical Research Centre of Finland. She received the MSc degree in information processing science in 2002 from the University of Oulu, Finland. Her research interests include quality driven design and analysis of software architectures, service oriented architectures and product families. The main topics in her current research projects are the quality analysis of service architecture and the methods to verify the reliability of architecture. She is also currently performing her PhD studies at the University of Oulu, Finland.

Mohamed Jmaiel obtained his diploma of engineering in Computer Science from Kiel (Germany) University in 1992 and his PhD from the Technical University of Berlin in 1996. He joined the National School of Engineers of Sfax (Tunisia) as Assistant Professor of Computer Science in 1995. He became an Associate Professor in 1997 and full Professor in January 2009. He participated to the initiation of many graduate courses at the University of Sfax. His current research areas include software engineering of distributed systems, formal methods in model-driven architecture, component oriented development, self-adaptive and pervasive systems, and autonomic middleware. He published more than 100 regular and invited papers in international conferences and journals, and has co-edited four conferences proceedings and three journals special issues on these subjects. More details are available on his home page: http://www.redcad.org/members/jmaiel/

Sofien Khemakhem (born May, 1973, Sfax-Tunisia) received the Engineering in Computer science from National School of Computer Sciences (ENSI TUNIS), in July 1998 and M.S. (DEA) degrees in Computer Science from National School of Engineers of Sfax (ENIS SFAX), in August 2001. Since November 2004, he prepared a PhD thesis at the Faculty of Economic Sciences and Management of Sfax (Tunisia) and the Laboratory for Analysis and Architecture of Systems (Frensh). He is since 2005, a researcher technologist in computer sciences at the Higher Institute of Technological Studies of Kairouan (Tunisia). Sofien KHEMAKHEM's research interests the discovery and the composition of software components. Sofien KHEMAKHEM is member of the program committees of the Integrated Intelligent Computing Conference. More details are available on his home page: http://www.redcad.org/members/khemakhem/

Chao-Sheng Lin received the BS degree in Architecture and Urban Design from Chinese Culture University, Taipei, Taiwan, ROC, in 1998, and the MS degree in the Department of Computer Science and Information Engineering from National Chung Cheng University, Chiayi, Taiwan, ROC, in 2007. He is now working toward the PhD degree in the Department of Computer Science and Information Engineering at National Chung Cheng University. He has two-year working experience in software engineering and had been the vice senior software engineer in Synchronous Communication Corp. in Taiwan. His research interests include formal verification, reconfigurable systems, and multi-core programming.

Shang-Wei Lin received the BS degree in management information system from National Chung Cheng University, Chiayi, Taiwan, ROC, in 2002. He is currently working toward the PhD degree in the Department of Computer Science and Information Engineering at National Chung Cheng University, Chiayi, Taiwan, ROC. He is a teaching and research assistant in the Department of Computer Science and Information Engineering at National Chung Cheng University. His research interests include formal verification, formal synthesis, scheduling, and object-oriented software synthesis.

Chun-Hsien Lu received the BS degree in Computer Science and Information Engineering from the National Chung Cheng University, Chiayi, Taiwan, ROC in 2006. He is studying for the PhD degree in Computer Science and Information Engineering from the National Chung Cheng University now. His main research interests include: reconfigurable computing, network on chip, multi-core systems.

Fergal McCaffery is a Lecturer at the Dundalk Institute of Technology. He is the leader of the Regulated Software Research Group in Dundalk Institute of Technology and a member of Lero. He has been awarded Science Foundation Ireland funding through the Stokes Lectureship and Principal Investigator Programmes to research the area of software process improvement for the medical device domain. Additionally, he has received EU FP7 research funding to improve the effectiveness of embedded software development environments for the medical device industry. Until January 2008, Dr. McCaffery was a Senior Research Fellow with Lero. He has both an industrial and academic background. His current research interests includes the development of a software development framework for the medical device industry, software process improvement frameworks and assessments, and global software development. He is currently the international project leader of a project to develop a software process assessment model for the medical device industry (Medi SPICE). He has published over 60 peer-reviewed conference and journal papers in the area of software process improvement and is a programme committee member and reviewer for a number of leading conferences and journals in this research area. Prior to joining Lero he worked in a research role for the Centre for Software Process Technologies at the University of Ulster for 3 years. Previously, he worked for 6 years as a Senior Team leader/Project Manager for Nortel Networks. This period in industry was preceded by 2 years as an academic member of staff at the University of Ulster, during which time he completed a D.Phil in Intelligent Adaptive Multimodal Interfaces.

Sanjay Misra obtained M.Tech. Degree in Software Engineering from Motilal Nehru National Institue of Technology, Allahabad India and D.Phil. from University of Allahabad, India. Presently he is Professor and Head of the Department of Computer Engineering, School of Communication and Information Technology, Federal University of Technology, Minna, Nigeria. He is a software engineer and previously held academic positions at Atilim University, Turkey, Subharati University, and UP Technical University India. His current researches cover the areas of: Software quality, software measurement, software metrics, software process improvement, software project management, object oriented technologies, XML, SOA, Web Services, and cognitive informatics. He published more than 60 papers in these areas. For his outstanding publications and research contributions, he has been awarded by TUBITAK(A Turkey Government Organization) and Atlim University several times. He chaired several international workshops (Software Engineering Process and Applications 2009 and 2010 (Springer), Tools and Techniques in Software Development Process 2009, 2010, (IEEE), Software Quality 2009 (IEEE), and Software Metrics and Measurement 2009(IEEE)) in area of Software Engineering. Presently, he is chief editor of "International Journal of Computer Science and Software Technology" (IJCSST) and serving as editorial board member of several journals of international repute.

Nikolaos Mittas was born in Kavala, Greece. He received his BSc degree in Mathematics from University of Crete, his Msc in Informatics from Aristotle University of Thessaloniki (AUTh) and his PhD in Informatics from Department of Informatics, AUTh. His doctoral dissertation has the title: "Statistical and Computational Methods for Development, Improvement and Comparison of Software Cost Estimation Models". His research interests involve application of statistics, especially computational statistics, to cost estimation of software projects and generally to data from software projects. He teaches mathematics and statistics as a visiting assistant professor in Technological Educational Institute of Kavala.

Eila Ovaska obtained the MSc degree in 1995 and the PhD degree in 2000 in information processing science from the University of Oulu, Finland. She has worked over thirty years in the embedded software research area at VTT Technical Research Centre of Finland. She led the Software Architectures Group at VTT until September 2002. Since 2001, she has been working as a research professor at VTT and since 2002 also as an adjunct professor of software architectures and components at the University of Oulu. She has acted as a reviewer for scientific journals and books, and as a member of many conference program committees. Quality-aware architecting and service architectures of pervasive computing environments based on ontology oriented design are her recent research interests. She has (co)authored more than 100 scientific publications and is a member of the IEEE and the IEEE Computer Society.

Baris Ozkan is a doctoral student in the Information Systems Department at Middle East Technical University (METU). He is a member of Software Management Research Group at Informatics Institute, METU. He holds a BSc degree in Industrial Engineering and an MSc degree in Software Management from METU. His work focuses on software measurement and metrics, software effort and cost estimation, software project management, software processes and process improvement. He worked in a number of software product development and IT/software process improvement projects as a consultant. Contact him at bozkan@ii.metu.edu.tr.

George A. Papadopoulos (PhD) holds the (tenured) rank of Professor of Software Engineering in the Department of Computer Science, University of Cyprus. His research interests include component-based systems, mobile computing, e-health, e-learning, open and distance learning, distributed systems, service oriented computing, and cooperative systems. He has published over 100 papers as book chapters or in internationally refereed journals and conferences and he serves in the Editorial Board of 5 international journals. Professor Papadopoulos is a recipient of a 1995 ERCIM-HCM scholarship award. He has been involved or is currently participating, as coordinator or partner, in over 50 internationally and nationally funded projects with a personal funding of more than 5 MEUR. He is the Director of the Software Engineering and Internet Technologies (SEIT) Laboratory (http://www.cs.ucy.ac.cy/seit).

Kai Petersen is an industrial PhD candidate at Ericsson AB and Blekinge Institute of Technology. He received his Master of Science in Software Engineering (MSc) from Blekinge Institute of Technology. Thereafter, he worked as a research assistant at University of Duisburg Essen, focusing on software product-line engineering and service-oriented architecture. His current research interests are empirical software engineering, software process improvement, lean and agile development, and software measurement.

Mario Piattini is full professor at the UCLM. His research interests include software quality, metrics, and maintenance. He holds the PhD degree in Computer Science from the Technical University of Madrid, and leads the Alarcos Research Group at the Universidad de Castilla-La Mancha. He is CISA, CISM e CGEIT by ISACA. Contact him at Escuela Superior de Informática, Paseo de la Universidad 4, 13071-Ciudad Real, Spain.

Minna Pikkarainen has graduated from University of Oulu and has a PhD in improving software development mediated with CMMI and agile practices. Dr. Pikkarainen has been working as researcher, project manager and senior research scientist in VTT Technical Research Centre of Finland since 1997.

During that time she has worked in 18 industrial driven research projects doing close industrial collaboration with more than 15 organizations in Finland, Ireland and Belgium. Minna's research has been published in 28+ journal and conference papers in the forums like ICSE, ICIS and Empirical Software Engineering Journal. So far Minna has provided trainings, workshops and invited talks for more than 10+ different industries related to agile methods and participated in several conference program committees. Minna has been member of Lero, The Irish Software Engineering Research Centre between 2006-2009 and Sirris, The Collective Center for the Belgian technological industry since 2010. For the past five years, her work and publications have been focused on research in the area of agile development. Recently she has focused her research in the area of software innovation and software variability management.

Ricardo Pérez-Castillo holds the MSc degree in Computer Science from the University of Castilla-La Mancha, and is currently a PhD student in Computer Science. He works in Alarcos Research Group at the University of Castilla-La Mancha. His research interests include architecture-driven modernization, model-driven development and business process recovery. Contact him at Escuela Superior de Informática, Paseo de la Universidad 4, 13071-Ciudad Real, Spain.

Gregor Scheithauer works as a business engineering consultant at Opitz Consulting München GmbH in Germany. He holds a Diploma in business information systems from University of Bamberg, Germany, where he also pursued his PhD thesis about conceptual service modeling. Gregor is the author and co-author of several publications at international conferences and conducts reviews for an IEEE journal. His research interests comprise service descriptions, business process modeling, and automation, as well as service engineering. He participated in several national and international research and industry projects including the German Theseus research program. Additionally, Gregor is a member of ACM and GI (German Society of Computer Science).

Panagiotis Sentas was born in Thessaloniki, Greece. He received his BSc and PhD degree in Informatics from Aristotle University of Thessaloniki (A.U.Th.). The subject of his PhD dissertation was the application of statistical methods and models to the analysis and estimation of software management data. He published three papers in journals and four papers in conference proceedings. His research is focused on software cost estimation with advanced statistical methods like regression analysis, survival analysis and imputation of missing data, especially of categorical data. He has participated in two funded programs and he is currently working as a teacher in high school.

Murat M. Tanik is a professor at the University of Alabama (UAB) at Birmingham since 1998. Prior to joining the UAB faculty, he was an associate professor and the director of Software Systems Engineering Institute (SSEI) at the University of Texas at Austin and served as the director of Electronic Enterprise Engineering at NJIT. He is also the director and chief scientist of Process Sciences Laboratory, a think-tank of process-centered knowledge integration. Dr. Tanik has worked on related projects for NASA, Arthur A. Collins (developer of Apollo moon missions' tracking and communications systems), and ISSI. After Collins and ISSI, he joined SMU as an associate professor and the director of the Software Systems Engineering Technology (SEK) research group. Dr. Tanik is co-founder of the interdisciplinary and international society, Society for Design and Process Science. His publications include co-authoring six books, co-editing eight collected works, and more than 100 journal papers, conference papers, book chapters, and reports funded by various government agencies and corporations. Under his direction, more than 20 PhD dissertations and 25 M.S. theses have been completed. Dr. Tanik's research interests include philosophy of science, software systems engineering, embedded and intelligent software systems, wireless and time-critical software support, collaborative computing for domain specific applications, and integrated systems design and process engineering. His first principles research include the development of information theoretical foundations for computing.

Bedir Tekinerdoğan, received his MSc degree in Computer Science in 1994, and a PhD degree in Computer Science in 2000, both from the University of Twente, The Netherlands. Currently he is an assistant professor at Bilkent University in Turkey. He is the primary founder and leader of the Bilkent Software Engineering Group (Bilsen). He has more than 16 years of experience in software engineering research and education. His key research interests include software architecture design, aspect-oriented software development, model-driven software development, software product line engineering, global software development, and service-oriented computing.

Konrad Voigt has joined SAP Research in 2006 as PhD candidate. The topic he works on is two-fold. First, he is investigating model driven service engineering in enterprises. Second, he studies data integration via schema matching with a focus on graph-based algorithms. Prior to joining SAP, Konrad received his Diploma degree from the HU Berlin, where he focused his studies on model-driven architecture and meta-modeling repositories.

Liqiang Wang is an assistant professor in the Department of Computer Science at the University of Wyoming. He received the PhD degree in Computer Science from the State University of New York at Stony Brook in 2006, the MS degree in Computer Science from Sichuan University of China in 1998, and the BS degree in Mathematics from Hebei Normal University of China in 1995. His research focuses on analyzing concurrency-related errors in parallel programs and designing data-intensive parallel computing systems for better performance and dependability. His research has been supported by NSF, ONR, and NASA.

Matthias Winkler works as a researcher at SAP Research Center Dresden and is currently involved in the German Theseus TEXO project. He is currently finishing his PhD studies in collaboration with the Technical University in Dresden, Germany. His research interests include service engineering and SLA management. He obtained a B.S. degree in Media and Computer Science from the Technical University in Dresden as well as a M.S. degree in Interactive Systems Engineering from the Royal Institute of Technology in Stockholm, Sweden. Mr. Winkler holds several publications on national and international conferences. Prior to his current work he was involved in the project EMODE as well as in research projects in the area of Smart Items and multimodal user interfaces.

Kun Yang received his PhD from the Department of Electronic & Electrical Engineering of University College London (UCL), UK, and MSc and BSc from the Computer Science Department of Jilin University, China. He is currently a Reader in the School of Computer Science and Electronic Engineering, University of Essex, UK. Before joining in University of Essex at 2003, he also worked at UCL on several European Union research projects such as FAIN, MANTRIP, CONTEXT, et cetera, in the area of IP network management and service engineering. His current major research interests include wireless networks and communications, heterogeneous wireless networks, fixed mobile convergence, pervasive service engineering, IP network management, and network virtualization, which are supported by externally-funded research projects from EPSRC, TSB, industries and EC. He has published more than 50 journal papers. He serves on the editorial boards of both IEEE and non-IEEE journals. He is a Senior Member of IEEE.

Jiehan Zhou is currently working as a research scientist at Computer Science and Engineering Laboratory, University of Oulu. He obtained his PhD in manufacturing and automation from the Hua-Zhong University of Science and Technology, Wuhan, China in 2000. His current research interests include pervasive computing, service-oriented computing, ontology engineering, and semantic Web.

Index

A

academic exercises 2

accuracy (AE) 228, 230, 233, 234, 235, 236, 238

adopted search 196

agile hybrid assessment method fo the automotive industry (AHAA) 281, 282, 288, 289, 290, 291, 292, 293, 296, 298, 299, 300, 301, 303, 304, 305, 306, 307, 310

agile practices 281, 283, 285, 287, 288, 289, 290, 291, 305, 306, 307, 311

algebra 6

analysis of variance (ANOVA) 226, 228

application programming interface (API) 389

Architectural description languages (ADL) 53, 105, 106

architecture-centered verification method (ACV) 105, 106, 120, 121

architecture design 48, 49, 50, 51, 52, 53, 55, 56, 57, 58, 60, 62, 63, 64, 66, 67, 68, 69, 72, 73, 74

Architecture-Driven Modernization (ADM) 75, 76, 77, 80, 81, 82, 83, 85, 86, 87, 89, 90, 97, 98, 99, 100, 101, 102, 103

Architecture-Driven Modernization Task Force (ADMTF) 81, 82, 85, 86, 102, 103

architecture modeling 48, 49, 50, 52, 57, 60, 64, 65, 69

architecture models 104, 107, 108, 110, 111, 115, 118, 120, 121

architecture reliability modeling 51, 58

architecture transformations 51

arithmetic 6

Atlas Transformation Language (ATL) 342, 347

atomicity violation 380, 392, 394, 395, 396, 403, 408, 415

attribute-based classification 202

automatic-control mechanisms 7

Automatic Flight Control (AFC) 326, 327, 328

automatic generation 197, 198

Automotive SPICE 281, 288, 289, 290, 291, 306, 307, 308

automotive system development domain 295

AutoSoft 292, 293, 294, 295, 296, 297, 298, 299, 300, 301, 302, 303, 304, 307, 312, 313, 314

Average Monthly Work Rate (AMWR) 351

B

balanced cooperative modeling 154, 169

Base Functional Components (BFCs) 245

basic attribute-based classification 202

basic control structures (BCS) 265, 266, 267, 268, 269, 271, 272, 273, 277, 278

Bayesian multiple imputation (BMI) 224

Binary Decision Diagrams (BDD) 107

black box 200

bottom-up governance 315, 319, 320, 325, 330

British Telecom (BT) 333, 344, 347, 350, 354

Broadband Engine (BE) 382

BSC 265, 269

business knowledge 75, 76, 78, 84, 87, 92, 98, 99

business process modeling (BPMN) 163

business sciences 129

C

C++ 79, 98

calculus 6, 8